THE FORMS OF THE OLD TESTAMENT LITERATURE

1 and 2 Chronicles

SIMON J. DE VRIES

The Forms of the Old Testament Literature
VOLUME XI

Rolf P. Knierim and Gene M. Tucker, editors

WILLIAM B. EERDMANS PUBLISHING COMPANY
GRAND RAPIDS, MICHIGAN

To my Father
bĕ lēb šālēm mitnaddēb lĕ yahweh

1 Chr 29:9

Copyright © 1989 by Wm. B. Eerdmans Publishing Co.
255 Jefferson Ave., S.E., Grand Rapids, MI 49503

Library of Congress Cataloging-in-Publication Data
De Vries, Simon John.
1–2 Chronicles / Simon J. De Vries.
p.   cm.   — (The Forms of the Old Testament literature; v. 11)
Bibliography : pp. 3ff.
ISBN 0-8028-0236-2
1. Bible. O.T. Chronicles—Criticism, interpretation, etc.
I. One and Two Chronicles.   II. Title.   III. Series.
BS1345.2.D4 1989
222'.606—dc19   88-11268
CIP

Contents

Abbreviations and Symbols

I. MISCELLANEOUS ABBREVIATIONS AND SYMBOLS

BHmg	*Biblia Hebraica,* marginal notes
ca.	*circa* (about)
ch(s).	chapter(s)
ChrH	The Chronicler as historian, the Chronicles history
ChrR	The Chronicler as redactor, the Chronicles redaction
cf.	compare
cj.	conjecture
col(s).	column(s)
comm(s).	published commentary(ies) as listed in main Bibliography
Diss.	Dissertation
Dtr	Deuteronomic/Deuteronomistic
DtrH	Deuteronomistic Historian/history book
E	Elohist
ed.	editor(s), edited by; edition
Eng.	English
f(f).	following verse(s), pages(s), line(s)
fem.	feminine
Fest.	*Festschrift*
Gk.	Greek
H	Holiness Code
Hebr.	Hebrew
hiph.	hiphil
hith.	hithpael
hoph.	hophal
i.e.	*id est* (that is)
impf.	imperfect
impr.	imperative
Intro(s).	published *Introduction(s)* to the Old Testament
J	Yahwistic source

L	Lucian
lit.	literally
LXX	Septuagint
LXX^A	idem, Codex Alexandrinus
LXX^B	idem, Codex Vaticanus
m.	masculine
MS(S)	manuscript(s)
MT	Masoretic Text
n.	note
OT	Old Testament
P	Priestly source
p(p).	page(s)
par.	parallel in Samuel-Kings or Chronicles
part.	participle
pass.	passive
perf.	perfect
plur.	plural
P^s	Priestly supplement(s)
rev.	revised
s.	singular
S^A	Codex Ambrosianus
Sam Pent	Samaritan Pentateuch
Syr.	Syriac version
Tg.	Targum
tr.	translated by
v(v).	verse(s)
viz.	*videlicet,* namely
Vg.	Vulgate
VS(S)	version(s)
→	The arrow indicates a cross reference to another section of the commentary.
=	is equivalent to

II. PUBLICATIONS

AASOR	Annual of the American Schools of Oriental Research
AB	Anchor Bible
AcAnt	*Acta Antiqua*
AcOr	*Acta orientalia*
AfO	*Archiv für Orientforschung*

ABBREVIATIONS

AJSL	*American Journal of Semitic Languages and Literature*
AnBib	Analecta biblica
AnOr	Analecta orientalia
AO	Der alte Orient
AOAT	Alter Orient und Altes Testament
ArOr	*Archiv orientální*
ATAbh	Alttestamentliche Abhandlungen
ATD	Das Alte Testament Deutsch
AUSS	*Andrews University Seminary Studies*
BASOR	*Bulletin of the American Schools of Oriental Research*
BBB	Bonner biblische Beiträge
BethM	*Beth Miqra*
BEvT	Beiträge zur evangelischen Theologie
BHS	*Biblia Hebraica Stuttgartensia*
Bib	*Biblica*
BibOr	Biblica et orientalia
BJRL	*Bulletin of the John Rylands University Library of Manchester*
BKAT	Biblischer Kommentar: Altes Testament
BN	*Biblische Notizen*
BOuT	De boeken van het Oude Testament
BSac	*Bibliotheca Sacra*
BTB	*Biblical Theology Bulletin*
BWANT	Beiträge zur Wissenschaft vom Alten und Neuen Testament
BZ	*Biblische Zeitschrift*
BZAW	Beiheft zur Zeitschrift für die Alttestamentliche Wissenschaft
CBQ	*Catholic Biblical Quarterly*
CBQMS	Catholic Biblical Quarterly—Monograph Series
ConB	Coniectanea biblica
CTM	*Concordia Theological Monthly*
EncJud	*Encyclopedia Judaica*
ErIs	*Eretz Israel*
EstBib	*Estudios Bíblicos*
ETL	*Ephemerides theologicae lovanienses*
EvQ	*Evangelical Quarterly*
EvT	*Evangelische Theologie*
Exp	*Expositor*
ExpB	Expositor's Bible
FOTL	The Forms of the Old Testament Literature
FRLANT	Forschungen zur Religion und Literatur des Alten und Neuen Testaments
HAT	Handbuch zum Alten Testament

HKAT	Handkommentar zum Alten Testament
HSAT	*Die heilige Schrift des Alten Testaments*
HTR	*Harvard Theological Review*
HUCA	*Hebrew Union College Annual*
IB	*Interpreter's Bible*
ICC	International Critical Commentary
IDB	*Interpreter's Dictionary of the Bible*
IDBSup	Supplementary volume to *IDB*
IEJ	*Israel Exploration Journal*
Imm	*Immanuel*
Int	*Interpretation*
JANESCU	*Journal of the Ancient Near Eastern Society of Columbia University*
JAOS	*Journal of the American Oriental Society*
JBL	*Journal of Biblical Literature*
JBR	*Journal of Bible and Religion*
JJS	*Journal of Jewish Studies*
JNES	*Journal of Near Eastern Studies*
JPOS	*Journal of the Palestine Oriental Society*
JSOT	*Journal for the Study of the Old Testament*
JSOTSup	Journal for the Study of the Old Testament Supplement Series
JSS	*Journal of Semitic Studies*
JTS	*Journal of Theological Studies*
KAT	Kommentar zum Alten Testament
KEH	Kurzgefasstes exegetisches Handbuch zum Alten Testament
KHC	Kurzer Hand-Commentar zum Alten Testament
KS	A. Alt, *Kleine Schriften zur Geschichte des Volks Israel*
Leš	*Lešonénu*
MIOF	Mitteilungen des Instituts für Orientforschung
NCB	New Century Bible
OLP	*Orientalia lovaniensia periodica*
OTL	Old Testament Library
OTS	*Oudtestamentische Studiën*
OTWSA	*Ou-Testamentiese Werkgemeenskap in Suid-Afrika*
PEFQS	*Palestine Exploration Fund Quarterly Statement*
PEQ	*Palestine Exploration Quarterly*
PJ	*Palästinajahrbuch*
RB	*Revue biblique*
RHPR	*Revue d'histoire et de philosophie religieuses*
RivB	*Rivista biblica*
RSV	*Revised Standard Version*

RTP	*Revue de théologie et de philosophie*
SBLMS	Society of Biblical Literature Monograph Series
SBT	Studies in Biblical Theology
SEÅ	*Svensk exegetisk årsbok*
SNTSMS	Society for New Testament Studies Monograph Series
SonB	Soncino Bible
SOTSMS	Society for Old Testament Study Monograph Series
ST	*Studia theologica*
Tarb	*Tarbiz*
ThSt	*Theologische studiën*
ThStK	*Theologische Studien und Kritiken*
TLZ	*Theologische Literaturzeitung*
TQ	*Theologische Quartalschrift*
TRu	*Theologische Rundschau*
TynBul	*Tyndale Bulletin*
TZ	*Theologische Zeitschrift*
UT	C. H. Gordon, *Ugaritic Textbook* (AnOr 38; Rome: Pontifical Biblical Institute, 1965)
VT	*Vetus Testamentum*
VTSup	Vetus Testamentum, Supplements
WO	*Die Welt des Orients*
ZAW	*Zeitschrift für die alttestamentliche Wissenschaft*
ZDMG	*Zeitschrift der deutschen morgenländischen Gesellschaft*
ZDPV	*Zeitschrift des deutschen Palästinavereins*
ZkTh	*Zeitschrift für katholische Theologie*
ZTK	*Zeitschrift für Theologie und Kirche*

Editors' Foreword

THIS BOOK is the sixth in a series of twenty-four volumes planned for publication throughout the nineteen-eighties. The series eventually will represent a form-critical analysis of every book and each unit of the Old Testament (Hebrew Bible) according to a standard outline and methodology. The aims of the work are fundamentally exegetical, attempting to understand the biblical literature from the viewpoint of a particular set of questions. Each volume in the series will also give an account of the history of the form-critical discussion of the material in question, attempt to bring consistency to the testimony for the genres and formulas of the biblical literature, and expose the exegetical procedure in such a way as to enable students and pastors to engage in their own analysis and interpretation. It is hoped, therefore, that the audience will be a broad one, including not only biblical scholars but also students, pastors, priests, and rabbis who are engaged in biblical interpretation.

There is a difference between the planned order of appearance of the individual volumes and their position in the series. While the series follows basically the sequence of the books of the Hebrew Bible, the individual volumes will appear in accordance with the projected working schedules of the individual contributors. The number of twenty-four volumes has been chosen for merely practical reasons which make it necessary to combine several biblical books in one volume at times, and at times to have two authors contribute to the same volume. Volume XIII is an exception to the arrangement according to the sequence of the Hebrew canon in that it omits Lamentations. The commentary on Lamentations will be published with that on the book of Psalms.

The initiation of this series is the result of deliberations and plans which began some twenty years ago. At that time the current editors perceived the need for a comprehensive reference work which would enable scholars and students of the Hebrew scriptures to gain from the insights that form-critical work had accumulated throughout seven decades, and at the same time to participate more effectively in such work themselves. An international and interconfessional team of scholars was assembled, and has been expanded in recent years.

Several possible approaches and formats for publication presented themselves. The work could not be a handbook of the form-critical method with some examples of its application. Nor would it be satisfactory to present an encyclopedia of the genres identified in the Old Testament literature. The reference work would have to demonstrate the method on all of the texts, and identify genres only through the actual interpretation of the texts themselves. Hence, the work had to be a commentary following the sequence of the books in the Hebrew Bible (the Kittel edition of the *Biblia Hebraica* then and the *Biblia Hebraica Stuttgartensia* now).

The main purpose of this project is to lead the student to the Old Testament texts themselves, and not just to form-critical studies of the texts. It should be stressed that the commentary is confined to the form-critical interpretation of the texts. Consequently, the reader should not expect here a full-fledged exegetical commentary which deals with the broad range of issues concerning the meaning of the text. In order to keep the focus as clearly as possible on a particular set of questions, matters of text, translation, philology, verse-by-verse explanation, etc. are raised only when they appear directly relevant to the form-critical analysis and interpretation.

The adoption of a commentary format with specific categories for the analysis of the texts rests upon a conclusion that has become crucial for all form-critical work. If the results of form criticism are to be verifiable and generally intelligible, then the determination of typical forms and genres, their settings and functions, has to take place through the analysis of the forms in and of the texts themselves. This leads to two consequences for the volumes in the series. First, each interpretation of a text begins with the presentation of the *structure* of that text in outline form. The ensuing discussion of this structure attempts to distinguish the typical from the individual or unique elements, and to proceed on this basis to the determination of the *genre,* its *setting,* and its *intention.* Traditio-historical factors are discussed throughout this process where relevant; e.g., is there evidence of a written or oral stage of the material earlier than the actual text before the reader?

Second, the interpretation of the texts accepts the fundamental premise that we possess all texts basically at their latest written stages, technically speaking, at the levels of the final redactions. Any access to the texts, therefore, must confront and analyze that latest edition first, i.e., a specific version of that edition as represented in a particular text tradition. Consequently, the commentary proceeds from the analysis of the larger literary corpora created by the redactions back to any prior discernible stages in their literary history. Larger units are examined first, and then their subsections. Therefore, in most instances the first unit examined in terms of structure, genre, setting, and intention is the entire biblical book in question; next the commentary treats the individual larger and then smaller units.

The original plan of the project was to record critically all the relevant results of previous form-critical studies concerning the texts in question. While this remains one of the goals of the series, it had to be expanded to allow for more of the research of the individual contributors. This approach has proved to be important not only with regard to the ongoing insights of the contributors, but also in view of the significant developments which have taken place in the field in recent years. The team of scholars responsible for the series is committed to following a basic design throughout the commentary, but differences of emphasis and even to some extent of approach will be recognized as more volumes appear. Each author will ultimately be responsible for his own contribution.

The use of the commentary is by and large self-explanatory, but a few comments may prove helpful to the reader. This work is designed to be used alongside a Hebrew text or a translation of the Bible. The format of the interpretation of the texts, large or small, is the same throughout, except in cases where the biblical material itself suggests a different form of presentation. Individual books and major literary corpora are introduced by a general bibliography referring to wider information on the subjects discussed, and to works relevant for the subunits of that literary body. Whenever available, a special form-critical bibliography for a specific unit under discussion will conclude the discussion of that unit. In the outline of the structure of units, the system of sigla attempts to indicate the relationship and interdependence of the parts within that structure. The traditional chapter and verse divisions of the Hebrew text are supplied in the right-hand margin of the outlines. Where there is a difference between the Hebrew and English versification the latter is also supplied in parentheses according to the *Revised Standard Version.*

In addition to the commentary on the biblical books, this volume includes a glossary of the genres discussed in the commentary. Most of the definitions in the glossary were prepared by Professor De Vries, but some have arisen from the work of other members of the project on other parts of the Old Testament. Each subsequent volume will include such a glossary. Eventually, upon the completion of the commentary series, all of the glossaries will be revised in the light of the analysis of each book of the Old Testament and published as Volume XXIII of the series. The individual volumes will not contain special indices but the indices for the entire series will be published as Volume XXIV.

The editors wish to acknowledge with appreciation the contribution of numerous persons and institutions to the work of the project. All of the contributors have received significant financial, secretarial, and student assistance from their respective institutions. In particular, the editors have received extensive support from their Universities. Without such concrete expressions of encouragement the work scarcely could have gone on. At Claremont, the Institute for Antiquity and Christianity has from its own inception provided office facilities, a supportive staff, and the atmosphere which stimulates not only individual but also team research. Emory University and the Candler School of Theology have likewise provided tangible support and encouragement. Henry Sun and Tim Fearer carried the major load during the first round of the editorial process. Thereafter, Mr. Sun's prompt effort helped in bringing that process to its conclusion. Finally, Keith Eades and Marilyn Lundberg were of significant help in editing the galley proofs. To all these Old Testament students at Claremont Graduate School and research associates to the FOTL project at the Institute for Antiquity and Christianity the editors are greatly indebted.

ROLF P. KNIERIM
GENE M. TUCKER

Preface

SOME YEARS AGO Rolf Knierim flew out to Ohio to ask Ronald Hals and me to join the FOTL project. Professor Hals was to do Ezekiel and I was to do 1-2 Chronicles. "But," I protested, "I don't know much about Chronicles." "Neither does anyone else," Knierim replied, "but I need you because you have worked on narrative." Because of my high enthusiasm for the project as a whole, I suppressed my misgivings, and the present volume is its fruits. I have had two special benefits as my personal reward: I have had the opportunity to become intimately acquainted with a rich but generally neglected portion of Scripture, and I have had an opportunity to make extensive employment of an exegetical technique developed many decades ago by Gunkel, but not even now fully understood or effectively utilized.

Most of what I have known about Chronicles has been superficial at best and misguided at worst. Having now devoted a number of years to the research and writing for this volume, I regard Chronicles as one of the richest mines of spirituality in all of Scripture. A mine, yes; and as a miner must chop and toil to bring out shining nuggets, students of Chronicles must labor with care, diligence, and circumspection if their hope is to make this treasure theirs.

As has been remarked, the method of form criticism has been one of my own sharp tools, and I eagerly share it with everyone who is concerned to understand this method better. The need for it ought to be obvious, for the *way* the sacred word is presented (i.e., in its structure and genre) is equally vital to the communicative process as its substance or content (words, images, ideas). It is not just *what* Scripture says that matters, but *how* it says it as well.

Like the other volumes in this series, this commentary on 1-2 Chronicles concentrates on exegetical concerns that most other commentaries barely touch upon, if at all, and whose understanding of the biblical text has tended accordingly to be one-sided and shrunken. Devoted by design to "structure," "genre," "setting," and "intention," this commentary aims to fill a large, too-long tolerated gap. This is not to deny, however, that it has been vastly enriched by commentaries of the ordinary type, which actually do at times offer important insights into matters of form and tradition criticism, but which have been relied on here mainly for historical, textual, and philological analysis. We have freely borrowed from them and presuppose them in every instance. This is to urge the user of this commentary not to depend on it alone—just as, in using the more traditional commentaries, one should not neglect the new insights which a form-critical commentary can bring to the whole wide range of concerns within the demanding discipline of biblical interpretation. In not including in our treatment of the text an extensive discussion of textual problems or extended treatment of historical and philological problems, we urge the user also to consult the more traditional commentaries and related studies—to which we also have been heavily indebted, but which for the large part do not follow a complete methodology. Here we offer the user the extensive results of the presently most meaningful methodology for discerning the shape and impact of the Chronicles text. Though not to be used alone, it supersedes other commentaries even as it gratefully borrows from and relies upon them.

SIMON J. DE VRIES

1 and 2 Chronicles

Chapter 1
Introduction to Chronicles

BIBLIOGRAPHY

G. C. Aalders, *Oud-Testamentische Kanoniek* (Kampen: J. H. Kok, 1952); Y. D. Abramsky, "1 Chronicles" (Hebr.), *BethM* 25 (1980) 199-201; P. R. Ackroyd, *The Age of the Chronicler* (Auckland: Colloquium, 1970); idem, "The Chronicler as Exegete," *JSOT* 2 (1977) 2-32; idem, *I and II Chronicles, Ezra, Nehemiah* (Torch Bible Commentaries; London: SCM, 1973); idem, "History and Theology in the Writings of the Chronicler," *CTM* 38 (1967) 501-15; idem, "The Temple Vessels—a Continuity Theme," in *Studies in the Religion of Ancient Israel* (VTSup 23; Leiden: Brill, 1972) 166-81; idem, "The Theology of the Chronicler," *Lexington Theological Quarterly* 8 (1973) 101-16; W. F. Albright, "The Date and Personality of the Chronicler," *JBL* 40 (1921) 104-24; L. C. Allen, *The Greek Chronicles: The Relationship of the Septuagint of I and II Chronicles to the Massoretic Text* (VTSup 25, 27; Leiden: Brill, 1974); Y. Amit, "A New Outlook on the Book of Chronicles," *Imm* 13 (1981) 20-29; W. Bacher, "Der Name der Bücher der Chronik in der Septuaginta," *ZAW* 15 (1895) 305-8; M. Bailey, "Levitical Legend from the Persian Period," *JBL* 46 (1927) 132-38; W. E. Barnes, "The Midrashic Element in Chronicles," *Exp* 2 (1896) 426-39; idem, "The Religious Standpoint of the Chronicler," *AJSL* 13 (1896-97) 14-20; A. Bea, "Neuere Arbeiten zum Problem der biblischen Chronikbücher," *Bib* 22 (1941) 46-58; C. Begg, " 'Seeking Yahweh' and the Purpose of Chronicles," *Louvain Studies* 9 (1982) 128-42; W. H. Bennett, *The Books of Chronicles* (ExpB; London: Hodder and Stoughton, 1894); A. Bentzen, "Sirach, der Chronist, und Nehemia," *ST* 3 (1949) 158-61; I. Benzinger, *Die Bücher der Chronik erklärt* (KHC 20; Tübingen: Mohr, 1901); S. B. Berg, "After the Exile: God and History in the Books of Chronicles and Esther," in *The Divine Helmsman* (*Fest.* L. H. Silberman; ed. J. L. Crenshaw and S. Sandmel; New York: KTAV, 1980) 107-27; E. Bertheau, *Die Bücher der Chronik erklärt* (2nd ed.; KEH 15; Leipzig: Hirzel, 1873); J. A. Bewer, *The Literature of the Old Testament in its Historical Development* (New York: Columbia, 1922); G. Beyer, "Beiträge zur Territorialgeschichte von Südwestpalästina im Altertum. I. Das Festungssystem Rehabeams," *ZDPV* 54 (1931) 113-34; J. Botterweck, "Zur Eigenart der chronistischen Davidgeschichte," *TQ* 136 (1956) 402-35; R. L. Braun, "A Reconsideration of the Chronicler's Attitude Toward the North," *JBL* 96 (1977) 59-62; idem, "Solomonic Apologetic in Chronicles," *JBL* 92 (1973) 503-16; idem, "Chronicles, Ezra, and Nehemiah: Theology and Literary History," in *Studies in the Historical Books of the Old Testament* (VTSup 30; ed. J. A. Emerton; Leiden: Brill, 1979) 52-64; A. M. Brunet, "Le Chroniste et ses sources," *RB* 60 (1953) 481-508; 61 (1954) 349-86; idem, "La théologie du Chroniste. Théocratie et messianisme," in *Sacra Pagina* (ed. J. Coppens, A. Descamps, and E. Massaud; Paris: Gabalda, 1959) 1:384-97; M. Buber, *Die Schriftwerke verdeutscht von Martin*

Buber (4th ed.; Heidelberg: Schneider, 1976); H. Bückers, *Die Bücher der Chronik* (HThK IV/1; Freiburg: Herder, 1952); W. W. Cannon, "A Note on Dr. Welch's Article 'The Death of Josiah'," *ZAW* 44 (1926) 63-64; A. Caquot, "Peut-on parler du messianisme dans l'oeuvre du Chroniste?" *RTP* 99/2 (1966) 110-20; H. Cazelles, "Les livres des Chroniques," in *La Sainte Bible de Jerusalem* (2nd rev. ed.; Paris: Cerf, 1961); B. S. Childs, *Introduction to the Old Testament as Scripture* (Philadelphia: Fortress, 1979); A. Cody, *A History of the Old Testament Priesthood* (AnBib 35; Rome: Pontifical Biblical Institute, 1969); R. J. Coggins, *The First and Second Books of the Chronicles* (Cambridge Biblical Commentary on The New English Bible; Cambridge: Cambridge, 1976); idem, *Samaritans and Jews: The Origins of Samaritanism Reconsidered* (Atlanta: John Knox, 1975); F. M. Cross, "A Reconstruction of the Judean Restoration," *JBL* 94 (1975) 4-18; E. L. Curtis and A. A. Madsen, *A Critical and Exegetical Commentary on the Books of Chronicles* (ICC; New York: Scribner's, 1910); S. J. De Vries, "The Land's Sabbath in 2 Chronicles 36:21," *Proceedings, Eastern Great Lakes and Midwest Biblical Societies* 6 (1986) 96-103; idem, "The Schema of Dynastic Endangerment in Chronicles," *Proceedings, Eastern Great Lakes and Midwest Biblical Societies* 7 (1987) 59-77; idem, "The Forms of Prophetic Address in Chronicles," *Hebrew Annual Review* 10 (1986) 15-36; idem, "Moses and David as Cult-Founders in Chronicles," *JBL* (forthcoming); idem, *Yesterday, Today and Tomorrow* (Grand Rapids: Eerdmans, and London: SPCK, 1975); S. R. Driver, *An Introduction to the Literature of the Old Testament* (8th ed.; New York: Scribner's, 1898); A. B. Ehrlich, *Randglossen zur hebräischen Bibel, textkritisches, sprachliches und sachliches VII* (Leipzig: Hinrichs, 1914) 326-86; O. Eissfeldt, *Einleitung in das Alte Testament* (2nd ed.; Tübingen: Mohr, 1956); A. L. Elmslie, "The First and Second Books of Chronicles. Introduction, Exegesis and Exposition," *IB* III (New York-Nashville: Abingdon, 1954) 341-48; G. Fohrer, *Introduction to the Old Testament* (10th ed.; tr. D. E. Green; Nashville-New York: Abingdon, 1965); D. N. Freedman, "The Chronicler's Purpose," *CBQ* 23 (1961) 436-42; V. French, "The Speeches in Chronicles, A Reply," *Exp* 1 (1895) 140-52; M. Friedländer, *Genealogische Studien zum Alten Testament. I. Die Veränderlichkeit der Namen in den Stammlisten der Bücher der Chronik* (Berlin: M. Poppelauer, 1903); K. Galling, *Chronikbücher* (HAT 21; Tübingen: Mohr, 1955); G. Gerleman, *Studies in the Septuagint. II. Chronicles* (Lund: Gleerup, 1946); H. Gese, "Zur Geschichte der Kultsänger am zweiten Tempel," in *Abraham unser Vater: Juden und Christen im Gespräch über die Bibel (Fest.* O. Michel; ed. O. Betz, M. Hengel, and P. Schmidt; Leiden: Brill, 1963) 222-34; M. Gil, "Israel in the Books of Chronicles" (Hebr.), *BethM* 13 (1968) 105-15; J. Goettsberger, *Die Bücher der Chronik oder Paralipomenon* (HSAT IV/1; Bonn: Hanstein, 1939); J. Goldingay, "The Chronicler as Theologian," *BTB* 5 (1975) 99-126; H. Gressmann, *Die Schriften des Alten Testaments* (2nd ed.; Göttingen: Vandenhoeck & Ruprecht, 1925) II/3; H. H. Grosheide, "De dateering van de boeken der Kronieken," *Gereformeerde Theologisch Tijdschrift* 36 (1935) 170-82; T. D. Hanks, "The Chronicler: Theologian of Grace," *EvQ* 53 (1981) 16-28; R. K. Harrison, *Introduction to the Old Testament* (Grand Rapids: Eerdmans, 1969); W. R. Harvey-Jellie, *Chronicles* (NCB; Edinburgh: Jack, 1906); A. S. Herbert, "I and II Chronicles," in *Peake's Commentary on the Bible* (ed. M. Black and H. H. Rowley; London-Edinburgh: Nelson, 1962); F. von Hummelauer, *Commentarius in librum primum Paralipomenon* (Cursus Scripturae Sacrae; Paris: Lethielleux, 1905); S. Japhet, "Chronicles, Book of," *EncJud* 5 (Jerusalem: Keter, 1971) 517-34; idem, "The Ideology of the Book of Chronicles and Its Place in Biblical Thought" (Hebr.) (Diss., Hebrew University, 1973); idem, "Interchange in Verbal Roots in Parallel Texts in Chronicles" (Hebr.), *Leš* 31 (1966-67) 165-79, 261-79; idem, "The Supposed Common Authorship of Chronicles and Ezra-Nehemiah Investigated

4

Anew," *VT* 18 (1968) 330-71; E. Jenni, "Aus der Literatur zur chronistischen Ge-schichtsschreibung," *TRu* 45/2 (1980) 97-108; W. Johnstone, "Reactivating the Chronicles Analogy in Pentateuchal Studies," *ZAW* 99 (1987) 16-37; O. Kapelrud, *The Question of Authorship in the Ezra-Narrative* (Oslo: Dybwad, 1944); C. F. Keil, *The Books of the Chronicles* (Edinburgh: Clark, 1872); R. Kittel, *Die Bücher der Chronik* (HKAT; Göttingen: Vandenhoeck & Ruprecht, 1902); R. W. Klein, "New Evidence for an old recension in Reigns," *HTR* 60 (1967) 93-105 (response by L. C. Allen in *HTR* 61 [1968] 483-92; rejoinder by Klein in ibid., pp. 92-95); A. Kropat, *Die Syntax des Autors der Chronik verglichen mit der seiner Quellen* (BZAW 16; Giessen: Töpelmann, 1909); J. Lach, "Idea Boga w ksiegach Kronik," *Ruch Biblÿny i Liturgigiczny* 30/1 (1977) 18-26; R. LeDéaut and J. Robert, *Targum des Chroniques (Cod. Vat. urb. Ebr. 1)* (2 vols.; AnBib 51; Rome: Pontifical Biblical Institute, 1971); W. E. Lemke, "The Synoptic Problem in the Chronicler's History," *HTR* 58 (1965) 349-63; idem, "Synoptic Studies in the Chronicler's History" (Diss., Harvard, 1963); J. Liver, *Chapters in the History of the Priests and Levites: Studies in the Lists of Chronicles and Ezra and Nehemiah* (Hebr.) (Jerusalem: Magnes/Hebrew University, 1968); D. Mathias, "Die Geschichte der Chronikforschung im 19. Jahrhundert," *TLZ* 105 (1980) 474-75; F. Michaeli, *Les livres des Chroniques, d'Esdrae et de Néhémie* (Commentaire de l'Ancien Testament 16; Neuchâtel-Paris: Delachaux et Niestlé, 1967); K. Möhlenbrink, "Die leviti-schen Überlieferungen des Alten Testaments," *ZAW* 52 (1934) 184-231; J. A. Montgomery, "A Study in Comparison of the Texts of Kings and Chronicles," *JBL* 50 (1931) 115-16; S.K. Mosiman, *Eine Zusammenstellung und Vergleichung der Paralleltexte der Chronik und der älteren Bücher des Alten Testaments* (Halle: Kämmerer, 1907); R. Mosis, *Untersuchungen zur Theologie des chronistischen Geschichtswerkes* (Freiburger Theologische Studien 92; Freiburg-Basel-Wien: Herder, 1973); S. Mowinckel, "Erwägungen zum chronistischen Ge-schichtswerk," *TLZ* 85 (1960) 1-8; J. M. Myers, *I Chronicles* (AB 12; Garden City: Doubleday, 1965); idem, *II Chronicles* (AB 13; Garden City: Doubleday, 1965); idem, "The Kerygma of the Chronicler: History and Theology in the Service of Religion," *Int* 20 (1966) 259-73; B. Neteler, *Die Bücher der Chronik der Vulgata und des hebräischen Textes über-setzt und erklärt* (Münster i. W.: Theissing, 1899); J. D. Newsome, Jr., "Toward a New Un-derstanding of the Chronicler and His Purposes," *JBL* 94 (1975) 201-17; A. Noordtzij, "Les intentions du Chroniste," *RB* 47 (1940) 161-68; idem, *Kronieken* (Korte Verklaring der Heilige Schrift; Kampen: Kok, 1937-38); R. North, "The Chronicler: 1-2 Chronicles, Ezra, Nehemiah," in *The Jerome Bible Commentary* (ed. R. Brown, et al.; London-Dublin-Mel-bourne: Prentice Hall, 1968) 402-38; idem, *Israel's Chronicle* (Saint Marys, KS: St. Louis University School of Theology, 1963); idem, "Theology of the Chronicler," *JBL* 82 (1963) 369-81; M. Noth, "Das chronistische Werk," in *Überlieferungsgeschichtliche Studien. Die sammelnden und bearbeitenden Geschichtswerke des Alten Testaments* (1st ed.; Halle: Niemeyer, 1943; 2nd ed.; Tübingen: Niemeyer, 1957) 110-80; idem, *Das System der zwölf Stämme Israels* (Darmstadt: Wissenschaftliche Buchgesellschaft, 1966); W. O. E. Oesterley and T. H. Robinson, *An Introduction to the Books of the Old Testament* (New York: Mac-millan, 1946; London: SPCK, 1955); J. Osty and J. Trinquet, *Premier et Deuxième Livre des Chroniques* (Paris: Editions Rencontre, 1970); J. Barton Payne, "The Validity of the Num-bers in Chronicles," *BSac* 542-43 (1979) 109-28, 206-20; D. L. Petersen, *Late Israelite Prophecy: Studies in Deutero-Prophetic Literature and in Chronicles* (SBLMS 23; Mis-soula: Scholars, 1977); R. H. Pfeiffer, *Introduction to the Old Testament* (New York: Har-per, 1948); O. Plöger, "Reden und Gebete im deuteronomistischen und chronistischen Ge-schichtswerk," in *Festschrift für Günther Dehn* (ed. W. Schneemelcher; Neukirchen-Vluyn: Neukirchener, 1957) 35-49 (repr. in *Aus der Spätzeit des Alten Testaments* [Göttingen: Vandenhoeck & Ruprecht, 1971] 50-66); idem, *Theokratie und Eschatologie* (WMANT 2; 2nd ed.; Neukirchen: Neukirchener, 1959) = *Theocracy and Eschatology* (tr. S. Rudman; Richmond: John Knox, 1968); R. Podechard, "Les références du Chroniquer," *RB* 22 (1915) 236-47; K.-F. Pohlmann, *Studien zum dritten Esra. Ein Beitrag zur Frage nach dem ursprünglichen Schluss des chronistischen Geschichtswerkes* (FRLANT 104; Göttingen: Vandenhoeck & Ruprecht, 1970); R. Polzin, *Late Biblical Hebrew: Toward an Historical Typology*of Biblical Hebrew Prose (Missoula: Scholars, 1976); G. von Rad, *Das Geschichtsbild des chronistischen Werkes* (BWANT 3; Stuttgart: Kohlhammer, 1930); L. Randellini, "Il libro delle Cronache nel decennio 1950-1960," *RivB* 10 (1962) 136-55; idem, "Il libro della Cronache," in *La Sacra Biblia-Garofalo* (Turin-Rome: Marietti, 1966); M. Rehm, *Die Bücher der Chronik* (Echter Bibel 8; Würzburg: Echter, 1949); idem, *Textkritische Untersuchungen zu den Parallelstellen der Samuel-Königsbücher und der Chronik* (ATABh 13/3; Münster: Aschendorff, 1937); H. N. Richardson, "The Historical Reliability of Chronicles," *JBR* 26 (1958) 9-12; J. W. Rothstein and J. Hänel, *Das erste Buch der Chronik* (KAT 18/2; Leipzig: Reichart, 1927); K. Roubos, *I en II Kronieken* (2 vols.; De Prediking van het Oude Testament; Nijkerk: Callenbach, 1969, 1972); H. H. Rowley, *The Growth of the Old Testament* (3rd ed.; London: Hutchinson, 1967); W. Rudolph, *Chronikbücher* (HAT 21; Tübingen: Mohr, 1955); idem, "Problems in the Book of Chronicles," *VT* 4 (1954) 401-9; P. N. Schlögl, *Die Bücher der Chronik* (KAT I, 3, 2; Vienna: Mayer, 1911); S. Segert, "Textkritische Erwägungen in Margine des Kommentars zu den Chronikbüchern," *ArOr* 25 (1957) 671-75; J. R. Shaver, "Torah and the Chronicler's History Work" (Diss., Notre Dame, 1983); J. D. Shenkel, "A Comparative Study of the Synoptic Parallels in I Paraleipomenon and I-II Reigns," *HTR* 62 (1969) 63-85; I. W. Slotki, *Chronicles* (SonB; London: Soncino, 1952); R. Smend, *Die Entstehung des Alten Testaments* (2nd ed.; Stuttgart: Kohlhammer, 1981); C. Steuernagel, *Lehrbuch der Einleitung in das Alte Testament* (Tübingen: Mohr, 1912); W. F. Stinespring, "Eschatology in Chronicles," *JBL* 80 (1961) 209-19; M. A. Throntveit, "Linguistic Analysis and the Question of Authorship in Chronicles, Ezra, and Nehemiah," *VT* 32 (1982) 201-16; C. C. Torrey, "The Apparatus for the Textual Criticism of Chronicles-Ezra-Nehemiah," in *Old Testament and Semitic Studies (Fest. W. R. Harper; ed. R. F. Harper, et al.; Chicago: University of Chicago, 1908) 53-112; idem, "The Chronicler as Editor and as Independent Narrator," *AJSL* 24 (1908-1909) 157-73, 188-217; idem, *The Chronicler's History of Israel. Chronicles-Ezra-Nehemiah Restored to its Original Form* (New Haven: Yale, 1954); A. van den Born, *Kronieken uit de grondtekst vertaald en uitgelegd* (BOuT V/1; Roermond/Maaseik: Romen, 1960); P. Vannutelli, *Libri Synoptici Veteris Testamenti seu Librorum Regum et Chronicorum Loci Paralleli, quos Hebraice Graece et Latine Critice Edidit* (2 vols.; Rome: Pontifical Biblical Institute, 1931-34); R. de Vaux, *Ancient Israel, Its Life and Institutions* (tr. J. McHugh; New York-Toronto-London: McGraw-Hill, 1961); L. Waterman, "Some Repercussions from Late Levitical Genealogical Accretions in P and in the Chronicles," *AJSL* 58 (1941) 49-56; W. G. E. Watson, "Archaic Elements in the Language of Chronicles," *Bib* 53 (1972) 191-207; J. Weinberg, "Das Eigengut in den Chronikbüchern," *OLP* 10 (1979) 161-81; idem, "Die Natur im Weltbild des Chronisten," *VT* 31 (1981) 324-45; A. Weiser, *The Old Testament: Its Formation and Development* (tr. D. M. Barton; New York: Association, 1961); A. C. Welch, *Post-Exilic Judaism* (Edinburgh-London: Blackwood, 1935); idem, *The Work of the Chronicler, Its Purpose and Its Date* (London: Oxford, 1939); J. Wellhausen, "Die Chronik," in *Prolegomena zur Geschichte Israels*(3rd ed.; Berlin: Reimer, 1886) 175-235 = "Chronicles," in *Prolegomena to the History of Ancient Israel* (tr. Menzies and Black; repr. Cleveland-New York: World, 1965) 171-227; P. Welten, *Geschichte und Geschichtsdarstellung in den*

Chronikbüchern (WMANT 42; Neukirchen-Vluyn: Neukirchener, 1973); idem, "Lade-Tempel-Jerusalem. Zur Theologie der Chronikbücher," in *Textgemäss: Aufsätze und Beiträge zur Hermeneutik des Alten Testaments (Fest.* E. Würthwein; ed. A. H. J. Gunneweg and O. Kaiser; Göttingen: Vandenhoeck & Ruprecht, 1979) 169-83; W. M. L. de Wette, "Historisch-kritische Untersuchungen über die Bücher der Chronik," in *Beiträge zur Einleitung in das Alten Testament* I (Halle: Schimmelpfenning, 1806-7; Hildesheim-New York: Olms, 1971) 1-132; T. Willi, *Die Chronik als Auslegung. Untersuchungen zur literarischen Gestaltung der historischen Überlieferung Israels* (FRLANT 106; Göttingen: Vandenhoeck & Ruprecht, 1972); H. G. M. Williamson, *1 and 2 Chronicles* (New Century Bible Commentary; Grand Rapids: Eerdmans, and London: Marshall, Morgan and Scott, 1982); idem, "Eschatology in Chronicles," *TynBul* 28 (1977) 115-54; idem, *Israel in the Books of Chronicles* (Cambridge: Cambridge, 1977); R. R. Wilson, *Sociological Approaches to the Old Testament* (Philadelphia: Fortress, 1984); O. Zöckler, *The Books of the Chronicles Theologically and Homiletically Expounded* (New York: Scribner's, Armstrong, 1877).

THE EZRA-NEHEMIAH/CHRONICLES COLLOCATION

Structure

The collocation Ezra-Nehemiah/Chronicles (mentioned in this order because the Hebrew order is judged more original than the opposite order, followed by the LXX and English translations) presents what is the largest narrative block of distinctively postexilic Hebrew. Not everything here is, to be sure, of postexilic origin; we have only to think of the long stretches of narrative copied more or less exactly in ChrH's extracts from Samuel-Kings. On the other hand, there exist significant postexilic supplements in major preexilic compositions such as the Pentateuch (complete with P) and the various collections of prophetic literature. Beside this, there is much psalmodic material, the bulk of the wisdom books (Proverbs, Ecclesiastes), Esther, and the Hebrew sections of Daniel. In any event, the large bulk of narrative material in the above-mentioned collocation has drawn the interest of biblical scholars, particularly because so much of ChrH's own material alternates and intertwines with parallel narration borrowed from Samuel-Kings. Ezra-Nehemiah is naturally studied alongside 1-2 Chronicles because it seems to continue Israel's story where 2 Chronicles leaves off—at the end of the exile; also because it shares 1-2 Chronicles' concern for the temple, the priestly-Levitical clergy, the religious festivals, and the administration of the city of Jerusalem.

It is not surprising that special study has been given to the vocabulary, syntax, and ideology of "the Chronicler"—meaning the author mainly responsible for 1-2 Chronicles, identical with the final editor of Ezra-Nehemiah. In 1909 A. Kropat published his monograph *(Die Syntax)*. It was possible for S. R. Driver to use this study in his *Intro.* (rev. ed.; New York: Scribner's, 1913), 475, 506-7, 535-40; and so also Curtis and Madsen (ICC, 1910), 27-36. Watson ("Archaic Elements") has recently taken up the subject from a fresh point of view, searching for elements of "archaic" Hebrew in the midst of this admittedly postexilic literary complex.

Critical scholars since J. Wellhausen (1886) have been influenced toward a late date for 1-2 Chronicles because of the certitude that it had been composed by the editor of Ezra-Nehemiah, and he of course would have to be dated after the Persian king mentioned in that book, Artaxerxes I or possibly Artaxerxes II, ca. 397 B.C. Thus among the *Intros.*: J. A. Bewer (pp. 282ff.), before 300; S. R. Driver (rev. ed., pp. 516ff.), after 333; O. Eissfeldt (2nd ed., pp. 654ff.), ca. 350, with redaction ca. 190; G. Fohrer (10th ed., pp. 238ff.), 300; R. H. Pfeiffer (pp. 782ff.), 300-350; A. Weiser (pp. 323ff.), 300. Two conservative writers, G. Aalders (pp. 398ff.) and R. K. Harrison (pp. 1152ff.), have defended a date of 400. B. S. Childs (*Intro.*, 639ff.), cautious of the connection with Ezra-Nehemiah, is noncommittal. Some of the important articles and monographs have adopted a date for 1-2 Chronicles, and these range from 529-515 for Newsome (1975), to a definite 515 date for Freedman (1961), 400-350 for Albright (1921), the 4th century for Williamson (1977), 300-250 for Welten (1973), down to 200 for Noth (1943). It should be pointed out that neither the Newsome nor the Noth studies—occupying opposite ends of the chronological scale—accepts a common authorship for 1-2 Chronicles on the one hand and Ezra-Nehemiah on the other. Braun (VTSup) has written another important article denying the connection. To complete the picture, we add these dates as adopted by the leading comms.: Elmslie, Myers, 400; Ackroyd, Coggins, 350; Williamson, 350-325; Rudolph, 325-300; Michaeli, 330-250; Bennett, 300-250; Galling, 300-200; Curtis and Madsen, 300; Gressmann, 200.

Dating is not the only consequence of ascribing 1-2 Chronicles and Ezra-Nehemiah to a common authorship. Several scholars have extrapolated from the Nehemiah-Sanballat struggle a designedly self-coherent, anti-Samaritan polemic as a major theme in 1-2 Chronicles. So, among the *Intros.*, Bewer and Pfeiffer; among the monographs, Noth; and among the comms., Galling and Rudolph. Smend's *Intro.* is undecided. Voting a definite "no" on this issue are Welten's and Williamson's monographs and the comms. of Coggins and Williamson. The theoretical groundwork for this position is found in Coggins, *Samaritans and Jews*. However late 1-2 Chronicles, or 1-2 Chronicles together with Ezra-Nehemiah, need to be dated, the Samaritan separation can no longer be simplemindedly joined to Nehemiah-Sanballat or to any supposed polemic in 1-2 Chronicles. It is a rather obscure historical problem that must be solved in complete isolation from the literary problems surrounding 1-2 Chronicles and Ezra-Nehemiah.

We speak of a "collocation," which means that these two literary complexes have been more or less accidentally drawn together, without any organic interconnection, unifying literary design, or common authorship. It is not suitable to think of a closely knit school (cf. Dtr) either. Most of the linguistic, and even ideological, similarities may simply attest to the jointly shared literary and cultural complex of the early postexilic period out of which both corpora apparently come—a product both of the time and of the narrow confines of the Jerusalem/Judean enclave. It is quite obvious that no diaspora Jews, or even Palestinian Jews living outside the geographical region immediately surrounding Jerusalem, had a hand in composing either 1-2 Chronicles or Ezra-Nehemiah.

As has been shown, even some very recent studies have maintained the Chronicles-Ezra/Nehemiah connection, yet those who have followed the discussion realize that the past two decades have brought the weight of scholarship in favor of separation. Three scholars in particular have been responsible for this change of course. These are: S. Japhet ("Supposed Common Authorship"; "Ideology"), H. G. M. Williamson, and R. Braun (→ Bibliography). Each in his or her own way has begun to sap the foundations of the widely accepted common-authorship theory.

The main arguments for this theory have been the following. First, 2 Chr 36:22-23 ends the 1–2 Chronicles complex with words almost identical to the words with which Ezra begins (1:1-3). This is interpreted as a common author's device (wooden, but not too wooden for ChrH) for joining an account of preexilic history in 1–2 Chronicles to an account of postexilic history in Ezra-Nehemiah. This theory creates difficulty for explaining the (almost certainly original) precedence of Ezra-Nehemiah to 1–2 Chronicles in the Hebrew text; the LXX reversal of order may in fact be an attempt to erase this difficulty. One small point makes the Chronicles version look like a gloss, borrowed from Ezra and tacked on to the end of Chronicles' sad account of Judah's deportation. Ezra 1:3 makes Cyrus's edict express a wish, or perhaps a granting of permission: "Whoever there is of you, from his entire people, may *[yĕhî]* his god be with him, and let him go up!" Ezra expands this as an appropriate introduction to his ensuing narrative. The original text of Chronicles, on the other hand, has a form of the verb "to be" confessing firm belief in an established theocracy. Rather than merely hoping for a restoration, this text affirms God's being with his people as a certain and accomplished fact. This is not clear from the MT, which reads the Tetragrammaton, taking it as the subject of an independent noun clause. It is the LXX that has the original recasting of Ezra's jussive. Apart from a few MSS that show normalization to the Ezra reading, it reads "is/will be" in the verbal form, *yihyeh.* Its final *h* is confirmed by Chr MT "YHWH." This emphatic indicative has to be later than Ezra's jussive, without the *h.* It expresses the conviction of a pious glossator living later than the restoration period of Ezra, and certainly much later than the time of the historical Cyrus. In any event, it is implausible to try to explain the Chronicles gloss, with its indicative, as a functional literary connection forward to Ezra's historically oriented account containing Cyrus's meaningful jussive.

Another consideration that some have advanced in favor of unity of authorship is the rather disconcerting fact that a rival Greek text of Ezra-Nehemiah known as *1 Esdras* (Gk. *Esdras A'*) begins with a somewhat modified parallel to 2 Chronicles 35–36. Pohlmann has reasoned that both 1–2 Chronicles — reproduced the more accurately here in *Paraleipomenōn* (LXX)—and Greek Ezra-Nehemiah (= *Esdras B'*) are produced from this rival Greek document, which in turn shows a literary continuity from Chronicles to Ezra-Nehemiah. This view has been severely criticized by Williamson (*Israel,* and now in his comm.). Three things argue against any original interconnection between Chronicles, Ezra-Nehemiah, and *1 Esdras:* (1) *1 Esdras* tends to be highly paraphrastic even in those sections where the canonical books are somewhat fully reproduced; (2) it adds fanciful material such as the legend of Zerubbabel; and (3) it is eclectic, taking only 2 Chronicles 35–36 at the beginning and, at the end, choosing only ch. 8 out of the entire book of Nehemiah. The origin of the separate entrances of these three corpora into the LXX is another point. Chronicles and Ezra-Nehemiah already existed in their individual Hebrew *Vorlages,* and *1 Esdras* existed, probably in Hebrew, as a derivative from them.

What now is to be said of the linguistic evidence? Alongside the work of Japhet and Williamson, we must take careful note of studies by R. Polzin and M. A. Throntveit. These scholars have not been uncritical of one another, but they do seem to be producing a consensus. Working with morphology, grammar, and style, Japhet has shown a number of impressive items in which it would have been impossible for a single author to have composed Chronicles and Ezra-Nehemiah. Turning his attention to the lists in Driver and Curtis and Madsen, Williamson has argued that most of the individual items listed are common to late biblical Hebrew generally and, while characteristic of Chronicles and to a less extent of Ezra-Nehemiah, cannot support a common authorship for the two individual corpora. Polzin's contribution has been to show that both these corpora display a vital, living language rather than the artificial, archaizing Hebrew of Esther and Daniel. Polzin does not intend this as proof that Chronicles and Ezra-Nehemiah are from the same author, nor is this the opinion of Throntveit, who agrees that, in spite of all uncertainties, the weight of evidence is strongly against it.

Genre and Setting

By way of the Vulgate, Eng. 1–2 Chronicles falls midway between 1–2 Kings and Ezra-Nehemiah, thus following the LXX arrangement. With Esther, this completes the section of our OT known as "History." The creators of the LXX, the Bible of the early church, clearly intended 1–2 Chronicles to be read as a parallel or variant version of the history in 1–2 Kings, with Ezra-Nehemiah as its narrative (and historical) continuation. This is, to be sure, the arrangement demanded by the natural sequence of the events recorded: 1–2 Chronicles is preexilic, Ezra-Nehemiah is postexilic. This gives us no assurance, however, that the LXX translators found these respective corpora in this sequence, or that they were actually joined in any way prior to translation. We do have to account for the fact that the MT has the opposite order, with Ezra-Nehemiah following Daniel, and 1–2 Chronicles following Ezra-Nehemiah. A popular misconception regarding the canon-forming process supposes that the LXX order is original and that for some reason, perhaps ideological (cf. H. Cazelles in his review of Williamson's comm., *VT* 29 [1979] 379-80), the two were shifted in the developing Hebrew Bible. We do not know why Chronicles came to be placed at the end, but we can agree with Williamson in his claim (comm., 5) that "canonization [is] never a selective act, but rather a declaration of a work's inherent authority, already recognized by the religious community over a considerable period of time" (see also T. Willi, 180-81). Both Ezra-Nehemiah and Chronicles are implicitly granted this status in their translation into Greek. What happened prior to that we do not know. Having in all probability been composed earlier, Ezra-Nehemiah came earlier into "canonical" recognition. Chronicles was composed later and canonized later. The fact that it seemed to rival 1–2 Kings was perhaps an inhibiting factor in the process.

Taking the Hebrew corpus as the direct object of our study, we see that, more than for the Greek corpus, 1–2 Chronicles along with Ezra-Nehemiah deserve no more specific description than the one we have given: collocation. They stand together in the biblical text for no better reason than that they belong together in the same general historical period—being joined the most firmly at the artificial seam between the end of Chronicles and the beginning of Ezra. Both works reflect the culture and theology of postexilic Judaism (and that in spite of the fact that Chronicles' history is about the preexilic period). Little more can be said in comparing them. Little can be gained from Ezra-Nehemiah for an understanding of

Chronicles, although most definitely we must take into account for this under-standing the events recorded in Ezra-Nehemiah. Were we to pass this by, we would have virtually nothing to guide us in comprehending the peculiar and sometimes seemingly outrageous way in which Chronicles has manipulated the earlier history that it is now retelling. The ruling Persians and Greeks have left precious little record. Scripture outside these books is only tangentially suggestive. So the col-location is a good place to begin, even if a very poor place to end.

Intention

For the overwhelming majority who still hold that Chronicles and Ezra-Nehemiah are one work, it makes sense to look for clues to the intention of the collocation as a whole. This holds true also if we are thinking of two separate works by the same author, in which case Chronicles must be seen as an appendix to Ezra-Nehemiah, or Ezra-Nehemiah to Chronicles, depending on whose canonical arrangement we follow. Because our previous argument has made a search for intention on these terms extremely hypothetical, it is aimless to offer elaborate expositions; yet a sum-mary sketch is demanded out of fairness for the scholars whose views we oppose. There are three essential aims according to these writers: (1) to establish the post-exilic cultus on a solid theocratic basis; (2) to illustrate that divine retribution is meted out on the basis of one's personal failings and present willingness to repent; and (3) to display God's grand design amid all the twistings and turnings of Israel's history. Among the writings previously listed as advocates of the single author theory, the *Intros.* of Bewer, Pfeiffer, and Weiser make strong pleas for all three themes, and most of the others occupy themselves with one or two of them. We have seen that all the comms. except Williamson's are single-author advocates; Williamson expounds all three themes on the basis of 1–2 Chronicles alone, but Ackroyd, Bennett, Michaeli, and Rudolph are likewise concerned with all three, and all the others pay attention to one or two of them.

This is not the place in this special kind of commentary to discuss these three prominent themes. This must come when we discuss the "intention" of "the original version of Chronicles"—a separate subsection to follow. Williamson is not alone in interpreting them as belonging to Chronicles in its own right; an examination of the single-author treatments reveals that most do in fact take most of their material from Chronicles and not from Ezra-Nehemiah. For an exposition of the "intention" of that work, see *Ezra, Nehemiah* in this series (FOTL XII).

Since we cannot accept the view that Chronicles and Ezra-Nehemiah are a single work, or are even by a single author, and since the historical and canonical relationships between the two corpora remain uncertain, it is aimless to pick out items that the two have in common, such as their mutual emphasis on the theocracy and the priesthood, as constituting a joint program. They may have been shared very widely by the postexilic community. The glossator of 2 Chr 36:22-23, whose addition does express a unifying purpose, provides the clue to the intention of this collocation as a whole. According to the LXX order, his intention was to under-score the importance of Cyrus's decree, through virtual word-for-word repetition, for ending Israel's time of wrath (2 Chr 36:20-21) and for introducing a restoration in which Yahweh was once more employing kings for his people's salvation. The repetition seems clumsy and unimaginative, another good reason for accepting the

11

MT's order—with the gloss at the very end. In this arrangement, Cyrus's decree stands at the very beginning, ushering in the age of restoration, and also at the very end. This interferes with our comprehension of ChrH's view of postexilic history, which seems now to be beginning anew. The clue for understanding may be the rival *yĕhî* in Ezra and *yihyeh* (LXX *Vorlage*) in Chronicles: "may be" versus "is" or "will be" (see above). ChrH writes later than the events recorded in Ezra-Nehemiah. He recognizes that the restoration has come, yet the theocracy as he idealizes it is missing. As in Daniel 9, an imperfect age of restoration may have to be passed over as irrelevant. To ChrH, the years of Ezra and Nehemiah may be as unreal and incomplete as the years of the kings of Judah. The man who placed the gloss at the end of his book affirms that, according to history as ChrH has rewritten it, what Ezra and Nehemiah tried to do has come to reality, and that now truly "God is with" his people.

THE REDACTED VERSION OF CHRONICLES

Structure

The next most meaningful structural entity is Chronicles as we have it in our biblical text: 1–2 Chronicles. The separation into two books has no structural significance and has been done purely for convenience in handling. One must realize, however, that we are not now speaking about 1–2 Chronicles as it appears in any particular publication of the Bible—not even in the MT. The reason is that the MT has numerous mistakes and corruptions, and the scholar seeks to restore a probable original with the aid of 1–2 Samuel, 1–2 Kings, and all the ancient VSS—particularly the LXX. Yet this task is not so difficult as to leave us in a complete quandary over the structure of the redacted book of Chronicles. The point is that this hypothetically restored redactional version is structurally (and ideologically) without significance on its own. The redactional additions are like the flesh on a human body, revealing no other form than the outline of the bony skeleton beneath.

Various scholars working on 1–2 Chronicles have had widely disparate perceptions of just how much is flesh and how much is skeleton. Some do not discuss the problem at all and give the impression that they consider the book a unity. The following writers admit to only minimal supplements: Bennett, van den Born, Elmslie, Fohrer, Michaeli, Pfeiffer, and Weiser. Bewer and Harrison are unclear. Answering the question of secondary additions in the affirmative, but remaining unspecific about the nature and extent of these additions are: Aalders, Gressmann, Noth, Oesterley and Robinson, von Rad, Rowley, Smend, Steuernagel, and Welch. More specific are Curtis and Madsen, Myers, and Williamson, who stress that the additions are minor in proportion to the whole, and Galling and Rudolph, who attribute extensive materials to secondary writers.

Often several scholars agree on the identification of secondary passages, but it seems that the more secondary material a particular writer claims to see, the less chance he has to find others that agree with him. Galling and Rudolph, who have assigned long sections to supplementers, often fail to agree, and one will insist that what the other calls secondary is original. Many scholars seem inclined to amputate the genealogical section, 1 Chronicles 1–9. But this is a cheap surrender. These chapters are sacrificed because the scholar does not understand their purpose or the intent of their connection to the following book of narratives. Closely scrutinized, they show the same "Chronicles" linguistic traits, and their striking absorption with the Levites and the house of David is shared by the entire book. To make any headway, one must be ready to recognize (1) that the Chronicler as historian and redactor aims to amalgamate numerous contending ideas from his circle, and (2) that his original composition did attract secondary accretions, though not nearly so many as some have contended and generally with some specific purpose and distinctive point of view. Wary of erasing seemingly erratic but designedly intended items, our own critical scrutiny ought always to be based as much as possible on (1) linguistic incongruities and (2) inconcinnities in the structure of the text. Form criticism proves to be a big help, even when not presented in studies specifically dedicated to that approach.

The recent comm. of Williamson proves to be especially perceptive regarding form, and at the same time quite convincing in its identification of secondary items. The present commentary can often agree with it because it faithfully follows the rules of interpretation outlined above. We too see a variety of minor glosses (explicative or propagandistic notes, usually short) and a restricted number of real literary expansions, i.e., such as quite shatter the structure of the underlying text and have a significant structure of their own.

Here is a list of post-ChrH glosses: 1 Chr 5:6a-bβ; 16:5bα, 38b, 42b; 18:8b; 21:3aβ, 5bβ, 12aβ; 2 Chr 1:4; 8:14a; 11:14a; 15:1a; 25:24aα. They are casual and add nothing to a special profile for a redacted Chronicles.

The substantive expansions ought to be identified here, as well as listed, in order to give the reader a clear idea of what kinds of material were inserted:

1 Chr 2:34-41	Lineage of Sheshan
2:42-50aα	Genealogy of Caleb
2:52-55	Further Judahite genealogies
6:35-38	Genealogy of Aaron
15:23-24	Additional clergy
23:24b-32	Levitical job descriptions
24:1-19	Sons of Aaron
24:20-31	Expanded list of chief Levites
25:7-31	Rota of musicians
26:4-8	Obed-edomite gatekeepers
26:12-18	Merarite table of organization
27:1-34	Officers of the people
2 Chr 24:5b-6	Levite laxness
29:25	Levite authority
34:6-9, 11-16	Parallel Passover narrative

Setting and Intention

The very late editorial gloss at 2 Chr 36:22-23 does not belong on this list because it was added to the redacted version as we are discussing it. There is other editorial work to be seen, but it belongs to Chronicles and forms part of the Chronicler's original work. The foregoing list, then, gives the original book its redacted new structure. One sees that each bone of the skeleton remains in place and fulfills its original function. It is only a superficial change in appearance that these redactional expansions provide. Not always do they fit comfortably in their context; indeed, they tend to increase the difficulty of understanding the structure, and therefore the message, of the specific context in question. They tend to create more disharmony than harmony. It is plain that we can claim for them no exegetical or midrashic function. What then are they up to? Scanning them carefully, we can see that they converge around one of three identifiable *topoi:* (1) Judah and the Judahites; (2) the duties and prerogatives of the various orders of clergy; and (3) the Passover ritual. One suspects conflict. Because of the great prestige of the Davidic kingship, overlooked clans struggled for recognition. Because of a constant struggle to gain a higher dignity in the clerical orders, Levites, musicians, gatekeepers, and Aaronite priests listed new privileges and new responsibilities. Because the Passover was being transformed from a family ritual into a great temple festival, other ways arose of telling of its observance. Linguistic evidence is insufficient to tell us whether one, or a few, or many, wrote the above expansions. We cannot even say whether a single redactor put them in position. The redactor or redactors did seek out the most appropriate locus for each—that is clear—thus creating a smooth transition from one item to another. Maximum inclusiveness rather than greater harmony and lucidity was, nevertheless, their obvious goal.

THE ORIGINAL VERSION OF CHRONICLES

Structure

I. The genealogical materials: Ideal Israel's
   table of organization   1 Chr 1:1–9:34

II. The narrative framework: the history of Ideal
   Israel's completing its land's sabbaths   1 Chr 9:35–2 Chr 36:21

As has been mentioned, a number of critics have been inclined to relegate the genealogical section in 1 Chronicles to the status of secondary expansion. Apart from a few isolated birth and conquest stories, it contains no narrative whatever, so what is its organic connection, if any, with the lengthy, complex, organically constructed narrative that follows upon it? That narrative is, unmistakably, the core of the work. It could quite readily stand by itself, for it has a clearly marked theme beginning with the death of Saul and reaching to the exile of Judah under Nebuchadrezzar. But the genealogical introduction needs the narrative, for it has no meaning in itself.

Interpreters have puzzled over why the narrative begins just with Saul's death. Why not at least offer a synopsis of Saul's kingship, which could be obtained as readily from the Samuel *Vorlage* as the story of his death and the history of David? Furthermore, why does Chronicles ignore the abundant narratives concerning Israel's becoming Yahweh's people and taking possession of the land—the Pentateuch with JEDP, plus Joshua and Judges? The question is, in fact, the answer. The genealogical materials at the beginning stand for—substitute for—that narration in the intent of this particular writer. Not substitute in the sense of ignoring or rejecting, but in the sense of retelling and interpreting, just as with the histories of the kings borrowed from Samuel and Kings.

The best clue to the interrelationship between these two sections of Chronicles is the redactional summation at 1 Chr 9:1a, "So all Israel was enrolled by genealogies, and these are written in the Book of the Kings of Israel." The Chronicler means that, according to his lists, "all Israel" is now complete. But he proceeds in the remainder of ch. 9 to give us new lists—those of laymen and various orders of clergy who survived the Babylonian exile (v. 1b) and are now dwelling in the land once again. This is the postexilic community, and this is the "all Israel" that has been enrolled according to 1 Chronicles 1–8. Now the story of Saul's death may be told, with all the history that follows it. The logic of this structure seems to be: to tell first who Israel is, and then to tell what happened to it.

Genre

We will discover, as we proceed to scrutinize each individual pericope, that 1–2 Chronicles is rich in genres, subgenres, and genre elements. It would be pointless to anticipate these at this early stage of our study, but it is necessary to discuss the genre of the book and of its two major parts. The adjective "genealogical," as applied to Part I, is intended as a descriptive term, not as a genre. What is meant is that this section contains practically nothing else but genealogical information. Scholars like M. D. Johnson (*The Purpose of the Biblical Genealogies* [SNTSMS 8; Cambridge: Cambridge, 1969]) and R. R. Wilson (*Genealogy and History in the Biblical World* [New Haven: Yale, 1977]) have taught us to distinguish between the genre GENEALOGY and related forms, as well as between different types or subgenres of this genre. Looking at Part I as a whole, then, we may identify the source material belonging to this section as deriving from isolated LISTS. But the lists are not there for their own sake. That is what they were when they existed merely as source material — official records. Compounded together, they resemble a real genre that actually occurs within the book (1 Chr 23:3-24; 26:12-18), the (→) TABLE OF ORGANIZATION. 1 Chronicles 1–9 wish to tell us how Israel is organized —and thereby who and what it is.

We have called the second part of 1–2 Chronicles "narrative," but that cannot be its genre name. What is distinctive about narrative? As lists and other kinds of administrative records communicate facts or items, narrative communicates events. There are many kinds of narrative: some speak of historical events and others speak of imaginary events (G. W. Coats, "Introduction to Narrative Literature," in *Genesis; with an Introduction to Narrative Literature* [FOTL I; Grand Rapids: Eerdmans, 1983] 1-10). After 1 Chronicles 9, most (but not all) of the text is filled with narration. What kind of narration it is depends on whether the events recorded are historical. (When we say "historical," we mean in the writer's intention and not necessarily in objective historical occurrence.) To the extent that scholars are willing to accredit ChrH's source material as historical, a level of authentic historicity has been ascribed to his writings. This in no way alters the fact that his sources were "history," which, reproduced in his own way, makes his own composition "history" as well. However, ChrH often departs from his sources. When he does this, his tendency is to interject material laudatory to the Levites, to exaggerate the magnificence of Israel, or to magnify the element of the supernatural. This has led a number of scholars to define the book as "midrash," but the only thing 1–2 Chronicles has in common with the midrash we know from rabbinic literature is a tendency toward haggadic exaggeration. There is a genre MIDRASH in texts from ChrH, which we intend to discuss thoroughly in connection with our exposition of 1 Chr 5:1ff., but it is altogether inappropriate as a genre name for the book as a whole. (See also Willi, 54-55; but Willi errs in describing Chronicles as nothing more than an ongoing "exegesis" of pre-given biblical documents in the style of rabbinic Mishna.)

No less than Samuel-Kings, Chronicles deserves the genre name HISTORY (see B. O. Long, "Introduction to Historical Literature," in *1 Kings; with an Introduction to Historical Literature* [FOTL IX; Grand Rapids: Eerdmans, 1984] 1-10). The reader of 1–2 Chronicles may ponder how well this late biblical book fits Long's definition of HISTORY (p. 250):

> An extensive, continuous, written composition made up of and based upon various materials, some originally traditional and oral, others written, and devoted to a particular subject or historical period. The author of history links together his materials and unifies the whole by imposing overarching structural and thematic connections. History is dominated by a concern with chronology and cause-effect relationships; it seeks to place events and how they occurred within a framework of interpretation and in relation to the author's own time. For purposes of literary definition, it is not important whether, from our modern point of view, the events actually occurred as reported. . . . Writers of history intended to document, reflect on, and organize the past in order to understand, legitimate, or define in some way the institutional and social reality of their own time.

In this commentary, we will be continually using the symbol ChrH (= the Chronicler as historian) with the understanding that what he was writing was HISTORY. (Wherever he is redacting source materials, as in the genealogical section, the symbol will be ChrR [= the Chronicler as redactor], even though the writer be the same person.) In a certain sense, ChrR is ChrH because what is being redacted is source material for the history. The expectation is that this distinction between two separate literary procedures may be helpful for understanding the structure and intent of the whole.

Setting

The setting of ChrH must not be confused with the setting or settings of its source materials, canonical or otherwise. (ChrH's biblical sources, particularly the DtrH in Samuel-Kings, are evaluated in the books of this series that deal with them directly.) As an example, Nathan's promise to David in 2 Samuel 7 does not have the same setting (or intent) as the same promise in 1 Chronicles 17. Likewise, it must be stated that each of the expansions that make up the redacted version of Chronicles (see above) has a setting different from that of the original ChrH.

We need a date, but, after all the facts are evaluated, we can give only an approximate one, the 4th century B.C. This is the late Persian period and the beginning of the Hellenistic. Chronicles shows no awareness of the international upheavals accompanying the rise of the Achaemenids ca. 500 or those that characterized the third-century struggle between the Ptolemies and the Seleucids. Noth and Gressmann have dated the final redaction ca. 200, but mainly for ideological reasons. Welten *(Geschichte)* identifies Hellenistic military practices in parts of ChrH, but the dating he chooses is disputed. The chronology of Ezra-Nehemiah might determine an absolute date for the Chronicles except that a whole century (500-400 B.C.) is all that we can claim for the former. That ca. 400 is the *terminus a quo* for Chronicles is seen from three facts in particular: (1) as compared with relative harmony and simplicity in Ezra-Nehemiah, affairs of the clergy are strikingly complex and controversial in Chronicles; this is precisely what the historian would expect of a highly authoritarian religious system finding its way out of the groping naiveté of the period immediately after the return; (2) in Neh 8:1ff. Ezra brings the book of the law of Moses in codified form to read to the people, as though this were a novel—perhaps unprecedented—event, but Chronicles' references to "Moses" or "the law of Moses" or "the book of the law of Moses" imply laconically that this same book has always been at hand, authoritative to settle any conflict (so except in the Josiah story copied from 2 Kings, 2 Chronicles 34); (3) the strong move to ethnic purity in Ezra-Nehemiah, understandable as a restoration program, is completely nullified in Chronicles' effort to unify "all Israel" about the Jerusalem cultus, not excluding loyal adherents of the northern tribes who at that period happened to be citizens of the province of Samaria. From our meager sources we know that the 4th century was a time of growing cosmopolitanization, for Palestinian as well as for diaspora Judaism. Greater ethnic self-awareness and a more intense torah-righteousness appeared only toward the end of the 3rd century, with the rise of apocalypticism and the religious parties.

The wars of the Persians, the conquest of Alexander, and the wars of the Diadochi apparently did little to disturb the tiny subprovince of Judea, so that the 4th century was for them a time of tranquility and relative security. Life was frugal but stable. The surrounding peoples, by and large, no longer threatened. An exception was the kingdom of the Idumeans lying to the south and usurping a large segment of territory formerly belonging to the kingdom of Judah. Repeated references in ChrH to "Edom," "Mount Seir," and the "Meunites" suggest that this people was still a menace, a condition that persisted down to the Hasmoneans and Herod.

Intention

Why was ChrH written? What is it trying to say? A problem that comes immediately to mind is why it was needed alongside the clearly authoritative DtrH/Samuel-Kings. In copying or paraphrasing—yet often ignoring—large sections of that work, ChrH shows that the work was determinative for the sequence of Israel's preexilic narrative. He is not actually attempting to correct or improve DtrH, as some writers have suggested, nor—*contra* Willi—is he trying to exegete it. Two things we notice about ChrH's way of telling his story of the preexilic kingdom: (1) he seizes every opportunity to interject a direct supernatural message, whether of warning or of encouragement, and this is usually delivered by a prophet (cf. Petersen, *Late Israelite Prophecy;* S. J. De Vries, "Prophetic Address") in the form of what von Rad calls the "Levitical Sermon"; (2) the preexilic history has been made into a framework for presenting and arranging the entire cultic establishment:

17

"Israel" is now the worshiping congregation *(qāhāl);* the ark, temple site, and temple are put in place according to the Samuel-Kings sequence; the priests, Levites, and other orders receive their directions; and—finally—the festivals are ordained as if for eternity. It is fair to say, then, that while DtrH is *Israel's* history, ChrH is intended as *God's* history. Also, it is clear that ChrH is writing the story not of a nation but of a congregation.

In reaching these distinctions, we acknowledge indebtedness to G. von Rad's imposing monograph *(Das Geschichtsbild des chronistischen Werkes).* Von Rad has helped us see that there really are alternative ways of telling history. We could call the DtrH way the way of *Heilsgeschichte*—historical events revealing God's intent through the events themselves. There is also the apocalyptic way, which in effect ignores historical event in order to state God's final, overarching plan in history. There is also this middle way, seized upon by ChrH—telling Israel's history as it should have been or as it may yet be.

The exiles have now returned and have passed through the experimental period of the restoration. It has survived; Israel is still there. Like the God whom it worships, it is undying. But now its adherents are crowded into a tiny enclave. It has no king of its own. It is completely at the mercy of powerful international governments. How can it survive? What is its destiny? Israel is not yet ready for apocalyptic, the theology of historical despair. But it must know who it is. As has been stated, it has no kings (ChrH has no structural place for the office of kingship) even though ChrH affirms a continuity with the ideal of kingship under the theme of the Davidic promise. In spite of a sense of continuity with preexilic Israel, that is only a type of what Israel may now be.

Two things are certain: (1) ChrH's Israel does not consist of sects and parties *(contra* Plöger), for as Williamson *(Israel)* has clearly shown, it is an "all Israel" that aims at nothing less than complete inclusiveness; (2) ChrH's Israel is no conglomeration of pious individualists, but a holy congregation joined in joyful worship.

ChrH helps Israel say who and what it is by retelling the story of its national period as a *warning* and as a *promise.* Its God has not changed and it has not changed. Now we can understand why it begins with a lengthy section of genealogies. I have given this the title "Ideal Israel in the making." ChrH does not need to retell the pentateuchal narrative, for that has already been told. Rather, it gathers together the names of tribes and families to show that *Israel is now and ever will be complete.* The tribes are there; the Davidic tribe and family, symbol of the everlasting kingdom of God, are there; the clerical families are there. "So all Israel was enrolled by genealogies" (1 Chr 9:1a).

In the long narrative section of ChrH a cyclical rather than sequential arrangement prevails. Since ChrH is following the DtrH story throughout, the cyclical model is scarcely suspected to the very end, where, having reported the fact of Nebuchadnezzar's deportation and the exile "until the establishment of the kingdom of Persia" (2 Chr 36:20), ChrH interprets this punishment as the fulfillment of Jeremiah's prophecy (Jer 25:11-12; 29:10; cf. Zech 1:12; Dan 9:2, 24-27): "To fulfill the word of Yahweh by the mouth of Jeremiah, until the land had enjoyed its sabbaths. All the days that it lay desolate it kept sabbath, to fulfill seventy years" (2 Chr 36:21). The convention in effect here is to call a period of seventy years a "sabbath" by multiplying seven, the figure of absolute holiness, with the figure ten, the figure of absolute completeness. Years are the typological equivalent of weeks (cf. Leviticus 25, with its "sabbatical years" and its seven seven's introducing the jubilee and the restoration). We must not overlook the plur. "sabbaths" in ChrH's explanation. He says specifically that all the days of the exile fulfilled Jeremiah's seventy years, but that in doing so the desolate land was "sabbathing" *(šābātâ)*. That he is here thinking of Lev 25:2-8 is clear from the foregoing statement that the exile lasted "until the land enjoyed *[rāṣĕtâ]* its sabbaths," for it is only there that one reads of the plurality of "sabbaths" for the land. This seventy years until Cyrus equals a "sabbath" on the 7 × 10 model. But it does not stand alone: it brings to culmination a sequence of "sabbaths" prevailing until *('ad)* the land shall have fully enjoyed (i.e., gotten full benefit and restoration from) them. The only explanation that makes sense from this arcane symbolic language must be that the Babylonian exile is only the end and culmination of a long sequence of "sabbaths," leading, according to the jubilee-year pattern, and according to Daniel 9's pattern of 7 × 70 years = 490 years, to the final "sabbath" of the exile. ChrH sees the entire foregoing history from Saul to Zedekiah as a struggle of the sacred land to "enjoy" its sabbaths realized now in the final "sabbath" of the exile. If we give Saul 2 years, David 40 years, Solomon 40 years, Rehoboam to Ahaziah 90 years, Ahaziah to Samaria's fall 119 years, Samaria's exile to Jerusalem's first deportation 125 years, then 72 more years to Cambyses, when the first return most probably occurred, we reach a figure of 488 years. Variables are, of course, that the return may be reckoned in Cyrus's first year, 539; that Jeremiah's seventy years may be reckoned from the second deportation, 587; uncertainty whether account might be taken for accession-year variations, New Year dates, or coregencies; finally, whether ChrH would have been counting from the beginning of Saul's reign, ca. 1013, or its end, ca. 1011. The above figures are scientific figures (cf. S. J. De Vries, "Chronology of the Old Testament," *IDB* I:580-99), and there is no way of knowing whether ChrH had access to a scientific chronology. Anyway, the final figure is approximate, and by simply following the biblical figures, ChrH could have come close to his 490 years.

It remains a question whether ChrH was in fact thinking in terms of precise chronological dating. Knowing his adeptness at adducing fitting typologies, we should allow for the possibility that he was thinking of the numerous apostasies of the Judahite kings as "sabbaths"—times of desolation, growing worse and worse up to this final one. The wording of Lev 26:34-35, 41, 43, which ChrH alludes to here, identifies the time of the land's "sabbathing" (= *kol-yĕmê hoššāmâ*, "all the days/years of desolation") as the time when it also "enjoyed" or "received recompense for" the totality of its "sabbaths" (cf. Isa. 40:2), i.e., the times when the land had been abused rather than restored through the apostasies of its kings. 2 Chr 36:21 intimates that the period of "sabbathing," ruined and desolated through apostasy, has now run full circle. Ideal Israel is ready to enter into the perfect rest that its God has designed for it. No matter the sins of the past; retribution has been dealt out to people as well as to kings (cf. S. J. De Vries, "Land's Sabbath"). What lies ahead is uncertain, but not if this true Israel remains faithful to its God. Small may be strong if Yahweh fights for his people. "O Yahweh, there is none like thee to help, between the mighty and the weak. Help us, O Yahweh our God, for we rely on thee" (2 Chr 14:10 [*RSV* 11]).

Thus does ChrH tell who ideal Israel is, how it has suffered by not being true to its God, and how it will remain true Israel as and if it now trusts him whom it has so often forsaken.

ChrH fulfills two tasks. He tells (1) how the ideal Israel was shaped and formed, and (2) how Israel's land "enjoyed" or "received recompense for" its lost "sabbaths." The combination of genealogies and narratives is more than a "history" —it is a confession, an affirmation of faith, and a call to unswerving piety. ChrH's final dictum would be: *Israel may yet be what it is.*

Chapter 2

The Genealogical Materials: Ideal Israel's Table of Organization, 1 Chr 1:1–9:34

BIBLIOGRAPHY

M. Friedländer, *Genealogische Studien zum Alten Testament* (Berlin: Poppelauer, 1903); H. L. Gilbert, "The Forms of the Names in 1 Chronicles 1–7 Compared with Those in Parallel Passages of the Old Testament," *AJSL* 13 (1896-97) 279-98; N. H. Gottwald, *The Tribes of Yahweh* (Maryknoll: Orbis, 1979); F. von Hummelauer, *Das vormosäische Priesterthum in Israel. Vergleichende Studie zu Exodus und 1 Chron. 2–8* (Freiburg: Herder, 1899); S. Japhet, "Conquest and Settlement in Chronicles," *JBL* 98 (1979) 205-18; M. D. Johnson, *The Purpose of the Biblical Genealogies* (SNTSMS 8; Cambridge: Cambridge, 1969); G. Richter, "Untersuchungen zu den Geschlechtsregistern der Chronik," *ZAW* 34 (1914) 107-41; idem, "Zu den Geschlechterregistern I Chronik 2–9," *ZAW* 49 (1931) 260-70; 50 (1932) 130-41; J. P. Weinberg, "Das Wesen und die funktionelle Bestimmung der Listen in 1 Chr. 1–9," *ZAW* 93 (1981) 91-114; R. R. Wilson, *Genealogy and History in the Biblical World* (New Haven: Yale, 1977); idem, "The Old Testament Genealogies in Recent Research," *JBL* 94 (1975) 169-89; idem, *Sociological Approaches to the Old Testament* (Philadelphia: Fortress, 1984).

Structure

Israel, as ChrH actually knows it, consists mainly of two secular tribes, Judah and Benjamin, who have belonged together as citizens of the kingdom of Judah since the time of Rehoboam and have now returned together from the exile. There are also the "sons of Levi," comprising the priests ("sons of Aaron") and the Levitical order to which ChrH himself appears to belong. But this is not in itself the "all Israel" which constitutes God's ideal theocracy. Did not Yahweh create a nation of twelve tribes out of "Israel" (ChrH's regular substitute for "Jacob")? As we read 1-2 Chronicles carefully, we see that a place is always made for the tribes that went with Jeroboam. Most of the Israelites that fell captive to the Assyrians (722 B.C.) may have never returned to Yahweh's land, but refugees adhering to the temple in Jerusalem, and not to Samaria, deserve to be counted as part of ideal Israel along with Judah, Benjamin, and Levi.

In spite of what some critics have claimed, the only secondary material in 2 Chronicles 1-9 is the transitions and glosses for which ChrR is himself responsible. Every student of 1-2 Chronicles has attempted to explain the seemingly random way in which the various tribal records are presented in ChrR's reconstruction of "ideal Israel in the making." He starts in the center with Judah, swings south and east to take in the marginal tribes, then suddenly presents his material on Levi and an assortment of Galilean and central tribes, with Benjamin appearing twice. Benjamin at the end (8:1-40) counterbalances Judah at the beginning and Levi in the middle, but why the earlier material on Benjamin at 7:6-12? ChrR's fondness for chiasmus (crossing over) may perhaps account for placing Issachar and Asher at the outside of a special inclusio (Naphtali would not count since there is no actual tribal record for it), with Benjamin, Manasseh, and Ephraim in the center. Finally, we note that no place is made for Dan and Zebulun.

It is this writer's conviction that such an analysis is hazardous and quite hypothetical. Why after all do Judah, Benjamin, and Levi have to be placed either at the ends or at the center? Better sense may be obtained if we follow the evidence for a progressive development. This may be shown in a chart and justified in an explanation:

	Foundational elements	"All Israel" from records
A. The forefathers of Israel	1:1-54	
B. Judahite records		2:1-55; 4:1-23
C. The Davidic family		
1. Original	3:1-9	
2. Expansion		3:10-24

D. Records of Simeon		4:24-43
E. Records of Transjordan		5:1-26
F. The Levites		
1. Original	6:1-4a	
2. Expansions		5:27-41; 6:4b-66
G. Muster of Issachar		7:1-5
H. Muster of Benjamin		7:6-12
I. Records of Naphtali		7:13
J. Records of Manasseh		7:14-19
K. Records of Ephraim		7:20-29
L. Records of Asher		7:30-40
M. More records of Benjamin		8:1-40
N. Custodians of postexilic Jerusalem		
1. Original	9:2-17	
2. Expansions		9:1b, 18-34

Contrary to what Noth and other scholars have supposed, none of this material is fictional. ChrR obtains it entirely from records that are—or purport to be—historical. The difference is that in A, C.1, F.1, and N.1 he is reproducing scriptures from already accredited sources, whether by thematic selection, by alternative phrasing and recasting, or by verbatim quotation. All three methods are to be widely employed in ChrH, the narration to follow. The rest of the material has been added redactionally from records that make no special claim to prior authoritative acceptance. Of course, it is essential to begin with a sketch of "the forefathers of Israel"—including materials about Edom because it is a "brother" people, and perhaps because it remains in this time a rival and a menace (→ Chapter 1 above). ChrR copies or paraphrases genealogies, birth stories, and name lists from Genesis 5; 10:2-29; 11:14-26; 25:1-4, 11-15; 36:9-14, 20-43; the fact that he selects from J as well as from P shows that he has, more or less, the completed Pentateuch before him. He selects genealogical materials for the family of David from 2 Sam 3:2-5; 5:5, 14-16; this begins with the new rubric wĕ'ēlleh hāyû bĕnê . . ., "Now these were the sons of. . . ." He reproduces a genealogy of the Levites from Exod 6:16-19. Finally, he reproduces more or less literally the genealogical records of the returnees found in Neh 11:3-14. The arrangement of these selections is commonsense: the forefathers, the kingship, the Levitical order, the new "Israel." These are the foundational elements for a complete (→) TABLE OF ORGANIZATION.

ChrR next turns to a variety of tribal records that have somehow been preserved. It is no wonder that he finds so many of them for Judah and Levi, but also comes upon "more Benjaminite records" (8:1-40) after having dealt with Benjamin in 7:6-12. It is likewise no wonder that he can find nothing for Dan and Zebulun. He apparently found a document with the title "The Naphtalites" (7:13), but it seems to have been in such poor condition that all he could get from it was a list of clan chieftains. We shall discuss the genre of each pericope in the following chapter. Suffice it to say that the documents in question do have a variety of genres and that they all belonged to official (→) REGISTERS, but in a confused and disordered arrangement. Little wonder that ChrR complains at one point (4:22b), wĕhaddĕbārîm 'attîqîm, "But the writings are ancient." The usual way for a new record to begin is with bĕnê . . ., "The sons of . . . ," several times with prefixed *wĕ*, "and" (5:1, 11, 23; 7:20), or *wĕlibnê*, "and as for the sons of" (7:1). Benjamin's two pericopes have eccentric introductory rubrics; in 7:6 it is simply "Benjamin" and in 8:1 it is *ûbinyāmin hôlîd . . .*, "and Benjamin begat . . . ," using a styling peculiar to a special group of genealogies (2:36-41; 4:14; 5:30-43; 8:1, 32-37 [= 9:35-42]). Since on independent grounds we can determine that 5:1-26 constitutes a single document, it is appropriate to see the three tribal records of Reuben, Gad, and half-Manasseh joined by *ûbĕnê* at vv. 11 and 23. The *ûbĕnê* at 5:1 indicates, further, that the Simeon record was originally joined to this combination. This form at 7:20 is not surprising since Manasseh and Ephraim are customarily joined. The peculiar form at 7:1 may show ChrR's styling after the long intervening Levi section. But the *hôlîd* formula at 8:1 suggests that this new Benjaminite material may not have belonged with the rest of the records when they were first assembled.

It is easy to see that the Judah-Levi-Benjamin arrangement is not based on an ideology. First comes the indispensable "forefathers" prologue, followed by ChrR's transition in 2:1. Next must come Judah's records because ChrH's constant thematic concern for the Davidic royal line demands a firm genealogical setting. One who reads chs. 2 and 4 sees much confusion in the original records underlying the text as to just who Judah's sons were; various lists and various traditions compete with each other. Yet we see that the concern of ch. 2—and of most of ch. 4—is with the lineage of Hezron, culminating in the eight generations that led to David and the house of Jesse (2:9-17). The Hezron genealogy also spreads out to include rich material along collateral lines, including several of David's affiliated clans. ChrR might have inserted his foundational genealogy at 2:15, where David is mentioned by name, but the pericope spoils his chance by immediately telling about the progeny of Zeruiah and Abigail. He does not find another suitable place in ch. 2. 2:42-50a and 52-55 are post-Chronicles expansions. A good place presents itself in the original genealogy of Hur beginning at 2:50b-51 and carrying over to 4:2-4. It is structured with an inclusio containing the opening rubric "The sons of Hur the first-born of Ephrathah," together with the concluding rubric "These were the sons of Hur, the first-born of Ephrathah, the father of Bethlehem." What better place for ChrR to insert his "family of David" (3:1-8), concluded by ChrR's summation in v. 9 and a genealogy of Solomon in vv. 10-24? ChrR's list of Judahite tribal eponyms in 4:1 is his bridge back to the Hur genealogy and the remainder of the Judahite material.

Thus the genealogy of David accounts for Judah's priority in these lists. It is the Davidic kingship, not Judah's preeminence as a tribe, that forms one of the pillars of ideal Israel. But now the others must be fitted in. Probably following his fondness for inclusio—working inward from the perimeters—ChrR offers the records for Simeon and the Transjordanian tribes: south and east of the Jerusalem center. The records of the Simeonites are reproduced pretty much as ChrR found them. As we have suggested, this may have been joined to the Transjordan material in the original sources. This is certainly true of the Reuben-Gad-half-Manasseh sources, but ChrR inserts a narrative about a war that the three tribes carried out, placing this before the half-Manasseh report (5:18-22, 23-24), then adding the very first interpretative comment of the book, a remark about retribution for the three tribal units under the hand of the Assyrians (5:25-26).

ChrR clearly desires to make his "foundation" record for the Levites central to his entire list, and precisely here, with five secular tribes (Judah, Simeon, Reuben, Gad, half-Manasseh) covered, and six (Issachar, Benjamin, Naphtali, Manasseh, Ephraim, Asher) yet to come, is the place to put it. But ChrR has expanded the original record with a profusion of related materials. Because of the functional priority of the Aaronite priesthood, the whole section is introduced with their genealogies (5:27-41 [*RSV* 6:1-15]). The secondary nature of this entire section is betrayed first of all by an introductory rubric that is identical to that of the Levite list beginning in 6:1 (*bĕnê lēwî*), and second by the *hôlîd* formula extending from v. 30 to v. 40, contrasting with the *bĕnô* pattern which ChrR applies to the Levite clans in their own genealogies appearing in 6:4-15 (*RSV* 19-30). Thus far there is a structural parallelism between the Aaronite and the Levite sections (name list; genealogies). But this does not exhaust ChrR's intent. He has two large blocks of material concerning the Levites, and he pauses to introduce each of them with the phrase *wĕ'ēlleh* . . . , "Now these are. . . ." The first section presents a REGISTER of cultic functionaries (6:16-34 [*RSV* 31-49]); the second presents a CATALOGUE of dwelling places for the Levitical families, reworked from Josh 21:9-40 (6:39-66 [*RSV* 54-81]). This intends only to enrich the image of Levi as one of Israel's *tribes*. (Parallel material appearing at various places in the book authorizes and clarifies the *cultic* function of both groups, the Aaronites and the Levites, claiming descent from Levi.) A post-Chronicles expansion, introduced by *wĕ 'ēlleh,* offers a variant priestly genealogy (using the *bĕnô* style in place of the *hôlîd* style) from Aaron to Ahimaaz (6:35-38 [*RSV* 50-53]).

Next come the six records of 7:1-40. Apparently ChrR could not find much material for them, for all are short. None is so short, however, as the one for Naphtali (7:13), which begins with the usual *bĕnê* rubric but has nothing to offer except a list of four sons and the name of their mother. This is enough, however, to serve ChrR's purpose, viz., to include Naphtali in "all Israel."

As we have suggested, the varied Benjaminite records in 8:1-40 were added when the preceding list had been completed. We can conjecture that ChrR came upon them in some previously unexamined source and felt that they were too important to be omitted.

Having recorded all this material, ChrR wrote a closing rubric for it, 9:1aα, "So all Israel was enrolled by genealogies" *(RSV)*. We see that the groups listed in 9:2-32 constitute no separate tribal group, so the rubric is inclusive. But before proceeding to 9:2ff., ChrR continues with "and behold, they are written in the book of the kings of Israel" (some scholars include the following "and Judah"). With the fuller styling this frequently forms part of the REGNAL RESUMÉ (2 Chr 16:11; 25:26; 27:7; 28:26; 32:32; 35:27), but the form with "Israel" alone is found in 2 Chr 20:34 and 33:18. This is not the place to discuss ChrH's attribution of his sources, which will be taken up in Chapter 4 below. One should mention that the battle is fiercely fought between scholars who think there actually was such a book and scholars who believe it to be fictitious. The present writer takes it to be fictitious, for reasons that will be argued later. The matter is important here because 9:1aβ leaves the impression that all the foregoing material was written down in a special book, from which ChrR himself quoted. Theoretically, it makes little difference whether ChrR has copied material that another writer has compiled or has drawn up that material himself, for either way it provides the image of ideal Israel that he intends. We must understand, however, that the verb *yḥś* (hith.) has the meaning "muster" in the foregoing sections and ought so to be translated here. It has nothing directly to do with "genealogies." Furthermore, the subject "all Israel" is the antecedent of the *hinnēh*-clause and therefore of the second verb, "are written" (better translated, "are inscribed"). "All Israel" is/are inscribed in this book which ChrR adduces as his source. That means that they are all there, forming the ideal community whose history ChrH will now recount.

As has been stated, 9:2-17, closely similar to Neh 11:3-14, is another of ChrR's foundation elements. It receives ChrR's narrative introduction in 9:1b. V. 2, "Now the first to dwell again . . . ," conveys ChrR's conviction that the lists that follow represent only the "firstfruits" of the "all Israel" that will constitute the perfect community that God has designed.

After expanded lists in vv. 14-34, ChrR rounds off his presentation with the words *'ēlleh yāšĕbû bîrûšālaim,* "These dwelt in Jerusalem." This concluding rubric creates an inclusio with the words in v. 2 about dwelling (same verb: *yšb*) in the land of return. The concluding rubric makes it clear that Jerusalem is, and always will be, first in the land.

Genre

An identification of the various genres employed throughout this section will be provided in the following chapter. Does this "genealogical" section have its own genre? Before answering this question, it will be useful to review the various tribal lists according to content, as follows:

> JUDAH: 2 genealogical, territorial; 3 genealogical; 4 genealogical, territorial
> SIMEON: genealogical, territorial, military
> REUBEN: military, territorial
> GAD: military, territorial (appended BATTLE REPORT for the three Transjordanian tribes)
> HALF-MANASSEH: territorial, military
> LEVI: genealogical, territorial
> ISSACHAR: military
> BENJAMIN: military
> NAPHTALI: genealogical
> MANASSEH: genealogical
> EPHRAIM: genealogical, territorial
> BENJAMIN: 8:1ff., genealogical, military, territorial; vv. 33ff., genealogical, military.

The "foundation material" in chs. 1 and 9 is entirely genealogical.

While conceding that the tribal material was taken pretty much as found in the archival records, with only occasional redactional intrusions, we would claim that in the list as a whole the different types of content provide answers to three specific questions. The genealogical materials say who ideal Israel is. The territorial materials tell us where ideal Israel lives. The military materials help say who ideal Israel is, but say also how it functions and what it does (muster rolls, combining a genealogical with a military concern).

Let us not suppose that this is some sort of catalogue. The information it provides is far from complete. Even if ChrR had an exhaustive gazetteer for all inhabited sites, or exhaustive census lists for every generation since the patriarchs (which he surely did not), to list them all would be nothing but an exercise in erudition. What the names and places mentioned in chs. 2–8 do is provide a typological outline. The tribal entities are a skeleton which shows the Israel of the here and now, who it is, where it lives, and how it functions.

There is a suitable genre name for what ChrR has produced: TABLE OF ORGANIZATION. It has been suggested earlier, and now, upon examination of the evidence, proves to be entirely suitable. At our discussion of 1 Chr 23:3-24 a complete definition for this genre, which appears also at 1 Chr 26:12-18 and Neh 12:23-26, will be offered. In the passages mentioned a tightly drawn group is involved, but here the genre is utilized for the "all Israel" that ChrR has reconstructed. A TABLE OF ORGANIZATION lists individual positions or responsibilities within a given organization, relates these to one another, and assigns individual persons or groups to fill each position and carry out each specific responsibility. That is precisely what we have in 1 Chronicles 2–8. The tribal groups are placed in relationship to one another, their responsibility (cultic or military) is assigned, and tribes, clans, or individuals are identified for each slot. As has been said, the names tell who "all Israel" is, the territorial claims tell who owns the land, and the cultic and military structures tell what duties it must fill.

Setting and Intention

In Chapter 1 above a setting has been given for the entire book. It is for postexilic Israel that ChrR has been providing these lists—but it is not the xenophobic community of Ezra-Nehemiah nor the second-century Hasidic community, with its torah-righteousness based on circumcision, sabbath keeping, and dietary correctness (none of these items is required in 1–2 Chronicles). Here is a chastened Israel striving to define itself. Continuity with the preexilic nation of Israel is fragile. The genealogies in ch. 1, drawn from Genesis, tell of course how Israel came to be a nation; it is still that nation. The Davidic kingship is still an ideal reality, and apparently ChrR is able to trace it to his own time (3:10-24). There is a continuity in the lists of priests and Levites (5:27–6:66), but these do not satisfactorily bridge the gap of the exile, because at points they seem to contradict one another. In other words, the pedigrees are suspicious, though continuity with Levi as a tribal eponym is clear.

As has been said, most of the "genealogical" lists are suspicious, and this is not because they are fictitious or unhistorical but because they are incomplete. They are to be taken as typological fragments. Several are very old, going back in fact to the pre-settlement period, yet they help ChrR's "Israel" tell who they are and why they are here. In a few places ChrR tries to extend the historical time span of a particular tribe. He does this by picking up from 4:41, 43 the expression *'ad-hayyôm hazzeh,* "to this day," suggesting that the tribes in question still hold claim to the territories they long ago conquered. He seems to do this, too, with the references to "Tilgath-pilneser" in 5:6, 26, which suggest not only an exile but also a restoration.

ChrR's work is now complete and we begin to identify him with the symbol ChrH, "the Chronicler as historian" or "the Chronicles' history." We now know

27

who "Israel" is; we must next be told what happened to it as the land fulfilled all its sabbaths. Certainly that HISTORY would be incomplete without the "genealogical" materials that introduce it. On the other hand, 1 Chronicles 1–9 is a functionless collocation of random information without the history that is to follow.

We agree that the redactor and historian of this book must have been a member of the Levite order, but is this propaganda for the Levites? The answer is no; it was written for the entire Jewish community. The repeated lengthy digressions for explaining this or that matter of Levite policy mean only that the redactor/narrator considers it part of his history. Let us think of this as analogous to the extended expositions on whales and whaling in *Moby Dick;* in Melville's intention, these do not interrupt the narrative of Captain Ahab but make it understandable. Thus the lengthy chapter for the Levites in the "genealogical section" makes the other tribal records understandable by giving them perspective — the perspective of the centrality of the sacred over against the secular. (We shall reserve to our discussion of 5:27–6:66 our remarks concerning the Levites vis-à-vis the Aaronite priests.) It is the sacred that reveals the Godward side of the secular. More than anything else, it is the intention of ChrR/H to show that the ideal Israel of his time has sacrality at its core, and is therefore the "kingdom of priests and holy nation" of Exod 19:6. This book speaks to a theocracy, and about a theocracy, in which all secularity is taken up into sacrality, and in which the entire flow of "all Israel's" history belongs to the Israel of this period because "all Israel" is a timeless reality.

Chapter 3

The Individual Units

GENEALOGICAL LISTS OF THE FOREFATHERS OF ISRAEL, 1:1-54

Structure

A much discussed problem has been whether 2:1-2 does not properly conclude this pericope. It offers a list of "the sons of Israel," a natural continuation
from 1:34, "Esau and Israel." Vv. 35-54 do no more than present materials for Esau-
Edom. Nevertheless, two considerations argue that 1:54 marks the end of the

pericope. One is that "the sons of Judah," etc., is too abrupt for introducing the lengthy formal section terminating in the self-conscious rubric at 9:1a, and the second is that 2:1-2 is itself a formal opening rubric, mentioning the tribes whose records are to be presented and forming, with 9:1a, a grand inclusio characteristic of ChrR. Although the pronoun *'ēlleh*, "these," opens and closes short genealogical notices taken from Genesis (1 Chr 1:29, 31, 33, 43), at 2:1 it is nonderivative and functions to give added weight to what is to follow.

The main division within ch. 1 is clearly marked by ChrR's name lists at vv. 1-4, 24-27. The style is sharply asyndetic at both places except for ChrR's clarifying note, "Abram, that is, Abraham." Neither name list has an introduction and both are linear except for v. 4, "Shem, Ham, and Japheth." This collateral listing is designed to introduce genealogical materials for each Noachian son, as taken more or less literally from Gen 10:2-29. LXX[B] omits vv. 11-16, opening up the possibility that the Egypt and Canaan genealogies are a late addition to the Chronicles text. The order of vv. 5-23—Japheth, Ham, Shem—provides a chiasmus with v. 4, but the noticeable effect is to narrow down the lineage to Israel's immediate ancestors. Each genealogy within this section has syndetic styling ("X and X and X"), but with the asyndetic caption *běnê* . . . , "the sons of . . . ," at the head of new lists and syndetic "and the sons of . . ." internally. V. 7 has a pairing style, "Elishah and Tarshish, Kittim and Rodanim." From v. 8 onward ChrR employs a striking *yālad*, "he bore," form, which he borrowed from J in Gen 10:8, 13-18.

In spite of the fact that a five-generation Shem genealogy is offered in vv. 17-23, the second name list, with Shem at the head, appears at vv. 24-27 as a summary introduction for the Abraham genealogies that follow in vv. 28-37. As has been said, this marks a sharp division within the chapter, giving the first half to Adam and the second half to Shem (the Edomite lists in vv. 38ff. are to be viewed as structural expansions). Paralleling vv. 5-23 in the first half, the opening caption in v. 28 expands the preceding name list from the point where its last name is mentioned. Interestingly, that name list follows Genesis 11–16 in naming this patriarch "Abram," but, because his genealogies are to be taken from sections following Genesis 17, ChrR inserts an explanatory note, "that is, Abraham," and proceeds to name him so. In spite of the fact that the opening caption for the Abraham genealogies (v. 28) mentions only Isaac and Ishmael, a Keturah genealogy is included at vv. 32-33. Chiasmus again appears, creating an inclusio for the Keturah section, in presenting the Ishmael genealogy first and the Isaac genealogy last — the same technique as is used for Shem, Ham, and Japheth in vv. 4-23. That the Abraham section is ChrR's central point of concern is made clear from the formal rubric at the head of v. 29, *'ēlleh tōlĕdôtām*, "These are their generations." The simple *wāw* is used irregularly in the Ishmael and Isaac genealogies, but with complete regularity in the Keturah section. Concluding rubrics round off the Ishmael and Keturah sections (vv. 31, 33), but there is none for Isaac. On the other hand, the Ishmael genealogy lacks an opening rubric, while the *běnê*-headings introduce the descendants of Keturah and Midian at vv. 32-33. Borrowing the style of J, the Keturah genealogy has the fem. form of *yld*, and it is the narrative form of this same verb *(wayyôled)* that introduces the Isaac genealogy ("And Abraham begat Isaac," v. 34), effectively drawing the reader's attention back to the central line of pre-Israelite ancestors. Internally, it employs the *běnê*-form for Isaac, Esau, Eliphaz, and Reuel.

The Seir genealogy in vv. 38-42 is introduced by *běnê* . . . (so throughout), but the king list of vv. 43-51a and the concluding list of Edomite chiefs (vv. 51b-54) have special introductory formulas, and the latter has a concluding rubric as well. One readily sees that these are expansions of the foregoing Esau genealogy; they lay ready to hand with the latter in the text of Genesis 36. Disregarding Gen 36:20, which makes Seir a Horite, ChrR equates him with Edom (cf. Gen 36:8). All seven siblings are listed in the segmented genealogy, hence *RSV* "Dishon" in v. 42 should be "Dishan" (so Gen 36:30). "The sons of Anah" followed by a single name (so Genesis) seems incongruous but derives unquestionably from the structure of antique records, which listed rubrics to be filled out as names became available. It is a form that appears several times in the genealogical sections of Chronicles. The list of Edomite kings has a strikingly stereotyped form. For each king there is first the (→) succession formula, then a variety of identifying statements, including father's name and city, and in the case of the second Hadad (Genesis "Hadar"), a pedigree for his wife and a report of his death. The mistaken placement of vv. 47b-49a after v. 51a in LXX[B] is a classic case of homoioteleuton.

Genre

1 Chronicles 1 has subgenres, but the main genre is LIST. There are various kinds of lists. This can only be called a genealogical list because its effect is to trace genealogical connections from the first man to the immediate ancestors of Israel. Following Genesis, it records collateral branches, but the direction is unmistakably linear. As has been seen, it employs name lists to mark off the two main divisions, with genealogies following. Lists of kings and chiefs are added at the end. Here then is a series of similar items (names and family relationships) arranged according to the principle of their traditional order.

Verses 5-7, 8-16, 17-23, 29-31, 32-33, 34-37, and 38-42 all belong to the important genre GENEALOGY. In popular usage, this term has been widely misused. Much recent work on the biblical genealogies has helped clarify the genre and distinguish it from related genres (Johnson, 382; Wilson, *Genealogy,* 11-198; Coats, *Genesis,* 60-62, 69-72, 89-93, and passim). It is a special type of oral or written LIST that enumerates individual and tribal descent from an originating ancestor through intermediate persons down to the last. It is built on a system of enumeration rather than narration, though brief narrative items may be included (→ GENEALOGY). It may be linear, tracing descent from father to son, and so on for several generations (in this it differs from the genre [→] PEDIGREE, which moves backward from the present generation to the remote ancestor), or it may be segmented, identifying siblings and from them tracing collateral branches. Wilson (*Genealogy,* 203) demonstrates that, in spite of their stereotyped structure and content, there is marked fluidity within and among genealogies, with notable variations in their original functions and in their relationships to their respective narrative contexts.

The genre NAME LIST is simply a list of names, arranged either haphazardly or according to some systematic principle. The example in v. 9a is a list of brothers, that of vv. 1-4 is a list of ancestors branching out to include brothers, and that of vv. 24-27 is purely a list of ancestors.

Another sort of LIST is the KING LIST of vv. 43-51. It enumerates successive rulers in a particular state. It consists of royal names with certain additional elements, here with notice of succession and the identification of father and city (→

KING LIST). Some commentators have argued that these verses, with their counterpart in Genesis 36, do not belong to this genre because the names are of contemporaries and are artificially joined (so Bartlett). Nevertheless, the genre identification is secure because of the form. Functioning also as a KING LIST is the LIST of *'allûpîm*, "chiefs," in vv. 51b-54 since it designates a succession of rulers prior to the establishment of Edom as a dynastic state.

A short maternal PEDIGREE appears at v. 50b. A NAME ETIOLOGY, taken from Genesis, is in v. 19b (play on the name Peleg and on the verb *plg* [niph.], "to divide"). Finally, the aforementioned SUCCESSION FORMULA, identifying the person succeeding to the throne, introduces seven of the eight kings listed in vv. 43-51a.

Setting

ChrR reveals at the very beginning that he knows the biblical tradition at least partially in written form. We shall see that he uses nothing else from Genesis or the Pentateuch except such genealogical and related materials as he chooses. For what he does select, he has no order except that which is inherent in the nature of the material. This is why he picks out just this material and arranges it as he does. In the name lists he simply summarizes, then follows somewhat verbatim in the genealogies. His text is close to that of Genesis, but there are some striking discrepancies. Some scholars have interpreted this as implying that there was a prior document, from which both Genesis and Chronicles have drawn, but it is a priori unlikely that ChrR would have copied from such a source when Genesis—which must be earlier than Chronicles—was available to him. Besides, ChrR's method of selecting and handling material in this chapter is precisely his style throughout the book. He more often departs from Samuel-Kings than adopts it verbatim. A better explanation is that he is drawing on an earlier form of the Genesis text, i.e., a recensional variant existing prior to the rise of the LXX and other ancient versions. In addition, he does make his own adaptations, as we have seen.

Some scholars have interpreted ChrR's fondness for genealogical materials, and his complete neglect of pentateuchal narrative, as proof for his strong ideological affinity with P. He does cite the JP combination in this chapter, however. Naturally, there are many similarities with P, for the expanded form of P (not just the exilic narrative) belongs to the same general period and reflects many of the same conditions. But everything points to ChrR's possessing the entire Pentateuch, though perhaps in a precanonical form.

This pericope is one of ChrR's "foundation documents," along with the David genealogy in 1 Chronicles 3, the Levite genealogy in ch. 6, and the lists for restoration Jerusalem in ch. 9 (→ Chapter 1 above). These are the materials ChrR did not have to search for. We can believe that they had special familiarity within the entire postexilic community. They had Genesis, and no one had to show them who their ancestors were. This is a "given" which ChrR could use to trace who "ideal Israel" is and how it got to be what it is in its present condition.

Intention

The commentaries have argued back and forth whether ch. 1 was an original part of 1–2 Chronicles. The genealogies of chs. 2–8 are just for the tribes of Israel, and

2:1-2 seems a proper introduction for them. "So all Israel was enrolled by genealogies [mustered]" in 9:1a is the closing rubric, and it too mentions only Israel. Quite apart from our overall redactional concept, we can argue for originality from various linguistic traits in this chapter that ChrR/H continues to use throughout the book. It is a distinctive ideological trait of his that "Jacob" becomes "Israel" at 1:34, just as at 2:1. But if ch. 1 is original—in fact, one of ChrR's "foundation documents"—are we not to suppose that it also included an "Israel" genealogy, such as the one in Gen 46:8-25, before coming to be used as part of the framework for the filled-out chs. 2–8? A literary analysis of ch. 2 will show us that vv. 1-2 are direct from ChrR; they are his transition from ch. 1. This means that he did not intend to take any more material from Genesis, and intended to make *this* a conclusion and an introduction at the same time. All the same, we need to know why ChrR seems to slight the all-important genealogy of "Israel" while spending so much time gathering materials on Edom, who never figures throughout the book he is about to write, except as foe.

ChrR's intention in ch. 1 may become clear if we keep in mind how he has divided up the pericope (vv. 1-23, vv. 24-54), giving us a lineage of Adam and a lineage of Shem. The two sections have a short NAME LIST followed by a segmented GENEALOGY (the latter with expansions), which takes its point of departure from the last-mentioned item in the name list. Thus we understand that the second section is not for Abraham but for Shem—and this even though Shem was the last-treated member of the immediately preceding GENEALOGY. This understanding gives us a better concept of what ChrR was up to. His structures expand in breadth just at the point where length of derivation is no longer a consideration. It is apparent that ChrR thinks cosmically, and that he intends to place Israel within a framework of two far-extending dimensions: backward to Shem and to Adam; laterally to all peoples having blood affiliation with Israel. Wilson (*Sociological Approaches*, 54-66) explains that linear lists like those of vv. 1-4, 24-27, have the function of establishing legitimacy, while segmented genealogies like those in the rest of the chapter have the function of defining familial and intertribal relationships. This is why all that has been included has a place and function. Because the subject of the entire complex structure is *Israel*, we do not need a list of his sons and grandsons, but only of his parentage (establishing his legitimacy as son of Shem and son of Adam) and of his brother Esau's widely dispersed family (placing him and his nation within the framework of immediate blood relationship). Knowing what we do of the intrusions of the Idumeans in the postexilic period, there may be special irony in ChrR's inclusion of so much information about Israel's blood brother and twin, Esau.

Bibliography

J. R. Bartlett, "The Edomite King-List of Genesis XXXVI.31-39 and 1 Chron. I.43-50," *JTS* 16 (1965) 301-14; I. Ephal, " 'The Sons of Keturah' and 'the Sons of Ishmael'" (Hebr.), in *Bible and Jewish History* (Fest. J. Liver; Tel Aviv: Tel Aviv, 1971) 161-68; M. D. Johnson, *The Purpose of the Biblical Genealogies* (SNTSMS 8; Cambridge: Cambridge, 1969); E. Podechard, "Le premier chapître des Paralipomenes," *RB* 13 (1916) 363-86; R. R. Wilson, *Genealogy and History in the Biblical World* (New Haven: Yale, 1977); idem, *Sociological Approaches to the Old Testament* (Philadelphia: Fortress, 1984).

GENEALOGICAL LISTS OF ISRAEL'S ROYAL TRIBE, 2:1–4:23

Structure

The structure of this section has been elaborately dealt with in Chapter 1 above, and little of what has been said requires repetition here. 2:1-2 is ChrR's general introduction to chs. 2–8. The rest of ch. 2 and 4:2-23, minus post-Chronicles expansions, were more or less intact just as he used them. As has been said, he broke off the Hur genealogy at 2:51 in order to insert what he intended as his core material, the Davidic genealogy plus its Solomonic expansion, in ch. 3, inserting 4:1 as a device to continue the broken-off Hur material. By placing the Judahite genealogies first on his list, he gives expression to the essentiality of Judah as a tribe, Jerusalem as a city, and David as an eponym of the Israelite monarchy.

JUDAHITE RECORDS (I), 2:1-55

Structure

Verses 1-2 have *'ēlleh běnê yiśrā'ēl*, "These are the sons of Israel" (not "Jacob"), followed by ChrR's idiosyncratic list of tribal eponyms. The names do not consistently appear in the order of tribal records in chs. 2–8, to which this short editorial unit provides a transition.

In spite of the great diversity in ch. 2, it is parallel in structure to ch. 1. The order there was (1) sons of Adam; (2) sons of Seth, with expansions. The order here is (1) sons of Judah; (2) sons of Hezron, with expansions. Because of ChrR's redactional method (→ Chapter 1 above), the Hezron expansions continue in ch. 4 along with a new section on the sons of Shelah. The Judah section (vv. 3-8) functions as a genealogy, though it does not belong strictly to the genre (→) GENEALOGY, continuing in linear form to the third generation (Perez to Zerah to Hezron), with fragments of a fourth Carmi generation erratically inserted at v. 7 (cf. Brunet, "Chroniste," 492-93).

The opening formula for Hezron, *ûběnê ḥeṣrôn 'ăšer nôlad-lô*, "and the sons of Hezron that were born to him," is pleonastic in form but serves to draw attention to the Hezron section (vv. 9-55; 4:2-20), which is not only of great length and complexity but is clearly intended as the goal and fulfillment of the foregoing Judah genealogy. In spite of the order of the introductory name list, a genealogy for Ram follows first (vv. 10-17) because it leads directly to the family of David. This is followed by a list for "Caleb son of Hezron," including appended reports for Hezron (vv. 18-24), and then a complex list for Jerahmeel (not technically a genealogy but functioning as such), and concluding with the idiosyncratic rubric *'ēlleh hāyû běnê yěraḥmě'ēl*, "These were (became) the sons of Jerahmeel" (vv. 25-33). To this are attached two post-Chronicles expansions, the Sheshan list in vv. 34-41 and the genealogy of "Caleb brother of Jerahmeel" in vv. 42-50aα. A Hur genealogy is just introduced in vv. 50aβ-51, but is broken off by three post-Chronicles expansions in vv. 52-55 and ChrR's "foundation document" in ch. 3.

The rambling structure has given the critics much opportunity for speculation and conjectural emendation. The LXX and other ancient VSS have tried to improve the text, but their readings are generally based on simple misunderstanding. Rudolph (HAT) wants to place vv. 21-23 after v. 9, vv. 18-19 after v. 55, and v. 24 with 4:5-8; in addition, he views v. 20, vv. 34-41, and vv. 50aβ-55 as late expansions. Fohrer (*Intro.*, 244) sees all of 2:18–4:23 as a late expansion. (Besides the comms., see also Brunet, "Chroniste," 490-94; von Rad, *Geschichtsbild,* 72; Noth, "Chronistische Werk," 108.) But clearly tradition and form criticism must take precedence here over literary criticism. Most of the lack of coherence within the chapter has been created by the jumbling together of blocks from diverse traditions, most of it left unaltered by ChrR and by the traditionists who preceded him.

We encounter not only a disconcerting array of genres (see below) but also a mixture of styles. Narrative styling prevails in vv. 3-8, 17-19, 21-24, 25-33, 34-35, 42-43, 46a, 48-49. Contrariwise, genealogical lists with a remarkable *hôlîd* styling prevail in vv. 10-13, 18a, 20, 36-41, 44, 46b. The *hôlîd* styling is common in Genesis; it goes: "X *hôlîd* Y." It means, "so-and-so begat so-and-so," and its purpose is to express direct and continuous descent.

Still another peculiar styling is the form "X *'ăbî* Y," i.e., "so-and-so, father of so-and-so." It occurs in vv. 21-24 three times, in vv. 42-50 seven times, in v. 49 three times, and in vv. 50-52 four times; also three times in 4:3-4, twice each in 4:5-7 and 11-12, once in 4:14, four times in 4:17-18, once in 4:19, and twice in 4:21-23. Because many of the names listed in these sections are of towns and clans, it is apparent that "father of . . ." denotes territorial interdependence. Interestingly, the passages in question belong to the Caleb and Hur sections, from which we may conclude that this is a special, probably antique phraseology. Noth ("Eine siedlungsgeographische Liste," 101-23) is on weak ground, however, in basing a complete history of tradition development upon them. They are, in fact, random elements copied into ChrR's documentary sources.

Chiasmus appears not only at vv. 9ff. (see above) but at vv. 28-30 and 43 as well. A non-syndetic style in the Judah and Perez genealogies lends them greater prominence. Glosses appear at vv. 46b and 49b. Vv. 34-41, beginning with "Now Sheshan had no sons," is to be identified as a late literary expansion because it conflicts with the statement in v. 31 that Sheshan did have a son; it is in fact an *apologia* for allowing the Egyptian Jarha into what amounts to a pedigree for Elishama, v. 41. It is followed by the second, completely different, Jerahmeelite Caleb genealogy in vv. 42-50a; complete with its formal closing rubric, this too is a post-Chronicles expansion. Since the original Hur-Shobal genealogy continues in 4:2, v. 53, along with vv. 54 and 55, is revealed as still a further expansion.

Genre

As we have seen, vv. 1-2 are the transition to an EDITORIAL UNIT. Examples of the GENEALOGY proper (linear and segmented) are vv. 10-17, 25-33, 36-41, and 50aβ-55. Separate from or included in genealogies are the NAME LISTS (vv. 1b-2, 5, 6, 9b, 16b, 25b, 27, 28a, 30a, 31a, 47, 52). The BIRTH REPORT, often confused with

GENEALOGY, appears at vv. 3-4a (two times), 17, 18-24 (seven times), 26, 29, 34b-35, 46, and 48-49. It appears also at 4:6, 17-19; 7:14-17, 18, 23; 8:8-9, 11-13; 2 Chr 11:18-20; Gen 25:19-26; 36:1-5. This is a special kind of REPORT, substituting a brief narrative item for its equivalent item of factual information in the GENEALOGY. From the fact that wives and mothers figure large in this sort of report, it may be inferred that the mothers were the primary tradents, and that accordingly the form has a matriarchal rather than patriarchal bias, such as in the genealogies and related name lists. Related to the BIRTH REPORT are the notices of childlessness at vv. 30 and 32, though these now occupy a rung on the genealogical ladder. In view of the fact that many of the names actually represent towns as well as clans, it is not surprising to find at vv. 22-23 reports of land possession closely related to the (→) schema of territorial claim. The Ram genealogy concludes in vv. 13-15 with a list of Jesse's sons involving one of ChrR's favorite devices, the RANKING FORMULA. This formula has a proper name with the attributive adjective *běkôr*, "choice," "first," followed by other names with ordinals, usually from "second" to "eighth." This formula identifies the persons named while defining their rank among their fellows. This formula appears also at vv. 42-45 and 50-51. The TALLY, seen at vv. 4b, 6, 16b, and 23, is a cardinal number attached to genealogies, muster rolls, and related materials, recording the information offered by the RANKING FORMULA in summary form.

Setting

The use of Scripture in this chapter is far more eclectic than in ch. 1, in fact so much of a paraphrase or mere allusion in most cases as to suggest that oral tradition or early recensional material was being cited. No doubt this is what should be expected in pre-documentary tribal records. ChrR's introduction recalls such genealogical material as is found in Gen 35:23-26, but ChrR makes his own arrangement of the twelve tribal eponyms (cf. Noth, *Stämme*, 21, 123; Gottwald, *Tribes*, 275, 561-63; and the titles listed in Chapter 1 above). V. 3b recalls Gen 38:7; v. 6 is parallel to 1 Kgs 4:31 (*RSV* 5:11); v. 7 is parallel to Josh 7:1, 17ff.; and vv. 10-12 recall Ruth 4:19b-22a. The remainder of the chapter is without direct scriptural parallels.

All of vv. 10-55 is taken directly from clan records. There is much overlapping and variation in individual names and in family affiliations. Although it is difficult to judge the precise age of this material, it appears to date from premonarchical times to the early monarchy. Evidence for this may be seen especially in that Caleb is so prominent, that his clan genealogies vary so much (he is identified in three different ways in vv. 18, 42; 4:15; cf. Judg 1:13), and that he has not yet been thoroughly subordinated to Judah, as in Judg 1:8-15, or given a place in Joshua's conquest, as in Num 14:6; Josh 14:6-15. Connecting the genealogical with the territorial information in the Judah records, Noth ("Eine siedlungsgeographische Liste," 112-23) infers that the north was still pure Judahite at this period and the south pure Calebite, with overlapping in between and a mixing of Judahites with Canaanites in the Shephelah. The old Judah clans Er and Onan have disappeared; Judah is in the process of absorbing Danite territory; half-nomads have settled in the steppeland around Tekoa, and Ephrathah/Bethlehem is extending its influence. The "Siphrites" (MT *sōpěrîm*) may be Kiriath-sepher.

This section surely does contain old clan terminology. The common word for "clan," *mišpāḥâ*, is not found until vv. 53, 55. The prevalence of the *'ăbî* formula shows that as the clans grew the parent group (*'āb*) would retain supervisory rights over the descendant groups. As the people moved from a pastoral to a town economy, dependent villages came to be called *bānôt*, "daughters." Clan eponyms taking a subordinate group under their wing are depicted as entering into marriage; the formula "and her name was . . . ," vv. 26, 29, guards the rights of affiliation claimed by these new groups. The prominence of birth reports reflects this intra-familial connection while suggesting the possibility of a matriarchal order of descent (see above).

The genealogy for Jesse's family is quite different; it was taken from court records. The number of sons agrees with that given in 1 Sam 16:10, except that David is not included there in the seven mentioned. Hence we may infer that our Chronicles passage is very old and authentic. 1 Sam 16:10 and 17:12 reflect a later tradition in which the "seven" were construed as a unit not including David; in adding his name they increased the total to eight.

Intention

ChrR's willingness to give the tribe of Judah so much prominence, even though he was himself probably a Levite, is quite what we would expect of a writer to the postexilic Jewish (= Judahite) community, teaching them not from the entire broad history of all who called themselves Israelites but from the history of Judah. But not all claiming descent from the patriarch Judah interested him; he was interested in Hezron, ancestor of David, the king who established the kingdom of Judah. Perhaps the clan records for most of Judah's other sons had disappeared—and this because the non-Hezronite clans subsided into insignificance with David's rise to prominence. In any event, we are impressed with ChrR's diligence in searching for so many varied clan records, long ago legitimizing and identifying tribal inter-relationships, but now presented as an adornment to David's and to Judah's heritage.

Bibliography

L. Koehler, "Hebräische Etymologien, 9," *JBL* 59 (1940) 38-39; R. A. S. Macalister, "The Craftsmen's Guild of the Tribe of Judah," *PEFQS*, 1905, 243-53, 328-42; idem, "Some Further Observations . . . ," *PEFQS*, 1908, 71-75; J. M. Miller, "Geshur and Aram," *JNES* 28 (1969) 60-61; R. North, "The Cain Music," *JBL* 83 (1964) 373-89; M. Noth, "Eine siedlungsgeographische Liste in I Chr 2 und 4," *ZDPV* 55 (1932) 97-124; S. Talmon, "These are the Kenites who Came from Hammath, the Father of the House of Rechab" (Hebr.), *ErIs* 5 (1958) 111-13 (= *IEJ* 10 [1960] 174-80); R. de Vaux, "The Settlement of the Israelites in Southern Palestine and the Origins of the Tribe of Judah," in *Translating and Understanding the Old Testament* (*Fest.* H. G. May; ed. T. Frank and W. L. Reed; Nashville-New York: Abingdon, 1970) 108-34; H. G. M. Williamson, "Sources and Redaction in the Chronicler's Genealogy of Judah," *JBL* 98 (1979) 351-59.

GENEALOGICAL LISTS OF THE DAVIDIC FAMILY, 3:1-24

Structure

This "foundation document," expanded and inserted by ChrR, has two clearly defined sections. The first (vv. 1-9) is entirely collateral in its form of presentation, while the second (vv. 10-24) is basically linear. In the list of Hebron sons, the text of 2 Sam 3:2-5 is followed closely. It has three noteworthy characteristics: (1) clear demarcation as a new section through the use of the introductory rubric *wĕ'ēlleh hāyû bĕnê dāwîd 'ăšer* . . . , "Now these were the sons of David who . . . ," substituting for the narrative form in Samuel (for the unusual form with *hāyû* cf. 2:50); (2) the respective mothers are named, being introduced by *lĕ*, "belonging to," or *ben* . . . , "son of . . ."; (3) the sons are ranked, but with the numeral foremost. This section consistently uses the niph. perf. of *yld* (vv. 1, 4, 5) where Samuel has the narrative form (note also the pual perf. in 2 Sam 3:5b), together with the introduction, giving it the styling of a genealogical list instead of narrative exposition. V. 4a adds a TALLY to Samuel's concluding rubric. The two chronological notices that appear in v. 4 provide a transition from this Hebron section to the Jerusalem section to follow. V. 5 has a formal introduction similar to that of v. 1: *wĕ'ēlleh nûllĕdû-lô bîrûšālayim,* "And these were born to him in Jerusalem." Unlike the Hebron list, it gives no mothers' names except for the all-important "Bathshua" (= Bathsheba), credited with bearing three other sons in addition to Solomon. Then the others are listed (Eliphelet is listed twice) and the TALLY of nine is given. Quite a different style—that of ChrR —appears in the conclusion, which suggests that sons of concubines and the sister Tamar should be counted too.

Verses 10-24 have the styling of a linear GENEALOGY from Solomon to Josiah and from Jeconiah to Shealtiel. Here we find only the proper name followed by *bĕnô,* "his son," the antecedent being the immediately preceding king. In v. 16 and in several passages to follow, *bĕnô* applies to siblings who are listed one after another with this formula appended, the intention being to enumerate them all as sons of the father just mentioned (in the case of Zedekiah, v. 16, the genealogist shows confusion, since he should identify Zedekiah as Josiah's son; otherwise he is giving *bĕnô* the wider sense of "descendant"). In spite of the LXX and *RSV,* the fourfold *bĕnê* of v. 21 should not be emended to *bĕnô,* for the styling with *bĕnô* foremost is not commensurate with the standard styling with this word following the proper name. This leaves us with a text more difficult than before, but the problem can be solved by reading "the sons of Rephaiah; the sons of Arnan; the sons of Obadiah; the sons of Shecaniah"—regular introductions to a name list, which, however, is absent in these four instances because, presumably, no data were available. Unless we are to take "and the sons of Shecaniah" as a dittograph, it is possible to think of the genealogist as drawing here on an empty framework and then returning to his usual sources to supply a rubric with a single name (common in ChrR; → Chapters 1 and 2 above). If, on the other hand, we do read *bĕnô* in v. 21, we still get four generations in the list, and this seems more congruous with the structure of this genealogy than to take *bĕnô* as referring to four sons of Jeshaiah, who has just been mentioned with his sibling Pelatiah without this formula. Whether four generations appear here rather than one is, naturally, of great interest to historians.

We have seen evidence that ChrR was working with an imperfect text, and this has led to vexing variations in the ancient VSS, as well as perplexities for modern scholars trying to unravel them. It is not to our purpose to join in the discussion of them. In terms of structure, it is important to note that MT *ûben* in v. 10 must be emended to the usual *ûbĕnê* (so LXX, *RSV*) because this is needed in an opening rubric, and because the nominal-sentence style, "Now the son of Solomon was Rehoboam," does not fit the following *bĕnô* styling. ChrR must be responsible for adding the gloss on Shelomith in v. 19, which intrudes to allow a TALLY of five sons for Zerubbabel (v. 20), excluding the two mentioned in v. 19 (cf. ChrR's concern for adding female siblings in v. 9). This TALLY plus those of vv. 22, 23, and 24 may be ascribed to ChrR ("six" in v. 22 is an error unless one name has dropped out).

Genre

The main genre is LIST. The Hebron material was a royal (→) REGISTER that was expanded by the Jerusalem material and the transitional chronological notices. Vv. 10-24 are a GENEALOGY with NAME LIST, RANKING FORMULA, and TALLY. A RANKING FORMULA appears also at vv. 1-3, with the TALLY at vv. 4, 5, and 8. The list-

ings of royal children in vv. 1-3, 5-8, are too brief to exhibit the genre (→) BIRTH
REPORT (see above on ch. 2) and must be identified as BIRTH NOTICES. The
Jerusalem list appears to have belonged first to a set of archival notes before being
taken up into the foregoing REGISTER.

Setting

Even though ChrH uses Samuel material in the narrative sections, and we can be
certain that he knew 1-2 Samuel as a complete book, he did not as a redactor take
1 Chr 3:1-3 directly from that source but from a document that contained the source
of 2 Sam 3:2-5; this document was a royal REGISTER to which were attached the archival notes from which 2 Sam 5:5, 14-16 are drawn. (ChrR also borrows from this
source in 1 Chr 14:4.) This is apparent from the niph./pual styling and what appear
to be errors in vv. 6-8, but especially from "Bathshua," with a variant patronym, substituting for "Bathsheba." From this we can be sure that our royal register is very
early — possibly contemporary with the reign of David. This impression is
strengthened by the fact that the chronological notice of "seven years and six
months" for David's residence in Hebron (so 2 Sam 5:5) has escaped the eventual
reduction to seven years, seen in 1 Kgs 2:11 (cf. 2 Sam 5:4-5). Thus ChrR did not
take vv. 1-8 directly from Samuel. It was nonetheless available in easily accessible
form within ChrR's community, available to serve as his second "foundation document" (→ Chapter 2 above). The Solomon GENEALOGY must have been equally accessible. Contrary to what some scholars have thought, it was not concocted afresh
from Kings. This is apparent from the fact that Johanan is given as the name of
Josiah's firstborn. "Azariah" would have been changed to ChrH's usual "Uzziah" if
Kings had been the source here; the fact that it survives in this list is evidence that
ChrR was copying an independent document. In all probability it traces the
Davidic/Solomonic lineage to ChrR/H's own time, but this cannot be proven. In any
case, it is very late—at opposite poles to the birth notices of vv. 1-8.

Intention

The effect of vv. 1-8 is to put David and Solomon, founders of the dynastic line,
into a familial framework. It is the counterpart of 2:13-17, which showed David's
brothers and cousins. In vv. 1-3 the Hebron sons are given with the ranking formula, perhaps because they had a chance in the proper order of succession. This
section prepares for 1 Chronicles 11–12, which will be designed to feature David's
"march" from Hebron, the place of acclamation, to Jerusalem, the place chosen by
God for rule to be exercised over "all Israel." In 2 Sam 5:14-16 the list of David's
Jerusalem sons completes the author's image of the riches and honor to which he
had risen. Parallel material, added in ChrR's royal register in vv. 5-9, has two purposes: (1) to complete the enumeration and (2) to designate Solomon's position
within the royal family. Since ranking is missing here—being of no concern for
these late-born progeny—tallies are provided as a substitute. The mention of "Bathshua" (Bathsheba) as the mother of four, including Solomon, draws special attention to him. With his addition in v. 9, ChrR reveals a concept seen in a number of
passages within the HISTORY, viz., that numerous sons epitomize an abundance of
riches and honor, the sure sign of divine favor. This is what David's family was like

in incipio. The Solomonic genealogy, tracing the royal lineage to ChrR's time (if not his generation), shows what David's family became *in extenso.*

Bibliography

P. R. Berger, "Zu den Namen 'Sheshbaṣar' and 'Shin'aṣar,'" *ZAW* 83 (1971) 98-100; J. W. Rothstein, *Die Genealogie des Königs Jojachin und seiner Nachkommen* (Berlin: Reuther & Reichard, 1902).

JUDAHITE RECORDS (II), 4:1-23

Structure

As with ch. 2, the disorderly array encountered in this section has given rise to a variety of suggestions for rearrangement and elimination. Thus, for instance, Rudolph (HAT) would insert vv. 1-2 after 2:52-53, vv. 3-4 after 2:51a, vv. 5-8 after 2:50a, vv. 9-10 after 2:55a, vv. 11-12 after 2:55b, vv. 13-15 after 2:55, vv. 16-20 after 2:42-50aα, and vv. 21-23 after 2:3. Nothing commends such a resorting of the deck. It is one thing to be orderly and try to put things where they seem to belong; it is another thing to explain how materials belonging together got so dispersed in the first place.

The ancient VSS have been as mystified by this material as the modern reader is, but have augmented confusion in many of their emendations. It does seem advisable to follow LXX and Vg. in reading *bĕnê* for *'ăbî* in v. 3 since the foregoing *wĕ'ēlleh* requires a plur. predicate, and the MT reading can be explained as a scribal error from the three occurrences of *'ăbî* in v. 4a. On the other hand, LXX and Vg. (cf. *RSV*) err in adding "Meonothai" at the end of v. 13 in order to make a transition to v. 14; as we have seen, the formula *bĕnê* . . . often appears with a single name, and v. 14 does not offer a subsidiary segment but a completely independent list.

These are perhaps the two most serious points of textual confusion. Two features make it difficult to sort out the elements of a structural whole within this pericope. First, several genealogical items hang loose because the name of a father appears erratically, without prior introduction in a list of siblings. Second, a striking array of stylings is used: *hôlîd 'et* (vv. 2, 8, 13-14) and the like. It is apparent that we are dealing with ethnological data, including genealogical fragments, drawn haphazardly from clan traditions. The confusion is worse here than in ch. 2, because we are further removed from the central Hezron elements. V. 2 has two occurrences of *hôlîd* in a short series, as does v. 14; it switches over to a mixed *(û)bĕnê* and *'ăbî* subsection in vv. 3-4a and continues to combine these stylings in vv. 5-7, which also feature chiasmus in switching the places of Helah and Naarah. V. 8 has the *hôlîd* formula; then follows the entirely disparate Jabez anecdote, vv. 9-10. The following Recahite genealogy (vv. 11-12) combines *hôlîd* with the *'ăbî* formula. The section in vv. 13ff. begins with one of this pericope's rare segmented (two-generational) listings, alternating name list, genealogy, name list, and birth reports. The genealogy for "Caleb son of Jephunneh," with following name lists, vv. 15-17a, has the *ûbĕnê* styling. Narrative verbs prevail in the birth reports of vv. 17b-18. V. 19 is especially confusing because "sons" in the subject becomes "father(s) of" in the predicate. V. 20 has the copula with *bĕnê* in two lists of siblings, attaching them to the Hodiah list.

A new subsection begins at v. 21. Because it has to do with Shelah (cf. 2:3; Gen 38:5ff.; 46:12), it cannot belong to the Hezron materials since the latter is descended from Judah through Er and Perez (2:5, 9). The opening formula at v. 21 lacks the copula, showing that this is independent material; so also the title "Shelah son of Judah" — an expression found nowhere else among these genealogies. Though Er is Shelah's brother at 2:3, he is his son here—another mark of independence. The *'ăbî* styling appears in v. 21a. The rest of the section is concerned with dependent guilds and lacks our familiar genealogical expressions.

It is the beginning of the Shelah subsection that marks the main break within this pericope. Apart from v. 1, which is ChrR's editorial transition from ch. 3, all the rest is a continuation of the Hezron list in ch. 2, minus the expansion in 2:52-55. Instead of drawing a genealogy to Kiriath-jearim, as in 2:52ff., 4:2 continues the line of Shobal through Reaiah, concluding with a formal rubric indicating that this lineage comprised the *mišpĕḥôt*, "clans," of the Zorathites, i.e., occupying the town and territory of Zorah on Judah's Danite border. A formal rubric introduces the Etam genealogy at v. 3. Without attribution to Etam, Penuel's and Ezer's *'ăbî* genealogies follow. A concluding rubric in v. 4b, virtually identical to 2:50a, is designed to complete the Hur genealogy; with *'ēlleh*, it is an ending as in vv. 6 and 12, not a beginning. Since "Hur" is a short name for the "Ashhur" mentioned in 2:24, the Ashhur list in vv. 5-7, deriving from a clan fragment residing in the Tekoa region, is appended.

The materials in vv. 8-12 seem to have no internal connection. It might seem that the Jabez anecdote lacks even a thematic link, except for the fact that it functions as a clan etiology (Jabez is mentioned as the town where the "Siphrites" dwelt in 2:55). The Recahite genealogy (vv. 11-12) is unusual in presenting names only for the first and third generations. Vv. 13-15, containing name lists and genealogies, are structured as a unique inclusio, beginning with Kenaz as clan eponym and ending with Kenaz as grandson of Caleb. Not only does this section show unusual fluidity of tradition; it demonstrates also the power of Caleb's prestige in claiming a third genealogy while relating him to the non-Israelite Kenizzite group.

Quite without support from the ancient VSS, *RSV* takes the last clause from v. 18 and inserts it after the Ezrah name list in v. 17a, making it appear that Bithiah was the mother of Ezrah's sons. This has been done to ease the difficulty created by the lack of a mother's name in the birth notice of v. 17b, but this produces the unparalleled situation in which two separate lists are attributed to one mother, and certainly does not explain how v. 18b became dislocated from its original position. It is better to think of the original compiler overlooking the mother's name in v. 17b and appending a retrospective identification of her ("These are the sons of Bithiah . . ." attaches her to "Miriam, etc.") in v. 18b. We note that the Judahite wife of Mered likewise remains unnamed; an interesting problem is the lack of verbal parallelism between Bithiah's "conceiving" *(hrh)* and the Judahite wife's "bearing" *(yld)*.

A similar concern for the role of mothers appears in v. 19, a fragmentary BIRTH REPORT. The sons remain anonymous here, while the prominence of female figures demonstrates the concern to trace maternal lineage. "Sons of" cannot agree with the sg. *'ăbî,* hence it is best to take "sons" distributively and "father" elliptically for the "parents" of the two towns, Keilah and Eshtemoa (the latter is related to Ishbah in v. 17).

Genre

The genres of ch. 2 continue to appear in profusion and confusion. We identify the GENEALOGY in vv. 2, 4, 8, 11-12, 14-15, and 21a; the NAME LIST in vv. 1, 3, 7, 13, 16-17a, 19, 20, 22; the BIRTH REPORT in vv. 6, 17b-18, 19. V. 1 is a transition to an EDITORIAL UNIT in which ChrR puts the broken-off Shobal material in genealogical perspective by listing him, his father Hur, and the three remote ancestors of 2:5, 7, 9 as the five sons of Judah (cf. 2:4). V. 9b is a typical NAMING ETIOLOGY; it makes a bad pun because the word *'ōṣeb,* "pain," in the mother's explanation reverses the last two root letters in Jabez's name *(ya'ĕbēṣ).* Another instance of this genre is seen in v. 14, where a grounding clause, *kî ḥărāšîm hāyû* (a possible scribal gloss), explains the place-name *gē' ḥărāšîm,* "valley of craftsmen." Looking back at vv. 9-10, we identify not only an ANECDOTE but a CLAN ETIOLOGY. The ANECDOTE is a private, biographical report of an important event in the life of a person, in this case a certain Jabez; but this anecdote has been turned into an ETIOLOGY for this person's clan. As has been suggested, this accounts for its inclusion in the present context, although the birthing element relates it also to the birth reports present here. It begins with the narrative *wayĕhî,* "and it came to pass . . . ," and continues, "that Jabez was/became more important than his brothers/brother clans." This is a formula of eminence, or preeminence, and the ANECDOTE about his prayer and God's answer to it functions as an ETIOLOGY — a primitive explanation of how things got to be as they are.

We identify, finally, the genre PRAYER, a direct address to God in the second person. Jabez prays for four particular things: (1) blessing (= large posterity; cf. Gen 12:2-3); (2) territorial enlargement; (3) the divine power-presence ("hand"); and (4) protection. All are indispensable to the success of a clan group (see A. Kropat, *Die Syntax des Autors der Chronik,* 76).

Setting

Only a few of the personal names mentioned in this pericope appear elsewhere in the Bible, and it is clear that we are dealing here with the eponyms of clans, subclans, families, guilds, and towns. Towns familiar to us are Gedor, Ephrathah, and Bethlehem (v. 4), Tekoa (v. 5), Ziph (v. 16), Soco and Zanoah (v. 18), Keilah and Eshtemoa (v. 19), and Mareshah (v. 21), and scholars have attempted to identify others as well (cf. Noth, "Eine siedlungsgeographische Liste," 102-12). The names Geharashim, Beth-ashbea, and Bethrapha can only be names of towns. We are especially struck by the references to craftsmen's guilds in vv. 14, 21 (*bêt,* "house"), and 23. Of the potters mentioned in v. 23 it is reported that they dwelt in the towns Netaim and Gederah to perform the work of the king, i.e., to supply his regular requisitions. The king mentioned could be any king or several kings, for this guild apparently had permanent status (cf. Macalister, "Craftsmen's Guild"). Cozeba in v. 22 is evidently a town, as is "Lehem," an abbreviation for Bethlehem. The group or groups that "ruled" (i.e., governed, administered) in Moab cannot be identified or dated.

The Shelah lists in vv. 21-23 constitute an attached fragment, but must derive from the same historical and sociological situation as the Hezron lists commencing in ch. 2. We have perhaps a hint that most or all of these lists arose in the premonarchical or early monarchical periods in v. 10's reference to "the God of Israel." Though Yahweh is meant, he is not named. One's impression is that Jabez may be a convert, that in appealing to *Israel's* God he gained status among the already committed clans.

Intention

4:2-20 completes the Hezron lists, forming an inclusio with ch. 2 for the redactionally inserted David and Solomon genealogies. A vast array of names surrounds the royal family, giving it a breadth commensurate with its length. (Ash)hur and Caleb continue in prominence. The Shelah listings in vv. 21-23 were probably added because its guilds were important to the royal establishment.

Bibliography

R. A. S. Macalister, "The Craftsmen's Guild of the Tribe of Judah," *PEFQS*, 1905, 243-53, 328-42; M. Noth, "Eine siedlungsgeographische Liste in I Chr 2 und 4," *ZDPV* 55 (1932) 97-124; P. Welten, *Die Königs-Stempel* (Abhandlungen des Deutschen Palästinavereins; Wiesbaden: Harrassowitz, 1969).

TRIBAL RECORDS OF THE SIMEONITES, 4:24-43

Structure

Five tribal eponyms are listed, then the linear descendants of the last named, Shaul, and finally the sons of the last-named descendant. Although the names in vv. 25-26 are followed by *běnô*, "his son," in v. 25 this expression refers back to the immediately preceding name, and in v. 26 it jumps back over siblings to the parent of them all. Needless to say, in some passages this is likely to cause confusion and uncertainty (so already in ch. 3). Though it is in expository style, v. 27 attaches directly to the last-given name, Shimei, whose many sons and daughters are mentioned as an exception to the general rule that his brother clans did not have many "children," leading to a final unfavorable comparison with prolific Judah (v. 27b). Reading *mišpaḥtām* (MT, *RSV*; LXX plur.), we should interpret the final clause of this verse as a retrospective conclusion, meaning that, even while counting Shimei's numerous progeny, the Simeonites as a group could not keep pace with their Judahite rivals.

The archive turns from clan and family names to settlements, distinguishing between *'ārîm*, "cities," and *ḥăsērîm*, "villages." There are thirteen "cities," identified as the places where "they" (all the Simeonites) dwelt. The dating formula in v. 31b (*'ēlleh* refers back to the thirteen cities) continues in close syntactical connection with a list of four (not five because Ain plus Rimmon is a single place-name) villages; the plur. possessive pronoun probably refers to the tribe, as in the preceding "their cities." An ancient glossator miscounted the four as five, designating them as "cities" (v. 32b), then adding a generalizing statement that there were still other villages surrounding these cities—which now means the four villages/cities of v. 32 and not those of vv. 28-31. V. 33 is an original closing rubric in which the term *môšěbōtām*, "their settlements/residences," includes both the cities and villages listed (*zōʾt*, a demonstrative pronoun, points to a generalized, unspecified antecedent such as "record"). Authentication for such a record is intended in the phrase *wěhityaḥśām lāhem*, which does not mean "and they kept a genealogical record" (*RSV*), but "and they were placed on the muster roll." In addition to authenticating the list, however, it prepares for the MUSTER ROLL to follow.

The major break within the pericope seems to come here because of the foregoing closing rubric, so that vv. 34-43 must be viewed as an appendix. V. 34 is closely attached to those verses by the copula, but it introduces an afterthought in the genealogist's composition. We have here a MUSTER ROLL of Simeonite leaders —the tribal militia. This consists, first, of a lengthy name list, now for the first time with three pedigrees, one having five names. Their rank (*nĕśî'îm*, "chieftains") is given in v. 38b; the phrase *habbā'îm bĕśēmôt*, like *hakkĕtûbîm bĕśēmôt* in v. 41, means "those expressly mentioned/inscribed." V. 38b appears to contradict v. 27, but *bêt 'ăbôtêhem* is a technical phrase for the muster roll and means "ancestral family(ies)," a category for enrolling members of the militia.

The appearance of this muster roll at the head of two short accounts of territorial conquest (vv. 39-41, 42-43) seems far more logical than many of the connections made in chs. 2 and 4. Each account appears in narrative styling. Vv. 39-41 relate why the Simeonites needed new territory, how they found it and drove out its former occupants, then took permanent possession of it. "Their tents" in v. 41 has to refer back to the Hamites mentioned in the grounding clause of v. 40b, but Meunites were there too, perhaps as clients or errant wayfarers. The narrator unexpectedly gives us two historical reference points: Hezekiah's reign as the time of conquest, and sometime thereafter (*'ad hayyôm hazzeh*, "to this very day") as the time of writing. A second grounding clause in v. 41b, "because there was pasture there for their flocks," is probably intended as an inclusio with v. 39.

The thematic word in vv. 39-41 is *yšb*, "dwell." So too in vv. 42-43. Strikingly, it too has *'ad hayyôm hazzeh*, but at the very end. This account gives us the name list and tally for a small offshoot of the Simeonites, records dispersal of some Amalekite refugees (persons displaced from their accustomed territory), and records that the Simeonites took permanent possession.

Genre

Familiar to the reader of these chapters are the genres GENEALOGY, found in vv. 25-27, and NAME LIST, found in vv. 24, 28-31a, 32a, 34-37, and 42b. Those of vv. 28-31, phrased in outright geographical terminology, do not differ substantively from those we have seen in 2:3–4:23, because many names there are actually of towns and geographical regions. Thus Rudolph and Noth are mistaken in identifying this section as secondary, and Williamson (comm.) is wrong in regarding the authentication notice at the end of v. 33 as ChrR's device for artificially placing vv. 28-33 on equal footing with the "authentic" list in vv. 25-27. V. 42a shows us the TALLY placed in narrative context, a variation of the original form. A form related to the GENEALOGY is the PEDIGREE, which appears in vv. 34-37. The latter is the precise opposite of the GENEALOGY, which proceeds linearly or collaterally from the early to the late, from the ancestor to the descendant. In the PEDIGREE a descendant traces his direct lineage to a remote ancestor, naming all the males in the direct line of descent. Its purpose is less identification than authentication. The regular formula is "X son of A, son of B, son of C, etc." Joshah's pedigree goes back one generation, Jehu's goes back three generations, and Ziza's goes back five generations. (The often-occurring patronymic formula, "X son of Y," is based on the PEDIGREE.) New here, but occurring frequently in the following sections, is the genre MUSTER ROLL. Easily confused with the GENEALOGY, this is in fact a list of effective fighting forces kept as a record to be used in preparation for battle. It showed, not individual names, but clans, subclans, and families serving as military units. The personal names that are given are those of eponymous ancestors; even when these would be long dead, their units would identify themselves by their names. The technical name for such units was *bêt 'ābôt*, "ancestral house" (v. 38b). In this genre, the APPELLATION and the RANKING FORMULA are often seen.

The identification of vv. 34-38 as a MUSTER ROLL is assured by its narrative attachment to the following examples of the BATTLE REPORT. This is a subgenre of one of ChrH's favorite genres, the REPORT. This is a brief, self-contained prose narrative, usually in third-person style, about a single past event, with no developed plot or imaginative characterization. Such are vv. 39-41 and vv. 42-43, recording settlement in new territory by Simeonite groups. Here one identifies the SCHEMA OF TERRITORIAL CLAIM, seen also in Deut 2:22 and 2 Kgs 16:6. Each of these passages contains the time expression *'ad–hayyôm hazzeh*, "until this day." This is no casual formulation, for it appears as a technical element in the (→) ETIOLOGY, and generally concludes passages establishing the antiquity of peoples, cities, rituals, monumental constructions, territorial claims, laws and customs, and political affiliations. The SCHEMA OF TERRITORIAL CLAIM, as we see it in vv. 39ff., 42f., establishes the following points: (1) the dispossession of the original inhabitants, who are mentioned by name; (2) an affirmation that the claimant groups have settled on the land and have dwelt *(yšb)* there; (3) an indication that this occupation is presently in force, having been continuous from the beginning. That this schema is devoid of any theological or political ideology is seen in the fact that 2 Kgs 16:6 applies it to territory seized from the Judeans by the Edomites.

The genre of the pericope as a whole is LIST with appended REPORT. The genealogist is clearly moving beyond the question of Israel as a people and nation to that of Israel in possession of a land.

Setting

Noth ("Chronistische Werk," 118, 120) regards vv. 24-33 as original and, with Rudolph, vv. 28-31 as secondary. Certainly there is no post-Chronicles expansion here, nor is ChrR's editorial hand evident. The authenticating formula in v. 33, *wěhityaḥśām lāhem*, is not ChrR's mark (cf. 1 Chr 9:1a), but an ancient tribal locution. It is true that several of the tribal records (Levi/Aaron, 1 Chr 5:27; Issachar, 7:1; Naphtali, 7:13; Manasseh, 7:14; Asher, 7:30; Benjamin, 8:1) start with a list of tribal eponyms, as here, and these are evidently taken from some common genealogical summation, but not necessarily from Numbers 26. It will be seen, in fact, that the genealogy of vv. 25-27 does not agree with Num 26:12 (cf. Gen 46:10), though interdependence of some sort is apparent. The list of towns and villages has a less expansive structure than parallel material in Josh 19:4-8a, which may date from the late monarchy. The fact that Josh 15:26-32, 42 gives several of these Simeonite towns to Judah explains both the complaint about Simeon's sparse population in relation to Judah (v. 27) and the dating formula given at the end of v. 31. Intense rivalry between these two tribes is reflected here; as it became consolidated, Judah usurped many sites previously claimed by Simeon.

It has been suggested that v. 38 is not in conflict with v. 27 because it belongs to a MUSTER ROLL and pertains to militia substructures rather than to individual ethnic groups. Although there is nothing that would keep vv. 34-38 from being contemporary with vv. 24-33, the reference to "the days of Hezekiah" definitely marks the date of the seizure of Gedor (Gerar?), and the *'ad-hayyôm hazzeh* formula in v. 41 has to refer to some date subsequent to this, though not necessarily the time of ChrR. It is tempting to view the tale of conquest in Mount Seir as very early because of the reference to "the remnants of the Amalekites," which may be related to Saul's action against this tribe (1 Samuel 15). This is not made impossible by the "to this day" formula in v. 43, which, as part of the SCHEMA OF TERRITORIAL CLAIM, would pertain to the date of the given record, not necessarily to the date of the foregoing report. Another possible consideration in favor of an early date is the fact that Edom became independent long before the time of Hezekiah (cf. 2 Chr 21:8), and probably would not have tolerated the presence of any Israelite group after that date. It is the pre-Chronicles genealogist who put vv. 39-41 and vv. 42-43 in narrative sequence, and he may have had no awareness of the actual historical circumstances underlying each report.

Intention

Having disposed of his material on Judah, ChrR arranges the rest of his material and prepares to present it in an appropriate order. Since Simeon had long since been absorbed into Judah, it naturally occupies second place. Because its territory lay on the southern fringe of Judah, ChrR will next take up Reuben and the other Transjordanian tribes, lying to the east. At that point he will give up his circuitous arrangement because he decides that the Levites must be presented. Nongeographical considerations will determine the order of the remaining tribes.

As has been seen, the Simeon materials presented in 4:24-43 date from the time of David until long after the time of Hezekiah—perhaps the Babylonian exile or even the postexilic period. ChrR has a special concern for the remnant of the Simeonites and is anxious to ensure them a place among the tribes constituting his ideal Israel, because Simeon did in effect become an important ethnic category with the restored Judah that he knew. It is quite unlikely that he had direct personal acquaintance with their original settlements because in his time these lay well within the territory of the Idumeans, which reached northward as far as Mareshah and Beth-zur. ChrR was a Jerusalem man "born and bred," and even if political conditions would have permitted an inspection tour, he would have preferred an examination of his records to the arduousness of an actual journey. What he took from these records had little historical interest for him. He was concerned only for the theological witness that they bore.

Bibliography

Y. Aharoni, "The Negev of Judah," *IEJ* 8 (1958) 26-38; J. B. Bartlett, "The Land of Seir and the Brotherhood of Edom," *JTS* 20 (1969) 1-20; B. S. Childs, "A Study of the Formula, 'Until this Day'," *JBL* 82 (1963) 279-92; M. D. Johnson, *The Purpose of the Biblical Genealogies* (SNTSMS 8; Cambridge: Cambridge, 1969) 38-82; Z. Kallai-Zimmermann, "The Town-Lists of Judah, Simeon, Benjamin and Dan," *VT* 8 (1958) 134-60; N. H. Tur-Sinai, "On Some Historical References in the Bible" (Hebr.), *ErIs* 5 (1958) 74-79.

RECORDS OF THE TRANSJORDANIAN TRIBES, 5:1-26

Structure and Genre

I. Records for Reuben	5:1-10
II. Records for Gad	5:11-17
III. Battle report: Transjordanian war	5:18-22
IV. Records for Half-Manasseh	5:23-24
V. Statement of common destiny	5:25-26

The opening identification, *ûbĕnê rĕ'ûbēn*, attaches 5:1-10 directly to the preceding Simeon pericope, and a similar syndetic styling connects vv. 11-17 to vv. 1-10, and vv. 23-24 to vv. 11-17. The whole is the work of the early genealogist, who evidently wanted to present these as a separate and complete entity. They share much the same structure with one another. Reuben's MUSTER ROLL leads into a BATTLE REPORT, just as in the Simeon material. Gad's MUSTER ROLL introduces territorial claims, while half-Manasseh's territorial claim is followed by its MUSTER ROLL. At 5:18-22 the series of tribal listings is interrupted by a report of a war against the Hagrites. Although this war is said to have involved all three tribal groups, it intrudes at the completion of the Reuben-Gad pairing, perhaps because these tribes overshadowed the half-Manassites in importance. The Hagrite war report is followed by the tribal record for half-Manasseh, which leads in the conclusion, 5:25-26, to a theological reflection on transgression and punishment, not only for the half-Manassites but for all three tribes together. The structure of 5:1-26 points to the form of EDITORIAL UNIT (see on vv. 25-26).

Setting and Intention

The combination as it now stands is unmistakably the work of ChrR. It is his language and ideology that one recognizes at vv. 20, 25-26. V. 20b has three of his familiar themes: crying to God in battle, the granting of his people's entreaty, and trust. Vv. 25-26 have other characteristic locutions of ChrH: transgression against the ancestral God ("God of their fathers" is his special term), playing the harlot like the peoples destroyed (borrowed from DtrH), "stirring up the spirit." ChrR apparently desired to account for the dearth of representatives from these Transjordanian tribes in the "Israel" reunited under Hezekiah and now reconstituted in the restoration community of his own time. This dearth was because of this early, and severe, offense. Here for the first time ChrR/H introduces the theme of exile. Although he attaches his theological reflection to the record of half-Manasseh, the parenthesis of v. 26, "namely, the Reubenites, the Gadites, and the half-tribe of Manasseh," assures that all three groups receive the blame. This is no doubt also the reason why the Hagrite war account has been inserted into an already completed combination. In ChrR's intention, it is weighted on the side of the half-Manassites in giving them a close connection to the dominant, more senior tribes, who as prime leaders in war were also prime seducers into sin.

I. RECORDS FOR REUBEN, 5:1-10

Structure

In the traditional lists, Reuben is always mentioned as the eldest of all tribal eponyms. The title *bĕkôr,* "firstborn," must have been one that this tribe continued to insist upon in spite of their decreasing importance within the tribal system in the process of settling down upon the land, so much so that the genealogist (or perhaps ChrR) has to interrupt the intended name list for Reuben's clans with a midrashic explanation that this tribe does retain the right to this title despite the fact that (1) the *bĕkōrâ,* "birthright," pertaining to his status was transferred to Joseph's sons, and (2) Judah became the strongest tribe and produced a *nāgîd,* "ruler," over them. V. 3a is a reprise of v. $1a\alpha^1$ (cf. 9:35-44; 21:20), redirecting the writer's presentation to its intended course. The name list (v. 3b) opens out into a linear genealogy for the Joelites, to which is appended the unparalleled explanation that the last of the line was exiled by the Assyrians (vv. 4-6a). This leads directly into a tribal muster listing the just-mentioned Beerah as *nāsî',* "chief," with three "brothers," i.e., clan fellows, as lieutenants, for the last of whom a statement of territorial possession is given (vv. 6b-8). So far, the syntactical structure remains cohesive, but a major structural break comes at v. 9, where an unmentioned subject (undoubtedly Reuben as a tribe, in spite of the singular verb) introduces a statement of the tribe's territorial expansion. V. 10 continues in narrative styling and with a plur. verb without subject (= Reubenites), telling of occupation of Hagrite land through conquest during the days of Saul.

This short pericope is a model for the entire genealogical section (see Chapter 2 above), and indeed for the entire 1-2 Chronicles, in its concern for (1) ethnic,

(2) military, and (3) territorial matters. It already raises ChrH's essential issues: the people, the land, the organization for perfecting the people within the land.

Genre

The basic genre of vv. 1-8 is LIST; vv. 9-10 are a BATTLE REPORT. GENEALOGY appears in vv. 4-6, with NAME LIST at vv. 3, 7-8. V. 1 has a fragment of the RANKING FORMULA ("chief" in v. 7 is an APPELLATION). There is a four-generation PEDIGREE in v. 8. The MUSTER ROLL appears at vv. 6-8. Vv. 9-10 display the SCHEMA OF TERRITORIAL CLAIM seen in the Simeon pericope, lacking only the statement of perpetual occupation. It has (1) a statement that the land eastward to the Euphrates was not sufficient for Reuben's cattle, (2) the report of a successful war against the Hagrites, and (3) a statement that they occupied (yšb) the entire territory of Gilead.

The genre of vv. 1-2 is MIDRASH. In essence, MIDRASH is an exposition of the authoritative word of Scripture according to the needs and viewpoint of later times (cf. A. G. Wright, *The Literary Genre Midrash,* p. 74; hence the dictum, "Midrash . . . is a literature about a literature," p. 67). Pre-rabbinic examples may be the "Midrash of the Passover Haggadah," the Qumran pěšārîm and Genesis Apocryphon, the homilies in Wisdom 11–19, and some passages in the NT and 4 Ezra. Rabbinic Judaism gave midrash wide application, both as a form and as a method. We are looking at it here as a form, not intending to deny the relevance of its development as a method. As a form, it falls midway between Targum, in which speculative reapplication is directly incorporated into an expanded scriptural translation, intended for liturgical use, and Mishna, a discursive, systematic exposition with no formal attachment to the scriptural text. Even in midrashic expositions that grow into extensive works, two characteristics are always important: (1) each individual segment of MIDRASH is a logically independent unit, and (2) the exposition may range from literal, grammatical explanation to unsupported philosophical speculation.

We will see in Chapter 4 that some scholars have claimed that ChrH is a "midrash" on Samuel-Kings, or even that ChrH had access to an unnamed "midrash" which was utilized for the non-synoptic passages. We will argue that the "midrashim" of 2 Chr 13:22 and 24:27, cited as sources for a given king's reign, are fictional; nevertheless this manner of reference shows that in ChrH's time the term did designate a specific kind of literature. But those who claim that Chronicles is a midrash or utilizes midrashim are thinking of the method known from rabbinic literature, which might be seen in isolated passages (cf. Seeligmann, "Beginnings"), though certainly not as extensively as claimed by M. D. Goulder (*Midrash and Lection in Matthew* [London: SPCK, 1974] 223-24). ChrH rewrites Israel's history but he does not comment upon it. Like DtrH, he extracts information from court annals, collections of prophetic legend, and the like—but this is not midrash.

We should not expect to find within the canonized OT an example of full-formed midrash, yet 1 Chr 5:1-2 and 27:23-24 show that this genre was coming into use in the time of 1–2 Chronicles. When we try to account for these two passages, we find that each lies loosely attached to its context. Each attempts to expound a solution to some serious problem arising within the received scriptural tradition as utilized by ChrR/H. Although we would not be justified in speaking of a fully canonized Scripture, the biblical texts in question plainly do possess a high level of authority. Each passage borrows from remote scriptural allusion or from unknown, independent oral tradition—a form of early *haggadah*. The passages mentioned are similar enough, both in form and intention, to justify applying to them the genre name MIDRASH.

The genealogist who has compiled these tribal records has been following the lists of Numbers 26, or an abstract or recensional variant of it. He comes upon the opening rubric, "The sons of Reuben the first-born of Israel." Before going on to list Reuben's sons in v. 3, he pauses to reflect on the problem that the *bĕkôr*, "first-born," gets the *bĕkōrâ*, "birthright," yet Reuben has in fact become one of the least of the tribes. MIDRASH provides the answer from Scripture and oral tradition, showing how the firstborn did in fact lose his birthright. In terms of content, then, this passage has an etiological function, explaining how this striking phenomenon came about (→ ETIOLOGY).

Setting and Intention

As with all these lists, the genealogy and name lists for Reuben are only representative and symbolic, for they span only a few generations and must reach from at least the time of Saul (v. 10) to the time of "Tilgath-pilneser" (mid-8th century). The new thing about this pericope is the midrash on "Reuben the first-born of Israel." Reuben apparently remained an effective tribe at least to the time of the Assyrian invasion, occupying a vast tract reaching as far as the Euphrates (v. 9), yet the land was empty steppeland and trackless forest (Gilead). They had some success in battle against the Hagrites (descendants of Hagar, Abraham's wife), but vv. 18-19 reveal that the Gadites and half-Manassites had to help, and even then victory would not have come except for some other unidentified assistance ("they received help against them"). In any event, the Reubenites occupied the eastern steppeland and were far distant from the center of political control, whether Samaria or Jerusalem. An etiological MIDRASH is needed to explain, then, why Israel's *bĕkôr* has lost his rightful birthright, his double portion of power, riches, and honor. The situation is the same as with Esau, who dwelt in the eastern steppeland opposite "Jacob," and for whom the etiology of Gen 25:29-34 provides a similar answer to the same question.

The MIDRASH builds on and interprets Scripture. It is clear why Israel's *bĕkôr* lost the *bĕkōrâ:* he lay with his father's wife (Gen 35:22; 49:3-4); this is a haggadic inference because Gen 49:4 threatens Reuben only with the loss of *yeter*, "preeminence." To whom, then, was the *bĕkōrâ* given? "To the sons of Joseph," says the MIDRASH, working only from Gen 48:5b, which speaks of their reception as two tribes in the place of one, and from Gen 48:15-16 and 49:22-26, which speak of a blessing and not a birthright. This is etiological also for Manasseh and Ephraim, Joseph's "sons." Since they received a double portion among the twelve tribes, they received the birthright. The midrash wants us to understand that this included the territory once occupied by Reuben—the central hill country—from which he has been forced to move to a region more barren and remote. A final question is, "Was the birthright not given to Judah?" The answer is that, though he is strongest and has the "prince," the birthright is Joseph's because of his two tribes.

Bibliography

R. Bloch, "Midrash," *Dictionnaire de la Bible, Supplement* V (Paris: Letouzey & Ane, 1957) cols. 1263-81; R. Le Déaut, "A propos d'une définition du midrash," *Bib* 50 (1969) 395-413; M. D. Goulder, *Midrash and Lection in Matthew* (London: SPCK, 1974); M. Kadushin, *A Conceptual Approach to the Mekilta* (New York: Jewish Theological Seminary of America, 1969); J. Neusner, *Midrash in Context* (Philadelphia: Fortress, 1983); I. Seeligmann, "The Beginnings of Midrash in the Book of Chronicles," *Tarb* 49 (1979/80) 14-32; idem, "Voraussetzungen der Midraschexegese," *Congress Volume: Copenhagen 1953* (VTSup 1; Leiden: Brill, 1953) 150-81; H. L. Strack, *Introduction to the Talmud and Midrash* (Philadelphia: Jewish Publication Society of America, 1945); G. Vermes, "Bible and Midrash: Early Old Testament Exegesis," in *Cambridge History of the Bible* I (Cambridge: Cambridge, 1970) 199-231; A. G. Wright, *The Literary Genre Midrash* (New York: Alba, 1967).

II. RECORDS FOR GAD, 5:11-17

Structure

A.	Tribal chiefs	11-12
	1. Introduction to name list	11
	2. Name list proper	12
B.	Muster roll of the families	13-15
	1. Introduction	13aα
	2. Name list with tally	13aβ-b
	3. Pedigree of Abihail	14
	4. Ahi as interfamilial chieftain	15
C.	Report of territorial claims	16
D.	Dates of mustering	17

Scholars are suspicious of the originality of this material. Willi *(Auslegung)* thinks *migrāšîm*, "pasture lands" (v. 16), is late, as in ch. 6, and hence he goes with Galling (ATD) in dating it post-ChrR. Noth ("Chronistische Werk," 120) agrees, but adds vv. 18-26 to the expansion, and Fohrer *(Intro.,* 244) dates all of vv. 11-41 after ChrR. These scholars may have been misled by two glosses at the beginning (v. 11), *lĕnegdām,* "over against them," and *yāšĕbû bĕ'ereṣ habbāšān 'ad-salĕkâ,* "they dwelt in the land of Bashan as far as Salecah." The original list simply began with the genealogical rubric *ûbĕnê-gād,* intending to continue with the name list in v. 12, but the compiler of this section of Transjordanian materials added the first gloss in order to bond this tribal record more closely to that of Reuben. Because the second gloss drastically reduces the territorial claim in v. 16 by restricting Gad to Bashan, it may be attributed to ChrR, who supposed that the first three words needed filling out. Once we recognize these intrusions, we see that this pericope is structured much like those of Simeon and Reuben. The muster roll in vv. 13-15 employs the usual terminology. *wa'ăḥêhem lĕbêt 'ăbôtêhem* has no proper antecedent in the preceding name list with ranking formula because the latter are tribal chiefs given in order of authority and not "brothers" in a genealogical sense. But the expression in question is normal in a muster roll and means "clan associates listed according to ancestral families." These are named and tallied, and then are identified as "sons" of Abihail, whose pedigree is traced back seven generations. Though not included in the tally, a certain Ahi is next identified as *rōʾš*, "leader," among the "ancestral families" just mentioned; he is given a pedigree of three generations (v. 15).

Turning now to the tribe as a whole: the original record informs us where they dwelt *(yšb)*: Gilead, Bashan, and Sharon (v. 16). Here we are led to understand that Gad shared Gilead with Reuben, which seems to be supported by the statement in vv. 18ff. that Gad shared in the war against the Hagrites, according to v. 10 the former inhabitants of Gilead. Sharon is the Transjordanian region mentioned in the Moabite Stone, line 13. "To their limits" (v. 16) gives *'ad* [LXX] *tôṣě'ôtām* a territorial meaning, but the semantic range of the verb *yṣ'* would allow "as they were opened up," i.e., settled. Finally, "all these" in v. 17 introduces a summarizing conclusion, in which *yḥś* (hith.) has the meaning "were enrolled in the muster," rather than *RSV*'s "inscribed in a genealogy." Because Jotham (750-742) was not contemporaneous with Jeroboam II (792-752), two separate musterings must be intended.

Genre

The basic genre is LIST. The NAME LIST in vv. 11-12 has the RANKING FORMULA, while that of v. 13 has the TALLY. Vv. 13-15 constitute a MUSTER ROLL. The PEDIGREE appears in vv. 14 and 15. V. 16 shows the influence of the (→) SCHEMA OF TERRITORIAL CLAIM, but its genre is REPORT.

Setting and Intention

Since the name lists do not draw an unbroken line of descent, this pericope can neither be dated nor used for historical reconstruction. All we have to go by is the genealogist's dating formula at the end, placing him—not the tribal leaders—later than the middle of the 8th century B.C., and ChrR's note in v. 11 restricting them to Bashan. As a traditional son of the by-wife Zilpah, Gad appears in various tribal associations, especially with Asher (whose territory is far removed from his), and gradually fades from the scene of nation-making activity. In the postexilic period few remnants of this population remained, while Gad's traditional territory lay far outside the land of Judah. All the same, ChrR has a place for him within the framework of his ideal Israel.

Bibliography

K. Elliger, "Gad," *IDB* II:333-35; J. P. Weinberg, "Das *bēit 'ābōt* im 6.-4. Jahrhundert vor unserer Zeit," *VT* 23 (1973) 400-414.

III. BATTLE REPORT: TRANSJORDANIAN WAR, 5:18-22

Structure

A. The battle	18-20
1. Muster roll of the fighting force	18
a. Tribal identities	18aα
b. Fighting qualities	18aβ
c. Tally	18b
2. The fighting	19-20
a. Attack on the allied tribes	19
b. Victory	20a
1) Arrival of timely help	20aα
2) Total conquest	20aβ
c. Theological explanation	20b
B. The prizes of war	21-22
1. Living beings	21-22a
a. Tally of livestock	21a
b. Tally of human captives	21b
c. Conclusion	22a
1) Numerous casualties	22aα
2) Theological explanation	22aβ
2. Occupation of captured territory	22b

Rudolph (HAT) sees this pericope as a late addition to v. 10, which also mentions war against the Hagrites; but then why should the editor not have placed it there? As we have argued, it is an independent tradition chosen by ChrR for insertion at this spot. The participating tribes are mentioned. Then, to show that only fighting men were involved, *min*, i.e., "some" (or "only out of . . ."), then specifies the fighting branches (light infantry: "carrying shield and sword"; archers: "drawing the bow") and lists the appellations (*benê-ḥayil*, "distinguished soldiers"; *lĕmûdê milḥāmâ*, "trained in fighting"; *yōṣĕ'ê ṣābā'*, "effective army-men") of this force (→ APPELLA-TION). Fantastic tallies are given, as in the list of plunder in v. 21, but this is characteristic in ancient battle reports. In the list of adversaries, only "Hagrites" is a gentilic; it is followed by proper names belonging to three client peoples, mentioned as "all who were with them" in v. 20 (cf. W. G. E. Watson, "Archaic Elements in the Language of Chronicles," *Bib* 53 [1972] 192 n. 1). No details of the battle are given except for the fact that they received unexpected help at the critical moment, resulting in total victory (v. 20a). Though the ancient record undoubtedly meant allied military forces, ChrR seizes upon this opportunity to interject his explanation that (1) God was the one who helped; (2) this was because of their cry/entreaty; (3) this was evidence of their trust in him. Vast numbers of *miqnêhem*, "their livestock," and *nepeš 'ādām*, "human beings," were taken captive (v. 21), and this grand success is explained in another ChrR gloss (v. 22a), adding two items of interpretation to the preceding, viz., that the victory was possible because many *ḥălālîm*, "wounded, killed," had fallen, and that this was "because the war was of God" (both themes are familiar in ChrH's highly schematic depictions of the holy war). V. 22b provides a brief statement of occupation with the dating formula.

Genre

The main genre here is the BATTLE REPORT, but it clearly exhibits the SCHEMA OF TERRITORIAL CLAIM, omitting the element of the search, emphasizing the element of armed conflict, and briefly noting that the victors dwelt *(yšb) taḥtêhem*, "instead of them" (v. 22)—no specific place being mentioned. Also, the element of continuous occupation is included in the phrase "until the exile." V. 18 is a MUSTER ROLL; the TALLY appears at vv. 18 and 21. V. 18 illustrates the APPELLATION (see above). V. 20 has the very familiar CONVEYANCE FORMULA, "given into their hands"; cf. the more secular "fell by their hand" in v. 10. "For many fell slain" in v. 22a rephrases the genre CASUALTY REPORT.

Setting and Intention

There is little to date this account except for the fact that "dwelt instead of them" in v. 22 sounds more permanent than "dwelt in their tents throughout . . . Gilead" in v. 10. Perhaps the Hagrites had been intruding in Gilead until the Reubenites drove them out, but they remained such a vexation that Reuben summoned Gad and half-Manasseh to drive them from their own homeland, which "they"—meaning all three tribal groups—then occupied until the "exile." The exile mentioned need not be the Babylonian captivity of the 6th century. It may have been the result of the defeat inflicted by the Arameans in the time of Hazael and his son, mentioned in 2 Kgs 13:3 (cf. especially ". . . escaped . . . dwelt in their homes as formerly," v. 5). Otherwise it could have been part of Pul's first invasion, 2 Kgs 15:19. In any event, this mention dates the genealogist, who must have worked after this memorial event.

IV. RECORDS FOR HALF-MANASSEH, 5:23-24

Structure

A. Statement of territory		23
1. Half-Manasseh in Transjordan		23a
2. Expansion to northern frontiers		23b
B. Muster roll		24
1. Introduction		24a
2. Name list: family chieftains		24bα
3. Appellations		24bβ

The genealogist does not employ the usual caption, "and the sons of X," perhaps because he has a *běnê* caption for "Manasseh" in 7:14. Attached here to the name of a tribal unit, not of the patriarchal eponym, *běnê* (v. 23) means "people of." There is no genealogy, only an historical statement with two narrative verbs, *yāšěbû*, "they dwelt," and *rābû*, "they increased" or "spread." The "land" (omitted in LXX) is not named, but must be Transjordan, the same region occupied by Reuben and Gad (cf. v. 22). The structure of v. 23 is unusual, with prepositional phrases relating to geographical territory foremost, then the emphatic personal pronoun, *hēmmâ*, "those ones," followed by the perfect verb. *wĕ'ēlleh* introduces the formal caption for a muster roll, including the general title for the leaders of militia, *rā'šê bêt-'ăbôtām*, which appears in almost identical form at the end of a name list with the appellations *gibbôrê ḥayil*, "powerful champions," and *'anšê šēmôt*, "distinguished soldiers."

Genre

The MUSTER ROLL with NAME LIST and APPELLATION is familiar. A new genre is the STATEMENT (v. 23), a brief prose word which simply notes or describes a situation or circumstance. Characteristically, the verbs are in the perfect—stating mere facticity — rather than in the narrative imperfect. The main genre of this brief pericope is REPORT.

Setting and Intention

We are to see historical progression in the statement about half-Manasseh's territory. From merely sharing the territory occupied by Reuben and Gad this group expanded to the outer fringes of the Holy Land, taking in Bashan, Senir, Hermon, and (LXX) Lebanon itself. Though the (→) SCHEMA OF TERRITORIAL CLAIM is not evident, the verb *yšb* assures that this REPORT does lay claim to the region described.

V. STATEMENT OF COMMON DESTINY, 5:25-26

Structure

A. Transgression		25
B. Punishment		26
1. Assyrian invasion		26aα
2. Permanent exile		26aβ-b

The narrative sequence of this pericope is carried by a series of verbs in the *wāw*-consecutive impf.: *wayyim'ălû*, "and they offended," *wayyiznû*, "and they prostituted themselves," *wayyā'ar*, "and he aroused," *wayyaglēm*, "and he deported them," *waybî'ēm*, "and he brought them." It is obvious that a sequence—not just a series—of events is intended. With the initial occurrence of the pronoun suffix, a parenthesis with ChrR's *lĕ* styling specifies by name that all three tribal groups are intended.

Genre, Setting, and Intention

This interpretative STATEMENT draws together the entirety of 5:1-26 into ChrR's EDITORIAL UNIT, which is defined as two or more independent pericopes drawn together under a new framework of interpretation. In view of the prominence of the SCHEMA OF TERRITORIAL CLAIM throughout this section, whose intent has been to ensure territorial rights, and in which the dating expression *'ad hayyôm hazzeh* normally occurs, ChrR's own use of this expression at the very end of v. 26 must be seen as nullifying the claims of these particular tribal groups, while consigning them to distant and permanent exile.

This is the first place where ChrR uses the familiar DtrH language of apostasy to condemn a particular group. Since the Transjordanians must have been among the first to suffer the effects of Assyrian invasion (cf. 2 Kgs 15:29), ChrR applies his doctrine of retribution, arguing from effect to cause; if they were singled out to suffer under Pul/Tilgath-pilneser, logic argues that they must have been more idolatrous than the rest. We cannot be certain that ChrR was not simply citing oral tradition here, rather than Samuel-Kings, for he misnames the Assyrian king, conflating the two forms of his name and the two reports of his invasion (cf. 2 Kgs 15:19ff., 29ff.), adding reports about Samaria's exile (cf. 2 Kgs 17:6; 18:11) that the biblical record does not directly apply to the tribes of Transjordan.

LISTS OF THE LEVITES AND AARONITES, 5:27–6:66
(*RSV* 6:1-81)

Structure

I. Lineage of Levi	5:27–6:38 (*RSV* 6:1-53)
II. Catalogue of dwelling places for the descendants of Levi	6:39-66 (*RSV* 54-81)

As has been mentioned above in Chapter 2, the Levite lineage given in 6:1-15 is one of ChrR's "foundation documents." Its original independence is revealed by the asyndetic heading *běnê lēwî*, a form copied by an early supplementer at 5:27 who insisted not only on including the Aaronites but also on giving them priority over the lower-ranking Levites. The form and content argue against those critics (Noth, "Chronistische Werk," 146; Rudolph, HAT) who take this supplement as a post-Chronicles expansion; so too the fact that 6:35-38, beginning with the asyndetic rubric *wě'ēlleh* and clearly an expansion later than ChrR, repeats part of its genealogy. Nevertheless ChrR himself has been at work, first in appending his involved list of cultic functionaries, also introduced with *wě'ēlleh* (6:16-38), and second in attaching a catalogue of dwelling places (vv. 39-66).

I. LINEAGE OF LEVI, 5:27–6:38 (*RSV* 6:1-53)

Structure

A. The priestly line	5:27-41
1. Tribal name lists through Aaron	27-29
a. First generation: sons of Levi	27
b. Second generation: sons of Kohath	28
c. Third generation: sons of Amram	29a
d. Fourth generation: sons of Aaron	29b
2. Genealogy: high priests from Aaron	30-41
a. Thirteen generations: Eleazar to Azariah	30-36

The main break in this section comes at the transition from the Aaronite to the Levite lineage, as explained above. But within each main section there are two separate subsections. The Aaron lineage has first a tribal genealogy with each generation introduced by *bĕnê . . . ûbĕnê . . . ûbĕnê . . . ûbĕnê. . . .* This is followed by a linear list of persons who occupied the high-priestly office up to the exile, with consistent *hôlîd* styling except where the narrative form, *wayyôled,* resumes the genealogy at the end of a first explanatory note (5:36b [*RSV* 6:10b]), which states that the second-named Azariah was Solomon's officiating priest, though this would have to have been his grandfather of the same name, a contemporary of the first-named Zadok. ChrR may have been responsible for the explanatory note at the end of this list (5:41 [*RSV* 6:15]), stating that the last-named person was exiled by Nebuchadnezzar. The second main division (6:1-15 [*RSV* 16-30]) has first a name list with the customary *bĕnê* styling (see another lineage for Merari in 1 Chr 15:6). The second element in this section is the genealogy (6:4b-15 [*RSV* 19b-30]) introduced by *wĕ'ēlleh mišpĕḥôt hallēwî la'ăbôtêhem,* "And these are Levi's clans according to their fathers' houses," listing Samuel along with Gershon, Kohath, and Merari. (The spelling "Gershom" is a mistake that ChrR/H eventually corrects.) On v. 6, see Watson ("Archaic Elements," 3.6 [Lexicography]); on Samuel's three generations, see Johnson (*Genealogies,* 289).

Rudolph (HAT) and von Rad (*Geschichtsbild*, 102-3) argue that vv. 16-32 are post-Chronicles; the former adds vv. 33-38 to this. But it is only vv. 35-38 that is secondary; its opening rubric, *wĕ'ēlleh*, identifies it as quite separate from what immediately precedes. Only this time it is no new group that is so dramatically introduced, but the *bĕnê 'ahărôn*, "the sons of Aaron," or "Aaronites." But a great point had been made to introduce the Aaronite line of Levites back in 5:27ff. (*RSV* 6:1ff.), and this new genealogy only repeats part of that. This is a literary expansion that can be explained from the anxiety of a postexilic Aaronite priest who thought that *bĕnê lēwî* (ethnological) in 5:27 could too readily be confused with *bĕnê lēwî* (vocational) in 6:1. To make sure that no one could confuse the pushy Levites of his day with the proper Aaronite priests, he added this new list. (See Williamson, comm., 74; *contra* Willi, 214; cf. also Möhlenbrink, 204-5.)

Introduced by *wĕ'ēlleh*, this section gives not a nominal predicate but a relative clause describing the duties of the group designated. These are the singers, whose roster follows. This lists the entire group according to the three eponyms that have just been mentioned (in a different order) in the foregoing genealogy for the Levites. Yet these singers are not actually Levites, if we are to judge from v. 33, where the work of the Levites is listed as quite separate, along with that of the Aaronite priests. For the Kohathites, Gershonites, and Merarites, the present ruling authority is given (Heman, Asaph, and Ethan, respectively) and then their respective pedigrees.

II. CATALOGUE OF DWELLING PLACES FOR THE DESCENDANTS OF LEVI, 6:39-66 (*RSV* 54-81)

Structure

The opening rubric, *wĕ'ēlleh môšĕbôtām lĕṭîrôtām bigbûlām*, "Now these are their settlements, i.e., their encampments, within their boundaries," marks a very abrupt transition to the second main section within this pericope. Anomalies like the double mention of Hebron as an Aaronite city, the designation of the Levitical cities in Judah-Simeon-Benjamin and in Ephraim as *'ārê hammiqlāṭ*, "cities of refuge," and the double listing of territory for "some of the Kohathites," the Gershonites, and "the rest of the Merarites" can be resolved only by recognizing that ChrR or an earlier compiler had the text of Joshua 21 before him and was making a free adaptation of it. This does not preclude the possibility that the Joshua text was not entirely identical to the MT; the detailed study made by W. F. Albright ("List") argues persuasively that it may have been from an earlier Hebrew text, as attested in Joshua LXX[BA], that ChrR worked.

In any event, we are not to be persuaded by the ingenious argument of A. G. Auld ("Levitical Cities") to the effect that the Joshua text was derived from Chronicles. It is his view that the Chronicles text developed quite independently of Joshua 21 (which in fact did not yet exist) in a process of internal expansion, as follows: (1) a list of Aaronite cities, vv. 39-45; (2) expansion by a list of the tribes making allotments of territory to the three Levitical families, vv. 46-49, with the addition in v. 45, "and from the tribe of Benjamin"; (3) a pedantic note in v. 50; (4) a name list of Levitical cities, as handed over to the respective Levitical families by the various secular tribes, vv. 51-66; (5) the insertion of tabulations in vv. 45, 46, 47, and 48, making the total of forty-eight—a tally that does not appear in Chronicles but has been supplied by the composer of Josh 21:41. Somewhat later, according to Auld, a pre-Masoretic form of the Joshua text reworked a pre-Masoretic form of Chronicles—or at least of the genealogical list which ChrR copied—moving in the direction of greater congruity by performing the following procedures: (1) creating a more logical arrangement by drawing forward ChrR's item 2, the list of tribal allotments (Josh 21:4-7), and rephrasing in v. 8 the summary of 1 Chr 6:49; (2) providing a complete list of tallies for ChrR's items 1 and 4, correcting the Aaronite list of names (11 in Chronicles) to correspond to the required 13 and adding the comprehensive total in Josh 21:41; (3) creating a narrative framework in vv. 1-2 and vv. 43-45, respectively.

Auld's thesis challenges the theory espoused by the majority of scholars to the effect that ChrR was drawing from Joshua 21. Certainly little progress is to be seen in various efforts to argue from the confused texts of these two rival passages, or in dealing decisively with the complex topographical and historical problems created by inconsistencies among the respective city names. It may be observed that current scholarship is generally moving away from the Alt-Noth view that the lists reflect the period of Josiah. Many commentators believe that they derive ultimately from the actual situation of the united monarchy, the only time prior to the Maccabean era when the Galilean and especially the Transjordanian cities were under the central control of Jerusalem. Because the Levitical cities lie in border areas, B. Mazar's view ("Cities") that they were a group of loyalist "colonies" established in politically or religiously endangered areas has received careful attention. There is nothing to bring into question the theoretical possibility that an original arrangement of Levitical cities could have existed in Solomon's, or even David's, time. The question is when the primary text was composed. Perhaps this did occur in Josiah's time, as programmatic material for that king's reform. But this does not solve the question of textual priority, which cannot be settled on the basis of Auld's theory.

Joshua 21 does indeed represent a higher level of reflection and normalization at certain points, but in this case it is precarious to argue from the general rule that the shorter and most disordered text (Chronicles) must be the basis of the text that proves to be more sophisticated and complete (Joshua). Auld overlooks an essential clue to ChrR's dependence on Joshua: the phrase in v. 50, which Auld calls a pedantic note, he'ārîm hā'ēlleh 'ăšer-yiqrā' [Chronicles plur.; LXX[B] sg.] 'ethem bĕšēm [Chronicles plur.; LXX[B] omits], "these cities which one/they mentioned by name(s)." The Chronicles' reading, bĕšēmôt, does seem more pedantic than Joshua's bĕšēm, but this could represent a late scribal alteration.

The main point to observe is that this phrase in 1 Chr 6:50 cannot be part of a retrospective note, for the locution qārā' bĕšēm demands an explicit list of names, not the mere tabulations of vv. 46-49. It cannot refer proximately forward to the names given in vv. 51ff., for the text states that the referent has to be associated specifically with "the tribe of the sons of Judah and the tribe of the sons of Simeon and the tribe of the sons of Benjamin" (MT's locution). Eight Simeonite plus Judahite cities are named in vv. 42-45, and, with explicit reference to "the tribe of Benjamin" (sic MT), three Benjaminite cities are named in v. 45a; cf. Josh 21:17. (The tally of 13 for both groups in v. 45b is inexplicable unless viewed as a scribal correction from Josh 21:19.) But it is only in Josh 21:9a that "from the tribe of the sons of Judah and the tribe of the sons of Simeon" (sic MT) appears at the head of the first (Judahite/Simeonite) list of cities, Josh 21:13-16, congruently in position though not in locution with the heading for the Benjaminite cities in the second list, Josh 21:17-18. Most importantly, this is followed in Josh 21:9b by the clause "they gave these cities, which they mentioned by name" (see above). Unless Josh 21:10-12 (par. 1 Chr 6:39b-41) is recognized as the intrusion from a broken list that it is, the plur. "cities" and the double listing of Kiriath-arba = Hebron have no explanation. But the clear intent of Josh 21:9 is to provide the preface to vv. 13-16, omitting vv. 10-12. 1 Chr 6:50 refers back to it in its slightly modified equivalent, *he'ārîm 'ăšer yiqrĕ'û 'ethem bĕšēmôt,* intending to ensure that the just-mentioned allotments to the "Levites" (v. 49) should be understood to include the Aaronite cities listed in vv. 42-44 and not just the cities allotted to "the rest of the Kohathites," the Gershonites, and the Merarites, vv. 46-48.

There is no escaping the conclusion that ChrR was using Joshua 21 or its close prototype. Since the earlier chapters of Joshua, set at a public assembly with Joshua as arbitrator, are commonly recognized as belonging to DtrH (see the comms.), and since Josh 21:1-42 implies a private conference between the Levite representatives on the one side and Eleazar with Joshua and the tribal chiefs on the other side, this passage must be recognized as a post-Dtr addition (the original DtrH account continues in 21:43-45). Following a narrative introduction, Josh 21:1-3, a brief list of the four major Levitical groupings ("sons of Aaron the priest," "the remaining Kohathites," the Gershonites, and the Merarites), including the names of the donor tribes and tallies of the cities, is given (vv. 4-8). Here—just following the sectional conclusion of v. 8—is found the pericope's main structural break. Vv. 9, 13-40 proceed to elaborate this short list with another that specifies first the respective Levitical groupings, next the donor tribes, next the city names, and finally the tally for each tribal grouping and a final tally for all the cities together, vv. 41-42. As has been argued, vv. 10-12 are an intrusion from a broken list, whose inclusion gives rise to the double listing for Hebron. ChrR copies it just as it is.

Evidently wishing to give greater prominence to the Aaronite contingent within the Kohathite family (which he has just mentioned in 1 Chr 6:34 [35-37 are a post-Chronicles gloss; see above]), ChrR omits Joshua's narrative introduction, defers Joshua's short list (21:4-8) to vv. 46-49, and places the equivalent of Josh 21:10-19 forward, just after his opening rubric, "And these are their dwelling places according to their settlements within their borders" *(wĕ'ēlleh môšĕbôtām lĕṭîrôtām bigbûlām),* vv. 39-45. To get congruity with the tribal specifications of the expanded list, vv. 51-66 (par. Josh 21:20-40), ChrR adds his explanatory note in v. 50, and from there he proceeds with his version of the expanded list, omitting, however, the tallies from the Joshua parallel. Why he omitted them we cannot guess; it is possible that they were introduced secondarily into a Joshua text unavailable to ChrR.

Still further discrepancies are present, but they are not of such importance as to affect our analysis of the structure of this city list from ChrR. "To the rest of the

Merarites" in 1 Chr 6:62 is an obvious corruption from "and to the rest of the Levites, the Merarite families" in Josh 21:34. It is not apparent why ChrR avoids the peculiar locution of Josh 21:4, 13, *běnê 'ahărōn hakkōhēn*, "descendants of Aaron the priest" (cf. *běnê 'ahărōn*, v. 10, *běnê 'ahărōn hakkōhănîm*, v. 19), unless it is because he prefers his own phrase, *běnê 'ahărōn*, which elsewhere identifies the priests in 1–2 Chronicles, in distinction from the Levites. We leave aside too the problem of ChrR's references to "cities of refuge" (*'ārê hammiqlāt*), except to remark that his apparent identification of all the Judahite-Simeonite-Benjaminite cities—not just Hebron—as such in vv. 42-45 can have no other source than the similar designation of Hebron, but not of the entire list, in Josh 21:13. So also ChrR's designation of the entire list of remaining Kohathite cities as cities of refuge, drawn from the reference to Shechem as the one city of refuge in Josh 21:21. These represent obvious confusion or misunderstanding on ChrR's part; but it is not clear why he does not join Joshua 21 in identifying three additional cities, Golan, Kedesh, and Ramoth-Gilead, as cities of refuge (vv. 27, 32, 38), or why he avoids Joshua 21's peculiar locution (not taken from Josh 20:1), *'îr miqlāt hārōṣēaḥ*, "city of refuge for the slayer." (Josh 20:8 adds Bezer to the list of cities of refuge, placing it within a symmetrical pattern of six; cf. also Num 35:9-15; Deut 4:41-43; 19:11-13.)

Genre

The basic, overall genre of this pericope is LIST, but it contains the GENEALOGY (5:30-41; 6:4b-15, 35-38), the NAME LIST (5:27-29; 6:1-4a, 10, 42-45a, 51-66), the RANKING FORMULA (6:13, 24a, 29a), the PEDIGREE (6:18b-23, 24b-28, 29b-32), and the TALLY (6:45, 46, 47, 48), already familiar to us. A dating formula, *mimměnôaḥ hā'ārôn*, "since the ark came to rest," appears in 6:16. A new genre, seen in 6:18-32, is the ROSTER, a list of all the names within a governmental or ecclesiastical group, along with the duties or offices assigned to each; it occurs almost exclusively in late literature. This genre is closely related to the (→) CATALOGUE, seen in 6:39-66. This is a LIST that enumerates or labels specified items or names according to a particular system of classification. This is also the apparent genre of Joshua 21, which our present cataloguer strives to bring to a more ideological arrangement.

We take note, finally, of the (→) AUTHORIZATION FORMULA in 6:34b. This is found frequently in 1–2 Chronicles and, appealing to the authority of Moses, David, or the prophets, aims to legitimize a specific cultic event or procedure. (See S. J. De Vries, "Moses and David as Cult-Founders.") In this instance "Aaron and his sons" are authorized to serve at the altars of burnt offering and incense on every sacred occasion (*lěkōl měle'ket qōdeš*) to atone (*kpr*) for Israel, a duty required by "Moses the man of God."

Setting

Those scholars prone to smooth things out have applied their scalpel here: thus Fohrer (*Intro.*, 244) omits 6:5-33, 39-66; Rudolph (HAT) omits 6:10-13, 33-38, 39-66; Willi (p. 195) also omits vv. 39-66. More helpful than this literary tossing of balls into the air is the patient effort of notable scholars to place these variegated materials within a proper framework of cultic tradition. We may mention especially Möhlenbrink's study of the Levite genealogy, of the roster of the singers, and of the genealogy of Aaron ("Levitische Überlieferungen," 199-203, 229, 204-5); also von Rad's work on the clan genealogies (*Geschichtsbild*, 101, 105-6, 109-10, 127); also Johnson's (*Genealogies*, 71-73, 270) and Lefèvre's ("Note d'exégèse," 289) observations about the Kohathites; finally, Gese's brilliant analysis of the "singer" tradition ("Zur Geschichte der Kultsänger"), especially at p. 224, where he summarizes its three stages as reflected within the book of 1–2 Chronicles (cf. Williamson, comm., 71-72, 121).

It is natural that this pericope should quote or closely rely on parallel materials in the P strand of the Pentateuch. With 5:27-29 compare Gen 46:11; Exod 6:16, 18, 20, 23; Num 3:17, 19, 20-32; 26:57-62. With 6:1-15 compare Exod 6:16-19; Num 3:17-37. With 6:33-34 compare Lev 1:3-9; Num 4:5ff.; 18:1-7. Vv. 39-66 are, of course, closely dependent on Joshua 21, as we have seen. There are, in addition, several cross-references within 1–2 Chronicles and Ezra-Nehemiah; for the singers, cf. 1 Chr 15:16ff., 23-26; 2 Chr 35:3.

Without question this pericope has many parallels within 1–2 Chronicles, as well as in Ezra-Nehemiah. Here is a breakdown of the regulatory passages in 1–2 Chronicles, including the one we are presently concerned with:

1 Chr 5:27–6:66	Aaronite lineage
	Levite lineage
	Roster of singers
	List of Levitical dwelling places
1 Chr 9:10-34	Priestly lineage
	Levite lineage
	Job description for gatekeepers
	Job description for singers
1 Chr 15:4-14	Levite roster
	Levite purification ritual
	Roster of singers/musicians
	Expansion: gatekeepers
	Expansion: priestly trumpeters
1 Chr 16:4-43	Ordering of the service
	Expansion: gatekeepers
1 Chr 23:2-32	Levite census
	Levite table of organization
	Expansion: Levite job description
1 Chr 24:1-31	Expansion: roster of Aaronites
	Expansion: roster of Levites
1 Chr 25:1-31	Roster of singers
1 Chr 26:1-32	Roster and rota of gatekeepers
	Expansion: table of organization for gatekeepers

Now the impression that ordinary readers receive, to the effect that 1–2 Chronicles indulges in numerous and unmotivated repetitions with respect to the Levites and other clergy, can readily be corrected. There is very little actual repetition, and almost everything is well motivated in terms of narrative contexting. Here all but the roster of singers finds a proper place as a key link within the tribal review.

In 1 Chronicles 9 everything helps draw a picture of the restoration community. Rosters, ritual, and the ordering of the service surround the narrative of the entrance of the ark in 1 Chronicles 15–16. Everything in 1 Chronicles 23–26 (census, table of organization, rosters, rota) is placed where David completes his preparations for the building of the temple. Various proper names will be repeated at times, not only because of the fluidity of the tradition, but also because they are eponymous, not always belonging to individual persons living at the time. Naturally, there is a reflection of progression and competition, and this will be seen especially in those sections that have been labeled (on independent literary grounds, to be argued at the passages concerned) as expansions. As will be seen, they reveal an anxiety to be recognized, especially on the part of gatekeepers, Aaronites, and new generations of Levites.

It is not our task to enter into the complicated and inconclusive question of the Israelite priesthood (see the major studies of recent date by Cody, Gunneweg, Liver, and Möhlenbrink). We refrain from indulging in any general speculations; we wish only to interpret these materials as part of 1–2 Chronicles. Nevertheless, we must point out the two hypothetical lines of development that may explain the evident drive of the Levites and associated groups to rival the Aaronite priests. The first possibility is that the Levites were the once-dominant group but have been degraded, and now are scrambling to hold on to whatever prerogatives the priests will allow them. The second possibility is that the Levites were originally a minor, obscure group who have taken advantage of the chaotic postexilic situation and are now threatening to supplant the Aaronites as priests.

To explain briefly the first hypothesis: Judges 18 shows that the Levites were once favored priests, but they lost out, first to the Ahimelech-Abiathar family, then to the Zadokites. Deuteronomy 18 shows a concern to make a place for them alongside the dominant priesthood at the closing down of the country shrines where they had been officiating. Ezek 44:10-14 (early restoration) subordinates them to the Zadokites, who claim to be a branch of "Levi" (40:46; 43:19; 44:15). In Ezra-Nehemiah the Levites are definitely subordinated to the priests, and a third group, the nĕtînîm, are added (Ezra 2:43; Neh 7:46; cf. 1 Chr 9:2). In 1–2 Chronicles the order is always first priests, then Levites, showing the latter's subordination, but with some cautious criticism of the priests in relation to the Levites at 2 Chr 30:3, 15; 35:14. 1–2 Chronicles drops virtually all reference to Zadokites, preferring the title bĕnê 'ahărōn, "Aaronites" or "sons of Aaron." It is apparent from 1 Chr 5:27ff. that this group claimed descent not only from Aaron but also from Levi (6:39ff. distributes cities according to the ancestral clans of Levi, 6:1ff., not according to the Aaronite genealogy in 5:27ff.; 6:35-37), revealing that Levi once had priority over "Aaron" as a clerical order, as well as a tribal group. Be that as it may, 6:34 is an anxious claim on the part of the Aaronites to perform the sacrifices, a right 1–2 Chronicles always allows them to retain (cf. 1 Chr 28:13; 2 Chr 30:17; 35:10-11). As here, the Aaronites always claim authority from Moses, showing the influence of P, whereas Levitical authority is always drawn from David.

The alternative hypothesis goes like this: Like the early Aaronites, the Levites always were an isolated and powerless group, but when the Zadokites lost control at the time of the exile (see 1 Chr 5:41; Ezekiel's propaganda on their behalf was ineffective), the Aaronites took control of the office of kōhănîm, claiming Mosaic authority (P's effort to associate Aaron with Moses as his brother is part of this same propaganda), while the Levite order simply took over the important nonsacrificial positions, leaving various menial tasks to the *nĕtînîm.* Both groups claimed to be *bĕnê lēwî,* but one claim or the other was a usurpation. To judge from the structure of 5:27ff.; 6:1ff. (see above), the Aaronites did the usurping. Furthermore, in 6:39-66 (cf. Joshua 21) the Aaronites look suspicious in claiming cities as part of the Levite genealogical pattern. In sum: both groups started at a lowly station but the Aaronites came out on tòp. The Levites crowded them, but the Aaronites were able to hold onto the office of *kōhēn* by usurping descent from Levi and the Levitical genealogy.

A study by H. J. Katzenstein ("Some Remarks") shows that, while the Zadokite lineage had lost out in the postexilic period, they continued in high respect (a certain Azariah is distinguished with the title *kōhēn hārō'š lĕbêt ṣādôq,* "high priest of the house of Zadok," 2 Chr 31:10). This is evident in the genealogy of 1 Chr 5:30ff., which omits Jehoiada and Hilkiah, so prominent in the ensuing narrative, presumably because they were not Zadokites. The Azariah of 2 Chr 26:17 is apparently on this list. It is evidently a genealogy solely of Zadokite priests, terminating at the exile, and our genealogist has no list like it continuing up to his own time. It has notable gaps and duplications; Josephus and the Talmud mention eighteen high priests from Solomon to the exile, some of which, however, may not have been Zadokites. Within 1–2 Chronicles the high priest is seldom mentioned, and then it is with a variety of titles showing a development of tradition. Jehoiada is called *hakkōhēn* in 2 Chr 22:11; 23:8, 9, 14; 24:2, 20; also *hārō'š* in 24:6. Azariah is *hakkōhēn* in 26:17 and *kōhēn hārō'š* in 26:20. The Zadokite Azariah is also *kōhēn hārō'š* in 31:10, and Hilkiah is called *hakkōhēn* in 34:14, 18 and *hakkōhēn haggādōl* in 34:9.

An important barrier-breaking study of recent date has been H. Gese's "Zur Geschichte der Kultsänger." Gese has helped us reconstruct the tradition history behind the various references to the singer group, and has clarified literary relationships within the book of 1–2 Chronicles. Since this study is too rich to be discussed or even summarized here, we take the liberty of reproducing the following schematic diagram of Gese's thesis from Williamson's comm. (p. 121):

I.   At the return from the exile, the singers are simply called "sons of Asaph," and are not yet reckoned as Levites (Ezr 2:41; Neh 7:44);

II. Neh 11:3-19 and 1 Chr 9:1-18, from Nehemiah's time. The singers are now reckoned as Levites, and are in two groups, (1) the sons of Asaph, and (2) the sons of Jeduthun;

IIIA. 1 Chr 16:4ff.; 2 Chr 5:12; 29:13f.; 35:15. The Levitical singers are now in three groups: (1) Asaph, (2) Heman, and (3) Jeduthun;

IIIB. 1 Chr 6:16ff. and 15:16ff. Jeduthun is replaced by Ethan, and Heman is now more prominent than Asaph.

Gese (p. 224) wanted to date stage IIIA with ChrR, identifying IIIB as a later level of development, but Williamson (comm., 120-22) argues that IIIB is from the time of ChrR. His argument seems superior, and will be followed in our own presentation.

Intention

In 1–2 Chronicles the Levites accept the priority of the Aaronite priests, even though (especially in the post-Chronicles expansions) the latter seem at times to be nervous in guarding their prerogatives. The book as a whole focuses on the Levites' duties, organization, and responsibilities. It is clear that the Levites as a sacral order will provide the heart of the new Israel that the nation is striving to become.

ChrR is eager to show that Levi is not only an order of clergy but one of the eponymous tribes possessing territory of their own. In this respect, it overshadows Aaron, who claims ethnic identity but cannot claim an eponymous ancestor belonging among the original twelve sons of Israel.

A final word about the singers: great aspirations for this group are revealed in that it claimed to have been appointed by David, in that the singers are "brothers" to the Levites, and in that they had rendered faithful service in the tabernacle until Solomon built the temple (1 Chr 6:17). Such a claim is designed to (1) give the singers royal legitimation, (2) place them on a par with a more prestigious order, and (3) guarantee them great antiquity.

Bibliography

W. F. Albright, "The List of Levitic Cities," in *Louis Ginzberg Jubilee Volume* (ed. S. Liebermann, et al.; New York: American Academy for Jewish Research, 1945) I:49-53; A. Alt, "Bemerkungen zu einigen judäischen Ortslisten des Alten Testaments," *ZDPV* 68 (1951) 193-210 [= *KS* II:289-305]; A. G. Auld, "The 'Levitical Cities': Text and History," *ZAW* 91 (1979) 194-206; A. Cody, *A History of Old Testament Priesthood* (AnBib 35; Rome: Pontifical Biblical Institute, 1969); H. Gese, "Zur Geschichte der Kultsänger am zweiten Tempel," in *Abraham unser Vater: Juden und Christen im Gespräch über die Bibel* (*Fest.* O. Michel; ed. O. Betz, M. Hengel, and P. Schmidt; Leiden: Brill, 1963) 222-34; A. H. Gunneweg, *Leviten und Priester* (FRLANT 39; Göttingen: Vandenhoeck & Ruprecht, 1965); M. Haran, "The Levitical Cities: Utopia and Historical Reality," *Tarb* 27 (1957-58) 421-39; idem, "Studies in the Account of the Levitical Cities," *JBL* 80 (1961) 45-54, 156-65; M. D. Johnson, *The Purpose of the Biblical Genealogies* (SNTSMS 8; Cambridge: Cambridge, 1969) 37-82; H. J. Katzenstein, "Some Remarks on the Lists of the Chief Priests of the Temple of Solomon," *JBL* 81 (1962) 377-84; A. Lefèvre, "Note d'exégèse sur les Généalogies des Qehatites," *Recherches de Science Religieuse* 38 (1950) 287-92; J. Liver, *Chapters in the History of the Priests and Levites. Studies in the Lists of Chronicles and Ezra and Nehemiah* (Hebr.; Jerusalem: Magnes, 1968); B. Mazar, "The Cities of the Priests and the Levites," *Congress Volume: Oxford 1959* (VTSup 7; Leiden: Brill, 1960) 193-205; K. Möhlenbrink, "Die levitischen Überlieferungen des Alten Testaments," *ZAW* 52 (1934) 184-231; M. Noth, "Überlieferungsgeschichtliches zur zweiten Hälfte des Josuabuches," in *Alttestamentliche Studien F. Nötscher gewidmet* (ed. H. Junker and J. Botterweck; BBB 1; Bonn: Hanstein, 1950) 152-67; G. von Rad, *Das Geschichtsbild des chronistischen Werkes* (BWANT 3; Stuttgart: Kohlhammer, 1930); L. Waterman, "Some Repercussions from Late Levitical Genealogical Accretions in P and the Chronicler," *AJSL* 58 (1941) 49-56; W. G. E. Watson, "Archaic Elements in the Language of Chronicles," *Bib* 53 (1972) 191-207; A. J. Welch, *Post-Exilic Judaism* (Edinburgh-London: Blackwood, 1935); T. Willi, *Die Chronik als Auslegung* (FRLANT 106; Göttingen: Vandenhoeck & Ruprecht, 1972).

MUSTER ROLLS OF ISSACHAR, 7:1-5

Structure

This pericope has been fair game for those looking for distinct literary levels: Noth ("Chronistische Werk," 118) eliminates vv. 2-5; Rudolph (HAT) vv. 2b, 4-5; Fohrer (*Intro.*, 244) vv. 2-11. But tradition development rather than literary expansion accounts for this pericope's unevenness. The compiler of the tribal lists is apparently responsible for the unusual introduction, *wĕlibnê* . . . , "Now as for the sons of . . . ," phrased to show a mental pause at the end of the lengthy Levite list and a turning of one's attention to the former scheme of listing tribal lists seriatim. Following the usual list of tribal eponyms, the leading clan of Tola is listed, with appellations and tally, then the twin clans of Uzzi and Izrahiah, with title, organization, and tally. Finally comes the enrollment of tribal groups not already listed.

Genre

As explained in Johnson (*Genealogies*, 67-68) this is another MUSTER ROLL — apparently the only sort of tribal record available to our genealogist. The genre NAME LIST appears four times and the TALLY five times. The APPELLATION appears once. V. 2b has a dating notice explaining a given tally.

Setting

One immediately observes that geographical proximity has been given up as the principle for presenting the various tribes, and it appears that these will now be given alternately as northerly (Issachar, Naphtali, Asher) versus southerly (Benjamin) groups, a sort of inclusio for the central tribes, also presented in northerly-southerly order (Manasseh, Ephraim). (As explained in Chapter 2 above, 1 Chronicles 8 was added as an appendix, and hence would not reckon directly in this scheme.)

For his tribal eponyms our genealogist has sources available in Gen 46:13;

Num 26:23-24 (on Tola, Judg 10:1). Apart from vv. 1 and 5, this pericope is really a list for Tola, segmented to include separate lists for his descendants Uzzi and Izrahiah. None of these lists is in any way a genealogy, for the names are those of militia leaders within the separate Issacharite clans and subclans. V. 2, "Tola had mighty warriors *[gibbôrê ḥayil]* in each generation *[lětōlědôtām]*," shows that Tola is here no historical individual but a clan perpetually bearing his name. We assume, of course, that this is true of the other names as well. In v. 3 the number five is an error if it refers directly to the "sons" of Izrahiah, but the latter may be included in the tally of "chief men" *(rā'šîm);* see the fuller form, *rā'šîm lěbêt 'ăbôtām,* "chiefs of their ancestral families," in v. 2; cf. v. 4. Each of the *tōlědôt,* "generations," was called upon to raise a military levy "according to their fathers' houses." Among the Uzzites these levies were organized as *gědûdê ṣěbā' milḥāmâ,* "troops within a military force"—capable perhaps of offensive as well as defensive operations. The Uzzite tally is given as 36,000, an unusually large force explained from this clan's numerous wives and sons. It has been generally recognized, however, that *'elep* is not a mere numeral but serves as the designation for a major military unit ("thousands, hundreds, fifties, tens" might be comparable to our "regiments, battalions, companies, platoons"), and just as modern units often are far below authorized strength, especially under battle conditions, the Hebrew "thousand" may be little more than an organizational shell. In this interpretation, Tola would have had twenty-six "regiments" and six "battalions," etc.

Together, all the families *(mišpěḥôt)* of Issachar are mustered at eighty-seven "thousands," a remarkable increase from the time of David (v. 2). They too are given the appellation "mighty warriors." Since it is "every" family that is enrolled, it is not certain whether the Tolaites and Uzzites are excluded or included in the term *'ăḥêhem,* "their brothers" (v. 5). Since the tally of v. 5 probably existed independently of the musters in vv. 2-4, this tally is probably for all, but of course only if it is from the same period. One notes that the tally of Num 26:25, possibly from after the exile, is 22,700 lower than this figure. As is usual in these ancient muster rolls, *yḥś* (hith.) means "enroll for war" (cf. v. 7).

Intention

The MUSTER ROLL has lost its original function. In ChrR's era Issachar probably no longer existed as a separate tribe, and certainly no longer maintained either a muster roll or a body of men to fill it. For ChrR it does two important things: (1) maintains a place for Issachar as an ethnic unit within "ideal Israel," and (2) presents the ideal of a skeleton force as part of the organization needed to maintain its claim to Israel's land.

Bibliography

M. D. Johnson, *The Purpose of the Biblical Genealogies* (SNTSMS 8; Cambridge: Cambridge, 1969) 37-82.

MUSTER ROLL OF BENJAMIN, 7:6-12

Structure

"Benjamin" stands alone at the head of this list, lacking the genealogist's usual *ûbĕnê*, which is, of course, suitable to a proper genealogy, which this pericope definitely is not. It shows the clear, and probably original, form of the MUSTER ROLL, without modifications toward the (→) GENEALOGY, and the asyndetic proper name apparently stood alone as a title. In all likelihood, it belonged to a collection of such lists, quite separate from the Benjaminite materials recorded in ch. 8. Apparently because that chapter gives fuller information, some scholars view this as a secondary addition (Noth, "Chronistische Werk," 122; Rudolph, HAT), though others consider v. 12 as original but garbled (cf. Noth, 118). After the title, three names are given, without mention that they are sons. Unusual is this form with the tally, "three." This list is also unusual in that it proceeds to offer name lists for each person listed at the head, though in the case of Jediael, who has only Bilhan, it is the latter's name list that is given. Still another unique feature is the statement of inclusiveness: "All these were the sons of Becher" (v. 8) and "All these were the sons of Jediael" (v. 11). In v. 7, where "mighty warriors" have just been tallied, and in v. 9, listing another group of "mighty warriors," *yḥś* (hith.) can have no other meaning than "muster for service." The evidence we have already seen is now fully confirmed regarding this expression. We are looking at certain proof that it is a *terminus technicus* for the tribal militia and a set formula belonging to the genre MUSTER ROLL.

Verse 12 is a stray fragment having nothing to do with the muster roll. The VSS have been perplexed, and modern scholars given to free emendation have had a field day. Noth ("Chronistische Werk," 118-22) is among those who would somehow restore the text to make room for Dan, who, like Zebulun, has been omitted from these genealogical records. "Shuppim and Huppim" may be a wordplay; cf. the gloss at 7:15; also Gen 46:21, 23; and Num 26:39-42. Above all, the text must not be emended to read *bĕnê dān haššēm bĕnô 'aḥēr*, "The sons of Dan: his son's name was Aher," favored by several scholars, for the simple reason that this is no census, no genealogy, but a muster roll (there is nothing like this in 1 Chronicles 1; 2:1-2; 4:24; 5:3; 7:13, 30).

1 AND 2 CHRONICLES

Genre, Setting, and Intention

The main genre is MUSTER ROLL; the NAME LIST appears at vv. 7, 8, and 10 (twice). The TALLY is at vv. 6, 7, 9, and 11. The APPELLATION is seen at vv. 7 and 11 (*gibbôrê ḥăyālîm*, "mighty champions," is a superlative, seen also at v. 40; *yōṣĕ'ê ṣābā' lammilḥāmâ*, "military man effective for combat" [v. 11], is peculiar to this muster roll; it is another superlative).

Since the days of Saul, the Benjaminites (*bĕnê yĕmînî*, "my right-hand men") always had a reputation for ferociousness in battle. After Rehoboam, this tribe became part of the kingdom of Judah and played a major role in all its military undertakings. More about Benjamin as an ethnic unity will be offered in ch. 8, but here its central role as part of the operational organization of the ideal Israel comes to expression.

Bibliography

W. Bacher, "Zu I Chron. 7, 12," *ZAW* 18 (1898) 236-38; F. Delitzsch, *Die Lese- und Schreibfehler im Alten Testament* (Berlin-Leipzig: de Gruyter, 1920) 102-25; A. Klostermann, "Chronik," in *Realencyclopädie für Theologie und Kirche* IV (3rd. ed.; Leipzig: Hinrichs, 1898) 84-98; M. Noth, "Die chronistische Werk," in *Überlieferungsgeschichtliche Studien* (Tübingen: Niemeyer, 1957) 118-22; H. G. M. Williamson, "A Note on 1 Chronicles VII 12," *VT* 23 (1973) 375-79.

TRIBAL RECORDS OF THE NAPHTALITES, 7:13

Structure

I. Name list: sons of Naphtali	13a
II. Ethnological attribution	13b

Genre, Setting, and Intention

The genre is NAME LIST, with the echo of a (→) birth report, narrated in Gen 30:7-8 and recorded in Gen 46:25. Our genealogist evidently had nothing more for Naphtali than four eponyms, borrowed from Gen 46:24 or Num 26:48-50—or possibly an independent tradition agreeing with them—in addition to the attribution to Bilhah as tribal mother. Nothing out of this brief LIST could have had significance to ChrR except that it filled a lacuna in his comprehensive image of the ideal Israel.

Bibliography

M. Noth, *Das System der zwölf Stämme Israels* (BWANT 4/1; Stuttgart: Kohlhammer, 1930).

TRIBAL RECORDS OF THE MANASSITES, 7:14-19

Structure

The asyndetic form *běnê . . .*, seen also in the Asher section commencing at v. 30, indicates an independent listing for this pericope, which, however, is syndetically attached to the Ephraim pericope, vv. 20-29, by its introduction with the copula, *ûběnê*. Although the genealogical introduction provides a plur. subject, we find no name list as a predicate, but only the single name Asriel, which is then modified by a series of verbal clauses. The pericope has narrative styling throughout, but there are so many loose ends that it has been suggested that most of it consists of disconnected glosses (cf. Fohrer, *Intro.*, 244). One may agree that "for Huppim and Shuppim" in v. 15 is a gloss, influenced no doubt by v. 12. It seems so arbitrary that we speculate for a rational explanation. Perhaps the glossator was convinced that the Benjaminites mentioned in v. 12 lacked a family and hence gave them one here. The locution *lāqaḥ 'iššâ* (should be *nāšîm*, plur.) signifies contracting a marriage for oneself; hence v. 15 refers to Machir's own marriage. Our glossator, in borrowing Maacah for Huppim and Shuppim, evidently changed "the name of his wife" to "the name of his sister" to avoid confusion about who got married. The formula "and the name of . . . ," seen at 2:26, 29, 34, appears four times in vv. 15-16, twice with reference to females and twice with reference to males; its function is to preserve the identity of a minor clan subgroup. The appearance of a single name after *ûběnê* in v. 17 is common; the formal rubrics are preserved in oral tradition even when a number of clan names are lost. The concluding rubric in v. 17 inappropriately summarizes the preceding material. Gilead got left stranded back in v. 14.

Genre

The main genre is again LIST, but it contains a series of notices exhibiting the genre BIRTH REPORT, with the NAME LIST (four times) in vv. 16-19. The word "second" in v. 15 belongs to the RANKING FORMULA, and the PEDIGREE appears at v. 17b.

Setting

The information offered here has parallels in Num 26:19-34; Josh 17:2-3; cf. Gen 46:20b (LXX). Our pericope is a veritable scramble of random ethnological information, in comparison with which the Numbers passage is a model of organization; it is for that very reason primitive. A few of the names in the present list are mentioned in Numbers but the majority are not. Loose ends frustrate the establishment of firm genealogical lines. "His sister" in v. 15 is ambiguous; so are "the second" in the same verse and "his sister Hammolecheth" in v. 18, as well as the fact that the Shemida of v. 19 is related to none of the preceding. It is certainly odd that Maacah is mentioned both as Machir's sister (v. 15) and as his wife (v. 16). This list seems to compass five generations from Manasseh to Bedan, as compared with the six generations from Manasseh to Zelophehad's five daughters in Num 26:29-33 (cf. Num 36:11). (The fact that our text cannot give the names of these daughters is another clue to its relative primitiveness.) Genealogical fragments for Hammolecheth (v. 18) and Shemida (v. 19) are left dangling.

We must point out the similarity of this pericope to other ethnological recitals in making much of female ancestors. There is Manasseh's Aramean concubine, Maacah in her dual role, Zelophehad's daughters, and Hammolecheth. A probable explanation for this phenomenon might be the prevalence of matriarchal descent within such groups, but we must also take account of the fact that materials drawn from birth reports naturally give priority to the mother. A patriarchal system seems to be taking over in the loss of the names of the Aramean concubine and of Zelophehad's daughters—and this in spite of the repeated use of the expression "and the name of . . . ," mentioned above. This intent to preserve identity (at least in the case of the females) may actually reflect the growing preponderance of the patriarchal over the matriarchal system.

Study of the Samaritan ostraca has revealed a number of Manassite clan names, two of which, Asriel and Abiezer, appear in our text. A. Lemaire ("Asriel") has cogently argued that "Asriel" is the original "Israel." His argument is worth summarizing for our purposes. Ostraca 42 and 48 associate a šr'l with a city yšb, corrupted to yōšĕbê (but cf. LXX) in Josh 12:7. There is a town Yassuf near Tappuah, between Ephraim and Manasseh (cf. Josh 17:7-8), south of Nablus and east of the main highway. Since the root yšb means "dwell," the original meaning may be "colony." Ostracon 42, line 3, mentions 'šrt, evidently el-Asharat, one kilometer southwest of Yassuf, close to Wadi el-Bucharat. This was the area occupied by the clan bĕnê 'aśrî'ēl, and this received a normalized verbal form in yiśrā'ēl, from the root śrr, "command," "dominate." Eventually this clan name became the name of an entire people and nation, though first it was associated with the "house of Joseph" (Ephraim and Manasseh); cf. the presence of the bĕnê yiśrā'ēl in the region of Shechem (Genesis 34). The southern limit of the clan Asriel was Shiloh, where a common sanctuary (with its cult object, the ark) drew Manasseh and Ephraim together.

Intention

ChrR's purpose in writing down this information is identical to that of the others: to secure for Manasseh a firm place within the territory and the ethnic stock of his ideal Israel. Although at his late date he could have known nothing of what archeology has informed us concerning the remote origins of Manasseh or of Israel, his instinct is unerring in giving this tribe a position of crucial centrality.

Bibliography

Y. Aharoni and M. Avi-Yonah, *The Macmillan Bible Atlas* (New York: Macmillan, 1968), nos. 65, 137; M. D. Johnson, *The Purpose of the Biblical Genealogies* (SNTSMS 8; Cambridge: Cambridge, 1969) 52-53; A. Lemaire, "Asriel, šr'l, Israel et l'origine de la confédération israélite," *VT* 23 (1973) 239-43; J. Wellhausen, *Prolegomena to the History of Ancient Israel* (tr. Menzies and Black; repr. Cleveland-New York: World, 1965).

TRIBAL RECORDS OF THE EPHRAIMITES, 7:20-29

Structure

I. Genealogy: from Ephraim	20-21aα
to Shuthelah: eight generations	
II. Report of Beriah's birth	21aβ-24
A. Ezer and Elead die at Gath	21aβ-b
B. Birth report: Beriah as their substitute	22-23
1. Ephraim comforted	22
2. Beriah's conception and birth	23a
3. Naming etiology	23b
C. Name list: his daughter and her cities	24
III. Genealogy: from Rephah to Joshua: eight generations	25-27
IV. Possessions and settlements	28-29
A. Name list: boundary cities	28
B. Enclaves on Manasseh's northern border	29
1. Name list	29a
2. Joint possession by Josephite tribes	29b

As has been noted, the introductory rubric *ûbĕnê* . . . joins this Ephraim material to that of Manasseh—not surprising in view of the fact that these were brother tribes and jointly "sons of Joseph"; cf. v. 29b. In spite of the plur., only one Ephraimite son, Shuthelah, is named, and from him a linear genealogy is drawn, using the *bĕnô* . . . *bĕnô* styling. Abruptly, without copula or relative, the text switches over to a narrative account of Beriah's birth (vv. 21aβ-23), followed by a name list for this person's daughter. Almost as abruptly, though with the copula, this leads into a linear genealogy styled exactly like the first but having no apparent connection to it (vv. 25-27). In v. 28 the copula introduces a list of *their* possessions and settlements, but the antecedent is obscure and can surely not be just the men of the immediately foregoing genealogy. We have become accustomed to severe dislocation in this ancient material, but perhaps we should allow the hand of a redactor as our solution, inserting the Beriah narrative between the two genealogies so as to allow the mention of the famous Joshua to stand next to the reference to Ayyah (Ai), which he is reported to have conquered (the other cities mentioned in vv. 28-29 may also have been conquered by him, even though the Bible gives no report of this). Of course, "Joshua" may have been a clan just like the rest.

The events reported in vv. 21-23 likewise involved clans and not just individual historical persons. Ezer and Elead are "slain" (a word used for violent actions, such as battles) at Gath by those born (*yld,* niph. part.) there, i.e., its original possessors and not transients. The former were the aggressors, having come to make a raid. A series of narrative verbs tell how Beriah became their substitute: Ephraim mourned . . . was comforted by his brothers . . . went in to his wife; she conceived . . . bore . . . called him. . . . The naming etiology of v. 23 intends to explain the name Beriah from the evil event that had led to his birth ("because evil had befallen his house"), but the text allows an exceedingly bad pun *(bĕrî'â kî bĕrā'â hāyĕtâ bĕbêtô).* The close similarity between *bĕrî'â* and *bĕrā'â* is the basis of the pun, so possibly we should identify the *b* before *bêtô* as a copyist's error, or otherwise just accept the bad pun as it stands and read, "Beriah, because 'in disaster' was in his house."

The antecedent of "his daughter" (= dependent clan or town) is uncertain (v. 24). It can be either Ephraim or Beriah, depending on this verse's original connection to vv. 21-23. In any event, this daughter group is said to have built (or rebuilt) the two Beth-horons, so famous in biblical history, and an Uzzen-sheerah, perhaps modern Beit Sira. The pun on the mother's name is obvious.

Equally uncertain as to grammatical antecedent is the reference to "their" possessions and "their" settlements in v. 28. We can guess that the whole Ephraimite populace is meant because the list that follows covers the entire territory claimed by Ephraim. The expression *'ăḥuzzātām ûmōšĕbôtām* seems to leave open the question whether certain sites were actually settled, or just conquered. Famous cities are included, the chief of them being Bethel. Boundary cities are Gezer at the west, Shechem at the north, and Naaran (cf. Josh 16:7, Naarah) at the east. "Daughters" (dependent villages) are also mentioned. Such "daughters" are likewise listed for the four well-known cities mentioned in v. 29. These lie along the Jezreel Valley. Apparently, they were shared by all the "sons of Joseph, son of Israel."

Genre

The main genre here is LIST with narrative modifications. Vv. 20-21 and 25-27 exhibit the genre GENEALOGY. The NAME LIST is seen in vv. 24, 28, and 29. Vv. 22-23 constitute a BIRTH REPORT, with elements of the FAMILY (→) SAGA, which is a narrative account of the events that compose the past of a family unit. The NAMING ETIOLOGY is featured as the climax of the birth report, v. 23b (→ "Structure" above).

Setting and Intention

This pericope provides essential historical information but is hard to interpret. Though the names of the cities are familiar to us, we know but few of the personal names. We cannot be sure that the "Joshua" of the genealogy is the great champion of the Israelite conquest, and it is unclear whether the genealogy of vv. 25-27 should follow in direct sequence from vv. 20-21, for if that were the case, Joshua would have lived some sixteen generations later than the patriarchs. Allowing a minimal twenty-five years per generation, this would have required approximately four hundred years, and even on the basis of the hypothetical early date for the exodus (ca. 1400 B.C.) there would not be time enough to fit in a conquest many years prior to the rise of the monarchy, ca. 1000. Even worse, it would make shambles of the concept of a forty-year stay in the wilderness between exodus and conquest. If, on the other hand, we take Joshua's genealogy separately, we still have a problem, though not so severe, in reconciling it with the normative historical traditions.

We are on firmer ground when we study the city lists of vv. 28-29, for they tell us some important, otherwise unknown facts: (1) Dan had already moved out and had left Gezer to Ephraim; (2) Benjamin had not yet become strong enough to contest the region about Naaran (perhaps Ain Duq near Jericho); (3) Ephraim was claiming Shechem in spite of Manasseh's presence in that region (see above); and (4) the most powerful Canaanite city-states in the Jezreel Valley region were claimed equally by Ephraim and Manasseh—a most remarkable fact in the light of the former's remoteness from this area.

There is little reason to suppose that ChrR was the redactor responsible for repositioning the second genealogy—if that is what actually happened. ChrR offers this material to assure Ephraim's place in his new Israel. He is also interested in an ideological claim to Ephraim's vital, centrally located territory. In his history, when proselytes to Jerusalem are mentioned, Ephraim and Manasseh are always the first to be named, for as possessors of the birthright (1 Chr 5:2-3), the heart of the land of Israel belonged to them.

Bibliography

B. Mazar, "Gath und Gittaim," *IEJ* 4 (1954) 227-38.

TRIBAL RECORDS OF THE ASHERITES, 7:30-40

Structure

I. Genealogy of Asher		30-33
A. Name list for first generation: children of Asher		30
B. Name list for second generation: sons of Beriah		31a
C. Third generation		31b-32
1. Son of Malchiel		31b
2. Name list: children of Heber		32
D. Fourth generation		33
1. Name list		33a
2. Conclusion		33b
II. Muster roll for the tribal militia		34-40
A. The family units		34-39
1. Name list: Shemer		34
2. Name lists: Helem and Zophah		35-37

This pericope occupies last place in the original genealogical collection. It begins with the asyndetic introduction, *běnê 'āšēr*, and immediately proceeds to offer a true genealogy, showing linear descent through four generations. Siblings are mentioned, but there is no segmentation, i.e., a breakdown into collateral lines. Not the entire genealogy but only the fourth-generational name list has a concluding rubric, "These are the sons of Japhlet."

Not until the end does one realize that vv. 34-40 are a list of an entirely different character. This is the tribal muster roll segmented into four distinct and underived clan units listed in direct parallelism, but with a separate listing for the eleven-member subclan of Zophah, vv. 36-37. The word *'āḥîw* in v. 35 means "his fellow clan member" (a technical term in the muster), but *'āḥî* in v. 34 has to be taken as a proper name, giving the pairing, "Ahi and Rohgah, Jehubbah and Aram." The name list of vv. 36-37 is broken into groups of five and six by the dropping of the copula before "Bezer," for a reason we cannot guess. The concluding rubric at v. 40, *kol 'ēlleh běnê 'āšēr*, "All these are sons of Asher/Asherites," belongs not to the pericope as a whole but just to this muster roll, as can be seen in the qualifying phrase *rā'šê bêt-hā'ābôt*, "chiefs of the ancestral clans"—another technical expression in the muster. This time we see the enrollment statement in narrative form: *wěhityaḥśām baṣṣābā' bammilḥāmâ*, "And one enrolled them for service in battle." The concluding tally has the unique heading *'ǎnāšîm*, "men/soldiers." As has been previously mentioned, *'elep* may mean a military unit rather than the numerical quantity "thousand."

Genre, Setting, and Intention

The kind of literary surgery that consigns disconnected elements to late levels of secondary expansion (e.g., Rudolph, HAT, rejecting the totality; Noth, "Chronistische Werk," 118, keeping only v. 30) is quite discredited by our form-critical analysis, which identifies the whole as a LIST, but vv. 30-33 as a GENEALOGY and vv. 34-40 as a MUSTER ROLL. The NAME LIST appears in every verse but the last, where occur the familiar genres APPELLATION and TALLY. The appellations are unusual: *bārûr* means "elite"; *gibbôr ḥǎyālîm* means "mighty champion" (cf. vv. 7, 11); *rō'š hanněśî'îm* means "chief of officers."

The list of Asher's sons reflects Gen 46:17; Num 26:44-46. The other names are strange to us, though one should take note of sisters named in vv. 30 and 32, and v. 31's "father of Birzaith"—a phrase seen often in chs. 2 and 4 and designating the founder of a town or city.

Asher's territory was remote and certainly lay far outside the province of Judah in the time of ChrR. Like Naphtali, it represented for the latter the far northern extension of Israel's proper territory. ChrR cannot use this material to illustrate prolific ethnicity, but its clear and strong system of military organization can typify its ideal structure.

Bibliography

F. M. Abel, "Une mention biblique de Birzeit," *RB* 46 (1937) 217-24; M. D. Johnson, *The Purpose of the Biblical Genealogies* (SNTSMS 8; Cambridge: Cambridge, 1969) 37-82.

MORE BENJAMINITE RECORDS, 8:1-40; 9:1a

Structure

Because this material is so long and involved, it is best to present an outline of its structure in segments. Our verse listings from 29 to 38 will show the parallel verses in the reprise of 9:35-44, avoiding the necessity of replicating the identical outline for that passage.

Verses 1-5 constitute a genealogy of two generations, each with names of siblings. Only the Benjamin list has the *hôlîd* styling; the Bela list begins with the narrative form *wayyihyû bānîm lĕbāla'*, "and Bela had sons," and continues with the proper names. Nothing more is heard of any of the names mentioned. The Ehud list in vv. 6-7 has the formal introduction *we'ēlleh bĕnê . . .*, but the names are held back for a parenthesis indicating that the sons to be named had been chiefs of the Geba garrison but had been relocated (*glh*) to Manahath. The parenthesis makes use of a locution found also in v. 13: *'ēlleh hēm rā'šê 'ābôt lĕyôšĕbê geba'*, "As for these, they were chiefs of ancestral families for the residents of Geba," which is to say that they were the ones properly so designated, an important point in the light of their reassignment to Manahath. A first generation is given, then a second is introduced with *wĕhôlîd*, a narrative form related to the regular genealogical formula. A narrative *hôlîd* (v. 8), followed by *wayyôled* (v. 9), introduces the unnamed Moabite sons of Shaharaim and the five sons born of Hodesh, respectively; as the Moabite sons remain anonymous, the names of the two divorced wives are presented in another parenthesis. This segment has the formal conclusion *'ēlleh bānāyw rā'šê 'ābôt*, "These were his sons, ancestral chiefs."

Verses 11-13 give us the genealogy of this family by another mother, Hushim. Two sons are named for the first generation, then the lineage is drawn from the second named (Elpaal), but in two groupings. We are given the names belonging to the first group, and this is followed by a parenthesis indicating that Shemed was their place of residence. We are then given the second list, and another parenthesis mentions that *hēmmâ rā'šê hā'ābôt lĕyôšĕbê 'ayyālôn*, "These were ancestral chiefs for the inhabitants of Aijalon" (same locution as in v. 6); also that they dispossessed the residents of Gath.

Verses 14-27 give us a series of name lists for five other clans. The form is quite regular throughout. We cannot be sure whether the conclusion in v. 28 pertains just to the five mentioned or to all the Benjaminites, though the first is more likely since it places those referred to in Jerusalem, while the aforementioned groups seem to be garrisons placed in Manahath and Aijalon, respectively. We only hesitate because the first and all subsequent clan lists are attached syndetically to what immediately precedes, giving the impression that vv. 14-27 are only part of what is included in *'ēlleh* with the appellations and *'ēlleh* with the residence notation in v. 28.

The section about the garrison at Gibeon (vv. 29-32) stands in direct juxtaposition to the Jerusalem notice, with *ûbĕgib'ôn*, "And in Gibeon," foremost. The syntax of this section is excessively disjointed. After the prepositional phrase comes *yšb* (plur. perf.), but there is no named subject ("Jehiel" is a gloss to the parallel list in 9:35), only a predicate in the s., *'ăbî gib'ôn*, then the nominal clause with a s.

pronoun suffix, *wĕšēm 'ištô ma'ăkâ*. This continues (v. 30) with *ûbĕnô*, "and his son," but this is followed by a plur. list. Unless we are to resort to radical emendation, we should read this difficult text as follows: "And in Gibeon dwelt [plur.]: the patriarch of Gibeon (now the name of his wife was Maacah); also his sons [plur.], the *bĕkôr* Abdon, etc." The two name lists in vv. 30-31, 32a suggest a genealogy, but the mention of a mother suggests rather a rudimentary birth report, in which case the Miqloth of v. 32a is a second wife (read *ûmimmiqlôt*, "and from Miqloth"), a possibility favored by the fact that Miqloth is a fem. name and by the fact that the locution "and the name of his wife was . . ." has been seen only in birth reports and related folk materials.

Verse 32b, an evident conclusion to the Gibeon section, is difficult. It seems to make self-contradictory statements, which may have been occasioned, however, by tradition developments over a period of time. The statement *wĕ'ap hēmmâ neged 'ăhêhem* probably means "Now even these were closely adjacent to their fellow clansmen." Possibly *neged* could be given a more confident translation if only we were familiar with the circumstances. We may be quite sure, however, that it is not equivalent to the following clause, *yāšĕbû bîrûšālaim 'im 'ăhêhem*, "They dwelt in Jerusalem with their fellow clansmen."

The radically different styling, with the paternal name foremost and the regular repetition of the *hôlîd* or *ûbĕnê* formulas, shows that vv. 33-40a are an appendix to the relatively closed-off complex just preceding. In spite of the fact that ChrR has copied it again at his reprise in 9:39-44, there is no reason to agree with Rudolph (HAT) in identifying it as a literary addition, for it simply shows that ChrR kept on adding new information on the Benjaminites, as he had done in adding 8:1ff. to his former list at 7:6-12. Here is a straight linear genealogy, reaching back two generations before Saul and extending to many generations after him. Then, in v. 38, ChrR adds a name list for the fourteenth generation, beginning with *ûlĕ'āṣēl . . . bānîm wĕ'ēlleh šĕmôtām*, "And Azel had . . . sons; and these were their names." Because Azrikam is listed as *bĕkôrô*, "his first-born" (MT *bōkĕrû*), a glossator has inserted "six" in the introduction, but there are only five. Perhaps so many sons were seen as a remarkable novelty, leading the genealogist to conclude, *kol-'ēlleh bĕnê 'āṣēl*, "All these were sons of Azel." Having said this, the genealogist turns immediately to another name list, in which rankings of first, second, and third are given; it is closely joined to the Azel list by the notation that Eshek, the father, was a fellow clansman *('āḥ)* of Azel. Appellations are given for the firstborn, Ulam; his "sons" were *'ănāšîm*, noted as *gibbôrê ḥayil*, "brave warriors," and as *dōrĕkê qešet*, "drawers of the bow"— a special attribute of the warlike Benjaminites.

Verse 40b intends to serve as the conclusion to the entire pericope, but the phrasing *kol-'ēlleh mibbĕnê binyāmin*, "All these belong among the Benjaminites," shows that no claim is being made that it offers a complete census. In fact, to be a "Benjaminite" was more qualitative than quantitative; i.e., the attributes and the fighting qualities mean more than the count of tribal members.

We have previously had opportunity to discuss the meaning and bearing of 9:1a. It is ChrR's own summation, closing off his extended array of tribal listings. Quite apparently, he employs *yḥś* (hith.) in a way somewhat different from its use in the tribal musters. There it means "enroll for battle"; ChrR gives it the new nuance "inscribe in a genealogy." The muster rolls have an organizational function, but ChrR is interested in recreating a people. (On ChrR's intent, see Williamson, *Israel*, 106; Liver, *Chapters in the History*, 234-48; cf. 2 Chr 16:11; 20:34; 25:26; 27:7; 28:26.)

Genre

The main genre is of course the LIST. GENEALOGY is the genre of vv. 1-5, 6-7, 11-13, and 33-37. The BIRTH REPORT appears in vv. 8-10, 11, 30-31. The NAME LIST is common: vv. 7, 9b-10a, 12a, 13a, 14-27 (here with names foremost followed by "sons of X"), 30-31, 32a, 38a, 39b. The MUSTER ROLL is found at vv. 38, 39-40a. The RANKING FORMULA is found in vv. 1-2 (with ordinals "first" to "fifth"), 38a ("first"), and 39b ("first" to "third"). The APPELLATION occurs at vv. 6, 13, 28, and 40, with the TALLY also at v. 40.

Setting

ChrR's collection of genealogical records had apparently included Benjamin materials only at 7:6-12, hence, in adding this pericope, he first supplied (cf. Gen 46:21-22 and Num 26:38-41) the names of the patriarch's sons, which do not agree with those of ch. 7. What he then goes on to add has nothing to do with 7:6-12. Benjamin's son Bela, the *bĕkôr*, is listed with four others in order of rank (vv. 1-2);

compare Bela with two others in 7:6. The nine sons of Bela listed in 8:3-5 are definitely not the same as the five sons of Bela listed in 7:7. Besides Bela, a few other names correspond. The Ehud of 8:6 is probably not the Ehud, son of Jediael, in 7:10, but apparently, judging by the appearance of the name Gera (twice) in the list just preceding, the Ehud son of Gera of Judg 3:15-30, the famous fighter against the Moabites. If the Hushim of 8:11 is the same as the Hushim of 7:12 (where the text seems badly confused), it is strange that the identification is feminine here but apparently masculine there.

The interpreter of this material must certainly make allowances for the different genres involved: 7:6ff. is a muster roll, 8:1ff. is a series of genealogical fragments with birth reports. It is impossible for us, with our limited knowledge, to distinguish historical individuals from clan eponyms and/or the leaders of militia. A heroic individual such as Ehud tends to grow into a tribal unit bearing his name, and our problem is that we cannot know at which end of the developmental process a given text stands. Within this particular pericope, we seem to range in time from the era of the judges to the end of the Judahite monarchy, for the Ner genealogy brings us that far. There is nothing to help us put most of the individual items, including the muster rolls tacked on at the end (vv. 38-40), in any certain sequence.

Our attention is drawn especially to the references to strong Benjaminite garrisons in Jerusalem and at strategic sites nearby, Aijalon, Manahat, and Gibeon. At Gibeon, famous as a shrine site but noted here as a garrison town defending Jerusalem, there was a functionary (no individual name is given, despite 9:35) called *'ăbî gib'ôn*, which may perhaps mean "commandant" rather than "patriarch." The "sons" assigned to this anonymous figure are, of course, military subalterns. They commanded an important garrison, stationed there "over against" or "in cooperation with" the garrison in Jerusalem. The Jerusalem Benjaminite contingent consisted of five separate clan groups, to judge from 8:14-28. As has been mentioned, v. 32b may intend to include in this Jerusalem contingent the Aijalon garrison (v. 13) and other Shaharaimites, who could have been transferred there as the original Geba garrison had been resettled in Manahath (v. 6). 8:32b probably indicates that the Gibeon garrison also came to be transferred to Jerusalem.

All the cities mentioned lay at strategic sites. Aijalon is Bronze Age and is to be identified with Yalo near Emmaus in the Aijalon plain. Of Benjaminite cities, it alone occupies a place on the list of Rehoboam's fortified cities, 2 Chr 11:6-10, justifying the statement there that "he held Judah and Benjamin" (v. 12). (If our conjecture that the Aijalon Benjaminites came to serve in Jerusalem has validity, it could be that Rehoboam stationed Judahites there.) Gibeon lies seven miles northwest of Jerusalem, and is well known from archeological excavation as well as from random biblical texts. There is no need to think of native Gibeonites (cf. Joshua 9) as serving in the Benjaminite militia; their traditional servant status argues quite against it. Geba lies northeast of Jerusalem close to the famous Michmash pass (cf. 1 Samuel 13–14). The Manahath of our pericope is not the Edomite town of that name (cf. 1 Chr 1:40) but the town mentioned in 2:52, 54, a Bronze Age site now lying within the western limits of the city of Jerusalem. From the fact that major Benjaminite contingents have been placed in and near Jerusalem, we have to deduce that Benjamin had been merged with Judah, their military forces serving together, as in 2 Chr 11:1. The time is that of the kingdom of Judah. It is not the time of David, with Saul's forces joining his (1 Chr 12:1-7), because under the united kingdom Benjamin was still being administered separately from Judah; cf. 1 Chr 27:21. Some elements, like the Ehud genealogy, could have been quite ancient; others, like the Ner genealogy, may have come from the end of the kingdom.

Intention

This pericope was added by ChrR to his former collection. It is not a secondary literary expansion (Fohrer, *Intro.*, 244; Rudolph, HAT; Noth, "Chronistische Werk," 122). By adding this material, ChrR certainly gives greater prominence to Benjamin, but this serves to balance the extended Judah material in chs. 2–4, reflecting the close pairing of the two groups within the kingdom of Judah. It also helps in drawing a proper image of ChrR's ideal Israel, which cannot be close to historical reality unless it reflects the fact that the totality of one-time Benjaminite territory was now included in Yehud, the province occupied by the people of the restoration.

Bibliography

A. Bartel, "Tradition über das Los der Gibeoniter in 1 Chr 8, 6f" (Hebr.), *BethM* 39 (1969) 24-27; J. Blenkinsopp, *Gibeon and Israel. The Role of Gibeon and the Gibeonites in the Political and Religious History of Early Israel* (SOTSMS 2; Cambridge: Cambridge, 1972) 100-108; A. Demsky, "The Genealogy of Gibeon: Biblical and Epigraphic Considerations," *BASOR* 202 (1971) 16-23; J. Liver, "And All Israel Were Reckoned by Genealogies" (Hebr.), in *Studies in Bible and Judean Desert Scrolls* (Jerusalem: Magnes, 1971) 234-48; idem, *Studies in the Lists of Chronicles and Ezra and Nehemiah* (Jerusalem: Magnes, 1968); B. Z. Luria, "Adasa, a City in the Territory of Benjamin" (Hebr.), *BethM* 25 (1979) 63-65; J. Simons, *Handbook for the Study of Egyptian Topographical Lists Relating to Western Asia* (Leiden: Brill, 1937) 117; J. Schäfers, "Studie zu 1 Chr 8, 6-9a," *BZ* 7 (1909) 279-84; H. G. M. Williamson, *Israel in the Books of Chronicles* (Cambridge: Cambridge, 1977).

LISTS OF THE CUSTODIANS OF POSTEXILIC JERUSALEM, 9:1b-34

Structure

Inasmuch as vv. 17ff. are an enlargement of the original core, we shall present the structure of each segment separately.

There are some who wish to attach "and Judah" (v. 1b) to the title of ChrR's hypothetical source document, "the book of the kings of Israel," because "and Judah" is sometimes included. On the other hand, it also appears just as here, without the addition. If ChrR/H has no difficulty in consigning his Judahite kings to a "book of the kings of Israel," identifying their kingdom as "Israel," how much more so in the concluding rubric to his long genealogical introduction, where "Israel," if not "kings," has been the subject. Besides, it is absurd to think of ChrR introducing a whole new pericope with a subjectless verb. It does not matter that *hoglû* is plur., because "Judah" can be distributive. When all is said, we identify a dramatic resumptive introduction, "Now Judah had been exiled because of their corruptness."

What follows is no narrative of the return, but a complex noun clause whose subject is "Now the first to dwell *[yšb]* in their possessions, in their cities," and whose predicate is the four (or three) generic groups: "Israel" (i.e., the laity), the priests, the Levites, and the "servants" *(hannětînîm)*. The priests are probably to be taken out of this list as a gloss from vv. 10ff. because *hakkōhănîm* is asyndetic with the following *halwîyim*, requiring us to read the questionable "Levitical priests," and because the reversal of these two names in LXX[B] suggests that one of

89

them is an intrusion. We would choose the Levites as original (1) because of ChrR/H's constant attention to them, and (2) because a priestly redactor's hand is seen elsewhere correcting the omission of the priests (cf. 6:35-37; 24:1-19).

These verses are a prologue to vv. 3ff., introduced by "and in Jerusalem" foremost. It is readily recognized that here ChrR takes up one of his "foundation documents" (see Chapter 2 above), a list closely related to, but not identical with, Neh 11:3-18. Throughout this section ChrR's styling is to introduce the various groups with *ûmin*, "and some of . . ." (cf. Nehemiah). The verb *yšb*, v. 3, governs all. The first group represents "all Israel" (*RSV* "the people" is explicative), coming from his favorite tribes, Judah, Benjamin, Ephraim, and Manasseh. The last two are joined without *ûmin* and, because no actual names for them are mentioned, may represent little more than a symbolic presence. What follows in vv. 4-9 is more a list of families or clans than of historical individuals, whatever they may have been in the Nehemiah list. The reason for saying this is that vv. 6 and 9 have the locution *wa'ăḥêhem*, lacking in Nehemiah, and v. 9 even adds *lĕtōlĕdôtām*, "according to their generations," indicating a generational descent from the persons mentioned. We are to suppose that, in the time of ChrR, Judah and Benjamin had received "brothers" not mentioned here. The Judah group is introduced asyndetically. Pedigrees to Perez (on to Judah), to Shelah (not MT "Shilonites"; cf. Num 26:20; 1 Chr 4:21-23), and to Zerah indicate the three main clans. The Benjaminite list (vv. 7-9) is introduced with *ûmin bĕnê binyāmin*, "and some of the Benjaminites." Pedigrees trace four leading clans to Hassenuah, etc. The conclusion is a tally with title, something new for ChrR. It is cast as a concluding rubric, *'ēlleh 'ănāšîm rā'šê 'ābôt lĕbêt 'ăbôtêhem*, "These were troopers [?], ancestral chiefs, even [emphatic *lĕ*; cf. Watson, "Archaic Elements," 8.1] according to their ancestral families." Since the form of the muster roll is being emulated, *'ănāšîm* refers to members of the militia, here restored in the ideal, if not in reality.

The priestly list begins with ChrR's *ûmin*, "And some of. . . ." It refers to *hakkōhănîm*, Nehemiah's term (ChrR prefers *bĕnê 'ahărôn*, "Aaronites"), but differences in individual names as well as in structure strengthen the impression that ChrR is not working directly from Nehemiah but from a list common to both. For instance, ChrR lists the anonymous kinsmen (*'ăḥêhem;* cf. vv. 6, 9) only after the families and individual names (v. 13), not after each family, as in Nehemiah. He gives us a short name list of priests without patronym, then three pedigrees. The remote ancestor Ahitub (v. 11) is mentioned with the title *nĕgîd bêt hā'ĕlōhîm*, "ruler of God's temple" (cf. Neh 11:11). The anonymous kinsmen are given the title *rā'šîm lĕbêt 'ăbôtām*, "chiefs of their ancestral families," and then tallied. That this is a title and not an appellation is seen in the fact that v. 13b does give an appellation—a most remarkable one—*gibbôrê ḥayil* [MT *ḥēl*] *mĕle'ket 'ăbôdat bêt-hā'ĕlōhîm*, "mighty warriors working in the service of God's temple," indicating that the image of military organization has carried over to the realm of the sacral.

"And some of the Levites" introduces vv. 14-16. Our outline lists the Levites as "associate clergy" because ChrR's source intends to give them, and them alone, a status of high sacrality alongside the priests. As our continuing outline will show, ChrR's expansion in vv. 17-33 intends to give the gatekeepers and singers Levitical status, so that the title "Levites" covers them all. As in the Nehemiah parallel, there is no reference here to "kinsmen," only to three chief families with pedigree ("from the Merarites" is ChrR's addition), with the insertion of three names without patronym, and finally Berechiah's name with pedigree and the indication that he dwelt *(yšb)* in the "villages" of the Netophathites — a reference omitted in Nehemiah and seemingly in contradiction to the apparent intention to place these priests and Levites in Jerusalem.

That ChrR turns now to another source is evidenced by a departure from the *ûmin* styling to the simple rubric *wĕhaššōʿărîm*, "As for the gatekeepers." This introduces a subject that will occupy most of the pericope. An introductory rubric, *wĕʾēlleh hamšōrĕrîm*, "And these are the singers," does mention a parallel order of minor clergy (v. 33), but ChrR mentions them in order to make a clean sweep in the concluding rubric to his Levite section (*ʾēlleh rāʾšê hāʾābôt lalwîyim lĕtōlĕdôtām*, "These were the ancestral chiefs for the Levites throughout their generations," v. 34a). ChrR has a final rubric also (v. 34b) for the entire collocation of groups listed in vv. 3-33: *rāʾšîm ʾēlleh yāšĕbû bîrûšālāim*, which is best translated—if *rāʾšîm* is not a gloss (it cannot be rationalized as such, for what function would it have?)—"Chiefs were these; they dwelt in Jerusalem."

No comment is needed on v. 33, where the singers are mentioned only for completeness; they had in fact been dealt with in 6:16ff. and were scheduled for further treatment in 15:16-24; 25:1-31. (Cf. A. Kropat, *Syntax*, 76.) Vv. 17-33—about the gatekeepers—may seem a hopeless jumble. Quite understandably, the ancient VSS make as many errors as they correct and can seldom be relied upon. We need to recognize that ChrR is using sources, and that here, more than in most passages, he gives free rein to his unorthodox syntax. Besides, he is introducing a new genre, the JOB DESCRIPTION (see below), at vv. 17-23, 24-27, and 28-32. The first passage is ideological, assigning the gatekeepers to "the camp of the Levites." The second translates this in more realistic terms as a charge over the foregoing, viz., "the house/temple of God." The third specifies this group's general supervision.

Looking carefully at vv. 17ff., we see that first a list of four names is given, with Shallum being specified as chief, and a nonsacral locale, "the king's gate" on the east, being specified as their previous post of duty. In contrast, we are told in v. 18b that *hēmmâ haššōʿărîm lĕmaḥănôt bĕnê lēwî*, "These are (in fact) of the camp of the Levites," a claim that is explicated in vv. 19ff. First we are told that the above-mentioned Shallum, himself from Korah, along with the entire Korahite family, is involved. Their ancestors, in the first instance with Phinehas as chief, guarded the camp in the wilderness (cf. Exod 32:25-29), Yahweh being with him (note the traditional use of "Yahweh," which ChrR usually avoids). A certain Zechariah (cf. 26:2, 14) is apparently now in charge of *ʾōhel môʿēd*, "the tent of meeting," typological for the temple. But *kullām*, "all of them," have been chosen to serve; a tally stresses the number 212 by placing it foremost, and we are told that these are "enrolled [*yḥś*, hith.] in their villages" (a contradiction of vv. 3, 34b). Authorization from David and Samuel is claimed for this (v. 22), posting them (*hēm ûbĕnêhem*, "them and their posterity") over the house of Yahweh (v. 23a). To ensure that the typological association is clear, ChrR adds *lĕbêt hāʾōhel*, i.e., "the tent shrine."

Verse 24 starts out afresh, listing the posts of each eponymous group at the four temple gates (foremost for emphasis). Contradicting vv. 3, 34b once again, v. 25 specifies how relief for duty personnel is to be brought in from the surrounding villages, apparently with a double shift for the sabbath. Vv. 26-27 tell us how the *gibbōrê haššōʿărîm*, "duty chiefs," are to guard the temple at night and open it

92

from morning to morning (a gloss in v. 26a retains this for the "Levites," specifically claiming Levitical status for this group).

Verses 28-32 are the most difficult to make sense of. A new phrase, *ûmēhem*, "and some of them" (not the *ûmin* of vv. 10, 14), details a certain group to supervise the holy services in v. 28, and a second group, specially appointed *(mĕmunnîm)* to guard the secular utensils, the sacred utensils, and the foodstuffs intended for the offerings. ChrR probably intends vv. 30-32 to be included in this same job description, but he switches to a rather puzzling syntax. He has here to do with the baking procedures; there are three groups to be supervised: "some of the *bĕnê hakkōhănîm* [priestly group] who mixed the spices, Mattithiah, who makes the flat cakes, and some of the *bĕnê haqqĕhātî min 'ăhêhem* [Kohathites, i.e., some of their kinsmen]." With the first and the third group, *ûmin* refers to those supervised, not to the supervisors. The term *be'ĕmûnâ* means "faithfully," "regularly," in vv. 26 and 31.

Genre

The main genre is LIST. There are no genealogies, but the PEDIGREE occurs at vv. 4, 7, 8 (three times), 11, 12 (twice), 14, 15, 16 (twice), 19; also the RANKING FORMULA in vv. 5, 17, 31; the NAME LIST at vv. 5, 17; the TALLY at vv. 6, 9, 13, and 22; and an eccentric, ideological APPELLATION at v. 13. Not seen before are the ASSISTANCE FORMULA ("I am with you," with variations) at v. 20 and the SCHEDULE, correlating persons, times, and tasks, at v. 25. As has been noted, the genre JOB DESCRIPTION occupies the entire space given in this pericope to the gatekeepers. Another example appears at 1 Chr 23:25-26, 28-32. The purpose of this genre is to detail work assigned to a group or individual, keeping each worker to his proper task, preventing disputes among the various workers, and assuring that every responsibility is properly assigned and adequately covered.

Setting

As v. 2 intends us to understand, the first returnees were the promise of more to come. The list may not have originally included the priests (see above), but it did include the *nĕtînîm*, which, according to Watson ("Archaic Elements," 11.1), may have been "guilds" (cf. Ugaritic *ytnm, UT,* 301:I:1); but cf. Blenkinsopp (*Gibeon,* 106-8). Some scholars (Rudolph, HAT; Gese, "Kultsänger," 224) think this entire list is an addition, but it is suffused with ChrR's linguistic peculiarities, and it would be difficult to conceive of ChrR bridging the gap from his genealogical to his narrative section without it. As we have seen, there is a close correlation with Neh 11:3-18, but plainly each text has gone its own way, and ChrR's stress on "their kinsmen" (vv. 6, 9, 13, 19) indicates that the original list from which both Nehemiah and ChrR have borrowed applies here to the families and clans that have developed from them. Both Levites (v. 16) and gatekeepers (vv. 22, 25) have at least some of their personnel in outlying villages such as Netophah, near Bethlehem. The important thing is that the gatekeepers, originally probably a lay group or subordinate order of minor clergy, to whom the Levites may have assigned their special task, are now plainly attempting to claim the status of Levite (cf. Watson, "Archaic Elements," 10.52). The relationship between Levites and priests is not at issue, yet v. 30 shows us that even the priests were not exempt from the general supervision assigned to the gatekeepers, now raised to Levitical status. In short, all the problems and tensions that might arise in the development of a new sacrificial cultus, claiming continuity from that which had gone before, have come to appearance in this pericope.

Intention

It is at least clear from the way of referring to these clerical groups as clans, employing some of the traditional nomenclature of the MUSTER ROLL, but especially from v. 13's appellation, "mighty warriors in the work of the service of God's house," applied to the priests, that ChrR conceives of the new clergy as a warrior host. Whom they have to fight against is not clear, but they are definitely organized like an army. ChrR will depend for the security of the "new Israel" more on them than on the tribal groups mentioned in vv. 4-9—and rightly so, for the struggle will now be not against a military host but against spiritual forces.

Probably the "gatekeepers" were actually armed in some way, and, like the Swiss Guards at the Vatican, offered physical force against every intruder and every offender. The JOB DESCRIPTION is definitely an instrument for keeping them to their task, and, as such, keeping the theocratic government in order. We can understand why ChrR wants to include them among the Levites (v. 34a), for they were required to supervise the Levites and the priests. It is also understandable that he insists (v. 34b) that they too "lived" in Jerusalem. It is where a man does his duty that he fulfills the purpose of his life, wherever he may lay his head at night to sleep (vv. 13, 22, 24).

That the use of armed force may have been one of the prerogatives of the gatekeepers is underscored by the reference to Phinehas as their previous leader (nāgîd... lĕpānîm; cf. v. 18) in v. 20. This man is reported in Num 25:7-8 as taking a spear and piercing an Israelite man and his Midianite wife. Vv. 19ff. constitute a strongly typological *apologia* for identifying the gatekeepers of this generation with the Levites of before. The typology is along two axes: (1) between the wilderness camp, with its tent of meeting, and Yahweh's temple; and (2) between the ancient Levites and the gatekeepers who have come to be part of them. The temple is the camp, the gatekeepers are the Levites. A similar typology has been found for the singers in 1 Chr 6:16-17 (*RSV* 32-33). Thus does ChrR bind postexilic Israel with ancient Israel, articulating the ideology which requires an extended genealogy, chs. 1–9, showing who ideal Israel is, as the proper prologue to his history, showing how and why the historical Israel has not yet become the ideal Israel that it has been designed to be.

Bibliography

J. Blenkinsopp, *Gibeon and Israel* (SOTSMS 2; Cambridge: Cambridge, 1972); B. Jacob, "Miszellen zu Exegese, Grammatik und Lexicon," *ZAW* 18 (1898) 290; S. Japhet, "The Supposed Common Authorship of Chronicles and Ezra-Nehemiah Investigated Anew," *VT* 18 (1968) 330-71; U. Kellermann, "Die Listen in Nehemia 11 eine Dokumentation aus den letzten Jahren des Reiches Israel?" *ZDPV* 82 (1966) 212-13; B. Levine, "The Nŭtînîm, " *JBL* 82 (1963) 207-12; G. von Rad, *Das Geschichtsbild des chronistischen Werkes* (BWANT 3; Stuttgart: Kohlhammer, 1930); H. G. M. Williamson, *Israel in the Books of Chronicles* (Cambridge: Cambridge, 1977).

Chapter 4

The Narrative Framework: The History of Ideal Israel's Completing Its Land's Sabbaths, 1 Chr 9:35–2 Chr 36:23

BIBLIOGRAPHY

P. R. Ackroyd, "The Chronicler as Exegete," *JSOT* 2 (1977) 2-32; idem, "History and Theology in the Writings of the Chronicler," *CTM* 38 (1967) 501-15; idem, "The Theology of the Chronicler," *Lexington Theological Quarterly* 8 (1973) 101-16; W. E. Barnes, "The Midrashic Element in Chronicles," *Exp* 2 (1896) 426-39; idem, "The Religious Standpoint of the Chronicler," *AJSL* 13 (1896-97) 14-20; C. Begg, " 'Seeking Yahweh' and the Purpose of Chronicles," *Louvain Studies* 9 (1982) 128-42; S. B. Berg, "After the Exile: God and History in the Books of Chronicles and Esther," in *The Divine Helmsman (Fest. L. H. Silberman; ed. J. L. Crenshaw and S. Sandmel; New York: KTAV, 1980) 107-27; J. Botterweck, "Zur Eigenart der chronistischen Davidgeschichte," *TQ* 136 (1956) 402-35; R. L. Braun, "A Reconsideration of the Chronicler's Attitude Toward the North," *JBL* 96 (1977) 59-62; idem, "Solomonic Apologetic in Chronicles," *JBL* 92 (1973) 503-16; idem, "Solomon, the Chosen Temple Builder," *JBL* 95 (1976) 581-90; idem, "Chronicles, Ezra, and Nehemiah: Theology and Literary History," in *Studies in the Historical Books of the Old Testament* (VTSup 30; ed. J. A. Emerton; Leiden: Brill, 1979) 52-64; A.-M. Brunet, "Le Chroniste et ses sources," *RB* 60 (1953) 481-508, continued in *RB* 61 (1954) 349-86; idem, "La théologie du Chroniste. Théocratie et messianisme," in *Sacra Pagina* (ed. J. Coppens, H. A. Descamps, and E. Massaud; Paris: Gabalda, 1959) 1:384-97; K. Budde, "Vermutungen zum Midrasch des Buches der Könige," *ZAW* 12 (1892) 37-51; A. Caquot, "Peut-on parler du messianisme dans l'oeuvre du Chroniste?" *RTP* 99 (1966) 110-20; W. Caspari, "Der Anfang von II Chron und die Mitte des Königsbuches," *ZAW* 39 (1921) 170-74; S. J. De Vries, "The Land's Sabbath in 2 Chronicles 36:21," *Proceedings, Eastern Great Lakes and Midwest Biblical Societies* 6 (1986) 96-103; idem, "The Schema of Dynastic Endangerment in Chronicles," *Proceedings, Eastern Great Lakes and Midwest Biblical Societies* 7 (1987) 59-77; idem, "The Forms of Prophetic Address in Chronicles," *Hebrew Annual Review* 10 (1986) 15-36; idem, "Moses and David as Cult-Founders in Chronicles," *JBL* (forthcoming); idem, *Yesterday, Today and Tomorrow* (Grand Rapids: Eerdmans, and London: SPCK, 1975); S. R. Driver, "The Speeches in Chronicles," *Exp* 1 (1895) 241-56, 286-308; D. N. Freedman, "The Chronicler's Purpose," *CBQ* 23 (1961) 436-42; M. Gil, "Israel in the Books of Chronicles" (Hebr.), *BethM*

13 (1968) 105-15; J. Goldingay, "The Chronicler as Theologian," *BTB* 5 (1975) 99-126; T. D. Hanks, "The Chronicler: Theologian of Grace," *EvQ* 53 (1981) 16-28; S. Japhet, "The Ideology of the Book of Chronicles and Its Place in Biblical Thought" (Hebr.) (Diss., Hebrew University, 1973); W. E. Lemke, "The Synoptic Problem in the Chronicler's History," *HTR* 58 (1965) 349-63; idem, "Synoptic Studies in the Chronicler's History" (Diss., Harvard, 1963); D. J. McCarthy, "Covenant and Law in Chronicles-Nehemiah," *CBQ* 44 (1982) 25-44; R. Micheel, *Die Seher- und Prophetenüberlieferungen in der Chronik* (Beiträge zur biblischen Exegese und Theologie 18; Frankfurt a/M: Land, 1983); J. A. Montgomery, "A Study in Comparison of the Texts of Kings and Chronicles," *JBL* 50 (1931) 115-16; S. K. Mosiman, *Eine Zusammenstellung und Vergleichung der Paralleltexte der Chronik und der älteren Bücher des Alten Testaments* (Halle: Kämmerer, 1907); R. Mosis, *Untersuchungen zur Theologie des chronistischen Geschichtswerkes* (Freiburg: Herder, 1973); J. M. Myers, "The Kerygma of the Chronicler," *Int* 20 (1966) 259-73; J. D. Newsome, Jr., "Toward a New Understanding of the Chronicler and His Purposes," *JBL* 94 (1975) 201-17; R. North, "Theology of the Chronicler," *JBL* 82 (1963) 369-81; D. L. Petersen, *Late Israelite Prophecy* (Missoula: Scholars, 1977); O. Plöger, "Reden und Gebete im deuteronomistischen und chronistischen Geschichtswerk," in *Aus der Spätzeit des Alten Testaments* (Göttingen: Vandenhoeck & Ruprecht, 1971) 50-66; idem, *Theocracy and Eschatology* (tr. S. Rudman; Richmond: John Knox, 1968); G. von Rad, *Das Geschichtsbild des chronistischen Werkes* (BWANT 3; Stuttgart: Kohlhammer, 1930); idem, "The Levitical Sermon in I and II Chronicles," in *The Problem of the Hexateuch and Other Essays* (tr. E. W. Trueman Dicken; New York: McGraw-Hill, 1966) 267-80; I. L. Seeligmann, "Der Auffassung von der Prophetie in der deuteronomistischen und chronistischen Geschichtsschreibung," *Congress Volume: Göttingen 1977* (VTSup 29; Leiden: Brill, 1978) 254-84; idem, "Voraussetzungen der Midraschexegese," *Congress Volume: Copenhagen 1953* (VTSup 1; Leiden: Brill, 1953) 150-81; J. R. Shaver, "Torah and the Chronicler's History Work" (Diss., Notre Dame, 1983); J. D. Shenkel, "A Comparative Study of the Synoptic Parallels in I Paraleipomena and I-II Reigns," *HTR* 62 (1969) 63-85; W. F. Stinespring, "Eschatology in Chronicles," *JBL* 80 (1961) 209-19; G. Vermes, "Bible and Midrash: Early Old Testament Exegesis," in *The Cambridge History of the Bible* (ed. P. R. Ackroyd and C. F. Evans; Cambridge: Cambridge, 1970) I:199-231; J. Weinberg, "Das Eigengut in den Chronikbüchern," *OLP* 10 (1979) 161-81; A. C. Welch, *Post-Exilic Judaism* (Edinburgh-London: Blackwood, 1935); idem, *The Work of the Chronicler, Its Purpose and Its Date* (London: Oxford, 1939); J. Wellhausen, "Chronicles," in *Prolegomena to the History of Ancient Israel* (tr. Menzies and Black; repr. Cleveland-New York: World, 1965) 171-227; P. Welten, *Geschichte und Geschichtsdarstellung in den Chronikbüchern* (WMANT 42; Neukirchen-Vluyn: Neukirchener, 1973); idem, "Lade-Tempel-Jerusalem. Zur Theologie der Chronikbücher," in *Textgemäss (Fest. E. Würthwein;* ed. A. H. J. Gunneweg and O. Kaiser; Göttingen: Vandenhoeck & Ruprecht, 1979) 169-83; T. Willi, *Die Chronik als Auslegung* (FRLANT 106; Göttingen: Vandenhoeck & Ruprecht, 1972); idem, "Thora in den biblischen Chronikbüchern," *Judaica* 36 (1980) 102-5, 148-51; H. G. M. Williamson, "The Accession of Solomon," *VT* 26 (1976) 351-61; idem, "Eschatology in Chronicles," *TynBul* 28 (1977) 115-54; idem, *Israel in the Books of Chronicles* (Cambridge: Cambridge, 1977).

Structure

I. Account of establishing Yahweh's nation
   and temple   1 Chr 9:35–2 Chr 9:31

It is clear that the narrative sections of 1-2 Chronicles follow the structure of 1 Samuel 31–2 Kings 25, but with numerous additions, alterations, and omissions. Mosis (*Untersuchungen*, 17-43), followed by Williamson (comm.), has given us the answer to why ChrH starts with Saul's death; it provides a grand inclusio with 2 Chronicles 36, for Saul's death and the dispersal of his people are a type and model of the death and exile of Judah and its last kings. The Saul story is a null-point pointing to the terminal null-point that comes at the end of the long and dismal history of Judah's kings. ChrH is interested in telling nothing more about Saul than his ancestry (the reprise of 8:36-38 in 9:42-44) and his death.

An important difference between this history and that of DtrH is that ChrH does not allow the Babylonian exile to be the end of the story. Whether or not 2 Kgs

25:27-30 hints at a renewal through Jehoiachin and his posterity, the conclusion of DtrH gives the impression of unrelieved gloom; the entire nation is guilty, the entire nation perishes. ChrH has a different plan. He does intend to tell of the nation's downfall, but first he wants to assure that there are three things that will survive the exile and go on forever: the Davidic kingship, the cultic establishment, and the temple itself. Thus he sets up his HISTORY in two main parts. He will first tell how Yahweh established his nation and temple (1 Chr 9:35–2 Chr 9:31), and then he will tell how Solomon's successors brought wrath on the temple and the nation (2 Chr 10:1–36:23). David and Solomon have no part in this wastrel behavior; DtrH's complaints about each of them are passed over in silence. David built the nation and established the ministry, at the same time making every preparation for the temple. For this, Yahweh establishes his permanent kingship in his son Solomon, who brings the temple to reality. The first ACCOUNT of Part I concerns the consolidation of David's rule; the second ACCOUNT tells of the building of the temple.

There is a lot to tell about the temple, which is clearly the focal point of Part I. But there is much to say as well about how David consolidated the kingdom that he received from Saul. This is vital because without the nation and the kingship, the cultus would have no function. But, as ChrH tells it, it is also important because the power and the wealth that David acquired were employed in two preliminary events leading up to—and vital for—the building of the temple: (1) the installation of the ark and the preparation of a clergy to serve it in Jerusalem (1 Chr 13:1-14; 15:1–16:42), and (2) the obtaining of a special site for the temple (21:1-27). The order in which ChrH tells about David follows generally the sequence of 2 Samuel 5–24, but the order as he modifies it makes good sense in his design. "All Israel" comes together to make him king; Jerusalem is captured; his army, consisting of his old guerrillas and representatives of Saul's old forces, is described; the narrative of the ark's entrance is encapsulated with information of David's political and military successes, then with reports of his establishment of the clergy and ordering of worship. Next we find the narrative of the dynastic promise, taken over almost word for word from 2 Samuel 7. This is followed by a collection of reports of the various battles in which David extended his political control while building up a rich treasure of booty to be used in building the temple. The theme of military might suggests the census of ch. 21, which forms the transition to ChrH's version of David's purchase of the threshing floor on the holy mount, above the "city of David."

Our reconstruction of the "Account of the building of the temple" might be challenged from two angles, but neither complaint would be valid. First, one observes that 1 Chr 21:28-30 continues the scene of Ornan's threshing floor, and hence ought to be attached to the preceding. The syntactical structure tells against this. We have first the temporal phrase *bāʿēt hahîʾ*, "at that time," introducing a distinctly new, though related, item. Next comes a temporal clause that summarizes what has just been told, providing a superfluous identification of the threshing floor. Then follows a narrative sequence, recounting new and radically different cultic actions on David's part. This cannot be the structure of a conclusion, but needs to be the introduction of a section sharply new.

The other objection might be that too much is included in an account of the temple building. It is easy to be misled by the clean way this is presented in 1 Kings

4–8. ChrH proceeds from David's dedicatory declaration in the passage just discussed to a detailed account of David's preparations, then to the lengthy section (1 Chr 23:1–29:30) about the transfer of the kingship to Solomon (including a report of David's death), and finally to the actual account of how Solomon built the temple and dedicated it to Yahweh's service.

From the point of view of structure, one will have to concede that the account of David's preparations must belong here if 1 Chr 21:28–22:1 is the formal introduction. The rather wordy section about Solomon's investiture (1 Chr 28:1–29:35) has to belong, for it is the narrative transition from David to Solomon. Thematically speaking, the complex materials in chs. 23–27 are appropriate, too. Before Solomon can begin the great task of building Yahweh's temple, three things have to occur: (1) David must make preparations; (2) the clergy must be ordered for this new specific task of ministering in the temple; and (3) David must hand over power and responsibility to his son Solomon.

The account of the actual building of the temple is itself long and complex. Here again, ChrH usually follows the sequence of Kings, but with a rather surprising amount of recasting, addition, and omission. One would readily concede that 2 Chronicles 3–7 is about the building of the temple plus the account of its dedication, necessary for putting it into use. But more is added. This material is placed inside another inclusio, i.e., framed at the beginning with an account of Solomon's own preparations (2 Chr 1:18–2:17) and at the end by a section on sanctifying the land for worship (8:1–16). 8:16a is intended as a final rubric for the section 3:1–8:15: "Thus was accomplished all the work of Solomon from the day the foundation of the house of Yahweh was laid until it was finished"; the concluding rubric for the entire inclusio beginning at 2 Chr 1:1 is 8:16b, šālēm bêt yahweh, "Perfected was Yahweh's house."

Lest it be thought that 1:1–17—about Solomon's dream—and 8:17–9:31—about the Queen of Sheba and Solomon's magnificence — have no structural relationship to the temple pericope (having been borrowed from Kings), one should be prepared to identify here still another of ChrH's inclusios. In matter of fact, both these sections speak about God's three great gifts to Solomon: riches, honor, and wisdom. The first section conveys them; the last section celebrates them; the long central section displays them and puts them to good effect.

A (→) regnal resumé is provided for Solomon (2 Chr 9:29-31), as had been provided for David (1 Chr 29:26-30), bringing to an end ChrH's first main section, "Establishing Yahweh's nation and temple." With Solomon's death, the book has reached an ideological and a structural climax. On the first, see below on "Intention." As for the second, the important thing to observe is that, amid the continuity provided by regular introductory and concluding regnal summaries for each successive king, these will now include the mostly negative theological appraisals found in Kings, beside numerous incidents of misbehavior by the kings and stern words of reprimand from the prophets. The concluding rubric for this long section is provided by 2 Chr 36:15-16: "Yahweh, the God of their fathers, sent persistently to them by his messengers, because he had compassion on his people and on his dwelling place; but they kept mocking the messengers of God, despising his words, and scoffing at his prophets, till the wrath of Yahweh rose against his people to the point where there was no remedy." Clearly it is all downhill from here on. David started the upward climb; Solomon reached the climax; now, even though there will be good kings, and bad kings, and good kings that do some bad, and bad kings that do good, the downward trend will be irresistible. And lest superficial readers imagine that it is only faithless kings that bring retribution, let them observe that the people usually share directly and responsibly (not just by way of corporate identification) in that faithlessless and therefore in that retribution.

The kings of Judah have been placed in chronological order. As though the story were already told, 2 Chronicles 36 barely mentions Judah's last four kings. And of course ChrH attempts no synchronistic interweaving for the stories of the northern kings, like DtrH (cf. the discussion of parataxis in Long, *1 Kings; with an Introduction to Historical Literature* [FOTL IX; Grand Rapids: Eerdmans, 1984] 22-23). ChrH brings the latter into his account only where the kings of Judah deal directly with them.

Most of the narratives about the respective Judahite kings are simple REPORTS (Abijah, Jehoram, Ahaziah, Joash, Amaziah, Uzziah, Jotham, Ahaz, Manasseh, Amon), but the narrative about Asa is a CHRONICLE, consisting of several independent reports; and the narratives of Rehoboam, Hezekiah, and Josiah (heroes to ChrH as to DtrH) are likewise complex structures requiring the name ACCOUNT. The interlinked narrative of Jehoshaphat's endangered progeny (21:1–23:21) is also a complex ACCOUNT. Usually the individual kings are linked together through the REGNAL RESUMÉ at the end, which normally includes a SUCCESSION FORMULA naming the successor. Because he died in disease and dishonor, Asa's narrative names no successor, and the equivalent of the succession formula appears instead in the introduction to the reign of Jehoshaphat. Because this good king ends up doing bad (20:32, 35-37), the succession is similarly named in the introduction to the reign of his son, Jehoram (21:1). With Jehoram commences the SCHEMA OF DYNASTIC ENDANGERMENT, terminating with the STORY of Athaliah's death and Joash's investiture; its discussion belongs below, under "Intention," but we can see that ChrH added some features—such as the murder of the royal princes in several generations—and reconstructed DtrH's account of the death of the Omride kings so as to throw greater blame on the house of Ahab. The REPORT of the reign of Joash begins in the normal fashion, and is not a structural part of the Athaliah story. "Hezekiah's reforms" is lengthened from the DtrH *Vorlage,* but "Hezekiah's deliverance" is much shortened, with heavy theological interpolations. Most of the ACCOUNT of Josiah's reign follows Kings, with extra years for doing good provided by putting his reform in the twelfth year of his reign. He is clearly ChrH's darling, for perpetual laments for his death (35:24-25) are required for him alone among all the kings that have died. Jeremiah's saying a lament for Josiah foretokens the imminent death of the nation and desolation of the land, predicted by this same Jeremiah (36:21).

Genre

In Chapter 1 above it was stated that ChrH as a whole belongs to the genre HISTORY. If that definition is accurate for the whole work, including the genealogical materials alongside the narrative materials, it is certainly true of the narrative section standing by itself. As has been shown, ChrH does not intend for the narratives to stand alone thematically; but strictly in terms of genre, the narrative section is a HISTORY.

Borrowing once again Long's definition (*1 Kings,* 250-51), we can show how this fits:

"An extensive, continuous, written composition": ChrH originated in writing; it is long (58 pericopes) and without gaps.

"Made up of and based upon various materials": ChrH copies, adapts, or simply alludes to previously given materials.

"Some originally traditional and oral, others written": ChrH follows a lengthy document such as DtrH, but also reproduces shorter oral and written materials.

"Devoted to a particular subject or historical period": ChrH's subject is ideal Israel fulfilling the land's sabbaths, and its chosen period is the era of the Judahite monarchy.

"Links together . . . materials . . . by imposing overarching structural and thematic connections": ChrH joins reign to reign, creating a grand inclusio from Saul to Zedekiah; his theme is the establishment of land and temple under David and Solomon, followed by their ineluctable decline under Solomon's successors.

"Dominated by a concern for chronology": though this is weaker in ChrH than in DtrH, the former does offer a chronology in the length-of-reign formulas for the successive kings.

"And cause-effect relationships": ChrR is much concerned to show not only how the kings receive the reward or retribution appropriate to their behavior, but also the ways in which given reigns are affected by those that precede them.

"It seeks to place events . . . within a framework of interpretation": a hallmark of ChrH is its repeated interruption of its narration with theological interpretation.

"In relation to the author's own time": in this narrative section, ChrH does this implicitly; for this it depends mainly on the genealogical section that precedes it, and especially on 1 Chronicles 3 and 9, where the postexilic context is made explicit.

As our analysis of "Structure" has shown, this HISTORY is made up of other genres: REPORT, ACCOUNT, and CHRONICLE. Individual pericopes offer a great variety of other genres, together with formal schemata and formulas. These will be defined or described at the first place where they appear.

Our review of ChrH's narrative structure must take notice at this point of a number of formal schemata (schema, s.) which this writer employs in extending his major themes over one narrative to another, effectively integrating materials of various origins and representing a variety of diverse genres. A schema is not a genre, it is a pattern—a pattern that tends to replicate itself from one narrative of a given genre to another of the same genre, or possibly that defines one specific genre in and of itself. It is more than a pattern of words, themes, or motifs, however. A schema as we have defined it also has *structure,* and its discussion clearly belongs in this section.

All interpreters of ChrH have observed his theme of reward and retribution, but it has not been recognized as one of the schemata that we are here discussing.

Scholars have been unaware of the others on our list as well. The four that we have identified are: (1) a SCHEMA OF REWARD AND RETRIBUTION; (2) a SCHEMA OF REVELATIONAL APPEARANCES; (3) a SCHEMA OF DYNASTIC ENDANGERMENT (alluded to above), and (4) a FESTIVAL SCHEMA. Each of these schemata is ChrH's own creation, not taken from his sources.

It will be seen that for the period from Saul to Zedekiah ChrH systematically applies the 'SCHEMA OF REWARD AND RETRIBUTION: virtue, reward; apostasy, retribution. Each king except David and Solomon occupies a place in the pattern that alternates the elements of this schema. Prophetic speeches are interspersed for warning against wickedness or encouraging repentance and righteousness. After Ahaz, these disappear. Another embellishment is an event of warfare, either (1) to elicit the monarch's faith, or (2) to punish his wrongdoing. Functionally eccentric are the addresses of 2 Chr 28:9-11, 13, in which punishment on the Judahites provokes a confession of common guilt and an appeal for brotherhood among the northern Israelites. This late, common involvement in guilty behavior is meant as a prolepsis of the national calamity to be recounted in 36:15-16.

The SCHEMA OF REVELATION APPEARANCES applies to the entire period after Solomon and takes in every prophetic and quasi-prophetic personage except Hezekiah's Huldah. All but the last, who is taken more or less intact from Kings, are products of ChrH's creative imagination, as a form-critical analysis of their various speeches will show (see De Vries, "Prophetic Address"). The foundational element in this schema is that it has the bringers of revelation offering assurance and encouragement to the good kings, but warning and condemnation to the bad kings (→ SCHEMA OF REWARD AND RETRIBUTION). Toward the end, ChrH grows paradoxical in the application of this schema, for instance encouraging Jehoshaphat while also chiding him (19:1-3), allowing a northern prophet to rebuke the northern people (28:9-13), or putting in the mouth of a foreign king Yahweh's revelation to Josiah (35:21). Although most speakers are prophets or seers, Asa's (14:10 [*RSV* 11] and Jehoshaphat's (20:5-12) prayers, along with Abijah's sermon (13:2-12), are also revelations of Yahweh's will for pious kings. Under the circumstances, the priest's warning shout of 26:18 is equivalent to the voice of God. Special gravity lies in the fact that Elijah's message comes in the form of a letter (21:13-15).

We have previously mentioned the next of ChrH's schemata, the SCHEMA OF DYNASTIC ENDANGERMENT. A detailed analysis appears in De Vries, "Dynastic Endangerment." This features tensions between two rival and mutually destructive forces: (1) the dynastic promise to David, brought to realization in the succession of the Judahite kings; and (2) an insatiable lust for blood among the Baalist Omrides and among members of the Judahite royal family affiliated with them or influenced by them. The climax of Athaliah's grisly deed is prepared for in the following steps: (1) Rehoboam and Abijah are models of fecund prosperity, richly confirming the dynastic prospect, yet an element of tension intrudes in the text's uncertainty about primogeniture in 11:18-23; (2) Jehoshaphat's consent to family affiliation with an Omride (18:1-2) brings the threat of wrath, to be fulfilled in his sons (19:2); (3) Jehoram's massacre of all his brothers (21:2-4), his Omride ways and marriage (v. 6), and the kidnapping of all his sons but the youngest (21:16-17; 22:1) provoke ChrH's assurance that David's "lamp" has not yet gone out (21:7); (4) Ahaziah, having adopted Omride ways and affiliations (22:2-4), is murdered by Jehu along with his royal cousins (vv. 7-9), leading Athaliah to murder all the remaining Davidides except Joash (vv. 10-12); (5) Joash himself succumbs to Baalist apostasy (24:17-18), justifying his own assassination (vv. 25-26); but the cycle is not complete until the instruments of endangerment, including Athaliah (23:15) and Joash's assassins (25:3), are themselves removed.

Finally we identify the FESTIVAL SCHEMA. It offers a common pattern, with variations, for Solomon's dedication feast (2 Chronicles 7) and Hezekiah's rededication feast (ch. 29), Asa's victory feast (ch. 15), and the Passover festivals of Hezekiah (ch. 30) and Josiah (ch. 35). The Solomonic pattern is likely to be the model for the others because it is directly adapted from 1 Kgs 8:65-66 and because it has the simplest development. The Asa and Hezekiah accounts have eccentric additions, while the Josiah narrative makes an eccentric deletion. In the Solomon story we find (1) a notice of the date, (2) a naming of the participants; (3) a description of the ceremonies; and (4) a notice of joyful celebration at the end. The Asa, Hezekiah, and Josiah narratives have the notice of date foremost, except that the Asa and Hezekiah stories preface it with an item about the participants and (in reverse order from each other) a notice of the preceding purification. The Hezekiah Passover narrative adds an additional purification notice after the date, and this is where we find the Josiah narrative's long section on ritual preparations. All five narratives come next with the climactic section on the actual ceremonies; the Asa narrative mentions no time frame, the Josiah narrative mentions seven days, and the narratives in ch. 7 and ch. 30 have seven days followed by a second seven-day celebration. At the end, we have the report of the joyful celebration that concludes the festival (this appears as thematic to ChrH), except in the Josiah narrative, which substitutes a closing notice of date. This is ChrH's FESTIVAL SCHEMA. While we need not doubt that the basic pattern of ritual is taken directly from ritual performances in ChrH's own experience, an ideological element is apparent in the attempt to model Asa, Hezekiah, and Josiah on the premier cultic celebrant, Solomon.

There are in ChrH, in addition to the above schemata, a number of noteworthy compositional patterns. One has already been taken note of, for it provides the inclusio framework for the entire work. This is the pattern of exile for apostasy, applied not only to Saul at the beginning and Zedekiah at the end, but as hints and prolepses at several places in between, e.g., the deportation of the Judahite captives in 2 Chr 28:8ff. and the menace of the Edomites and Assyrians in 28:16ff. (This pattern is forecast already in 1 Chr 5:6, 26, referring to the deportation of the Transjordanians.) The preceding should be seen as a pattern, not as a schema, for it neither has structural elements shared from passage to passage nor constitutes such a structural element in itself. So also for the following.

There is a meaningful pattern also in the account of David's rise to power, symbolized in his progression from Hebron to Jerusalem. In 1 Chr 11:1-2 "all Israel" gathers to make David "shepherd" and "prince"; in v. 3 the elders covenant themselves and make him king. Then in v. 4 David and "all Israel" march up to Jerusalem, to take possession of it. Strangely, the narration brings David back to Hebron in 12:38-40, which tells of the warriors who are identified in 11:10–12:37 coming together to that city to make David king, being joined by "all the rest of Israel." The apparent overlap cannot be due to a conflation of sources, for in 12:38ff. ChrH is composing freely. To make sense out of the narrative transition from 11:1 to 12:38, it is necessary to translate the second passage in the pluperfect; this is not foreign to ChrH's intent, for he intends the two Hebron pericopes as an inclusio for

104

what lies in between. In terms of his major thematic development it is important because it gives emphasis, right at the beginning of the account of David's rule, to the concept that "all Israel"—north and south—is united by and in the kingship of David, with Jerusalem as its central point of focus. Here is a pattern, then, that gives expression to the unity of nation, land, and kingship.

More than mere typology is involved in a pattern that equates David with Moses and Solomon with Joshua. It appears in 1 Chronicles 22; 28–29, where Solomon's investiture repeats in a number of details the succession of Joshua. We are indebted to R. Braun ("Solomon") and H. G. M. Williamson ("Accession") for bringing this to the fore. We shall have an opportunity to examine it closely when the mentioned passages come up for individual analysis.

Williamson (comm.) calls attention to another important pattern. It concerns ChrH's handling of the division of the kingdom under Rehoboam. The narrative of the confrontation at Shechem is repeated pretty much as it stands in 1 Kings 12, and ChrH makes no special point of holding either Rehoboam or Jeroboam guilty for what happened. It soon appears, however, that both Jeroboam and the northern Israelites are committing grievous sin in not returning to heal the breach. This is expressed emphatically in Abijah's speech of 2 Chronicles 13. Nevertheless ChrH continues to hold out the possibility of individual northerners affiliating themselves once again with Jerusalem, and he insists on referring to Judah as "Israel." He follows Kings in making Jehu's son Jehoahaz the instrument of bringing one of Judah's apostate kings, Amaziah, to account (2 Chr 25:17-24). Although the two kingdoms are never reunited, ChrH allows the division to be healed in principle when he places in the mouth of a northern prophet the charge that "the fierce wrath of Yahweh" upon the northerners makes them no better than the Judahites whom Ahaz has caused to go into captivity (28:9-10). In response certain Ephraimite chiefs forbid the enslaving of the captives, confessing, "Our guilt is already great, and there is fierce wrath against Israel" (v. 12). ChrH knows how the Assyrians brought the northerners into exile, but in this they only share a common fate with Judah under the Babylonians. With Samaria destroyed, nothing appears to stand in the way of the remaining northerners returning to Jerusalem. Hezekiah effectuates this when he sends "to all Israel and Judah" (here "Israel" means the northern kingdom), specifically writing letters to Ephraim and Manasseh, inviting all to be present at the Passover he has prepared (30:1). Thus Hezekiah fulfills the typology of Solomon, who brought the nation, the kingship, and the cultus to perfect oneness.

In his comm. on 7:14 (pp. 225-26) Williamson finds in ChrH's modification of 1 Kgs 8:35 a significant pattern of repentance (see above on SCHEMA OF REWARD AND RETRIBUTION) that provides the model for all the narratives of repentance to follow. The text reads, "If my people who are called by my name humble themselves, and pray and seek my face, and turn from their wicked ways, then I will hear from heaven, and will forgive their sin and heal their land." Thus the four specific ways of returning to God are (1) humility, (2) prayer, (3) proper ritual, and (4) a change of behavior.

These constitute the most important elements of "structure" in ChrH. One should add to them a number of *topoi*, such as "building the walls" (Welten, *Geschichte*, 42-52) and "foreign invasion," together with many striking motifs (e.g., peace, rest, joy) that help ChrH bring his concept to full expression. These are thematic rather than structural elements, however, and will be discussed at the relevant passages.

Setting

It will not be useful to repeat here our remarks on "Setting" (→ Chapter 1 above) regarding the entire, unredacted book. As we said there, ChrH's community is Palestinian Judaism living in the 4th century B.C. This is ideal Israel in search of its identity. In spite of the rebuilding of the temple and the work of Ezra and Nehemiah, it still lies between exile and restoration. That is, "ideal Israel" remains an ideal. It does not yet experience the fulness of a perfect union with God or a perfect realization of its own peoplehood and nationhood. ChrH's community's choice seems to lie between taking in too many or too few, between undue permissiveness and undue rigidity. The unifying element of the Davidic kingship has not been put into effect through a resumption of political independence, and the royal heirs of this late date are kings in title but not in reality. The temple, the ritual, and the cultic establishment are present, but can they provide the unity and the identification that are required?

Thus ChrH's community abides in tension. The future remains open to fulfill the restoration that he contemplates, but the gap between the actual character of the Jerusalem community and the full realization of that vision leaves him in continual anxiety. If this quandary is to be resolved, it will be necessary for "ideal Israel" to identify and submit fully to an authority that can ease quarrels, suppress rivalries, and resolve disputes. It is ChrH's lasting contribution in writing this book that he does identify, more clearly than ever, where that authority lies.

For ChrH the sources of authority are (1) "the God of the fathers"; (2) the cultic establishment of priests, Levites, and minor clergy; and (3) Scripture. We put these in the order of rank that ChrH himself accords them. The ancestral God has now become more definitely the God of heaven, and absolute obedience to his direction is required. Characteristically, ChrH refers to him as Israel's king, and to the Davidic kingship as his kingship. (As we have previously remarked, Israel's history is also his history.) In theory, no member of the postexilic community would question the divine authority, but how does God impose his authority and how does he make his will known? Since God now resides in heaven, he is accessible to his people in the temple services, and therefore the clergy possess the authority of guarding those services through careful performance and through proper instruction. But the priests and Levites cannot follow merely their own tradition, but must themselves be led by Scripture. By this term we mean Scripture in the making, for, in spite of the etymology, Scripture was not yet entirely reduced to written form— or let us say, not yet rid of rival recensions and put into a single, standardized book. But the concept was clear: God had spoken in the past, and many of his words had been preserved in such a form (oral or written) as to serve as a permanent record of his self-revelation.

Eventually ChrH's own writing—known to us as 1–2 Chronicles—would be admitted into the sacred body of Scripture. His book does not in any way replace the Scriptures that already exist, nor, in spite of Willi (*Auslegung*, 53-69), is it a mishnaic exegesis of Scripture. Nor is there truth in the once popular view that it is a midrash, or rabbinical homily, based on Scripture. We repeat this from Chapter 1 above: it is a retelling of Israel's story based on selected parts of Scripture and designed to clarify it for this new day.

What then are the Scriptures as ChrH knew and used them? Starting from the latest sections of the OT because with them we can be brief, we find that he knows at least some of the psalms (1 Chr 16:8-36; 23:25; 28:2-3; 2 Chr 6:41-42) and some of the prophets, "major" and "minor": Isaiah (2 Chr 16:7; 20:7-8, 17, 20), Jeremiah (2 Chr 15:2; 16:10; 36:21), Ezekiel (2 Chr 31:3), Joel (2 Chr 20:13), and Zechariah (2 Chr 16:9). This does not mean that ChrH necessarily knew these books in their complete content or in their present arrangement; although on other grounds it is likely that each was already substantially as we know it now.

We can be equally brief in our comments about the Pentateuch, Joshua, and Judges. We may assume that ChrH knew and accepted Joshua and Judges, especially because he draws much of the Moses-to-Joshua investiture pattern, discussed above, from the book of Joshua. Genesis is of course quoted and adapted in the genealogies of 1 Chronicles 1. The exodus-settlement theme found in Exodus-Numbers is so well known and accepted that it requires no comment from him. So likewise the priestly ritual code (P) of these pentateuchal books. Whenever ChrH describes the clerical establishment or the festival ritual, he simply states, without description, whatever is prescribed in this code (e.g., the procedure for offering a sacrificial animal, found in Leviticus 1ff.). "Moses" is often mentioned as the authority for new cultic regulations (→ AUTHORIZATION FORMULA), just as in the Pentateuch. It must not be thought, however, that ChrH's preference for P ruled out other legislative portions of the Pentateuch. J. Shaver ("Torah," 184) has shown us that ChrH leaned the most heavily on Deuteronomy, and that he also follows certain rules laid down in Exodus in preference to the more formal collocation of Leviticus-Numbers. It may well be that, though ChrH accepts the authority of P, it had not in his time been integrated into the Pentateuch as a literary document.

This brings us to ChrH's major source document, the DtrH, or, as we know it, Samuel-Kings. As any reader can recognize, this fully dominates the structure of ChrH's own narrative. For reasons previously given, ChrH does not begin to work from it at its own beginning, but once he takes it up, he stays with it till the end. We cannot assume that ChrH was reading the Hebrew text as we know it in the MT. Allen *(Relationship)* and Lemke ("Synoptic Problem") have studied this problem in the light of the Qumran discoveries and have shown how often the LXX has a text more ancient, and possibly more authentic, than that of the MT. This must make scholars more cautious of basing their analyses purely on the MT, and it shows them that Samuel-Kings as well as Chronicles has passed through a long and complex process of development.

In the course of our treatment of individual passages the various techniques by which ChrH adapted DtrH to his own use will become apparent. Willi *(Auslegung,* Part II) has enriched this whole field of study through his insightful analysis. But we are more involved here with the question of how ChrH used this literary source than with the matter of technique. It is, after all, the content of the tradition as an element of "setting" with which we are concerned.

Let us list then four distinct methods by which ChrH cites Samuel-Kings and makes it part of his own narrative: (1) exact or very close (remembering our caveat about the text) reproduction; (2) radical recasting and/or minimal reproduction; (3) substitution of a specially designed substitute; and (4) complete omission. All these methods effectuate ChrH's purpose—even omission. Exact or very close replication can be seen mainly in the so-called "synoptic" passages (Vannutelli, Lemke). Though it would not be to the point to list all these, we can see that they are, in general, the passages providing material that ChrH wants to have and cannot obtain elsewhere. Here is a list of the most characteristic or most prominent: Saul's death on Gilboa (1 Samuel 31); David's anointing and capture of Jerusalem (2 Sam 5:1-10); the roster of his chief warriors (2 Sam 23:8-39); the retrieval and installation of the ark (2 Samuel 6); David's victories and external politics (2 Sam 5:11-12; 8; 10:1–11:1; 12:26-31; 21:18-22); the Nathan oracle with David's prayer for his dynasty (2 Samuel 7); the census, pestilence, and purchase of the threshing floor (2 Samuel 24); the regnal resumés for David (1 Kgs 2:10-12) and his successors (but not for most of the totally bad kings!); Solomon's dream and most of Kings' varied assortment of notices concerning this king's honor, riches, and wealth (1 Kings 1–4; 10); preparations for and building of the temple and fabricating its appurtenances (1 Kings 5–7); the dedication of the temple, with Solomon's address and lengthy prayer (1 Kings 8); renewal of the Gibeon revelation with threat for apostasy (1 Kgs 9:1-9); the schism under Rehoboam (1 Kgs 12:1-24); military alliances with foreign kings, such as those of Asa and Ben-hadad (1 Kgs 15:16-22) and of Jehoshaphat with Ahab (1 Kgs 22:1-38); Jehoram's and Amaziah's wars against Edom (2 Kgs 8:20-22; 14:7); Joash's investiture and Athaliah's execution (2 Kings 11); Amaziah's execution of his father's assassins (2 Kgs 14:5-6); his war with Joash of Israel and his own assassination (2 Kgs 14:8-22); Amon's reign (2 Kgs 21:19-26); the finding of Josiah's lawbook and Huldah's prophecy (2 Kings 22); Jehoahaz's accession and deportation (2 Kgs 23:31-34). In taking up these materials, with numerous insertions, alterations, and expansions, ChrH is making them part of his own story, not just exegeting them (*contra* Willi, *Auslegung*, 53-69). The liberties he takes in reproducing them are justified by his intent to tell the story his own way. When he leaves them almost entirely intact (1 Chronicles 17; 2 Chronicles 18; etc.), it is because they make their statement just as ChrH wants it.

Here is a list of the main materials from Samuel-Kings which ChrH subjects to radical recasting: Rehoboam's contact with Shishak (1 Kgs 14:25-28); Ahaziah's death at the hand of Jehu (2 Kgs 8:28–9:28); the reign of Joash (2 Kings 12); the notice of Uzziah's (Azariah's) leprosy (2 Kgs 15:5); the reign of Ahaz (2 Kings 16); Hezekiah's reforms, Passover, deliverance from the Assyrians, illness, and sign (2 Kgs 18:9–20:21); Manasseh's reign (2 Kgs 21:1-18); Josiah's reform, Passover, and death (2 Kings 23); the reigns of the last four kings and Judah's deportation (2 Kgs 24:1–25:21). While it is certain that ChrH is reading the Kings text for these items, he departs so widely from them at certain vital points (again, by alteration, subtraction, or addition) that we must speak of his composition as a creative and original process. Here the underlying text does not say enough to express ChrH's meaning, or says it in a way that is inadequate to his purpose.

ChrH also employs substitution as a compositional method, but this is rare. It occurs when this writer has a complete narrative at hand which must be used to take the place of one that ChrH finds objectionable or inadequate. This occurs in 2 Chronicles 20, telling of aggression on the part of Moab and its allies against Jehoshaphat. It takes the place of the narrative of Jehoshaphat's aggression against Moab in 2 Kings 3, which ChrH declines to use because it again involves

Jehoshaphat in an Omride alliance and because it does not fit the pattern of the defensive holy war.

There are also elements in the Samuel-Kings tradition that ChrH declines to reproduce in any form. This is more through ideological objections on his part than through his inability to see any value in them. This is apparent in the list of his major omissions: the narrative from Samuel to Saul (1 Samuel 1–30); David's rivalry with the Saulides (2 Samuel 1–4), including his kindness to Mephibosheth (2 Samuel 9); the Bathsheba affair and strife with Amnon, Absalom, and Sheba (2 Samuel 11–20); Solomon's foreign marriages (1 Kgs 3:1; 11:1-13); the harlots incident and details of the administration of Solomon's kingdom (1 Kgs 3:16-28; 4:1–5:14); Solomon's palace (1 Kgs 7:1-12); adversaries against Solomon (1 Kgs 11:14-40); Jeroboam's religious reforms (1 Kgs 12:25-33) and all matters pertaining to the northern kings; the Elijah and Elisha narratives (1 Kings 17–2 Kings 13); most of the Jehu accession history (2 Kings 9); the downfall of Samaria, with DtrH's theological interpretation (2 Kgs 17:7-41); DtrH's condemnation of Manasseh (2 Kgs 21:10–16; 23:24-27; 24:3-5, 20); Gedaliah's governorship and the fate of Jehoiachin (2 Kgs 25:22-30). ChrH believes that Yahweh directly appointed David (1 Chr 10:14), making any notice of the latter's rivalries with Saul and the Saulides irrelevant. Attention to David's adultery and family strife would tarnish his image; so likewise any reference to Solomon's marriage and to political opposition against him. The stories of the northern kings are a sideshow and detract from the image of the ideal Davidic kingship. Most of the prophet narratives mentioned concern only the north. ChrH would agree with most of 2 Kings 17, but his concern is restricted to condemnation upon Judah. DtrH's censure of Manasseh fails to accord with ChrH's image of this king as one who repented and made reforms. By these omissions, therefore, ChrH shapes his message to a more unified, concentrated rehearsing of the biblical tradition that provides the ultimate message for the time in which he lives.

A discussion of ChrH's tradition is incomplete without some observations regarding the literary sources that are named in the various regnal resumés. Readers are advised that they may find more information about a certain king by referring to such a source. These are of three kinds: (1) a "History of the Kings of Israel" (sometimes "and Judah" or "Judah and Israel," but never "of Judah" alone); (2) Histories/Prophecy/Chronicles/Midrash (lit., "investigation")/Writing/Vision of a variety of prophets and seers; (3) a "Midrash of the Book of the Kings," 2 Chr 24:27. Scholars have argued whether these were authentic or fictitious. Some have dismissed the alleged prophetic sources, but have taken the reference to a midrash or midrashim as evidence for a book from which ChrH took most of his nonsynoptic narratives. But the persistence of a characteristic ChrH style throughout these sections undermines this theory. Whatever the term *midrash* means at this stage in the development of Judaism, the term as used in the passages mentioned is plainly on a par with the prophetic sources. These are, in fact, neither independent nor real. They always appear at the precise place—and only here—where ChrH takes his regnal resumés from Kings, and this tells us simply that this writer uses them as variations for his other alleged source, "the History of the Kings of Israel," which in turn is a substitute for Kings' "Chronicles of the Kings of Israel/Judah." We may speculate as to why ChrH adduces such questionable sources. Many of the prophetic personages mentioned are scriptural, several are not. All may in fact be historical, but did they in fact write books about the kings? Where are these books, and why has ChrH himself not incorporated some of their material in his own document? The answer is that there were no such books, though the prophets in question did exist. The reason why ChrR was interested in them is that he rightly saw DtrH as a prophetic book, one of the "former prophets." Since his own book is a recasting of DtrH, prophecy continues in his own narration.

These alleged prophetic sources are surrogates for "the History of the Kings of Israel," as can be seen in 2 Chr 32:32, where "the vision of Isaiah" is said to be "in the Book [= history] of the Kings of Judah and Israel." As has been stated, this in turn is tantamount to Kings' "Chronicles." Though these are cited for further reference (also in Kings), it all stands for "Scripture as ChrH knows it." This means basically Samuel-Kings, with perhaps other recensional material. Let us recall from our discussion in Chapter 2 that 1 Chr 9:1b puts all the genealogical materials that have been collected into the same alleged "Book of the Kings of Israel." This is not part of Scripture as we know it, but had to be part of the "Scripture" that ChrH had at his disposal. In inventing titles, he probably intended only to mark certain sections of his scriptural tradition as relevant to the subject in hand. (Thus Chronicles of Samuel, Nathan, and Gad, whose order shows us that these were sections of Samuel in the order known to us [1 Chr 29:29].) Certainly ChrH did not mean to support the sections he wrote himself with these citations.

Intention

In Chapters 1 and 2 above the basic intention has been identified as showing the postexilic Jewish community the "ideal Israel" that it ought to strive to become. Through the tribal lists of 1 Chronicles 2–8 a symbolic or typological concept is provided of what ideal Israel is in its ideal organization, and in ch. 9 "the first to dwell again in their possessions" following the return from the Babylonian exile —"Israel, the priests, the Levites, and the temple servants" (v. 2)—stand for all members of these groups who are destined to make up the "ideal Israel" of Chronicles. But ChrH does not proceed with a narration of postexilic Jewish history. Instead, he writes a new HISTORY covering the period from Saul to the exile, telling the following truths: (1) in spite of its disunity, "ideal Israel" is, and always will remain, one; (2) its sovereignly transcendent God was, is, and always will be the same; (3) God appointed the Davidic dynasty to the office of kingship, and it will continue to represent divine kingship in the midst of Israel; (4) the temple, with its clergy and its ritual, offers ideal Israel permanent, unbroken access to its God; (5) God speaks through the prophets of the past and through "prophetic" singing in the temple liturgy; (6) though punishment for apostasy remains a threat, it is now more clear than ever that God's desire for Israel is a repentance and a fidelity to which he will ever respond in continuous blessing and protection; (7) the restoration will be complete when the Israel that now is becomes fully and perfectly the "ideal Israel" that God has designed.

Several articles and monographs have recently been occupied with ChrH's "intention," and few treatments of 1–2 Chronicles in commentary form have failed to give it attention. We are in the advantageous position of being able to coordinate it with our foregoing analysis of "structure" and "genre." We find it convenient to clarify our own summary by itemizing in the paragraphs that follow what has already been stated.

Israel. We have stated many times our complete agreement with Williamson's argument (*Israel;* comm., 24-26) that the united kingdom of Saul, David, and Solomon constitutes Israel. We must not be misled by the fact that the history of the northern kings is ignored, or that occasionally the northerners are called "Israel" over against "Judah." We intend to call special attention to these instances in our analysis of the individual narrative passages. Occasionally the Davidic kings are referred to as "kings of Israel." "All Israel" rejects Rehoboam at Shechem, yet "Rehoboam reigned over the people of Israel who dwelt in the cities of Judah" (2 Chr 10:16-17), meaning that the Judahites are part of Israel and remain "Israel." Eventually northerners return, restoring the ideal unity of one Israel. The work of David in building up the nation, together with the work of Solomon in constructing the temple, gives "all Israel" a political and cultic center; the northern kings and northern cult centers do not count. The northerners still have the gift of prophecy (Elijah, 2 Chr 21:15; Oded, 2 Chr 28:9), and still have the opportunity to repent (13:4ff.). Translating this typology into postexilic realities, we perceive that ChrH welcomes northerners to his spiritual community, whatever political separations may still remain.

God. Occasionally ChrH slips back into the old terminology and names God "Yahweh," but his preference is for *'ĕlōhîm,* "God," even in passages where he borrows directly from Samuel-Kings, where "Yahweh" prevails. There can be no question but that this betokens a weakening of the exodus-Sinai traditions. No doubt ChrH is anxious to show that Israel's God is more than a national deity; he is the God of the nations, the God of heaven and earth. Nevertheless, ChrH has a peculiar and frequently repeated usage, *'ĕlōhê hā'ǎbôt,* "the God of the fathers," i.e., "the ancestral God," which is especially important to him because he is trying to assure the Jews of his time that their God is the same as the God of the patriarchs and the God of David and Solomon. ChrH's God spans all the chaotic history in between, just as he fills the heavens along with all the earth. And not only does he fill Israel's history, along with the cosmos; he stands in continual sovereignty and active superintendency over it. The truth of God's continual, purposeful presence in every historical event is expressed in many ways: in prophetic oracles, in Solomon's prayer (2 Chr 6:18-40), in the great psalm of praise of 1 Chr 16:8-36, in the narrative of Hezekiah's response to the taunt of Sennacherib, 2 Chr 32:14ff. It is also expressed in numerous statements of God's direct intervention, and in a variety of theological reviews appearing throughout the book. In some stereotyped formulas such as the ASSISTANCE FORMULA ("I am with you") and the REASSURANCE FORMULA ("Be not afraid") this theology is put to dramatic effect. One is especially impressed, however, by ChrH's own programmatic statements placed at strategic places in the story, which have been given the genre name DESCRIPTION OF YAHWEH:

> "Let me fall into the hand of Yahweh, for his mercy is very great" (1 Chr 21:13)
>
> "Yahweh the God of Israel has given peace to his people; and he dwells in Jerusalem forever" (1 Chr 23:25)
>
> "Yahweh searches all hearts, and understands every plan and thought. If you

seek him, he will be found by you; but if you forsake him, he will cast you off for ever" (1 Chr 28:9)

"Thine, O Yahweh, is the greatness, and the power, and the glory, and the victory, and the majesty; for all that is in the heavens and in the earth is thine; thine is the kingdom, O Yahweh, and thou art exalted as head above all. Both riches and honor come from thee, and thou rulest over all. In thy hand are power and might; and in thy hand it is to make great and to give strength to all" (1 Chr 29:11-12)

"I know, my God, that thou triest the heart, and hast pleasure in uprightness" (1 Chr 29:17)

"O Yahweh, there is none like thee to help, between the mighty and the weak" (2 Chr 14:11)

"The eyes of Yahweh run to and fro throughout the whole earth, to show this might in behalf of those whose heart is blameless toward him" (2 Chr 16:9)

"O Yahweh, God of our fathers, art thou not God in heaven? Dost thou not rule over all the kingdoms of the nations? In thy hand are power and might, so that none is able to withstand thee" (2 Chr 20:6)

"God has power to help or to cast down" (2 Chr 25:8)

"Yahweh our God is gracious and merciful, and will not turn away his face from you, if you return to him" (2 Chr 30:9)

Kingship. Very much is made of the founding, the ascendancy, and the decline of the dynasty established from the loins of David. Its continuity is axiomatic. This may not be an eternal kingship, but it surely is a perpetual kingship. Individual kings come and go, but the kingship survives. Some are apostate; others are righteous but fall into serious error. Repentance benefits the individual king, but its absence does not disrupt this perpetual kingship. Not even the destruction of nation and temple under Nebuchadrezzar has been able to do that; they needed to be rebuilt, but all the while it remained intact. This last observation gives us insight into what was really unique about the Davidic kingship. It was not simply the power to hand on from father to son the administrative authority of a political jurisdiction, including all the pomp and circumstance pertinent thereto. No, it was the ideal of authority, derived directly from Yahweh the heavenly king and raised up to symbolize the very structure of authority within the reality of Israel, coming to manifestation as a nation. A nation—particularly Yahweh's nation—must have a regal head. This is needed to give it a sense of oneness and self-identity. It is needed to help it function the way Yahweh designed it—to fulfill his mission in the world. The point to remember, though, is that all does not hang on one single king, not even David. David cannot do it all; he passes his task on to Solomon. But even with the two of them as a joint ideal of kingship, all the other kings contribute to the image. There is no real problem with the role of the kingship in the postexilic period. We know that no king reigned in Jerusalem at that time, yet he was honored in principle. More than ever, he was needed for symbolizing the unity of the nation and the sovereignty of God. Even if no Davidide ever did succeed in regaining the crown, this ideal helped Israel know who and what it was. No matter, then, that so many preexilic kings besmirched the image of Davidic kingship; the image remained pure and intact, now when no king of David's lineage sat upon the throne no less effectively than when the apostate monarchs were still around to defile it.

Cultus. Leaving the topic of "kingship," we are reminded to say that except in the covenant ritual (2 Chr 34:31), the Davidic kings had no special cultic function. Numerous references to kings making sacrifices (e.g., 1 Chr 21:28) must be understood to mean that they presented the sacrificial animals and priests carried out the actual ritual. ChrH has much to say about regulations for priests and Levites, but nothing whatever for the king. Nevertheless, the king is given an august place of importance as the founder, the patron, and the supervisor of temple and ritual. We think especially of David and Solomon, of Asa and Jehoshaphat, of Hezekiah and Josiah. In ChrH priests are given priority but little is said about them, suggesting that their cultic role must have been accepted and firmly fixed. It is different with the Levites and the lesser orders who apparently were endeavoring to achieve Levitical recognition. That ChrH gives so much space to the Levites betrays his anxiety that these struggles might be brought to a resolution. It is interesting to note that in his use of the AUTHORIZATION FORMULA, ChrH appeals to Moses for the priests (influence of P!), but to David for the Levites. (For expansive supporting argument see De Vries, "Moses and David as Cult-Founders.")

As we have noted, the temple dominates the entire book. David prepares for it and Solomon builds it. Early Israel's cult objects and cult traditions are drawn up into it: ark, tabernacle and tent of meeting, altar of the holocaust, Moriah. Solomon dedicates it, Ahaz defiles it, Joash, Hezekiah, and Josiah repair it and cleanse it, Nebuchadrezzar destroys it. ChrH allows others to tell how it was rebuilt, but the very way in which he specifies the temple duties of the Levites and other orders shows that it surely existed in his time. He was also concerned to imply that it could again be consecrated, repaired, defiled, or destroyed. The religious festivals, including the Passover, were now pilgrim feasts and were celebrated at the Jerusalem temple. Attendance at the festivals was motivated by sincere piety, and always resulted in profound joy (→ FESTIVAL SCHEMA). About the Passover: the obvious Hezekiah/Josiah versus David/Solomon typology is intended to put attendance at this festival on a plane with honor to the temple itself; by telling of two successive Passovers, ChrH shows postexilic Israel that this is the premier time—and the temple the premier place—for "ideal Israel" to realize its unity and worship its God.

Prophecy. Though 1–2 Chronicles has been relegated to the kĕtûbîm, the third section of the canon, it remains in many ways a prophetic book. This point has been strongly brought out by Petersen (*Late Israelite Prophecy*, 55-96). As we have seen, ChrH claims to draw from prophetic documents, and he repeatedly introduces prophetic spokesmen (→ SCHEMA OF REVELATIONAL APPEARANCES), but in truth these elements are largely fictional. Willi (*Auslegung*, 215-20) wants us to suppose that 1–2 Chronicles achieved canonical status because of this purported prophetical element. Not so: it eventually was canonized because it fulfilled the "intention" we have described: to show Israel who and what it is. Nevertheless, we can see that ChrH understands itself as resting firmly on the classical prophetic foundation. One important difference is that the messages it composes for its prophetic spokesmen betray a postexilic setting by echoing the prevailing pattern of promise common to the canonical prophets of this period, not the pattern of doom so common among the preexilic prophets. It is also apparent that in ChrH's time lay prophecy was dying out, for "prophesying" was now a service performed by a suborder of the clergy (1 Chr 25:1, 5). (See further De Vries, "Prophetic Address.")

Reward and retribution. The SCHEMA OF REWARD AND RETRIBUTION has been shown to be an important structural element in ChrH. In demonstrating how this works out for each individual king, ChrH follows Samuel-Kings but is not bound by it. At times he allows his imagination to help him make his point. Here is his rationale for Rehoboam: (1) he foolishly disrupted the nation; (2) he ruled with the aid of the Levites and of numerous sons, strengthening the Davidic dynasty; (3) his repentance brought divine favor. For Abijah: (1) he set the terms for the reunification of the nation; (2) his model rule (Solomonic) set the pattern for others to follow; (3) he was rewarded with many sons. For Asa: (1) trust in Yahweh brought him victory; (2) a foreign alliance provoked wickedness; (3) his unrepentance was punished by disease. For Jehoshaphat: (1) he organized the religious and the secular order for the "ideal Israel"; (2) a foreign alliance was reproved; (3) trust in Yahweh brought victory. For Jehoram and Ahaziah: marriage with the Omrides threatened the Davidic dynasty. For Joash: (1) this "brand plucked from the fire" gave hope that the endangered dynasty should continue; (2) his unparalleled wickedness, provoking his assassination, foreboded the nation's ultimate ruin. For Amaziah: (1) a shadow-figure of his father, his initial dealing with the regicides promised good; (2) his thoroughgoing wickedness made himself the victim of regicide. For Uzziah: (1) his model rule was spoiled by his gross impiety; (2) this led to his ignominious sickness and death, a forecast of Israel's ruin. For Jotham: he was a model of what might and should have been, but even his perfect piety could not save Israel from the folly of future kings. For Ahaz: (1) his unrelieved wickedness (idolatry!) marked the nation for ineluctable doom; (2) the exile he provoked was balanced by the return of the exiles and the reunification of the nation. For Hezekiah: (1) his vast and exemplary good extended the day of divine patience; (2) but since the nation was doomed, his peccadillo—even with his repentance—kept the nation on its fateful path; (3) nevertheless, he firmly set in place the model for the restoration of Israel's cultic life. For Manasseh: (1) his serious wickedness led to his own exile, foreboding that of the nation; (2) though his repentance was accepted, the nation continued unrepentant. For Amon: (1) his father's repentance was insufficient to save either son or nation; (2) his emulation of his father's sins showed his own unrepentance and that of the nation. For Josiah: (1) his many good deeds saved neither him nor the nation; (2) at this late hour, he worked to consolidate the proper cultus and to promulgate the law by which the nation should again live. For the sons of Josiah: (1) all hastened to doom; (2) yet the divine plan was to restore.

Although ChrH does not preach the doctrine of corporate doom, he clearly believes in the solidarity of king and nation. The many variations in which he presents the SCHEMA OF REWARD AND RETRIBUTION intend to demonstrate only that God is free to forgive and that man is free to repent. This concept gives ChrH the character of (→) parenesis, urging restoration Israel to repent and be faithful. It is not doomed by the sins of its fathers, but is free to become the ideal Israel that they failed to be. The past offers various examples of piety and impiety, but the past is only prologue. The new Israel must decide for itself whether the fateful pathway of doom has finally come to an end (Deut 30:15-16).

Eschatology. Much study has been given to the question of the existence of eschatology in ChrH, with positions taken on both sides. From what has been presented here, it is necessary to conclude that ChrH and his community cherished what may be called a "realized eschatology." We borrow this expression from christological discussions, which have appropriate analogies with what we observe here. In NT theology it means that the coming of Jesus brought the messianic hopes to fulfillment, while the era of the church is the perfection of that fulfillment. In the Jewish community of ChrH, the eschatology of restoration had been fulfilled in the partial return from exile and the partial reconstruction of "ideal Israel." ChrH's prospect for the future is to perfect that restoration and reconstruction. The big question is, God allows it, will Israel choose it? So far as we can see, there is no militant messianism, no apocalyptic, no sign of disaffected parties. Very likely the community is apathetic. It needs help to choose and to act. More than ever there must be faithfulness to God's commandments, emulation of the piety of the fathers, and a sense of authentic oneness, even in the face of imperfections and incompletion. This is ChrH's eschatology. It is not for some distant future, but for "today."

There are concrete things for "ideal Israel" to do besides pray and attend the festivals and be pious, of course. These are not directly enjoined on the people— as in DtrH—but secured through illustrations in Chronicles' HISTORY. We hint at only a few. One thing is possessing the land, not through military conquest but through settlement, cultivation, and organization. Another thing is continuous care for the temple and provision for the clergy, exemplified particularly in the stories about Hezekiah, Josiah, and especially Solomon. Finally there is the defensive holy war, a frequent theme in the HISTORY. Despite our ignorance of the period in question, we can readily suppose that the fear of foreign attack must have been constantly present. This could not be resisted by a strong army, for there was none. But Jerusalem's defenses could be built and strengthened—a familiar theme in the HISTORY—and above all the people could cultivate a greater sense of fidelity and trust. That, above all, is what Chronicles' HISTORY should have taught them. As the prophet long ago said (2 Chr 15:2): "Yahweh is with you, while you are with him. If you seek him, he will be found by you, but if you forsake him, he will forsake you." The future remains open, but the conditions remain unchanged. Israel may become more fully "Israel" if it remains faithful to the God whose faithfulness never changes and whose purpose never fails.

Chapter 5

The Individual Units

ACCOUNT OF ESTABLISHING YAHWEH'S NATION AND TEMPLE, 1 CHR 9:35–2 CHR 9:31

Structure

I. The consolidation of David's rule	1 Chr 9:35–21:27
II. The building of the temple	1 Chr 21:28–2 Chr 9:31

THE CONSOLIDATION OF DAVID'S RULE, 1 CHR 9:35–21:27

Structure

I. Report of Saul's Removal	9:35–10:14
II. Report of David's confirmation in the kingship	11:1-9
III. Report of David's army	11:10–12:41 (*RSV* 40)
IV. Account of the installation of the ark	13:1–16:43
V. Report of the dynastic promise	17:1-19
VI. Accounts of warfare	18:1–20:8
VII. Historical story: obtaining the temple site	21:1-27

The report of Saul's removal is, as we have seen (→ Chapter 4 above), a preface to the entire HISTORY. It is also a preface to the narrative of David's establishment in his rule. Although there are no formal transitions between the various units of this structure—they have been taken more or less intact from synoptic material in Samuel—there is a remarkable thematic unity. The ACCOUNT of the installation of the ark and the HISTORICAL STORY about obtaining the temple site occupy the positions of penultimate and ultimate climax, making it clear that David's political success is ancillary to his efforts toward the building of the temple.

116

REPORT OF SAUL'S REMOVAL, 9:35–10:14

Structure

I.	Saul's kinship: reprise	9:35-44
II.	The kingdom passes to David	10:1-14

ChrH sees fit to introduce the figure of Saul, who appears only to be dismissed in favor of David, with a reprise (virtual word-for-word repetition of previous material) of 8:29-38. The structure is (1) genealogy of the Gibeon militia, 9:35-38; (2) genealogy of Ner, vv. 39-43; (3) family of Azel, v. 44 (for detailed structural and genre analysis, see Chapter 3 above on this passage). This is not idle; it is not the work of a lazy man. Rather, it is designed as an effective transition from the genealogical section, chs. 1–9, to the narrative section to come. The reprise brings to convergence the Ner genealogy, producing Saul, Israel's first putative claimant to the kingship, and, in repetition, marking him as a man doomed for rejection. The account of Saul's death that follows, 10:1ff., is ChrH's very first borrowing from Samuel-Kings, but it is used only to make way for David. We might say, "The king is dead; long live the king!" Only, for ChrH, Saul is no true king.

THE KINGSHIP PASSES TO DAVID, 10:1-14

Structure

I.	The Saulides die on Gilboa	1-7
	A. Battle report: Israel's defeat	1-2
	1. The fleeing army slain	1
	2. Saul's sons slain	2
	B. Death report: Saul's death	3-5
	1. Wounded by archers	3
	2. Double suicide	4-5
	C. Summary: end of Saul's dynasty	6
	D. Philistines occupy abandoned cities	7
II.	Exploit report: Jabeshites honor Saul	8-12
	A. Philistines display trophies	8-10
	B. Heroism of the Jabeshites	11-12
	1. Rescue of the corpses	11-12a
	2. Burial and fasting	12b
III.	Theological appraisal (accusation)	13-14a
	A. Charge of infidelity	13-14aα
	1. Disobedience	13a
	2. Apostasy	13b-14aα
	a. Consulting a medium	13b
	b. Neglecting Yahweh	14aα
	B. Death penalty	14aβ
IV.	Conclusion: opportunity for David's succession	14b

The main division within the narrative itself is marked by the temporal phrase *wayĕhî mimmāḥărāt,* "And it happened on the morrow." The first section builds up tension, from the first report of general defeat and the slaying of Saul's sons (vv. 1-2) to Saul's wounding and suicide (vv. 3-5), to the climactic summary in v. 6 and an anticlimactic statement of the defeat's widespread consequences in v. 7. The second section of the narrative, rising to a new climax in the original Samuel version, but repeated here mainly to record Saul's utter debasement and the fact of his burial (vv. 8-12), finishes off the narrative and makes way for ChrH's appraisal of Saul (vv. 13-14a) and statement of the results of Saul's death in terms of Yahweh's intent to turn the kingdom over to David.

Verses 1-8 give us our first opportunity to observe ChrH's method in adapting Samuel-Kings, his major written source (see Ackroyd, "Exegete," 3-9). In these verses ChrH follows Samuel closely for the main part; the entire structure and most of the phrasing are taken verbatim from this source document. Although allowance must be made for the possibility that, in places, the Chronicles text follows a superior Hebrew *Vorlage* than the one Samuel was following (cf. Lemke, "Synoptic Studies," on vv. 9, 10, 12, 14), many of the minor changes are due simply to ChrH's manner of rendering his source according to his own taste and to express his own ideology. Willi *(Auslegung),* who has taken pains to record ChrH's various "exegetical" methods, finds normalizing in v. 2, conjecture in v. 7, interpretation in vv. 8-10, omission and archaizing in vv. 11-12 (cf. pp. 49, 101, 109, 128, 138-39, 143, 149). ChrH makes of v. 6 an even greater climax than in 1 Sam 31:6 by adding "and all his house," but his ultimate climax comes in the theological appraisal and conclusion.

Genre

ChrH makes wide use of the genre REPORT, a brief, self-contained prose narrative (see B. Long, *1 Kings; with an Introduction to Historical Literature* [FOTL IX; Grand Rapids: Eerdmans, 1984] 5-6). Not always is it so brief as a mere (→) notice, however. Often it is long, composite, and carrying diverse contents. We have seen only one report thus far—the battle report of 1 Chr 5:18-22—and now our second example likewise belongs to the subgenre BATTLE REPORT. Our battle report, in turn, encompasses the subgenre DEATH REPORT, in which all interest is focused on a violent death, following the schema: (1) causes, (2) death, (3) effects. Saul's death as ChrH tells it departs from the rule that heroic deaths or battle deaths do not belong to this genre because such notices are structural elements in the BATTLE REPORT (→ DEATH REPORT). The reason is that here Saul is no hero, and the battle with the Philistines is only instrumental to his death and departure. Vv. 8-12 contain an EXPLOIT REPORT, featuring the heroism of the Jabeshites. In this we see how ChrH alters not only the phrasing but the genre and intent, even while keeping the structure essentially the same (see "Structure" above). As I have explained elsewhere *(Yesterday, Today and Tomorrow* [Grand Rapids: Eerdmans, and London: SPCK, 1975] 106-7), 1 Samuel 31 is a HEROIC SAGA, with the Jabeshites as tradents, having been expanded at vv. 1, 7 as part of the Davidic accession history, with "on the morrow" as a redactional gloss in v. 8 and "and all his men" in v. 6 as an interpretative addition. As often with narratives of this genre, *bayyôm hahû',* "on that day," makes v. 6 an epitomizing conclusion (→ EPITOME). ChrH regularly omits the phrase wherever it appears in his source, having no conception, apparently, of its original force, and he omits it here.

The genre ACCUSATION is in vv. 13-14. This provides the legal basis by which an offender such as Saul is condemned, in this case consisting of a charge (*ma'al*, "infidelity," "betrayal") followed by specifications of apostasy: he did not keep the word, i.e., instruction or command, that Yahweh had given him; he visited a medium (*'ôb*) in search of an oracle; he did not try to get an oracle from Yahweh.

Setting and Intention

ChrH needs a rationale for dismissing Saul and his entire lineage in the history he is about to recount, thereby assuring for David the position of eponymous king of Israel. We immediately see that this writer expresses his view just as effectively in the passages he omits as in those he modifies or quotes more or less verbatim. He will hear nothing of Saul's rise, of his long struggle to eliminate David, or of David's own struggle against Ishbosheth. Not too much must be made of this human, worldly contest; for, rather, it is a matter of Yahweh judging Saul and thereby clearing the way for David.

This is the one and only place where we read that Yahweh directly intervenes to substitute one king for another: "Therefore Yahweh slew him and turned the kingdom over to David the son of Jesse" (v. 14b). We can discern that, quite apart from Saul's relatively inoffensive life as recorded in Samuel, he is needed here to serve as the prototype of all the evil and wayward kings that shall arise in the history of the kingdom. It is important to interpret his death as retribution, and thus to start afresh with David as the prototype of all good rulers.

In Chapter 4 above we mentioned ChrH's basic schema, the SCHEMA OF REWARD AND RETRIBUTION. To see how Saul stands at the head of this schema, we take this opportunity to present a chart showing how every king except David and Solomon did righteousness or wickedness, bringing reward or retribution on themselves and/or their people. The chart will also show the presence of prophecy as a guide, and the setting of warfare (the latter is important because it serves as an opportunity for good kings to do good or as part of the divine punishment against evil).

		Good				Evil		
War	Prophecy	Repentance	Reward		Prophecy	Wickedness	Retribution On King	On people
			SAUL					
•					•		•	
			REHOBOAM					
•	•		•		•	•	•	•
			ABIJAH					
•			•					
			ASA					
•	•		•		•	•	•	
			JEHOSHAPHAT					
•	•		•			•		

•				JEHORAM		•	•		
				AHAZIAH		•	•		
•				JOASH		•	•		
	•	•	•	AMAZIAH		•	•		
•		•	•	UZZIAH			•		
•		•	•	JOTHAM					
•				AHAZ	•	•	•		
•		•	•	HEZEKIAH		•	•		•
		•	•	MANASSEH		•	•		
				AMON		•	•		
•		•		JOSIAH	•	•	•		
				JEHOAHAZ		•			
				JEHOIAKIM		•	•		
				JEHOIACHIN		•	•		
				ZEDEKIAH		•	•		•

Good Kings were destined to do good, and sometimes evil. Evil kings were destined to do evil, and sometimes good. There would be few who were all bad and few who were all good. None would be quite like David and his son Solomon, who would set a model for them all. We know from the prominent place accorded the tribe of Benjamin, and the family of Ner in the genealogies, that Benjamin had been a valued element in the kingdom of Judah throughout its history, and appreciation for it must have continued in postexilic Yehud. It is perhaps paradoxical that none of the northern kings was from Benjamin, and that Benjamin was not willing to reassert Saul's claims when the disruption under Rehoboam came. Apparently the Benjaminites' self-esteem was even at that time able to accept ChrH's later dictum, to the effect that Yahweh had rejected their kinsman Saul in favor of David. After all, Saul was the first Israelite king before Josiah to be killed in foreign combat. Josiah was a good king, of course, and scarcely deserved such a fate; but who says Saul was really bad? He made some miscues, as did Josiah—particularly that of ignoring revelation (1 Chr 10:13; cf. 2 Chr 35:21-22). Josiah's sin was bad enough to nullify the good of his administration, preparing the kingdom for a quick and sudden doom under Nebuchadrezzar. How much more the sin of Saul!—serious enough to justify displacing Benjamin forever as the bearer of Israel's monarchical dignity. In the ideal Israel, even Benjamin must accept that Yahweh had done justly in pushing their kinsman aside and giving his place to one more worthy than himself.

All the misbehavior of the wicked kings and all the misdeeds of the good kings are to be rehearsed in ChrH's history for the purpose of warning the ideal Israel how easy it is to go astray and fall under God's wrath. How much more so the waywardness of Saul! The fatal charge against him is *ma'al,* "infidelity," which is mentioned a number of times with particular reference to religious infidelity (2 Chr 26:16, 18; 28:19, 22; 29:5-6, 19; 30:7; 33:19; 36:14). As betrayal of trust and violation of responsibility, it is the most heinous sin that Israel's leaders can commit, and they ever need to be warned against it. Then, as we have seen, Saul is accused of a number of specific offenses, the first of them being failure to "keep the command of Yahweh." Commentators have speculated as to just which command had been violated, whether that of 1 Samuel 13, or 15, or 22. But, as Williamson points out (comm., 95), ChrH may mean Saul's entire life and reign. Inasmuch as an honorable and abundant life is often held by ChrH to be the specific reward of doing Yahweh's commandments (cf. 2 Chr 12:1, 4; 13:11, 13ff.; 14:4-5; 33:8; 34:2; 36:16), the gruesome way in which he met his death simply proves that he had not been obedient to God. Similarly, Israel had "died" at the hand of Nebuchadrezzar; but now, revived again, it must be reminded that the commandments are still there to be obeyed, and that divine wrath still threatens any who would disobey.

Another specification against Saul is that he consulted the medium; because of the syntax, Ackroyd ("Exegete," 8) calls this a gloss, but we ask how ChrH could have overlooked the offense of 1 Samuel 28. One should weigh the reference to Manasseh's sin in 2 Chr 33:6, more heinous than all the sins of which the Judahite kings are normally accused because it specifically included the ritual consultation of the dead. Students of religious history know that occult rites continued in prominence in the imperial age, just at the time when biblical religion was rising to more extreme forms of transcendentalism. To the restored Israel, for whom prophecy was gradually dying out, the temptation must have been strong for believing that revelation through the dead and through occult spirits was better than no revelation at all; but Saul's fate is here offered as a stern warning against it.

A final specification against Saul is also intended for the restored Israel: *lō'-dāraš běyahweh.* This phrase means "seek an oracle from Yahweh," as regularly in the older writings, and stands in contrast to "He consulted a medium, inquiring for an oracle" (v. 13b). ChrH comes to use it with some frequency in a much broader meaning, "to devote oneself to Yahweh." Echoing the first meaning in the reference to the woman of Endor (ChrH is not concerned about Dtr's explanation, 1 Sam 28:6, that Saul was forced to go to the medium because Yahweh *would* not give him revelation), ChrH imperceptibly merges it into the later meaning, using this as still another warning and admonition for the Israel of his own generation. Their chief duty is *děrôš yahweh,* "inquiring for Yahweh," thus to know and perform his will. This requires a deep interiority in their piety, which alone can guarantee the fidelity, trust, and obedience that truly pleases God and assures his blessing on them as his people.

We may agree with Williamson (comm., 94 and passim) that the majority of interpreters have gone astray in treating the episode of Saul's death as simply a

121

prelude to David's reign, or as the typological foil to David's brilliant success (cf. von Rad, *Geschichtsbild*, 79; H. J. Boecker, *Die Beurteilung der Anfänge des Königtums* [Neukirchen-Vluyn: Neukirchener, 1969] 61-88). He believes that Mosis (*Untersuchungen*, 17-43) has exhibited a unique brilliance of insight in interpreting Israel's forsaking their cities and fleeing (v. 7) as thematic for the whole book. This first fleeing under Saul is a preview of many exiles, but especially of the last terrible exile under Nebuchadrezzar. Thus Saul, as "the king who never should have been," is not the only symbol offered in this pericope. The exile of a people who followed after a godless king is a symbol just as powerful. Although this verse is taken directly from Samuel, ChrH endows it with a special message for his generation. Here is the root cause of exile. Those who forsake the way of Saul and follow in the way of David shall never experience it again.

Bibliography

P. R. Ackroyd, "The Chronicler as Exegete," *JSOT* 2 (1977) 2-32; J. Botterweck, "Zur Eigenart der chronistischen Davidgeschichte," *TQ* 136 (1956) 12-31; K. Koch, "Das Verhältnis von Exegese und Verkündigung anhand eines Chroniktextes," *TLZ* 90 (1965) 659-70; W. E. Lemke, "The Synoptic Problem in the Chronicler's History," *HTR* 58 (1965) 349-63; R. Mosis, *Untersuchungen zur Theologie des chronistischen Geschichtswerkes* (Freiburger Theologische Studien 92; Freiburg: Herder, 1973); T. Willi, *Die Chronik als Auslegung* (FRLANT 106; Göttingen: Vandenhoeck & Ruprecht, 1972).

REPORT OF DAVID'S CONFIRMATION IN THE KINGSHIP, 11:1-9

Structure

I. Anecdote of David's anointing	1-3
A. "All Israel" announces its fealty	1-2
1. Assembly at Hebron	1a
2. Affinity saying	1b
3. David's previous designation	2
a. Generalship under Saul	2a
b. Yahweh's promise of future kingship	2b
B. Israel's elders confirm his kingship	3
1. Assembly at Hebron	3aα
2. Ceremony of investiture	3aβ-b
a. David offers a covenant	3aβ
b. Elders anoint him king (fulfillment formula)	3b
II. Report of Jerusalem's capture	4-9
A. David and "all Israel" march to Jerusalem	4
B. Battle report: the city's capture	5-6
1. David confutes the Jebusites' boast	5
a. Boast of invulnerability	5a
b. Epitome of David's success	5b
2. Joab accepts David's challenge	6

As Williamson has shown (comm., 105) 11:1-3, 10-40; 12:1-41 are arranged in a striking chiasmus constructed to feature Hebron, after Saul's death the administrative center of "all Israel," as the place to which troops come from various rallying points in order to march with David to take possession of Jerusalem (→ Chapter 4 above). The chiasmus goes:

Hebron
    Ziklag
        Hammĕṣad
    Ziklag
Hebron

This weighs against those critics (Rudolph, HAT; Noth, "Chronistische Werk," 116; Fohrer, *Intro.*, 244) who hold 12:1-24 to be secondary, leaving the Hebron pericope, 12:25ff., as original. The problem of why there are two separate assemblies at Hebron is left unresolved by this excision, for the second Hebron assembly has no explanation in a temporal sequence of events. Williamson must be credited with an original and illuminating insight, for his identification of the chiasmus shows how, in ChrH's methodology, form and ideology take first place over a concern for temporal ordering. Another chiasmus, assuming the deletion, with the sequence Hebron-Jerusalem-Hebron, might make sense except for the fact that each Hebron episode speaks of David being made king (11:3; 12:39). The installation of David in Jerusalem just after the first Hebron assembly (11:3ff.) can have only one explanation: ChrH wishes to underscore that the "all Israel" that swore their fealty to David at Hebron (11:1ff.) demonstrated their loyalty to him by marching up with him to capture Jerusalem ("David and all Israel," v. 4). The function of Hebron in the chiasmus is plainly to be the assembly point for the whole nation. Otherwise it has no interest for our historian, for the true center of the nation can only be Jerusalem, henceforth to be the residence of all the Davidic dynasty and, eventually, of "all Israel" itself.

The story of Jerusalem follows the Samuel account with some freedom (cf. Botterweck, "Eigenart," 409-11; Watson, "Archaic Elements," 2.3), yet ChrH's theological evaluation in v. 9 can find no better words than those of 2 Sam 5:10, quoting the usually avoided *yahweh ṣĕbā'ôt* (cf. Japhet, *Ideology*, 27-29). A problem arises with respect to the abrupt statement *wĕyô'āb yĕḥayyeh 'et- šĕ'ār hā'îr* (v. 8), not found in the Samuel parallel and seemingly making little sense here. If it is not ChrH's own comment, it is a gloss, but of uncertain meaning. The usual *(RSV)* rendering, "And Joab repaired the rest of the city," plainly contradicts the foregoing statement that David "repaired" *hā'îr missābîb min-hammillō'*, "the city all around beginning with the Millo." The verb for Joab's action is not *bnh*, as with David, but *ḥyh* (piel). Can stones and mortar be said to "be made alive"? Or is this metaphor? If so, why is David not included in this action, for was not his "building" as much a "reviving" as what Joab did? The glossator must be thinking of the stern Joab as a threat to the life of the inhabitants of Jerusalem (called Jebus in another gloss at v. 4; cf. 2 Sam 5:6), who customarily carried out David's bloody deeds but is here said to have "left them alive."

Anticipating much of the narration that is to follow in coming chapters, ChrH repeats Samuel's epitomizing summary in v. 9b, to the effect that "David became greater and greater."

Genre

Genres already familiar to us are the REPORT (vv. 4-9) and the BATTLE REPORT (vv. 5-6). There is the NAMING ETIOLOGY in v. 7, where Jerusalem's by-name, "the city of David," is explained from the fact that the Jebusites had said that he could not enter, yet he captured the Zion stronghold. V. 9b has the ASSISTANCE FORMULA ("I will be with you"), in narrative form. Otherwise forms rarely seen heretofore, or not at all, appear. Vv. 1-3 constitute an ANECDOTE, a narrative report of a single event in the life of an individual, in this case, David. The words of fealty in v. 1, "Behold, we are your bone and flesh," is a set formula, the AFFINITY SAYING. In v. 2 "all Israel" repeat a PROMISE, a genre employed regularly in behalf of the Davidic house, as here. The end of v. 3 has the FULFILLMENT FORMULA (created here by ChrH and not in Samuel), which makes explicit reference at the end of a narrative sequence to a previous prophetic announcement, claiming that the event in question is the intended fulfillment of what had been predicted; Willi (*Auslegung*, 172) can think of this only as a "reflexion." What the Jebusites say in v. 5a is a BOAST, an utterance which appraises some person or thing as superior to another. In this case, the Jebusites are bragging, puffing up themselves while belittling David. At the same time, the words *lō' tābō' hēnnâ* (v. 5a) fit perfectly the pattern of the PROHIBITION, a direct forbiddance of an action or thing, usually based on authority, but in this case on military force.

"Nevertheless David took the stronghold of Zion" (v. 5b) and "So David became greater and greater" (v. 9a) belong to the genre element EPITOME. This is a succinct distillation and summation through authoritative interpretation, stating the deepest meaning and lasting significance of the event in question. In this passage the EPITOME of capturing Jerusalem is ancillary and instrumental to the EPITOME of David's increasing in greatness. Both items are vital to ChrH: the Davidic kingship hangs upon the occupation of Jerusalem, while Jerusalem's greatness depends on the king who resides within it.

Setting

ChrH passes over 2 Samuel 1–4, but the omission tells us David's seven-year stay in Hebron had no significance for his ideal kingship. This brings the narration to a slightly altered duplicate of David's accession and subsequent installation in

Jerusalem, as told in 2 Sam 5:1-10. Opinions are fairly evenly divided as to whether the Samuel text or the Chronicles text deserves preference. In vv. 1-3, Lemke ("Synoptic Studies," 18) is quite prepared to attribute all the differences to what he calls ChrH's "pan-Israelite tendency," but he is prepared to give Samuel the priority in vv. 4-8 (idem, 20-23; cf. Allen, *Relationship*, I:129-30), and some commentators (H. W. Hertzberg, *I & II Samuel* [tr. J. Bowden; OTL; Philadelphia: Westminster, 1964] 266-70; Y. Yadin, *The Art of Warfare in Biblical Lands* [New York: McGraw-Hill, 1963] 267-70; Williamson, comm.) think that ChrH had an independent tradition for v. 6 that enabled him to illumine his obscure and somewhat damaged Samuel *Vorlage*. As has been noted, ChrH has added the FULFILLMENT FORMULA at v. 3b and a glossator—possibly ChrH himself—is responsible for the Joab notice in v. 8b.

The possession of Jerusalem and the installation of the Davidic dynasty were as much a part of ChrH's program for restoration Israel as they had been during the period of the monarchy. Throughout the lengthy account of the preexilic monarchy, for which this is the necessary introduction, these will remain the two foci around which the entire account will revolve. The city's restoration is seen as a token of God's intent to raise up the house of David, even in this late time of imperial domination, if not as independent rulers, then as the symbolic leaders of God's people.

Intention

David's years at Hebron may be counted in genealogies (3:4) and regnal resumés (29:27), but they are ignored here because in postexilic times Hebron lay outside the border of Yehud; and besides, they symbolized the disunity of Israel rather than the unity of Israel. Hebron is on the fringe, serving only as the rallying point for "all Israel" and a mustering place from which this entire united nation might march up to conquer Jerusalem. How different from Samuel's account of this affair! There it was the march of David's private army, and it was he—not the nation—that turned it into his capital. ChrH tells it in such a way as to suggest that David was being passively obedient to Yahweh's appointment, 10:14b, and submissive to the nation's initiative. The old promise is given renewed force: "You shall be shepherd of my people Israel, and you shall be prince over my people Israel" (11:2). And not only is there this promise; there was also prophecy—symbolized though not articulated in the actions of Samuel reported in 1 Sam 16:1-13.

Verse 8 contains a very old and no doubt historical statement about David "building" (probably restoring) the "city" (probably the walls) in all directions, with the Millo as the center point. This reference is surely treasured by ChrH and becomes a dominant *topos* (Welten, *Geschichte*, 42-52) throughout his history of the kings; cf. 2 Chr 11:5-12; 14:5-6; 17:12-13; 26:9-10; 27:3-4; 32:5-6; 33:14. In addition to this notice, only that of 2 Chr 11:5-10 (with ChrH expansion in vv. 11-12) can be identified as historical. The others, based on fiction and conjecture, show what the successive kings *should* have done in strengthening the walls, even if historical records to that effect are wanting. Restoration Judaism was quite understandably obsessed with the necessity of rebuilding the walls of Jerusalem (cf. Neh 2:11–6:15). In the ideology of ChrH, Jerusalem could not serve as the capital of the nation, as the residence of the Davidic family, or as the site of the temple, without walls constantly repaired and strengthened. This was not only for military defense; it was also for architectural adornment (note the "New Jerusalem" of Rev 21:17-18). ChrH's images of wall building do reflect to some extent the historical expansion of the city in preexilic times (so also "city of David," "Millo," "Ophel"; cf. Welten, 197-98), but they express more of ideology than of historical actuality.

"So David became continually greater" may be a better translation of *wayyēlek dāwîd hālôk wĕgādôl* (v. 9a), because to ChrH it expresses the notion that this was a process extending throughout his lifetime and extending through the whole line of kings calling themselves "David" and reaching down even into the present. "David" was destined to govern "all Israel" unto perpetuity (*'ad 'ôlām*). By themselves, the people, the land, and the temple were incomplete, without visible token that the God of Israel was in their midst. "David" would be forever needed because "Yahweh Sebaoth was *with* him" (v. 8b).

Bibliography

A. Alt, "Jerusalems Aufstieg," *KS* III (Munich: Beck, 1959) 243-57; C. E. Hauer, "Jerusalem, the Stronghold and Rephaim," *CBQ* 32 (1970) 571-78; K. M. Kenyon, *Digging up Jerusalem* (New York: Praeger, 1974); H. J. Stoebe, "Die Einnahme Jerusalems durch David und der Ṣinnôr," *ZDPV* 73 (1957) 73-99; P. Welten, *Geschichte und Geschichtsdarstellung in den Chronikbüchern* (Neukirchen: Neukirchener, 1973).

REPORT OF DAVID'S ARMY, 11:10–12:41 (*RSV* 40)

Structure

Because of the complexity of this outline, it is best to offer it in two major segments.

I. David's chief warriors	11:10-47
A. Introduction	10
1. Opening caption	10aα
2. Their purpose to make David king	10aβ
a. Loyal to his kingship	10aβ1
b. "All Israel" collaborates	10aβ2
3. Fulfillment formula	10b
B. Roster of David's warriors	11-47
1. Among the three	11-14
a. Introduction	11a
b. Jashobeam	11b
1) Provenance and rank	11bα
2) Exploit report	11bβ
c. Eleazar	12-14
1) Provenance and rank	12
2) Anecdote of victory over the Philistines	13-14
a) Battle situation	13aα
b) Solitary defense of battlefield	13aβ-14a
c) Epitome: theological interpretation	14b

This passage is taken directly from 2 Samuel 23, usually with its exact wording and certainly in its order of sequence. In the context of such precision, the merging of Samuel's Eleazar and Shammah exploits is surprising, but the text may be corrupt at this point (vv. 13-14). Since Samuel's list already begins with a formal rubric, *wĕ'ēlleh šĕmôt,* "Now these are the names" (2 Sam 23:8), altered by ChrH as *wĕ'ēlleh mispar,* "Now these constitute the roster . . ." (1 Chr 11:11), v. 10 presents itself as ChrH's special prologue, beginning with the rubric *wĕ'ēlleh rā'šê haggibbôrîm 'ăšer lĕdāwîd,* "Now these are the chiefs of the warriors who adhered to David," but then names no names directly, offering instead the statement that they supported (*ḥzq,* hith.) the effort to make David king, along with the same "all

Israel" of vv. 1 and 4. This is just a transition, though, for surely all the chiefs and soldiers would have been included in "all Israel," and that is why v. 10 gives us the heading for a list but no list. The list is, of course, the roster of vv. 11-47. This is needed, along with 12:1-23, to prepare for ChrH's illogical, highly ideological inclusio putting all the troops back in Hebron for the great festival of enthronement (12:24-41).

11:11-25 is a ROSTER, but only of chiefs. Only four are named: Jashobeam, Eleazar, Abishai, and Benaiah (2 Sam 23:9b-11 adds Shammah). When we consider that a rather lengthy anecdote intrudes at vv. 15-19, we find that we have another of ChrH's impressive inclusios, with two heroes at the beginning and two heroes at the end. The styling for the four is much the same. We are given name, patronym, gentilic, rank, and then, in narrative styling, the exploit or exploits that entitled them to be included among "the three" (Jashobeam, Eleazar) or "the thirty" (Abishai, Benaiah). Abishai is given no patronym (elsewhere he is named as son of Zeruiah, his mother), but here his famous brother, Joab, is mentioned (cf. 2:16; strangely, Joab is not listed among these heroes). For Abishai (cf. Watson, "Archaic Elements," 7.1) and for Benaiah (cf. Willi, *Auslegung*, 117), a rather involved apologia is given (vv. 20b-21, 24-25a) to the effect that each achieved great renown among the thirty but failed to gain inclusion among the three. The report on Benaiah is especially remarkable. Not only is he credited with three separate exploits (vv. 22b-24), but he alone is given honorific appellations: *'îš ḥayil*, "mighty warrior," *rab pĕ'ālîm*, "master of exploits." Each individual exploit is introduced by the independent personal pronoun, *hû'*, and a participle or perfect verb. For Eleazar (vv. 13-14) and for Benaiah (v. 23), concrete details modify mere reports as anecdotes. The only theological note appears for Eleazar in v. 14b, conflated from Samuel's Eleazar and Shammah reports: *wayyôša' yahweh tĕšû'â gĕdôlâ*, "and Yahweh performed a great victory" (cf. Willi, 139; also De Vries, *Yesterday, Today and Tomorrow*, 94-96).

The anecdote of the water from Bethlehem is a virtual copy of its Samuel equivalent (cf. Willi, 140, on its styling). It is in narrative style throughout and includes discourse in David's speech, vv. 18b-19a. This, with the anonymity of the three warriors who perform the exploit, shows us that the anecdote is really about David, in spite of the concluding rubric *'ēlleh 'āśû šĕlōšet haggibbôrîm*, "These things [plur.!] did the three warriors" (v. 19b). The general situation is that the three warriors seek David at a rocky promontory near the cave of Adullam, while the Philistines occupy the valley of Rephaim, the main approach to the central highlands. This is made more specific by two circumstantial clauses beginning with *'āz*, "at that time" or "under those circumstances," telling us that David was in his *mĕṣûdâ*—evidently holed up with sparse rations—while an enemy garrison occupied Bethlehem (v. 16). This explains David's wish, interpreted by the three as a challenge, perhaps the more so since David may have in fact been testing them as newcomers. Their exploit of obtaining Bethlehem water by force of arms proves them worthy, all the more so because the well is *by* the gate if not *within* it (*baššaʿar*). David's refusal is not willful, as it might seem to the superficial reader, but a solemn act of solidarity with his valiant supporters. He pours the water out as a libation to Yahweh, swearing an oath of refusal, explaining that this water is tantamount to heroes' blood, fit as a worthy sacrifice, but not for human lips. Willi's claim (p. 172) that David's words are mere reflexion does less than justice to a cun-

ning structure, in which *lō' 'ābâ* (v. 18) creates a striking chiasmus with *lō' 'ābâ* at
the end (v. 19).

Verses 26ff., continuing the ROSTER, have the opening rubric *wĕgibbôrê
haḥăyālîm*, "Now the mighty warriors were. . . ." What follows is drawn from
2 Sam 23:24-38, except for vv. 42-47, for which ChrH has an independent source.
Avoiding absolute regularity, this list gives the proper name, the patronym or name
of a brother, a gentilic, and/or a place of origin. There is no tally, as in 2 Sam 23:39.

As "chiefs of David's mighty men, who gave him strong support in his kingdom," the warriors mentioned in 11:10-47 are to be kept in strong contrast to the persons mentioned in 12:1-23. The former are understood to be included among the "all Israel" that made him king in Hebron and helped him capture Jerusalem. The latter are those who joined (had joined) him at Ziklag and the wilderness fortress (*mĕṣād*). The crucial word throughout this section is '*zr,* "help." The accession of three different tribal groups is stated, with a special anecdote intruding in vv. 17-19, leading to the generalizing conclusion of v. 23, "Indeed, almost daily they would come to David to help him, eventually constituting an army of enormous size" (*maḥănēh 'ĕlōhîm,* lit., "an army of God"; cf. Watson, "Archaic Elements," 10.3, p. 192 n. 1; B. Jacob, "Miscellen zu Exegese, Grammatik und Lexicon," *ZAW* 18 [1898] 290-91). The reports of the three contingents have a generally similar structure, with a statement of David's situation (vv. 1a, 9a, 20-21a), then a description of their qualities, abilities, and/or affinities (vv. 1b-2, 9), and either a roster (vv. 3-8, 10-15) or a name list with designation of rank and statement of appointment to service (vv. 21-22); cf. P. Joüon, "Notes de lexicographie hébraïque," *Bib* 18 (1937) 205. Along with the customary appellations are statements of rank in vv. 3, 10-14, a special notice for Ishmaiah as leader over the "thirty," fanciful titles for the Gadites (v. 9b), and a narrative statement of a famous exploit by the

Gadites in v. 16, introduced by the phrase *'ēlleh hēm*, "These were those very ones"; cf. Watson, "Archaic Elements," 3.8.

Scholars who have looked for secondary elements have attributed all or most of this material to a writer later than ChrH (Rudolph, HAT; Noth, "Chronistische Werk," 116; Fohrer, *Intro.*, 244). Rothstein and Hänel (KAT, 242-43) rearrange these verses as follows: (a) 17-19; (b) 9-16; (c) 1-8; (d) 20-22. We on our part are quite certain that ChrH's language and style are evident here, and that Williamson is right in insisting that the chiasmus Ziklag-*mĕṣād*-Ziklag gives it an overall unity in spite of the diverse source materials that are in evidence (" 'We are Yours, O David,' " 169ff.). The fact that in vv. 20-22 David is only on the way to Ziklag would make no difference to ChrH's scheme.

Somewhat parallel in structural position to the anecdote of 11:15-19, and expressing the same theme of David's testing for genuine affinity, is the anec-dote of 12:17-19. Elsewhere in this chapter the question of Saul's kinsmen show-ing their support for David comes to the fore (cf. vv. 2b, 30), but here it is ab-solutely crucial. A certain "thirty" (cf. v. 19; not that of ch. 11), consisting of deserters from Benjamin and Judah and led by a certain Amasai, approach David's stronghold (cf. Watson, 10.3). He will not allow them in until he tests their loyalty, and meets them outside. The phrase *wayya'an wayyō'mer*, "And he replied, saying . . . ," implies a foregoing discussion, and we are to take David's admonition of v. 18 as his final position. Cast in the *'im* . . . *wĕ'im* style, it of-fers *lēbāb lĕyāḥad*, "the spirit of unity," for peace and help, at the same time ap-pealing to the ancestral God (*'ĕlōhê 'ăbôtênû*) to witness ("see") any hidden dis-loyalty and smite them for it (cf. Watson, 4.3). In poetic lines reflecting ancient usage (cf. Watson, 5.5; Ackroyd, comm.; Williamson, "We are Yours," 172) and comprising the genre AFFINITY SAYING (cf. 2 Chr 10:16), Amasai, "clothed" *(lbš)* by the spirit, declares an unbreakable loyalty, confirmed by the blessing of God on David.

Verses 24-41's muster of the troops in Hebron seems, on the face of it, to con-tradict the statement in v. 39 that *kol-'ēlleh*, "all these," i.e., the foregoing contin-gents, marched *(bō')* to Hebron to make David king (Noth, "Chronistische Werk," 115, identifies the muster as secondary). This is surely fictional, being based on Numbers 1 and 26, but in the logic of ChrH's overall inclusio, which repeats the event of David's coronation, it has to be imagined as occurring during David's seven-year residence in Hebron prior to his investiture by all Israel. This is, of course, the militia, drawn from all the tribes, who would have been dispersed after having been enrolled in the muster. Be this as it may, we are here given an ideal-ized review of all the tribal contingents. In form, this is the report of a muster but no actual (→) muster roll. Twelve tribal units are given, but none of the clan names or actual appellations that are proper to that genre. Instead, we find descriptive comments about features of special interest to ChrH, with tallies that have little claim to be historical. A blunder is made in v. 32, where half-Manasseh, included at v. 38, stands alongside Ephraim. Quite otherwise than in the genealogical sec-tion, Issachar and Dan are included, thus bringing the tribal total to twelve. As many agree, vv. 27-28 are a late priestly expansion.

The structure of vv. 39-41 contemplates two separate actions: (1) the coronation march, and (2) the joyful feast. In attendance are *kol-'ēlleh*, meaning all the tribes and their total number. They come to Hebron *bĕlēbāb šālēm*, "with

131

unanimous intent," to crown David—which is tantamount to saying that they actually crowned him (hedging in view of 11:3). A clause with *wĕgam,* "and indeed," states that all the rest of Israel, evidently those outside the military muster, were of *lēb 'eḥād,* "a single mind," in support of this action. In v. 40 the adverb *šām,* "there," stresses that the feasting took place where the coronation occurred. A time indicator, "three days," is given. The mustered troops were continually eating and drinking, and there was enough because the *'aḥîm,* "fellow clansmen," prepared for them. In v. 41 another *wĕgam* introduces the remarkable fact that *haqqĕrôbîm,* "adherents," from three distant tribes brought all manner of provision. All is summed up in the interpretative epitome, *kî śimḥâ bĕyiśrā'ēl,* "Indeed, joy was in Israel!"

Genre

Most of the formal elements are already familiar to us. The main genre is REPORT (11:10-47; 12:1-23, 24-41). The ROSTER is seen at 11:11-47; 12:3-8, 10-15 (cf. 6:18-33); it is a list of all the names within a related group, along with the duties and offices assigned to each. The ANECDOTE appears at 11:13-14, 15-19, 23; 12:17-19. Closely related is the EXPLOIT REPORT, seen at 11:11, 22b-24; 12:16. This is a brief note drawn from an original anecdote reporting a heroic exploit. Lacking narrative development, it mentions the hero's name and parentage, rank and standing, plus the exploit itself. It originates within organizations of fighting men but eventually becomes part of the court record, as reflected in 2 Samuel 23 (and par.). 12:25-38 is no proper (→) muster roll but an imaginary LIST drawn from a CENSUS roll. A final genre is the AFFINITY SAYING, seen in 12:19. This is a clipped, rhythmic affirmation making an enthusiastic commitment and lending itself to being remembered, repeated, and actuated. It is the precise functional opposite of the (→) repudiation saying. Additional minor genres are those seen at 12:18-19, the CALL TO LOYALTY, which is a challenge delivered by a leader to those offering to be his followers, and the BLESSING ("Peace, peace to you, and peace to your helpers!"), a pronouncement designed to release the inherent power of the spoken, performative word. The CALL TO LOYALTY in v. 18 includes an example of the genre ADMONITION, which is designed to dissuade an individual or group from a certain type of conduct (→ EXHORTATION).

Most of the fixed formulas and genre elements seen in this passage are already familiar; they include the EPITOME (11:14b; 12:14b; see our comments at 11:5 and the discussion in De Vries, *Yesterday, Today and Tomorrow,* 94-96), the FULFILLMENT FORMULA (11:10b; 12:24b), the WISH (11:17), the OATH (11:19a), the RHETORICAL QUESTION (11:19a), the RANKING FORMULA (11:20a, 25; 12:10-14), the APPELLATION (11:22a; 12:2a, 9a, 22), the NAME LIST (12:10-14, 21), the ASSISTANCE FORMULA (12:19a), and the TALLY (12:25-38). Like the example in 11:3, the fulfillment formulas in 11:10 and 12:24 cite no specific prophecy, but seem to take ChrH's own statement of the divine intent concerning Saul in 10:13-14 as having predictive force, finding fulfillment in the narration of David's rise to power. The WISH is a form of speech in which one expresses a strong desire to have something or see something happen. The oath of 11:19 has the form of a self-cursing. The RHETORICAL QUESTION, which occurs frequently in ChrH, is asked for its rhetorical or telling effect and does not seek information.

Setting

The roster of David's warriors is copied with slight modifications from 2 Sam 23:8-39. Its position in 1-2 Samuel may suggest that it applies to David's military organization during his actual rule, but everything—especially the Bethlehem water anecdote—suggests that it describes the warrior bands that followed him in the Negeb and Shephelah as he fled the wrath of Saul, and possibly the inchoate army that he organized in Hebron, prior to the consolidation of the kingdom. An exceedingly helpful study is B. Mazar, "Elite"; cf. also K. Elliger, "Helden Davids," 62ff. A commentary on Chronicles is hardly the place to discuss this, since ChrH simply borrowed from Samuel and may not have had accurate knowledge of what the various designations meant. Suffice it to say that "the thirty" was an early Israelite organization of freebooters and appears not only in 2 Samuel 23 but also in 2 Sam 10:7; 16:6; 20:7; 1 Kgs 1:8-10; 2:32. The first thirty names in the list of 2 Sam 23:8-39 par. 1 Chr 11:26-47 were of Judahites or of men living nearby, whereas the remaining names in Samuel are from distant regions, from indigenous populations, or from mercenary units. 1 Chr 11:42ff. adds fourteen more names, mostly of men from Transjordan, and almost certainly these are from later than David's time. According to Mazar (pp. 315-20), "the three" represent commanders of a regimental-style organization consisting of from four hundred to six hundred men, with each "hero" commanding one of two line battalions or a battalion in reserve (cf. 1 Sam 25:13; 27:2). Solomon must have eliminated all of this—perhaps because of their spirit of proud independence—relying instead on fortresses and chariots (but cf. Neh 3:16). In ChrH's time whatever military personnel existed must have enjoyed the status of guard and police—no more.

As has been stated, there is no reason whatever to regard 12:1-23 as secondary. Certainly, the reports of the various accessions pertain to groups that came to David in his flight from Saul, but, from ChrH's point of view, they belonged to the period prior to David's coronation in spite of 11:1-9—which was true equally of the warriors mentioned in 11:10ff., even though the list in Samuel is placed late in David's reign. Little can be said in favor of A. Zeron's view ("Helpers of David") to the effect that the traditions involved concerned Absalom rather than David. Everything points, rather, to the authenticity of this material, particularly the anxiety that pervades it all for David's safety in the face of Saul's persecution. The Benjaminites play a prominent role, for their loyalty is crucial if David is to take Saul's place upon the throne.

So much cannot be said for the highly stylized muster in 12:24-38, culminating in the enthronement at Hebron, vv. 39-41. The muster is clearly based on those of Numbers 1 and 26, even though ChrH arranges the tribes in a different order. ChrH's number is twelve, but he keeps Levi as a secular tribe while giving Ephraim and half-Manasseh (otherwise combined as "Joseph") separate places, resulting in the necessity of dumping all the Transjordanians (with half-Manasseh repeated) into the twelfth slot. There are tallies characteristic of the (→) muster roll, but what might otherwise be appellations are ChrH's arbitrary descriptive comments. With the evidence of such disarrangement at hand, one should not quibble that Levi is given a main force, and then two separate contingents under Jehoiada and Zadok (vv. 28-29). Mendenhall's study ("Census") of census lists in Numbers 1 and 26 is of no particular help except in arguing a now widely conceded point, to the effect that the word *'elep* is a fixed unit of militia organization and not a literal thousand, hence the tallies in these passages and in 1 Chronicles 12 are excessive because the totals counted this word as the numeral "thousand," rather than recognizing its signification as a military unit. Mendenhall argues that Numbers 1 is older than Numbers 26 because the total of its troops is smaller. Mendenhall reasons that in 1 Chronicles 12 the tally of units (329) and soldiers (2300) is rudimentary and early because it is much smaller than the figures in Numbers. This implies that ChrH had a primitive and authentic source, but we may be sure that the alleged rudimentariness of his list is due to arbitrariness and schematicism, rather than to an early origin.

Intention

1 Chronicles 11–12 cannot be explained without taking account of a decisive element of resumptiveness and prolepsis. The resumptiveness is seen especially in 11:10ff., which is not dated earlier or later than the coronation and march to Jerusalem narrated in 11:1-9, but which recalls the strong support that David received, mainly from Judah, in the effort to give him the kingdom. Thus the opening rubric at 11:10, "Now these are the chiefs of David's mighty men, who gave him strong support in his kingdom"—i.e., in his accession to the kingship. The inclusio by which David comes twice to Hebron for enthronement has the effect of dating this list both after and before his coronation. That is to say, they were there before, and they were there after. The pattern we are seeing is like that of the "second coming" of Christ, a problem that has continued to vex Christian eschatologists. Christ is long expected, and when he has died and risen to heaven he is expected again. The best typological explanation suggests that the *parousia* is a transhistorical and transtemporal event, not one fixed at a single time and place. So here: David is crowned at Hebron, marches to Jerusalem, his kingdom's center, and returns to Hebron to be confirmed in his kingship before counseling with his people about taking measures to bring up the ark. The very group of warriors that had brought him to Hebron at the first join him at Hebron at the last. His earliest supporters, they are his latest supporters as well.

Repetition of the phrase "all Israel" lays stress on the unity and unanimity of the nation in giving the kingdom to David. The mustering related in 12:24ff. only underscores this. No tribe of Israel is to be left out, not even if two and a half of them have to be squeezed into a single unit in order to fit them to the twelve-tribe scheme (v. 38). The fact that accessions from Benjamin are twice identified (12:1-8, 17-19) and that the Benjaminites are pointedly referred to as "Saul's kinsmen" shows that ChrH, in his late age, shares the anxiety that the historical David would have felt in trying to claim Saul's kingship, as promised in 10:14. Yahweh had turned Saul out and let David in—but did the Benjaminites know and accept this, and was there enough support from Judah and the other tribes to overcome Saulide opposition? Though the parlous days of which the text speaks are now long past, the question remains real and existential for ChrH, for without actual occupation of the throne due to Persian imperialism, the dynasty of David still living remains vulnerable to challenge from other groups within restoration Israel. With neither throne nor crown nor scepter, the question might seem trivial, yet in ChrH's ideology the ideal Israel requires a symbolic head, and that head has to be "David." It is ChrH who declares with Amasai (12:19), "We are yours, O David; and with you, O son of Jesse!"

Bibliography

J. Botterweck, "Zur Eigenart der chronistischen Davidgeschichte," *TQ* 136 (1956) 411-12; S. J. De Vries, *Yesterday, Today and Tomorrow* (Grand Rapids: Eerdmans, and London: SPCK, 1975) 94-96; K. Elliger, "Die dreissig Helden Davids," *PJ* 31 (1935) 29-75 (= *KS* [1966] 72-118); J. A. R. Mackenzie, "Valiant Against All," *Int* 22 (1968) 18-35; B. Mazar, "The Military Elite of King David," *VT* 13 (1963) 310-20; G. E. Mendenhall, "The Census Lists of Numbers 1 and 26," *JBL* 77 (1958) 52-66; H. G. M. Williamson, " 'We are Yours, O David.' The Setting and Purpose of 1 Chronicles 12:1-23," *OTS* 21 (1981) 164-76; A. Zeron, "The Helpers of David in I Chr XII, 1-22" (Hebr.), *Tarb* 46 (1977) 8-16: idem, "Tag für Tag kam man zu David, um ihm zu helfen, 1. Chr. 12, 1-22. Ein versprengtes Stück einer Abschalom-Tradition?" *TZ* 30 (1974) 257-61.

ACCOUNT OF THE INSTALLATION OF THE ARK, 13:1–16:43

Structure

I.	Report of bringing the ark to Obed-edom	13:1-14
II.	Report of David's growth in power and honor	14:1-17
III.	Report of preparing the clergy	15:1-24
IV.	Report of ritual: entrance ceremony	15:25–16:3
V.	Report of ordering the regular service	16:4-43

Following a transition from chs. 11–12, ChrH paraphrases the *hieros logos* of 2 Samuel 6 to the point where the ark is deposited in the "house" of Obed-edom. He then shifts back to 2 Sam 5:11-25 to pick up important details concerning homage received from Hiram, David's growing family, and his victories in the vale of Rephaim. This provides a basis for enabling David to prepare a suitable shrine for the ark, and once the Levites have been instructed in carrying the ark and the singers in making melodious music, the entrance and installation, adapted from 2 Sam 6:12-23, is recounted. After David arranges for the regular service before the ark, the ceremony is concluded and the people are sent home.

Genre and Intention

Combining various materials exhibiting several different subgenres, this entire pericope constitutes an ACCOUNT, similar to but longer and more complex than a (→) report. Often consisting of reports, statements, descriptions, or fragments of a story, but organized upon a common theme, an account may aim at explanation rather than a mere chronicling of events. This account depicts an important second phase in David's kingship. The first was to get crowned and capture Jerusalem. This second phase brings the tribal cult object, the ark, into Jerusalem and provides for a regular worship in its presence. This, though, is but preliminary to the construction of the temple, to whose preparation the remainder of ChrH's David narrative is to be devoted.

I. REPORT OF BRINGING THE ARK TO OBED-EDOM, 13:1-14

Structure

A. Agreement of purpose — 1-4
  1. Editorial transition — 1
  2. Proposal to the assembly — 2-3
    a. Summons to absent Israelites — 2
    b. Retrieval of the ark — 3
  3. Approval — 4
B. The return of the ark (report of ritual) — 5-8
  1. "All Israel" summoned — 5
  2. "All Israel" transports the ark from Kiriath-jearim — 6-7
  3. "All Israel" makes holy noise — 8
C. Temporary deposit in Obed-edom's "house" — 9-14
  1. Uzzah's transgression — 9-11
    a. Touches the ark — 9
    b. His death — 10
    c. David's anger — 11a
    d. Change of place-name (naming etiology) — 11b
  2. David arrests the procession — 12-13
    a. David's complaint — 12
    b. Deposit in Obed-edom's "house" — 13
  3. Three months of divine favor — 14

Willi (*Auslegung,* 172) speaks of vv. 1-4 as a mere reflection on ChrH's part, but it is plain to see that these verses tie directly back to chs. 11–12. They are, in fact, a necessary and well-designed continuation and culmination. Since v. 2 introduces David's actual speech, we can take v. 1 as an editorial transition, aimed at giving the impression that David first broached his proposal to the military leaders who had surrounded him at Hebron before presenting it to the *qāhāl* of Israel. Wherever ChrH mentions the *qāhāl*, it is in a liturgical setting —and so here. Although ChrH does not identify Hebron as a shrine site (this would violate his adherence to the theory of Jerusalem's monopoly), and the "Israel" who is there for his coronation feast is in a secular rather than a sacral role, its imminent participation in the ritual act of bringing up the ark automatically turns it into a "congregation." David hedges his proposal with the double condition, "If it seems good to you and it pleases Yahweh our God" (v. 2). God, people, king, cultus: these must be kept together in unanimity for so portentous an act as this (cf. Watson, "Archaic Elements," 7.9). So David proposes to summon two groups: (1) kinsmen living throughout the territory of Israel who could not be present at the coronation, and (2) priests and Levites. Willi (p. 195) wants to remove v. 2aβ, like similar references in ch. 6, because these clergy did not have pasturelands of their own in the time of ChrH; but he fails to do justice to ChrH's powers of ideologizing, in this instance following pentateuchal prescriptions that were long superseded. Apparently, ChrH does not introduce the priests and Levites at this point in order to have them present for carrying the ark, for he follows Samuel in giving this task to Uzzah and Ahio from the "house," i.e., shrine of Abinadab. The Uzzah incident demonstrates what happens when ignorant officiants, not of the priestly or Levitical order, are allowed to accompany the ark, and this in turn is intended as the justification for 15:1-15, specifically assigning this task to the Levites. Now we are able to understand why ChrH breaks off the Samuel account where he does: he must allow Obed-edom's three months for David to make more thorough preparations to receive the ark (14:1–15:1); but, more importantly, he must ensure that the clergy are more thoroughly prepared (15:2-24), so that no new disaster shall occur.

ChrH copies Samuel fairly closely in 13:2-14, but Lemke ("Synoptic Studies," 28-29) allows for the possibility that Chronicles is following an old Palestinian text superior to that of Samuel. Certain slight changes are very revealing. V. 3, "We neglected it in the days of Saul," seems to assign a blame to Saul that is certainly not implied anywhere in Samuel; it is ChrH's own ungracious comment, strengthening his censure of Saul and further glorifying David. ChrH surely knows his Bible, for he has to take the reference to Kiriath-jearim from 1 Sam 7:1, not from the parallel in 2 Sam 6:3 (an unlikely alternative is that he is drawing upon an independent source). Very striking is his threefold phrase "David and all Israel" in vv. 5-8, far transcending the thirty thousand chosen men of 2 Sam 6:1. In v. 12 ChrH breaks his rule of not repeating *bayyôm hahû'*, "on that day," in his sources (cf. De Vries, *Yesterday, Today and Tomorrow* [Grand Rapids: Eerdmans, and London: SPCK, 1975] 100-101); for him it has none of its original epitomizing function. (On the styling of this entire section, cf. Willi, 140, 145, 147.) In v. 14 ChrH changes his source in such a way as to avoid giving the impression (so Samuel) that the ark may have been placed in an illegitimate shrine *(bēt)*, writing *wayyēšeb 'ărôn hā'ĕlōhîm 'im-bêt 'ōbēd 'ĕdōm bĕbêtô* [not a gloss] ... *wayĕbārek yahweh 'et-bêt 'ōbēd-'ĕdōm wĕ'et-kol-'ăšer-lô,* "And the ark of God remained in the house of Obed-edom, even in his house, ... and Yahweh blessed the house of Obed-edom and all who pertained to him."

Genre, Setting, and Intention

Here the main genre is REPORT. Vv. 12-13 have a proposal for a LITURGICAL SUMMONS, an urgent invitation to a religious ceremony, in this case consisting of (1) a call for the *qāhāl* to issue a summons, (2) a proposal to assemble, and (3) a further proposal to bring up the ark. Vv. 5-8 have the genre REPORT OF RITUAL, a brief description of procedures followed in public worship, regulated by formal ritual. V. 11b repeats from Samuel a NAMING ETIOLOGY on the root *prṣ*, "break out." V. 12 has a COMPLAINT, a statement which describes personal or communal distress, often addressed to God in vivid language and in the form of a question, "why" or "how."

Interpreters have little trouble identifying the intention of this passage from those special features that ChrH has added. The ark story, familiar to his readers, merely advances the action to the coming episodes, and this shows little special ideology. It is in the proposal to the assembly, which now becomes the *qāhāl*, "congregation," and in the threefold repetition of "all Israel" as associates of David (vv. 2-8), that ChrH shows the intention, not only of this passage, but of his entire history (cf. Lemke, 27ff.; Botterweck, "Eigenart," 412-14). Vv. 2 and 5 definitely place the narrative in another time than that of David, viz., a time when "all Israel" included dispersed brethren within "all the land of Israel" and living "from the Shihor of Egypt to the entrance of Hamath"—thus far beyond the narrow confines of Yehud (cf. Watson, "Archaic Elements," 7.9; Williamson, *Israel,* 124). No one is rejected, out of all the ancient tribes, who is willing to participate in making Jerusalem the shrine where Yahweh meets his people. This is the paradox of biblical universalism defined by ritual particularism. The blessing that came on Obed-edom's "house" came only because it was a way station on the march to Jerusalem. Thus it is a prolepsis of the far greater blessing that awaits all who refuse to tarry on the road, but hasten to complete their pilgrimage to the city that God has chosen.

Bibliography

J. Botterweck, "Zur Eigenart der chronistischen Davidgeschichte," *TQ* 136 (1956) 402-35; W. E. Lemke, "Synoptic Studies in the Chronicler's History" (Diss., Harvard, 1963); P. Welten, "Lade-Tempel-Jerusalem. Zur Theologie der Chronikbücher," in *Textgemäss (Fest.* E. Würthwein; ed. A. H. J. Gunneweg and O. Kaiser; Göttingen: Vandenhoeck & Ruprecht, 1979) 169-83; H. G. M. Williamson, *Israel in the Books of Chronicles* (Cambridge: Cambridge, 1977).

II. REPORT OF DAVID'S GROWTH IN POWER AND HONOR, 14:1-17

Structure

Although at vv. 8, 12, a superior ChrH *Vorlage* may account for minor differences from Samuel, Lemke ("Synoptic Studies," 31-33) attributes other differences to the pan-Israelite tendency of ChrH. Willi sees a historicizing interest in v. 12 (p. 153) and ChrH's special styling in vv. 14-15 (p. 140). All is taken pretty much in order, but with elements of ChrH's peculiar diction, from 2 Sam 5:11-25; and, because the two battle accounts are out of order in Samuel's ancient accession history, what used to be the epitomizing conclusion to that entire history now serves only as an intermediary reflection at 1 Chr 14:2. There are three brief reports in this chapter, vv. 1-2, 3-7, and 8-17 (cf. Botterweck, 414-16). The first and the last are clearly marked off by formal concluding statements, the first of which is this fossilized epitome. It is understood that everything reported occurs within the three months during which the ark is at Obed-edom's: the Phoenician embassy, the family review, and the two battles. In actuality, much longer time periods would have been required, especially for the begetting of so many children (vv. 3ff.), but we must understand that ChrH is again dealing in his familiar practice of retrospect and prolepsis, as in chs. 11-12 (on the additional wives and children, see Watson, "Archaic Elements," p. 201 n. 2). Welten ("Lade-Tempel-Jerusalem," 173ff.) correctly perceives that the victories at Rephaim were recounted here as the indispensable preliminaries to installing the ark in Jerusalem. There is no hint of this in Samuel, nor does ChrH make it explicit, yet the positioning makes the intent apparent. Both Samuel and Chronicles use the account of the Rephaim battles for the sole purpose of glorifying David, whose accession to the kingship was a menace to the Philistines (v. 8), and whose victory gave him international fame (v. 17a) while filling the nations with a dread of him that came from Yahweh (v. 17b). The Philistine idols that David's men took as trophies in the historical report of 2 Sam 5:21 are burnt in ChrH's report (v. 12).

From the way these reports hang together in ChrH's account, we are to understand the numerous children and the two victories as evidence for, and the outworking of, v. 2, David's confirmation in the kingship. The three reports together reveal that Obed-edom's blessing has spread to David, thus theoretically securing both termini in the sacred route over which the holy ark must pass.

Genre

The main genre is REPORT. The BATTLE REPORT occurs in vv. 9-12, 13-16. Vv. 3-7 comprise a BIRTH REPORT with NAME LIST. Familiar formulas are the NAMING ETIOLOGY, punning once again on the root *prṣ*, "break out" (v. 11), and the ASSISTANCE FORMULA (v. 15b), modified as "God has gone out before you." Vv. 10 and 14 have the genre ORACULAR INQUIRY, which includes the genre ORACLE. The ORACULAR INQUIRY includes a report that an oracle is being sought, usually at the request of a military leader, and then the ORACLE itself. Usually this is being sought from a priest or a prophet, but in our text we are told only that David inquired (*šā'al*) of God. V. 10 tells us what he asked: "Shall I go up . . . ? Wilt thou give them into my hand?" (the CONVEYANCE FORMULA). The ORACLE is affirmative in the first instance, and in the second instance is negative to David's proposal but offers an alternative plan of victory (→ ORACLE; ORACULAR INQUIRY; CONVEYANCE FOR-MULA). Perhaps deliberately ambiguous is the INTIMIDATION FORMULA of v. 17 (not found in Samuel), *wĕyahweh nātan 'et-paḥdô 'al-kol-haggôyim;* it could mean, "So Yahweh placed his own fear on all the nations," or it could mean, "So Yahweh placed his [David's] fear. . . ." It probably means the former because in 2 Chr 14:13; 17:10; 20:29 it is Yahweh's/God's fear or dread that is mentioned. This interpretation is entirely in line with ChrH's overall ideology, which makes God the actual fighter in Israel's battles (→ INTIMIDATION FORMULA; QUASI-HOLY-WAR STORY).

Setting and Intention

Hiram's decision to exchange ambassadors (not "messengers") with David, lead-ing to an agreement to furnish materials and artisans for constructing a worthy palace *(bêt)* for himself (v. 1), led David to "know" that Yahweh had in fact estab-lished him as king over Israel (v. 2). In other words, all that had gone before was symbol; this was fact. Or we can put it thus: God had a plan for David—David now accepts (and actuates) that plan. On this key word *kûn,* cf. Willi (pp. 186-87). With respect to the David dynasty, ChrH uses the qal in 1 Chr 17:12, 14, 27; 22:10; 28:7; 2 Chr 17:5; the niph. in 2 Chr 8:16; 29:35; 35:16; the hiph. in 1 Chr 15:1, 3, 12; 2 Chr 1:21; 31:11; 35:20; with respect to the temple, it is used in 1 Chr 22:3, 5; 28:2; 29:2-3, 16, 19; 2 Chr 2:6; 3:1. As the fossilized epitome of 1 Chr 14:2 phrases it, we are given to understand that a higher divine purpose lies behind this establishing of David: it is that the "kingdom" *(malkût)* might be raised exceeding-ly high "for the sake of *[ba'ăbûr]* his people Israel." Paraphrasing, we can say that David's glory is for the kingdom, and the kingdom's glory is for God's people (al-ways in personal possessive relation to him), Israel. Because God is faithful, Israel endures; because it endures, the kingdom abides, and with it, the Davidic kingship.

Bibliography

J. Botterweck, "Zur Eigenart der chronistischen Davidgeschichte," *TQ* 136 (1956) 402-35; P. Welten, "Lade-Tempel-Jerusalem," in *Textgemäss (Fest.* E. Würthwein; ed. A. H. J. Gun-neweg and O. Kaiser; Göttingen: Vandenhoeck & Ruprecht, 1979) 169-83.

III. REPORT OF PREPARING THE CLERGY, 15:1-24

Structure

This pericope does not advance the narrative of the ark's entrance except in offering further details about preparations for it. This is quickly taken care of in vv. 1-3, where David prepares the place of deposition, the Levites are designated as bearers, and the people are summoned (they have presumably scattered to their homes during the ark's three-month stay at Obed-edom's). On the syntax of v. 1, cf. Watson ("Archaic Elements," 10.51). The reader should not miss the strong contrasts that ChrH intends in both vv. 1 and 2. Following the lead of 14:1, ChrH reports that David had built "houses," i.e., palaces for himself (all in this three-month period!) but had only established (*kûn*, hiph.) a *māqôm*, "shrine," and a tent at that, for the ark ("of God," "of Yahweh," seems arbitrary); so also at vv. 3, 12. This is an imaginative expansion of 2 Sam 6:17. There it was a pragmatic necessity, but here it expresses a basic principle of ChrH's ideology, for none might build a *bēt* for Yahweh except Solomon (cf. ch. 17). In v. 2 the contrast is between the *'āz*, "then," at the beginning and the *'ad-'ôlām*, "perpetually." David ordered (*'mr*) that only the Levites should carry (*nś'*) the ark and minister (*šrt*) to it. In spite of Num 4:4-15, 1 Chronicles 13 has shown that this must be something new, and the two time designations underscore this as a radically new departure. Heretofore others carried the ark; *'āz* marks the moment of authoritative intervention, which will have effect from now and *'ad-'ôlām*.

At the same time that David was making a congregation (*qhl*) of "all Israel" again (v. 3), he assembled (*'sp*) the Levites for organization and authorization (vv. 4-15). Though this hardly advances the narrative action, it is a strategic place for

ChrH to introduce this matter because they will be called upon in vv. 12ff. to perform their traditional duty of bearing the ark into the sanctuary. (Williamson, comm., 121-22, argues that pre-Chronicles traditions are involved.) Other scholars (Willi, 196; Noth, "Chronistische Werk," 116; Fohrer, *Intro.*, 244) think vv. 4-24 is a post-ChrH expansion; Galling (ATD) identifies vv. 4-10, 16-24 as secondary; von Rad (*Geschichtsbild*, 105, 117-18) views vv. 16-24 as secondary. But those who would omit at least vv. 11-14 from the original text would be hard put to explain why ChrH cut off the ark story just after the report of Uzzah's death and temporary deposit in Obed-edom's "house." As ChrH sees it, this was not because the ark was inherently dangerous, as in the original *hieros logos*, but because Uzzah was not properly qualified and ordained for the task.

Interruption of narrative sequence is no sufficient reason for automatically assigning vv. 4-24 to a secondary layer, yet there are glosses and expansions here. Williamson (comm.) has shown that, at various places throughout the book, adherents of the priestly (not Levitical, as some interpreters would have it) party have corrected what they considered to be excessive claims on the part of the Levites. That references to the priests are secondary can be discerned from their intrusion at improper places. In v. 4 the "sons of Aaron" are mentioned before the Levites, but the roster that follows is purely that of the Levites (cf. 6:16-30). In v. 11 David summons "the priests Zadok and Abiathar," along with six Levites, but in addressing them he says, "You are the heads of the fathers' houses of the Levites," which might conceivably include the priests as descendants of Levi through Aaron; but carrying the ark is exclusively the duty of the Levites according to Numbers 4, hence we are surprised to read that the priests as well as the Levites sanctify themselves for bringing up the ark (v. 14), yet immediately read that it is solely the Levites who did the carrying (v. 15), plainly marking the references to priests in vv. 11, 14 as glosses. We must point out the prolepsis in v. 15 which reports that the Levites carried the ark prior to the narrative of the fetching of the ark in vv. 25-28.

Another pro-priestly gloss is the mention of the priestly trumpeters in v. 24a. This appears in a literary expansion, vv. 23-24, which designates Berechiah and Elkanah as "gatekeepers" for the ark, adds the item about the trumpeters, and then, as a correction from v. 18, repeats that Obed-edom and Jehiah (v. 18, Jeiel) were the ark's gatekeepers.

In vv. 5-10 the six chief branches of the Levites are listed, each with the name of the chief who was serving at the time, plus a tally of *'eḥāyw*, which would have meant "fellow clansmen" in the muster rolls, but here evidently refers to the various family groups doing service in the temple. Vv. 11-14 is a brief narrative having no connection to vv. 1-3, 25ff., but which clearly harks back to ch. 13 in its reproach to the Levites for not preventing the Uzzah disaster. David's command is a noun clause followed by imperatives; it identifies the addressees as responsible heads authorized by David, then orders them to sanctify themselves (a special rite often mentioned in liturgical contexts) and bring up the ark. The *RSV* in v. 13 is a makeshift translation occasioned by ChrH's lapidary style (cf. Watson, 10.3): David is blaming these chiefs for not carrying the ark in the first place and he shares the blame of all for not "seeking" (*drš*) Yahweh as prescribed. In the report of compliance (v. 14) it is the *lĕwîyim* (omitting the gloss) who sanctify themselves, but in the out-of-sequence narrative of v. 15 it is the *bĕnê-halwîyim* (a term implying an extension of the original group of Levites) who do the actual carrying, this time with Mosaic authorization and with specific mention of carrying poles, so as to avoid the sin of Uzzah.

Like 6:1-15, 15:4-15 identifies the original order of Levites (with changing personnel brought up to date in 9:14-16). As with the gatekeepers, the singers/musicians were striving for inclusion in the Levitical order, as can be seen in 6:16ff. and here in vv. 16-24. They are here authorized by David, but under specific order of the "chiefs of the Levites" (cf. Kropat, *Syntax*, 77), indicating clearly that their service was at the sufferance of the superior order. What we are offered here is a duty ROSTER, somewhat different from the ordinary roster of 6:16ff. The Levites appoint (*'md*, hiph.) them as "brethren/kinsmen" to their various tasks. There are three groups, the singers accompanied with cymbals, the harpists, and the lyre players (Alamoth and Sheminith, acronyms for special songs or tunes, may indicate certain keys or styles of music). In 6:18 Heman is chief and represents the Kohathites, in 6:24 Asaph is on his right—next in rank—and represents the Gershonites, and in 6:29 Ethan is on his left and represents the Merarites. Here in 15:17 these three are placed in a first order of singers (on Kushaiah, cf. Peiser, 348), while a second order of singers (*'ăḥêhem hammišnîm*) is listed, along with the cymbal players. The harpists and lyre players appear to come from this second order of singers/musicians, for seven of the first and five of the last are drawn from v. 18 (leaving out Maaseiah). The original list is complete with the mention of Chenaniah, the director (v. 22). It is not entirely clear why he is called a *śar halwîyim* (same title as in vv. 5-10). Also, there has been dispute over what is meant by *běmaśśā'*. Some (Petersen, *Late Israelite Prophecy*, 63; von Rad, *Geschichtsbild*, 110) say this is a temporal term and means "at the carrying (of the ark)," but this is part of a duty roster of uncertain date. It is better to follow the immediate context and translate "in the music" *(RSV)*.

Genre

The main genre for this pericope is REPORT. David's words in v. 2, "No one but the Levites shall carry the ark of God," exhibit the genre EDICT, which is a proclamation carrying the force of law, issued by an authority acting in an executive capacity. Though in this instance it is the area of the strictly sacral that is being regulated, the proper installation of the ark is a matter of prime concern to the nation and to David as king; at the same time, this edict sets the typology by which all ritual matters mentioned in ChrH find their authority (→ AUTHORIZATION FORMULA). We find two examples of the ROSTER, at vv. 5-10 and at vv. 16-24. The first mentions the chief of each group with a TALLY (six times) of authorized kinsmen. The second lists distinct functions, followed by six (including secondary additions) examples of the NAME LIST, which also appears in v. 11. In v. 12, David's words "Sanctify yourselves" constitute the genre ORDER, a forthright, direct expression of personal will addressed to persons under authority. It is closely related to the genre COMMAND, a direct commission based on custom, law, or decree; though our passage lacks this in verbatim form, there is a REPORT of such in the narrative transition at v. 16. V. 13 has the genre REPROACH, in this instance directed first against the Levites and then against the whole company. The REPROACH, virtually synonymous with the REBUKE, criticizes an indecorous or blameworthy performance, and implies authority on the part of the speaker over those under his direction. The

AUTHORIZATION FORMULA in v. 15b claims Mosaic precedent along with direct divine revelation. We mention, finally, the single word at the end of v. 13, *kammišpāṭ*, "according to ordinance." This is the REGULATION FORMULA, very similar in form, ideology, and intent to the AUTHORIZATION FORMULA. The former focuses on correct cultic procedures rather than on assuring that these have been fully sanctioned and authorized. In simple terms, the AUTHORIZATION FORMULA blesses a given procedure, while the REGULATION FORMULA assures that such a procedure shall be fully and correctly carried out. The REGULATION FORMULA may be compared to a rubric in the Missal, as compared with the rule in canon law endowing it with papal authority. For further details → REGULATION FORMULA. Both of these formulas appear with frequency in ChrH. For further details see De Vries, "Moses and David as Cult-Founders."

Setting and Intention

As has been noted, the intention of this pericope is to bring forward the narration of the ark's entrance by introducing the clergy that are to be involved in the ritual. The original Levites stand in the center, while the priests appear only in secondary intrusions. The singers/musicians are also put in place—both according to family and to function—while both their subordination to the Levites and their effort to be recognized as part of them come to the fore. Williamson (comm.) is almost certainly correct in recognizing vv. 5-10 as a roster of the Levites as they existed prior to the intrusion of the singers and doorkeepers. On the contrary, the duty roster of the musicians, vv. 16-24, represents a far-advanced stage of the development of this group. More and more scholars are being persuaded by H. Gese ("Zur Geschichte") to the effect that ChrR/H plus Nehemiah-Ezra reveal a number of stages in the postexilic tradition development of the singer/musician group. Though this has been mentioned previously, it is useful to restate the essential outline, which is as follows:

First stage: Ezra 2 par. Nehemiah 7
Second stage: Neh 11:3-19; 1 Chr 9:1b-18
Third stage: A. 1 Chr 16:4-42; 2 Chr 5:12; 29:13f.; 35:15
               B. 1 Chr 6:16-32; 15:16-24

The singers were a preexilic group, and are mentioned ca. 515 B.C. in Ezra-Nehemiah. The Asaph group, with the title *ḥōzeh*, "seer," are preexilic according to 1 Chr 25:1-3. In the Ezra-Nehemiah list, the singers are not included among the Levites, but precede the doorkeepers. The *běnê-'āsāp* of 2 Chr 35:15; Ezra 3:10 claim descent from Asaph, who in 2 Chr 29:30 is titled *ḥōzēh*, "seer." This is the early stage. A second stage arises ca. 450, in Nehemiah's time, with the citizen lists of Neh 11:3-19; 1 Chr 9:1b-18, and now the temple personnel are the priests, Levites, and doorkeepers, with the singers already belonging to the ranks of the Levites. A certain Jeduthun ranks alongside Asaph. A third stage is reached ca. 350-300, wherein our Levitical singers are now divided into three groups: Heman, Asaph, and Ethan. 1 Chr 16:4ff. subordinates Heman and Jeduthun to Asaph (cf. 2 Chr 5:12; 29:13f.; 35:15). 2 Chr 35:15 calls Jeduthun *ḥōzēh hammelek*, "the king's seer." A later tradition puts Heman foremost, over Asaph and Jeduthun

(1 Chr 6:16-32 [*RSV* 31-47]; 15:16-24). In 2 Chronicles 20 the Korahites appear alongside Asaphite "prophets." In 1 Chronicles 15–16—our text—Tradition A of this third stage has the order Asaph-Heman-Jeduthun, which will be altered in Tradition B (ca. 300) to the order Heman-Asaph-Ethan, thus sacrificing the historical preeminence of Asaph. At this late date Ethan has taken the place of Jeduthun and has become the *hērōs eponymos* of the Heman group of singers (cf. 1 Kgs 5:11; *RSV* 4:31). Another late development will be the expansion of the fourteen temple musicians listed in our passage, 1 Chronicles 15, into twenty-four courses of singers in 1 Chronicles 25, copying the twenty-four priestly classes.

According to Gese, the Jeduthun group arrive late, since in Ezra's time all singers were called *běnê-'āsāp*. Asaph was, of course, the eponym of the entire singer guild. New groups arrived, with no claim to Asaphite genealogy (hence the artificial name "Jeduthun," from the root *ydh*, "praise") and membership remained fluid, with rivalry between these singers and the doorkeepers. When the Asaphites began to lose prestige, the old Levitical genealogy was stretched to make a place for this "Jeduthun," deriving him from Merari. This group remained subordinate to Heman but claimed equality with the Asaphites. When the Korahites emerged to prophesy with the Asaphites, "Jeduthun" had disappeared, but this is only because Korah, with a genealogy taken from Num 26:58, had become the preferred, more prestigious name for this group.

Scholars like Petersen (*Late Israelite Prophecy*, 61) have suggested minor modifications in this scheme, but in basics it is sound. It can afford the student of Chronicles a sure guideline through the tangled trail of tradition development coming to manifestation in individual passages within ChrH. It can be safely said that, if 1 Chronicles 15–16 represent the very latest stage of the development of the singers within this history, it is remote in time from that of David and his ark. From the historian's point of view it might seem an intrusion and imposition. From the viewpoint of ChrH himself, however, it is altogether fitting that the very singers of his own time should be symbolically and typologically present to participate in this first stage toward the development and perfection of the temple cult.

Bibliography

M. J. Buss, "The Psalms of Asaph and Korah," *JBL* 82 (1963) 382-92; H. Gese, "Zur Geschichte der Kultsänger am Zweiten Tempel," in *Abraham unser Vater: Juden und Christen im Gespräch über die Bibel* (*Fest.* O. Michel; ed. O. Betz, M. Hengel, and P. Schmidt; Leiden: Brill, 1963) 222-34; F. E. Peiser, "Miscellen," *ZAW* 17 (1897) 348-49; D. L. Petersen, *Late Israelite Prophecy* (SBLMS 23; Missoula: Scholars, 1977); J. R. Shaver, "Torah and the Chronicler's History Book" (Diss., Notre Dame, 1983).

IV. REPORT OF RITUAL: ENTRANCE CEREMONY, 15:25–16:3

Structure

A. Preparation   25-27
  1. Procession to Obed-edom's house   25
  2. Levites offer sacrifice   26

ChrH's narrative of the ark's installation resumes with a transitional *wayĕhî*, "And then it happened . . . ," but there is no narrative verb to carry the action forward unless we read the m. plur. part. of *hlk* without the article, as in LXX^A (so *RSV*). Closely following 2 Sam 6:12-19, ChrH divides the action into four brief scenes: (1) preparation, (2) entrance, (3) dedication, and (4) celebration. The act of dismissal with which the *hieros logos* of 2 Sam 6:19b-20 concludes is deferred to 1 Chr 16:43 so that the appointment of Levites to praise may be included.

The same assemblage that took a leading part in the events of 11:3; 12:38; 13:1 proceed to Obed-edom's house *bĕśimhâ*, "with rejoicing"—a common note in ChrH's liturgical reports (v. 25). The Levites, now duly installed, take a foremost role in the rites that follow. Employing classical Hebrew syntax beginning with another *wayĕhî*, v. 26 inserts a highly ideological circumstantial clause, *be'zōr hā'ĕlōhîm 'et-halwîyim nōś'ê 'ărôn bĕrît-yahweh*, "Inasmuch as God had helped the Levites (to become) bearers of the ark of Yahweh's covenant," and then proceeds to narrate that they offered the sacrificial animals. This was David's privilege in 2 Samuel, but it is no surprise that ChrH should take it away from a secular leader and give it to clergy; only, they ought to be priests *(kōhănîm)* in normative ideology. It will not do to read the verb *wayyizbĕhû* with an indefinite subject, involving the entire party in the sacrificing, because then the circumstantial clause would have no point. The solution is that 2 Samuel makes no mention of priests, hence ChrH neglects them too. He is concerned only about exalting the Levites. V. 27 is an appendage, employing a participle and a noun clause to tell how David and the clergy were clad (observe the inclusio: David-Levites [etc.]-David).

In the entrance scene "all Israel" once again participates. All that is said here is that this totality *'lh* (hiph.) the ark with all sorts of music and shouting. The verb is participial and is by no means synonymous with the *nś'* which the Levites do; hence we must take this as a resumptive clause, stating the action and result of the entire installation. The equivalent of 2 Sam 6:15, v. 28b is certainly not a literary expansion, as Willi claims (p. 195). V. 29 could make a better claim for secondary status because it interrupts the action to tell us about the attitude of Michal; but of course this is in the Samuel *Vorlage*. Evidently this is a matter of great concern for ChrH, but I have explained elsewhere (*Yesterday, Today and Tomorrow* [Grand Rapids: Eerdmans, and London: SPCK, 1975] 212-16) that the original *hieros logos* was interrupted at this point by a redactor wishing to make a strong anti-Saul polemic, and for him the introductory verb, *wĕhāyâ*, would be the normal form, rather than ChrH's *wayĕhî*. (Thus 2 Sam 6:16 should be read, "Now when the ark of Yahweh had come . . . while Michal was looking out . . . that she saw . . . and despised.") In other words, the original syntax of Samuel makes this a quite detached event. In ChrH it remains part of the main action. The deposition of the ark in the tent follows; for some reason, ChrH omits reference to this being at a *māqôm*, "shrine site," as in 2 Sam 6:17; 1 Chr 15:1, 3.

Since the verb *qrb* usually means "offer sacrifice"—a priestly prerogative—we are somewhat surprised that in 16:1b ChrH gives this action to the people, and in v. 2a to David. This time there is no mention of Levites. Has he suddenly lost his fastidiousness, or does he intend the readers of this already familiar story to assume that priests were present to do the actual sacrificing, with Levites to help them?

The king's blessing on the assemblage now has special force. Yahweh is present in power in David's city. ChrH normally avoids the divine name Yahweh, but here he allows David to bless the people *bĕšēm yahweh*, "in Yahweh's name," avoiding the epithet of 2 Samuel, "Yahweh Sebaoth." Finally, David's gifts: they are the same as in 2 Samuel, and we cannot expect that ChrH would have known enough about ancient Hebrew rites to recognize that there is a Baalistic element in them. What we can say with some assurance is that the gifts that David here presents are intended as another subtle inclusio with the gifts brought him at Hebron, 12:40. ChrH sharpens 2 Sam 6:19, *hā'ām lĕkol-hămôn*, "the people, even the entire multitude," by changing it to *lĕkol-'îš yiśrā'ēl*, "even every man of Israel" (16:3).

Genre

Although "I am/will be with you" is the usual form of the ASSISTANCE FORMULA, the verb *'zr* in the circumstantial clause of v. 26 produces a variation of this formula, in which the divine presence is acknowledged to be active in enabling the Levites to carry out their ordained office, viz., to bear the sacred ark. The pericope as a whole exhibits the genre REPORT OF RITUAL, which is a brief description of procedures followed in the performance of public worship. Although in this instance the REPORT OF RITUAL has been directly adapted from 2 Samuel 6, it is a favorite of ChrH elsewhere (2 Chr 1:2-6; 7:3-10; 15:10-15; 20:18-19, 26, 28; 29:20-33; 35:10-15). Although only priests may perform ritual, ChrH intends his reports of ritual to be normative for the "ideal Israel."

Setting and Intention

In 2 Sam 6:12-19 the cult object in question is called *'ărôn yahweh* four times and *'ărôn hā'ĕlōhîm* twice—a variation seen also in 1 Samuel 4 – 6. This reflects simply the instability of terminology still prevalent in premonarchical Israel, but ChrH reflects the effect of the ark's longtime domicile in the temple in his preference for a deuteronomistic locution, *'ărôn bĕrît-yahweh*, "ark of Yahweh's covenant" (four times), varied perhaps for style as *hā'ārôn* (once) or *'ărôn hā'ĕlōhîm* (once). ChrH frequently takes this liberty with his *Vorlage*, and there is little reason to suppose that he is reading a different text.

The pan-Israel *Tendenz* seen in chs. 11–13 comes strongly to the fore in 15:25, 28; 16:2b-3 (cf. Lemke, "Synoptic Studies," 36), but even more noticeable is the strong emphasis on the privilege of the Levites in 15:26 (Lemke, 37; Willi, 125), superseding in this instance even the priority of the priests. As has been pointed out

147

in the section on "Structure," this text allows even the congregation to offer sacrifices on this occasion (16:1b), sharing with David a privilege (16:2a) that he alone had enjoyed in 2 Sam 6:17, and which he again carried out when dedicating the altar at Ornan's threshing floor, according to 1 Chr 21:26. Rather than suppose a theological quirk in allowing the congregation to sacrifice (Willi, 127), it is better to assume that ChrH misunderstands the verb *wayĕkal* as seen in the Samuel *Vorlage*. There it functions as a transition from the actual sacrificing, 2 Sam 6:17b, and the blessing of the people that follows. The sentence has a resumptive quality that escapes ChrH's understanding, and he assumes that the congregation first had to sacrifice in order for David to "complete" the process. All the same, the absence of priests and Levites at this point is an odd deficiency, and can be accounted for only on the supposition that their participation would have been assumed. It is to be assumed, furthermore, that in ChrH's mind the people and David did not perform the actual ritual, but presented the victims to the proper, unnamed officiants.

The wearing of the linen is rephrased from Samuel. Lemke (p. 38) suggests a possibly superior Chronicles text, but Willi (p. 140) is on a more certain track when he suggests that 15:27 shows normal ChrH styling. Agreeing with this, we lay heavy emphasis on the David-Levites-David inclusio, marking the Levites as the visible, authorized representatives of a prerogative which at first David held as a right of his kingship. (On Chenaniah's function as director of the music *[hammaśśā']*, see above on 15:22; *contra* Petersen, *Late Israelite Prophecy*, 63-64.)

G. von Rad (*Geschichtsbild*, 100) makes much of the entrance of the ark, and the singing that accompanied it, as crucial to ChrH's entire philosophy of history. This is correct, because to ChrH the cult is the foundation of Israel's new society, and singing, rejoicing, is both the basis and the effect of cultic worship. We shall have other occasions to observe that the king is constantly called upon to foster this joy by adding his personal blessing, and at the same time by providing gifts of food for feasting, as here in 16:2b-3. This marks an ideal, harmonious relationship. Our text allows the incident of Michal's disdain to mar that harmony for only one purpose: to show that Yahweh did right, after all, in deposing the house of Saul and installing David (ChrH pointedly alters Samuel's references to David's participation in Baalistic symbolism—the original reason for Michal's offense; cf. Willi, 117). Michal and the house of Saul are, in effect, banned from the celebration and ignored in the future life of the ideal Israel.

V. REPORT OF ORDERING THE REGULAR SERVICE, 16:4-43

Structure

A. Roster of liturgists	4-6
1. Their task	4
2. Name list: rank and position	5
3. Priestly trumpeters	6
B. Appointment of praise psalms	7-36
1. David's innovation	7
2. Examples	8-36a
3. Popular approval	36b

It has become customary for venturesome commentators to eliminate portions of this pericope; thus Willi (p. 196) omits all of vv. 4-38, 41-42; Noth ("Chronistische Werk," 116) omits the same except for v. 4; Galling (ATD) omits vv. 5-6, 37-38, 41-42; Fohrer (*Intro.,* 244) omits vv. 5-38, 41. There are, to be sure, a few glosses: all the names in v. 5 except those of Asaph and Zechariah; the reference to Obed-edom and Hosah as gatekeepers in v. 38b; the names Heman and Jeduthun in v. 42a; the reference to the' sons of Jeduthun in v. 42b. These were all added in the interests of rival groups at a later time. Otherwise, this pericope is suffused with ChrH's ideology. We can, as a matter of fact, scarcely conceive of him passing up so excellent an opportunity for rationalizing David as the originator of the praise psalm. Williamson (comm., 185-86) is surely right in identifying 16:7-36 as the framework introduction to an inclusio ending in David's own grand psalm of praise at 1 Chr 29:10-13.

It is obvious that this pericope advances the ark narrative not a whit; i.e., not until ChrH borrows from Samuel in v. 43 to have "all the people" go home and David return to his own house. V. 4 does begin in narrative, but without David as the identified subject. Rosters for Levites dedicated to praise (vv. 5-6) and priestly trumpeters (v. 6) are given. The task of these Levites is *lĕhazkîr ûlĕhôdôt ûlĕhallēl,* "to memorialize and to thank and to praise," Yahweh as the God of Israel, and the persons named are to play all sorts of musical instruments for this. Although the reference to the priestly trumpeters invites excision as a pro-priestly gloss, the adverb *tāmîd,* "continuously," seen also in the reference to priestly sacrificing at Gibeon (v. 40), makes it likely to be original. From the point of view of syntax, vv. 5-6 contain the direct object of the opening verb in v. 4. The two original Levite names are offered with a statement of their rank ("first," "second") and balance off the two names given for the priestly trumpeters.

Verse 7, with the hymnic material that follows, invites criticism as a secondary addition because it restates that David appointed "Asaph and his brethren" to sing praise to Yahweh. This is especially suspicious because "his brethren" looks like a generalizing repetition of vv. 4-5. Its function is, rather, resumptive. V. 7 begins with an unparalleled collocation of time words: *bayyôm hahû' 'āz . . . bārō'š,* "on that day, then . . . at the beginning." Awkward as this may seem, it makes quite clear what ChrH intends. It is that on the occasion of the ark's entrance, not before and not afterward, David authorized and ordained this elemental feature of Israel's cultic life. Thus we translate: "On that day, even then, David arranged for the very first time that Yahweh should be praised under the auspices of Asaph and his kinsmen." Abruptly asyndetic are the actual words of some examples (vv. 8-36a). These are extracts from Psalms 105; 96; and 106. One has to assume that ChrH is thinking of David's reciting, though the possibility remains that he is thinking of

Asaph and his kinsmen doing this. The point is moot, because now and forevermore this group will sing psalms of praise, and they will do it solely and strictly upon his authority. Anyway, when the liturgist in question is done, all the people will say "Amen" and "Praise to Yahweh!" (v. 36b).

ChrH wants to make clear that such an act of praise did not occur solely on this occasion but is perpetual. The verb '*zb*, "leave," brings this out: David went home by-and-by, but when he did, he left behind the persons named in vv. 37-38a to minister to the ark *tāmîd*, "continuously" (cf. vv. 6, 40). Not only so: their ministry was to be *lidbar-yôm bĕyômô*, "taking care of each day's affairs on the day ordained" (v. 37). These were the Asaphites and the Obed-edomites (the latter's eventual claim on another function is reflected in the gloss at v. 38b; cf. 26:4-8).

All along, ChrH has been speaking of Jerusalem, but suddenly he recalls that Gibeon was still Israel's great shrine. His *wĕ'ēt* at the beginning of v. 39 does not indicate the object of the verb *wayyittēn* at the beginning of v. 4, but, in familiar ChrH styling, requires the translation "Now as for. . . ." What follows in vv. 39-42 is a complex nominal sentence specifying who were still in service at Gibeon, their duty, and the conditions of that duty: (1) *tāmîd* (perpetually the same), (2) *labbōqer wĕlā'āreb*, "morning and evening," and (3) "according to everything written in Yahweh's Torah." The latter was not just some reference guide but a rule imposed by God himself. This side-glance at what was going on at Gibeon does not disturb ChrH's line of presentation because Jerusalem was not at this stage a regular place of sacrifices. All the same, ChrH hints that Gibeon will eventually be closed down in favor of Jerusalem by stating (vv. 40-41) that some unneeded Levitical musicians, Heman and Jeduthun, were sent over to see to it that the Zadokite priests had plenty of praise-music to accompany their sacrificing. "and with them" (*wĕ'immāhem*) at the head of vv. 41, 42, secures a bond between Gibeon and Jerusalem that will never be severed.

Genre

Verses 4-6 constitute another ROSTER, including NAME LIST and RANKING FORMULA. Vv. 7-36 have a composite HYMN OF PRAISE, a psalm which extols and glorifies God. Unparalleled is the LITURGICAL PARAPHRASE in v. 36b. The genre involves a deliberate recasting of a standard liturgical model, in this case Ps 106:48b, which has its own concluding liturgical command, *wĕ'āmar kol-hā'ām 'āmēn*, "And let all the people say 'Amen,'" and then the editor's refrain, a plur. impr., *halĕlû-yāh*, "praise ye Yahweh!" ChrH paraphrases, *wayyō'mĕrû kol-hā'ām 'āmēn wĕhallēl lĕyahweh*, "And all the people said 'Amen' and 'Praise to Yahweh!'" (→ LITURGICAL PARAPHRASE). Another example of this genre is *kî lĕ'ôlām ḥasdô*, "for/indeed forever is his fidelity," seen as an antiphonal response in Ps 118:1-4, and as a closing refrain in Ps 118:29 (cf. also 2 Chr 5:13; 20:21).

The TALLY appears in modified form at v. 38, and the AUTHORIZATION FORMULA at v. 40. The main genre for the entire pericope is REPORT.

Setting and Intention

Gese's reconstruction of the tradition history of the singers' guild ("Zur Geschichte"; see on 15:1-24) proves its usefulness here. Asaph is on top and Heman has lost status, to regain it at a later date. This is stage IIIA, 350-300 B.C. Here it is not a matter of the singers accompanying the investiture of the ark but of perpetual service to it; and the David who once supervised the ceremony of installation stands as perpetual supervisor of those who serve it.

It is naturally the praise hymn of vv. 8-36a that has attracted the most comment. Not only has ChrH taken excerpts from three well-known psalms; he has in places altered the wording and the internal arrangement (see Watson, 2.7, 3.7, 5.6, 7.3 on vv. 13, 19, 29, 31, 37). J. A. Loader ("Redaction and Function") would correct the sequence to read 30a, 31b-30b, 31a-32a, 32b-33a, 33b, giving us the structure: Stanza A, vv. 8-22; Stanza B, vv. 23-33b; Stanza C, vv. 34-36a (see his chart on p. 71). The common, unifying theme is "Israel among the nations." Subthemes are: A, "The preservation of Israel among the nations"; B, "The universal acknowledgment of the God of Israel"; C, "Tense relations between Israel and the hostile nations." Of course, these three stanzas are equivalent to Ps 105:1-15; 96:1-13a; and 106:1, 47-48, extracted by ChrH for his purposes. He uses the first citation solely to prepare for vv. 16ff., breaking off his citation where it leaves the theme "Israel among the nations." The citation from Psalm 96 is the heart of the matter, extolling the particularism within which ChrH and his community operate. This is contemporized, and to the prayer of Psalm 106 ChrH adds the particularistic prayer of v. 35. The overall viewpoint is that Israel must remain the chosen, a fact which the heathen nations will be forced to acknowledge. The hymn ends in a prayer, in which Yahweh is asked to save Israel from the surrounding enemies. T. C. Butler, who has made a similar analysis of this psalm, brings out the intriguing thought that this is propaganda suitable to the last postexilic period. Political conditions had made the strident nationalism of the psalms a practical impossibility, hence ChrH arranges and adapts the preexilic poems as vehicles for bolstering the people's faith that some day they may yet become what the psalms say they are.

Bibliography

M. J. Buss, "The Psalms of Asaph and Korah," *JBL* 82 (1963) 382-92; T. C. Butler, "A Forgotten Passage from a Forgotten Era," *VT* 28 (1978) 142-50; J. A. Loader, "Redaction and Function of the Chronistic 'Psalm of David,'" *OTWSA* 19 (1976) 69-75.

REPORT OF THE DYNASTIC PROMISE, 17:1-27

Text

Alongside treatments in commentaries, synoptic comparisons, and special studies (e.g., J. A. Bewer, "Textkritischen Bemerkungen zum Alten Testament," in *Festschrift für A. Bertholet* [ed. W. Baumgartner, et al.; Tübingen: Mohr, 1950] 74-75; S. Merenef in *AJSL* [1936-37] 47), a thoroughly exhaustive text analysis has been prepared by H. van den Bussche. Lemke ("Synoptic Studies," 40-46) attributes divergences from Samuel to ChrH's ideology, rather than to disturbances in the original texts.

Structure

Because this chapter follows 2 Samuel 7 with a high level of verbal fidelity, there has been none to deny it to ChrH. It is that very same trait, however, that has enabled readers to compare Samuel and Chronicles and observe ChrH's late and distinctive style (so S. R. Driver, "Speeches"). Yet Watson (5.4, 6.2, 7.9, 10.1, 10.3, p. 200 n. 3) has identified touches that might be called antiquarian in vv. 5, 12, 13, 16, 18, 26, and 27 (cf. Kropat, 77, on v. 27b). No reasonable person expects ChrH to make no changes (cf. von Rad, *Geschichtsbild*, 123-24; Williamson, "Eschatology"; Botterweck, 421-23). T. Willi has a field day in demonstrating ChrH's various types of "exegesis": vv. 1 and 10 show normalizing (p. 143), v. 11 is a specification (p. 105), vv. 12-13 show historicizing (p. 143), vv. 17-19, 22 show theologizing (pp. 130, 154), v. 21 is conjectural (p. 117), v. 23 is another case of normalizing (p. 147), and v. 14 promotes the interests of the theocracy (p. 131). In spite of this evidence that ChrH does go his own way, linguistically and ideologically, the commentators often seem bent on making this passage conform to Samuel, sometimes through conjectural restoration, but usually through straight textual criticism. Lemke (pp. 40-46) finds little basis for testing the relative merits of the two texts because ChrH is so obvious in the explication of his personal ideology. He and most scholars would find van den Bussche far from the track in claiming that ChrH is original in omitting Samuel's reference to Solomon's chastisement, 2 Sam 7:14. Nothing can overthrow the argument that ChrH could have had this in his *Vorlage* but passed it by because it denigrates his super-hero, Solomon.

The outline we propose is inevitably the same that would apply to 2 Samuel 7 (see De Vries, "Prophetic Address," 18-20). The three main divisions are determined by the change of setting. Scene I has David getting approval for a temple from Nathan; scene II finds Nathan receiving a revelation in bed, which he delivers to David in the morning; scene III has David sitting (*yšb*) before Yahweh doing nothing but making one long, convoluted prayer. Since v. 1 begins with a circumstantial clause, *wayěhî ka'ăšer yāšab dāwîd běbêtô,* "Now it happened, just as David was sitting/dwelling in his house," a deliberate inclusio with the *yšb* of v. 16 is probably intended—though of course the inclusio is already in Samuel. David apparently puts emphasis on this sitting or dwelling, for he calls Nathan's attention to it in his opening speech, v. 1. The ark's situation, next mentioned, is expressed in the dependent noun clause that follows. Nathan's imperative to go ahead is based on a truth for which there is now abundant evidence, viz., that "God is with you" (v. 3). We note that Samuel's reference to David's enemies being subdued is repressed, for, as ChrH intends to tell it, there are still many enemies for David to subdue.

The second scene presents the temporal phrase "that night" in good classical style. Here appears the one major break within the narrative. Unexpectedly, a revelation occurs, jarring in its abruptness, putting a sudden end to David's plans and turning completely around the questions, (1) who shall build the "house," and (2) what kind of "house" is it going to be. The recipient of this revelation is David, of course; Nathan is only the messenger. Yahweh's speech is concerned first to correct David's faulty (and perhaps egocentric) notion that Yahweh wants a house, i.e., temple; Yahweh never had one, and he does not need one now. The second part of Yahweh's message, beginning in v. 7, says that Yahweh does want a "house" after all, but that Yahweh and the man he shall choose will build it. Here we begin to flounder in double entendre. This divinely built "house" is a dynasty, the first scion of which is to build God his "house," i.e., temple. Each part of the revelation, vv. 4-6 and 7-14, respectively, is presented as a separate oracle introduced by the MESSENGER FORMULA that was to become commonplace in classical prophetism. Thus the revelation contains two separate messages which are joined in v. 7 by the expression wĕ'attâ, "so now," relating the second message logically rather than temporally to the first (De Vries, *Yesterday, Today and Tomorrow*, 41-42). In v. 4 ChrH's emphatic prohibition, lō' 'attâ tibneh-lî, "It is not you who shall build me," replaces Samuel's rhetorical question: "Shall you indeed build?" In vv. 5-6 a grounding clause beginning with kî underscores the foregoing prohibition. This clause affirms the fact that, since the exodus, Yahweh has been perfectly content to go about from tent to tent (v. 5) and then (v. 6) launches out into a rhetorical question asking whether he, Yahweh, has ever complained about not having a temple while travelling about with the judges (šōpĕṭîm; not šibāṭîm, "tribes," as in LXX^BA, Samuel).

Thus the first message concludes with a historical review. Back to back with it, and joined by wĕ'attâ, is a second historical review, but one that pertains to Yahweh's previous dealings with David (vv. 7-8). A foremost 'ănî stresses that in David's own experience Yahweh has always taken the initiative. An important problem is whether to keep all the verbs in v. 8, and also those in v. 9, in the past tense, or to identify a shift to the future in v. 8's wē'āśîtî. But wā'ehyeh and wā'akrît may be read as wāw-consecutive imperfects, putting all of Yahweh's acts on David's behalf in the past tense. V. 8b, introduced by a perfect with wāw, ought not to be put into the future and made part of the promise because the promise to David actually begins with the imperfect with conjunctive wāw (wā'aggid) in v. 10b. But wĕ'āśîtî in v. 8b, if taken futuristically, cannot follow in proper syntax from the foregoing wāw-consecutive imperfects, so this clause must be taken resumptively, meaning that Yahweh's taking David, being with him, and cutting off his enemies has resulted in Yahweh's "making" him a name like those of the great ones of the earth.

The break between the past and the future has to come with wĕśamtî, "and I will appoint," because wĕlō' yirgaz 'ôd wĕlō'-yôsîpû bĕnê-'awlâ lĕballōtô has the simple imperfect, and because the comparative clause, "as formerly," and the temporal clause, "from the time when I appointed judges over Israel," contrast Israel's previous distress with the peace and prosperity that they shall now experience.

Although otherwise Yahweh speaks of himself in the first person, when his promise shifts to David in v. 10b he speaks of himself in the third person, but as subject of the action, retained to final position in the syntactical structure: wā'aggid *lāk ûbayit yibneh- lĕka yahweh,* "And I announce to you that also a house shall build for you Yahweh." This is obviously the point of highest emphasis. Perhaps Nathan is to be understood as shifting over for the moment to an objectifying form of speaking about God, but the stress is clearly on the fact that Yahweh, not David, will do the building. Immediately the text returns to first-person styling to explain that, once David is dead and gone, Yahweh will do the following: (1) raise up one of David's sons; (2) establish *(kûn)* his kingdom (v. 11). With emphatic *hû'* at the beginning of v. 12 and *'ănî* at the beginning of v. 13, Yahweh next specifies what each shall do for the other, and what their relationship (father-son) to each other shall be. Then Yahweh states that this appointive—rather, adoptive—prerogative that Yahweh intends to exercise will preclude the possibility that Yahweh might remove his *ḥesed,* "covenant fidelity," from this new king, as in the case of Saul. Dynastic continuity from David through Solomon is forever secure. Because *'md* (hiph.) means "appoint to an official position," we are to understand *bêtî* in v. 14, parallel to *malkûtî,* not as "my dynasty" but as "my temple." In other words, Yahweh appoints Solomon to two areas of supervision, the temple and the kingdom. This is to be *'ad-hā'ôlām,* implying that David's son will be the first of an unbroken line of kings like himself. Instrumental to all this happening is the climactic promise, *wĕkis'ô yihyeh nākôn 'ad-'ôlām.* The imperfect of *hyh* with *nākôn* implies that his throne will exist in the distant, and not just the immediate, future.

The reader gets the impression of extreme wordiness in the promise to David, but ChrH is simply repeating verbatim much of what he finds in Samuel, and many critics agree that DtrH has expanded the original narrative in 2 Sam 7:13-15, as also in 2 Sam 7:22-24. Quite unmotivated, both in the Samuel and in the Chronicles text, is the final scene in which "King David" makes a long, involved prayer for what he has just been promised. The theology of whining about for what God has already freely given is highly questionable, to say the least. The writer's own explanation is that the original story in Samuel is a prophet legend in which Yahweh promises David a permanent hold on the kingdom by assuring dynastic perpetuity, rather than by allowing him to glorify himself by building a temple. To this a redactor within David's court has added the aimless, anxiety-ridden prayer.

The independent origin of this material is certainly suggested by its strong preference for the divine title *'ădōnāy yahweh,* 2 Sam 7:18, 19 (twice), 20, 22, 28, 29. Naturally, ChrH has obscured much of this, preserving it only in 1 Chr 17:16, 17. If he had so desired, ChrH could have omitted this prayer, and if he had done so, it would not have been because he was unhappy about its structure or its ideology. He does in fact use it, and for the probable reason that he was delighted to be able to present David as such a pious, prayerful fellow, supporting so strongly the divine intentions for the permanence of his dynasty. "King David's" approach is lowly ("Who am I . . .?"). "My house" now means David's family. The rhetorical question is made more rhetorical by contrasting Yahweh's saving acts, previous and future. David is honored in Yahweh's promises, and David can account for this honor solely out of two possible motivations: (1) "thy servant's sake," i.e., free, un-merited grace; and (2) "thy own heart"—i.e., the hidden impulses of God's own design. V. 20 has a unique parallelism: "there is none like thee; there is none be-side thee." In other words, this is a confession of Yahweh's incomparability along-side a confession of his solitary uniqueness (cf. the first and second commandments of the Decalogue).

Next David rehearses, in rhetorical-question form, the uniqueness of Yahweh's people, for whom Yahweh has performed numberless acts of might (v. 21), entering with them into a covenant (v. 22), by which they became his people *'ad-'ôlām* and Yahweh became their God. Having recited these remarkable deeds of divine grace, David prays that on the basis of them *(wĕ'attâ)* three things may be permitted to happen: (1) let the dynastic promise be confirmed (*'mn*, niph.) perpetually (*'ad-'ôlām);* (2) let action be according to the divine word; and (3) let the divine name be confirmed (*'mn*, niph.) and glorified according to the confession "Yahweh Sebaoth the God of Israel *is* Israel's God," assuring that the "house" (dynasty) of David will truly be established (*kûn*, niph.) before him (vv. 22-23). In retrospect of vv. 11-14, David now makes his actual request (vv. 25-27). David has found courage to pray it because God has revealed *(glh)* that he intended to build a "house" for him. That this is definitely the dynasty and not the temple is certain from v. 27, where David asks Yahweh to bless it in terms of perpetual survival. He asks this on the basis of the divine promise (v. 26), and confesses (v. 27b) that what Yahweh blesses is blessed *'ad-'ôlām,* "forever."

Genre

The main genre is REPORT, but a special prophetic genre, PROPHETIC COMMISSION REPORT, appears in vv. 3-15. V. 4 has our second occurrence of the PROHIBITION (cf. 11:5). In vv. 5 and 7-8 we encounter the genre HISTORICAL REVIEW, which is the rehearsing of salient facts in the past experience of Israel or an individual person, closely associated with the (→) testimony and the (→) farewell speech, generally with a strong parenetical concern. V. 6 echoes an imaginary COMPLAINT, which is a statement describing personal or communal distress or injustice ("Why have you not built me a house of cedar?"). Vv. 9-14 contain the genre PROMISE, in which the maker's word assures a gift or the performance of a desired action. V. 15, the narrative conclusion to scene II, paraphrases the revelation that Nathan has received for David in the form of an OFFICIAL REPORT, which ordinarily presents in literal and official form information or a message, duly authorized and dispatched by the sender; our author's summary lumps the entire report under the headings "words" and "vision." Vv. 16-27 contain our first example of the genre PRAYER, which is any communication to God in direct, second-person address. V. 16b is a CONFESSION OF GUILT, a statement in which one acknowledges his guilt, discloses his actions, or explains his circumstances. Another genre is v. 20's DESCRIPTION OF YAHWEH, which is a laudatory declaration briefly setting forth one or many of Yahweh's attributes or actions; it compares closely with the (→) incomparability statement, which pertains generally to human beings or earthly things. V. 24 contains a PRAISE SPEECH, usually a brief but highly formulaic utterance offering praise and thanksgiving to God, but here simply confessing, "Yahweh Sebaoth, the God of Israel, is (indeed) Israel's God." The end of v. 27 has the DOXOLOGY, no description of Yahweh (see above), but a pithy, highly lyrical acclamation of the divine glory (*'attâ yahweh bĕraktā ûmĕbōrāk lĕ'ôlām,* "Thou, O Yahweh, hast blessed and art forever blest!").

Among stereotyped formulas we have the following: the ASSISTANCE FORMULA in vv. 2, 8; the MESSENGER FORMULA in vv. 4, 7; the WORD FORMULA in vv. 3, 7; the RHETORICAL QUESTION in v. 6; the ADOPTION FORMULA in v. 13; the SELF-

ABASEMENT FORMULA in v. 16; and the COVENANT FORMULA in v. 22. All but the first appear here for the first time. The WORD FORMULA is found frequently in prophetic revelations in the form "The word of Yahweh came," and the like. The HERALD FORMULA is used even more frequently, always in the form "Thus says Yahweh." The ADOPTION FORMULA, based on Egyptian models copied for the divine protocol in Ps 2:7, is applied in 1 Chr 17:13 par. 2 Sam 7:14; 1 Chr 28:5 to Solomon as Yahweh's "son." The verb is no longer *yld*, "beget," as in the psalm, but *hyh*, "be/become," or *bḥr*, "choose." There is no notion of actual generation. Yahweh *adopts* the new king; thus it is the intimate mutuality of the relationship that is stressed.

The SELF-ABASEMENT FORMULA makes the speaker less significant or less worthy than he actually is because he measures himself over against some greater and more worthy person. The COVENANT FORMULA, as seen in v. 22, expresses a mutuality similar to that of the (→) adoption formula, being two-sided in expressing that Yahweh is Israel's God, while Israel is Yahweh's people.

Setting and Intention

Although it is necessary to disregard the role of this material in the setting it has been given in Samuel, it does have a somewhat similar role here in ChrH. There it serves to bind together the Davidic accession history, with the ark story attached, and the succession history that is about to be presented (2 Samuel 9 is a Dtr intrusion). Here it makes an ideological, not a literary, link: David is secure on his throne and the ark has been installed, but this chapter is needed as a prognosis, both of what is to happen with David's throne once he has passed away, and with the Jerusalem shrine which David has only begun to prepare. As in Samuel, *bēt*, "house," is deliberately ambivalent, carrying both the meaning "temple" and the meaning "dynasty." Though Yahweh's oracle emphatically corrects David's initial proposal for the former, promising rather the latter, an innuendo is carried throughout to the effect that the temple goes along with the dynasty. ChrH cannot think of a reconstructed, ideal Israel without both of them together.

In our structural analysis we have remarked about the apparent senselessness of having David make a long, convoluted prayer for the divine blessing and for dynastic perpetuity when the oracle had already promised this to him. Samuel apparently does not blink at this, but for ChrH it may have had some special sense. All his genealogies and histories lie outside the linear time orientation, anyway, and the fulfillment that was expected for the kingdom of Judah, having been wasted in the misconduct of her kings, is now prayerfully awaited in the ideal Israel that he contemplates for those restored from exile. We can say it simply: the promises have become promises again; the ideal future is still the ideal future. Hence what David does in first receiving the promise, and then praying that he may receive it, is the exact model of how Israel possesses the divine promise but must ever and again pray to possess it. As ChrH experiences it, the temple is again with Israel, but not in its full Solomonic glory. Just so, the line of David survives, but not in full possession of its regal power. ChrH does not expect God to repeat the promise once given through Nathan, for all the misconduct of the kingly line has not rendered it void. There has been a long, harsh exile from the land, yet God has brought his people back, and among them are members of the Davidic family.

Under the conditions of Persian and/or Hellenistic imperialism, the promised throne must still have some meaning. Since the precise realization of that promise remains far from clear, David's prayer of vv. 16-27 gains an even greater urgency. One thing is certain: the Solomonic temple must play a vital role in the real and final restoration of that kingship—perhaps not so much in architectural splendor as in the perfection of the liturgy and the service of the clergy that have been devoted to serve it.

It would be quite impossible to discuss the numerous and varied interpretations that scholars have attempted to apply to Nathan's promise for the Davidic dynasty. Many go astray in one way or another. It is no better with H. Kruse's article ("David's Covenant"), for his hypothetical reconstruction of an "original" oracle underlying both biblical versions fails to assess what both Samuel and ChrH intended in the renderings they have offered. It can scarcely be disputed that Solomon is intended in the words "He shall build a house for me," in 1 Chr 17:12a, carrying out the divine initiative declared in v. 10. The important difference between Samuel's expectation and that of ChrH is that the former gives the promise directly to David (2 Sam 7:16, wĕne'man bêtĕkā ûmamlaktĕkā 'ad-'ôlām lĕpāneykā, kis'ăkā yihyeh nākôn 'ad-'ôlām, "And assured is thy house and thy kingship forever, thy throne will endure forever"; 1 Chr 17:14, wĕha'ămadtîhû bĕbêtî ûbĕmalkûtî 'ad-'ôlām, wĕkis'ô yihyeh nākôn 'ad-'ôlām, "And I will appoint him over my house and over my realm forever, and his throne will endure forever"). For ChrH, the promise is for Solomon, not for David; but, most importantly, the "house," whether the temple or the dynasty, belongs to Yahweh and not to David. Thus, whatever may actually happen to the lineage of David, a greater King preserves his proprietary right to the institution of the kingship and to the temple that shall be built. The Davidic line may somehow perish, and even the restoration temple may be destroyed, yet the God of Israel will remain. Permanence is the main point, hence the repeated use of 'ad-'ôlām. But real permanence resides only in God and his promises.

All is expressed in the closing doxology: "For what thou, O Yahweh, hast blest is blest forever" (v. 27). While paraphrasing the royal promise from Nathan's oracle, contemplating that every appearance was against the likelihood of a Davidic scion ever again actually taking the throne, the words that ChrH must have clung to most confidently were those that directly reflected the character of God: "I will not take my ḥesed from him." Everything else aside, God's covenantal fidelity was what mattered the most (v. 13)—that and the promise made specially for Israel as a nation (v. 9), promising that he would assign them a place (māqôm), where they might be planted (nṭ'), so that they might dwell (škn) in a place they could call their own and be wasted by violent men no more. Even more than the symbol of Davidic rule, the forlorn residents of Yehud (Persian name for Judah) needed territory and security, benefits that could no longer be obtained by their meager weaponry, but only as gifts secured by Yahweh's promise.

Bibliography

R. L. Braun, "Solomonic Apologetic in Chronicles," *JBL* 92 (1973) 503-16; S. R. Driver, "The Speeches in Chronicles," *Exp* 1 (1895) 241-56, 286-308; H. Gese, "Der Davidbund und die Zionserwählung," *ZTK* 61 (1964) 10-26; T. Ishida, *The Royal Dynasties in Ancient*

Israel (BZAW 142; Berlin: Töpelmann, 1977) 81-117; S. Japhet, "The Ideology of the Book of Chronicles and Its Place in Biblical Thought" (Hebr.) (Diss., Hebrew University, 1973); H. Kruse, "David's Covenant," *VT* 35 (1985) 139-64; T. N. D. Mettinger, *King and Messiah: The Civil and the Sacral Legitimation of the Israelite Kings* (ConB 8; Lund: Gleerup, 1976); E. von Nordheim, "König und Tempel," *VT* 27 (1977) 449-53; H. van den Bussche, "Le texte de la prophétie de Nathan sur la dynastie davidique (I Samuel VII–I Chronicles XVII)," *ETL* 24 (1948) 354-94; H. G. M. Williamson, "The Dynastic Oracle in the Books of Chronicles," in *Sefer Yitshaq Aryeh Zeligman* III (ed. A. Rofé; Jerusalem: Rubinstein, 1983) 305-18; idem, "Eschatology in Chronicles," *TynBul* 28 (1977) 115-54.

ACCOUNT OF WARFARE, 18:1–20:8

Structure and Genre

I. Reports of victories and their results	18:1-17
II. Historical story: the Ammonite-Syrian war	19:1–20:3
III. Report of duels with the Philistines	20:4-8

This is an ACCOUNT made up of three clearly defined subunits, each of which is introduced by a temporal expression to produce a temporal sequence. Thus *wayĕhî 'aḥărê-kēn*, "And it happened after this," introduces 18:1, 19:1, and 20:4, reproducing materials taken from 2 Samuel 8; 10–12; and 21. The various incidents have been arranged to depict victories on the north, east, south, and west. Some commentaries have claimed that ChrH was interested in repeating this material merely for the purpose of showing how David collected the rich treasures that he would be giving for the temple-building project. While that is indeed one of his purposes, military security for the nation of which David had just become king is another of his considerations. Diverse as this material is, it is united in theme. The abruptness with which the story of acquiring Ornan's threshing floor is introduced in 1 Chronicles 21 emphasizes that our battle complex adheres together and serves as a bridge to that new subject.

Setting and Intention

1 Chronicles 17 already communicates the notion that God has no destiny for David as a person except to pass the kingdom on to Solomon. Thus 1 Chronicles 17 lies at a watershed. This is not how it had seemed in the earlier chapters, where David rises to the kingship and then installs the ark, ultimately to be the most sacred item in the temple, at the same time laying down strict regulations to guide the Levites in attendance on that ark. But the very provisionality and portability of the ark should have warned David that his own kingship was provisional and temporary—temporary not in the sense of time, but in terms of its bearing less than lasting significance in God's grand design. As we say, 1 Chronicles 17 designedly takes what had been David's promise in Samuel and gives it to Solomon. David becomes an abettor and not a fulfiller. Clearly, his rise to kingship, the capture of Jerusalem, and the installation of the ark prepared for the kingship of Solomon and all the kings descended from his loins, with the installation of Yahweh in all his glory in the temple.

159

We need to keep this in mind in the present account of warfare. We have mentioned two of ChrH's obvious themes, but let us not wonder at how closely he sticks to his *Vorlage* in hurrying on to the new topic of the threshing floor. This is because he is not interested in the subject in itself, and would be wasting no time to tell it, except that the themes of riches and protection are needed as background for the installation of Solomon and the construction of the temple. Here too, it may be added, ChrH will find material to justify his portrait of David as a "man of blood," destined to be used as the reason why Yahweh prevented him from building the temple and gave this privilege instead to Solomon. The model of military security comes in for elaborate use in the way in which ChrH will tell of defensive wars to the north, south, east, and west (cf. Welten, *Geschichte,* 166-72), revealing the anxiety which the restoration community felt toward hostile neighbors. To inspire ideal Israel in defending its little piece of "Israel," these wars of David would have had typological significance. Yet David is restricted to the secular realm, while Solomon becomes the paragon of the sacral. How ironic, then, the shedding of blood that David did! It did good in protecting the boundaries of ideal Israelite territory, but disqualified him for supervising the realm of the sacral.

I. REPORTS OF VICTORIES AND THEIR RESULTS, 18:1-17

Structure

A special discussion is devoted to this section in Botterweck ("Eigenart," 423-26). The material is taken almost verbatim from 2 Sam 8:1-18, Dtr's summary of David's warfare drawn by Dtr from annalistic sources available to him. There are some interesting textual divergences between Samuel and Chronicles. Lemke ("Synoptic Studies," 47) considers the omission of David's harshness to the Moabites, as reported in Samuel, a pro-David gesture on the part of ChrH, but he views the latter as having a superior text in v. 4 (see also Ap-Thomas, "Numerical Poser"). Lemke (p. 48) lays emphasis on the fact that the longer LXX text is preserved in Qumran and Josephus. It is different in v. 8b, where Samuel states simply that the booty of bronze was dedicated to Yahweh, whereas ChrH states specifically that it was used in Solomon's temple for the sea, the pillars, and the bronze utensils. Willi (p. 174) attributes this longer text to ChrH as one of his "reflections." To accept this is better than to go along with Galling (ATD) in removing it as a late gloss; it is in any event supported by *Basileiōn* and Josephus, which may be reading a longer Hebrew text lost in Samuel but preserved in ChrH, who certainly has lent it his styling.

The section of battle reports concerning Philistia, Moab, and Zobah is straight narrative, with no discourse. The structure of each report is similar, but with increasing content. The fighting is not described; all we have is the verb (three times) *wayyak*, "and he smote," followed by *wayiqqaḥ*, "and he seized" (v. 1), by *wayyihyû*, "and they became" (v. 2), or by *wayyilkōd*, "and he captured" (v. 4). In v. 1 it is a city and its villages that were seized. In v. 2 (ignoring the terrorizing execution described in Samuel), it is a matter of forcing the Moabites into vassalage and putting them under tribute, according to Willi (p. 117) ChrH's humane but conjectural substitution. In vv. 3-6a ChrH is still resorting to conjecture, according to Willi (p. 120); ironically, David subjects Hadadezer to defeat just as he journeys to his Euphrates boundary to set up his proprietory stele. When the Damascenes come to help, David slays twenty-two thousand (likely an exaggeration) of them, placing garrisons in their land and laying them under heavy tribute. The unity of this report of three victories is underscored by the theologizing EPITOME of v. 6b (see v. 13b): *wayyôša' yahweh lĕdāwîd bĕkōl 'ăšer hālāk*, "And Yahweh gave victory to David everywhere he marched." This is meant to summarize what has just been reported, and does not suggest that David continued his aggressions after these campaigns had been completed (→ EPITOME).

Verses 7-11 constitute another of ChrH's inclusios: booty/Tou's embassage-treasure. All is in narrative form, but the stress is on the precious objects. The account of booty reads like a checklist, with the two kinds of precious metals, gold and bronze (Samuel adds silver and gold to the bronze list in v. 8). The gold comes from Hadadezer, the bronze from Tibhath and Cun; each is alike destined for the temple that Solomon will build.

With the embassage of Tou comes a new movement in the narrative. Here is a willing ally who congratulates David on Hadadezer's defeat and presents gifts of gold, silver, and bronze (Willi, 143: a normalization to the list of v. 8). This is tribute, not booty, but the coming temple needs them both. V. 12 lists five hostile nations who are coerced into this project: Edom, Moab, Ammon, Philistia, Amalek. The mention of Ammon is proleptic of ch. 19, but the inclusion of Amalek is un-motivated in this account.

The Edomites, ancestral enemies of Israel, come in for rough treatment in the attached battle report of vv. 12-13. Eighteen thousand (another exaggeration?) are slain in the valley of Salt, where they had perhaps taken the path of aggression against Israel. But who is the Israelite conqueror? Samuel says David, but this may be a normalization to the context; Ps 60:2 (*RSV* superscription) says Joab; ChrH says Abishai (we have seen in 11:20 that ChrH favors Abishai rather than Joab, and he may be usurping Joab's glory here, so that the original hero was Joab after all). After this massive defeat David puts garrisons in Edom and lays vassalage upon them. The conclusion is a repetition of the epitome of v. 6b, stating that this was all from Yahweh.

As in Samuel, a list of high officials is added to the summary of David's reign (vv. 14-17), not because there was any temporal or logical connection to the victories just recorded, but because of Dtr's drive to complete his account of this king. Starting out this section with the narrative verb *wayyimlōk* makes it appear as if David's reigning came as a consequence of the victories that Yahweh gave him—an impression that runs contrary to chs. 11–12, and is of course false. Yet there is some logic in this arrangement, for the ideal state of monarchy as here depicted would never have been possible without the prior securing of peace out-side his borders. The fact of David's ruling is stated (v. 14a), and then his major and all-inclusive duty: *wayĕhî 'ōśeh mišpāṭ ûṣĕdāqâ*, "and he was/became the one administering justice and establishing just laws." The officials who assisted him are listed in a ROSTER, as follows (note the chiasmus):

Joab ben Zeruiah	a	Over the army
Jehoshaphat ben Ahilud	b	Recorder
Zadok ben Ahitub	c	Priest
Ahimelech ben Abiathar	c'	Priest
Shavsha	b'	Secretary
Benaiah ben Jehoiada	a'	Over Cherethites and Pelethites

2 Sam 8:18 adds: "David's sons—priests," but this so offends ChrH that he offers a substitute, "and David's sons were the chief officials in the service of the king" (*ûbĕnê-dāwîd hāri'šōnîm lĕyad hammelek*). On the list as a whole, with special em-phasis on the apparently Egyptian secretary (without patronym), cf. Cody ("Titre égyptien," 381ff.), Mettinger (*Solomonic State Officials*, 7). Lemke ("Synoptic Studies," 53-56) suggests that the Chronicles text may be, after all, correct. Since everyone else on this roster is named, it does seem odd that the "sons of David" are

listed anonymously. It seems advisable to keep them off the roster as such, reading v. 17b as a concluding qualification: "But David's sons (remained) the chief persons at the hand of the king"—that is, his intimate advisors and associates.

Genre

The main genre is REPORT, including the BATTLE REPORT at vv. 1-6 and vv. 12-13. Typical examples of the CASUALTY REPORT are seen at vv. 5, 12. We are to think of these as founded on an OFFICIAL REPORT coming from one engaged in the fighting. One prominent feature is an unbounded exaggeration of enemy losses, as here. Tens or even hundreds of thousands are reported slain in battle. The CASUALTY REPORT is placed at the end of the BATTLE REPORT, and as such it regularly has an epitomizing function (→ EPITOME), summing up the action, and accordingly the function of the entire affair. The time expression *bayyôm hahû'*, "on that day," frequently found in the early texts, is missing here and is usually ignored in ChrH's battle reports (→ CASUALTY REPORT).

As has been said, vv. 6b, 13b have the EPITOME in identical form. Like the CASUALTY REPORT, this form stands at the end of a narrative; its purpose is to distill the qualitative significance of the event in question. Another clearly defined genre is the ROSTER of vv. 15-17. The genre NAME LIST is a functional part of the ROSTER. Another sort of LIST is seen in v. 10b.

Setting and Intention

For these elements, see the discussion under this heading in the parent pericope above, "Account of Warfare," 18:1–20:8.

Bibliography

D. R. Ap-Thomas, "A Numerical Poser," *JNES* 2 (1943) 198-200; A. Cody, "Le titre égyptien et le nom propre du scribe de David," *RB* 72 (1965) 381-93; T. N. D. Mettinger, *Solomonic State Officials. A Study of the Civil Government Officials in the Israelite Monarchy* (ConB 5; Lund: Gleerup, 1971).

II. HISTORICAL STORY: THE AMMONITE-SYRIAN WAR, 19:1–20:3

Structure

A. The provocation	19:1-5
1. Succession formula: a new king in Ammon	1
2. David's embassage	2a
a. Resolve of loyalty	2aα
b. Dispatch of messengers	2aβ
3. Mistreatment by the Ammonites	2b-5
a. Arrival of the ambassadors	2b
b. Counselors plan suspicion	3

All the episodes of this story are closely knit together, in terms of both time sequence and topographical location. The introductory transition from the list of David's officials in 18:15-17, which hardly advances the narrative from 18:12-13, Abishai's victory over Edom, is *wayĕhî 'aḥărê-kēn,* "and after these things." The first episode, the provocation, takes place in Jerusalem, then in Ammon, and again in Jerusalem (19:1-4). The second episode, the preliminaries, has David in Jerusalem, the Israelite troops confronting the troops of the Ammonite-Syrian alliance outside Rabbah, and Joab's return to Jerusalem following the withdrawal of these troops (vv. 6-15). The third episode is climactic: it tells of the entrance of a famous general with powerful allies on the Syrian side and David himself on the Israelite side (vv. 16-19). All this takes place in a first year; a second year is introduced by the phrase *wayĕhî lĕʿēt tĕšûbat haššānâ lĕʿēt ṣēʾt hammĕlākîm,* "And at the time of the turning of the year, at the time when kings venture out" (20:1). This fourth episode is anticlimactic; it tells of the capture of Rabbah, the taking of spoils and enslavement of captives, with a final return to Jerusalem. Samuel and Chronicles differ somewhat in details, here and previously in the story, but it appears that David is absent from the actual combat while present for the taking of spoils.

The close dependence of Chronicles on Samuel in this passage gives Willi another opportunity to dissect ChrH's exegetical methods, as follows: v. 3, explication (p. 140; cf. Watson, 10.3); v. 4, generalizing (p. 100) (*mipśāʿâ,* "hidden parts," for Samuel *šĕtôt,* "buttocks"; cf. L. Köhler, 228); v. 5, explication (p. 103); vv. 6-7a, conjecture (p. 120); vv. 7b, 9, generalizing (p. 101); vv. 16-19, conjecture (pp. 98-99); v. 18, normalizing (p. 143); v. 19, theologizing (p. 130); 20:1, specification (p. 108) and normalizing (p. 143). Watson finds more archaic elements in Chronicles at v. 3 (10.3) and v. 13 (10.1). Textual matters of moment are the following: since Joab and Abishai are to render each other mutual assistance while attacking the separate Syrian and Ammonite forces (19:10ff.), it does not make sense that the Syrians should be positioned so far away from the capital as Medeba, hence the latter name should be changed to read *mê-rabbâ,* "the waters of Rabbah." *wayyaʿărōk ʾălēhem* in v. 17a, not read by LXX[A] or Vg., should be removed as a dittography from the following clause. As Horn explains (170-80), what David places upon his head according to 20:2 is the precious stone, not the heavy golden crown of the king of Ammon. The abrupt introduction of David at this point can be explained from the fact that it is just here that the Samuel *Vorlage* is picked up again after having been abandoned in order to omit the Bathsheba incident, which ChrH omitted because it was unflattering to his hero David. The statement in 20:3b, "Then David and all the people returned to Jerusalem" (also in Samuel), brings the king back to Jerusalem, where the next narrative about him, ch. 21, is to take place.

Genre

This is the first time we have seen the genre HISTORICAL STORY. This is the self-contained narrative recounting a particular event with more detail and sophistication than a simple (→) report. There is a rudimentary plot running from a cause of tension to its resolution (→ STORY), along with dialogue and imaginative touches. A familiar genre, BATTLE REPORT, appears at 19:14-15a, 16-19; 20:1-2. 19:1 has the SUCCESSION FORMULA. David's instructions to the ambassadors in 19:5 constitute a COMMAND, while Joab's instruction to Abishai in 19:12 is an ORDER. V. 13 belongs to the genre SUMMONS TO WAR, including the call to fight and a motive of resignation to the will of God concerning the outcome: "May Yahweh do what seems good to him." At v. 18 we see the genre CASUALTY REPORT with its typical exaggerated count of the dead.

Setting and Intention

Apart from ChrH's fondness for huge numbers (19:7, 18), the main ideological difference to observe in ChrH's alteration of this passage is the greater role he gives to David. In the provocation scene Samuel/Chronicles keep David in Jerusalem. In 1 Chr 19:8 David receives intelligence of the mustering of his enemies (cf. 2 Sam 10:6), not of their tactical movements, as reported in v. 9 (so ChrH; but v. 9, adding the allies, contradicts v. 7). David has no further direct role in this scene. It ends indecisively as the Syrians flee, the Ammonites hole up in their walled city, and Joab returns to Jerusalem. His return is meant as the direct transition to the climactic battle episode. Rather pointedly, David is brought into the fighting to counterbalance the appearance of the notorious Syrian general, Shophach, whose coming is reported to David in v. 16. The texts of Samuel and Chronicles contradict each other in v. 17: Samuel reports that the Syrians attack David, but ChrH reports that David took the initiative in attacking the Syrians. In v. 19, the defeated Syrians sue for peace from David (not "Israel": Samuel). In 20:1 it is expressly stated that David remains in Jerusalem; Samuel has a statement that David sends Joab, but this is omitted in ChrH. Samuel has Joab seizing the crown, but in 1 Chr 20:2 it is David himself who does this. As has been explained, this inconcinnity is due to ChrH's omission of the Bathsheba incident.

The statement *wattĕhî 'al-rō'š dāwîd* is not to be translated "And it was placed on David's head" *(RSV)*, as though David was adorned with this trophy right there on the battlefield, but "And it was (eventually/indefinitely) on David's head," i.e., made part of his crown. David's forced labor imposed on the Ammonite captives is surely to be understood according to the text of 2 Sam 12:31, avoiding the quite incomprehensible and entirely unmotivated "sawing" of human flesh reported in Chronicles. In 1 Chr 20:3b, "Thus did David to all the cities of the Ammonites" is added to the received text in order to indicate that the entire nation, not just the capital city, was forced to suffer the consequences of this defeat. Unquestionably, the greater role given David in this ChrH version has the intention of underscoring the portrait of him as a "man of blood."

Bibliography

S. H. Horn, "The Crown of the King of the Ammonites," *AUSS* 11 (1973) 170-80 (plates 17-20); L. Köhler, "Hebräische Vokabeln III.2," *ZAW* 58 (1940-41) 228.

III. REPORT OF DUELS WITH THE PHILISTINES, 20:4-8

Structure

A. Exploit report: Sibbecai against Sippai	4
1. Warfare at Gezer	4a
2. Victory	4b
B. Exploit report: Elhanan against Lahmi	5
1. Renewed warfare	5a

A transitional *wayĕhî 'aḥărêkēn,* "and it happened after this," shows that this report of combats with Philistine heroes is part of the "Account of Warfare," chs. 18–20. What is told here is not so much battles as duels. In each case, the situation is very similar to that of 1 Samuel 17. We are told in three cases that there was warfare against the Philistines, and in vv. 4 and 6 the place is named. Next we are told the name of the Israelite hero, after which comes the name of the Philistine champion, except in v. 6, where he remains nameless, but his unusual physical attributes (huge stature, twenty-four digits) are noted instead. It is said of this man that he was descended from the giants *(hārāpā'),* but this is said of all the Philistine champions in v. 8. Certainly the Lahmi of v. 5 must have been huge (Chronicles states that he was the brother of Goliath, but in the Samuel par. this is Goliath himself). The results are always favorable for the Israelites: in v. 4, after Sippai, one of the giants, is slain, all the Philistines are subdued *(kn');* Elhanan slays Lahmi; the giant who taunts Jonathan is slain by him. A summarizing conclusion tells us that (1) all the victims were descendants of the giants in Gath; (2) all were killed by David (either because he took credit for what his men did or as a dislocated tradition from the event of 1 Samuel 17) and his servants.

Genre

The main genre is REPORT, but this consists of the EXPLOIT REPORT in vv. 4-5 and an ANECDOTE in vv. 6-7.

Setting

This passage is a virtual word-for-word facsimile of 2 Sam 21:18-22, but the differences that do exist between Chronicles and Samuel have given rise to various efforts to emend our text. Lemke ("Synoptic Studies," 57) remains uncertain as to which text of v. 5 is authentic. In v. 6 Chronicles repeats the word *'eṣbĕ'ōtāyw* only once, where Samuel has it twice; ChrH is either abbreviating or has a defective text. In any event, one has to gather from the total, "twenty-four," that this means toes as well as fingers. Minor points in which Willi (pp. 100, 120) identifies ChrH's method in altering the Samuel *Vorlage* are at vv. 4, 5, and 6.

Intention

The Philistines were the first to attack David after his accession (ch. 12). He cannot be secure upon his throne until ChrH includes this old list of how even the greatest of their champions was subdued.

Bibliography

J. Botterweck, "Zur Eigenart der chronistischen Davidgeschichte," *TQ* 136 (1956) 416-27.

HISTORICAL STORY: OBTAINING THE TEMPLE SITE, 21:1-27

Text

Although the structure of this pericope follows that of 2 Samuel 24, Chronicles has a longer text and has idiosyncratic insertions of his own. The general trend among textual scholars has been to favor the Samuel text as the more original, explaining Chronicles as arising from its well-known theological motifs and from its familiar exegetical techniques. F. M. Cross has shown, however, that Chronicles approaches the old Palestinian text discovered among the documents of Qumran (*The Ancient Library of Qumran* [Garden City, NY: Doubleday, 1958]; on vv. 16, 20, cf. p. 294). Although Cross has not published all the material available, his pupil, W. E. Lemke, has commented extensively on the bearing of Cross's fragment ("Synoptic Studies," 62-74), emphasizing throughout his discussion that Chronicles' peculiarities may in many, or even most, cases represent the ancient text from which Samuel and Chronicles are drawn. With so little actual manuscript material at our disposal, Lemke is himself cautious in promoting a general priority for Chronicles, yet we do have evidence that ChrH is a document composed in its own right, and neither a jumbled reconstruction of Samuel-Kings nor a midrashic exegesis upon it (Willi).

Structure

I. David brings pestilence on Israel	1-15
A. The transgression	1-6
1. The king's instructions	1-4a
a. Satanic incitement	1
b. David's order	2
c. Disputation: Joab's remonstrance	3
1) Positive considerations	3a
a) Wish for divine increase	3aα
b) Rhetorical question: assurance of total loyalty	3aβ
2) Negative considerations	3b
a) Purposelessness	3bα
b) Peril of transgression	3bβ
d. David's truculence	4a
2. Joab's census	4b-6

168

The great theme of this chapter is the peril into which David's sin has put the Israelite people, and how his purchase of a site for the temple averts their complete destruction, thus identifying this site henceforward as the choice place for repentant prayer and divine absolution. The "angel of Yahweh" who figures in 2 Sam 24:16 as the instrument of destruction is given thematic importance in the playing out of the several episodes of the story as ChrH tells it. He comes in at the same point where he appears in Samuel, i.e., after David has committed his sin, and then taken one of the penalties God offers him. We are to think that David expected greater leniency in submitting himself and his people to three days of "the sword of Yahweh" (v. 13); he in fact avers that "his mercy is very great." The Lord's sword is in the hand of a destroying angel, who shows what a menace he is (1) by allowing a pestilence to slay seventy thousand Israelites (a large portion of those put under the census, v. 5), (2) by refraining from destroying Jerusalem only when Yahweh stays his hand, and (3) by standing, ready to destroy further, at the threshing floor of Ornan (v. 15). Here is the main point of division within the story, with the angel whom David's choice has summoned ready to carry further his bloody work.

The second main episode includes two effective actions on the part of David: a prayer for mercy (vv. 16-17), and sacrificial worship upon the altar that David erects on Ornan's threshing floor (vv. 18-26). Let us not overlook how v. 16 motivates these actions. Not until this moment, we are to assume, has he become fully aware of the potential consequences of the choice he has made. This comes when he lifts his eyes to see the angel, who, though waiting at the threshing floor, hovers aloft with sword drawn, pointing it toward Jerusalem. (The standing at the threshing floor and the standing between heaven and earth conflict unless we realize that the former concludes the first episode, pointing forward to the second episode, while the latter introduces David's prayer and subsequent actions.) David prays his prayer under this threat, and under this same threat he moves to build and sacrifice upon this new altar. This episode is concluded in v. 26 in the report that "Yahweh answered him with fire from heaven upon the altar of burnt offering" that he had constructed.

There is one more verse, but it stands structurally alone (v. 27). Yahweh had previously told the destroying angel to stay his hand because it was already quite a lot *(rab)*, v. 15, but the angel had remained on station for any further command. Now there is no further use for the angel's sword, so Yahweh commands him to put it back into its sheath. Structurally this is climactic, articulating the relief of anxiety-filled suspense that had threatened throughout the entire narrative.

It is in the census episode, in references to the threatening angel, and in the conclusion, where David builds and worships upon the altar, that ChrH shows the greatest degree of independence over against the story in Samuel. In vv. 1-4 five items are drawn from Samuel: David's incitement, his command to Joab and the army commanders, Joab's remonstrance, David's stubbornness, and the census itself. The first item is needed here at the beginning if the reader is to understand at all why this good David suddenly does something that puts into motion the entire course of action that will lead in the end to his building and sacrificing upon this new altar. Unwilling to follow Samuel in making Yahweh himself responsible for inciting David, ChrH brings in the Satan known from Job 1-2 and Zechariah 3 as the one who "stands up" against God's people as the ultimate instigator of David's deed. David issues a command that "Israel" (not "Israel and Judah" as in Samuel), "from Beersheba to Dan" (ChrH's southerly orientation; cf. 1 Chr 13:5; 2 Chr 19:4) is to be numbered. We are to suppose from Joab's reply that worldly pride is David's motivation, and accordingly the source of the sin that he confesses, vv. 8, 17. Willi (pp. 131, 140, 155, 171) explains ChrH's alterations from his ideas of demonology, theocracy, and desire for explication. But Lemke (p. 72) insists that ChrH's angelology and demonology do not differ from that of his source material. Be that as it may, he does depict David as more rationally insistent in the course he has chosen. Joab offers the wish of a hundredfold increase as God's gift, if that is what David wants (*kullām la'dōnî la'ăbādîm*, "all of them to my lord are [faithful] servants," is a gloss; cf. *Paraleipomenōn, Samuel, Basileiōn*). Rhetorical questions in v. 3 stress the negative side: the census has no useful purpose, but it does put David in peril of bringing *'ašmâ* ("guilt") on Israel—the kind of guilt that hazards severe penalties and cannot be lightly atoned for. As in Samuel, David's word is firmer *(ḥzq)* than Joab's, v. 4 (this becomes a favorite locution of ChrH in descriptions of Judah's kings, especially when used in the favorable sense of being firm or loyal toward Yahweh). ChrH skips the fine details of Joab's census taking, stating merely that he reports to David when it is accomplished. Since "all Israel" is a term that includes the tribe of Judah in ChrH's usage, and since Judah is not mentioned separately in v. 2 (contrariwise Samuel), but must be included under the locution "from Beersheba to Dan," it is clear that the separate tally for Judah in v. 5bβ is another gloss. ChrH means it to Joab's credit when he explains in v. 6 that his abhorrence of the command has led him to exclude Levi and Benjamin from the total he gives for Israel. The figure of 1,100,000 is almost certainly schematic. Counting Ephraim and Manasseh as separate tribes, omitting Benjamin, and not counting Levi as a tribe, his reckoning is for 100,000 for each tribe (cf. Williamson, comm., 145).

A discursive style prevails in vv. 7-12. By way of summary introduction, we are told two things: (1) that this thing displeased Yahweh, and (2) that as a result he smote *(wayyak)* Israel (v. 7). This is ChrH's prolepsis for the entire section, for, while David may have been so conscience-stricken that he was aware of Yahweh's attitude (Joab had warned him of this in v. 3), Yahweh had not yet sent his angel when David began to pray. In his prayer he does seem to take the responsibility upon himself, yet *ḥāṭā'tî mĕ'ōd*, "I have erred seriously," in his confession, and especially *niskaltî mĕ'ōd*, "I have acted very foolishly," in the request for absolution (v. 8), hardly express the kind of repentance that can avert the severe penalty that his transgression has earned. Yahweh replies to David's prayer (vv. 9-11), but we note that he speaks only indirectly, through Gad (here called David's seer, some kind of official intermediary). First Yahweh instructs Gad, summarizing David's situation as having to choose his own punishment; he is responsive to David's plea only in making him who has "erred" and "done foolishly" decide his own destiny. In passing on this revelation to David, Gad makes clear what his actual options will be (vv. 11b-12a). Their duration plus their apparent severity are offered so as to seem to make David's choice an easy one: three years, three months, or three days; famine, fleeing enemies, or "the sword of Yahweh" ("pestilence upon the land" is a gloss from Samuel, while "the angel of Yahweh, etc.," is an interpretative gloss from the sequel; cf. Syr.). In his answer (v. 13), David never seems to consider the first penalty; for him it is a choice of falling into the hand of Yahweh rather than into the hand of man. That Yahweh's mercy *(raḥămāyw)* is great is indeed a pious confession, and one that one does well to rely upon—but in our story God's mercy is no idle whim, mitigating the forthcoming penalty, but is his surprising willingness to be mollified by an appropriate cultic initiative.

The "sword of Yahweh" turns out to be a pestilence *(deber)* killing an appallingly large number of Israelites — seventy thousand. Symbolizing his power to destroy Jerusalem itself, Yahweh sends a destroying angel *(mal'āk hammašḥît)* whose sword is stayed only when Yahweh "repents" *(nḥm*, niph) and declares that the destruction is already *rab*, "great." Ending the episode (vv. 14-15), ChrH leaves this angel, now called "the angel of Yahweh," waiting at Ornan's threshing floor to see what David may yet do to stay the sword of vengeance (to Willi, 126, 141, v. 15 is explication and articulation of ChrH's angelology).

As we have seen, the second episode (vv. 16-26) begins with David becoming aware of the threatening angel; this is a new exposition, summarizing what has just been narrated. Instinctively he and certain sackcloth-clad "elders" fall to the earth. At length, realizing the seriousness of the choice that he has made, David asks God to lay the responsibility on him with a rhetorical question, "Was it not I . . . ?" and a direct affirmation, "It was I." The reference to the people as *'ēlleh haṣṣō'n*, "these sheep," plus the reading of the Qumran fragment published by Cross (see above, "Text"), require that we translate David's plea as follows: "And I am he who has sinned; yes, the shepherd [*wĕhārō'eh* (MT *wĕhārēa'*, "and the evildoer")] has done evil *[hărē'ôtî]*." The king as shepherd is an ancient and widespread image. Because it implies official irresponsibility, David's prayer is that Yahweh's hand may be on him and his paternal house, leaving the innocent free.

Avoiding the directness of Samuel, ChrH next employs Gad for a new errand, to tell David to erect an altar on Ornan's threshing floor. This is what Yahweh really wants; this alone will keep those innocent Israelites alive while shriving David—and the paternal house that he has just mentioned—from further guilt. There is no report of Gad telling David this, only the statement that David did what Gad said, recognizing that it had been spoken through divine authority, *bĕšēm yahweh*, "in Yahweh's name." In v. 20 *RSV* translates MT *hammal'āk*, "the angel," and this should not be emended to *hammelek*, "the king" (Samuel, LXX, MSS), because v. 21 states that Ornan "looked and saw David." The point of v. 20 is that it presents Ornan and his sons as suddenly seeing the destroying angel (cf. v. 15). Ornan next sees David, makes proper obeisance, and, probably more from fright of the angel than out of goodwill to David, enters into the climactic negotiation, vv. 22-24. As in Genesis 23, whose influence is strongly present here, Ornan's impromptu generosity is no more than custom; he would ordinarily expect to bargain on until a satisfactory price had been agreed upon. Here, however, Ornan is given no opportunity to make an introductory speech, as in Samuel (cf. Watson, 5.6). David makes his demand (v. 22), *tĕnâ-lî mĕqôm haggōren*, "Give me this threshing site." It is not just the threshing floor *(gōren)* that David wants, as in Samuel, but the entire ground that is destined to become Israel's temple complex. David also tells Ornan the purpose he has in mind: *wĕ'ebneh-bô mizbēah lĕyahweh*, "so I may build an altar for Yahweh." Its price is not to be some figure arrived at after hard bargaining, but *kesep mālē'*, "full money," an amount repeated in v. 24 and turning out in v. 25 to be not Samuel's relatively meager figure but six hundred golden shekels. This figure would have been far out of proportion for a peasant's threshing floor, but the very telling of it is a testimony to the grandeur that the temple and the temple area would eventually come to have.

According to Willi (pp. 103, 148, 157-58) this passage demonstrates ChrH's techniques of explication, normalizing, and typology. David is urgent in demanding the site so that the projected altar may avert further plague from the people (v. 22). As insistent as Ornan is in giving all the implements as well as the whole site *(māqôm)*, David's "no" is final (v. 24). David asserts that Ornan can have no part in the giving—perhaps because in Israelite tradition no foreigner could claim any credit for it, but especially because any burnt offerings that he intends to offer to avert Yahweh's wrath must not be somebody else's but his own. "I will not . . . offer burnt offerings that have cost me nothing" *(lō' . . . hinnām)*.

Various interpreters, such as von Rad (*Geschichtsbild*, 101) have taken vv. 26-27 with 21:28–22:1 as the foundation narrative for the new sanctuary, but as we shall see, vv. 28ff. constitute a separate pericope. The present story concludes with the dismissal of the threatening angel, though only through David's immediate actions in building an altar *šām*, "there" (at that very site), then offering to Yahweh the *'ōlôt ûšĕlāmîm*, "whole burnt offerings and fellowship offerings." The response of divine acceptance comes in the form of fire from heaven consuming the gift on the altar (cf. Lev 9:24; 1 Kgs 18:38; 2 Chr 7:1).

Genre

Like 19:1–20:3, this is a HISTORICAL STORY employed as a framework for an altered HIEROS LOGOS in vv. 18-26. In terms of traditional structures, this pericope has a richer variety than anything seen thus far. V. 2 has the genre ORDER—direct instructions from a superior to a subordinate. V. 3 has the genre DISPUTATION, defined as a dispute between two or more parties expressing contending points of view. In this passage (not in Samuel), the subordinate party is forced to obey the order but connives to hedge on its complete fulfillment (v. 6). Joab's response in v. 3 contains the RHETORICAL QUESTION. Vv. 5-6 have the OFFICIAL REPORT of a census (not a → muster roll because this is a one-time, complete count): this is defined as the representation of the transmission of information by a person duly authorized. It includes the TALLY and the APPELLATION (so again the gloss in

v. 5bβ), which this time is the unusual expression *šōlēp ḥereb*, "one trained to draw (and use) the sword." V. 8 has the genre PRAYER, which in this instance includes the CONFESSION OF GUILT, a statement formally acknowledging guilt and often disclosing the guilty action with its circumstances, together with a SHRIVING PETITION, an impassioned plea for divine forgiveness without consideration for one's worthiness. In addition to the MESSENGER FORMULA, "Thus says Yahweh," seen in vv. 10 and 11, v. 9 has the introduction to a unit, vv. 9-12, exhibiting the genre PROPHETIC COMMISSION REPORT, which tells of God commissioning a prophet to bring a message. The content of the message in this case is a double COMMAND (*bĕḥar lĕkā*, "choose," v. 10, and *qabbel-lāk*, "Take for yourself," v. 11b), followed by the three choices (*'im . . . 'im . . . 'im . . .*) in v. 12, and a renewed COMMAND, *wĕ'attâ rĕ'ēh mâ-'āšîb 'et- šōlĕḥî dābār*, "So now decide what reply I shall bring to him who sent me." (For further details see De Vries, "Prophetic Address," 20.)

David's choice in v. 13 is guided by a brief DESCRIPTION OF YAHWEH, which in this instance is *kî-rabbîm raḥămāyw mĕ'ōd*, "Indeed, very great/many are his deeds of compassion." This is so short and so axiomatic as to qualify also as an APHORISM, a pithy, commonsense statement in common speech. V. 15 has Yahweh's ORDER to the angel, *'attâ herep yādekā*, "Now withdraw your hand." Because it is argumentative and not a simple plea, David's speech in v. 17 should be assigned to the genre ADDRESS, in which the hearer is expressly named. David's words exhibit the SCHEMA OF REPRIEVE, a pattern describing penitence following an event of divine punishment; in a stereotyped way David confesses his sin, asks that "these sheep" be held innocent, and takes the penalty on himself. David's address also includes a RHETORICAL QUESTION ("Was it not I . . . ?") and a modified PLEA OF INNOCENCE.

Verse 18 presents a new COMMAND, but in a third-person report. It includes INSTRUCTION (a genre that gives guidance to an individual or group) respecting the building of an altar. V. 19 reports in third-person style the essence of the AUTHORIZATION FORMULA, which ChrH so often uses to validate cultic matters. All of vv. 20-25 belong to the genre NEGOTIATION, which is defined as a kind of conversation marked by exchange of speeches moving toward agreement or disagreement and focused upon a particular issue. V. 26, finally, is a REPORT OF RITUAL, a brief description of procedures followed in the performance of public worship, all of which is regulated by ritual.

Setting

Commentators have been inclined to make much of ChrH's angelology on the basis of this passage because it so strikingly expands the role of the heavenly destroyer in 2 Sam 24:16-17, who is introduced rather suddenly there and is called "the angel" three times, in one occurrence with the appellative *hammašḥît*, "the destroyer/destroying one." He is also once called "the angel of Yahweh." By comparison, 1 Chr 21:15-27 speaks seven times of this apparition, and in v. 16 removes him from terra firma, where angels have always been found in older biblical documents, and makes him stand "between earth and heaven." This invites the interpretation that ChrH has been strongly influenced by the burgeoning angelology of late Judaism, particularly in its tendency to make semi-divine beings of a great horde of angels and make heaven their proper home (cf. especially *1 Enoch, Jubilees*).

But several considerations may hold us back from this conclusion. Now certainly—as we have stressed under "Structure"—the angel of our story is thematic. But let it be observed that he does nothing in the Chronicles passage that he does not also do in Samuel, except command Gad concerning the building of the altar (v. 18), a role occasionally given to angels in the prophetic tradition, though not in Samuel. The standing between earth and heaven is supported by Cross's fragment, 4QSam[a] (see above, "Text"), which means that it may have been in Samuel's source and hence is no invention of ChrH. When we study the references in 1 Chronicles 21, the multiplicity of occurrences is seen to have a greater syntactical integrity than in Samuel, suggesting the possibility that Samuel may have lost, or deliberately dropped, certain materials common to the *Vorlage* from which both accounts have been drawn. Thus in v. 15 it is not "the angel" but "an angel" (thus far unidentified) whom God sends. He is identified in both documents with the appellative "the one destroying," but it is reasonable to suspect the addition *bāʿām*, "on the people" (2 Sam 24:16) as explicative. This apparition is identified in the same position in both documents with the traditional title "the angel of Yahweh" (v. 15), and this carries over into the next two references, vv. 16, 18; but we note that this full title functions in vv. 15-16 to identify, first as subject and then as object; in v. 18 the full form is used as subject and with the apparent purpose of identifying the source of Gad's revelation, whose inspiration is held to be so important by David in v. 19. In vv. 20 and 27, where the apparition is referred to objectively, it is simply "the angel." Referring back to our pericope, v. 30 purposefully uses the full title, "the angel of Yahweh."

When all is told, the only point at which ChrH goes beyond the angelology of Samuel is in making the same "angel of Yahweh" who destroys also the revelational authority for the command to build the altar (v. 18). ChrH does mean to place cultic indifference under the severe ban. As Yahweh once sent his angel to destroy Israel's enemies (2 Kgs 19:35; Isa 37:36; 2 Chr 32:21), he stands ready to send a destroying angel on anyone guilty of showing disdain to this, his holy place. The imagery may have changed from that of the seven executioners of Ezekiel 9, but the threat is the same.

No more than its angelology has this pericope's demonology made the radical advances that many interpreters have attributed to it. The most striking difference between Job 1:6ff. and Zech 3:1ff. on the one hand and this passage on the other hand is that there the determinative with *śāṭān* identifies this figure as a functionary, whereas the absence of the determinative here turns this into a proper name, as in late Judaism. As in the Zechariah passage, the setting is that of a court of judgment because "Satan" is "standing up" against David—a technical term meaning to appear as a formal accuser. We have noted ChrH's alteration from Samuel; he needs someone, but not Yahweh himself—to bring the guilt for which pestilence will be the penalty, and the new altar the place of atonement. We take note of the additional point that ChrH is guarding David's reputation along with God's: in spite of his contriteness, David is never punished and, apparently because of his prompt willingness to buy the site and build the altar, comes through with the reputation of model blamelessness. At the same time one should take note of the fact that ChrH allows his Samuel source to lead him into a drastic modification of the concept of repentance that governs his entire history of the Hebrew kings, viz., never requiring cultic sacrifice as a condition for their restoration.

175

Interpreters have been in a quandary as to why David should have been punished for taking his census, especially in the light of the fact that God specifically commands censuses in Exod 30:12; Num 1:2; 26:2. Furthermore, the muster tallies of Chronicles' early chapters are direct evidence that men were indeed counted for the purpose of organizing for war. One thing to remember is that the muster tallies are early and historical, while the passages in the Pentateuch are all late—as late perhaps as Chronicles—and highly ideological. All the same, ChrH follows Samuel in his condemnation and goes so far as to have Joab warn David that it would be an *'ašmâ*, "guilty thing," requiring atonement. Probably the best way to resolve this apparent enigma is to understand that both Samuel and ChrH are reasoning in retrospect. The goal of both versions is the threshing floor and the altar; it must have been necessary because of the pestilence, which must have come because of guilt, which presupposes sin and error. Who caused that is, of course, Samuel's and ChrH's basic point of disagreement.

Our story brings to expression the standard Hebraic doctrine of retribution; yet, as has been mentioned, neither David nor his "father's house" personally suffers. We may perhaps speak of corporate guilt, but not of corporate punishment. On the other hand, there is corporate atonement, both for the Israelites who escape the angel's sword and for David's family, present and future. It is with the latter, no doubt, that ChrH is chiefly concerned. If any of his posterity do, in fact, transgress—and many of them will—it will be for their own sin that they are punished, and not for anything David did.

David plays an exceedingly ambivalent role throughout this story, and every change in his situation is directly caused by a decision he has made. With Satan's incitement, he wills to make the census over Joab's protestation. When confronted by God's three choices, he decides without hesitation, yet for something that he understands not. When the plague comes, he offers to shield the people by taking the blame himself, yet how eager he is to escape the blame is revealed by the alacrity with which he seeks out Ornan and by how extravagantly generous he is. There is typological significance in each of these roles: David the determined transgressor; David the decisive dispenser of justice; David the willing substitute; David the diligent and enthusiastic worshiper.

We should not overlook the enigma of prayer as it comes to expression in this story. David is quick to pray, v. 8, but not until the very end does Yahweh answer, v. 26. The teaching, no doubt, is that God does not answer prayer until he is ready to answer it. In this story, the person doing the praying must first meet the condition set by God. There is a mystery in God's compassion, in which David places so much confidence (v. 13). God is indeed compassionate, but not in the way David reckoned on. Yahweh was certainly not compassionate to the seventy thousand, yet he did at last stay the angel's hand, saving 1,500,000 left over from David's census. In reducing the census, Yahweh is perhaps showing David that he will number Israel as he will, and the mercy is that there is any Israel at all.

Various interpreters have noted that David's negotiation with Ornan is closely modeled after Abraham's negotiation with Ephron the Hittite in Genesis 23. Both stories intend to secure absolute rights for plots of ground within the domain of foreigners. The P story in Genesis uses the burial place at Hebron as a symbol of Israel's eventual proprietorship over the entire land. Going beyond Samuel in his intent, ChrH uses the symbol of Ornan's threshing floor as the surety of the

176

temple complex under the proprietorship and supervision of David and his father's house.

Another typological parallel may be seen in the legend of Gideon's altar, Judges 6 (cf. Williamson, comm., 148). At the angel's instruction, Gideon prepares a sacrificial meal, which Yahweh's fire consumes. This leads him to build an altar and dedicate it to "Yahweh Shalom," v. 24. In our story the altar is all-important because it sanctifies every offering made upon it in Yahweh's name. We would be mistaken to interpret the answer by fire as some kind of proof of God, as most interpreters of 1 Kgs 18:38 would claim; rather, it is the visible token of his abiding presence. This is definitely the intent here and in 2 Chr 7:1, but it is true also in the Elijah story, where the real question is not "Is Yahweh God, or Baal?" but "Is Baal truly present, or Yahweh?" Fire and light are standard biblical representations for the true God, who appears in the fire on the mountain, as a pillar of fire leading Israel to the promised land, and as a token of his abiding presence in their sanctuary (Exod 40:34-38).

Intention

ChrH has skillfully adapted another passage from Samuel to articulate his concept of David's career as a preparation for the erection of the temple under Solomon. David proceeds step by step to all that he can do. Step one was to capture Jerusalem; step two was to install the ark. This is step three: gaining free title to a *māqôm*, "site," for the temple; and, as earnest for it, building upon it the altar where sacrifices are already acceptable to Yahweh. Thus to ChrH this story is absolutely programmatic—no mere appendage, as in 2 Samuel 24. This story makes a big stride in advancing ChrH's major ideological concern. It does not monopolize everything, to be sure, for ChrH continues to develop the parallel themes of (1) preparing the clergy and (2) gathering the materials. The story in 2 Samuel 24 was no doubt the original *hieros logos* for the sacred site, but it must not be interpreted, as K. Rupprecht argues *(Der Tempel von Jerusalem)*, as a disguise for the existence of an already-standing Jebusite shrine taken over by David (for full refutation see De Vries, *1 Kings* [Word Biblical Commentary 12; Waco, TX: Word Books, 1985] 97-98). ChrH has no independent knowledge, as Rupprecht claims, that a Jebusite shrine was there first (cf. 2 Chr 3:1). Ornan (Samuel: Araunah) had a *gōren*, "threshing floor," which at times could be identified as a place of revelation (cf. Judg 6:36-40; 1 Kgs 22:10 par. 2 Chr 18:9). When purchased for lavish money as a *māqôm*, "site," for the temple, it served the purpose of revealing God's favor (v. 26), but when the temple itself would come to occupy that site, it would have been built, not by Ornan, not by David, but by Solomon.

A final note about this pericope is that it already articulates ChrH's ideology that the temple would be the place of atonement par excellence. When ChrH takes over Solomon's dedicatory prayer in 2 Chr 6:18-39, he underscores through repetition that the temple is not to be thought of as a house for God to dwell in, but as the place from which effective prayer must come. Here in ch. 21 ChrH is anxious to teach that divine forgiveness is to be sought at the temple—a lesson emphasized again and again in the stories of the Judahite kings, whose repentance is in every case tested by their subsequent behavior with regard to that temple.

Bibliography

W. E. Barnes, "The Midrashic Element in Chronicles," *Exp* 2 (1896) 426-39; idem, "The Religious Standpoint of the Chronicler," *AJSL* 13 (1896-97) 14-20; J. Botterweck, "Zur Eigenart der chronistischen Davidgeschichte," *TQ* 136 (1956) 427-30; A. Garcia del Morel, "La Sagrade Escritura y la aplícación de technicas estadísticas al pueblo de Dios. Reflexiones pastorales sobre 2 Sam 24 y 1 Chron 21," *Communio* 3 (1970) 1-28; G. von Rad, *Das Geschichtsbild des chronistischen Werkes* (Stuttgart: Kohlhammer, 1930); K. Rupprecht, *Der Tempel von Jerusalem, Gründung Salomos oder jebusitisches Erbe?* (BZAW 14; New York-Berlin: de Gruyter, 1977).

THE BUILDING OF THE TEMPLE, 1 CHR 21:28–2 CHR 9:31

Structure

I. Report of David's preparations	1 Chr 21:28–22:19
II. Account of the transfer of the kingship	23:1–29:30
III. Account of the building of the temple	2 Chr 1:1–9:31

Up to this point the narrative has been about "David consolidating his rule," leading to his supreme and final act, in his regal capacity, of acquiring a site where the temple might be built. ChrH is prepared now to tell how the resources of David's kingdom, sacred and profane, would be mobilized for the actual occurrence of this supreme event. In the first part of a rather long and involved ACCOUNT, David makes certain declarations and gives certain exhortations regarding the temple site (1 Chr 21:28–22:1), his own contribution (22:2-5), the duty of his son Solomon (22:6-16), and the task of Israel's leaders (22:17-19). The second part of the account is fairly simple in its outline, but complex in detail. The reason for this is that secondary additions have been made in chs. 23–27. Without them, this is a section in which David organizes the clergy for temple service before actually turning the kingship over to Solomon. The last is told with fondness and some eloquence in chs. 28 and 29. This brings us to the third section of the account, 2 Chronicles 1–9, the climactic part that tells of the temple being built, but not without a sufficiency of details concerning the person of Solomon. Although far less space is devoted to Solomon than to David, every reader recognizes this as climactic. David is the man whom Yahweh has chosen (1 Chr 10:14), but it is Solomon who will enjoy the status of God's son (22:10).

REPORT OF DAVID'S PREPARATIONS, 21:28–22:19

Structure

I. Exclusive worship at Ornan's threshing floor	21:28–22:1
A. David acknowledges its legitimacy	28
1. A place of benign revelation	28a
2. Response of sacrificial worship	28b

Because of the subject matter, it might be thought that 21:18–22:1—or at least 21:28-30—should be attached to the preceding altar story, but these verses actually constitute a rather formal introduction to the entirety of ch. 22, and accordingly to the entire section, chs. 22–29. This decision is not made arbitrarily, but with close attention to three points: (1) the joint between 21:27 and 21:28, (2) the structural and thematic connection of 21:28–22:1 to 22:5ff., and (3) the final break for the pericope as a whole.

Occasionally, ChrH uses time designations like *bā'ēt hahî'*, "at that time," as formal transitions to new material, and that is what he is doing here. 21:28–22:1 contains this expression of contemporaneity in two positions: foremost in 21:28 for emphasis on the fact that what David was about to decide occurred at the same time (or in the same situation) as the building of the Jerusalem altar; also in subordinate position in v. 29 to indicate the simple fact of the coexistence of the Gibeon sanctuary. Following the initial *bā'ēt hahî'* in v. 28, we encounter a circumstantial clause, "when David saw . . . ," concluded with a subordinate result clause in narrative style, *wayyizbaḥ šām*, "so that he sacrificed there" (cf. *šām* in v. 26). The entirety of v. 29 is a noun clause, with a finite verb only in a relative clause qualifying *ûmiškan yahweh*, "and Yahweh's tabernacle." V. 30 offers a verb in the imperfect, *wĕlō'-yākōl*, "but he was not able" (a durative action), in a circumstantial clause balancing off the preceding noun clause; it includes a grounding clause with *kî* and the niph. of *b't*, "for he was terrified in the presence of Yahweh's angel." That is to say, the angel of Yahweh remained present though unseen, ready to strike down anyone who might desecrate, or even disregard, the altar on Ornan's threshing floor, and this is weighty enough cause to justify David's no longer patronizing the Gibeon shrine with its Moses-made tabernacle. Finally at 22:1, we encounter the first independent narrative verb in this entire sequence, *wayyō'mer dāwîd*, "and David said." We must understand, then, that everything that precedes, the time designation, the noun clause about the Gibeon shrine, the circumstantial clause about David not going there, and the grounding clause about fearing the angel, explains and motivates what David says. Rather, we should read, "what David directs or commands," for that is the meaning of *wayyō'mer dāwîd* wherever it is used in this pericope (vv. 2, 5, 6, 7). 22:1 is, in fact, a formal DEDICATORY DECLARATION, one to be spoken at the actual dedication ceremony, but borrowed here for the narrator's purpose: *zeh hû' bêt yahweh hā'ĕlōhîm wĕzeh-mizbēaḥ lĕ'ōlâ lĕyisrā'ēl*. The double *zeh*, in foremost position, clarifies that the Jerusalem shrine is sharply in contrast to Gibeon. The parallelism of *bêt yahweh hā'ĕlōhîm* with *mizbēaḥ* expresses David's decision to make this particular altar into a temple— not just any temple or another temple, but "the temple of Yahweh God." *lĕ'ôlâ*, "for sacrificing," indicates its specific purpose; and "for Israel" shows that it is to be no private shrine but the supreme (if not exclusive) place for Yahweh's worship.

This is a drastic declaration indeed. To go against age-old Mosaic tradition and set up a rival and exclusivistic shrine is a move that no one, however power- ful or however holy, would dare make on his own initiative. But to ChrH there is nothing presumptuous in this declaration. If 21:28–22:1 constitutes an involved conditional sentence—and it does—vv. 28-30 is the protasis and 22:1 the apodosis. The "then" of David's decision is only the logical consequence of the "becauses" that precede it. Those are Yahweh's "becauses." At Ornan's threshing floor he "answered," i.e., gave revelation, hence this was to be for always *the* place of revelation. Accompanying this motive of believing expectation is the motive of fear—fear of a destroying angel who might destroy again if Yahweh's will were not heeded.

What follows in ch. 22 is directly governed by David's momentous decision. ChrH means David's commands to various persons who would be involved in the construction of the temple, or in preparations for it (vv. 2-5, 6-16, 17-19), to be un- derstood as direct consequences of David's declaration. Each section begins with a narrative introduction including *wayyō'mer dāwîd*, "and David directed," or *wayĕsaw dāwîd*, "and David commanded," v. 17. Each section but the last, then, has discourse introduced anew by the formula *wayyō'mer dāwîd* (all of vv. 17-19 except the intro- ductory words is in direct discourse). With a narrative conclusion in v. 5b, the section vv. 2-5 is an inclusio with narrative at the beginning and end, telling what David provided for and donated, and a short consultation with himself in the middle dis- course section, where he cites Solomon's immaturity as reason for him to provide so much himself. Vv. 6-16 have only a short narrative introduction, stating that David called Solomon shortly before his death (v. 5), commanding him (*swh*, piel) to build the temple. All that follows is in discourse. David tells Solomon that it was his own intent to build this temple (v. 7), but countering it have been Yahweh's own words, which David next quotes (vv. 8-10), to the effect that: (1) Yahweh declared him unfit; and (2) Yahweh designated Solomon to be the builder. Here ChrH repeats the basic items of ch. 17 (cf. Williamson, "Eschatology," 136-37; Willi, 193 [normalizing]): a son of peace to counter David's blood; a son to build Yahweh a "house"; adoption to be Yahweh's "son"; and the dynastic promise, securing his throne forever. Having quoted Yahweh to the end, David next (*'attâ bĕnî*, "Now my son . . .") offers Solomon his paternal advice (Williamson, comm., 155-57: "installation charge"); citing the revelation just repeated (*ka'ăšer dibber 'āleykā*), David expresses the hope that Yah- weh may truly be with him (*yĕhî yahweh 'immāk*) so that he might succeed (*slḥ*, hiph.) and build (*bnh*) the temple. David also hopes for the gifts of *śēkel*, "wisdom," and *bînâ*, "understanding," by which alone Yahweh's law may be obeyed (v. 12). Vv. 13- 16 contain David's concluding ADMONITION, enumerating David's gifts and urging Solomon to emulate his generosity in making gifts of his own (there is a chiasmus in this arrangement: fine to rough, v. 14; rough to fine, vv. 15-16a; cf. Curtis and Mad- sen, ICC, 258), then commanding Solomon to act (though not necessarily right now; cf. v. 19), repeating from v. 11 (inclusio) the wish, *wîhî yahweh 'immāk*, "And may Yahweh be with you!"

It is not necessary, with Rudolph (HAT), to view vv. 17-19 as a secondary addition because of the change of the operative verb to *ṣwh* (piel). At this point ChrH has dropped his monotonous repetition of *'mr,* and in any case *ṣwh* (piel) is more appropriate, since "deciding" and "directing" are what a man does for himself and his son, but "commanding" is what he does for subjects. In any event, ChrH has not forgotten that the whole nation has a stake in the temple-to-be, and that its *śārîm,* "officials," need a command, and not just an invitation, to participate. The basis of this participation is determined by the infinitive of *'zr,* "help," so prominent in ch. 12. As soldiers there came from many tribes to assist David in gaining the kingship, prominent men are here summoned to help David's son in building the temple. In the first of two rhetorical questions, David affirms what he had only hoped for Solomon, that Yahweh was with them! In a second question, followed by direct affirmations, David then points out that there are no wars to fight (that had been *his* duty, "bloody man" that he was!), and that they as leaders have full power over the land's original inhabitants, the Canaanites, so that the land is subdued. In v. 19 (cf. v. 11), *'attâ,* "so now," draws a connection from these affirmations to the consequences that David expected to see come from them. The first concerns internal spirituality, and without it there could be no second; it is that these leaders should set heart and mind to the duty of seeking *(drš)* Yahweh their God— a familiar phrase of ChrH, for whom it means nothing less than making Yahweh the sole and full object of religious devotion. The second consequence—actually the purpose for which the first has been demanded—is that these leaders might join in building a *miqdaš,* "sanctuary," into which a "house built for the name of Yahweh," the ark and "the holy vessels of God"—presumably the articles mentioned in 2 Chr 5:1—might be brought. "Arise and build" (v. 19) need not imply that David expected direct and immediate compliance, any more than he expected this in saying "Arise and be doing" to Solomon in v. 16. That would be impossible on the presuppositions of ChrH's own sequencing, which envisaged many things yet to be told, including Solomon's investiture and David's death. The effect is, rather, of ignoring temporalities and making David present at the dedication of the temple. "Arising and doing" is, in any event, a state of mind before it can issue forth into practical performance.

Genre

The main genre of this pericope is REPORT. It is not long or complex enough to be called an (→) account. Notice has been taken of the impressive DEDICATORY DECLARATION in 22:1. In this genre solemn words of dedication and/or consecration, cast in exalted, easily remembered poetic form, mark the transition of the previously profane into the realm of the holy (cf. Gen 28:17; Exod 32:29; 1 Kgs 8:12-13 par. 2 Chr 6:1-2). Although we are not to allow the mention of David's providing temple materials before his death *(lipnê môtô),* v. 5, to denominate what he next says to Solomon, vv. 6-16, as a FAREWELL SPEECH, that is its actual genre, in spite of the appearance of another like it at a more appropriate place, 28:1-10 (not being aware of the demand of modern logic to the effect that farewell speeches should take place at a farewell, ChrH probably intended this action to be contemporaneous with that of v. 1 and of vv. 2-5; yet this speech is "farewell" in the sense that it expresses what is ultimate in David's mind for Solomon). Like 28:9-10, it is also a

VOCATION ACCOUNT II. There are several examples of this genre in the OT. It is defined as a first-person styled speech reported to have been delivered near the time of one's death. Admonitions and other directives are typical of its contents, as here. Vv. 8-10 belong to the genre ORACULAR REPORT, a message of Yahweh quoted or closely paraphrased in a direct-address report made by the original receiver to an interested third party. It may be mainly concerned with the receiver, the person being addressed, or both. It differs from the (→) prophetic commission report in that the reporter is the original recipient of the oracular words (see 1 Kgs 8:16, 18-19 par. 2 Chr 6:5-6, 8-9).

We notice many other formal structures in David's speech to Solomon. V. 8a has the WORD FORMULA, "The word of Yahweh came to me." V. 8aβ-γ, "You have shed much blood and have waged great wars," though spoken by Yahweh, has the form of a short INDICTMENT SPEECH, which is properly a formal declaration handed down by a judicial authority charging a person with committing a punishable act. "You shall not build a house to my name" in the same verse is a PROHIBITION with a grounding clause. The PROHIBITION is a direct forbiddance of an action or thing, usually based on custom, law, or decree, but here uttered by Yahweh as a penalty for the previously mentioned wrongdoing. V. 9 first promises that Solomon will be 'îš měnûḥâ, "a quiet man," but in a grounding clause with kî it announces that his name would be called šělōmōh because Yahweh promises to give šālôm wāšeqeṭ, "peace and repose," upon Israel. This is a classic NAMING ETIOLOGY.

Verse 10a has the ADOPTION FORMULA, here phrased "He shall be my son and I shall be his father." V. 10b has the dynastic PROMISE. Vv. 11-16 constitute a PARENESIS, which is defined as an address to an individual or a group which seeks to persuade toward a definite goal, in this case getting Solomon to build the temple. In v. 11 the familiar phrase "Yahweh be with you" is the ASSISTANCE FORMULA; so too in v. 16b. "Succeed and build" is a COMMAND. "As he has spoken concerning you" is the familiar FULFILLMENT FORMULA. V. 12 contains a WISH. Vv. 13-16 relinquish PARENESIS and take on the genre INSTRUCTION, a genre that gives guidance to an individual or group, setting forth values, giving rules of conduct, or answering questions. In v. 13 it includes a short ADMONITION, a speech designed to dissuade an individual or group from a certain kind of behavior—in this case, indifference in keeping Yahweh's law. This verse also includes the REASSURANCE FORMULA in emphatic form: "Be strong and of good courage; fear not, be not dismayed." In v. 14b "To these you must add" constitutes another COMMAND. V. 16 has an EXHORTATION, "Arise and be doing!" It makes no particular assumptions, unlike the ADMONITION. The latter is basically negative, the former is positive. This EXHORTATION, however, includes an ORDER to take action, together with the ASSISTANCE FORMULA.

Verses 17-19 include another example of INSTRUCTION. Both the ASSISTANCE FORMULA and the CONVEYANCE FORMULA ("give into your hand") are in v. 18. V. 19, finally, is another ADMONITION; it assumes duties on the part of the parties addressed, and while it contains another ORDER ("Arise and build") to do what is expected of them, it intimates the misgiving that these persons may not in fact do what is demanded.

Setting and Intention

One can hardly overestimate the significance of this passage for the postexilic community for whom ChrH was speaking. As a narrative it has lacunae and inconcinnities: the assumption that until his death David worshiped at the threshing floor, ignoring not only the Gibeon shrine but the Jerusalem tent shrine which he himself had dedicated for the ark; the making of a farewell speech to Solomon before it was time for a farewell; the urgent commands of vv. 16 and 19, implying that there would be an immediate response because everything was on hand for Solomon to work with, and that the absolute peace that reigned in the countryside had taken away every hindrance to the *śārîm* helping. We cannot, therefore, praise this pericope from a strictly literary point of view. What can be said in a positive way has been said: that ChrH has succeeded (though not to the satisfaction of many modern interpreters) in tying it all together as a meaningful and effective pericope. Three sections of discourse (vv. 5, 7-16, 17-19) disclose how the three most affected parties (David, Solomon, the officials) responded to the decisive dedicatory declaration in v. 1. As we have seen, these are not to be read necessarily in temporal sequencing, but they make good sense as crucial elements in bringing the temple to reality. The thing for us to perceive is how they each retained that function in holding the postexilic community to the task of restoring the temple first built by Solomon.

In each section we can see how ChrH contemporizes the past and the future. He does not leave the threshing-floor tradition as an isolated block, like Samuel, but immediately makes it permanent by showing (1) that Yahweh makes clear that this is where he wants his temple, and (2) that all rival traditions, like that of Gibeon, have been invalidated. We do not know a great deal about the Gibeon shrine (cf. Blenkinsopp, 100-105) except that it definitely enjoyed high prestige in the days of Solomon (cf. 1 Kings 3 par. 2 Chronicles 1). We can well understand why this shrine did not survive into the period of the Hebrew kings, and eventually disappears from living tradition. Once the Solomonic temple was built, it was too small and too close to the temple to compete, and it survived, if at all, solely as one of the *bāmôt,* "local shrines," which were doomed in Josiah's time to be completely suppressed. Perhaps in ChrH's time a contingent of Benjaminites had returned to restore continuity with the Gibeonites of (→) 1 Chr 8:29-32, but if they still made Mosaic claims for their shrine (Galling, ATD, views v. 29 as a secondary expansion, which assumes that these claims were being made even after ChrH's time), ChrH is able to brush the authority of tradition aside with his claim that Yahweh's answer by fire, together with the dread of the destroying angel, simply invalidated such a claim. If the returned exiles needed to be reassured that the ruined Jerusalem temple definitely was the sanctuary where Yahweh wanted to be worshiped, they had, alongside the authoritive declaration of Israel's "first" and most prestigious king, ChrH's clarification that Yahweh had indeed given his clear sign that this was where he was to be worshiped, along with the warning that his wrath still threatened any who might follow other impulses and disregard it.

Verses 2-5 continue the theme illustrated in David's paying six hundred shekels of gold—twelve times what Samuel said it was worth—for the threshing floor. The essential concept is articulated in v. 5, where David explains why he had gathered great quantities of various material: "The temple that is to be built for Yahweh must be exceedingly magnificent, of fame and glory throughout all lands." A cautious literary criticism in 1 Kings 6–7 reveals that the historical temple was rather small and plain (cf. S. J. De Vries, *1 Kings* [Word Biblical Commentary 12; Waco, TX: Word Books, 1985]), and that the profuse references to goldwork are secondary in the text. Yet, as such, the concept of a golden temple, assumed also in 2 Chronicles 3–4, is motivated directly by the same ideology just cited from David, viz., that since this was the sanctuary that Yahweh himself had chosen, it must be of unrestricted grandeur. As we know, the Babylonians thoroughly stripped the temple of all its gold, silver, and other precious metals (2 Kgs 25:13-17), the bulk of which must have stayed in foreign possession in spite of Ezra 1:4. As we read in Hag 2:3, what the returned exiles saw upon returning to Jerusalem was "as nothing," having been robbed of "its former glory." Yet the oracle through Haggai promises what David, *apud* ChrH, intends: "I will shake all nations, so that the treasures of all nations shall come in, and I will fill this house with splendor. . . . The silver is mine, and the gold is mine. . . . The latter splendor of this house shall be greater than the former, says Yahweh Sebaoth" (Hag 2:7-9). David's words, then, are ChrH's. His having "aliens," Sidonians and Tyrians, assist in assembling the materials expresses the ideal of making foreign nations acknowledge the superior magnificence and prestige of Yahweh's temple. If Haggai's prophecy yet remained unfulfilled, the words with which David expresses his intent would have held up to ChrH's community a concept which they were obliged once again, and forever, to strive to fulfill.

Verses 6-16 draw heavily on 2 Samuel 7 par. 1 Chronicles 17 for the commissioning speech to Solomon (cf. Josh 1:1-9; 1 Kgs 2:1ff.). This is programmatic material for ChrH, and will be repeated in 1 Chr 28:1-10; 1 Kgs 8:16-21 par. 2 Chr 6:5-11. All the concepts articulated in vv. 9-10, the rest, the *bêt* that is a dynasty as well as a temple, the adoption as Yahweh's son, and the everlasting rule, though lost with Nebuchadrezzar's deportation into Babylon, fill out the model of the ideal ruler that remains with restoration Israel. The call to resolution and exhortation of vv. 13 and 16 recalls a Joshua typology as articulated in the deuteronomistic language of Deut 31:23; Josh 1:6, 9. But as interiorized by postexilic Judaism, it is not enough to hear "Be strong and of good courage. Fear not, be not dismayed" (v. 13). With good purpose does v. 14 have David enumerate the tremendous amount of gold and precious metals he has amassed, concluding with the command *wa'ălêhem tôsîp*, "Now to them you must add." (For archaic elements, cf. Watson, 5.1; Rudolph, HAT, identifies editorial changes in v. 14.) This is parenesis for the post-kingdom generation. What the kings had done to glorify Yahweh's temple had been very much indeed, yet it had not been enough. To what remained over they must surely now add what they could. Hence the command to Solomon, *qûm wa'ăśēh*, "Get to work!" and a fervent wish for the divine presence, *wîhî yahweh 'immāk*, "and may Yahweh be with you," were also directed to them.

In the instructions to the leaders in vv. 17-19, while recalling how David had once had to rely on the "help" of numerous others (1 Chronicles 12), ChrH's own contemporaries are exhorted to "help" their own "Solomon." What David says to the chiefs is surely true of the leaders in ChrH's own community: they had the divine presence; they had rest from warfare; they had control over the inhabitants of the land. For them and for "all Israel" it was a duty of the heart (seat of the will and affections) and of the soul (seat of intellect and spirituality) to *drš* (seek) Yahweh as their God by building what had been ruined and by bringing in what had been scattered.

Bibliography

P. R. Ackroyd, "The Temple Vessels—a Continuity Theme," in *Studies in the Religion of Ancient Israel* (VTSup 23; Leiden: Brill, 1972) 166-81; C. Begg, "'Seeking Yahweh' and the Purpose of Chronicles," *Louvain Studies* 9 (1982) 128-42; S. B. Berg, "After the Exile: God and History in the Books of Chronicles and Esther," in *The Divine Helmsman (Fest. L. Silberman*; ed. J. L. Crenshaw and S. Sandmel; New York: KTAV, 1980) 107-27; J. Blenkinsopp, *Gibeon and Israel* (SOTSMS 2; Cambridge: Cambridge, 1972); J. Botterweck, "Zur Eigenart der chronistischen Davidgeschichte," *TQ* 136 (1956) 430-31; R. L. Braun, "Solomonic Apologetic in Chronicles," *JBL* 92 (1973) 503-16; A.-M. Brunet, "La théologie du Chroniste. Théocratie et messianisme," in *Sacra Pagina* (ed. J. Coppens, et al.; Paris: Gabalda, 1959) 1:384-97; H. G. M. Williamson, "The Dynastic Oracle in the Books of Chronicles," in *Sefer Yitshaq Aryeh Zeligman* I (ed. A. Rofé; Jerusalem: Rubinstein, 1981) 305-16; idem, "Eschatology in Chronicles," *TynBul* 28 (1977) 115-34.

ACCOUNT OF THE TRANSFER OF THE KINGSHIP, 23:1–29:30

Structure

I. Title	23:1
II. David's court	23:2–29:30
A. The organization of clergy and laity	23:2–27:34
1. Register of Levites and priests in the temple	23:2–24:31
a. Census and organization of the Levites	23:2-24
b. Job description of the Levites	23:25-32
c. Report concerning the sons of Aaron	24:1-19
d. Expanded list of Levites	24:20-31
2. Register of musicians	25:1-31
3. Register of guards and custodians	26:1-32
4. Register of the officers of the people	27:1-34
B. Solomon's investiture	28:1–29:25
1. Report of the gathering at Jerusalem	28:1
2. Report of introductory charges	28:2-10
3. Report of instructions concerning temple plans	28:11-21
4. Report of David's farewell speech	29:1-9
5. Report of David's prayer	29:10-19
6. Report of ritual: the investiture	29:20-22
7. Report: Solomon initiated into the kingship	29:23-25
C. David's regnal resumé	29:26-30

It is not difficult to understand why some interpreters want to deny the section 23:2–27:34 to the original work of ChrH. It consists of lists, lists, lists. Some materials concerning Levitical personnel conflict with some sections on the Levites and other clergy elsewhere in the book. Most important, 23:1 states flatly that David made Solomon king over Israel, a summarizing introduction that finds its narrative continuation in 28:1ff. On two assumptions we would be obliged to agree that this entire section has been added to the inauguration account: (1) that all of it is of the same age, i.e., later than ChrH; and (2) that it really does shatter the narrative continuity of the inauguration account. We shall dispose of the first objection in the analysis to follow, where we shall show that there are, in fact, a number of late additions. With respect to the second objection, it should be pointed out first that David's words to Solomon in 28:21 clearly presuppose at least some of the lists of chs. 23–27: "And behold the divisions *[maḥlĕqôt]* of the priests and the Levites for all the service of the house of God," confirming the narrative statement in v. 13 to the effect that David had in fact given this information to Solomon as part of his plan for the temple. Another point to consider is the difference in structure between what seem to be parallel introductions to the investiture in 23:1 and 28:1. 28:1 is structured in normal narrative style, *wayyaqhēl dāwîd 'et-kol-śārê yiśrā'ēl*, "Now David assembled all the officials of Israel." After going on to specify the various types of officials that were included in this designation, the narrative sequence continues: *wayyāqām dāwîd . . . wayyō'mer . . . ,* "And David arose . . . and said . . . ," introducing his address of vv. 2-7. Appropriate discourse and narration continues to the end. 23:1, however, begins with a noun clause with subject foremost, *wĕdāwîd zāqēn wĕśāba' yāmîm,* and this is followed with a *wāw*-consecutive imperfect which draws out in normal Hebrew syntax the consequence of the noun clause: *wayyamlēk 'et-šĕlōmōh bĕnô 'al-yiśrā'ēl.* This should properly be translated, "Now when David had grown old and sated with years he crowned his son Solomon as king over Israel." Although this might well serve as a summary introduction to 28:1ff., we need to observe that 28:1 is itself an expository introduction to the address of 28:2ff.; hence it is possible but not likely that 23:1 is a summary introduction to 28:1ff. On the other hand it will not do to make 23:1 the exposition for 23:2, for the assembly told of there has to do with a meeting to appoint the Levites and other clergy. The solution is to identify 23:1 as the title to the whole section. It does not involve abbreviation, like our modern literary titles, but it does involve synopsis, as in the titles to some of the Psalms, e.g., 7; 30; etc. Our verse is not to be taken as part of the narrative, therefore, but as a title that could cover seemingly irrelevant materials such as the lists of chs. 23–27—because ChrH understood them as a necessary part of what was to be included under this title. The title is appropriate because the noun clause about David in his old age covers also his last official acts respecting the organization of the clergy, and forms a transition to the succeeding narration in which he turns over the kingship to his son.

The formal summary of David's reign, 29:26-30, forms a pericope in its own right, but it is included in this section and is covered by its title because it provides a final and definitive expression to the subject "David in his old age turning the kingdom over to Solomon."

Because of the extreme complexity of the material in 1 Chr 23:2–29:30, we present separate structural outlines for: "A. The organization of clergy and laity" (23:2–27:34), "B. Solomon's investiture" (28:1–35), and "C. David's regnal resumé" (29:26-30).

A. THE ORGANIZATION OF CLERGY AND LAITY, 23:2–27:34

Structure

Apart from those commentaries that insist on attributing every word to ChrH, one expects to find one suggestion or another for identifying secondary material in this section. It is not just that such a variety of subjects is treated, but that they are jumbled together and so full of apparent contradictions. Many identifications that have been made prove, on close scrutiny, to be erroneous and subjectivistic. The scholarly world is fortunate that, just recently, an eminent scholar on the book of Chronicles, H. G. M. Williamson, has offered a well-reasoned and eminently justifiable analysis that does concede the presence of certain secondary elements in this section, while defending its originality as a whole. This is in his comm. (pp. 157-78), but especially in his article "The Origins of the Twenty-Four Priestly Courses." In most, not in all, details, the present writer accepts the literary criticism at which Williamson has arrived. Eschewing any preconceived notion of what would or would not have been included in ChrH's original text, Williamson relies completely on internal evidence. The only thing that surprises us is that such a heavy volume of secondary material is identified. Yet that will not seem strange if we keep in mind that it is precisely the passages regulating the Levites, such as chs. 6 and 16, that have been expanded the most. Whoever the secondary writer was who interpolated his material in chs. 23–27, he saw this as his last chance and made the most of it.

The formal appearance of the original material in 1 Chr 23:2–27:34 featured solely the Levites and other sub-orders associated with them, as follows:

I. Levites in the temple	23:2-24
II. Musicians	25:1-6
III. Guards and custodians	26:1-3, 9-11, 20-32

There is a minimal narrative framework that holds this concatenation together as an ACCOUNT: 23:2-6: "David assembled. . . . The Levites . . . were numbered. . . . David said. . . . And David organized them in divisions. . . ." 25:1a: "David and the chiefs of the service also set apart for the service. . . ." 26:32: "King David appointed him and his brethren to have the oversight . . . for everything pertaining to God and for the affairs of the king." Perhaps we should include certain other verses employing passive verbal constructions, but at least there is some apparent function in these sparse but well-distributed references to David taking authoritative action. It is enough to remind us that action is going on, that this is still Episode One in the account of Solomon's investiture.

In other words, ChrH does not at all mean these details about the organization of the Levites as a sidetrack or diversion. The Levites were present when David took his first official action as king—at the entrance of the ark. From ChrH's point of view, the regulations of chs. 15–16 were promulgated especially for that occasion, not in the sense that they would cease to have any bearing once the temple was built, but in the sense that more complete regulations would now be necessary with Solomon's coming to the throne and the building of the temple. ChrH is thorough if anything; he will not let an opportunity like this go by. It is in this sense that these regulations are an essential part of the investiture narrative.

All this might be much clearer to us if certain redactors into whose hands ChrH's history fell had not felt it necessary to make extensive revisions. The ones that can be identified with some certainty are the following:

1. An Aaronite supplement, 23:25-32 (perhaps including the gloss in v. 24b), reducing the Levitical age from 30 (v. 3) to 20 (vv. 24, 27), cancelling David's statement in 15:12 and ordering the Levites to serve the Aaronites (vv. 28-29), and laying down specifically just what duties the Levites did have (vv. 30-32).

2. Genealogies and a rota for the Aaronites, 24:1-19, which priestly priority over the Levites would not have allowed to have been placed in this secondary position if it were original.

3. An extended roster with genealogies (24:20-31) introduced abruptly by the rubric *wĕlibnê lēwî hannôtārîm,* "Now as for the Levites left over," contradicting the genealogies of 23:2-24 in several details and duplicating it in others.

4. The rota for the musicians in 25:7-31, emulating the rota for the priests, 24:6b-31. Its secondary character can be seen from the fact that the order Asaph-Heman-Jeduthun in the original material has been altered to Asaph-Jeduthun-Heman in v. 6b, an order that is also reflected in the rota of vv. 9-31 (see below).

5. An intrusive claim of the Obed-edomites, otherwise known as gatekeepers (cf. 26:15; 16:38; but cf. 16:5), to belong among the singers, 26:4-8.

6. A table of organization for the gatekeepers, 26:12-18, misspelling the "Meshelemiah" of vv. 1, 2, 9 as "Shelemiah."

7. The record of secular officials in 27:1-34, with its unparalleled, expansive introduction, competing with 26:29-32 in usurping outside duties assigned to the Levites, introducing matters not covered in the original introduction at 23:3, where David's speech makes it clear that he has the Levites, and them alone, in view. This list also lies outside the narrative framework that we have identified. Like some of the other secondary materials listed here, it may contain ancient traditions, or even go back to authentic records, but it was not in the original version of ChrH.

In order to be helpful, a structural outline of these chapters ought to show the interweaving of original with secondary materials:

	Original	Expansions
1. Register of Levites and priests in the temple		
a. Census and organization	23:2-24	
b. Job descriptions of the Levites		25-32
c. Report concerning the sons of Aaron		24:1-19
d. Expanded list of Levites		20-31
2. Register of musicians		
a. Introduction	25:1a	

I. REGISTER OF LEVITES AND PRIESTS IN THE TEMPLE, 23:2–24:31

Structure

(continued on p. 195)

Following on from the title of 23:1, in which David is the acting subject, ChrH adds a new active verb in v. 2, assuming David as subject. The verb is from the root *'sp,* "gather," instead of *qhl,* "assemble," perhaps with the meaning that the persons mentioned were merely summoned to witness what would be done, rather than expected to take an active part in it (cf. *qhl* in 13:2). There is a question whether *hakkōhănîm,* "the priests," has come into the text by the same hand as added vv. 13b-14 and vv. 24b-31, reconstructing the normal locution, "the priests and the Levites." Since everything in this section that has directly to do with the priests proves to be secondary, it is easy to argue for this position, in which case the only persons present would be David, *kol-śārê yiśrā'ēl,* "every official of Israel," and the Levites. A passive verb, the niph. of *'sp,* tells us that on this occasion, and in this assemblage, the Levites thirty years old and upward were counted *(spr),* with the result that their number, i.e., counting every person (a ChrH locution, *lĕgulgĕlōtām,* uses *lĕ* as the sign of the definite object; lit., "every skull," i.e., "head"), but only *ligĕbārîm,* "grown-ups" (again with *lĕ* used as sign of the definite object), was 38,000. On the purpose of this census and the meaning of these numbers, one should consult von Rad *(Geschichtsbild,* 90); but it is immediately evident that the tallies as well as the proportions are schematic, perhaps representing the maximums that each subgroup, and the Levites as a whole, were allowed to have in the ideal Israel.

The *RSV* gives the mistaken impression that David is mentioned in the Hebrew text as ordering the arrangements of vv. 4-6. This impression is created by the phrase *'ăšer 'ăśîtî lĕhallēl,* "which I made for praise." But the reading is dubious (cf. LXX[B] and Vg.) and may have been scribally altered to the first person from the third person, with a probable indefinite subject, because someone—presumably David—seems to be speaking. As a matter of fact, the authoritative person giving these instructions can be no other than ChrH, for David is not introduced as the speaker. Perhaps ChrH wishes to attribute the arrangement into *maḥlĕqôt,* "functions," "positions," to David, but dares not take the liberty of citing actual words from him. Be that as it may, the summary in v. 6a informs us that this affair has only the appearance of a census. We read there *wayḥallĕqēm* [MSS, LXX, Vg., Tg., over against MT niph. passive] *dāwîd maḥlĕqôt,* "So David assigned them to positions." The word *maḥlĕqâ* is explicated by the enumerated offices: temple servants (*'al- mĕle'ket bêt-yahweh,* "in charge of caring for Yahweh's temple"), officers and judges, gatekeepers, praise-musicians. This informs us that ChrH definitely included these sub-orders among the Levites. At the same time, however, the traditional Levites, the twenty-four thousand, retained control of supervising the temple service. As v. 4 states, the service of all the *maḥlĕqôt* was to be forever (*lĕnaṣṣēaḥ*).

What follows in vv. 6b-24a is a genealogical list for the three major branches or "families" of the Levites. It starts out (vv. 6b-7) in characteristic ChrH diction, *lĕ* being used as sign of the definite object, or a determinative, rather than in the traditional dative function. We are to translate, "Sons of Levi: Gershon, Kohath, and Merari [this order is retained in what follows and serves as a formal subtitle]; Gershonites: Ladan and Shimei." But immediately ChrH departs from this styling and surrenders to the common *bĕnê . . . ûbĕnê . . .* patterning of the traditional genealogies. For arguments in support of the originality of this entire list, cf. Williamson ("Origins," 30). The styling and diction is definitely ChrH's. G. von Rad (*Geschichtsbild,* 96-98) interprets it as a program for Levitical holiness typical of ChrH.

This list is unlike most of the genealogies that ChrH has offered in that it aims at a fully collateral structure, filling in with narrative exposition whenever it has gaps in its tabulations, as in v. 11, "Jeush and Beriah had not many sons, therefore they become a father's house in one reckoning"; also in v. 17, "Eliezer had no other sons, but the sons of Rehabiah were very many"; again in v. 22, "Eleazar died having no sons, but only daughters; their kinsmen, the sons of Kish, married them." These are all fully integrated into the genealogical list, and are original, but vv. 13b-14, stating the prerogatives of the Aaronites and emphatically identifying Moses' sons as Levites, fits ill into its context, showing itself to be an ideological gloss. Otherwise the list is well in order, drawing out the genealogical connections to the second, third, fourth, and even fifth generations. Regularly the NAME LIST, TALLY, and RANKING FORMULA appear. To the superficial observer, the recurrent tallies might be interpreted as an effort to explicate the census figures in vv. 4-6, but this is wrong because, as we will show under "Genre," each of these is actually a TABLE OF ORGANIZATION, in which both the census figures and the tallies are schematic and ideal. It is not unusual to see genealogical listings with only one name, but it does seem strange to find two single names with the title *hārō'š* normally used where a list of ordinals follows to produce the RANKING FORMULA.

Unparalleled in this document is the summary in v. 9b, *'ēlleh rā'šê hā'ābôt lĕlaʿdān.* It does not seem reasonable to take this as an original element in the list from which ChrH was working and then argue that "Shimei" in v. 9 or v. 10 is a scribal error for some other name, as some scholars have claimed. It is true that when a name list is given, not every sibling need be given a separate new segment, but the point that has to be made is that no names are given a new genealogical segment except such as have already been listed, making it very unlikely that some other name originally stood where either occurrence of "Shimei" now stands. It seems that the Shimei list in v. 9a, with the Ladan summary, is an interpolation. This does not mean that the names given in v. 9a have to be unhistorical. They do differ from those in v. 10, but our interpretation is that the "sons" are actual families whose tenure in the Shimei list has varied in the course of time (we note that a Shimei with his brother Libni [= Ladan?] is listed in 6:2 as a son of Gershon, but in 6:14-15 as a son of this "Libni," who is a grandson of Merari).

Lest one imagine that the genealogical list just discussed is intended to cover the entire 38,000 of v. 3, it should be seen that the closing rubric of v. 24a specifically states that they are equivalent only to the original Levites of v. 4a, whose task was to be *ʿal-mĕleʾket bêt-yahweh,* "in charge of caring for Yahweh's temple." This conclusion is quite particular in specifying to whom the list pertains. It begins, *ʾēlleh bĕnê- lēwî lĕbêt ʾăbōtêhem,* "These are the Levites according to their ancestral families"; it continues, *rāʾšê hāʾābôt lipqûdêhem,* "ancestral chiefs according to their enrollment"; and then, *bĕmispar šēmôt lĕgulgĕlōtām,* "as they were assigned individually to a name"; and finally, *ʿōśê* [MSS, LXX, Vg., Tg.] *hammĕlāʾkâ laʿăbōdat bêt yahweh,* "performing the supervision for the worship in Yahweh's temple." The recurrence of the unusual *gulgĕlôt,* "heads," lit., "skulls," from v. 3 is assurance that ChrH is still at work in spite of the fact that this rubric pertains only to the first group of Levites. One should note, however, that *mispār* no longer means "count," "number," but "enumeration" or "assignment"—a subtle but important difference. The only words in v. 24 that confuse this explication are *mibben ʿeśrîm šānâ wāmāʿlâ,* "from twenty years and up." This is a gloss similar to v. 27, correcting v. 3 and introducing the Aaronite addition of vv. 25-32.

Genre

The main genre here is REGISTER; this is defined as an administrative writing which officially records items or persons with regard to the identifying characteristics by which they are subject to administration by institutions or corporate bodies. It does not matter that, in this case, the REGISTER is introduced by narration. ChrH's own words make the statement that 38,000 Levites were counted, but, as we have seen, vv. 4-5a are in a form of discourse which may intend to express David's will, but have to have been spoken by another person—perhaps by ChrH himself. In any case, the form of this section is that of INSTRUCTION, informing the hearers of something they need to know for their own functioning or well-being. To the TALLY of v. 3, giving the total counted, the INSTRUCTION adds specifications, to wit, further tallies of 24,000 for the temple supervisors, of 6,000 for officers and judges, of 4,000 for the gatekeepers, and of 4,000 for the musicians. Inasmuch as vv. 4-6a are not cited as a quotation (in spite of *RSV*), there can be no objection to taking this as a special genre, TABLE OF ORGANIZATION. This is defined as an administrative instrument in which the several different jobs or responsibilities within an organization are listed in relationship to one another, accompanied by an identification of the person or group assigned to fill each position. Our passage gives a specific name for such positions: *maḥlĕqôt* (v. 6a), from the verbal root *ḥlq,* "divide," "distinguish." No proper names are given, but rounded-off numerals, and yet the numerals are assumed to apply to individual persons because v. 3 (cf. v. 24) specifically states that their *mispār* (numbering or assignment) was to be by individuals *(lĕgulgĕlōtām).* The TABLE OF ORGANIZATION differs from the (→) roster, whose main concern is to identify persons, linking each with his function or office, and it differs from the (→) job description, which details the various aspects of a job-holder's responsibility.

In our discussion of the structure of vv. 6b-24a, hints were made that, in spite of appearances, this was no proper GENEALOGY because of the unparalleled use of the TALLY and the RANKING FORMULA. Outside of vv. 4-6a, the former is found in vv. 8, 9, 10, 12, 23; the latter is found in vv. 8, 11, 18, 19, 20. The NAME LIST occurs at vv. 7, 8, 9, 10, 12, 15, 16, 17, 19, 21 (twice), and 23. These verses actually display another form of the TABLE OF ORGANIZATION, but one that follows a genealogical rather than functional principle. The genealogical interrelationship is the pattern, but the names assigned to each eponymous ancestor are those of family groups (*bêt 'āb;* cf. v. 11, s.) who are assigned to various *maḥlĕqôt,* but are expected to follow the genealogical precedence of this ancestral list. This may explain why v. 10, with Jahath, Zina, Jeush, and Beriah, represents perhaps a later— or else earlier—listing of names than those of Shelomoth, Haziel, and Haran, named as Shimei's sons in v. 9. The introduction to this second TABLE OF ORGANIZATION is in v. 6b and has the form of a title: "Levites: Gershom, Kohath, and Merari." As we have seen, the concluding rubric in v. 24a puts all who are covered by this title under the *maḥlĕqâ* of temple supervisors, i.e., the Levites in the proper sense. This does not rule out the possibility that genealogical considerations had a role to play in organizing the other *maḥlĕqôt,* the officers and judges, the gatekeepers, and the musicians, although, because those occupying those positions appear to have gained Levitical recognition only gradually (→ 9:17-32), one would expect their sense of genealogical identification to be weak. It seems quite certain, therefore, that the TABLE OF ORGANIZATION of vv. 4-6a was for the expanded Levitical circle, laying stress on different duties, while the TABLE OF ORGANIZATION of vv. 6b-24a pertained only to the original elite—those who could trace their ancestry from Levi.

Setting and Function

On the subject of "setting" there is little to say. We have seen that this pericope is a continuation of the David narrative, but there can be no question that these administrative lists belong, not in the time of David, but in ChrH's own time. Comparison with ch. 9 shows a progression from the situation in which Levites were listed separately from gatekeepers and singers, so it seems reasonable to date our pericope late. The attribution of this material to David accords well with the ideology of chs. 15–16. As we have opportunity to scrutinize examples of the AUTHORIZATION FORMULA in the course of this study, we shall find that the Levites and related subgroups appeal to the authority of David on several occasions (1 Chr 9:22; 2 Chr 23:18; 29:25; 35:15). Although in ritual matters they acknowledged the authority of Moses, David was their special *hērōs eponymos.* It would be no exaggeration to say that ChrH makes a *pontiff* out of David and his successors, with the

Levites as his special "Swiss Guard." Although the Aaronite priests had charge of the sacred ceremonies, all else was under the care of the Levites. We can well imagine, then, that if the historical David were actually living in the time of ChrH— or vice versa — he surely would have numbered, categorized, and checked the credentials of this all-important group.

Bibliography

A. H. Gunneweg, *Leviten und Priester* (Göttingen: Vandenhoeck & Ruprecht, 1965); J. Liver, *Chapters in the History of the Priests and Levites* (Jerusalem: Magnes, 1968); K. Möhlenbrink, "Die levitischen Überlieferungen des Alten Testaments," *ZAW* 52 (1934) 184-231; G. von Rad, *Das Geschichtsbild des chronistischen Werkes* (Stuttgart: Kohlhammer, 1930); H. G. M. Williamson, "The Origins of the Twenty-Four Courses: a Study of 1 Chronicles xxiii-xxvii," in *Studies in the Historical Books of the Old Testament* (VTSup 30; ed. J. A. Emerton; Leiden: Brill, 1979) 251-68.

I. REGISTER OF LEVITES AND PRIESTS IN THE TEMPLE, 23:2–24:31, continued

Structure

B. Job Description of the Levites	23:25-32
1. David's assignment of new duty	25-31
a. Dedicatory declaration	25
1) Israel's God gave rest	25a
2) Description of Yahweh: dwelling perpetually in Jerusalem	25b
b. Levitical portering obsolete	26
c. David's final instruction	27-31
1) Introduction	27
2) Assistants to the Aaronites	$28a\alpha^1$
3) Custodial responsibilities	$28a\alpha^2$-29
a) List: temple worship, courts, and chambers	$28a\alpha^2$
b) Purification	$28a\beta$-29
(1) List of holy things	$28a\beta$
(2) Worship duties in temple	28b
(3) Sacred bread	29a
(4) Weights and measures	29b
4) List of occasions for attendance at worship	30-31
a) Daily morning service	30a
b) Daily evening service and at burnt offering	30b-31a
c) Regulation formula	31b
2. Instruction concerning Levitical custody	32

a. Service of "the tent of meeting" $32a\alpha^1$
b. The holy things $32a\alpha^2$
c. The behavior of the Aaronites $32a\beta$-b

(continued on p. 198)

Were it not for the summarizing character of v. 24 (without the gloss changing the age to twenty), the reader might imagine that vv. 25-32 are an original continuation; that is in fact what the supplementer wants to suggest as he draws David back from vv. 2-6 for the purpose of extending his intervention into the affairs of the Levites. The introductory *kî* can be rendered "but," "for," "moreover," or "however"—but it introduces a new command *('mr)* in the form of a DEDICATORY DECLARATION (cf. 22:1): *hēnîaḥ yahweh 'ĕlōhê–yiśrā'ēl lĕ'ammô wayyiškōn bîrûšālaim 'ad-lĕ'ôlām,* "Yahweh the God of Israel gave his people rest; and he made his residence *[škn]* in Jerusalem unto eternity." V. 26 draws the immediate conclusion (emphatic *wĕgam lalĕwîyim),* "So definitely the Levites . . ." *(lĕ* as determinative). A noun clause with infinitive states that the Levites are no longer to carry the *miškān* or any of the implements appropriate to its service. The reference is to the Pentateuch, with the background of the wilderness wandering; hence such a duty would have been obsolete long before the historical David. The point can be seen in a pun on the word *miškān,* from the root *škn,* used in the preceding verse of Yahweh. In that Yahweh now dwells permanently in Jerusalem, he has no need of a *miškān,* lit., "place to dwell." Still, this pericope keeps up the imagery of the desert shrine, assigning the Levites in v. 32 to attend the *'ōhel–mô'ēd,* "tent of meeting"—an alternative name for the tabernacle.

This said, David presumably continues speaking in vv. 27ff. But before David can speak, he is interrupted by a gloss that comes apparently from the same hand as the last four words of v. 24; the glossator insists that these regulations pertain to twenty-year-olds, not only to those older than thirty, and he appeals to David's authority by stating that these were David's last words, i.e., his final and irrevocable instruction. V. 28, the beginning of the original instruction, is in chiasmus with v. 32, the last verse. Since v. 25b negated the Levites' previous duty of portering, *kî* in v. 28 means "but"; it is followed by the phrase *ma'ămādām lĕyad–bĕnê-'ahărōn,* "Their position shall be in attendance on the Aaronites." The word *ma'ămād,* from the root *'md,* "stand," is used regularly in ChrH and means a "position" for performing a role within the ritual. Thus the Levites' chief duty is to assist the priests, but vv. 28-29 go on to specify the entire range of their responsibilities. The syntax is difficult to disentangle: *lĕ* with the direct object pertains to the temple worship, *'al . . . wĕ'al . . . wĕ'al* governs the courts, chambers, and purification *(lĕkol- qōdeš)* of various kinds of sacred food or bread *(lĕ . . . lĕ . . . lĕ . . . lĕ).* V. 28b, "and any work for the service of the house of God," is a generalizing gloss. Without any formal break, vv. 30-31 list the various times when the Levites will be required to be in attendance *(wĕla'ămōd):* it is to be mornings, day by day, and similarly *(kēn)* at evening, but also while burnt offerings are sacrificed at any of the holy days. V. 31b sums this up with the phrase *bĕmispār kĕmišpāṭ 'ălêhem,* meaning "by duties [not "number," *RSV*] as assigned them." As has been suggested, v. 32 is in chiasmus with v. 28, yet it has its own distinctive structure and intent. It speaks of the Levites' duty of watching, guarding, regulating (Hebr.

196

šmr). The word for what is being watched, *mišmeret*, is from the same root, and this verse uses this to distinguish the three special objects of their vigilance: (1) the "tent of meeting," a metaphor for the temple; (2) the *qōdeš*, "purification rites," and (3) "how the Aaronites perform worship in the house of God."

Genre

The main genre of this pericope is JOB DESCRIPTION. As seen in 1 Chr 9:14-33, this is a detailing of work assigned to a group or individual. Hypothetically, it is David who makes the determination. As has been noted, v. 25 is a DEDICATORY DECLARA-TION, with a DESCRIPTION OF YAHWEH in v. 25b. Vv. 27-28a, including the gloss, belong to the genre INSTRUCTION; so too v. 32. The genre LIST is identified three times in vv. 28-31. V. 31b, finally, has the REGULATION FORMULA, which assures that a sacrosanct procedure is fully and correctly carried out. It differs from the (→) authorization formula, which blesses and certifies a given procedure. The DED-ICATORY DECLARATION of v. 25 borrows heavily from 1 Chr 22:9, 18; Psalm 132.

Setting and Intention

It is in Numbers 4 that Levites in service are required to be thirty years old, as in 1 Chr 23:3. Elsewhere in Numbers the age is reduced to twenty-five, while in the glosses in our chapter, vv. 24 and 27, plus 2 Chr 31:17; Ezra 3:8, it is allowed to be twenty. Although it is difficult to date these passages, the trend seems to be toward the lower age. This apparently reflects a situation in which either there were too many unemployed Levites, or the age had to be lowered in order to fill the depleted ranks.

Some friction with the Aaronite priests is evident here, but it is not a priest or someone pleading for their cause who has added this new material. Rather, this addition expresses the desire of a writer later than ChrH to accomplish two things: (1) assure that the Levites would retain their standing next to the priests, and (2) spell out completely the duties, places, and times of their service. The statement that the Levites are to serve *lĕyad*, lit., "at the hand of," the priests is no disparage-ment but an assertion of their privilege. What is surprising, perhaps, is the injunc-tion in v. 32, to the effect that their overall responsibility of supervision must in-clude also the performance of the priests in their leadership of worship within the temple. This stance resembles more than anything else the attitude toward the priests reflected in such criticism as in 2 Chr 30:15-17.

Bibliography

K. Möhlenbrink, "Die levitischen Überlieferungen des Alten Testaments," *ZAW* 52 (1934) 184-231; G. von Rad, *Das Geschichtsbild des chronistischen Werkes* (Stuttgart: Kohlham-mer, 1930) 90, 107-8.

I. REGISTER OF LEVITES AND PRIESTS IN THE TEMPLE, 23:2–24:31, continued

Structure

(continued on p. 201)

Verse 1a is actually a title: *wĕlibnê 'ahărōn maḥlĕqôtām;* again reading *lĕ* as a determinative, this should be rendered, "Now as for the Aaronites [sons of Aaron]: their assignments." In narrative form we are told (1) why there were only two Aaronite families when Aaron had four sons; and (2) how the priests belonging to the two surviving families were organized with use of the lot. Knowing Lev 10:1-3 and Num 3:4, the readers know very well why Nadab and Abihu died, leaving no children, so that Eleazar and Ithamar were left to serve as priests (verb: *wayĕkahănû,* v. 2b). Eager to include also the priests in David's assignments (23:2-6a), the narrator states (v. 3) that David did organize them (*wayyeḥolqēm . . . lip-quddātām ba'ăbōdātām,* "in their enrollment within their (respective) service." *RSV,* "with the help of Zadok . . . and Ahimelech," is wrong; the reading should be "with Zadok representing the Eleazarites and Ahimelech representing the sons of Ithamar." That is to say, these two well-known priestly figures from David's time now serve to represent the two families.

Next the narrator states (v. 4) why, in the allotment, there would be twice as many (16) to represent the Eleazarite branch as those representing Ithamar (8); it was because the former had more *rā'šê haggĕbārîm,* "chiefs of the prominent men." So they appointed them *(wayyaḥlĕqûm)*—so many—as *rā'šîm lĕbêt-'ābôt,* "chiefs for each ancestral family," sixteen and eight. This might seem a just principle to follow, but vv. 5-6 take pains to state that the lot for the rota was carried out fairly and in due proportion. The principle is: *'ēlleh 'im 'ēlleh*, "this one equal with that one" —though of course in the proportion of two to one. Furthermore, since both families had *śārê-qōdeš wĕśārê hā'ĕlōhîm*, the lot was to favor neither the one family nor the other (there is no agreement among scholars as to the distinction of "chiefs of the holy" from "chiefs of God"). A Levite, Shemaiah son of Nethanel—otherwise unknown, but evidently a person of high integrity—recorded the lot as it was taken, and this was witnessed by an impressive company of authorities, starting with the king himself. They all saw to it that ancestral families were chosen in proper alternation (since Eleazar had to come out with twice as many positions as Ithamar, "one for Eleazar ... and one [MSS, LXX^BA, Vg., S^A] for Ithamar" has to mean that neither family took two lots when it should have been one).

Finally, the actual ROTA is given in the style of a narrative, telling how the lot came out (vv. 7-19). Except for the first course, that of Jehoiarib, the order is simply: proper name, ordinal, up to twenty-fourth. These courses were either for half-months or for two weeks. The concluding rubric of v. 19 is ponderous. Referring back to v. 3, the text tells us that *'ēlleh pĕquddātām* [LXX, Vg., plur.] *la'ăbōdātām*, "These were their enrollment for their service." Their service was, of course, *lābô' lĕbêt-yahweh*, "to enter Yahweh's house/temple." This agrees with OT tradition in general, giving the priests the exclusive right actually to enter into the temple. By the ROTA that had now been given, this "entering" was to be restricted to the periods assigned. Authorities for this rule were Aaron their father, and Yahweh, the God of Israel.

Genre

The main genre of this pericope is REPORT; but, though it is cast in narrative style, it is meant as regulation. There is a NAME LIST in v. 1b agreeing in substance with 5:29. A new genre in this pericope is the ROTA, defined as a rudimentary calendar fixing the order of rotation for a particular group, in this case the Aaronite priests. The duties of individual members of the rota are not stated, only the names and order of service. Other rotas will be seen in 25:8-31 and 27:2-15.

Along with several examples of the AUTHORIZATION FORMULA, we have seen one example of the REGULATION FORMULA. For a detailed discussion of the differences between these two formulas, (→) AUTHORIZATION FORMULA; REGULATION FORMULA. The latter is like a marginal rubric guiding the performance of a modern liturgy, its purpose being to assure that a given rule is carried out according to regulation. The former is more like canon law, authorizing a given change in procedures. When a specific person is named in the REGULATION FORMULA, this is solely for historical orientation. Thus v. 19aβ, *kĕmišpāṭām bĕyad 'ahărōn 'ăbîhem*, "according to their rule as carried out by their father Aaron," a REGULATION FORMULA, states that the twenty-four courses of priests are to "enter" Yahweh's temple by regulation —the one employed by their eponymous ancestor Aaron. But the text concludes with *ka'ăšer ṣiwwahû yahweh 'ĕlōhê yiśrā'ēl*, "just as Yahweh God of Israel commanded." This is the AUTHORIZATION FORMULA, stating by whose authority and command the practice in question proceeds.

Setting and Intention

The GENEALOGY of 5:27-32 names Aaron's four sons as they are named here, but it does not mention the death of Nadab and Abihu, nor does it offer the lineage of Ithamar. The list of high priests that it offers is, then, exclusively from the line of Eleazar. Our present passage clearly favors Eleazar in its 16:8 proportion, but the fact that it at least offers one third of the priestly assignments to Ithamar shows that this priestly family remained intact long after the return from exile. Scholars speculate about the bitter fate of Nadab and Abihu. They are somehow remembered in the list of family eponyms, yet the claim that they were both childless — a coincidence that strains the imagination — can reasonably be explained from the supposition that they lost out in the competition, and that all records and memories of their respective posterity were lost or died away. About Zadok and Ahimelech (v. 3): from the court record of 18:16 our redactor knows that they lived together in David's court and served jointly as his priests. As a descendant of Eleazar, only the former gets mention in 5:27ff., but in a confused list that mentions the names "Zadok" and "Ahitub" several times. It is evident that our redactor shares with ChrH a specially high regard for this priest, and only for the reason that he was at David's court. In 15:11, Abiathar is Zadok's companion in office, but perhaps the tradition of 1 Kgs 2:26-27, to the effect that David banished Abiathar, has led him to make Ahimelech the son of Abiathar to serve here alongside Zadok.

The giving of the first lot to Jehoiarib has led some scholars to suggest that since a person of this name was the ancestor of the Maccabean family, this must be propaganda, at least reflecting greater prestige gained by this priestly course during the Hasmonean ascendancy. But there is nothing to prove such a connection, and in any event, propaganda for Jehoiarib is not apparent in this passage. There has been, naturally, a great deal of discussion about the origin of the twenty-four priestly courses, but most of the evidence adduced comes from rabbinical sources. Avi-Yonah ("Caesarea Inscription") has found inscriptional evidence dating back to the period of the second temple—the period of ChrH. What can be read corresponds to the list given here. Though what survives agrees with our list, this does not, according to the author, prove its historicity.

Recalling what has been said previously, this pericope must be a secondary addition to 23:2-24a (also to vv. 25ff.) because the Aaronite priests would never have appeared in a secondary position if it were original. The order is ever: "priests and Levites." But in 23:2ff. ChrH undertakes to regulate only the Levites, and it is a later hand that adds 24:1-19. It has three main purposes: (1) to explain the ROTA into twenty-four courses; (2) to validate this rule by adducing David's supervision; and (3) to legitimize the ancestral division of present-day priests, in the proportion of 2:1, by giving both Eleazar and Ithamar direct access to David.

Bibliography

M. Avi-Yonah, "The Caesarea Inscription of the Twenty-Four Priestly Courses" (Hebr.), *ErIs* 7 (1964) 24-28; J. Liver, *Chapters in the History of the Priests and Levites* (Jerusalem: Magnes, 1968); H. G. M. Williamson, "The Origins of the Twenty-Four Priestly Courses. A Study of 1 Chronicles xxiii-xxvii," in *Studies in the Historical Books of the Old Testament* (VTSup 30; ed. J. A. Emerton; Leiden: Brill, 1979) 251-68.

I. REGISTER OF LEVITES AND PRIESTS IN THE TEMPLE, 23:2–24:31, continued

Structure

This section has a new title: *wĕlibnê lēwî hannôtārîm,* "Now as for the remaining Levites." A ROSTER by families is then given, and it includes registers for Kohath's four sons, Amram, Izhar, Hebron, and Uzziel, but then goes on to give listings (vv. 26-27) for Kohath's brother Merari. Down through v. 25 the structure is clearly stereotyped; for each listing there is (1) the name of the chief representative of a family group and (2) the name of a descendant of that group — presumably the contemporary chief. V. 21 has a different form: "To Rehabiah (of the sons of Rehabiah) Isshiah as chief." It is probable that this group is to be included among the Amramites, just mentioned. V. 23, like v. 27 and v. 30, gives an ancestral NAME LIST, but only in v. 27 are the names placed in order with use of the RANKING FORMULA. In v. 26 Jaaziah is named twice, and the reading cannot be brought in order without viewing v. 27 as a genealogical gloss that strives to make sense out of a garbled text in v. 26. As in 1 Chr 23:21, Merari's two sons are named, breaking the pattern of naming only one heir. V. 28 notes only, in agreement with 23:22, that Eleazar son of Mahli was childless; but v. 29 states that Kish, who is said to have married Eleazar's daughters, was the father of Jerahmeel.

The roster concludes with the names of the three sons of Mushi, the second son of Merari (v. 30a; cf. 1 Chr 23:23). The ending has the concluding rubric that one would expect: "These are the Levites according to their ancestral families."

The redactor shows how much of an epigone he is in adding a note in v. 31; it states: (1) that these also *(gam-hēm)* cast lots; (2) that this was just as with their brothers *('ăḥêhem)* the Aaronites (cf. 24:6ff.); (3) that this was in the presence of the same dignitaries as in 24:6a; and (4) that in this procedure the ancestral chief *('ābôt hārō'š)* was treated just like *(lĕ'ummat)* his young brother *('āḥîw haqqāṭān)*. Finally, we should mention that from a genealogical aspect, this list is linear with collateral branches. Unusual is v. 25, where Isshiah in named as a brother *('āḥ)* of, rather than son *(ben)* of, Micah. Since the VSS support the MT here, we must explain the Micah reference as collateral to the line of Micah, just preceding, and this procedure parallels the collateral treatment of Mahli and Mushi in vv. 28-30. This is further evidence that we are not dealing here with an actual genealogy, which would not name a sibling as *'āḥ* except for purposes of identification (cf. 2:42).

Genre

This LIST exhibits the specific genre of ROSTER, which is defined as a list of all the names within a related group, along with the names of duties or offices assigned to each. In this example, the position in question is service as family eponym. Specific individuals are assigned to represent a given family within the overall genealogical structure. The NAME LIST, showing the whole pattern of sibling relationships, is found only for Hebron, for Merari, and for Mushi. Its irregular and nonfunctional appearance suggests that it is not integral to the ROSTER as such. The RANKING FORMULA, which appears in vv. 21, 23, is another non-essential embellishment in this particular passage.

Setting and Intention

The close relationship of this pericope to 1 Chr 23:6b-24a is apparent from the fact that it copies some material from it word for word, and that everything it copies is in the same order. As has been noted, it takes its material solely from the Kohath and Merari segments of that passage. Perhaps the supplementer had no interest in the Gershonites, or else he found it accurate and had no new material to add. He has an item for Amram (v. 20), but mentions a different line of descent than that of the famous Moses and Aaron; cf. 23:13-15. In v. 22 he draws the descent of Shelomoth from Izhar, but in a different structure; cf. 23:18 ("Shelomith"). In v. 23 he repeats the entire NAME LIST of Hebron from 23:19, including even that passage's RANKING FORMULA. In v. 24 Shamir becomes a descendant of Uzziel, representing the family of Uzziel, and in v. 25 Isshiah is named as the brother of Micah (see above); this differs from 23:20, where Micah and Isshiah are named as "chief" and "second" among the sons of Uzziel. V. 26a takes Merari's Mahli and Mushi from 23:21, with the genealogical note of v. 27 adding other sons. In vv. 28-29, 23:21-22 is paralleled rather freely, and with the addition of the name of Jerahmeel. The Mushi list in v. 30a, finally, is identical to 23:23.

The differences we have seen in comparison with ChrH's original material in 23:6b-24a can be explained mainly from the fact that this is a ROSTER and has a slightly different interest and intent than 23:6ff., and from the surmise that, being a later correction and/or addition, the passage of time had allowed certain names —mainly eponymous in which individuals stand for families—those that were currently in operation in place of those in the earlier document. The purpose is much the same: to assure a secure standing, on a genealogical basis, for the individuals and families mentioned.

Although 23:3-6 suggests that the persons named in the second TABLE OF ORGANIZATION in 23:6b-24a were assigned to their respective positions by direct decree from David, our secondary author takes pains to state that the Levites were appointed by lot, just as the Aaronites were in the first addition (v. 31). If this were ChrH himself writing, we would expect more consistency with regard to the appointment of the Levites. The supplementer of the present segment may be appealing to the Aaronite precedent of resorting to the lot as lending a greater level of authority to the persons on his list, for the lot is a very old device in which the direct will of God is brought to bear, and must therefore outrank the fiat of an earthly king.

II. REGISTER OF MUSICIANS, 25:1-31

Structure

Evidence that vv. 7-31 are a secondary addition to vv. 1-6 is seen primarily in the fact that v. 7 begins with the formula *wayěhî mispārām,* "and their roster was," just as in v. 1. In v. 1 this introduces a list of the chief representatives of the three main groups of singers/musicians, each structured similarly with name list (tally), a statement of whose direction each group served under, and a statement of each director's reputation. Though the tallies of six and fourteen are given, respectively, for the Jeduthunites and Hemanites, there is none for the Asaphites even though four names are recorded. It is pure speculation whether the sum, twenty-four, is supposed to correspond to the twenty-four courses in vv. 9-31, even though most of the names are the same. V. 7, on the other hand, follows the *wayĕhî mispār* formula with a statement that the total was two hundred eighty-eight, which is the product of 24 times 12, this being the figure for the number of courses, multiplied by the twelve assigned to each. Not only are we surprised at the statement that the same personnel who were assigned to genealogical groupings in vv. 2-6 were then later put into a priest-like rota of biweekly (or twice monthly) rotation; we are suspicious also that the twenty-four have swelled out to 288. The introduction to the rota in v. 7 states that their number was "with their brethren trained in music for Yah-weh" *('im-'ăhêhem mĕlummĕdê-šîr lĕyahweh)*. The figure of 288 is next said to apply to *kol-hammĕbîn,* "everyone properly trained," which would include the twenty-four of vv. 2-6 plus 264 others, perhaps as apprentices. The arrangement does not seem unreasonable, but the differences in structure in vv. 1-6 and vv. 7-31, respectively, beside the fact that each is introduced by the *wayĕhî mispār* formula, makes it virtually certain that the latter is an expansion or adaptation of the original material in the earlier verses. V. 1 seems to be using *mispār* in a sense different from its usage in v. 7. In v. 1 it seems to mean "assignment," and not much, in fact, is made of tallies in this section. In v. 7, on the other hand, where tallies are all-important, it clearly means "number." Add to this the fact that the sequence of names in the rota is definitely constructed with vv. 1-6 in mind, and one has strong evidence for the secondary character of vv. 7ff. Perhaps the most important argument is the unlikelihood that, in a genealogically oriented arrangement, there would be exactly eleven apprentices to attach themselves to each of the twenty-four chief singers.

In making these comparisons, one should not overlook the high degree of artificiality. The narrative framework begun in 1 Chr 23:2 reasserts itself with the statement (25:1) that David divided up tasks *(wayyabdēl . . . la'ăbōdâ)* between the three singer eponyms and the groups naming themselves after them: Asaph, Jeduthun, and Heman (cf. 6:16-34, where Heman's lineage is traced to Kohath, Asaph's lineage is traced to Gershon, and Ethan [Jeduthun?] traces his lineage to Merari—making them all Levites in a genealogical sense). Military terminology is used in describing those who aided David *(śārê haṣṣābā',* "commanders of the army")*. Either Asaph, Heman, and Jeduthun, or those who were being set aside, are said to be "prophesying" (so Qere, LXX, Vg., Tg.; Ketib "prophets") under the influence of musical instruments. Then follows the assignment to the descendants of the three eponymous musicians. The Asaphites served according to the Asaphite order, etc. Asaph is said to have prophesied *'al- yĕdê hammelek,* meaning perhaps, "by royal commission." Jeduthun is said to be the one who used the harp to "prophesy" (MT "prophet") in special praise and thanksgiving hymns to Yahweh. Heman is said to be *hōzēh hammelek,* "the royal visionary." V. 6 summarizes all that has been stated about these musicians: (1) they performed according to the order set down by their eponymous father; (2) they made instrumental music in the temple; and (3) it was at the king's command *('al yĕdê hammelek)* that these three groups performed.

The casual reader will notice the unusual length of the Heman NAME LIST, v. 4; but the truly striking thing is that it has been arranged as a kind of rebus, though designed for worship and not for entertainment (cf. Watson, "Archaic Elements," 206 n. 1; H. Torczyner, 247-49; comms. by J. Myers; Curtis and Madsen; Williamson). As most contemporary scholars would agree, after the first five names, the names begin to hang together syntactically, producing, with justifiable emendations, the following:

ḥānēnî yāh ḥānēnî	"Be gracious to me, Yahweh, be gracious to me";
'ēlî 'attâ	"My God art thou";
giddaltî wĕrōmamtî 'ôzrî	"I have magnified and will exalt my Helper";
yōšēb qāšâ mallôtî	"Dwelling in adversity I have spoken":
hôtîr maḥăzî'ōt	"Be generous with revelations."

It may also be, as Myers (comm.) has suggested, that these five lines are actually the incipits, or first-line titles, of five psalms.

A few words yet about the structure of the ROTA: this is strikingly stereotyped, but not as rigid in the Hebrew text as the translations seem to suggest (cf. Peterson, *Late Israelite Prophecy*, 67). Since the names in the rebus of v. 4 reappear here, one might question whether anything so artificial could be based on historical actuality. To show that the fabricator of this rota is as schematic as the writer of v. 4, we present the following diagram:

Asaph	*Jeduthun*	*Heman*	
1. Joseph	2. Gedaliah		
3. Zaccur	4. Izri		
5. Nethaniah		6. Bukkiah	
7. Asharelah	8. Jeshaiah	9. Mattaniah	
	10. Shimei	11. Azarel	
	12. Hashabiah	13. Shubael	
	14. Mattithiah	15. Jeremoth	
		16. Hananiah	17. Joshbekashah
		18. Hanani	19. Malloti
		20. Eliathah	21. Hothir
		22. Giddalti	23. Mahazioth
		24. Romamti-ezer	

This shows that the casting of the lot is an artifice, and that the order of vv. 1-6, Asaph-Jeduthun-Heman, strictly governed the arrangement of names within this rota. It is especially noteworthy that the indented names (nos. 16-24), all of which belong to Heman, are the same ones used in v. 4 but appear here in alternating order. Like Heman's own name, they appear together at the end.

Genre

The main genre of this pericope is REGISTER. It is based, however, on a ROSTER in vv. 1-6 and on a ROTA in vv. 9-31. As part of the ROSTER, the NAME LIST appears in vv. 2, 3, and 4. Vv. 3, 5, and 7 have the TALLY. In v. 5b the formula "according to the promise of God to exalt him" is the familiar FULFILLMENT FORMULA. One new formula, one that appears regularly in vv. 9-31, is the FAMILY FORMULA, "and his sons and his brothers," standing for lineal plus collateral relatives, respectively. The order may be reversed or the formula modified. It appears also at 26:8.

Setting and Intention

Most of the scholarly discussion of this pericope has centered on matters of linguistics and literary criticism. We may mention particularly Petersen (*Late Israelite Prophecy*), who discusses the names of vv. 2-4 (pp. 91-92) and the redaction and tradition history of the whole (pp. 64-68); also von Hummelauer (pp. 254ff.), who makes a careful study of the order of names in vv. 1-6 and vv. 9-31, respectively. There is no good reason to deny the ROSTER of vv. 1-6 to ChrH (one notes the narrative of David ordering it in v. 1), but for reasons previously stated, the ROTA with its narrative introduction, vv. 7-31, has to be a secondary expansion, but evidently one from within the same circle of musicians. The list of names is not the same as in 6:16-32, and it has no equivalent in 15:16-24 except perhaps "Mattithiah." This must mean that ch. 25 represents a different period than chs. 15–16.

Drawing once again upon Gese's seminal study, "Zur Geschichte der Kultsänger," we see that we have come here to a point of transition. Gese's Stage III-A has the order Asaph-Heman-Jeduthun. (The order of names is an indication of rank.) This arrangement is thought to be contemporary with ChrH; it is found in 1 Chr 16:37-42; 2 Chr 5:12; 29:13-14, and 35:15. We note that our passage, 1 Chr 25:1-6, has modified this order by assigning Heman to last place, after Asaph and Jeduthun; yet there are three things that create an *apologia* for his priority, suggesting that this is just a temporary arrangement: (1) he holds the high distinction of serving as the king's visionary; (2) his advancement stands as a special promise from God; and (3) he is blessed with the fourteen sons from whom the rebus of v. 4 is taken, and who of course end up having fourteen out of the twenty-four courses, with the nine names of the rebus at the end (vv. 23-31); the mention of three daughters alongside these fourteen sons only throws greater weight upon them. The conclusion is that Heman, though temporarily demoted, is on the rise, and in Gese's Stage III-B (ca. 300) the order becomes Heman-Asaph-Ethan (alternate name for Jeduthun, which, after all, is an artificial contrivance from *ydh*, "praise"). In 1 Chr 6:16-32 and 1 Chr 15:16-24 (not necessarily later than the work of ChrH but late from a tradition-historical perspective) this new ranking appears. Heman has come to the top, fulfilling the promise of 25:5.

Since it is evident that Heman's genealogical NAME LIST can be treated artificially and schematically — not to say playfully — it is hard to lend historical credence to the ROTA. Not only is it an imitation of the Aaronite rota in 24:7-31; it actually fixes the last nine allotments to match the last nine of Heman's offspring. More than anything else, this is evidence of a primitive tendency to midrash, in which entities are interpreted more in line with what they ought to mean than for what they mean in normal, descriptive discourse.

This is not the place for an extended discussion of prophecy in ChrH. S. Mowinckel ("The Prophetic Word in the Psalms and the Prophetic Psalms," in *The Psalms in Israel's Worship* [tr. D. R. Ap-Thomas; Oxford: Blackwell, and Nashville: Abingdon, 1962] II:53-73) had claimed that the prophets had a regular place in Israel's cult from the beginning. But the identification seems to come here at the end, rather than at the beginning, of that institution's development. Here it is the Levitical singers who are said to "prophesy" and to serve as *ḥōzēh* at the king's command. D. L. Petersen (*Late Israelite Prophecy,* 62) refutes Mowinckel while demonstrating the affinities between the late canonical prophets and these singer-prophets of ChrH. A valuable addition to this discussion is found in Th. Booij (*Godswoorden in de Psalmen*), explaining from the structure of several psalms how the Levitical singers went about performing a quasi-prophetic function in the Jerusalem liturgy.

Bibliography

J. Boehmer, "Sind einige Personennamen 1 Chr 25, 4 künstlich geschaffen?" *BZ* 32 (1934) 93-100; Th. Booij, "Prophetische elementen in de tempelzang," in *Godswoorden in de Psalmen: Hun functie en achtergronden* (Amsterdam: Rodopi, 1978) 63-77; H. Gese, "Zur Geschichte der Kultsänger am zweiten Tempel," in *Abraham unser Vater* (*Fest.* O. Michel; ed. O. Betz, et al.; Leiden: Brill, 1963) 222-34; P. Haupt, "Die Psalmverse in 1 Chr 25:4," *ZAW* 34 (1914) 142-45; P. F. von Hummelauer, "1 Chr 25: Ein Beitrag zum Gebrauch des Loses bei den Hebräem," *BZ* 2 (1904) 254-59; T. Kahane, "The Priestly Courses and their Geographical Settlements" (Hebr.), *Tarb* 48 (1978-79) 2-29; S. Mowinckel, "Kultprophetie und prophetische Psalmen," in *Psalmenstudien* III (repr. Amsterdam: Schippers, 1961) (= "The Prophetic Word in the Psalms and the Prophetic Psalms," in *The Psalms in Israel's Worship* [tr. D. R. Ap-Thomas; Oxford: Blackwell, and Nashville: Abingdon, 1962] II:53-73); D. L. Petersen, *Late Israelite Prophecy; Studies in Deutero-Prophetic Literature and in Chronicles* (SBLMS 23; Missoula: Scholars, 1977); H. Torczyner, "A Psalm by the Sons of Heman," *JBL* 68 (1949) 247-49.

III. REGISTER OF GUARDS AND CUSTODIANS, 26:1-32

Structure

This is the third and last section of the major division "Organization of Clergy and Laity," 1 Chr 23:2–27:34, i.e., not counting the many intrusions. Even this pericope has been expanded. The Obed-edom section, vv. 4-8, was not present in ChrH's work because this person is not listed either for the family of Meshelemiah, vv. 1-3, 9, or for the family of Hosah, vv. 10-11. A second intrusion is vv. 12-18, which inserts names chosen at random from vv. 1-11 or other sources, substituting "Shelemiah" for "Meshelemiah," and giving *maḥlĕqôt*, already defined in vv. 1ff., a quite different bearing. Vv. 1-11, actually a ROSTER, has the title *lĕmaḥlĕqôt lĕšōʿărîm*, "As for the assignments of the gatekeepers," and this agrees with the terminology of the conclusion in v. 19: *ʾēlleh maḥlĕqôt haššōʿărîm libnê haqqorḥî wĕlibnê mĕrārî*, "These are the assignments of the gatekeepers belonging to the Korahites and the Merarites" — which covers the two families described in the preceding original material. The expansion in vv. 12ff. makes *maḥlĕqôt* tantamount to *mišmārôt*, "watches"; one should translate v. 12: "For these [the persons mentioned in the roster] there were guard stations, i.e., according to the chief dignitaries, even watches on behalf of their kinsmen."

The original material in this pericope is divided up into three groupings. There were, first, the regular *šōʿărîm* or gatekeepers, vv. 1-3, 9-11. Next there were Levites who had charge of the two treasuries, vv. 20-28. Third, there were two special groups of Levites who were in charge of the public administration, vv. 29-32. Taking the "gatekeepers" first, we find that their ancestral families were the Korahites and the Merarites, but the fact that each eponym is represented by only one person, Meshelemiah and Hosah, respectively, may reflect a process in which each of these gatekeeper families chose a tribal eponym at the time when the gatekeepers gained Levitical status. Meshelemiah's pedigree from Asaph, chief singer, cannot be accounted for; perhaps another man with this name is intended. Since Kore is also named, the gatekeeper in question may be the same as the Shallum ben Kore of 9:19. His sons are given with a NAME LIST and rank in vv. 2-3. Hosah's sons in vv. 10-11 also have these formal elements, and we can be quite sure that the explanatory clause about Shimri in v. 10b, telling us that even though he had not been *bĕkōr*, "first-born," his father elevated him to the rank of *rōʾš*, "chief," is a gloss. Since *rōʾš* is very common in these late ranking formulas, a variant tradition would hardly cause this change in terminology, and it must be viewed as a random midrashic annotation.

The title of the section beginning in v. 20 is simply *wĕhalwîyim ʾăḥêhem* (LXX; MT: "Ahijah"), "As for their kinsmen the Levites." Without any kind of structural cue, this pericope is divided up among names belonging to two of the chief Levitical eponyms, Gershon (vv. 20-21) and Kohath (vv. 22-28), and from the latter, the Izharites through Shelomoth (cf. 23:18). V. 23, listing the four Kohathite families, seems to say that, among Kohathites, they were represented by Shebuel, whose pedigree is given from Moses, to be "chief officer in charge of the treasuries," with the title *nāgîd*, "supervisor." Zetham and Joel from Jehieli, from Ladan, from Gershon, were, on the other side, in charge only of the treasuries of Yahweh's temple (v. 22). We take note of Zetham and Joel's joint tenure, as though the one was needed to keep check on the other. We note also that Shebuel, the general fiscal chief, likewise has "brethren" (v. 25), but from the passed-over son of Levi, Eliezer (Eleazar), who probably had a similar responsibility toward him. In v. 26 we read that *hû' šĕlōmôt*, "this (same) Shelomoth," likewise had "brethren" to share the responsibility for the other treasury — the one where booty and dedicatory offerings, listed as if from an inventory, were kept.

Though a new area of responsibility is touched upon in vv. 29-32, the title is simply: "As for Izhar" and "As for Hebron." Among the Izharites (already included among temple treasurers; cf. above), the family of Chenaniah is appointed *lammĕlā'kâ haḥîṣônâ 'al-yiśrā'ēl*, "for external duty on behalf of Israel." Two further words, *lĕšōṭĕrîm* and *lĕšōpĕṭîm*, explain what is meant: they were to serve as administrators and as judges in the public domain (cf. Deut 17:8ff.). In the section on the Hebronites, similar duties are assigned but in different regions. There are two families, the sons of Hashabiah and the sons of Jerijah; for each group there is a tally, an assigned territory, and a statement of the areas of responsibility. The Hashabiahites number 1,700 and have oversight of Israel west of the Jordan. The Jerijahites number 2,700 and supervise the Transjordan (Curtis and Madsen, comm., 288, takes this disproportion as an indication of a Maccabean date, which is not probable, even though no alternative explanation seems readily available). V. 31a takes pains to tell us that Jerijah was *hārō'š*, "the chief," of all the Hebronites *lĕtōlĕdōtāyw lĕ'ābôt*, "in all their ancestral generations"—which can only mean that his name was continuingly eponymous. Taking up the narrative once again at v. 31b, ChrH mentions a search for *gibbôrê ḥayil* ("mighty warriors" in military jargon, but "competent men" here) as far as Jazer in Gilead, where apparently Jerijah was discovered. It was he and his "brethren," then, whom David appointed to serve as his 2,700 *rā'šê hā'ābôt*, "ancestral chiefs," in the two and a half tribes. Duties for Hashabiah and for Jerijah, respectively, are given in slightly different phrasing but with the same apparent meaning. The former must serve *lĕkōl mĕle'ket yahweh wĕla'ăbōdat hammelek*, "in all Yahweh's affairs and in the service of the king" (v. 30). The latter must serve *lĕkol-dĕbar hā'ĕlōhîm ûdĕbar hammelek*, "in every divine matter and in the king's business" (v. 32). Whether this be real or visionary (it certainly does not date from David's actual fortieth —his last—year), we see here a blatant theocratic theology in which clerical personnel are at the same time in charge of ecclesiastical and secular affairs.

As has been stated, the Obed-edom section is an unquestioned intrusion— but one that makes a forcible self-representation. Obed-edom had eight sons through God's blessing (vv. 4-5). Several sons and grandsons are named, but the total of the whole lot was sixty-two (v. 8), as compared with the measly eighteen of Meshelemiah and thirteen of Hosah (vv. 9, 11). One is particularly struck by the large number and variety of appellations claimed by the Obed-edomites: *mimšālîm lĕbêt 'ăbîhem*, "rulers in their ancestral family" (v. 6); *gibbôrê ḥayil*, "mighty warriors" (v. 6); *bĕnê ḥāyil*, "worthy men" (v. 7); *'îš ḥayil bakkōaḥ la'ăbōdâ*, "worthy man, mighty in service" (v. 8). Occasionally these appellations derived from the military appear in these chapters, but never with such profusion as here. This comes near to bragging, and one suspects a readiness of self-assertion that manifests itself otherwise in pushing Obed-edom's claim in contexts where he does not belong (so here and in 1 Chr 16:5, 38). The final family tally seems large (62), but is less than the 68 claimed in 16:38.

In the secondary section, vv. 12-18, the wording for casting lots sounds so similar to that of 25:8 that identity of authorship has to be suspected. As one sees, the structure for the assignment of the four sides of the temple is not thoroughly congruous. The east and the north are assigned each to one person, though it does seem strange that one is given to a father and another to a son (assuming that "Shelemiah" is the same as "Meshelemiah," v. 2). Obed-edom gets the south side, but with two extra places for his sons, who guard a storehouse. Two worthies—only one of whom has been mentioned—get the west, with its "Shallecheth" gate. The phrase *mišmār lĕ'ummat mišmār* probably means that there were congruous watches on each of these sides. The tally of guards (vv. 17-18) may be realistic, but one notes that Obed-edom, with his four at the south, plus two and two at the storehouse, has managed to get more positions than anyone else.

Genre

The main genre is REGISTER, but each section has its own genre. Vv. 1-11 is a ROSTER, a list of all the names within a related group, along with the duties or offices assigned to each. The duties or offices in question here are to function as family representatives in a specific duty. This implies that we are not to take the personal names as those of individuals, but generally they stand for a family "slot" which unnamed individuals are to fill. In this case, there is no (→) rota or (→) schedule governing just who does what, and where.

The expansion in vv. 12-18 has the genre TABLE OF ORGANIZATION. It lists the various jobs or responsibilities and then joins to this the names of the persons who are filling each spot. Vv. 20-28 is another ROSTER, but it clearly distinguishes between the job of guarding the treasury of Yahweh's temple and the job of guarding the "holy things," in this case booty from warfare and dedicated offerings from individuals. Vv. 29-32, finally, are still another ROSTER. This too is very explicit in adding to the names (1) the territory of operation, and (2) the double duty of guarding God's interests while seeing to the affairs of the king.

Again we are obliged to comment on military images employed in these regulations for the restoration temple. Phrases and formulas from real military documents are used profusely, but especially in the Obed-edom section, vv. 4-8: RANKING FORMULA, vv. 2-3, 4-5, 10-11, 31; NAME LIST, vv. 1-3, 7, 10-11 (see Watson, "Archaic Elements," 205 n. 6), 22-25; APPELLATION, vv. 6, 7, 8, 9, 14, 30; TALLY, vv. 8, 9, 17-18, 30-32; FAMILY FORMULA (→ 25:9-31), vv. 8, 9, 11.

Setting and Intention

Nothing of what is recounted here could have taken place in David's time. We are looking at rules contemporary with ChrH, for which he wished to claim, in a typological sense, Davidic promulgation and authorization. We do learn some important things about the postexilic Levites' duties outside their work in the temple service, as assistants to the priests. To them fell the responsibility of supervision in three areas not covered by the list of 23:28-32. The first one—to guard the gates and utilitarian structures like the temple storehouses—was assigned to the Levites in general, but to the gatekeepers in particular. The ROSTER of family slots for this responsibility is given in vv. 1ff., with Obed-edom's intrusion of vv. 4-8 claiming a distinction not afforded him in the original form of the text. The second Levitical responsibility was to keep tabs on the two treasuries (vv. 20-28); they apparently held not only lock and key, but pad and pen as well, for discharging this all-important responsibility. The third responsibility was to function as public administrators and as judicial officers, watching over religious matters along with the secular. We have mentioned the strongly theocratic character of this arrangement—but this passage is perhaps a rare clue of what may have been an originally secular context for the work of the Levites. However, the day seems to be past for giving sacral matters to one group of professionals and secular matters to another group entirely distinct from them.

IV. REGISTER OF THE OFFICERS OF THE PEOPLE, 27:1-34

Structure

Rudolph (ATD) identifies this entire pericope as later than ChrH. Williamson (comm.) seems to agree chiefly on the ground that 1 Chr 23:3 has only the Levites in mind. We have added to this consideration the fact that 27:1 is much longer and more complex than ChrH's own introductions, the fact that the Davidic framework ends in 26:32, and the fact that 27:25-34 competes with 26:30, 32, which put two Levites in charge of the affairs of the king. An epigone apparently believes that the secular order must be organized as well as the sacred. There is to be a twelve-month rota of cadres to work for the king, modeled perhaps after 1 Kgs 4:7-19, but certainly influenced by the priestly rota of 1 Chr 24:7-18 and the singers' rota of 25:9-31.

The introduction begins *ûbĕnê yiśrā'ēl lĕmispārām,* "Now as for the Israelites: their assignments/numbers." Their leaders are to be: (1) "the ancestral chiefs"; (2) "the commanders of thousands and hundreds"; and (3) "the responsible administrators for the king in every matter concerning the cadres *[hammaḥlĕqôt],* their enlistment, and their mustering out *[habbā'â wĕhayyōṣē't]."* This was to be month after month throughout the year, and each cadre was identical in number: twenty-four thousand.

Verses 2-15 give us the ROTA, then, first with the leader's name and provenance, whether a clan or a town (see the style of the roster in 11:26-47). The rota is numbered, first to twelfth, is given the month numbered, and is concluded by the statement that the tally comes to twenty-four thousand. There is an explanation about Jashobeam in v. 3, about Benaiah in v. 6, and about Joab's brother Asahel in v. 7. As there were 288 singers among the Levites (1 Chr 25:7), there are now 288,000 Israelites to do the king's work out in secular society. Nothing specific is said about what they are to do. There is no work mentioned; this is just organization for organization's sake.

But Israel can be organized a different way—the tribal way (vv. 16-22). One *nāgîd,* "chief" or "prince," is over each tribe. The tribal name comes first, then the name of the *nāgîd.* Though similar to the list in Num 1:5-15, the present list's order is unique. It has "Manasseh" and then two "half-Manassehs"; also, it has no Asher or Gad. The order is: Reuben, Simeon, Levi, Judah, Zebulun, Naphtali, Ephraim, Manasseh, half-Manasseh, half-Manasseh in Gilead, Benjamin, and Dan. The concluding rubric is in v. 22b: *'ēlleh śārê šibṭê yiśrā'ēl,* "These are the chiefs of Israel's tribes."

Quite unexpectedly, vv. 23-24 interrupt at this point to talk about David's census of ch. 21. This is a piece of primitive MIDRASH that will be explained below.

It is the census in 2 Sam 24:5-8 that set the writer to thinking about it in connection with the tribes. In Samuel, Joab is described as actually journeying from place to place throughout the realm. This is the point of departure—one might say, the text seeking an explication—for the midrash to follow.

Verses 25-31 are an ancient record that has the look of basic authenticity. It follows the proper order for the ROSTER, with the duty listed first and then, as in a ledger, the name of the person performing it (besides the name, we find either a patronym or a gentilic, i.e., the name of the town of one's origin). This is a much more practical way of organizing the king's work, and probably dates from the time of the united monarchy. (On Joab's count, cf. Watson, "Archaic Elements," 7.7; 11.3 on the fieldwork designated in vv. 26-28; cf. a ration list for fieldworkers in *UT*, 2013.) The concluding rubric for this ancient roster is: *kōl-'ēlleh śārê hārĕkûš 'ăšer lammelek dāwîd*, "All these are/were in charge of the property of King David." In the ROSTER of vv. 32-34, the proper name comes first and then the job or title. Both Jonathan, David's *dôd* (uncle or lover?), and Ahithophel are designated as *yô'ēṣ*, "counselor"; there are comments on Jonathan's qualifications, as if he were relatively unknown, and on the fact that he shared with Jehiel the task of tutoring the king's sons (v. 32a). Hushai the Archite is "the king's friend" *(rēa' hammelek)*, a kind of chief executive. Some interpreters think that the reference to Joab is a gloss, but what would be the glossator's purpose? His isolation at the end, following explanations about Jehoiada and Abiathar, may be in fact climactic—particularly if we consider that our interpolator may have wished to make a handy introduction to 28:1 and the scene of all the administrators, officials, and officers gathered for Solomon's coronation.

Genre

The main genre is REGISTER. The pericope contains a ROTA, vv. 2-15, and three examples of the ROSTER, vv. 16-22a, vv. 25-31, and vv. 32-34. The one in vv. 25-31 shows the purest form, and is likely to be the most authentic in terms of historical fact. The next most factual is the ROSTER in vv. 32-34—though, as it now stands in the text, it shows a branching out to regular narrative styling. The roster with tribal content in vv. 16-22 has so artificial an arrangement of the tribes that the names that go with them are suspect. ChrH wishes to perpetuate the notion of the twelve-tribe union as the basis for Israel's corporate structure, and has given it his best backing in the genealogical chapters, where he offered materials for all the tribes except Dan and Zebulun. The present ROSTER, undoubtedly from ChrH's redactor, picks those two tribes up, but has to sacrifice Asher and Gad, just to stick to the twelve-tribe scheme, which for reasons known only to him had already been filled out through the inclusion of two half-Manassehs when Manasseh had already been listed. The ROTA emulates 24:7-18 (which may be historical) and 25:9-31, but has an extravagant, meaningless structure. A grand TALLY of 24,000 appears in this contrived structure at v. 15 (cf. the twenty-fours at 1 Chr 24:18; 25:31).

Verses 23-24 constitute our second example of primitive MIDRASH within 1–2 Chronicles. The previous example was at 1 Chr 5:1-2, where a discussion of midrash in general, and in ChrH specifically, is to be found (→ 5:1-2). We may say in brief that the principle of MIDRASH as a biblical genre is that it (1) starts from a well-known but difficult biblical passage, and (2) explicates it on the basis of biblical and oral tradition, combined in reasoning from general theological principles to a conclusion that may make no sense historically, but that satisfies the sensitivities of the writer and his audience. The basic biblical text here is 1 Chr 21:2-6, ChrH's version of David's census. The subject comes naturally to mind just here because the redactor has recorded his roster of the twelve tribes—all Israel. Seemingly out of the blue, he states, "David did not number those below twenty years of age." He gets this from 23:24b, 27, and he means this as a scriptural mitigation of David's census. What could have moved David thus to diminish the upshot of his census? The answer is: Yahweh promised to make Israel "as many as the stars of heaven." This is taken from Gen 15:5 and seems to be implied in Joab's rhetorical question at 1 Chr 21:3a. Leaving aside the point of neglecting the underage Levites, the midrash draws in another consideration, to wit, Joab's incomplete count. It is unnecessary to adduce 21:6, to the effect that (1) Levi and Benjamin were left completely out, and (2) Joab found David's decree abhorrent, because two things in fact did happen: wrath came on Israel anyhow, and the number that Joab presented was not entered in "the chronicles of King David." This final conclusion is what the redactor is interested in because he needed a rationale to explain why the order of the tribes on the one hand, and the tallies of the cadres on the other, seemed to be so disparate.

Setting and Intention

Whether the redactor made up the MIDRASH himself, or took it over from another, we cannot tell. He seems to be on flimsy ground in his ROTA with its twelve cadres, particularly because the large work force seems to have had nothing to do. His tribal ROSTER is also quite contrived. What he seems to be trying to say is that Israel as a nation and Israel as a tribal confederation are perfect in their ideal organization. He uses a ROSTER of royal administrators, vv. 25-31, that hypothetically fit the very time of David's rule; so too the ROSTER of court officials in vv. 32-34.

In these chapters, we have become so suffused with clerical ideology that we may venture to believe that the redactor did some good in balancing off the clerical with the secular. We stand at the point of taking up a very secular—yet enigmatically sacred—affair, the coronation of David's son, who shall be builder, dedicator, and guardian of Yahweh's temple and all that pertains to it.

Bibliography

T. N. D. Mettinger, *Solomonic State Officials* (ConB 5; Lund: Gleerup, 1971); H. Seebass, "Erwägungen zum alttestamentlichen System der zwölf Stämme," *ZAW* 90 (1978) 196-220.

B. SOLOMON'S INVESTITURE, 28:1–29:25

Structure

IV. Report of David's farewell speech	29:1-9
V. Report of David's prayer	10-19
VI. Report of ritual: the investiture	20-22
VII. Report: Solomon initiated into the kingship	23-25

This section is so complex that it will be helpful to analyze the structure of the major segments separately.

I. Report of the gathering at Jerusalem	28:1
A. Introduction	1aα
B. Specifications	1aβ-b
II. Report of introductory charges	2-10
A. Address to the officials	2-8
1. David prevented from building the temple	2-3
a. Introduction	2aα
b. Call to attention	2aβ
c. Plans and preparations	2b
1) Plans	2bα
2) Preparation	2bβ
d. Oracular report of divine prohibition	3
2. The divine choice	4-7
a. Of David	4
1) A perpetual rule	4aα
2) Selection of tribe, family, individual	4aβ-b
b. Of Solomon	5-7
1) Chosen to the throne from many sons	5
2) Oracular report	6-7
a) Solomon appointed as temple builder	6a
b) Adoption formula	6b
c) Conditional promise	7
(1) Perpetual rule	7a
(2) Conditioned on keeping the law	7b
3. Parenesis	8
a. The forum: "all Israel"	8aα
b. Exhortation to fervent piety	8aβ
c. Promise of the "good land"	8b
1) For present hearers	8bα
2) For posterity	8bβ
B. Vocation account	9-10
1. Admonition to wholehearted devotion	9
a. Command to know and serve God	9aα
b. Rationale: description of Yahweh	9aβ
c. Aphorism on the divine reaction	9b
2. Command to build the temple	10
a. Solomon as the divine choice	10a
b. Call to valorous performance	10b

Scholars have noted the close similarity between 28:1ff. and 22:6-19. The ideology and much of the thematic language are identical; it is only the narrative setting that is different. Certainly ChrH is composing here with that passage in mind. A difference in arrangement is that in 22:7-16 David speaks, apparently in private, while in vv. 17-19 he addresses Israel's leaders. Here in ch. 28 David first addresses the assembly, vv. 2-8, and then speaks to his son, vv. 9-10. We would call this a chiasmus if the passages were not so far separated from each other. Also, the report that David gives to Solomon in 22:7-10 of Yahweh's revelation (blood makes David unfit; Solomon is chosen to build the temple and occupy an eternal throne) is here reported instead to the assembly (vv. 3-4, 6-7), very much as in 1 Kgs 8:18-19 par. 2 Chr 6:8-9. That David now goes public with a secret which he had shared only with Solomon is appropriate to the situation. He is not now just preparing his son and the leaders to build the temple, but actually handing over the public administration. Having finished with the business of ordering the Levites (chs. 23–26), David is ready for the last act to be played out. A great assembly is called; the verb is *qhl* because the business at hand is both secular and sacred (cf. 13:2, 5). A whole list of specific officers is mentioned: tribal and regal administrators, commanders of major military contingents, stewards over the king's property and family, and all the veteran soldiers of high standing (v. 1). "King David" in v. 2 is his honorific title and is quite appropriate to this occasion. Though old (see 1 Kgs 1:1-4), he rises to full height to stand on his feet (v. 2a). He addresses his audience with affection: *'aḥay wĕ'ammî,* "My brothers and my people."

David begins his discourse by revealing the contrast between what he had intended and what God did about it (vv. 2b-3): both *'ănî,* "I," and *hā'ĕlōhîm,* "God," are foremost for emphasis. The reason for God's refusal, viz., that David was "a warrior and [had] shed blood," is drawn in abbreviated form from 22:8. Having revealed God's refusal to let him build a temple, David next explains how God got around to Solomon instead. There were two moments of divine choice *(bḥr):* first, when he selected him, v. 4, and second, when he selected Solomon, v. 5. Braun ("Temple Builder," 582) sees vv. 4-5, 8 as a secondary expansion, but one should note the typical ChrH chiastic structure:

a   David's perpetual rule (4aα)
  b   David's selection by tribe, family, individual (4aβ-b)
  b'   Solomon's selection out of numerous sons (5)
a'   Solomon's perpetual rule (7a).

A contrast to note is between David's ruling over "all Israel," v. 4, and Solomon's reign over "the throne of the kingdom of Yahweh over Israel," v. 5. It is also worthy of note that David's selection by tribe, then family, then individual directly reflects the traditional pattern of lot casting, though beyond doubt ChrH here has the story of 1 Samuel 16 in mind. Yahweh *bāḥar* ("chose") David, v. 4; he *bāḥar* Solomon to sit on David's throne, v. 5; he *bāḥar* him also to be his son, v. 6b. In vv. 6-7 David divulges to the assembly God's revelation to him about Solomon. "He said *['āmar]* to me" means "He commanded me." It was not a matter of discussion or dispute, but something fixed forever in God's purpose. Putting the object foremost for emphasis, Yahweh declares that Solomon is the designated temple builder *(šĕlōmōh binkā hû'-yibneh . . .).* In a grounding clause with *kî* Yahweh goes on to ratify the adoption in which Solomon is to be Yahweh's son and Yahweh his father (v. 6). This means a perpetual rule for Solomon, in which Yahweh promises to establish *(kûn)* his throne forever, but on one condition: *'im- yeḥĕzaq*. The verb *ḥzq*, "be firm, resolute," assumes an attitude or stance that is always held up to Israel/Judah's kings by ChrH to depict their proper behavior over against the Deity, often with the law and commandments as specific object, as here. That v. 7 sets the model for all the kings after Solomon is made clear by Yahweh's final words, *kayyôm hazzeh*, "as on this day," suggesting that this day of transition from David's rule to Solomon's is a model of perfect order, with Solomon committed to an attitude of perfect submission.

Having cited Yahweh's own words, David turns back to the assembly with the transitional word *wĕ'attâ*, "So now. . . ." He has a command for them in this situation. Witnesses are summoned, with different images to suggest the attention they must give (v. 8). "All Israel," also called the *qĕhal-yahweh*, "congregation of Yahweh," must *see*; Yahweh will *hear*. The exhortation is to *šmr* and to *drš* the commandments. This is interesting because the deuteronomistic language that ChrH is emulating regularly uses *šmr*, "keep," as the governing verb when the law or commandment is the object, while *drš*, "seek," "pursue," is a term that ChrH himself prefers. As is usual, the command to obey the commandments comes with a promise, but here it is with a telescoped time frame in which David's hearers are promised something that was promised by Moses and Joshua to the Israelites about to enter the promised land; i.e., they would *yrš*, "take possession of," this good land, leaving it as an inheritance *(nḥl*, hiph.) to succeeding generations forever. In other words, David and his company stood as Joshua, having conquered the promised land through the faithful performance of their duties in getting the city and the shrine site and the building materials ready for a new entering in. What they had done was an inheritance for future generations—all on condition that Yahweh's law be obeyed.

David now turns directly to Solomon in words that closely resemble 22:6-16: "And as for you, Solomon my son." Two things need to be laid upon his heart. The first is wholehearted devotion. David commands Solomon to know *(yd')* and to serve *('bd)* the ancestral God *('ĕlōhê 'ăbōteykā* [LXX; MT: *'ābîkā*]). A grounding clause with *kî* gives the rationale for this command: "Yahweh searches *[drš]* every heart, and he comprehends every impulse of one's imaginations." David follows this with an APHORISM, a ready saying that asks to be quoted by everyone and lived by always: *'im-tidrĕšennû yimmāṣē' lāk wĕ'im ta'azbennû yaznîḥākā lā'ad*, "If you seek him he will surely be found, but if you leave him he will cast you away forever."

But this matter of the heart is preparatory to the ultimate, decisive command to Solomon (v. 10): "Take heed now." Another grounding clause with *kî* reminds him that he is indeed Yahweh's choice to build his temple. No matter that David is disappointed that it could not have been he. No matter if some in the company might prefer another of David's sons, or think Solomon too young and inexperienced. Yahweh has said clearly what he wants. What is needed now is resolution, and David's command to him is *ḥăzaq wa'ăśēh*, "Pull yourself together and do it!" (see 1 Chr 22:16, 19).

III. Report of instruction concerning the temple plans   28:11-21
  A. Presentation   11aα

Having informed the assembly why Solomon would be the one to build the temple (vv. 1-8), and having exhorted Solomon to be strong and forthright in accepting his responsibility (vv. 9-10), David makes a move of strategic importance in getting the work started (vv. 11-21). He hands over three plans for the temple's preparation. ChrH is here no doubt under the influence of P's image of the tabernacle, also called a *tabnît*, as found in Exodus 25–31 (cf. 25:8), which the people were then later obliged to bring to reality (see von Rad, *Geschichtsbild*, 130). There is no enumeration of three separate plans, but *tabnît* is used in v. 11 for the central sanctuary, in v. 12 for the courts, clerical duties, and vessels, and in v. 13 for the cherubim's chariot (cf. Ackroyd, "Temple Vessels"). Some scholars who have not otherwise been eager to excise secondary materials are suspicious here. Willi (p. 196) identifies vv. 12b-13a, 14-18 as secondary. Braun ("Temple Builder," 581) supports this opinion. Galling (ATD) views just vv. 14-18 as an addition. The reference to the priestly and Levitical cadres as part of a so-called "plan" may seem strange; but now we know why ChrH has insisted on inserting his regulations for the clergy into his narrative of the investiture. As he sees it, Solomon's temple must be more than buildings and sacred vessels: there must be priests and Levites there to bring it alive. We may also consider it strange that no fewer than five and a half verses should be devoted to the weights of precious metal to be used for the vessels and furniture (cf. 1 Chr 22:15), but ChrH surely intends to depict David in this way as having a hand in everything, so that the temple will be truly his as well as Solomon's (on the "pure gold" of v. 17, cf. Watson, "Archaic Elements," 3.2). Perhaps ChrH's meaning is not that David hands over three separate designs, but just one having three individual sections, the third of which is for the cherubim's chariot, v. 18b (cf. Ezek 10:19). V. 19 is an authorization statement (cf. Watson, 9.1). It tells how Solomon will be able to execute so detailed a plan, and by whose authority his father David gives such precise instructions. There was a writing from the "hand of Yahweh"—in other words, a revelation to David written down as fast and secure as the Decalogue given to Moses (Exod 32:16). David is not speaking here, yet the MT adds *'ālay,* "upon me," an interpretative gloss; cf. LXX. The final phrase, *hiśkîl kōl mal'ăkôt hattabnît,* "It [the writing from God's hand] clarified all the work according to the plan."

The next move is introduced by "Then David said" in v. 20. His speech to Solomon is first EXHORTATION (v. 20) and then INSTRUCTION. The EXHORTATION (cf. Watson, 6.1) is first a COMMAND to be strong, be brave and act, accompanied by reassurance and a statement of the divine presence, all of which is concluded with the promise of continual help from God: "He will not let you down and will not leave you until the completion of [ChrH: *'ad liklôt*] every work for the sacred service in God's temple." The INSTRUCTION (v. 21) is to make generous use of three groups. The first are the priests and the Levites, who can be counted on, on their own initiative, to take care of all the service of the temple. The second group are the artisans who will share, with Solomon as chief architect, the actual construction of the temple: *wě'immĕkā bĕkol-mĕlā'kâ lĕkol-* [ChrH] *nādîb bahokmâ lĕkol-'ăbôdâ,* "And with you in every task will be everyone ready to use his knowledge in whatever kind of service." The third group consists of the general populace, chiefs and laymen, who may be called upon whenever Solomon shall summon (*lĕkol- dĕbāreykā*).

IV. Report of David's farewell speech	29:1-9
A. Call to consecration	1-5
1. Narrative transition	1aα
2. Solomon's need	1aβ-b
3. David's testimony	2-5a
a. Former provision for God's temple	2
b. Donation of private treasury	3-5a
4. Challenge to piety	5b
B. Response of the assembly	6-9
1. List of participating officials	6
2. List of donated metals	7
3. Conveyance of precious stones	8
4. General rejoicing	9
a. By the people	9a
b. By King David	9b

The reference to the availability of skilled volunteers and to the willingness of officers and people alike to be of help (1 Chr 28:21) is the link to this new section, which features an appeal for generous giving. 1 Chr 29:1 makes the transition, facing David ("David the king" identifies him in his authoritarian capacity) back to the *qāhāl* once again. (Galling, ATD, views this entire section as secondary. Driver, "Speeches," 247ff., 292ff., makes a special analysis of the address in vv. 1-2.) In his address David follows the principle of lesser/greater. The lesser in this instance is Solomon, whom David indeed identifies as the chosen one of God, standing all alone. In contrast, the work is great, all the more so because *habbîrâ* (late word, found in Chronicles, Nehemiah, Esther, Daniel, meaning the "palace") which he is charged to build will not be for man's use but for God's (v. 1). David intends to use this gross incongruity as the basis for an appeal to the assembly (v. 5b), but in order to motivate them further he first bears testimony to two ways in which he himself has poured out his riches. In v. 2 he says, *ûkěkol-kōḥî hăkînôtî lěbêt- 'ělōhay*, "and to the limit of my ability I have provided for the house of my God"; he then goes on to list the rich things he has given. In v. 3 he adds, *wě'ôd birṣôtî běbêt 'ělōhay yeš-lî sěgullâ*, "and besides, I have private funds which I may use at my pleasure for the house of my God." From this he has set apart a large amount of gold and silver, specifically for the purpose of overlaying the walls (v. 3). In v. 4 David actually divulges the exact amount, specifying that besides being used to adorn the walls, it is to be used for various artifacts of gold and silver (v. 5a). David concludes, *ûmî mitnaddēb lěmallō'wt yādô hayyôm lěyahweh*, "So who will come forward to be consecrated to Yahweh today?" The expression *mālē' yād*, normally referring to an ordination to holy office, here suggests that those laymen who give all they have to God's work have thereby set themselves apart in a very special way. (On vv. 3, 4, cf. Watson, 3.4, 10.51.)

In telling about the response to David's appeal, ChrH first lists all the rankings of those who made freewill offerings (*ndb*, hith.), v. 6; he then lists the weight (and thereby the value) of gold, silver, bronze, and iron that they gave (v. 7). Perhaps gems were especially scarce and precious; v. 8 uses the niph. part. of *mṣ'* as subject of a sentence stating that those owning them brought them to Jehiel the Gershonite for deposit in the treasure house of the temple (something of an anachronism since the temple had not yet been built; cf. 1 Chr 23:8; 26:21-22; cf. Watson, 7.2). Rejoicing (*śimḥâ*) is the result, v. 9, an inclusio telling first that the people rejoiced and then also (*wěgam*) "King David" — in his case with *śimḥâ gědôlâ*, "a great joy" (cf. Kropat, *Syntax*, 77).

2. Request for Israel's purity of heart   18aβ-b
3. Request on Solomon's behalf   19
   a. Steadfastness in keeping the law   19a-bα
   b. Success in building the temple   19bβ

On the structure of David's prayer, one may consult Driver ("Speeches," 247ff., 292ff.) and Plöger. Williamson (comm., 185-86) performs a valuable service in showing two essential things about the structure. First, the psalmodic anthology in 1 Chr 16:8-36 is paralleled segment by segment in this prayer: 16:8-22 dwells on the theme of the landless patriarchs, and so also David, especially in vv. 14-16; 16:23-33 celebrates the kingship of God, and so also David in vv. 11-12; 16:35 contains a petition, just as here in vv. 18-19. As Williamson explains, these two pericopes together provide a framework for the entire narrative of David's preparations for building the temple, chs. 17–29. It is indeed appropriate that having done everything in his power to dedicate his own resources, the people's resources, and Solomon's heart and strength to this grand purpose, he now turns in prayer to God. This is the last thing for him to do before actually handing the kingdom and the building of the temple to his son.

Verse 10a is a major transition, for it first informs us of what David will do —bless Yahweh—before it begins to cite that blessing. This is a great congregational prayer, for David stands "in the presence of all the assembly" (*qāhāl*). His prayer is tantamount to what C. Westermann (*The Praise of God in the Psalms* [tr. K. Crim; Richmond: John Knox, 1965] 116-61) would call "descriptive praise." All is in flowing poetic parallelism. First comes the blessing (v. 10b), then a richly articulated ascription of greatness, majesty, riches, and power—mentioning for contrast that God alone has strength to give to those without it (cf. Watson, 7.3, 10.1), vv. 11-12. In v. 13 there is attestation that "we" are now totally dedicated to thanking and praising God's name. The "blessed art thou" second-person formula may be a late development in the liturgical usage of the OT (otherwise only at Ps 119:12) because the third-person usage ("Blessed is the Lord, etc.") is seen more often and in earlier texts (1 Kgs 8:15; Ps 41:14 [*RSV* 13]; 72:18; 106:48). Without allowing for the fact that he is citing the Mishna and medieval Jewish liturgy, Finkelstein claims that David dared to use the second-person address because he was outside the temple and was not a priest. As a layman reciting a benediction outside the temple, David would have had to use two preliminary words before the divine name, and that is what he in fact does here. But a more spontaneous, less punctilious impulse is seen by those who read the Scriptures from a historical viewpoint, refusing to assume that the people of the Bible acted from the rules of a postbiblical community.

Verses 14-17 constitute a confession, not of guilt, but of utter dependence on the Yahweh whose greatness has been extolled in vv. 11-12. David begins this section with a statement of SELF-ABASEMENT, "But who am I, and what is my people?" It is no wonder that he and Israel have been motivated to give so freely because in giving their riches they have only been giving what God has already given them (cf. Watson, 7.3, p. 200 n. 3). That they amount to paupers in their own resources is underscored (1) by recollection of the fact that from patriarchal times they were strangers and sojourners (*gērîm . . . wĕtôšābîm*), and (2) by confessing a fact that is true of all mankind, viz., that life is like a shadow (*ṣēl*), without hope (*miqweh*).

In v. 16 David makes the words of v. 14 more specific by referring directly to the temple, and in v. 17, having confessed ("and I know") that God searches man's intentions, he first flatly states that he himself has been generous in giving *běyōšer lěbābî*, "in the rectitude of my heart," so that now *(we'attâ)* he has had the satisfaction of seeing God's people emulating his generosity, and doing so with joy *(běsimḥâ)*. In v. 18 he invokes the ancestral God, using the language of the patriarchal tradition: "Yahweh, God of Abraham, Isaac, and Israel, our forefathers" ("Israel" is ChrH's constant substitute for "Jacob"). He petitions that the people may ever keep this purpose, and that Solomon might be enabled to keep the law *lēbāb šālēm*, "with a perfect heart," in this mind turning to the work of building "the palace" *(habbîrâ)* for which David has made provision.

VI. Report of ritual: the investiture	29:20-22
A. First day: sacrificial preparation	20-21aα¹
1. David's ritual command	20a
2. The assembly worships	20b
3. Offering of sacrifices	21aα¹
B. Second day: ceremony of investiture (transition formula)	21aα²-22
1. Renewed sacrifices	21aα²-b
2. Epitome: joyful feasting	22a
3. Installation	22b
a. Solomon made king	22bα
b. Solomon anointed	22bβ
VII. Report: Solomon initiated into the kingship	23-25
A. Solomon acts as David's successor	23a
B. Universal pledge of loyalty	23b-24
C. Encomium on his unparalleled magnificence	25

It is not a problem to identify where the investiture section begins. Having concluded his prayer, David gives the ritual command, *bārěkû-nā' 'et-yahweh 'ělōhêkem*, "Now bless Yahweh your God," and the congregation *(qāhāl)* does so (v. 20). The question is, following this opening ritual, whether everything narrated in vv. 21-22 immediately follows. Beecher argued for a major break at v. 22a, separating the people's feasting from Solomon's investiture (so *RSV*), but this leaves the time designation in these two verses unexplained. It is above all necessary to recognize that the clause with *bayyôm hahû'* is a perfect example of the EPITOME, summing up what has happened with a statement of the essential quality of this day. In *Yesterday, Today and Tomorrow* (pp. 115-16) I explain that this ceremony requires two separate days, as follows:

Day 1: The ritual of blessing; the people worship Yahweh *(wělammelek,* "and the king," is a gloss; it is wanting in LXX^BA, Syr.), v. 20; they sacrifice *(zbḥ)* sacrifices *(zěbāḥîm)* to Yahweh, v. 21aα¹.

Day 2: "On the morrow of that day" *(lěmāḥŏrat hayyôm hahû')* they offer up *('lh,* hiph.) so many animals with their appropriate drink offerings *(niskêhem)*, v. 21aα²; then they make abundant sacrifices *(ûzěbāḥîm lārōb)* on behalf of "all Israel," v. 21b; then they eat and drink before Yahweh "on that day" *(bayyôm hahû')*, v. 22a.

This arrangement makes sense of the time designations and produces a meaningful sequence. It also avoids giving the impression that sacrificing (*zbḥ*) was done twice on the same day. At the termination of these acts of worship the people crowned Solomon (*šēnît*, "a second time," is not attested in LXX^BA and is a naive effort to harmonize this statement with 1 Chr 23:1) and anointed him to serve as *nāgîd*, "leader," to Yahweh ("and Zadok as priest" overlooks 1 Chr 15:11; it is a gloss later than the latest pro-priestly expansion in this book).

Verses 23-25 should not be joined to v. 22, as in *RSV,* because the action moves on from the day of investiture to a statement that the goal of this entire preceding account has been realized. One should note the language: "And Solomon sat on Yahweh's throne [not "David's"] as king in the place of David his father, and he prospered *[wayyaṣlaḥ],*" v. 23a. To show how he prospered, ChrH states that "all Israel" obeyed him, while the leaders, men of influence, and even the rest of David's sons pledged their loyalty (*nātĕnû yād taḥat*) to Solomon as king, vv. 23b-24. The account concludes with the statement that Yahweh gave Solomon unparalleled magnificence (v. 25); cf. 2 Chr 1:1. "Than any king before him" is a careless remark on the part of ChrH because it would put Solomon up for comparison with any king who may have reigned on earth; hence the gloss (missing in LXX^BA) "over Israel."

Genre

In a passage where the major theme has an intricate array of variations one can more or less count on a proliferation of formulas and formal genres, and so it is here. The main genre is ACCOUNT, and the genre of the segment 28:1–29:19, varied thematically but united by the image of David standing in place and speaking continuously, is REPORT. The next two segments are also of the genre REPORT: first, 29:20-22, where new action is introduced in the people's sacrificing and the investiture of Solomon; second, in 29:23-25, a REPORT of how and in what fashion Solomon took possession of the kingdom.

Coming back to the beginning of the ACCOUNT: 28:2-8 is best defined as an ADDRESS, which is a speech to an audience, usually named in the vocative, as here ("Hear me, my brethren and my people"), on a political, military, or religious topic. Williamson (comm.) would prefer to call ChrH's speeches by kings, prophets, or Levites by von Rad's term, "Levitical sermon," but it is questionable whether calling this passage a (→) sermon is suitable because the latter is defined as taking place specifically in a cultic gathering; though cultic activity does indeed take place at the end of this first REPORT, i.e., in David's prayer, 29:10-19, and in the ceremony of investiture, 29:20-22; and although religious topics are repeatedly brought into the various speeches covered by the REPORT, the people whom David gathers to Jerusalem according to 28:1 represent Israel mainly as a political entity. All the same, we can say that David's opening ADDRESS does set the model for the so-called "Levitical sermon." Von Rad ("Levitical Sermon") tries to show that the SERMON in 1–2 Chronicles tends to develop three parts: (1) *doctrina,* (2) *applicatio,* and (3) *exhortatio.* The general impulse is to reach back to the ancient words of Scripture, and that is what, in fact, David does in citing Ps 132:7 in our passage. Von Rad admits, however, that this form becomes neglected or confused in some passages, to the point where the name "Levitical sermon" becomes of questionable application. Our practice will be to choose the genre name SERMON only in passages where the cultic setting is primary, and where the full, three-part development is clear.

Within David's ADDRESS we take note of a number of formal elements. V. 2 has the CALL TO ATTENTION, a formula which opens a public presentation or address and intends to attract the attention of the hearers to the speech which follows. Vv. 3, 6-7 have the ORACULAR REPORT, with essentially the same content that we have observed in 1 Chronicles 22. In v. 3 this contains a divine PROHIBITION, and in vv. 6-7 a PROMISE featuring the ADOPTION FORMULA, "I have chosen him to be my son, and I will be his father." V. 8 is PARENESIS, defined as an address seeking to persuade to a goal by exhorting, admonishing, commanding, or prohibiting; in this verse there is the EXHORTATION to "observe and seek out" and the PROMISE of the land.

Verses 9-10 display the genre VOCATION ACCOUNT, which normally has the pattern: (1) call to attention; (2) commission; (3) objections and reassurance; and (4) commitment. The first two elements are apparent in this section; the objections are not spoken, but are implied in the reminder that Yahweh searches every heart, and will be found if Solomon seeks him, but will cast him off forever if he forsakes him. We see here also the genres ADMONITION (v. 9), COMMAND (v. 9a), DESCRIPTION OF YAHWEH (v. 9a), and APHORISM (v. 9b). The ADMONITION is, "If you seek him, he will be found by you; but if you forsake him, he will cast you off forever" (see above under "Structure"). An APHORISM is a terse saying, embodying a general truth or a characteristic typical of the addressee. The VOCATION ACCOUNT concludes with a COMMAND instructing Solomon what he has to do and urging him to do it.

Verses 11-21a are an example of INSTRUCTION, a genre that gives guidance, setting forth values or rules of conduct or answering questions. David's giving of the three plans—or three parts of a single plan—instructs Solomon in detail how he must prepare the temple and its service. It exhibits the genre LIST, seen in vv. 11, 12-13a, and 13b-18, respectively. In addition, this section contains an EXHORTATION (v. 20), including a COMMAND to be strong and act, the REASSURANCE FORMULA ("Fear not, be not dismayed"), the ASSISTANCE FORMULA ("Yahweh my God is with you"), and a PROMISE ("He will not fail you or forsake you"). It concludes with another example of INSTRUCTION, in which Solomon is informed about the help he might expect to receive.

This brings us to the FAREWELL SPEECH of 29:1-9. This genre is defined as a first-person speech delivered by a leader near to the time of his death, urging the hearers to carry out unfulfilled obligations; it often includes the speaker's testimony of personal blamelessness. Here David lays heavy emphasis on Solomon's need for help, and then, in a typical TESTIMONY, David points to two lists of items he has provided: the things he has purposely gathered for this work (v. 2) and the items he now bestows, as a last bequest, from his private property (vv. 3-5a). V. 5b shows a rare genre, CHALLENGE TO PIETY, which is defined as a call to the individual toward the performance of some very demanding action ("Who then will offer willingly, consecrating himself today to Yahweh?"); cf. Exod 35:5. The section on the leaders' response contains two LISTS: a LIST of participants (v. 6) and a LIST of materials provided (v. 7).

Verses 10-19 exhibit the genre PRAYER. It begins (vv. 10b-13) with a PRAISE

SPEECH, defined as a brief and somewhat elaborate formulaic utterance which offers praise and thanksgiving to God. The opening *bārûk ('attâ) yahweh* is characteristic. The ascription of divine majesty in vv. 11-12 is emphatically theocentric. As Seeligmann points out, all greatness and power is said to belong to God ("Für den Chronisten sind Kraft und Macht keine menschliche Eigenschaften, sondern ausschliesslich Gott vorbehalten"). So it is throughout ChrH, who receives this outlook from the classical prophets (p. 278).

The confession part of David's prayer begins with the SELF-ABASEMENT FORMULA ("But who am I, and what is my people . . . ?"). The second half of v. 5 is another APHORISM ("Our days on earth are like a shadow, and there is no hope" [*RSV* "abiding"]). V. 17 is a PLEA OF INNOCENCE, formally a statement by a defendant that he is not guilty of allegations made against him: David appeals to God, who discerns the hearts, to judge that there has been no untoward purpose in the work that he has done. This includes a DESCRIPTION OF YAHWEH. David's prayer concludes with two PETITIONS, one for the people (v. 18) and the other for Solomon (v. 19). The PETITION is a request or plea asking for some definite response, in this case the gift of firmness of commitment for the people and of a wholehearted dedication for Solomon.

Verses 20-22 have the genre REPORT OF RITUAL, beginning with the COMMAND, "Bless Yahweh your God." "On the morrow of that day" in v. 21 is a TRANSITION FORMULA moving from the events of Day 1 to those of Day 2 (see above under "Structure"). We have now seen several examples in ChrH of the EPITOME, a succinct distillation and summation stating the deepest and most lasting significance of the event in question, very often featuring the time expression "on that day": the people's eating and drinking before Yahweh with "great gladness" offers the most profound qualification of the day of Solomon's investiture.

Verse 25, "And Yahweh gave Solomon great repute in the sight of all Israel, and bestowed upon him such royal majesty as had not been on any king before him ['in Israel' is a gloss]," is our first example of the genre ENCOMIUM applied to the figure of Solomon (for passages, → ENCOMIUM). Related to the (→) praise speech, this is an oration, or a writing in oration style, exaggerating the subject's virtues to the point of wild adulation. Since the ChrH examples paraphrase or transcribe counterparts from 1 Kings, it is clear that Solomon had become the subject of the ENCOMIUM and attained the status of a legendary hero at least before the time of DtrH.

Setting

Let it be kept in mind that, apart from the "title" in 1 Chr 23:1, David is nowhere said to have actually worked to have Solomon replace him on the throne. To be sure, this is the effect of what he does in chs. 28–29, viz., get Solomon accepted as the designated temple builder. First, he tells the people of Yahweh's revelation that he was prevented from doing this because he was a "man of blood" and because Yahweh had expressly chosen Solomon to do this work in his place. Then he encourages the people and Solomon to give freely and work hard in order to get the temple built without delay, turning over to Solomon a revealed set of plans to go by. Then he prays an eloquent and moving prayer, to the effect that God will keep the people to their purpose and enable Solomon to make a perfect performance.

But for one who had not read 1 Chr 23:1 it might not be clear that David intended to include turning over the kingship. It comes, therefore, as something of a surprise to read in 29:20-22 that David called a great sacrificial feast, at the end of which "they" crowned Solomon king and anointed him as *nāgîd,* "leader." Since the account does not suggest that this was done against David's will or without his knowledge, the reader naturally tends to assume that David just got swept along by these stirring events and, as his last act, had Solomon crowned king. This, of course, is a naive and uninformed view, for (1) 1 Chr 23:1 is enough to cue him in on how to interpret what was happening, and (2) there have been plenty of hints that to be designated "temple builder" involves serving as king. ChrH believes in a kind of sacral kingship in which the monarch's chief task is not the administration of public affairs but oversight of spiritual institutions—specifically the clergy and the sanctuary.

The informed reader of this account is quite aware that it has virtually no contact with the account of Solomon's accession in 1 Kings 1-2. That account has David in his doddering old age, while here he still appears to be in his prime. There David is unable to choose who shall succeed him, and Solomon (so passive in ChrH) is able to wrest the succession out of Adonijah's hands only through the firmness, loyalty, and cleverness of his supporters; here, on the other hand, David speaks confidently to Solomon, as earlier in 1 Chronicles 22, not of an immediate succession but of a herculean task that would inevitably involve holding the kingship. In Kings there had been no talk of a temple until Solomon conceived of it himself, but ChrH makes this account the climax in a long series of acts by which David had prepared for the temple, from which pinnacle the next logical step—the investiture of Solomon—must lead swiftly to a frenzy of activity in actually bringing it to completion.

Braun ("Temple Builder") has drawn on three special biblical concepts in order to explain the relationship of Solomon to David. First, there is the concept of the "rest" *(hēnîaḥ, měnûḥâ)* which Solomon will bring (1 Chr 28:2; cf. 22:9), omitted by 1 Chronicles 17 in copying 2 Sam 7:1, 11, but emphatically connected with the name "Solomon" in 1 Chr 22:9. Second, there is the striking typology of Moses turning over the leadership to Joshua as a model for David turning over the leadership to Solomon; cf. the emphasis on the keeping of the law in Josh 1:7-8 with 1 Chr 22:12-13; 28:7; Ps 132:11-12; also the fact that only Josh 1:8 promises *ṣělaḥ,* "prosperity," fulfilled in Solomon according to 1 Chr 29:23; note also that the "reassurance formula," 1 Chr 28:20, occurs also in Josh 1:9; 10:4; Deut 31:6. Third, Braun argues that the word *bāḥar,* "choose," which refers to Solomon in 1 Chr 28:6, 10; 29:1, must be holding him up to high distinction because in Genesis through Kings this term never refers to Levites or kings after David. Thus there was an actual transferral of office from David to Solomon, and Solomon becomes, in Braun's reckoning, the prime model of Israel's king.

Lohfink, McCarthy, and Porter (→ Bibliography) have done work on this "Gattung der Amtsetzung," which Williamson ("Accession") prefers to call "the installation schema"; we have identified it at 1 Chr 22:6-16; 28:9-10 under the genre title VOCATION ACCOUNT. Williamson agrees that the Solomon narrative has been strongly influenced by the story of Joshua's succession. David is disqualified (1 Chr 22:6ff.; 28:2-8), just as Moses was according to Deut 1:37-38; 31:2-3; Solomon, a man of peace and rest (1 Chr 28:9, 18), takes his place (cf. Josh 11:23, etc.). The "installation schema" has three parts: (1) encouragement, (2) description of the task, and (3) assurance of divine aid; cf. Deut 31:23; Josh 1:6, 9b; 1 Chr 22:1-10; 28:20. Not enough attention is paid in Williamson's analysis to the actual structure of the ChrH passages as we have offered them, but he is quite correct in pointing to the characteristic phraseology: *ḥăzaq we'ĕmaṣ*, "Be firm and steadfast"; *'al-tîrā' wĕ'al-tēḥāt*, "Fear not nor be afraid"; *yahweh 'ĕlōhîm 'ĕlōhay 'immāk*, "Yahweh God, my God, is with you"; *lō' yarpĕkā wĕlō' ya'azbekkā*, "He will not let you down or forsake you." As Williamson sees it, the stress on keeping the law as a condition of kingship is characteristic (Deut 31:5; Josh 1:7-8; 1 Chr 22:12-13; 28:7-9). The pattern of first a private announcement (1 Chronicles 22), then a public announcement (1 Chronicles 28), is paralleled in Joshua 1; Deut 31:7. Rather than exalting Solomon at the expense of David (Braun), Williamson defines the purpose of this arrangement to be to weld David and Solomon together, identifying the two as closely as Moses and Joshua, "the second Moses." David's work builds up to this point, and Solomon's work carries it to its goal. The one cannot do without the other, for the two are really one.

We would like to underscore this perception by pointing again to the phraseology of 1 Chr 29:23, "And Solomon sat on the throne of Yahweh as king in the place of David his father." The throne belongs neither to David nor to Solomon; whoever sits upon it at the particular moment has been placed there by Yahweh. Yahweh gave David Saul's kingship (10:14; 11:3) because it was his to take away and bestow on another. Now the throne is not being taken away from David for unfaithfulness but —quite on the contrary—precisely because he has been so faithful in preparing for the great work of the one who shall succeed him. However many scions may arise to the house of David, this will therefore be called "the throne of David," since David was the one to secure it forever as the throne of Yahweh.

Inasmuch as the temple remains the focus of every brave and faithful effort throughout these chapters, we must observe carefully David's image of what it is to be. This is expressed particularly in 28:2, where he says, "I had it in my heart to build a house of rest *[bêt mĕnûḥâ]* for the ark of the covenant of Yahweh, and for the footstool of our God *[hădōm raglê 'ĕlōhênû]*." On this imagery cf. von Rad, *Geschichtsbild*, 127-30. It is apparent that ChrH has been strongly influenced by Psalm 132, according to H. J. Kraus (*Psalmen* II [BKAT XV; Neukirchen-Vluyn: Neukirchener, 5th ed., 1978] 1053-1066) a preexilic Levitical pilgrimage liturgy accompanying the periodic retrieval of the ark. The verses in question (vv. 7, 8, 14) read:

> Let us go to his dwelling place *[miškĕnôtāyw]*;
>> let us worship at his footstool *[lahădōm raglāyw]*
> Arise, O Yahweh, and go to thy resting place *[limnûḥātekā]*;
>> thou and the ark of thy might!

> This is my resting place for ever;
>> here I will dwell, for I have desired it.

The psalm also has much to say about choosing one of David's sons on the condition of his keeping the law (vv. 11-12), so that the imagery of finding Yahweh a resting place immediately elicits in David's mind the promise of a son. Further citation of Psalm 132 occurs at the end of the long account of building and dedicating the temple, 2 Chr 6:41-42.

A final thing to note regarding "setting" is the emphasis on the people's joy at the festival of investiture, 1 Chr 29:22. There is indeed a special FESTIVAL SCHEMA in 1-2 Chronicles (which we shall have opportunity in another place to study), showing that joy comes without exception at the conclusion of the great festivals. As our section on "Structure" has emphasized, the epitome that sums up the whole long and involved ceremony stresses this joy: "And they ate and drank before Yahweh in that day *[bayyôm hahû']* with great rejoicing."

Intention

This pericope represents the culmination of the entire preceding narrative. It is of crucial importance because it shows how Israel's God eases her over the gaps and the null points of history. There were to be many such in the history of the Judahite kings, up to the last of them. But what might look like decline from one point of view may be seen as preparation from another point of view; for instance, the wickedness of the last four kings and the exile that they provoked can be understood as the preparation for the new temple and the new Israel. So it was in the transition from David to Solomon. David's reign had been the preparation for the fulfillment that was to come under the kingship of Solomon. In this situation, the preparation was the effective cause of the fulfillment because the warring that David did in order to seize riches for Yahweh's forthcoming temple made him a "man of blood," thereby disqualifying him as temple builder and handing this privilege over to Solomon. This paradox of cause and effect was something that ChrH and his community could appreciate, for it applied also to their own times. The mystery that lay in it did not disturb them, for they were able to believe that somehow the throne was Yahweh's (1 Chr 29:23), and that he set first one man, and then another, upon it. We know that it was not possible for any of the surviving Davidides actually to take the throne during the Persian and early Greek periods, but this could not upset ChrH's aspirations for the ultimate fulfillment of the promise to David of an everlasting dynasty (cf. De Vries, "Dynastic Endangerment," 72-74). The throne belonged to Yahweh, and he could be trusted to dispose of it in his own inscrutable wisdom. Thus does ChrH's high theology remove the questionings and the doubtings of history. With perfect logic David declares in his prayer (29:11):

> Thine, O Yahweh, is the greatness and the power and the glory and the victory and the majesty; for all that is in the heavens and in the earth is thine; thine is the kingdom, O Yahweh, and thou art exalted as head above all.

To ChrH, God is not only *in* history (the classic Hebrew view), but *above* history. We need to see this to understand how and why this HISTORY was written. Israel already has a history of the kings (DtrH), so why does ChrH think he must write another? The answer: he is writing the history of the kingdom *as it should have happened*. 2 Samuel tells us nothing of David making extensive preparations for building the temple, but in ChrH's view he should have done so. 1 Kings 1-2 tell of a David heavy with age, irresolute about who should succeed him, or even whether there should be a succession; ChrH tells instead of a David in his vigor, single-mindedly going through an elaborate ceremony to hand over the succession to Solomon. 1 Kings also tells of a mean-spirited, revengeful Solomon killing off or expelling every rival, but to ChrH Solomon is immediately accepted, so much so that "all the sons of King David pledged their allegiance" (1 Chr 29:24). One way to understand Israel's history is the way of DtrH, but ChrH looks back and rewrites it according to the higher, more mysterious purpose that he believes Yahweh must have intended. This was a way of describing history that ChrH's community could appropriate better than the way of DtrH. That had been the HISTORY of despair and self-recrimination, but this HISTORY was filled with hope and optimism and expectation.

There has been extensive discussion about ChrH's eschatology, specifically whether he clung to some kind of messianism. Probably the best treatment of this subject is in Williamson's "Eschatology." From our own study we must agree with Williamson's conclusion that the postexilic community did cling to a certain hope for the Davidic family, but that this was strictly for the eventual restoration of Israel's throne to one of them. If there was an eschatology in this, it was a "realized" or this-worldly eschatology—not an expectation of a heavenly redeemer figure. This refutes Plöger's view that there is no eschatology whatever in ChrH. It refutes also the attempt of Cross, Freedman, and Newsome in seeing ChrH's hopes pinned on Zerubbabel. Williamson is leery also of Mosis's notion that Hezekiah fulfills the dynastic promises as a reincarnation of Solomon. The dynastic oracle is intended to apply perpetually—to the ongoing line, and not to one specific individual (see also Williamson, "Dynastic Oracle").

Let us review, then, what 1 Chronicles 28–29 must have meant to ChrH's community. One looks at David and then Solomon and understands that it will ever be the duty of whatever Davidides there are to prepare continually and work diligently for the greater beauty, influence, and effectiveness of Yahweh's temple. One looks at the behavior of the leaders, knowing that they are continually being called upon for generosity and willing volunteering; the typology of bringing gifts for the tabernacle (Exod 35:4-9) is repeatedly being fulfilled. One looks at the laypeople and understands that it will always be a duty for the humblest citizen to "bless God" and attend the sacred festivals "with great rejoicing." Change need not lead one to discouragement and despair. For those who believe that the "throne" is always Yahweh's, there is room only for happy joy. To them ChrH means to say (1 Chr 28:20): "Fear not, be not dismayed; for Yahweh God, even my God, is with you. He will not fail you or forsake you, until the work for the service of the house of Yahweh is finished."

Bibliography

P. R. Ackroyd, "The Temple Vessels—a continuity theme," in *Studies in the Religion of Ancient Israel* (VTSup 23; Leiden: Brill, 1972) 166-81; W. J. Beecher, "Note on the Proper Paragraph Division in 1 Chron xxix.22," *JBL* 5 (1885) 73-75; J. A. Bewer, "Textkritische Bemerkungen zum Alten Testament," in *Festschrift für Alfred Bertholet* (ed. W. Baumgartner, et al.; Tübingen: Mohr, 1950) 75-76; R. Braun, "Solomon, the Chosen Temple Builder: The Significance of 1 Chronicles 22, 28, and 29 for the Theology of Chronicles," *JBL* 95 (1976) 581-90; S. J. De Vries, *Yesterday, Today and Tomorrow,* 115-16; S. R. Driver, "The Speeches in Chronicles," *Exp* 1 (1895) 241-56, 286-308; L. Finkelstein, "The Prayer of King David According to the Chronicler" (Hebr.), *ErIs* 14 (1978) 110-16; N. Lohfink, "Die Darstellung des Übergangs der Führuing Israels von Moses auf Josue," *Scholastik* 37 (1962) 32-44; D. J. McCarthy, "An Installation Genre," *JBL* 90 (1971) 21-41; O. Plöger, "Reden und Gebete im deuteronomistischen und chronistischen Geschichtswerk," in *Aus der Spätzeit des Alten Testaments* (Göttingen: Vandenhoeck & Ruprecht, 1971) 50-66; J. R. Porter, "The Succession of Joshua," in *Proclamation and Presence (Fest.* G. H. Davies; ed. J. Durham and J. Porter; Richmond: John Knox, 1983) 102-32; G. von Rad, *Das Geschichtsbild des chronistischen Werkes* (Stuttgart: Kohlhammer, 1930); idem, "The Levitical Sermon in I and II Chronicles," in *The Problem of the Hexateuch and Other Essays* (tr. E. W. Trueman Dicken; New York: McGraw-Hill, 1966) 267-80; I. L. Seeligmann, "Die Auffassung von der Prophetie in der deuteronomistischen und chronistischen Geschichtsschreibung," in *Congress Volume: Göttingen 1977* (VTSup 29; Leiden: Brill, 1978) 267-80; H. G. M. Williamson, "The Accession of Solomon in the Books of Chronicles," *VT* 26 (1976) 351-61; idem, "The Dynastic Oracle in the Books of Chronicles," in *Sefer Yitshaq Aryeh Zeligman* I (ed. A. Rofé; Jerusalem: Rubinstein, 1981) 305-18; idem, "Eschatology in Chronicles," *TynBul* 28 (1977) 115-54.

C. DAVID'S REGNAL RESUMÉ, 29:26-30

Structure

I. The facts about David's reign	26-28
A. Epitomizing conclusion	26
B. Statement of length and place of reign	27
1. Total years	27a
2. Totals for Hebron and Jerusalem	27b
C. Death and burial formula	28a
D. Succession formula	28b
II. Source material (citation formula)	29-30
A. Documents	29
B. Contents	30

Genre

This is the first example in 1–2 Chronicles of the REGNAL RESUMÉ, invented by DtrH and copied by ChrH with some notable lapses. In Kings and generally in Chronicles there is an opening and a concluding section, bracketing the narration about a particular king and serving as a framework for delimitation of pericopes. Characteristic elements incorporated for David's resumé are the STATEMENT OF LENGTH AND PLACE OF REIGN, the DEATH AND BURIAL FORMULA (modified by omission of the burial notice), a SUCCESSION FORMULA for Solomon, and the CITATION FORMULA, "Now the acts of King David, from first to last, are written in. . . ." V. 26 is an EPITOME.

Setting

Verse 26 is not likely to be understood as saying that David continued to reign after Solomon had been installed on the throne, 29:23. It is true that 1–2 Kings provides evidence that for some time Solomon served simply as coregent and active administrator, but ChrH will have none of that. Solomon is now king, and ChrH wants to tell nothing more about David except his death. V. 26 is not constructed as narrative but as an epitomizing statement of fact, with the subject (name and patronym) foremost, next the perfect verb *mālak*, "he reigned," and then a limiting prepositional phrase, "over all Israel." This is not a part of the REGNAL RESUMÉ, but actually functions as a summary of the entire account of his career from 1 Chronicles 11 onward. It is important to read "over all Israel," for that epitomizes the whole significance of David's reign. David did what Saul could not do: unite "all Israel" under one king.

The STATEMENT OF LENGTH AND PLACE OF REIGN is taken from 1 Kgs 2:10-12. The STATEMENT OF DEATH, lacking a notice of burial, is unusual in that it summarizes both how David died and how he lived. He died in a good old age *(běśêbâ ṭôbâ)*, full of (surfeited with) days (= years), riches, and honor. In other words, he did not die untimely or in broken health; he did not die impoverished or dishonored. He had lived as long as any mortal man might expect to live, and when he died, all the riches and honor that he handed over to Solomon had not made him poor. The statement that Solomon his son reigned in his stead (the SUCCESSION FORMULA) can neither be taken to mean that Solomon took his place while he was yet alive, nor that Solomon did not begin his reign until after his death; it is simply the regular notice, borrowed ultimately from official archives, that Solomon was the next ruler after David.

The CITATION FORMULA is modeled after its counterparts in Kings, but there is less likelihood than with Kings that actual books are being referred to (→ Chapter 4 above). ChrH's summation of the contents of these alleged sources is fulsome, to say the least. They are said to offer three special kinds of information: (1) accounts of his rule and might; (2) the circumstances *(hā'ittîm,* late usage; lit., "the times")* that came upon him and upon Israel; and (3) those that came upon all the kingdoms of the countries.

Intention

It is the intention of this pericope to pay a last tribute to David before he passes from the scene. All that Israel has become, and all the potential greatness that resides in Solomon, is the achievement of this great man. Thus it is not sufficient to record the simple facts in the pattern of the REGNAL RESUMÉ. The citation of sources for further referral suggests that what has been recounted in ChrH is only a small part of what David actually accomplished. Books *(dibrê)* are ascribed to the three inspired figures, Samuel, Nathan, and Gad, who spoke definitive words about his career: picking him out, diverting him from erroneous actions, and directing him to actions that would fulfill God's plan for him. As has been suggested, it is highly unlikely that the prophets actually wrote books about David, but ChrH wants to make his readers think that they did, for their inspiration lends the aura of divine acceptance. (ChrH is in fact citing those sections of Samuel in which Samuel, Nathan, and Gad are active as "books," or simply, "words.") ChrH would have us understand that a life guided by the prophetic word is itself prophetic—that is, a word of God about the ways of God.

232

ACCOUNT OF THE BUILDING OF THE TEMPLE, 2 CHR 1:1–9:31

Structure

I. Report: Solomon confirmed in his rule   1:1-17
II. Account: Solomon builds the temple   1:18 (*RSV* 2:1)–8:16
III. Report: Solomon in his glory   8:17–9:31

The observations of Williamson (comm., 125) make plain how tightly drawn ChrH's account of Solomon's career is. 1:2-17 is set over against 8:17–9:29 so as to emphasize the attributes that enabled Solomon to build the temple and then profit from it. The chiasm as we are able to outline it here draws attention to the centrality of the temple:

a   Solomon's piety, 1:2-6
  b   Gift of wisdom (riches and honor consequential), 1:7-13
    c   Riches in trade of horses, 1:14-17
      d Solomon builds the temple, 1:18–8:16
    c′   Riches in gold through sea commerce, 8:17; 9:13-21
  b′   Wisdom revealed to Queen of Sheba, 9:1-12
a′   Wisdom, riches, universal honor, 9:22-28

Piety, wisdom, and riches were required for Solomon to become the builder of this one great unifying edifice, the temple. With the temple, Israel was able to share with Solomon the honor and admiration of all the nations of the earth.

Bibliography

W. Caspari, "Der Anfang von II Chron und die Mitte des Königsbuches," *ZAW* 39 (1921) 170-74.

REPORT: SOLOMON CONFIRMED IN HIS RULE, 1:1-17

Structure

I. Introductory summary with assistance formula   1
II. Report of ritual: worship at Gibeon's shrine   2-6
  A. The pilgrimage   2-3a
    1. Solomon speaks to "all Israel"   2
    2. Procession to Gibeon   3a
  B. Traditional accoutrements of worship   3b-5a
    1. "Tent of meeting" at Gibeon   3b
    2. The ark installed in Jerusalem   4
    3. Bronze altar at Gibeon   5a
  C. Performance of worship   5b-6
    1. Religious acts   5b

In 1 Kgs 2:12, where Solomon is introduced as his father's successor, the firmness of his tenure is stated in the words *wattikkōn* [niph.] *malkutô mĕ'ōd,* "And his kingdom was firmly established." In 2 Chr 1:1 it is not directly Solomon's kingdom that is said to be established, but Solomon in his kingdom (*ḥzq,* hith.). This is perhaps to remind the reader of 1 Chr 29:23, where it is emphasized that the throne is Yahweh's, and Yahweh allows him to rule upon it in the place of David. Thus the *RSV* in 2 Chr 1:1 may be somewhat misleading in translating, "Solomon . . . established himself." The middle meaning for the hith. is dubious, and in any case seems to clash with the concluding clause, which states that Yahweh made him great. An introduction to the story of his reign, this verse has the intent of summarizing the outcome and ultimate significance of Solomon's rule. What Solomon will do with the unparalleled opportunity of the ensuing narrative will demonstrate the extent to which this purpose and this qualification have already been fulfilled.

From ChrH's point of view it is important that Solomon show himself to be a king possessing piety, wisdom, and riches. This accounts for the structure of this chapter. In vv. 2-6 Solomon shows himself possessed of piety (cf. Williamson, comm., 193); in vv. 7-13 he chooses "wisdom" as a gift from God (cf. Williamson, comm., 195); and in vv. 14-17, especially transferred here from the end of

Solomon's reign as found in ChrH's source material, he displays his great riches and how he acquired them (cf. Williamson, comm., 196).

ChrH has passed 1 Kings 1–2 by, but stops at ch. 3 to extract from it the narrative of Solomon's dream at Gibeon. Travelling to Gibeon to worship will display Solomon's piety, and the revelation from God will display his wisdom. ChrH's account begins with only ephemeral allusions to the story in Kings, but in the revelation episode it adheres rather closely to the original. The story begins with Solomon addressing "all Israel," consisting mainly of the groups addressed in 1 Chr 28:1. Solomon's piety is not private but an act of devotion in which the entire nation shares. It has again become a *qāhāl* in the true sense of that word: a congregation gathered for worship. The shrine at Gibeon is still called *bāmâ;* we encounter in ChrH none of the Dtr animosity toward this kind of provincial shrine. All the same, v. 3 makes clear that this shrine had legitimacy because it possessed the very *'ōhel mô'ēd hā'ĕlōhîm,* "God's tent of meeting," which Moses the servant of God had made in the wilderness. This was evidently identical to the *miškan yahweh,* "Yahweh's tabernacle," v. 5, so there is no hint that a double shrine is meant. But before this tabernacle there was also Bezalel's bronze altar, another relic from the desert. There Solomon and his co-worshipers sacrificed a thousand burnt offerings (the impf. *ya'ăleh* in Kings is frequentative, and therefore more understandable than the narrative form, the *wāw*-consecutive impf., which implies one momentary act; the plur. may save the day by implying that such a great congregation added their numerous offerings to Solomon's). Our comment on v. 4 is that it sanitizes any implication of apostasy on Solomon's part by interjecting that the bringing of the ark into Jerusalem had long since demonstrated David's true goal in structuring Israel's worship (cf. Watson, "Archaic Elements," 7.2). Otherwise concerning the text: Lemke ("Synoptic Studies," 82) explains that ChrH's obvious "pan-Israelite" tendency accounts for any changes over against Kings, so that restoration from the one text or the other is precarious.

Then we come to the revelation, which in Kings is said to have come as a dream at night. Lemke (p. 80) discusses the text of this section, and on pp. 83-85 opines that there would have been no *Tendenz* in ChrH's omission of the dream element. We may agree, for ChrH is manifestly abbreviating. We must choose the term "epiphany" over against "theophany" in spite of *nir'â 'ĕlōhîm,* "God appeared," because the entire following proceeding is verbal and aural. The structure is very simple and forthright: (1) God offers; (2) Solomon requests; (3) God replies. The offer is very direct: *šĕ'al mâ 'eten-lāk,* "Ask what I shall give you," which only makes sense if it means that God is willing to give anything that Solomon shall ask. Following Kings, ChrH's version of Solomon's reply misses some fine nuancing in that source. True to Kings, he states that God did *ḥesed,* "faithful devotion," to David in getting Solomon crowned to the throne (v. 8). *'attâ,* "Now," at the beginning of vv. 9 and 10, draws direct consequences from that deed of *ḥesed.* In v. 9 it is that Solomon has thereby become the ruler of a people "as many as the dust of the earth." In v. 10, skipping the possibly demeaning reference to Solomon as a young child, ChrH draws the second consequence *('attâ),* asking for *ḥokmâ ûmaddā',* "wisdom and knowledge," to rule Yahweh's people, who without Solomon's intent have become very great. The kind of "wisdom" Solomon is asking for (this comes through in ChrH, as in Kings) is a practical shrewdness, with understanding intelligence. That point was perhaps clearer in 1 Kgs 3:9, where Solomon had described the Israelites as *'ammĕkā hakkābēd,* "your heavy [i.e., 'difficult'] people." We can understand why ChrH, who seldom disparages the people, much prefers to have Solomon say that he needed wisdom because they were so "great," i.e., so numerous, mighty, and notable. As the saying goes, prosperity requires as much skill to manage as poverty and meanness.

The Deity, in replying, identifies the basis for the gift that will be forthcoming. He commends Solomon for what he has asked (v. 11a) and commends him also for the things he has not asked (v. 11b). Wisdom in the sense of shrewdness or administrative skill is granted as requested (v. 12a). But there will be a *donum superadditum:* the riches and honor he has not requested, above every earthly ruler.

Verse 13 tells of the return to Jerusalem. This involves a departure—the final one—from the Gibeon "high place" (MT *labbāmâ* is explained as an archaism in Kropat, 77) and "from the presence of the tent of meeting," whose existence remained an embarrassment until the Levites started cultivating a terminology which made the Jerusalem temple the typological equivalent of the tent of meeting (1 Chr 23:26, 32).

The words of v. 13b, "And he reigned over Israel," must be taken as confirmatory. It is as if the test of the Gibeon revelation had confirmed Solomon in his kingship.

As has been said, ChrH found the content of vv. 14-17 in 1 Kgs 10:26-29. ChrH repeats this material in 2 Chr 9:25-28, at a place corresponding to the passage in Kings. His reason is transparent: he wishes to show the rich Solomon to complete this portrait of who Solomon was and what he was destined to become. The three items he brings in to demonstrate Solomon's riches were each independent of the others: information about the quartering of cavalry and chariots; an encomium on Solomon's wealth; information on how he carried out a trade in horses and chariots, with the wealth and power that they brought.

Genre

The following formulas occur in this pericope: ASSISTANCE, v. 1, "Yahweh his God was with him"; TRANSITION, v. 7, "In that night"; RHETORICAL QUESTION, v. 10, "Who can rule this thy people, that is so great?"; INCOMPARABILITY STATEMENT, v. 12, "such as none of the kings had who were before you, and none after you shall have the like." Resembling the (→) aphorism in pithiness, exaggeration, and concrete imagery, this last may be seen as a formula or, when occurring independently, as an independent genre (→ INCOMPARABILITY STATEMENT). Here it appears as part of an ORACLE and functions as a formula. In an ENCOMIUM, which is its usual context, it uses the syntax of the superlative, stretching all limits of metaphor in comparing the object or person being praised to whatever is being scorned.

Verses 2-6 comprise another example of the genre REPORT OF RITUAL; beside the eventual burnt offerings, Solomon's address and the religious pilgrimage to Gibeon are presented as part of a ritual. Although ChrH has removed "in a dream" (1 Kgs 3:5) and "Behold, it was a dream" (1 Kgs 3:15), he still places vv. 7-13 at night. Since 1 Kgs 3:1-15 has a DREAM REPORT, ChrH follows it closely enough to justify also calling his version of the narrative by this genre name, even though he has removed the expressions that explicitly identify it as such. A DREAM REPORT recounts the principal elements in a dream experience, in this instance the mysterious appearance of God, giving it great importance in articulating theological themes of canonical scope. This aspect carries the genre name DREAM

EPIPHANY, in which God gives a message or otherwise engages in dialogue with the recipient (→ DREAM REPORT; DREAM EPIPHANY). It is believed that the DREAM EPIPHANY derives traditio-historically from the genre ROYAL NARRATIVE, found mainly in ancient Egypt. Inscriptions of this genre regularly present the king as an ideal figure of strength, piety, and success. Literary context, form, and date vary considerably, but certainly this name would take in such a narrative as that of 1 Kgs 3:4-15 par. 2 Chr 1:7-13. It is true that this is the only biblical material fitting the description, but this is not surprising in the light of considerable evidence for close relations between Solomon and the Egyptian court (→ ROYAL NARRATIVE). Solomon's request in vv. 8-10 is another example of PETITION. The divine reply in vv. 11-12 is another ORACLE, in this case spoken epiphany-style and not through a prophet or priest. V. 12b is another example of PROMISE, announcing the consequence of the "wise and discerning mind" that God is just now giving; the PROMISE also comprises the INCOMPARABILITY STATEMENT identified above.

Verses 14-17 comprise a REPORT made up of two unrelated statements and an encomium. The STATEMENT of v. 14 tells (1) that Solomon built up a force of chariots and cavalrymen; (2) the tally of each; and (3) where they were stationed. The definition of STATEMENT as a genre is: a brief prose writing which simply notes or describes a situation or circumstance. A second example of this genre is in vv. 16-17, a somewhat lengthier report of Solomon's lucrative trade in horses and chariots. The ENCOMIUM in v. 15 is like that of 1 Chr 29:25 except that it shows exaggeration beyond all reality and focuses exclusively on Solomon's riches. The main genre, finally, is also REPORT.

Setting and Intention

The first chapter of 2 Chronicles offers a good example of how free ChrH is in following what appears to be his only written source, 1 Kings (DtrH). He adapts rather freely in vv. 2-6 because (1) he wants to identify the journey to Gibeon as a religious pilgrimage involving "all Israel" and not just Solomon as a private person; (2) he wants to identify the Gibeon shrine as important enough, with its "tent of meeting"/"tabernacle" and its great bronze altar dating from the time of Moses, to justify Solomon's pilgrimage there, when his father David had feared the angel of Ornan's shrine too much to venture there (1 Chr 21:28–22:1); cf. Blenkinsopp (*Gibeon*, 100-105); and (3) he wants to avoid the impression given by 1 Kgs 3:2-3 to the effect that Solomon went to a *bāmâ*, later much condemned by DtrH, merely because the temple had not been built and he could not wait; he does this by stating at the end of v. 5 that "Solomon and the assembly *[qāhāl]* sought *[drš]* Yahweh." That is to say, they marched to Gibeon in a positive spirit, with no other purpose in mind than to seek out the Lord and serve him with the purest devotion. ChrH's narrative is therefore highly creative, not the scribe-like effort at explicating the Kings version with which Willi (*Auslegung*, 141) credits it (on ChrH's tabernacle typology, cf. Willi, 174).

ChrH omits the end of Kings' account (1 Kgs 3:15b) for the obvious reason that the latter appears to be allowing Solomon to act as priest, standing before the ark to make sacrifices. Otherwise his account of the DREAM REPORT is closely similar to Kings. He does feel free to remove explicit references to the epiphany being a dream, perhaps because dream revelations had fallen into disfavor in his time (Lemke, 83-85, sees no theological *Tendenz* in the omission, but has no alternative explanation apart from the possibility that the text may be in error; cf. p. 80). It is in ChrH's vv. 9-10 that the most striking differences arise. ChrH is short; he actually paraphrases Kings. 1 Kgs 3:6-7 has Solomon complaining about how young and inexperienced he is, and how numerous the people whom he must govern are. In 1 Kgs 3:9 his petition is, "Give thy servant therefore an understanding mind *[lēb šōmēaʻ]* to govern thy people, that I may discern between good and evil; for who is able to govern this thy burdensome people *[ʼet- ʻammĕkā hakkābēd hazzeh]*?" In this version Solomon is asking for a very practical skill, involving open-mindedness and shrewdness, needed for determining "good" and "evil" in all the difficult cases that this "heavy," "burdensome" people are bound to bring before him. ChrH has been far too much under the influence of an image of Solomon as a wise man in the traditional sense to discern the real meaning of Solomon's plea in Kings, hence he substitutes "wisdom and knowledge" *(ḥokmâ ûmaddāʻ)* for *lēb šōmēaʻ* and forgets all about the complaint that the people are heavy or difficult. This suits ChrH's ideology very well, in any case: the people are not difficult—they are numerous and great; Solomon does not have to bother about a "receptive heart"—he is the perfect man of encyclopedic wisdom. ChrH makes a boast of Kings' complaint, but in the weighing he is the poorer for it.

As has been explained, ChrH has the equivalent of 1 Kgs 10:26-29 at 2 Chr 9:25-28, but he has brought it forward to this chapter, vv. 14-17, for the very apparent purpose of setting up the first part of an inclusio depicting Solomon as perfect in everything: perfect in piety, perfect in wisdom, perfect in riches. Solomon is far from passive in all this. He acts deliberately to "seek" Yahweh, and what he does on the pilgrimage to Gibeon will be seen magnified in the upcoming work of building and dedicating the temple. He seeks a revelation and gets it, and when God offers him a choice he makes the right one. Piety and wisdom together demonstrate the validity of his kingship (v. 13b). Wisdom above all else will be needed in building the temple. Solomon's riches come through diligence and shrewdness. They too will be needed; in fact, the temple that Solomon will build will display his riches and glory as much as the riches and glory of Yahweh.

Bibliography

W. F. Albright, "The High Place in Ancient Palestine," in *Volume du Congrès: Strasbourg 1956* (VTSup 4; Leiden: Brill, 1957) 243-45; W. B. Barrick, "What Do We Really Know About High-Places?" *SEÅ* 45 (1980) 50-57; J. Blenkinsopp, *Gibeon and Israel* (SOTSMS 2; Cambridge: Cambridge, 1972); S. I. Fernandez, "Geographica: 'El Gran Bamah' de Gabaón," in *Miscelanea Biblica B. Ubach* (Barcelona: Monasterio de Montserrat, 1953); S. Herrmann, "Die Königsnovelle in Aegypten und Israel," *Wissenschaftliche Zeitschrift der Karl-Marx Universität* 3 (1953-54); Y. Kaufmann, "The Opening of the Stories on the Reign of Solomon" (Hebr.), in *Sefer M. H. Segal* (Jerusalem: Kiryath Sepher, 1964) 87-93; P. Reymond, "Le rêve de Salomon," in *Maqqél shâqédh: La Branche d'Amandier. Hommage à W. Vischer* (ed. D. Lys; Montpellier: Causse Graille Castenau, 1960) 210-13; S. Zalevsky, "The Revelation of God to Solomon in Gibeon" (Hebr.), *Tarb* 42 (1973) 215-58.

ACCOUNT: SOLOMON BUILDS THE TEMPLE, 1:18
(RSV 2:1)–8:16

Structure

I. Report of preparations	1:18–2:17 (*RSV* 18)
II. Report of work on the temple and its appurtenances	3:1–5:1a
III. Account of the dedication of the temple	5:1b–7:22
IV. Report of sanctifying the land	8:1-16

Before discussing this outline, we need to get our bearings to see where it fits. We are in the second main section, composed of narrative materials: "Ideal Israel completes its land's sabbaths": 1 Chr 9:35–2 Chr 36:23 (see outline, on pp. 96–98). We are still under the first main subhead, "Establishing Yahweh's nation and temple," 1 Chr 9:35–2 Chr 9:31. The next subhead was "The building of the temple," 1 Chr 21:28–2 Chr 9:31, with its subhead, "Account of the building of the temple," 2 Chr 1:1–9:31. We have already covered the section "Solomon confirmed in his rule," 2 Chr 1:1-17, and a third coordinate section awaits us after we treat our present pericope: "Solomon in his glory," 8:17–9:31. From this review it can be seen that we are rapidly approaching the conclusion of the section "Establishing Yahweh's nation and temple," and that we are now right in the midst of the climactic part—the part where all preparation finds its fulfillment and the temple is actually built. A king as great as, or greater than, David has been installed, and according to ChrH this king moves immediately to obey his father David and get the work started on the temple. Bye and bye the construction will be completed, the temple dedicated, and regular services instituted for all time to come. Once the temple is in place and its service begun, ideal Israel will be what God's creation and all past history has destined them for: "all Israel" united in the worship of Yahweh at "the house where his name dwells," led in a perfectly ordered service by the priests and Levites whom he has ordained.

The structural outline that we have prepared follows a structure that involves the principle of chiasm within the wider inclusio of 1:1-17 and 8:17–9:28. The order for this inner chiasm would be the following:

a	Preparations
b	Work on temple and appurtenances
b'	Dedication of the temple
a'	Sanctifying the land

The core is the pericope about the work on the temple, with its outflowing consequence, its dedication. Surrounding it is the initial framework element about the preparations, and the concluding framework about sanctifying the land. These are two elements that are not thematically unrelated to each other, since at the beginning the land produces the things necessary for the temple building, and at the end the land is purified so that it may enter fully into the sanctity of the temple.

Borrowing from Kings, ChrH has been able to provide opening and closing rubrics as signals to this structure. They are the following:

1:18 (*RSV* 2:1) *wayyō'mer šĕlōmōh libnôt bayit lĕšēm yahweh ûbayit lĕmalkûtô,* "And Solomon purposed to build a house to Yahweh's name and a house for his kingdom."

3:1 *wayyāḥel šĕlōmōh libnôt 'et-bêt-yahweh* (etc.), "And Solomon began to build Yahweh's house" (etc.).

5:1a *wattišlam kol-hammĕlā'kâ 'ăšer-'āsâ šĕlōmōh lĕbêt yahweh,* "And all the work that Solomon performed for Yahweh's house was perfected."

7:11 *wayĕkal šĕlōmōh 'et-bêt yahweh wĕ'et-bêt hammelek wĕ'ēt kol-habbā' 'al-lēb šĕlōmōh la'ăśôt bĕbêt-yahweh ûbĕbêtô hiṣlîaḥ,* "and Solomon completed Yahweh's house and the king's house; all that came into Solomon's mind to do on Yahweh's house and on his house was successful."

8:16 *wattikkōn kol-mĕle'ket šĕlōmōh 'ad-hayyôm mûsad bêt-yahweh wĕ'adkĕlōtô šālēm bêt yahweh,* "and every work of Solomon, from the day that he founded the temple until its completion, was validated: he had made perfect Yahweh's house."

We do not intend to give ChrH more credit than he deserves for clever arrangement, particularly because we realize that he inserted most of these summarizing statements from the place in Kings from which he was working. 3:1; 5:1; and 7:11 are taken from 1 Kgs 6:1; 7:51; and 9:1, respectively. 8:16 echoes 1 Kgs 6:38 without its chronological elements, while it takes the words *šālēm bêt yahweh* from 1 Kgs 9:25. 2 Chr 1:18 (*RSV* 2:1) seems to have no Kings counterpart. ChrH ignores all the chronological data, also that in 1 Kgs 6:1, 37; 7:1, being far more interested in the place where the temple was built, as witness the expansive description of the site in 3:1. We can speculate on why this was: we see that ChrH has little concern for the history of the building of the temple and makes everything of the special sacrality of the holy place where it was built.

Not only is the centrality of the temple's construction apparent thematically (see above); the diction also bears this out in making the "house of Yahweh," without reference to any other building, parallel in 3:1 and 5:1a. The work starts with *ḥll,* "begin," and it ends with *šlm,* "be perfected." Although ChrH has no report on the building of Solomon's own palace ("house") or the other buildings described in 1 Kgs 7:1ff., he assumes that the reader knows about them from his mention of the palace in 8:1. Hence an outer circle beginning at 1:18 and ending at 7:11, just at the conclusion of the dedication festival, has summary statements mentioning both the temple and the palace (*bayit lĕmalkûtô,* 1:18; *bêt hammelek,* 7:11). In other words, Solomon planned for them both and completed (*kll*) them both. Thematically, however, the dedication is the counterpart of the completion of the temple, and 7:11 should not be seen as the formulaic counterpart of 1:18. Rather, this has to be seen in the ponderous declaration at 8:16. This allows a twenty-year passage of time in which both "houses" were built (8:1), the land was subjugated and organized (vv. 2-10), Pharaoh's daughter was put in residence outside Jerusalem (v. 11), and the clergy was put under a firm regulation for carrying out the sacrifices (vv. 12-15). This is to be understood as "all the work of Solomon." 8:16 measures the time span for this "from the day when Yahweh's house was founded [is this the same day as in 3:1?] until it was completed *[kll]*." Judging from the fact that this verse seems to summarize the contents of ch. 8, we must assume that ChrH is saying that the building process was not really finished until these things, too, had been carried out. This, then, would be the full meaning of *šālēm bêt yahweh,* "Perfected was Yahweh's house." And if so, this is intended as the full counterpart of 1:18, so that the overall formulaic structure would be:

a		Solomon intends to build temple and palace, 1:18 (*RSV* 2:1)
	b	Solomon begins to build the temple, 3:1
	b'	All the temple work is finished, 5:1
	b"	Solomon finishes the temple and palace, 7:11
a'		All of Solomon's work is completed, 8:16a
a"		The temple is perfected, 8:16b

I. REPORT OF PREPARATIONS, 1:18–2:17 (*RSV* 2:1-18)

Structure

A. Statement of Solomon's intention	1:18
B. Steps toward fulfillment	2:1-17
1. Report of cadres to prepare stone	2:1
2. Negotiation with Huram	2-15
a. Solomon's message	2-9
1) Introduction	2a
2) Historical preamble	2b
3) Plans for Yahweh's temple	3-5
a) Its purpose	3
(1) Dedication for every religious occasion	3a
(2) Authorization	3b
b) Its grand design	4-5a
(1) Commensurate with grandeur of Israel's God	4
(2) Rhetorical question: inadequate for containing him	5a
c) Rhetorical question and self-abasement formula	5b
4) Petition for an artisan	6
a) Job description	6a
b) Supervision for native artisans	6b
5) Petition for timber	7-8
a) Specifications	7aα
b) Preparation by skilled workmen	7aβ-b
c) Further specifications	8a
d) Purpose	8b
6) Specification of compensation	9
b. Huram's messenger speech	10-15
1) Introduction	10a

241

The external boundaries of this pericope are set by the report of Solomon's horse trade in 1:14-17 and by the report of the commencement of the temple construction in 3:1ff. Its own internal structure features two main sections of drastically unequal length, 1:18 (*RSV* 2:1) serving as the first main head and all the rest representing together the second main head. We have already given some attention to the statement of Solomon's intent: while serving to set the bounds for the enlarged temple pericope, it tells of Solomon's preparations as well, i.e., the determination that came into his mind once he saw that he was confirmed in his kingship (2 Chr 1:13b). Even though ChrH makes very little of the royal palace, it is not unnatural to read that Solomon includes it in his plan (note Huram's reply in v. 11, besides the formulaic mention in 2 Chr 7:11 and 8:1). There is no equivalent to this verse in Kings, hence it is Chronicler's creative transition, not the exegetical explication that Willi (*Auslegung,* 172) claims it to be.

Part II is in three main divisions that turn out to be another typical ChrH inclusio. For constructing the temple Solomon will need much stone and timber. In 2:1 (*RSV* 2:2) ChrH takes 1 Kgs 5:15-16 (*RSV* 5:1-2) to serve as the introductory framework, with a virtually identical framework statement in vv. 16-17 (*RSV* vv. 17-18), stating the number of men assigned to three specific tasks involved in the quarrying of stones: bearing burdens, quarrying, and overseeing. We shall comment further in taking up vv. 16-17.

The long central section, vv. 2-15 (*RSV* 3-16), is the center of the inclusio and the heart of the pericope. It contains the report of Solomon's agreement with Huram (Kings: Hiram) for obtaining timber. The entire pericope is in the form of a negotiation between the two kings, with no narrative statement at the end to express fulfillment. The form is that of a dialogue carried on by messengers and written correspondence on two matters: (1) whether and in what manner Huram would be willing to send the timbers that Solomon requires, and (2) what price will be paid. One takes note of the fact that there is no introductory embassage to Solomon, as in 1 Kgs 5:15 (*RSV* 5:1). There is simply Solomon's message, vv. 2-9, and Huram's reply, vv. 10-15. In v. 2a the expression *wayyišlaḥ* means "and he sent a messenger," who is charged to repeat Solomon's words (not clear in *RSV*). Lemke (pp. 87-88) discusses a problem in the text. In v. 2b *ka'ăšer* introduces a historical preamble alluding to Huram's trade with David according to 1 Chr 14:1, but the comparative sentence is not completed (cf. *RSV*); instead, Solomon tells his plans for a grand temple for Yahweh (Lemke, 88, claims ChrH's text is colored with his cultic bias). ChrH tells of its purpose in a long series of parallel statements, using alliteration: it will be dedicated to Yahweh (1) for the burning of incense of sweet spices, (2) for the continual offering of the showbread, and (3) for burnt offerings. The occasions when the last are offered are also mentioned: (1) regular morning and evening sacrifices; (2) sabbaths; (3) new moons; and (4) appointed feasts. These activities and these occasions are far from imaginary; in the section on Hezekiah, 2 Chr 29:18 and 31:3 refer specifically to them for the time of the Judahite kings, and they would surely have been in effect in the time of ChrH (see Williamson, *Israel*, 121-22). The authorization for the practices that ChrH is contemplating is stated in 2:3 in the words *lĕ'ôlām zō't 'al-yiśrā'ēl*, "From antiquity this has been imposed on Israel," with reference to Exod 30:1-10 and Lev 24:1-9. (Equally, the Hebrew could mean, "Unto perpetuity this has been imposed on Israel," but that way of understanding it would be meaningful only for ChrH's contemporaries, not for Huram, since he could be expected to have no sense of Israelite eschatology.) Solomon goes on to tell Huram some of his aspirations—and even ideology—for this temple. It has to be *gādôl*, "great," because "our God is greater than *[gādôl min]* all gods." Blanching at such an extravagant boast in a message to the adherent of a foreign god, Galling (ATD) would remove this "because" clause as a late intrusion, but he forgets that ChrH is no historian of religions, only a religious propagandist. This is the premise for his next two statements, to the effect that only heaven can contain this God, hence the most he can do is offer incense to him there.

If this were 1 Kings 5, Solomon would now request the timber, but that has to wait while ChrH adapts the description of Hiram in 1 Kgs 7:13-14 into a preliminary request (v. 6 [*RSV* 7]), which will be granted in v. 13 (*RSV* 14). Willi (p. 143) explains this intrusion as an editorial normalization. Lemke (p. 88) sees it rather as an example of ChrH's unrestrained cultic bias. It is neither, but an example of ChrH's imaginative inventiveness in bringing the two "Hurams" together and in magnifying Solomon's authority by obtaining two requests instead of one. In vv. 7-8 (*RSV* 8-9) Solomon makes his request for the timber, adding the gratuitous explanation, "for the house that I am to build will be great and wonderful *[gādôl wĕhaplē']*." (On the request for timber, cf. Watson, 2.1, 11.2.) According to Lemke (p. 90), it is the pious king theme that has led ChrH to add wine to the list of items promised in return (1 Kgs 5:25 [*RSV* 5:10]).

We get Huram's congenial reply in vv. 10-15 (*RSV* 11-16). Lemke (pp. 88-91) raises questions about the possible superiority of the Chronicles text in vv. 10, 14-15; he also opines that cultic bias reappears in v. 13 (p. 88). Willi (p. 121) considers v. 15 a conjectural emendation of Kings. It is natural that the verses concerned in these discussions deal with technology. Apart from them, however, the narrative flows smoothly. Huram is replying, albeit by letter (ChrH would have considered this a specially honorable and weighty way of replying to an Israelite king; cf. 21:13). He praises Solomon by saying that Yahweh must love his people to place Solomon over them (v. 10b), and then he launches into a fulsome blessing of the Israelite Deity in the language of their own theology, adding that the son whom Yahweh has given to David, full of wisdom, discretion, and understanding, is now at the point of building Yahweh's temple, as well as a palace for himself (v. 11). Being in this frame of mind, he appoints his man Huram-abi (the name, patronym, and qualifications are given; cf. Watson, 7.7, 5.1), lists his many skills, and gives assurance that he will work well with the native craftsmen over whom he is evidently to be placed (vv. 12-13). In vv. 14-15 Huram restates for clarification what the agreement will be: foodstuffs in the variety and quantity promised, to be delivered to Huram; as much timber as needed to be rafted to Joppa by the Phoenicians and dragged by Solomon's servants up to Jerusalem.

Verses 16-17 (*RSV* 17-18) repeat the substance of v. 1, completing the inclusio. Added is the statement in v. 16 that Solomon took a census separate from the one his father had taken (1 Chronicles 21), but just of aliens (*kol-hā'ănāšîm haggērîm*, lit., "all the men who were sojourners"), and found them to total 153,600. This idea of the impressment of foreigners (though not of *gērîm*, "sojourners," specifically) is found in 1 Kgs 9:20-21. ChrH seems to vacillate as much as Kings does, whether native Israelites or non-Israelites were to be employed in the work of the temple (it would have been an honor for Israelites to work on the temple, but the heavy labor would have been viewed as suitable only for non-Israelites). The total in v. 16 combines the tallies of v. 17 (cf. v. 1 [*RSV* 2]): burden bearers, 70,000; quarriers, 80,000; supervisors, 3,600.

Genre

The main genre of this pericope is REPORT. 2:1, 2-15, and 16-17 are also REPORTS. Vv. 2-15 are a NEGOTIATION, as is 1 Chr 21:20-25, even though no bargaining is reported. The initial verse, 1:18, is a STATEMENT. Vv. 2-9 and vv. 10-15 are of the genre MESSENGER SPEECH, an address from one person to another communicated by, or even spoken by, a specially designated and authorized intermediary (the messenger). This way of sending messages was much relied upon in the ancient world, and only gradually came to be supplanted by messages in writing, as in our v. 10 (a possible anachronism). The RHETORICAL QUESTION occurs twice in v. 5: "Who is able to build him a house . . . ?" and "Who am I to build a house for him?" The latter contains the SELF-ABASEMENT FORMULA, "So now send me. . . ." V. 6 is a PETITION, and so again v. 7. V. 9 gives a JOB DESCRIPTION, listing needed skills and the prospective manner of employment. V. 10b is a PRAISE SPEECH, while v. 11 is a BLESSING that turns into another PRAISE SPEECH. The TALLY is used in vv. 16-17 for the total of stone-workers and for each category of worker.

Setting

Except for the opening verse, this entire pericope relies heavily on 1 Kings 5. The negotiation with Huram (rather, "Hiram," as in Kings; more fully, "Ahiram," "My brother [deity!] is/be great") is altered from the Kings version to give less prominence to David. Everything that the Bible tells us, except Ezekiel's diatribes in chs. 27–28, regarding Israel/Judah's relationships with Tyre is favorable—too favorable in the case of Ahab's marriage to Jezebel, 1 Kgs 16:31-33. Hiram had previously entered into a trade agreement with David, 1 Chr 14:1; cf. 2 Sam 5:11-

12; it is not strange that, in beginning the work of building the temple, Solomon goes to him for a chief architect and timber. There would have been no harm in that from the viewpoint of the historical Solomon (he had many foreign alliances, which, however, ChrH deliberately neglects to tell us about). According to the most recent archeological and typological work, the Jerusalem temple was designed architecturally after the Phoenician temples (cf. Busink), which is what we should expect with Huram-abi (Kings: Hiram) as chief architect as well as master craftsman. Things were different in ChrH's own time. True, no military threat came from Phoenicia, yet ChrH and his community had grown measurably more xenophobic, distrusting especially that country's still rampant fertility worship. A number of touches in the present pericope tend to mitigate this offense. We note that Solomon, not Huram, takes the initiative, and tailors the proposal to his wishes. Huram almost fawningly answers back; ChrH touches up his greeting as found in 1 Kgs 5:21 (*RSV* 5:7) by making a virtual proselyte of him: "Blessed be Yahweh God of Israel" (cf. Ezra 1:2). He also fawns on Solomon with these words: "who has given King David a wise son, endued with discretion and understanding, who will build a temple (etc.)." This reference to Solomon's wisdom is, of course, a carryover from 2 Chronicles 1. The timbers are to be cut and transported as ordered, but instead of Kings "to the place you shall direct"—which in ChrH's viewpoint could have been someplace outside Israelite control—they are to be brought straight to Joppa. Solomon's servants would bring them up directly to Jerusalem.

Taking his cue from 1 Kgs 7:14, ChrH mentions that Huram-abi the artisan was half-Israelite, and therefore had a partial claim in the covenant community. The reference to the proselytes working on the stone-cutting, vv. 16-17 (*RSV* 17-18), added to a text that is here repeated from vv. 1-2 (*RSV* 2-3), intends perhaps to show that Huram-abi is not unique in working on the temple as a foreigner; all who have at least half a claim in Israel have a right (and duty) to help with the temple. We see from the JOB DESCRIPTION for Huram-abi in v. 8 (*RSV* 9) that he was to be modeled after the man who had crafted the tabernacle in the desert, Bezalel, of whom Exod 35:30-33 speaks: "See, Yahweh has called by name Bezalel . . . and he has filled him with the spirit of God, with ability, with intelligence, with knowledge, and with all craftsmanship, to devise artistic designs, to work in gold and silver and bronze, in cutting stones for setting, and in carving wood, for work in every skilled craft."

Verse 3 (*RSV* 4) begins with Solomon announcing to Huram the reason for the timber: "Behold, I am about to build a house for the name of Yahweh my God." This is entirely what the conversation requires, and is found in 1 Kgs 5:19 (*RSV* 5:5). But everyone who knows pentateuchal law recognizes that what Solomon says next (entirely inappropriate in address to a noncomprehending foreigner) is drawn from the legal codes of the Pentateuch—here, to be specific, from Exod 30:1-10 and Lev 24:1-9. It concerns the burning of incense and the display of the showbread, as regulated in those passages. This is not the first passage in ChrH that shows direct dependence on pentateuchal legislation; we saw this previously at 1 Chr 15:15, citing Num 4:4-15 regarding the duty of the Levites to carry the ark. We should proceed no further without pausing to raise the question of ChrH on the pentateuchal law in general. There have been numerous minor studies of this problem, but nothing so thorough as Shaver's dissertation. The aim of this study is to ascertain whether the various cult-oriented passages in 1–2 Chronicles cite or show special reliance on specific pentateuchal passages, and particularly whether they show preference for any specific literary strand. Arranging the relevant passages according to the pentateuchal strand on which they are dependent, we can summarize Shaver's work as follows:

JE	Exod 12:21	2 Chr 30:15, 17; 35:1, 6, 11	"killing Passover lamb"
Deut	16:1-16	2 Chr 8:13	three *ḥaggîm*
	24:16	25:4	limited execution (par. 2 Kgs 14:6)
H code	Lev 23:5	35:1	Passover date
	23:36, 39	7:8-10	post-Passover assembly
P code	Exod 30:1-10; Num 17:5 (*RSV* 16:40)	26:17-18	priestly privilege
	Exod 30:11-16	24:6	tax
	Num 4:4-15	1 Chr 15:15	Levites carrying ark
	9:6-11	2 Chr 30:15	Passover in second month
	Exod 12:8-9	35:13	roasting (Deuteronomy: boiling) Passover lamb
Pˢ	Num 29:35	2 Chr 7:8-10	post-Passover assembly
	28–29	31:3	burnt offerings
	Exod 30:1-10; Lev 24:1-9	2:3 (*RSV* 2:4)	incense, showbread in temple
Non-pentateuchal		30:16-17; 35:10-11	Levitical role in Passover
Ezekiel	45:17 "prince's" contribution	31:3	king's contribution

From this display it can be seen that ChrH cites from all the main strands of the Pentateuch, as commonly recognized; not surprisingly citing more often from P and Pˢ, who happen to be roughly contemporaneous with ChrH. This is the case with the reference to the incense and showbread in v. 3 (*RSV* 4) of our passage, which draws from two Pˢ passages. The important discovery of Shaver's work is that 2 Chr 30:16-17, citing the authority of "Moses the man of God," and 35:10-11, citing "Moses," cannot be associated with any passage in the Pentateuch; they in fact contain the AUTHORIZATION FORMULA, showing that the privileges they claim for the Levites in handling the sacrificial victims, over against the priests, whose prerogative they appear to be usurping, is needed for supporting a new practice.

But what is this "law of Moses" that justifies practices not recorded in the Pentateuch? Is the Mosaic legal code still fluid? Shaver had extended his analysis into Ezra-Nehemiah and found there still more passages that claim Mosaic authority for non-pentateuchal practices, to wit: Ezra 6:18, organizing the priests

246

and the Levites "as written in the book of Moses"; Ezra 10:3, demanding the dismissal of foreign wives and children "according to the law," defined also as "the commandment of our God"; Neh 8:15, giving instructions for gathering branches for constructing booths "as written" (cf. Lev 23:40); and Neh 10:35 (*RSV* 34), demanding a wood offering "as written in the law." One other passage in Chronicles that apparently claims Mosaic authority is 2 Chr 30:18, which mentions the proper way to eat the Passover "as written." The least that can be said about these citations is that they show that the Mosaic legal tradition had not yet assumed a final form. This last passage together with those from Ezra-Nehemiah all contain the REGULATION rather than the authorization formula (→ REGULATION FORMULA), being concerned not with the authority behind a given practice but with the correct way of performing the religious duties prescribed.

Intention

In recent scholarship there has been much discussion about rival concepts in ancient Israel concerning the function of the temple. These are (1) the notion that the temple is Yahweh's dwelling place, and (2) the claim that the temple is only the place where his "name" dwells, his true dwelling place being in heaven. ChrH allows the first to come to expression in his pericope about the dedication. This is apparently not his own true view, but since he is always acting creatively and responsibly in deciding what to repeat from his sources and what to omit, we must hold him at least partially responsible for allowing this view of the temple to come to expression. In 2 Chr 6:1-2 Solomon repeats from Kings the ancient hymn of dedication: "Yahweh has said that he would dwell in thick darkness. I have built thee an exalted house, a place for thee to dwell in forever." He suppresses the Kings ending of Solomon's long dedicatory prayer (2 Chr 6:41) and has him recite from Ps 132:8 the following words: "And now arise, O Yahweh God, and go to thy resting place, thou and the ark of thy might." It is true that these citations express the theology of the divine entrance into the sanctuary prepared for him, yet words like *mĕnûḥâ*, "resting place," *lahăḏōm raglāyw*, "footstool for his feet," and the very verb *yšb* suggest a permanent residence (cf. 1 Chr 28:2). By and large, however, ChrH takes over the theology of DtrH, which comes to emphatic expression in Solomon's dedicatory prayer. He has Solomon announce in 2 Chr 6:10 that he has built "the house for the name of Yahweh," thus showing ChrH's essential adherence to the "name" theology (cf. 1 Chr 28:3). A further purpose according to this passage is to contain the ark, which is not a "footstool for Yahweh's feet" but a receptacle for "the covenant of Yahweh which he made for the people of Israel" (v. 11)—in other words, the tablets of Moses' law (cf. 2 Chr 5:10). In repeating almost verbatim Solomon's prayer from Kings, ChrH adds his support to the interpretation of the temple as a place to which prayers must come— that is, where "Yahweh's name dwells," where he may be invoked.

Looking back at Solomon's announcement to Huram (2:4-6 [*RSV* 5-7]), we see that he supplements his statement that the house he plans to build must be great because his God is greater than all other gods (v. 5). He adds the double rhetorical question (v. 6) affirming that no temple can contain him since even the highest heaven cannot contain him, and that Solomon is too weak and insignificant to provide any other "house" than a *māqôm*, "shrine," for burning incense before him. This is no doubt an innuendo of the reference to Ornan's threshing floor as a *māqôm*

(1 Chr 21:22, 25) for calling on God, worshiping him, and receiving his answer. Doubtless this expresses ChrH's own opinion concerning the temple as it had been reconstructed in his own day. There were few anymore who believed that their Deity resided in the temple. It was, rather, the ordained *māqôm* from which Israel's prayers rose to heaven. But cf. 2 Chr 36:15.

Bibliography

T. A. Busink, *Der Tempel von Jerusalem* (Leiden: Brill, 1970); M. Kislev, "Towards the Identity of Some Species of Wheat in Antiquity," *Leš* 42 (1977) 64-72; J. Offord, "Archaeological Notes on Jewish Antiquities. 53. How Cedars Were Transported," *PEFQS* 50 (1918) 181-83; J. R. Shaver, "Torah and the Chronicler's History Work: An Inquiry into the Chronicler's References to Laws, Festivals and Cultic Institutions in Relation to Pentateuchal Legislation" (Diss., Notre Dame, 1983).

II. REPORT OF WORK ON TEMPLE AND APPURTENANCES, 3:1–5:1a

Structure

As we have previously noted, 2 Chr 3:1, "Then Solomon began to build . . . ," is the opening rubric for an innermost double inclusio concluded by 2 Chr 5:1a and 7:11. According to Lemke (pp. 93-94) ChrH's text is clear of tendential traits throughout the section 3:1–5:1. ChrH is much more interested in the place of building than in the time of building. Following 1 Kings, v. 2 does give a date for beginning, but measured in respect to the years of Solomon's reign and not in terms of Israel's departure from Egypt (1 Kgs 6:1). We note also that ChrH has no date of completion comparable to 1 Kgs 6:37-38, and the reason may be that he wants the building of the temple to serve as the one most important project of the twenty years of building that include the construction of the temple according to 2 Chr 8:1. ChrH evidently has a scheme of reckoning according to which the temple is not complete until everything needed to make it fully operable is done; cf. 2 Chr 8:16. He is very precise and emphatic about the site: it is in Jerusalem; it is on Mount Moriah (Gen 22:2); it is where Yahweh had appeared to David; it is at the place *(māqôm)* that David had appointed; it is at the threshing floor of Ornan the Jebusite.

In the report of the construction of the temple, 3:3-14, ChrH follows Kings rather closely, but with minor additions and omissions that are probably due to his fancy and not to problems in the text. The section on the measurements of the *bayit* (sanctuary) is structured with nominal clauses; the section on the sanctuary's adornments is based on verbal clauses; and the section on the holy of holies *(bêt qōdeš haqqŏdāšîm; dĕbîr,* "adytum," in Kings) combines verbal and nominal clauses. This entire section relies entirely on four verbs, *'śh,* "make," *ṣph,* "overlay," *ḥph,* "line," and *'lh,* hiph., "apply." Since the verbal form *wayya'aś* occurs thirteen times, Willi

(p. 96) claims that it is thematic, but this peculiarity is due instead to the reportorial nature of the writing. As compared with Kings, ChrH's description of the cherubim in vv. 11-13, all in nominal clauses, is strikingly prolix. Willi (p. 174) interprets the reference to the old-style cubit in v. 3 as based on an archeological notice. Watson ("Archaic Elements," 4.8) has a note on the nave, v. 5.

ChrH omits Kings' items about the temple court and about Solomon's various administrative and residential buildings, coming in 3:15-17 to the two pillars, Jachin and Boaz. This section is much simplified from the corresponding description in Kings; it is doubtful, indeed, that ChrH truly understood all the technical architectural terms in the text that lay before him. In any event, the style of writing changes somewhat as ChrH relies entirely on verbal constructions. The verbs used here are *'śh*, "make," *ntn*, "put," *qwm*, hiph., "raise," *qr'*, "name," and *nwḥ*, hiph., "secure." On providing the pillars with capitals, cf. Watson (4.2).

In 4:1 ChrH provides information lacking in Kings regarding the dimensions of the great bronze altar that stood before the temple. Although this was no doubt historical, and ChrH was evidently well informed, it is not likely that this notice stood in the original account as presented by Kings. There is little justification in Rudolph's claim (HAT) that the verse is a post-ChrH addition. ChrH returns to Kings for descriptions of the reservoir (sea) and the lavers, vv. 2-6. Here is rich detail, based no doubt on an architect's specification as available to the writer of Kings. As for the ten golden lampstands, the ten tables, the hundred golden basins, and the two courts with their doors (vv. 7-9), they come not from Kings but from ChrH's private sources, being based perhaps on observation of the temple of his own time (Willi, 121, claims that details about the courts are conjecture), with possible influence from Ezekiel 40ff. The note in v. 10 about positioning the reservoir at the southeast corner of the sanctuary repeats 1 Kgs 7:39, hence it is difficult to understand why Willi (p. 197) should consider it a post-ChrH addition. Vv. 11-22 are closely dependent on Kings (see Lemke, 96, on the text), hence it is hard to understand why ChrH could not himself have copied this material from Kings rather than attribute this, with Willi (Rudolph, HAT, vv. 11-14), to a post-ChrH redactor. Here is an inventory of Huram-abi's artifacts, vv. 11-16, and a statement about the manufacturing process, vv. 17-18. This is followed by another inventory, that of Solomon's work in gold, that is secondary to Kings, vv. 19-22 (cf. S. J. De Vries, *1 Kings* [Word Biblical Commentary 12; Waco: Word, 1985] 111).

The conclusion to this section is 2 Chr 5:1a, a framework-concluding rubric (see above): *wattišlam kol-hammĕlā'kâ 'ăšer-'āśâ šĕlōmōh lĕbêt yahweh*, "And perfected was all the work that Solomon did on the house of Yahweh." This is no doubt a pun on the name Solomon (cf. Willi, 185; cf. 143: a normalizing interpretation).

Genre

The main genre of this pericope is REPORT. 3:3-14 and 3:15–4:10 belong to the subgenre CONSTRUCTION REPORT, which is defined as a type of report which tells of building, manufacturing, or fabricating cultic and/or official state objects and edifices, along with descriptions of size, materials, ornamentation, etc. Archival records possibly stood behind these reports, but those who transcribed them did so with prescriptive overtones. In 4:11-22 we encounter two examples of the genre

INVENTORY. This is a special kind of list whose purpose is to simplify and regularize the public administration. In 2 Chr 4:11-16 (1 Kgs 7:41-44), the main concern is to number the objects of each kind. In vv. 19-22 (1 Kgs 7:48-50) the purpose is to assure that each object on the list is of the specified material (gold) and desired quality (*zāhāb sāgûr,* "pure gold," etc.). 4:17-18 belong to the genre STATEMENT. 4:7 has the REGULATION FORMULA: "And he made ten golden lampstands according to their official description *[kĕmišpāṭām]*"; cf. v. 20 (gloss).

Setting

Here is a listing of the major items that Solomon had made for the temple. As 5:1a declares, he "perfected" or "fulfilled" all his work. As we have noted, ChrH goes his own way with relation to the parallel passage, 1 Kgs 6:1-38; 7:15-50, adding or subtracting, and in some instances altering, what is found there, following perhaps a better text at times, or otherwise going by variant traditions, or simply his personal idea of how things should have been. But the main thing to remember is that in ChrH's understanding Solomon was not only completing or perfecting a great work (see also 1 Kgs 7:51), but a special plan *(tabnît)* that his father had given him (1 Chr 28:11-19), and which David had identified as revealed to him in a special writing received "from the hand of God." In other words, David—or Yahweh through David—was the actual architect and Solomon (with the help of Huramabi) only the builder. As we compare the contents of 2 Chronicles 3–4 with the itemization given in David's description, we see that the latter laid far more weight on the use of gold than of bronze; also that various structures are listed that are not mentioned in the construction report: vestibule, "houses," treasuries, upper rooms, inner chambers. The "holy of holies" of 2 Chr 3:8 had been called "the room for the mercy seat." On the other hand, the construction report mentions the pillars, the reservoir, and the lavers, which are not in David's *tabnît.* It would be idle to try to make something of these discrepancies. Back in 1 Chronicles 28 ChrH was composing in the impulse of spontaneity, expressing his own concept of what the temple ought to be, as he had heard of it from various historical sources and as he imagined it. When it came to writing an actual construction report he took the one that was in the Kings text before him, making the minor revisions that we have noted. ChrH had not forgotten the *tabnît.* The temple, as Kings reports Solomon's building it, expresses the typology of the *tabnît;* the process of history—especially the history of ChrH's own time—will shape the restored temple more and more to express this typology. A great temple with many, many chapels, corridors, and courts (cf. Ezekiel 40), all heavily adorned with gold and silver—this is the temple that ought to be, and which ChrH expects it to become!

To ChrH another vitally important aspect of Solomon's temple was the site on which it was built, as 2 Chr 3:1, analyzed under "Structure," so emphatically makes clear. At this site converge two significant elements from the cult traditions of the past. The first is "in Jerusalem on Mount Moriah." Here ChrH reaches back to the patriarch Abraham, who offered his son Isaac at this very place, and where God demanded that animal sacrifices be offered (Genesis 22). (Since ChrH does not mention Isaac—or Abraham for that matter—this cannot be taken to suggest the Isaac = Israel typology that became important in rabbinical tradition.) The second item to which ChrH refers is the revelation to David and his dedication of this site as Yahweh's preferred place of worship, 1 Chr 21:1–22:1. We can imagine David's words of dedication still ringing in his ears: "Here shall be the house of Yahweh God, and here the altar of burnt offering for Israel," 22:1. The altar is the root and core of Yahweh's ideal cult; little wonder, then, that ChrH inserts in the construction report, 2 Chr 4:1, an item wanting in Kings: the bronze altar. The Jerusalem temple may indeed be the place to invoke God, but it is also the place for burning incense and offering sacrifices, 2 Chr 2:5 (RSV 6). The fact that Yahweh accepts that incense and those offerings shows that he also receives his people's prayers. He had done that on the day when David purchased Ornan's threshing floor (1 Chr 21:26), and he will forever do that, so long as his people remain faithful and offer his sacrifices according to his law.

Whenever the Jerusalem temple is mentioned, ChrH is reminded about the tabernacle/tent of meeting at nearby Gibeon, with its prestigious altar of burnt offering (1 Chr 21:29; 2 Chr 1:3-6, 13). These had been sanctified because they were attributed to Moses and Bezalel. Strangely, ChrH appeals constantly to Moses' law when justifying cultic practices, but he ventures to set aside whatever authority Moses may claim with regard to the sanctuary itself. Moses' desert shrine is constantly promoted in P, and evidently in the completed Pentateuch. Both were championed by the postexilic priesthood, and evidently honored by the people. ChrH does not ignore this tradition in promoting his own temple ideology; according to 2 Chronicles he includes the tent of meeting among the holy objects brought into the temple on the occasion of its dedication (5:5, glossed into the text of 1 Kgs 8:4), thereby fusing the tent of meeting/tabernacle with the temple. There is little likelihood that Moses' desert shrine existed in historical reality, in spite of ChrH's Gibeon tradition; or if it did, the early historical sources outside the Pentateuch are remarkably silent about it, and it must have dropped out of view at some insignificant tribal site. In that case, the P document must have refurbished some ancient tradition on the experience of Solomon's historical temple. ChrH pays no more than lip service to the image that P has created, no doubt because to his way of understanding, the temple supersedes the tabernacle. It is difficult to trace this rivalry further; be it understood that for the postexilic priesthood as well as for ChrH, the (postexilic) temple is the reality and the tabernacle is only its image. The priestly tradition would add: model. But for ChrH, the *tabnît* of the temple is the one provided by revelation to David (1 Chr 28:19) and not the *tabnît* given to Moses on Mount Sinai. The most important divergence, however, is that for ChrH, David is the one who shapes and authorizes the new cult of Yahweh, not Moses.

Intention

In commenting on 2 Chr 3:1, von Rad (*Geschichtsbild,* 129-30) makes the claim that ChrH's intention is to identify David as the real temple builder. But there is no real evidence that ChrH wants to demean or minimize what Solomon does. Nevertheless, this verse does emphatically identify the work of David and the work of Solomon as one and the same. Solomon is in fact presented as David's alter ego, doing a work that David himself would gladly have done had he not been prevented from doing so by express revelation from God. At the same time, Solomon could not have built the temple if it were not for another revelation, the one of the *tabnît,* "plan." With all this emphasis on revelation, one would have to be blind not to see that, after all, Yahweh is the real temple builder. David and Solomon must be seen in tandem: father, son; preparer, perfecter. ChrH definitely wants to give both of them credit for doing a work that Yahweh himself had ordained, in a manner which he himself had specified.

When 2 Chr 5:1 reports that "all the work that Solomon did for the house of Yahweh was perfected," the reference is only to the actual work of construction. We have previously noted that 2 Chr 8:16 means to include more: "Thus was accomplished all the work of Solomon"—this includes the temple and palace, v. 1, the organization of the land, vv. 2-11, the starting of regular sacrifices, vv. 12-13, and the appointing of priests and Levites, v. 14—"from the day the foundation of the house of Yahweh was laid until it was finished," i.e., it was not fully finished until the twenty years of 8:1 were up and all the above matters were settled. This may seem like a very enigmatic and roundabout way of writing, but in all the paradox there is profound truth. ChrH means to say that the temple is not finished until it is *ready*, i.e., not only dedicated, but provided with perpetual sacrifices and served by a clergy well instructed and fully prepared. It may seem premature to mention ch. 8 at this particular point, but we do so in order to put chs. 3–4 in proper perspective. Solomon worked to perfect the temple, 5:1a; he did this according to the *tabnît* of his father David, and on the holy site that David had already dedicated. But David had done more: David had ordered the work of the priests and Levites (8:14; cf. 1 Chr 28:13, 21), as one sees especially in 1 Chronicles 15–16; 23–26. Without a perfectly regulated and energetic clergy to make it function for the glory of God and the edification of his people Israel, it remained incomplete and unfinished. Here ChrH makes plain his priorities. A temple without a faithful clergy and a worshiping congregation is only a beautiful building. The people need a temple, and a devout clergy to help, because this is the divinely appointed *māqôm*, "place," where the community may be held together by sanctified prayer and praise.

Bibliography

T. A. Busink, *Der Tempel von Jerusalem von Salomo bis Herodes* (Leiden: Brill, 1970); R. E. Clements, *God and Temple* (Oxford: Oxford, 1965); K. Möhlenbrink, *Der Tempel Salomos* (Stuttgart: Kohlhammer, 1932); J. L. Myers, "King Solomon's Temple and Other Buildings and Works of Art," *PEQ* 81 (1948) 14-41; J. Ouelette, "The Basic Structure of the Solomonic Temple and Archeological Research," in *The Temple of Solomon* (ed. J. Gutmann; Missoula: Scholars, 1976) 1-20; K. Rupprecht, *Der Tempel von Jerusalem. Gründung Salomos oder jebusitisches Erbe?* (Berlin: de Gruyter, 1977); H. Schmid, "Jahwe und die Kulttraditionen von Jerusalem," *ZAW* 67 (1955) 168-97; idem, "Der Tempelbau Salomos in religionsgeschichtlicher Sicht," in *Archäologie und Altes Testament* (Fest. K. Galling; ed. A. Kuschke und E. Kutsch; Tübingen: Mohr, 1970) 241-50; F. Stolz, *Strukturen und Figuren im Kult von Jerusalem* (BZAW 118; Berlin: de Gruyter, 1970); S. Yeivin, "Jachin and Boaz," *PEQ* 91 (1959) 6-22.

III. ACCOUNT OF THE DEDICATION OF THE TEMPLE, 5:1b–7:22

Structure

A.	Report of ritual: the ark's entrance	5:1b–6:2
B.	Report of Solomon's address	6:3-11
C.	Report of Solomon's dedicatory prayer	6:12-42
D.	Report of renewed theophany and sacrifice	7:1-10
E.	Report of a confirmatory dream revelation	7:11-22

The structural analysis of this complex ACCOUNT can best proceed by offering a separate outline of each of its segments.

A.	Report of ritual: the ark's entrance	5:1b–6:2
	1. Entrance of David's treasure	1b
	2. Fetching the ark	2-7
	a. Festal assembly in Jerusalem	2-3
	1) Leading men	2
	2) Citizenry	3
	b. Solemn procession	4-5a
	c. King and congregation sacrifice	5b-6
	d. Priests deposit the ark	7
	3. Descriptive statement	8-10
	a. Cherubim	8
	b. Poles	9
	c. Ark's contents: tables of the law	10
	4. Theophany report	11-14
	a. Priests emerge from the sanctuary	11a
	b. Description of worshiping clergy	11b-12
	1) Sanctified priests	11b
	2) Musicians	12
	a) Levites	12a
	b) Priests	12b
	c. The moment of glory	13
	1) Trumpets and instruments in unison	13aα
	2) Hymnic refrain: "Praise Yahweh, for he is good"	13aβ
	3) Theophany: cloud fills the temple	13b
	d. Priests awed at the cloud	14
	5. Dedicatory declaration	6:1-2

Except for vv. 11b-13a, which Galling (ATD), Willi (p. 196), and Noth ("Chronistische Werk," 117) regard as a post-ChrH addition, the text of this pericope follows Kings rather closely. That 5:1b introduces a new pericope is seen first from the fact that it has *bêt hā'ĕlōhîm,* "the house of God," in the place of *bêt yahweh,* "the house of Yahweh," in v. 1a (ChrH often interchanges these names, but as a rule in separate contexts). It is seen also in the fact that Solomon is introduced anew, but as subject of a new narrative sequence. As also in Kings this statement about Solomon depositing David's treasure is intended as an introduction to the narrative about the fetching of the ark; it is important that all the gifts dedicated for the temple be in place before the key object, the ark, is put in place. V. 1b is chiastically arranged, with the narrative verb *wayyābē'*, "And [Solomon] brought in," at the beginning of the first clause and the factitive perfect, *nātan*, "stored," near the end of the second clause; then also the object in general terms, *'et-qodšê dāwîd 'ābîw*, "the sanctified things of David his father," at the end of the first clause and the distributive object, "the silver and the gold and the vessels *[hakkēlîm]*," at the beginning of the second clause.

The episode about bringing in the ark is introduced by *'āz*, "then," as in 6:1, marking a decisive new initiative of Solomon. A festal assembly is gathered *(qhl)*. First mentioned are the leading men, designated as *ziqnê yiśrā'ēl*, "the elders of Israel," plus *kol-rā'šê hammaṭṭôt*, "all the chiefs of the tribes," which together constitute *hā'ābôt libnê yiśrā'ēl*, "the ancestral heads of the Israelites." This is one of the rare references to the tribes (absent in Kings), by which ChrH is now pointing to his genealogies of the tribes in 1 Chronicles 2–9 (see also 1 Chr 12:23-37) as representatives of the whole people. V. 2a states the purpose: to bring up the ark "out of the city of David, which is Zion" (cf. 1 Chr 11:5), that is, from Ophel to the temple mount, formerly the threshing floor of Ornan. In compliance, "all the men of Israel" —which is intended to include the leaders mentioned plus the common citizens— were assembled, or assembled themselves *(qhl,* niph.). The place: before the king; the time: at the feast of the seventh month (Tabernacles). Then the first mentioned elders started the procession, the Levites following after them carrying the ark (ChrH appears to have altered "priests" in Kings; cf. "priests and Levites" in v. 5b and "priests" in v. 7). While this is going on the king and *kōl-'ădat yiśrā'ēl*, "the entire assembly of Israel," performed uncounted sacrifices (cf. Watson, 5.2; on the leading men, 7.5). That the king is performing the important function of general supervision is shown especially in the title given him: "King Solomon." V. 5a, "And they brought up the ark (etc.)," is the conclusion of this narrative segment; v. 5b is resumptive and emphatic. As in Kings, the holy objects are (1) the ark, (2) the tent of meeting (glossed into Kings), and (3) the holy vessels that were in the tent (thus not the vessels deposited in the treasury, v. 1). V. 6, about the sacrificing, is circumstantial. V. 7 resumes the narration; here ChrH leaves out his favorites, the Levites, and allows the priests to deposit the ark (note that nothing is said about the tent of meeting and other vessels) in the most holy place within the temple.

ChrH follows Kings in the section giving statements of fact concerning the position of the cherubim, with the ark's carrying poles and the Mosaic tablets as contents, vv. 8-10. In v. 9 "ark" has been substituted for *haqqōdeš*, "the holy place" (so MSS, LXX, Kings); according to L. C. Allen ("Cuckoos in the Text Nest," *JTS* 22 [1971] 143-50), the former was in the margin and gradually displaced the latter, but it makes poor sense. In vv. 11-14 a new movement in the narrative begins with *wayĕhî* and the temporal phrase "as the priests were emerging from the holy place"; properly the narrative continues with a main clause, "then the house of Yahweh was filled with a cloud"—the shekinah of glory—as in Kings. There is an abrupt intrusion here, but it is ChrH's, not from a redactor or glossator. The particle *kî*, "for," marks the intrusion: it tells us about who was there, not distinguishing between priests who were just now coming out of the sanctuary and

Levitical singers with priestly trumpeters, who stood eastward of the altar to make praise to Yahweh with the music of the famous hymn, "Praise Yahweh, for he is good," Ps 118:1; 106:1; cf. 1 Chr 16:41; 2 Chr 7:3 (cf. Watson, 200 n. 4). The list of singers, with Asaph at the head, is from a tradition antedating ChrH, according to Gese's analysis, and this is one of the arguments against assigning this intrusion to a secondary expansion. Following Kings, ChrH next tells of the priests' fright (v. 14). To begin 6:1, another *'āz*, as in Kings, introduces another of Solomon's decisive actions, this time his official DEDICATORY DECLARATION, equivalent to 1 Kgs 8:12-13.

B. Report of Solomon's address 6:3-11
   1. Introduction 3
   2. Protocol of legitimation 4-10
      a. Blessing 4
      b. Oracular report: the divine choices 5-6
         1) Formerly neither city nor prince 5
         2) Now Jerusalem and David 6
      c. Redirection of David's plan 7-9
         1) Plan to build the temple 7
         2) Oracular report 8-9
            a) Commendation 8
            b) Solomon designated as builder 9
      d. Declaration of fulfillment 10
         1) Expressed generally 10a
         2) Expressed specifically 10b
            a) Solomon succeeds David 10bα
            b) Solomon builds the temple 10bβ
   3. Declaration of the ark's installation 11

Except in vv. 5b-6a and 11, ChrH here follows rather closely his *Vorlage* in Kings. The introduction in v. 3 marks a clear break in the action. Solomon faces about, i.e., turns from the spectacle of the cloud of glory, and, as the congregation (*qāhāl*) of Israel stands looking at him, gives them his blessing. The congregation is now called *qĕhal yiśrā'ēl*; cf. 2 Chr 5:6. The difference arises in ChrH's sources, 1 Kgs 8:5 and 14, which themselves are from different literary strands. Solomon begins his address with a BLESSING (cf. 1 Chr 29:20), *bārûk yahweh 'ĕlōhê yiśrā'ēl*, "Blessed be Yahweh the God of Israel," who is then praised for "doing with his hand" what "he promised with his mouth" in fulfilling the promise made to David. Next follow two oracular reports, quoting what Yahweh said to David about his choice, vv. 5-6, and what he said about appointing Solomon to be the builder of the temple, vv. 8-9. V. 5 does not omit Kings' reference to the exodus from Egypt, though ChrH does reject a similar reference in v. 11. In vv. 5b-6a ChrH expands Kings' statement that Yahweh chose no city, but chose David; he makes Yahweh say that Yahweh chose no city except Jerusalem and chose no leader except David —giving more prominence both to Jerusalem and to David—both important issues in ChrH's agenda (cf. Lemke, 97). Much emphasis is placed here upon the election (*bḥr*) of Jerusalem and David (cf. *bḥr* with reference to Solomon in 1 Chr 28:6). Repeatedly we hear also that the temple has been built "for the name" of

Yahweh, vv. 6, 7, 8, 10; cf. 1 Chr 29:16. V. 10 is naturally the climax, but this does not justify *RSV*'s "now," for no temporal designation is present. Rather, we have four somewhat alliterative *wāw*-consecutive impfs., the first one with Yahweh as subject, the others with Solomon as subject: *wayyāqem*, "and [Yahweh] has raised up/made stand/fulfilled"; *wā'āqûm*, "and I have arisen"; *wā'ēšēb*, "and I sit"; *wā'ebneh*, "and I built." The objects or modifiers of these verbs are, respectively, Yahweh's word of promise; the prepositional phrase "in my father David's place"; the prepositional phrase "on the throne of Israel"; the house or temple. The series of first-person verbs continues into v. 11, which is introduced by *wā'āsîm*, "and I placed," with "the ark" as object, and then a relative clause that defines the ark by what is in it, i.e., "Yahweh's covenant which he made with the people of Israel," by which is meant the tables of the law (2 Chr 5:10) on which the covenant is based. We must interpret v. 10 as a kind of protasis—a review of the conditions that have brought Solomon and his people to this situation—and v. 11 as its apodosis—the appropriate action that has followed from it. "And there" *(šām)* at the beginning of v. 11 is emphatic, as it is also in 1 Chr 21:28b, and as is *zeh hû'*, "right here," in 1 Chr 22:1. This underscores ChrH's emphasis on Ornan's threshing floor as the right place for building the temple in 2 Chr 3:1.

C. Report of Solomon's dedicatory prayer	6:12-42
1. Solomon's reverent posturing	12-13
a. Standing before altar, arms spread	12
b. Movement to bronze platform	13
1) Construction	13aα
2) Dimensions	13aβ
3) Action	13b
2. Prayer for Solomon's posterity	14-17
a. Praise speech	14-15
1) Description of Yahweh (incomparability statement)	14
2) Fulfillment of promise to David	15
b. Petition	16-17
1) Plea for fulfillment of dynastic promise	16
2) Plea for confirmation of promise to David	17
3. Prayer for acceptance of temple	18-40
a. Petition to hear Solomon's prayers	18-20
1) Denial that God resides in temple	18
2) Request for continual responsiveness	19-20
a) Plea for divine concern	19
b) Attentiveness to the temple	20
b. Prayer of intercession for those needing attention (casuistic review)	21-39
1) Plea for all Israel	21
2) Judging oaths in case of offenses	22-23
3) Restoring repentant Israel in defeat	24-25
4) Giving rain withheld as punishment	26-27
5) Relieving all manner of afflictions	28-31
6) Promote devotion by receiving foreigners	32-33

Verse 12 signals a new movement in the account by having Solomon now turn away from the *qǎhal yiśrā'ēl*, "congregation of Israel," toward Yahweh's altar, which, though not previously mentioned in Kings, is intended by ChrH to be the altar that David built on Ornan's threshing floor (1 Chr 21:26), reconstructed as the bronze altar of 2 Chr 4:1. According to v. 13, missing in Kings, an explanatory clause introduced by *kî* intrudes, telling of a bronze platform that Solomon had built and positioned on this spot. The verse continues in narrative form. He stood on this platform, then knelt down on it "in the presence of the entire congregation *[qǎhal]* of Israel"—i.e., where all could see him, and spread out his hands in a grand gesture of prayer. Although some interpreters view this as ChrH's interpretative intrusion, or possibly as a post-ChrH gloss, Lemke (pp. 99-100) argues that it was in the text original to both Kings and Chronicles, surviving in Chronicles but omitted in the Kings text by *homoioteleuton* (slip of the eye from the first to the second *wayyiprōś kappāyw,* "and [Solomon] spread forth his hands"). Then commences a long (→) PRAYER OF INTERCESSION, first for Solomon's posterity, vv. 14-17, then for the temple, vv. 18-40. This follows closely the DtrH prayer in 1 Kgs 8:23-61, although vv. 50b-53 (with 54-61) are omitted because of their heavy emphasis on Moses and the exodus, with a concluding plea for attention, v. 40, and a hymn of entrance, vv. 41-42, appearing in their place.

Since this passage is unique in having one text follow another for so long a space and with such precise reproduction, we should pause to offer a few representative examples of the changes that have appeared in the process of transmission, keeping in mind that, according to important recent studies, the Chronicles text may in places very well deserve preference over the text of Kings. These textual alterations are of six kinds: (1) alternative pointings; (2) alternative spellings, (3) transpositions, (4) omissions and additions, (5) altered grammatical forms, and (6) altered vocabulary.

The pointings are largely a matter of *plene* versus *defectiva*. The spellings are items like *yēdě'ûn* in 1 Kgs 8:38 versus *yēdě'û* in 2 Chr 6:29. An example of a transposition is found in 1 Kgs 8:47, *wěhe'ěwînû rāšā'nû,* "and we have acted perversely, have done wickedly," versus 2 Chr 6:37, *he'ěwînû wěrāšā'nû,* "we have acted perversely and have done wickedly." Omissions and additions are generally of miniscule importance; e.g., *nā'* in 1 Kgs 8:26 is omitted in 2 Chr 6:17; 2 Chr 6:26 omits the conjunction on *ûmēhaṭṭā'tām,* "and from their sin," in 1 Kgs 8:35; *yērāqôn 'arbeh ḥāsîl,* "mildew, locust, caterpillar," in 1 Kgs 8:37 becomes *wěyērāqôn 'arbeh wěḥāsîl,* "and mildew, locust, and caterpillar," in 2 Chr 6:28; *haššāmayim* in 1 Kgs 8:39 means the same as *min-haššāmayim,* "out of/from heaven," in 2 Chr 6:30. Examples of altered grammatical forms are the following: *těhinnat,* "supplication of," in 1 Kgs 8:30 becomes *tahǎnûnê,* "supplications of," in 2 Chr 6:21; *tihyeh,* "will be," in 1 Kgs 8:38 is corrupted in 2 Chr 6:29 to *yihyeh* (m. with fem. subject); *wěhabbayit,* "and the house," in 1 Kgs 8:48 is changed to the late postexilic form with *lĕ* determinative in 2 Chr 6:38, *wĕlabbayit*. Examples of altered vocabulary (and syntax) are seen in the following: *lĕpānay*, "before me," in 1 Kgs 8:25 becomes in 2 Chr 6:16 *bĕtôrātî*, "in my law"; *yihyeh šĕmî šām*, "my name will be there," in 1 Kgs 8:29 becomes in 2 Chr 6:20 *lāśûm šimkā šām*, "to put thy name there"; *lĕharšîaʿ rāšāʿ*, "to condemn the guilty," in 1 Kgs 8:32 becomes *lĕhāšib lĕrāšāʿ*, "to requite the [*lĕ* determinative] guilty," in 2 Chr 6:23; *ʾăšer*, "in case that," in 1 Kgs 8:33 becomes *kî*, "if," in 2 Chr 6:24.

If this sampling were directly intended as an elucidation of 2 Chr 6:12-39 we would need to make it more exhaustive. The point we are making is that these six kinds of textual alterations are found wherever ChrH closely copies Kings, if only for short sections. Our practice has been to cite textual variants which might have a direct bearing on the structure of a given pericope, and that is seldom the case. Our purpose here has been to show that even where the Kings text and the Chronicles text are very similar, ChrH shows whatever degree of freedom he desires to use. He may stick closely to his *Vorlage*, cite it very loosely or paraphrase, or ignore it altogether. This is not "exegesis," as Willi claims. ChrH is writing his own book. If it so happens that Kings is saying exactly, or almost exactly, what ChrH desires to say, he will let Kings say it for him, reserving the freedom to alter it where he will. It is Kings' word, but it is ChrH's word as well. ChrH would not deny that DtrH in Samuel-Kings is true history. It is only that ChrH is recreating that history, retelling it as it should have happened.

In the prayer for his own posterity, vv. 14-17, Solomon first praises Yahweh for keeping covenant and *hesed*, "devoted faithfulness," with his true servants and for fulfilling "this day" the promise to David. In v. 16 *wĕʿattâ*, "so now," introduces his petition based on this fidelity and this keeping of the promise to raise up a son to build the temple. The petition is that Yahweh might confirm the more extensive promise to keep a scion of David on the throne indefinitely, so long as David's posterity continues to walk in God's ways. Willi (p. 125) explains this as programmatic to ChrH's theology (which indeed it is), even though the words are taken directly from Kings. (On the emphasis on the keeping of the law in this passage, cf. von Rad, *Geschichtsbild*, 128-29; on confirmation of the promise to David, cf. idem, p. 126.) The placement of this petition before the petition for the temple, vv. 18-40, shows how centrally important the ideal-king concept is over against the ideal of the temple.

Verse 18 is parallel to 2 Chr 2:5 (*RSV* 6) in denying that the temple can be God's residence, i.e., actually contain him. Its purpose must therefore lie elsewhere, and in his entire long petition Solomon identifies the temple as a hallowed *māqôm*, "place," to which Yahweh "from heaven" pays close attention. Solomon prays (v. 20) that Yahweh's eyes (anthropomorphic symbol of all-seeing perceptiveness) may be open "day and night," i.e., continually, to "hear" (mixed metaphor) Solomon's own prayer and the supplication for forgiveness raised up by himself and his people Israel. Access to the temple, and thereby to Yahweh himself, is constantly needed both by the king and by the people. (Cf. Willi, 145, on the styling of this passage.)

Mention of the fact that the Israelite people will constantly need to make supplication at (or toward, vv. 26, 29, 32, 34, 38) this temple introduces in abrupt fashion a whole sampling of possible supplications. The whole series follows the casuistic style, with "when" or "if" introducing the situation or complaint, and "then hear thou from heaven and forgive" providing the request. The formulation varies. In vv. 22-23, 24-25 it is *(wĕ) 'im . . . wĕ'attâ*, "if . . . then thou." In vv. 26-27 it is *bĕ* with an infinitive and *wĕ'attâ*, "in case that . . . then thou." In vv. 28-31 one or another specific affliction is named, followed by *kî yihyeh* and *wĕ'attâ*, "if so-and-so happens . . . then thou" (cf. Watson, 3.9). Because the request is so remarkable, vv. 32-33 have *wĕgam 'el . . . wĕ'attâ*, "and indeed unto . . . then thou." In vv. 34 and 36, both of which introduce secondary additions in Kings, the formula is simply *kî*, "if," "when." Vv. 36-39 are a triply conditional sentence in which the first protasis is "if they sin," v. 36; it has two subordinate conditions, "yet if they lay," v. 37, and "if they repent . . . and pray," v. 38; the apodosis is v. 39, "then hear thou from heaven . . . and forgive."

Suddenly the casuistic review is broken off with a concluding plea for divine attention, v. 40. The poetic HYMN OF ENTRANCE in vv. 41-42, seemingly far less suitable than DtrH's original conclusion in 1 Kgs 8:50ff., has likely been chosen because it quotes (with some freedom) from Ps 132:8-10 because of its closing request, "Remember thy steadfast love for David thy servant." It can be justified only by ChrH's desire to make an inclusio with the first petition of vv. 14-17. On the *ḥasdê dāwîd*, "steadfast love for David" (cf. Isa 55:3), see von Rad (*Geschichtsbild*, 127), Welten ("Lade-Tempel-Jerusalem," 180-82), Gese ("Der Davidsbund und die Zionserwählung," *ZTK* 61 [1964] 10-26). On ChrH's deliberate elimination of the exodus and Moses references in his Kings source, cf. Williamson (*Israel*, 64-65; "Eschatology," 143-45).

"And when Solomon had ended his prayer," a circumstantial clause, is a clear transition to this new section. Otherwise than in Kings, it tells of a new theophany. Again, the cloud of glory (2 Chr 5:13) fills the temple, but in addition there is a fire that falls from heaven to consume "the burnt offerings and sacrifices." This is an obvious inconcinnity since ChrH has made no previous reference to them. The explanation is that he wants the fire to be understood as a token of divine acceptance, hence he borrows the offering, as well as the consuming fire, from 1 Chr 21:26. Williamson (comm.) is quite right to deny that 7:1-3 is secondary; it constitutes an inclusio with 5:13-14, bracketing Solomon's address and prayer. Barnes ("The Midrashic Element in Chronicles," *Exp* 2 [1896] 427) earlier claimed that the references here and in 1 Chr 21:26 to the fire constitute a midrash on 1 Kgs 18:38, but this only shows confusion about what midrash is and how it is structured (→ 1 Chr 5:1-2). Circumstantial clauses in vv. 2-3 depict the effect of the theophany on the priests and people; they are followed by a brief narration of the people worshiping, reciting the familiar HYMNIC REFRAIN, "For he is good (etc.)," completing the inclusio with the same hymn as in 5:13.

Galling (ATD) and Willi (p. 196) regard vv. 4-7 as a gloss from 1 Kgs 8:62-64, but there is no sufficient reason to deny this section to ChrH himself. A circumstantial clause with the participle states the situation, v. 4. Then, in v. 5, narrative sequencing tells of Solomon's generous act and, with astonishing brevity as in Kings, of the joint act of dedicating (*ḥnk*, hiph.) the temple. V. 6 (from ChrH; cf. Lemke, 105: "cultic bias") tries to dress out this brief statement with three participial clauses specifying the groups, priests and Levites, musicians, "all Israel," who participated in the ritual of dedication. V. 7, from 1 Kgs 8:64 (secondary in Kings; cf. De Vries, *Yesterday, Today and Tomorrow*, 110), tells of consecrating the middle of the court to accommodate the thousands of sacrifices that Solomon had offered.

The ceremony concludes with what the date given in v. 10 shows to be the Feast of Tabernacles, commencing on the fifteenth day of the eighth month and continuing for eight days according to Lev 23:34-36; Num 29:12-38. This was not the intention of 1 Kgs 8:65-66, whose mention of an eighth day nonetheless led ChrH to this identification (cf. Watson, 10.3). In a hyperbole that reminds us of David at the retrieval of the ark, 1 Chr 13:5-6, the "all Israel" that participates is called a "very great congregation" gathered from the most distant borders, Hamath on the north and the Brook of Egypt on the south. At the end, the people return to their homes with joy for Yahweh's great goodness, v. 10.

As has previously been mentioned, 7:11 is the concluding rubric for the inclusio beginning with 2 Chr 1:18 (*RSV* 2:1), with, however, a still more final rubric at 8:16. ChrH at the same time uses it to introduce the divine acceptance and warning, vv. 12-22, borrowed from 1 Kgs 9:1-9 (Dtr), pointing at the same time to the accomplishment of "all the work of Solomon" reported in 2 Chr 8:1-16. A subsidiary inclusio is created by the insertion of the epiphanous revelation containing the acceptance and warning, serving as a counterpart to the epiphany of 2 Chronicles 1. The divine address, which, according to Lemke (pp. 101, 103, 107), carries the same theocracy theme as is seen in 2 Chr 6:39–7:3, begins with Yahweh's declaration that he has accepted this *māqôm*, "place," as a "house of sacrifice," v. 12. Before copying further from Kings the promise that Yahweh chooses and consecrates this temple to bear his name perpetually, keeping his eyes and heart there forever (v. 16), ChrH makes the divine epiphany correspond closely with Solomon's lengthy prayer in 6:12ff. Vv. 13-14 paraphrase, in particular, 6:26-27, and repeat the pattern of conditional sentences found there. The heart of the matter is, of course, the repentance and prayer of the people, for this is ever the condition of divine forgiveness. Vv. 17-18 repeat the familiar condition and promise for the lineage of David (cf. Williamson, "Eschatology," 149-53). In v. 19 ChrH introduces from Kings (Dtr with exilic expansion) a terrible threat against the potential apostasy of the people. The penalty will be exile and loss of the temple, whose eventual ruin is portrayed in the image of idle passers-by asking in astonishment how it came to be that way and receiving the answer that its former devotees forsook the God of the exodus deliverance. "Therefore he has brought all this evil upon them" is the conclusion to the entire threat segment, vv. 19ff., because it refers directly to the apostate Israelites and not only to their temple.

Genre

As has been said, the main genre is ACCOUNT, longer and more complex than a (→) report. 5:1b–6:2 is a REPORT OF RITUAL, as are 6:12-13 and 7:1-10. 5:8-10 is a STATEMENT, a brief prose writing which simply notes or describes a situation or circumstance—in this case, details about the ark. A THEOPHANY, which by definition mentions both Yahweh's coming and some visible manifestation of his presence—in this case the cloud of glory and the consuming fire—is seen in 5:11-14 and 7:1-3. At 5:13 and again at 7:3, with a paraphrase at 7:6, is the genre HYMNIC REFRAIN, defined as an exalted ejaculation for confession and adulation in the midst of a liturgical service. 6:1-2 is a DEDICATORY DECLARATION, similar to David's in 1 Chr 22:1. 6:3-11 is a REPORT and at the same time an ADDRESS. Vv. 4-10 contain a PROTOCOL, which is defined as a solemn declaration made at the beginning of a king's reign, in which the task with which he is officially charged and the ways he plans to fulfill it—or has already fulfilled it—are set forth. 6:4 is another BLESSING, this time in the third person (cf. 1 Chr 29:20, second person). 6:4-5 and 8-9 belong to the genre ORACULAR REPORT.

6:12-42 is another PRAYER, with the PRAISE SPEECH in vv. 14-15, including a DESCRIPTION OF YAHWEH and the INCOMPARABILITY STATEMENT, "there is no God like thee in heaven or on earth" (cf. 2:4 [*RSV* 5]). The next prayer element is the PETITION in vv. 16-17, 18-20, then, in vv. 21-39, the PRAYER OF INTERCESSION, which in this passage is by Solomon on behalf of the temple and Israel. This is at the same time a unique example of the CASUISTIC REVIEW, which makes a list of hypothetical cases, arranging them in a series determined by similarity. 6:40 belongs to the genre CALL FOR DIVINE ATTENTION, which is defined as initiating or repeating a petition or prayer of intercession for special and direct help; here and in 1 Kgs 8:52 it belongs entirely to the future and the hypothetical because it applies to the hypothetical cases in the preceding CASUISTIC REVIEW. The genre HYMN OF ENTRANCE may be seen in 6:41- 42, which, taken from the liturgical Psalm 132, contains a plea for Yahweh, the ark, the priests, and all who are sanctified to take their places and do what the situation calls for.

Although 7:12, like 2 Chr 1:7, avoids stating that revelation came to Solomon in a dream, the reference to night indicates that 7:11-22 belongs to the genre DREAM REPORT, with the actual DREAM EPIPHANY in vv. 12ff. Everything beyond the narrative introduction, v. 12a, is in the form of an ADDRESS, with examples of the PROMISE in vv. 13-16, 18a, and the THREAT in vv. 19-22. The last is defined as a short speech, grim and menacing, spoken to or about the intended victim(s) by someone, usually God, who has the authority and the means for carrying it into action.

The portrayal of the strangers' amazement in 7:21-22 exhibits the QUESTION AND ANSWER SCHEMA seen in a number of prophetic passages; it is a literary device which projects a question and its answer as a means of describing a future situation, in this case the devastation of the temple and the desolation of the land. Skweres has compared biblical examples with three Neo-Assyrian texts, all of which have the schema: (1) experience or threat of devastation; (2) inquiry why; (3) answer: sin and guilt. Since the Neo-Assyrian texts have to do with political infidelity, Skweres chooses the name *Verweis auf Strafgrunderfragung*, "inquest into the grounds for punishment."

To make our survey complete, we must mention the TALLY of Solomon's offerings at 7:5 and the TRANSITION FORMULA, "at that time," in 7:8. There is, finally, the FESTIVAL SCHEMA of 7:7-10. This schema is shared by three other passages telling about a great religious festival presided over by a king, Asa in ch. 15, Hezekiah in ch. 30, and Josiah in ch. 35. The festivals in question are dated in the seventh, third, second, and first months, respectively, and correspond to Tabernacles, Weeks, and Passover (twice), respectively. The schema that is shared by all these passages has four elements: (1) notice of date, (2) identification of participants, (3) description of the ceremonies, and (4) note of joyful celebration. The last three passages are modeled on the account of Solomon's feast, as is evident from the fact that ChrH is here directly adapting 1 Kgs 8:65-66, and from the fact that they tend to add and rearrange elements in the schema. The theological significance of this schema is that these three kings (and perhaps others) consciously modeled themselves after Solomon.

Setting

Although 2 Chr 5:10 takes its notice of the contents of the ark from Kings, the statement that these were no other than the two tablets that Moses put there at Horeb (Exod 25:16) is essential to ChrH's familiar locution, "the ark of the covenant of Yahweh," and to the notion that the temple containing this ark was a guarantee and focal point for the covenant, which, of course, presupposes the repeated emphasis on the keeping of the law as the obligation of this covenant. The dominant theme of the prayer of dedication is that Yahweh really dwells in heaven, and that accordingly the temple is where Yahweh's "name" dwells—meaning that it is the place to which prayers may be directed, and to which he intends to pay constant attention; but it is also the depository for the ark, "in which is the covenant of Yahweh which he made with the people of Israel," 6:11.

Another expression of ChrH's temple ideology is the HYMN OF ENTRANCE in 6:41-42, a paraphrase of Ps 132:8-10 (or possibly from a variant textual tradition). It contains words and phrases loaded with ancient ideology, which still had relevance for ChrH's own time: the temple is Yahweh's resting place; it contains the ark of divine might (a memento from its use as a war palladium); the priests, parallel to the "saints" (ḥăsîdîm), are the embodiment of festive joy and bearers of the divine salvation; acts of steadfast fidelity for David (ḥasdê dāwîd), Yahweh's anointed and his servant, are here to be "remembered," i.e., brought back to living reality.

The theophany of the cloud of glory and later of the fire on the altar are drawn directly from Exod 40:34-38; Lev 9:23-24. Thus the tabernacle is the type and the temple the antitype, though ironically the P document from which this imagery is drawn seems to have borrowed heavily from the historical temple of Solomon. In any event, it is clear that for ChrH the temple supersedes the tabernacle, or tent of meeting (the two terms seem to be synonymous for ChrH, evidently because in his day the two traditions had long since coalesced). Although the reference to the tent of meeting being brought up with the ark and the holy vessels in 5:5 seems to be textually secure, the conclusion to be drawn from the dropping of further reference to it in the following verses has to be that this is ChrH's final gesture to the tabernacle/tent of meeting tradition. The temple itself is henceforth to be the tent of meeting. (We cannot credit the argument of R. E. Friedman, "The Tabernacle in the Temple," *BA* 43 [1980] 241-48, that the *'ōhel mô'ēd,* "tent of meeting," was actually set up in the *dĕbîr,* "adytum," of Solomon's temple.) ChrH solves the rivalry of cultic traditions by simply merging the unwanted one into the one that is dominant.

Attention has been called to the FESTIVAL SCHEMA shared by four separate passages in 2 Kings (see above). The Passover feasts of Hezekiah and Josiah, together with the Weeks festival of Asa, are based structurally on Solomon's Tabernacles festival in this passage, which is also the feast for the dedication of the temple. It is to the Holiness Code in Leviticus 23 that ChrH looks (see Shaver, 140-43). Sukkoth or Tabernacles had always been a feast of special joy for the Israelites. ChrH modifies the prescribed festival calendar in such a way as to bring "all the men of Israel," i.e., males prepared for the festival (cf. Exod 34:23), to Jerusalem "at the feast that is in the seventh month" (2 Chr 5:3), but he must mean that they came ahead of time, prepared for Tabernacles, because 7:8 reports that the dedication ceremonies lead into a "feast for seven days," which is explained in v. 9b as being for "the dedication of the altar, seven days," after which "the feast" (*ḥeḥāg;* cf. 5:3) is kept another seven days (successive, not contemporaneous), after which the "eighth day" came for the "solemn assembly" (*'ăṣāret;* cf. Lev 23:36). This brings us to "the twenty-third day of the seventh month," v. 10, the regular time for concluding Tabernacles.

Intention

As has been noted, ChrH takes liberties with the Kings version of the entrance of the ark. Although he allows the priests their uncontested privilege of carrying the ark into the sanctuary, 5:7, he has the Levites fetch it from the tent of David, v. 4 (v. 5b is a harmonization). ChrH can hardly be censured for this tampering with his text because carrying the ark had always been a duty assigned to the Levites (1 Chr 23:26), and they were here performing that duty, in ChrH's conception, for the last time (Lemke, 95, speaks of a Levitical bias; on the Levites' role with regard to the ark, see von Rad, *Geschichtsbild,* 99).

In this section ChrH is not as concerned to protect the prerogative of the Levites as to underscore the right to rule belonging to the lineage of David. Previously, at 1 Chr 17:9-14; 22:8-10; 28:2-7, he had spelled this out. It is also underscored in 2 Chr 6:16-17; it explains, too, why 6:4-10, 14-39, regularly has Solomon refer to David as "my father" (it matters not at all that these verses are borrowed from DtrH in Kings, for ChrH gladly chooses them to speak for himself), and why the Psalms quotation concluding with "Remember thy steadfast love for David thy servant" supplants the references to Moses in 1 Kgs 8:50b-64. Again it has been made clear that ChrH honors Moses only for his law, apart from which everything that he holds precious is derived from David.

To our explanations under "Setting" regarding the festivals, we may add one remark regarding intention: ChrH means his description to be prescriptive; i.e., Israel's greatest joy ought ever to be to journey to the temple and take part in the sacred festivals. This is experientially the highest point of biblical piety. ChrH envisages "a very great congregation" (7:8). Their coming "from the entrance of Hamath to the Brook of Egypt" is type and image of the congregation that will one day be gathered from the very ends of the earth.

In his time ChrH must have been quite aware that the threat of 7:19-22 was still in force—that the land and temple could again be destroyed if Israel should prove untrue. For present and future exiles he would also have held out the petition for leniency in 6:36-39. We should pay special attention to the two motive clauses in Solomon's prayer, 6:31, 33b (par. 1 Kgs 8:40, 43). For Israelites who sin and repent, and for foreigners who hear of Yahweh and pray to him, the aspiration is that they might "fear" *(yr')* God, with the result, in the first instance, that they might fulfill the deuteronomic promise of walking in God's ways throughout all their days in the promised land; and in the second instance, that they (the foreign proselytes) might know that the temple is called by Yahweh's name.

Finally, we take special note of the fact that ChrH has Yahweh repeat in 7:13-14 just that part of Solomon's prayer, 6:16-17, that is the most expressive of the divine promise to forgive. Williamson (*Israel*, 67) argues that this is programmatic for the entire pattern of God forgiving good kings who repent of wrongdoings in the succeeding history of the Judean kings. In copying so much of Kings in this context, ChrH is surely giving expression to his most pressing concern for post-exilic Israel. For them too the promise holds good. God may forgive the repentant sinner, with or without the temple; but the restored temple stands, like its predecessor, as the lasting symbol of God's will to forgive.

Bibliography

A. van den Born, "Zum Tempelweihespruch," *OTS* 14 (1965) 235-44; A. Gamper, "Die heilsgeschichtliche Bedeutung des salomonischen Tempelweihgebets," *ZTK* 85 (1963) 55-61; M. Görg, "Die Gattung des sogenannten Tempelweihespruchs," *UF* 6 (1974) 53-63; F. von Hummelauer, "Salomons Tempelweihe," *BZ* 1 (1903) 43-46; J. R. Shaver, "Torah and the Chronicler's History Work" (Diss., Notre Dame, 1983); D. E. Skweres, "Das Motiv der Strafgrunderfragung in biblischen und neuassyrischen Texten," *BZ* 14 (1970) 181-97; P. Welten, "Lade-Tempel-Jerusalem. Zur Theologie der Chronikbücher," in *Textgemäss* (Fest. E. Würthwein; ed. A. J. H. Gunneweg and O. Kaiser; Göttingen: Vandenhoeck & Ruprecht, 1979) 169-83; H. G. M. Williamson, *Israel in the Books of Chronicles* (Cambridge: Cambridge, 1977); idem, "Eschatology in Chronicles," *TynBul* 28 (1977) 115-54.

IV. REPORT OF SANCTIFYING THE LAND, 8:1-16

Structure

A. Statement about restoring cities — 1-6
  1. Rebuilding and settling Huram's towns (transition formula) — 1-2
  2. Capture of Hamath-zobah — 3
  3. Construction projects — 4-6
    a. Extraterritorial cities — 4
    b. Palestinian cities — 5-6a
    c. Construction for self-satisfaction — 6b
B. Statement about subjugating original inhabitants — 7-10

It is easy to see the boundaries of this pericope; it extends from the time reference in 8:1 (borrowed from 1 Kgs 9:10) to the concluding rubric in v. 16. It is more difficult to discern what holds the pericope together—what its common theme is—until one sees that ChrH has changed the reference to the removal of Pharaoh's daughter in 1 Kgs 9:24 by adding two grounding clauses with *kî*, "for," the first of which introduces Solomon as speaking a prohibition, and the second of which explains that she had to be removed to another "house," apparently built for her outside the city, since Jerusalem is one of those places made holy because Yahweh's ark had come to it (the PROHIBITION, banning this woman from "the house" of David king of Israel, makes no sense because she had not been David's wife and Solomon had installed her in a palace he himself had made, 1 Kgs 7:8; we can only suppose that ChrH misunderstood 1 Kgs 9:24, "from the city of David to her house which he had built for her," taking "David" as the antecedent of "he built"). This has to be the clue to ChrH's handling in vv. 1-10 of materials taken from 1 Kgs 9:10-14, 17-23, which concern restoring cities through purchase, capture, and reconstruction. This was all done to organize the land with its inhabitants so as to support the temple and share in its holiness.

It is probable that ChrH did not understand the reference to twenty years of building in 8:1, and took it over simply because it was in Kings. In v. 2 he shortens the reference in 1 Kgs 9:11-13 to Huram's cities so as to avoid embarrassment for Solomon. Lemke (pp. 110-12) judges ChrH's treatment of Kings so erratic as to prevent a close comparison of the two texts; his study of vv. 4-6 (pp. 114-15) leaves unsolved the question of whether Tadmor or Tamar (1 Kgs 9:18) is meant (cf. also Watson, 2.3). To avoid impairing Solomon's image, ChrH omits reference to the capture of Gezer, 1 Kgs 9:15-16. For further discussion of the list of captured cities, cf. Welten *(Geschichte,* 34-36). The statement in vv. 7-10 about setting up a permanent forced levy of surviving natives, with Israelites serving as officers over them, is taken pretty well intact from Kings, although one may note that v. 8, *lō'-killûm,* "they did not destroy *[kll]* them," has somewhat softened the harshness of 1 Kgs 9:21, *lō'- yākĕlû . . . lĕhaḥărîmām,* "they were unable *[ykl] . . .* to extirpate them," thereby enhancing Solomon's image. Lemke (pp. 115-16) sees a cultic bias in v. 11, but ChrH's alterations derive, rather, from the ideology that the whole land, and especially Jerusalem, must share in the temple's holiness (cf. Watson, 10.52). Willi (p. 172) is amiss in calling v. 11 a mere reflection.

Verses 12-15 develop 1 Kgs 9:25a, but they are all ChrH's own, in spite of the claim of Galling (ATD) that vv. 13-15 are secondary, and of Willi (p. 197, and Noth, "Chronistische Werk," 117) that vv. 14-15 are secondary. The whole section shows strong dependence on Deut 16:1-16 (Shaver, "Torah," 136-39). It is introduced by the temporal transition *'āz,* "then" (absent in 1 Kgs 9:25), followed by a factitive perf., "sent up" (*'lh,* hiph.), which, like *lō'sārû,* "they did not turn," in v. 15, is meant to give permanence to the action indicated. V. 13 tells us how often and on what occasions Solomon carried out this practice, listing the various festivals and adding that it was "as Moses commanded" *(kĕmiṣwat mōšeh).* In v. 14 the narrative verb *wayya'ămēd,* meaning "and he assigned/appointed to their posts," refers to two sorts of temple personnel, the Levites and the gatekeepers (the reference to the priests is a gloss because ChrH does not elsewhere refer to the assignment of priests), omitting the singers. This verse is to be compared to 1 Chr 16:4ff., where certain Levites are appointed to minister to the ark, once it was installed in the tent shrine. V. 15 makes it clear that these personnel function by David's—not Moses'—authority. This is made clear in the REGULATION FORMULA, *kĕmišpaṭ dāwîd-'ābîw,* "according to the regulation of David his father" (v. 14), and also in the grounding clause's *kî kēn miṣwat dāwîd 'îš- hā'ĕlōhîm,* "for thus was the command of David the man of God" (v. 14). A "man of God" is someone inspired (cf. 1 Chr 28:19).

Verse 16 is the summary. The second half of the verse, *šālēm bêt yahweh,* "was perfected Yahweh's house," contains a pun on the name Solomon (cf. 2 Chr 5:1a), but functionally it is an (→) EPITOME, summarizing the entire preceding account and forming a final inclusio with 2 Chr 1:18 *(RSV 2:1).* In the first half of this verse *'ad-hayyôm mûsad* has to be taken in the sense "back as far as the founding"; cf. LXX, Syr., Tg. This is suitable in a sentence that has an aspectual rather than a temporal bearing. It is to be translated: "And every work of Solomon was completed, from (what happened on) the day of the founding of Yahweh's house to its final completion." Everything recorded in the present pericope has been part of that work.

Genre

The main genre here is REPORT. Vv. 1-6 are a STATEMENT; so are vv. 7-10, 11, and 12-15. 8:1, "at the end of twenty years," is a TRANSITION FORMULA, but the transition is rough, with a perfect instead of the expected *wāw*-consecutive impf. and pleonastic references to Solomon. A NAME LIST occurs at v. 7, a TALLY at v. 10, and an EPITOME at v. 16b. Vv. 13-14 are a good place to study the difference between the often-encountered AUTHORIZATION FORMULA and the REGULATION FORMULA. Briefly, the function of the first is to establish the legitimacy of a certain practice, while that of the second is to assure that a practice is done according to the prescribed rule. Both have to do with the cult. In v. 13 Solomon follows a sacrificial calendar "according to the commandment of Moses" — an AUTHORIZATION FORMULA. In v. 14b, in the *kî* clause, Solomon's appointment of clergy to their respective offices is said to be authorized by "David the man of God" — another AUTHORIZATION FORMULA (the designation of David as "man of God" is unparalleled, and can only be explained from the inspiration claimed in 1 Chr 28:19). "According to the ordinance of David his father" is a REGULATION FORMULA in form *(kĕmišpāṭ)* and in function, assuring that what is here authorized will also be carried out as prescribed. The reference is, of course, to those chapters in 1 Chronicles (6; 9; 15–16; 23–26) where rules for the Levites and related orders are laid down. As a final genre in this pericope we mention the PROHIBITION in v. 11.

Setting and Intention

This pericope has to do with the accomplishing of all of Solomon's work *(mĕle'ket)*, v. 16a, without which it could not be said that *šālēm bêt yahweh*, "Perfected was/is Yahweh's house," v. 16b. "Thus was accomplished" refers directly to the *mĕle'ket*, but in ChrH's mind this refers also to the temple because, in spite of v. 6b, Solomon's only task and calling was to build the temple of Yahweh and prepare it completely for his perpetual service. What we might call secular works (8:1-11) were in the temple service because they made the land and people perfect for holiness. Besides this, Solomon's work had been constructing the sanctuary and its accoutrements (2 Chronicles 3–4), dedicating and praying for the temple (2 Chronicles 5–7), and establishing the perpetual service, with a fully authorized and regulated clergy to care for it (8:12-15). In this last we detect a prescriptive and parenetic appeal that the clergy of ChrH's own day might continue in the rule of David in order that the law of Moses might be fulfilled. The temple is a one-time (or, with the restoration, a two-time) concern. Once it is constructed, it is there. It can be defiled by Israel's own kings and ruined by foreigners, as ChrH already knew; but what was always at stake was whether the clergy — especially the temple's guardians, the Levites—would still be faithful to their task.

REPORT: SOLOMON IN HIS GLORY, 8:17–9:31

Text

This entire pericope closely follows 1 Kgs 9:26–10:29; 11:41-43, substituting stylistic changes rather than corruptions, with only occasional ideological changes (e.g., at 9:18). There are transpositions, variant grammatical forms, spellings, and lexicographical substitutions, plus occasional omissions for brevity or additions for explication (cf. Lemke, 120-27; → 2 Chr 6:12ff., "Structure").

Structure

I. Report of Solomon's magnificence	8:17–9:28
A. Statement: sea venture with Huram	8:17-18
B. Anecdote of the Queen of Sheba	9:1-12

Although this pericope has a tangible theme, it possesses little structure, consisting as it does of a variety of unrelated notices that go back ultimately to temple archives. The most cohesive element is the anecdote of the Queen of Sheba, which follows a meaningful narrative development from her coming in 9:1 to her departure in 9:12. This is broken, however, by a notice about import from Ophir in vv. 10-11, which must have been added to the Kings text after the Sheba anecdote was already in place. Intent on furbishing Solomon's image, ChrH omits 1 Kgs 11:1-40, which tell about this king's enticement by foreign wives and about unrest and incipient insurrection against his realm. This leaves him with no more information to pass on about Solomon except what is in his concluding summary, 1 Kgs 14:29-31, which he modifies for inclusion in 9:29-31.

A number of stylistic and textual peculiarities should be noted. In 8:17 the perf. of *hlk*, with Solomon as subject, indicates an established practice and not a separate instance. In 9:1, the first *wattābô'*, "and she came," is intended as an introductory summary with a purpose clause; the second *wattābô'* begins the actual narration. In v. 2b, "there was nothing hidden," and in v. 4b, "there was no more spirit in her," are circumstantial clauses. Vv. 5-6 have a pun on *'ĕmet*, "truth," and *he'ĕmantî*, "I believed," and at the same time these verses echo the leading terms of vv. 1-6, *bw'*, "come," *r'h*, "see," and *ngd*, "tell." On vv. 10-11 cf. Watson (2.1, 10.53). In v. 12 ChrH has tendentiously changed Kings, "whatever she asked besides what was given her," to "whatever she asked besides what she had brought to the king." Likewise tendentious is ChrH's omission of the reference to a calf's head as adornment to Solomon's throne, 1 Kgs 10:19 (cf. Willi, p. 129: theologizing; Watson, 3.1, 10.6; but to Lemke, pp. 120-21, the *Tendenz* is unclear).

Problems arise with respect to vv. 25-27; Rudolph (HAT) sees this as a gloss from Kings; Lemke (pp. 123-24) argues that ChrH misunderstands the Kings text; and Willi (p. 174) interprets v. 26 as a recasting of 1 Kgs 5:1 (cf. LXX). As for v. 29, Lemke (pp. 124-27) identifies the sources mentioned as ChrH's invention; cf. also Watson (2.8, 3.6).

Genre

The main genre is REPORT. Vv. 17-18 are a STATEMENT. The narrative is an ANECDOTE as it now stands, but is actually derived from a royal LEGEND, celebrating the unparalleled wisdom of the king. Vv. 5-8 contain an ENCOMIUM, an uninhibited adulation. The queen's gifts to Solomon, v. 9, inspire the INCOMPARABILITY STATEMENT, "There were no spices such as . . ."; other examples are found at vv. 11, 19, and 22. The genre STATEMENT is seen at 8:17-18; 9:10-11, 13-21. Vv. 22-28 are another ENCOMIUM with the INCOMPARABILITY STATEMENT. Vv. 29-31 are our second REGNAL RESUMÉ, with CITATION FORMULA, RHETORICAL QUESTION, STATEMENT OF PLACE AND LENGTH OF REIGN, DEATH AND BURIAL FORMULA (the burial is omitted, as with David), and the SUCCESSION FORMULA (cf. 1 Chr 29:26-30).

Setting and Intention

In our earlier discussion we expressed agreement with Williamson (comm.) to the effect that ChrH intends 2 Chronicles 9 to be the concluding counterpart to 2 Chronicles 1. In that chapter, vv. 14-17 were drawn forward from their position in Kings in order to complete a portrait of Solomon as one possessed with (1) piety,

(2) wisdom, and (3) riches and honor. 1:14-17 appears here in 9:25-27 as a reprise, with minor variations (see above the attempts to correct them). 1:22-28 speaks of Solomon's wealth and of his honor, while 8:17-18; 9:13-21 speak of his riches. Great riches are a factor in the anecdote of the Queen of Sheba, but here the main element is Solomon's wisdom. While the order of virtues appears in a sequence different from ch. 1, the intent of ch. 9 is clear, viz., to depict Solomon in all his magnificence as the perfect counterpart of the young Solomon of ch. 1. What was there promised him has here been perfectly fulfilled.

If Solomon is remembered for anything, even down to the present day, it is for his wisdom (ḥokmâ); cf. 9:22-23, "Thus King Solomon excelled all the kings of the earth in riches and in wisdom. And all the kings of the earth sought the presence of Solomon to hear his wisdom, which God had put into his mind." We can scarcely think of the earth's monarchs coming to Solomon for help in managing public policy in their respective realms. The text plainly means that Solomon was a Sirach in his bêt-hammidrāš (lit., "house of inquiry"), answering questions and uttering wise sayings for the earth's kings to take home with them. He was, in other words, the archetypal answer-man. His wisdom was encyclopedic and essentially intellectual. We can see that this concept of Solomon's wisdom had to be current already in the time of DtrH, for it is his book, Samuel-Kings, from which ChrH is quoting. Yet it is a serious question whether this image of Solomon's wisdom is historical. The latest tendency has been to affirm it, yet the wisdom which he requests in his Gibeon epiphany is plainly more pragmatic, offering Solomon lēb ḥākām wĕnābôn, "a wise and understanding heart" "to understand what is right" (1 Kgs 3:12, 11), or haḥokmâ wĕhammādda', "wisdom and knowledge" (2 Chr 1:12) "to go out and come in before this people" (v. 10). Even with the changes he had made, ChrH cannot get entirely away from the concept of "wisdom" as cleverness, skill, and perceptivity in the practical exercise of the duties of kingship. DtrH makes it clear that this is his understanding by inserting after the Gibeon account his folktale about the two harlots, 1 Kgs 3:16-28, which concludes with the statement, "and all Israel heard of the judgment which the king had rendered; and they stood in awe of the king, because they perceived that the wisdom of God was in him, to render justice" (v. 28). It is not surprising that ChrH, who is moving away from the pragmatic concept of wisdom, omits this narrative, yet it is enough to guarantee that this is the original portrait. See also David's description of Solomon as a "wise man" who will know how to deal with Joab, 1 Kgs 2:9.

Scott ("Solomon") has successfully traced the tradition history of this changing image of Solomon as the model wise man. According to Scott, there were three successive concepts: (1) wisdom as the ability of a successful ruler; (2) wisdom as the insight to distinguish right from wrong in administering justice; and (3) wisdom as intellectual brilliance and encyclopedic knowledge. The first two are pre-DtrH, while the third is mainly postexilic. Scott believes that this last originated with Hezekiah, since his reign—also the time of Isaiah, the prophet with the closest ties to the wisdom movement—was a time of international and intellectual wisdom (cf. Prov. 1:1; 25:1). ChrH naturally tends to credit Solomon with this intellectual kind of wisdom; even the promise of wisdom in 2 Chronicles 1, dependent for its context on 1 Kings 3, moves in this direction. Minor support for Scott's view may be seen in the fact that ChrH depicts Hezekiah as a second Solomon (2 Chr 32:27-31). It is a strange paradox that the figure of Solomon colors ChrH's portrait of Hezekiah, whereas it was probably the historical Hezekiah who decisively changed the original image of Solomon's wisdom.

We must also mention Braun's article, "Solomonic Apologetic." After comparing the contrasting portraits of Solomon in DtrH and ChrH, Braun summarizes by stating that (1) like David, Solomon is a king by direct divine choice in ChrH's understanding; (2) ChrH presents Israel as unanimous in supporting Solomon, as it had been in supporting David; and (3) it presents both kings as zealous patrons of the cult, i.e., the temple and the clergy to serve it. Braun points out that ChrH does not go beyond Kings in developing the promise to David for an everlasting dynasty, except as it pertains directly to Solomon himself (2 Chr 6:1-11 par. 1 Kgs 8:15-21). He also points out that the work of David and Solomon is seen as a unity, that "all Israel" reflects the united kingdom under David and Solomon, that Israel's enthusiasm for David and Solomon demonstrates recognition of the temple's unique position, and that ChrH reinterprets Solomon's activities at Gibeon, ignores DtrH's rejection of him, and persistently affirms God's choice of him as temple builder.

We note, finally, that the REGNAL RESUMÉ for Solomon departs from its *Vorlage* in 1 Kgs 14:29-31 in referring the reader, not to the "Chronicles of the kings of Judah"—which was probably an actual book—but to certain fictitious writings by the prophets (→ Chapter 4 above, under "Setting"). He thus continues the practice begun with David's summary, 1 Chr 29:26-30, where the *dĕbārîm*, "chronicles," of Samuel, Nathan, and Gad are mentioned. Here the prophets in question are Nathan, Ahijah the Shilonite, and an unknown Iddo; ChrH grows more imaginative in naming their writings *dĕbārîm*, "words," *nĕbû'â*, "prophecy," and *ḥăzôt*, "visions," respectively. The prophets in question are—or purport to be—from Solomon's time, but this does not demonstrate their historicity. It seems rather apparent that ChrH is using a fictitious device to gain credence for his own writing, but appeal to the prophets must have some deeper impulse. Here may be discerned an element of rivalry with the history of Dtr, almost certainly accepted by this time as a book of prophecy ("Former Prophets"). If ChrH's book cannot be accepted as a book of prophecy, its author wants to make a strong claim that prophets had a vital part in its production, endowing it thereby with an element of prophetic authority (cf. Petersen, *Late Israelite Prophecy*, 55-56).

Bibliography

R. L. Braun, "Solomonic Apologetic in Chronicles," *JBL* 92 (1973) 503-16; F. Canciani and G. Pettinato, "Salomos Thron, philologische und archäologische Erwägungen," *ZDPV* 81 (1965) 88-108; M. Noth, "Die Bewährung von Salomos 'Göttlicher Weisheit,'" in *Wisdom in Israel and in the Ancient Near East* (VTSup 3; *Fest.* H. H. Rowley; ed. M. Noth and D. Winton Thomas; Leiden: Brill, 1955) 225-37; D. L. Petersen, *Late Israelite Prophecy: Studies in Deutero-Prophetic Literature and in Chronicles* (Missoula: Scholars, 1977); R. B. Y. Scott, "Solomon and the beginnings of wisdom in Israel," in ibid., 262-79; E. Ullendorff, *Ethiopia and the Bible* (London: Oxford, 1968); idem, "The Queen of Sheba," *BJRL* 45 (1963) 486-504.

ACCOUNT OF BRINGING WRATH ON YAHWEH'S TEMPLE AND NATION, 10:1–36:23

Structure

I. Account of the reign of Rehoboam	10:1–12:16
II. Report of the reign of Abijah	13:1-23a (*RSV* 14:1a)
III. Chronicle of the reign of Asa	13:23b (*RSV* 14:1b)–16:14
IV. Account of the reign of Jehoshaphat	17:1–20:27
V. Account of fratricide among Jehoshaphat's Baalistic successors	21:1–23:21
VI. Report of the reign of Joash	24:1-17
VII. Report of the reign of Amaziah	25:1–26:2
VIII. Report of the reign of Uzziah	26:3-23
IX. Report of the reign of Jotham	27:1-9
X. Report of the reign of Ahaz	28:1-27
XI. Account of the reign of Hezekiah	29:1–32:33
XII. Report of the reign of Manasseh	33:1-20
XIII. Report of the reign of Amon	33:21-25
XIV. Account of the reign of Josiah	34:1–35:27
XV. Report: Judah fulfills its final sabbath	36:1-23

This is the anticlimatic section of ChrH's HISTORY (→ Chapter 4 above, under "Structure"). The section on "Solomon in his glory," following the account of his building and dedication of the temple, was the climax. Thematically speaking, that section defined, once and for all, how things ought to be in the perfect new Israel that ChrH hopes to see restored. But first the story of the Judahite kings, with their many failures and ultimate ruin of nation and temple, must be told. Its interest is less to inform than to exhort, so that the history of failure be not repeated. The fifteen (I-XV) main divisions of this second main section of the HISTORY will be treated in detail in what follows.

Genre

This whole long section is an ACCOUNT. The theme is "Bringing wrath on Yahweh's temple and nation," the counterpart of "Establishing Yahweh's nation and temple," 1 Chr 9:35–2 Chr 9:31. One should note the transposition of objects: David built first the nation, and then he and Solomon built the temple. Here the successive kings keep desecrating the temple until the nation is ruined. Ignoring the kings of the north, ChrH gives reports, accounts, and even a chronicle for the successive Judahite kings, taking much material from the parallel treatment in Kings but adding much of his own. Having already adopted the pattern of concluding reigns with the REGNAL RESUMÉ, he continues this, with only minor alterations, for all the kings up to Josiah, and then omits most of it for the last four kings (2 Chronicles 36) in order to hurry through to the bitter climax of the exile.

Although such persistent themes as the aspiration for security, rest, and peace bind together the story ChrH has to tell, a good part of the narrative is structured on a variety of special schemata, i.e., patterns that carry over from story to story.

These have each been described in (→) Chapter 4 above, under "Genre," but require further elucidation here.

First there is the SCHEMA OF REWARD AND RETRIBUTION. This concerns the repeated cycle of virtue and reward, of apostasy and retribution, applied not only to good and bad kings as marks on their entire individual reigns, but often characterizing "good" kings when they backslide or "bad" kings when they repent. ChrH systematically applies this schema from Saul to Zedekiah, omitting David and Solomon. ChrH introduces speeches by prophets or their equivalents in order to warn against wickedness or to encourage repentance, but after Ahaz (2 Chr 28:9ff.) the organs of revelation disappear. The introduction of warfare is an embellishment intended to elicit the monarch's faith or punish his wrongdoing. Functionally eccentric are the addresses of 28:9-11, 13, in which punishment on the Judahites provokes a confession of guilt among the northern Israelites and an appeal for brotherhood. Thus north and south share in the guilt that produces the ultimate national calamity, 36:15-16.

Another dominant pattern in this section is the SCHEMA OF REVELATIONAL APPEARANCES, which closely overlaps the SCHEMA OF REWARD AND RETRIBUTION in 1 Chr 10:13-14 and in 2 Chronicles 11–36. In this schema the bringers of revelation offer assurance and encouragement to the good kings, but warning and condemnation to the bad kings (or to good kings going bad). A pliable element is seen in that, while most speakers are prophets or seers, the prayers of Asa (2 Chr 14:11 [RSV 12]) and Jehoshaphat (20:5-12), together with Abijah's sermon (13:2-12), show that Yahweh may reveal his will for pious kings through their very own prayers and sermons. Various prophets appear in the citations for further reference that are part of the regnal resumés, creating the impression that ChrH draws material not only from the "prophetic" book, Samuel-Kings, but from other writings of the prophets—imaginary or real—that are presumed to be familiar to ChrH's readers.

The SCHEMA OF DYNASTIC ENDANGERMENT concerns chs. 11–25. ChrH has structured his narration concerning the monarchs from Rehoboam to Joash on a pattern of rivalry between the dynastic promise, brought to new realization in the succession of the Judahite kings, and the insatiable blood lust of the Baalistic Omrides, aided by certain members of the Judahite royalty who are affiliated with them. In this schema the situation grows steadily worse. The large families of Rehoboam and Abijah seem safe. Asa suppresses Baalism, removing even his idolatrous mother (15:16), but Jehoshaphat consents to a family affiliation with an Omride (18:1-2) and accompanies Ahab to battle (18:3ff.), being threatened by a "wrath" to be fulfilled on his sons (19:2). His son Jehoram massacres all his brothers (21:2-4) and adopts Omride ways (21:6), provoking the kidnapping of all his sons but the youngest (21:16-17; 22:1). That son, Ahaziah, enthusiastically adopts Omride ways and affiliations (22:2-4), but is murdered with his royal cousins by Jehu (22:7-9). Athaliah then murders all the remaining Davidide males, leaving only the baby Joash (22:10-12). Through the intervention of the high priest, Jehoiada, Athaliah is herself put to death (23:15), but when Joash becomes a man he himself resorts to the Baalistic apostasy (24:17-18) and ends up the victim of assassination (24:25-26). Ultimately his own assassins are executed (25:3), thus bringing full circle the pattern of apostasy and assassination. Cf. S. J. De Vries, "Dynastic Endangerment," 59-77.

The fourth important schema in this section is the FESTIVAL SCHEMA, which has already been observed in 2 Chronicles 7. With eccentric additions and re-arrangements, this schema is a stereotype of rigid procedures, based as much on the form of ritual as ChrH witnessed it as on any preconceived pattern of how things ought to proceed. The Solomon account in ch. 7 has its basis in 1 Kgs 8:65-66, from which it has been adapted. The others are modifications. Here is the outline of how the five festival accounts compare:

Ch 7	Ch 15	Ch 29	Ch 30	Ch 35
Solomon	*Asa*	*Hezekiah*		*Josiah*
Dedication (= Tabernacles)	Covenant renewal (= Weeks)	Rededication	Passover / Mazzoth	
7th month	3rd month	1st month	2nd month	1st month
	Purification, 8		Participants, 1-13a	
	Participants, 9		Purification, 14	
Date, 8a (5:3)	Date, 10	Date, 3a, 17	Date, 15a (2, 13)	Date, 1
Participants, 8b				
		Purification, 3b-19	Purification, 15b-20	
		Participants, 20		
				Preparations, 2, 15
Ceremonies, 9	Ceremonies, 11-14	Ceremonies, 21-35	Ceremonies, 21-24	Ceremonies, 16-18
7 days dedication			7 days Mazzoth	7 days Mazzoth
7 days feast			7 days feast	
Date, 10aα				Date, 19
Dismissal, 10aβ				
Celebration, 10b	Celebration, 15	Celebration, 36	Celebration, 25-26	
			Dismissal, 27	

From this it can be seen that (1) the opening notice of date, (2) the identification of the participants, (3) the description of the celebration, and (4) the notice of the joyful celebration at the end (except in Josiah's Passover) are common to all these narratives, and that they appear in an order that keeps the ceremonies and the celebration at the end but allows greater variation at the beginning. In the narratives of Solomon's and Josiah's festivals, purification is not a consideration, but it is very basic to the other three accounts. The annual festivals come, respectively, in the seventh, third, second, and first month, representing Tabernacles, Weeks, and Passover (twice). 2 Chronicles 29 is a remodeling of Solomon's dedication, and at the same time a shadow of Hezekiah's immediately following Passover (→ 2 Chronicles 29). The most notable feature of all but Josiah's celebration is the joyful feasting at the conclusion. It is clear that for ChrH ritual is no burden, but a constant delight. (Neh 7:73–8:18; 12:43 combine elements of the FESTIVAL SCHEMA, but without the clear patterning of ChrH — another consideration that weighs against the possibility of common authorship.)

These four schemata together provide most of the narrative structure for ChrH's overall account. They also carry the major themes: punishment and forgiveness, revelational supervision, victory over apostasy, and festal joy.

ACCOUNT OF THE REIGN OF REHOBOAM, 10:1–12:16

Structure

I. Historical story: Rehoboam's rejection	10:1-19
II. Report of security for three years	11:1-23
III. Report of Shishak's punitive raid	12:1-12
IV. Regnal resumé	12:13-16

The narration concerning the reign of the first of Solomon's successors, Rehoboam, is of sufficient complexity to warrant the genre name ACCOUNT. ChrH takes intact from Kings the story of Rehoboam's rejection by the northern tribes (= "Israel"), but composes the rest freely except for a few verses taken from Kings concerning Shishak's raid, which he interprets as a punishment from Yahweh. ChrH has been reluctant to report evil concerning the builder of the temple, Solomon, but he cannot avoid relating the crucial act of folly, Rehoboam's rejection by "Israel," with the resultant schism and its perpetual estrangement. ChrH will not comment on the text taken from 1 Kings 12; he will allow it to speak for itself. Where he does level blame against Rehoboam is in the context of Shishak's raid, which he interprets as Yahweh's disciplinary censure, offering this first king of separated Judah a crucial choice for or against submission to Yahweh's rule. ChrH needs a model for ideal piety among Judah's kings at the onset of its independent rule, but for this he must wait for the reign of Rehoboam's son, Abijah (ch. 13), whom he will depict as the prototypical champion of Yahweh's rule over his entire nation, now separated but ideally united.

The four main sections of this ACCOUNT will be discussed in detail in what follows.

I. HISTORICAL STORY: REHOBOAM'S REJECTION, 10:1-19

Structure

A. Negotiation: "all Israel" demands mitigation	1-5
1. Israel assembles to crown Rehoboam	1
2. Recall of Jeroboam	2-3aα
3. Their rebellious speech	3aβ-4
4. Rehoboam's request for delay	5
B. Rehoboam consults his veterans	6-7

Although the Chronicles text follows closely most of the Kings text in this passage, there are some significant differences. It is apparent from 1 Kgs 12:20 that Jeroboam took no part in the confrontation with Rehoboam, but was summoned to Shechem only after Rehoboam had returned to Jerusalem, v. 18. ChrH deliberately omits 1 Kgs 12:20, partly because he does not wish to record anything political about the northern kingdom, but mainly because he wants to make Jeroboam chiefly responsible for the rebellion (cf. 2 Chr 13:4-12). It is ChrH, therefore, who first inserted 10:2-3a, recalling Jeroboam from Egypt, but in an impossible sequence which first places Rehoboam and "all Israel" at Shechem (v. 1), next has the report of it come all the way to Egypt, then has Jeroboam make the journey back to Palestine, and lastly has Jeroboam called from wherever he was to Shechem (vv. 2-3aα). We can agree with Lemke (pp. 133-36) that this got copied into the Kings text as a gloss; cf. Watson (p. 201 n. 2). ChrH's omission of 1 Kgs 12:20, a definite conclusion to the original narrative, creates a situation in which the ending is somewhat uncertain because v. 19, "So Israel has been in rebellion . . . ," can be taken as the introduction to a final episode of the rebellion story, which would contain the Shemaiah incident and then conclude the entire story with the notice of 11:4, "So they hearkened . . . and returned and did not go against Jeroboam." This would have the effect not only of making Rehoboam seem less of a coward, but also of underscoring that Jeroboam was at the heart of the matter. This may have been what ChrH intended, but from a structural point of view it is better to keep the mangled rebellion story intact, allowing 10:19 to serve as the conclusion, and then taking 11:1-4 as the opening incident of a whole new section concerning Rehoboam's security.

This HISTORICAL STORY has a clearly defined plot. The nation is at a point of crisis. Solomon has died and the crown prince, Rehoboam, has travelled to Shechem, apparently still the political center for the ancient tribal league, to be crowned (v. 1). Since the principle of primogeniture seems by now to be firmly established, Rehoboam accepts the inconvenience, confidently expecting a smooth and brief ceremony. But the people ("all Israel") demand a prior concession. They complain that his father had made their yoke heavy, hence they propose what amounts to a conditional sentence, *wĕ'attâ*, "So now," with the imperative "lighten" (*qll*, hiph.), with the double object, "hard service" and "heavy yoke"; the apodosis is the promise "then we will be your servants" *(wĕna'abdekkā)*. We have no way of knowing whether the people's complaints are metaphor and exaggeration, but the existence of Solomon's corvées is confirmed by the behavior of Hadoram, v. 18.

The main tension in the story is created when Rehoboam fails to give an immediate answer to this eminently reasonable request. A three-day pause delays his answer as he deliberately moves to consult two distinct groups of counselors, the veterans or "elders," and the newcomers, or "young men." The first are the men who had served his father Solomon, the second are his court "buddies," destined for preferment in his own administration. From the way vv. 9-11 read, we would think that Rehoboam thought over carefully what the veterans advised him, rejected it, and then turned to the newcomers. This is, however, the narrator's design, aiming at creating a climax. We note also that there are two brief elements in the consultation of the veterans: request for advice and the giving of counsel. These provide the structure in the scene of consulting the newcomers, but each has been expanded, with a citation of the people's demand chiastically juxtaposed with a new citation in vv. 9b-10a. The veterans' counsel of kindness is cast as a condition, *'im* . . . *wĕhāyû lĕkā*, "if . . . then they will be to you," v. 7. The veterans' condition is essentially the same as that voiced by the people in vv. 3aβ-4; the newcomers do not consider it. By dropping out *hayyôm*, "today," from 1 Kgs 12:7 and changing "be a servant . . . and serve them" to "be kind . . . and please them," ChrH suggests kindness on the king's part as a permanent condition, sacrificing the more subtle point that the king should assume servant-like humility just on this occasion, in order to gain the people's allegiance permanently (see De Vries, *Yesterday, Today and Tomorrow,* 226). In v. 10a, abruptness in the citation of the people's demand suggests rudeness and disrespect on the part of the newcomers, a deliberate impression that is strengthened by the twofold aphorism that the latter would place in Rehoboam's mouth.

The scene of the fateful confrontation seems almost anticlimactic. We are told that Rehoboam follows the newcomers' advice, threatening a heavier yoke and repeating the second of their aphorisms. The conclusion, "So the king did not hearken to the people," is followed by an interpretative declaration, to the effect that God was behind all this, to bring to fulfillment the prophecy of Ahijah the Shilonite. ChrH does not have this; it is in 1 Kgs 11:31ff. ChrH simply assumes that his readers know that passage. ChrH repeats from Kings "all Israel's" reaction: their perception of Rehoboam's ill will, the recitation of a political ditty (REPUDIATION SAYING), their dispersal, and their rough treatment of Adoram (ChrH "Hadoram") and of Rehoboam himself (cf. Williamson, "Israel," 108-9; Willi, p. 145; Watson, 10.51).

Genre

10:1-19 is an HISTORICAL STORY, defined as a self-contained narrative concerned mainly to recount what a particular event was and how it happened, but with more literary sophistication than is evident with a simple (→) report. It runs from tension (here the threat to Rehoboam's kingship, and later of Shishak's invasion) to resolution (fortresses, family, adherence of northerners, and repentance); a subplot is Rehoboam's pride, leading first to disruption and then to apostasy. Within the revolt episode, the main genre is NEGOTIATION. In vv. 10, 11, 14 we see the genre APHORISM ("My finger is thicker than my father's loins"; "My father chastised you with whips, I will chastise you with scorpions"). The last saying is also a THREAT. V. 15 has the FULFILLMENT FORMULA, "that Yahweh might fulfill his word which he spoke by Ahijah." V. 16 has a REPUDIATION SAYING, a rhythmic political ditty designed to make the maximum possible impact on the person being repudiated. The precise opposite of the (→) affinity saying (1 Chr 11:1), it is full of rhetorical questions and taunting imperatives: "What to us any portion in David? . . . To your tents, O Israel! Now look to your own house, O David!" The revolt episode is concluded by the EPITOME, "So Israel has been in rebellion against the house of David to this day."

Setting and Intention

"So Israel has been in rebellion against the house of David to this day," 10:19, defines much of the tension that is destined to characterize the stories of the Judahite kings, down to the last. The ideal kingdom of David and Solomon, united around the temple and their kingship, has been shattered, and will remain shattered, until both north and south are lost. That Rehoboam allowed it to happen is presented straightforwardly and is seen as a fault. But the trouble is Israel's trouble. Rehoboam has done wrong but he rights himself with God by humbling himself. The question arises whether the throne in Jerusalem, occupied by the house of David, is still "Israel," or part of "Israel." In telling the story of the revolt at Shechem, ChrH takes his cue from the Kings text, referring with almost perfect consistency to Rehoboam's antagonists as "all Israel" (10:1, 3, 16a, and 16b). But it was only Rehoboam's intransigence that made them antagonists; ChrH has regularly called the assembled nation "all Israel." In the verses that show Rehoboam's disdain (10:5, 6, 7, 9, 10, 12, 15) they are referred to as presumptuous individuals: "the people," "this people," "all the people." "So all [Kings omits] Israel departed to their tents," v. 16b, does not refer to the sometime kingdom of Israel, which was not at that moment in existence, but to Israel as an organized whole. In other words, Rehoboam was not repudiated by a political entity antagonistic to him, but by his own proper people. But this "all Israel" was still represented by "the people of Israel who dwelt in the cities of Judah," v. 17. The "people of Israel" whom Hadoram tried to coerce were evidently individuals, or a group of individuals, living outside Judah, and not under Rehoboam's rule (v. 18).

Bibliography

A. M. Dubarle, "Le jugement des auteurs bibliques sur le schisme de Jéroboam," in *Miscelanea Biblica Andres Fernandez* (ed. J. Sagues; Estudios Eclesiasticos 34: Madrid: Selecciones Graficas, 1961) 577-94; D. G. Evans, "Rehoboam's Advisers at Shechem and Political Institutions in Israel and Sumer," *JNES* 25 (1966) 273-79; B. Halpern, "Sectionalism and the Schism," *JBL* 93 (1974) 519-32; A. Malamat, "Kingship and Council in Israel and Sumer: A Parallel," *JNES* 22 (1963) 247-53.

II. REPORT OF SECURITY FOR THREE YEARS, 11:1-23

Structure

We are told in 10:17 that there were "people of Israel who dwelt in the cities of Judah." They were certainly not among "the people of Israel" who stoned Hadoram to death, 10:18. The latter constitute "Israel" as a political entity, whose rebellion has been against "the house of David," i.e., the Davidic royal establishment. In 11:1 we are told that Rehoboam assembled *(qhl)* "the house of Judah and Benjamin," meaning these two tribes as political entities, to the number of 180,000, whose task it was to fight against "Israel," i.e., the separated northern kingdom, in order to restore, i.e., to reunite, Rehoboam's proper kingdom. Shemaiah's countering revelation interrupts these intentions (vv. 2-4a). "They," i.e., Rehoboam and his army, hearken to or obey *(šmʿ)* this prohibition as the word of Yahweh and refrain from attacking Jeroboam and his supporters, much in contrast to the fact that Rehoboam is said to have refused to hearken to/obey "all Israel's" demand in 10:15, 16.

This Shemaiah episode is now structurally a part of the "security" section because the report of Jeroboam's accession has been sacrificed and 2 Chr 10:19 serves as an epitomizing conclusion to the revolt narrative. Besides, the willingness to heed the voice of prophecy sets the tone for the "security" theme: Rehoboam shows that he gives priority to a prophetic word over the opportunity to employ 180,000 soldiers. This makes him spiritually and militarily strong. The next subsection, 11:5-12, will show how he prepares a system of effective defense for the territory still loyal to him. This will be followed by a section, vv. 12-17, that tells of important accessions from the renegade north. It will be followed by a section, vv. 18-23, that will show how Rehoboam becomes strong in and through his own family.

The Shemaiah incident has a definite conclusion in v. 4, *wayyāšubû milleket 'el-yārobʿām*, "and they returned from marching on Jeroboam" (better than *RSV*, "and returned and did not go against Jeroboam"). The fortress section that follows has a possibly intentional pun: *wayyēšeb rĕḥabʿām bîrûšālāim*, "So Rehoboam dwelt/stayed in Jerusalem" *(šwb; yšb)*. Thematically the difference is important, of course: Rehoboam moved from an aggressive to a defensive posture, and it is this that makes him militarily strong. He did not hole up in Jerusalem, but built fifteen fortress cities on the fringes of his territory; these are named in a circuit from southeast to south to southwest to west, with only Hebron—for some reason—out of order. The text says that these cities were "in Judah and in Benjamin," which is wrong, except for two possibilities: (1) that the former Danite towns of Zorah and Aijalon had been abandoned by the Danites and taken over by Benjaminites (cf. 1 Chr 8:13), or (2) that the expression "Judah and Benjamin" was now the common territorial-geographical title for the region under Rehoboam's control, hence it mattered not whether any of the cities named were actually in the traditional tribal district of Benjamin.

Following Ackroyd (comm.) and Williamson (comm.), we identify the expression in v. 12b, *wayĕhî-lô yĕhûdâ ûbinyāmin*, "So Judah and Benjamin were his," as the resumptive introduction to vv. 13-17. It tells of accessions from "all Israel," which now means the former united kingdom apart from the territory directly under Rehoboam's control. Because he has identified the word *migrāšîm*, "pasture lands" (v. 14), as a mark of the post-Chr redactor, Willi (p. 195) considers the entirety of vv. 14-15 a gloss. Williamson (comm.) takes v. 14a as a gloss because it breaks the connection between the reference to the priests (with Levites in secondary position) in v. 13 and the notice in v. 14b that Jeroboam would not have them as Yahweh's priests. In v. 16 "and after them" makes a transition to another group, evidently laymen, whose description is: *hannōtĕnîm 'et-lĕbābām lĕbaqqēš, 'et-yahweh 'ĕlōhê yiśrā'ēl*, "those who gave their hearts to seek Yahweh the God of Israel." They came to Jerusalem to sacrifice to the "God of their fathers"—the ancestral god equivalent to "Yahweh, God of Israel." We are not informed whether such persons came only for the festivals, but, as v. 17 tells us, the effect of their coming was to strengthen (*ḥzq*, piel) Judah and support ('*mṣ*, piel) Rehoboam. The duration of three years is mentioned, and is then repeated in the grounding clause (*kî*) that states that he (LXX; MT "they") all the while behaved himself like David and Solomon. The reason for this emphatic reference to the three years will be seen in 12:2, where mention is made of a period of general infidelity leading to Shishak's invasion in the fifth year.

Some scholars (Rudolph, HAT; Noth, "Chronistische Werk," 143) regard the section vv. 18-23 as a post-ChrH addition. There is a problem here, but it could just as well be with his source material as with ChrH. The problem is with the appointment of Abijah as crown prince, v. 22, when Maacah his mother is identified as becoming Rehoboam's wife later than ('*aḥăreyhā*, "after her") Mahalath (v. 20). The suspicious thing here is that the principle of primogeniture is by now supposed to be firmly established, and that, although we cannot show that Mahalath had all her four sons before Maacah had her first, viz., Abijah, the normal thing would have been to present Abijah with his mother first if he was in fact the firstborn. This suspicion is strengthened by the *apologia* that seems to be made in mentioning the special love that Rehoboam had for Maacah "above all his wives and concubines," who are then tallied to emphasize the distinction. Furthermore, v. 22 has language that strongly suggests that Rehoboam made a definite move to give Abijah the preference over whoever may have been the actual firstborn: "And Rehoboam appointed as chief *[wayya'ămēd lārō'š]* Abijah the son of Maacah in order to *[kî]* make him king" ("as prince among his brothers" is an explicative gloss). V. 23 might seem to duplicate, or possibly even to contradict, vv. 11-12, but it is in fact a useful notation giving more information about the royal family and how

Rehoboam managed it. We are told, *wayyāben wayyiprōṣ mikkol-bānāyw . . .*, "And he cleverly dispersed some of his sons. . . ." The cleverness *(byn)* lay not so much in the fact that Rehoboam made good use of his sons' talents and loyalty by turning over to them the command of certain fortresses, so much as in his keeping them away from Jerusalem, where they might make a plot to vent their resentment about being passed over in favor of Abijah. To keep them happy, Rehoboam provided them with abundant provisions and even got them wives (emendation of corrupt MT v. 23, "and he asked for a multitude of wives").

Genre

The section on "security" is a REPORT, filled with information from diverse sources. 11:1 speaks not only of a huge number but uses the APPELLATION *'ōśēh milḥāmâ,* "professional soldier," thus underscoring Rehoboam's threat to Jeroboam. Vv. 2-4a contain a PROPHETIC COMMISSION REPORT. The PROPHETIC SPEECH itself contains the WORD FORMULA, "the word of Yahweh came to Shemaiah . . ."; the COMMISSION, "Say to Rehoboam . . . and to all Israel"; the HERALD FORMULA, "Thus says Yahweh"; a PROHIBITION, "You shall not go up or fight"; and a COMMAND, "Return every man to his home," with a grounding clause, "for this thing is from me." See S. J. De Vries, "Dynastic Endangerment," 66; idem, "Prophetic Address," 25, 32.

11:6-10 contain a NAME LIST. "And after them" and "and after her" in vv. 16 and 20 show the TRANSITION FORMULA. Vv. 18-19 and v. 20 belong to the genre BIRTH REPORT, giving the wife's name, the name of her parents (only the father in the case of Maacah), and the names of sons. V. 21 has a TALLY and v. 22 the RANKING FORMULA (*rō'š,* "chief").

Setting and Intention

Shemaiah's commission "to Rehoboam . . . and to all Israel in Judah and Benjamin," 11:3, has seemed tendentious to scholars who have preferred the reading in 1 Kgs 12:23, "to Rehoboam . . . and all the house of Judah and Benjamin, and to the rest of the people." But ChrH's alteration is consistent, for he persists to the end in referring to the adherents of the Judahite kings as "all Israel" (see Williamson, comm., 239-40; idem, *Israel,* 97-101, 103, 108-9; Japhet, "Ideology," 178ff.; Lemke, 136; *contra* von Rad, *Geschichtsbild,* 18-37). As a partisan of Rehoboam, ChrH quickly seeks items that will tend to lighten Rehoboam's blame and shift it to the north. He obeys Yahweh's prophet (11:4) even though he would not hearken to the people (10:15)—from the theocratic point of view a most commendable choice. In 11:13-16 he welcomes the priests and Levites who had once lived throughout the tribes of Israel (1 Chronicles 6), but who would now make Judah and Jerusalem their home (cf. 13:9). In 11:16-17 he welcomes the "God-seekers" who know that Yahweh the God of Israel, "the God of the fathers," can be worshiped only in Jerusalem (this is deuteronomistic cultic exclusivism rather than an anti-north polemic). These newcomers strengthen Rehoboam and make him secure (though for only three years), so that we are inclined to think of them as permanent residents and not as festival pilgrims. Unfortunately, "all Israel"—surely including native Judahites and not just (at all?) these proselytes—join Rehoboam at the end of the three years in forsaking Yahweh's law, 12:11.

Bibliography

G. Beyer, "Beiträge zur territorialgeschichte von Südwestpalästina im Altertum. I. Das Festungssystem Rehabeams," *ZDPV* 54 (1931) 113-34; V. Fritz, "The 'List of Rehoboam's Fortresses' in 2 Chr 11:5-12," *ErIs* 15 (1981) 46*-53*; Z. Kallai, "The Kingdom of Rehoboam" (Hebr.), *ErIs* 10 (1971) 245-56; P. Welten, *Geschichte und Geschichtsdarstellung in den Chronikbüchern* (WMANT 42; Neukirchen-Vluyn: Neukirchener, 1973) 42-52.

III. REPORT OF SHISHAK'S PUNITIVE RAID, 12:1-12

Structure

Here the action moves on smoothly, but with a pause in vv. 5-8 to allow for Shemaiah's oracle and its effect, leading to an EPITOME in v. 12. In v. 1, the strength and stability of Rehoboam's rule produce a pride that manifests itself in a universal forsaking *('zb)* of Yahweh's law (cf. Kropat, 78). Yahweh's reaction against this first apostasy of his kings is swift and severe, yet restrained upon the evidence of repentance (Willi, 173, 175, calls this a reflection on 1 Kgs 14:25-28, the parallel passage). As in chs. 13, 14, etc., large numbers are given for the opposing army; Shishak comes with 600 chariots and a hundred times more cavalrymen, with uncounted allied infantrymen from the countries of northwest Africa (so in ch. 14). They swiftly capture all the fortresses that Rehoboam had just built and then come *(bw')* to, i.e., besiege, Jerusalem, v. 4. This is the signal for Shemaiah to intervene with another divine message. Gathered because of Shishak are the king and the *śārê yĕhûdâ,* "princes/officials of Judah." Shemaiah's accusation and announcement are memorable: *'attem 'ăzabtem 'ōtî wĕ'ap-'ănî 'āzabtî 'etkem,* "You have forsaken me, so I have also forsaken you" (chiastic arrangement).

As in 2 Chr 11:4, the response is swift and positive. The princes and king (chiasmus with v. 5a) humble themselves *(kn'),* lit., "kneel down," and confess, *ṣaddîq yahweh,* "Yahweh is in the right!" (v. 6). A modifying revelation comes to Shemaiah (there is no report that he passed this on), vv. 7-8. Yahweh saw the *kn',* and now because of the *kn',* three things will (or will not) happen: (1) he will not destroy *(šḥt,* hiph.) them; (2) he will give them *kim'aṭ liplêṭâ,* "a little escape" or "escape for a while"; and (3) he will not allow his wrath *(ḥămātî)* to be poured out on Jerusalem—a grim prolepsis of 34:25; cf. 36:16. Nevertheless, they have sinned, and Yahweh will use this to teach them a lesson, v. 8. "They shall be servants (vassals) of him," i.e., Shishak, so that they may know (by harsh experience) two things: "my service" and "the service of the kingdoms of the countries." In other words, they must choose to be loyal servants of the one lord or the other; if not Yahweh, then the harsh kings of the earth. V. 9 reports: "so Shishak . . . came up *['lh],*" i.e., attacked, Jerusalem. His booty was the temple and palace vessels and *hakkōl,* "everything." Specifically, ChrH names the golden shields of Solomon, v. 9, and then copies from Kings how Rehoboam manufactured and employed substitute shields of bronze, v. 10. V. 12a is an EPITOME: "So when they humbled themselves *[kn']* Yahweh's anger *['ap]* turned back, and it did not come to absolute devastation *[wĕlō' lĕhašḥît lĕkālâ]*"; this tells the whole story in a nutshell. V. 12b, "Conditions remained good in Judah," summarizes the whole reign of Rehoboam and provides a transition to the REGNAL RESUMÉ (vv. 13-16).

Genre

The section about Shishak's raid is a REPORT, with the subgenre BATTLE REPORT in 12:2-4. Otherwise than in 11:2-4 (copied from Kings), 12:5-6 is the REPORT OF A PROPHETIC WORD, defined as a narrating genre developed in the exilic period and found frequently in the prose tradition of Jeremiah and Ezekiel, reflecting the belief that the word of a prophet must be understood as growing out of a particular historical situation (this late derivation fits well with ChrH's postexilic situation, though presumably not with that of the historical Shishak). Apart from the MESSENGER FORMULA, Shemaiah's new message has only a REPROACH ("You have forsaken me, so I have forsaken you"), defined as a sharp criticism for indecorous or blameworthy behavior. V. 6, "Yahweh is in the right," is a CONFESSION OF GUILT, a genre in which a defendant or defendants formally acknowledge his/their guilt, being the virtual equivalent of the (→) plea of guilt. Introduced by the WORD FORMULA, vv. 7-8 have the genre ORACLE, which in this instance comprises Yahweh's disclosure to Shemaiah of his intentions, without any report that the prophet actually communicated this to the people. (On this passage see further De Vries, "Prophetic Address," 25, 32-33.) Vv. 9-11, taken from Kings, are a bare STATEMENT. V. 12a is an EPITOME, summarizing and characterizing the entire event.

Setting

The pattern of Rehoboam's reign is (1) failure, (2) success, (3) disaster (Williamson, comm., 238). What he took confidence in is, ironically, quickly taken from him. He relied on a chain of strategically placed and effectively manned fortresses (see Welten, *Geschichte,* 11-15, 194-95, who argues for an historical core in this list; cf. also the territorial-geographical analyses of Beyer, Kallai, and Fritz); he relied also on a large family, the sure sign of divine favor. But he forsook Yahweh, so Yahweh forsook him. ChrH provides a theology for the brief notice about Shishak in 1 Kgs 12:25-26. Yahweh brings him to teach Rehoboam that those who refuse to acknowledge servitude to him must experience servitude to the great rulers of the earth, 12:8. The fortresses do no good; Shishak plunders Jerusalem anyway. And the many sons? Not now, but later, the seeds of envy and mistrust that Rehoboam has sown in elevating Abijah over his brothers will sprout, and the SCHEMA OF DYNASTIC ENDANGERMENT will play its important role.

Perhaps the most important theological statement in this entire account is 12:6, "Righteous is Yahweh!" Even in humbling himself at Shemaiah's reproach, this meant that Rehoboam could not escape Shishak. The principle of divine righteousness governs ChrH's entire pattern of coming punishments on apostasy.

Intention

The ideal kingdom was shattered. Like a rejected lover, ChrH tries to ignore the estranged partner, refusing to tell of the northern kings. Yet we shall see many signs of his longing for a reunion. After the exile, the "two sticks" of Ezekiel 37 are still not joined, but this, if anything, is at the top of ChrH's eschatological agenda. As of now, it must be said, "So Israel has been in rebellion against the house of David *to this day.*"

It must be said that ChrH is harsher with Rehoboam than Kings is; he may have, after all, harbored resentment against him for letting the kingdom fall apart. 1 Kgs 14:22-24 tells in detail of the abominations that prevailed in Judah during his reign, but leaves the impression that, apart from not doing something effective to suppress them, he was not personally involved. But ChrH does not even mention these abominations. Rather, 12:14 seems like a mere slap on the wrist: "He did evil, for he did not set his heart to seek Yahweh." In other words, he was wishy-washy. But at least he followed ChrH's great cure-all remedy: repentance, humbling himself. He may have been foolish and proud, but he did respect the prophets; and when they said "humble yourself," he humbled himself.

It is again quite clear how highly ChrH regarded the prophets. There could not have been many real prophets in his postexilic community, however. Various things give this away. One is that the genre REPORT OF A PROPHETIC WORD is comparatively late (exilic and postexilic), yet it is employed for Shemaiah's oracle in 12:5. Another is the fact that after 11:2 (from Kings), Shemaiah is no longer called "man of God" but "prophet" (12:5, 15). ChrH was able to draw narrative materials about the historical prophets in earlier passages from Kings (1 Chronicles 17; 21), but we shall now see prophets appear regularly whose historical existence may be seriously doubted. With respect to structure, they appear like puppets making their entrance on a stage. This may speak poorly of ChrH's reputation as an historian, but it speaks very highly of his reverence for the bearers of divine revelation.

We have previously mentioned the SCHEMA OF REVELATIONAL APPEARANCES. To show how ChrH intends to have his prophets appear we offer this chart:

Encouragement	*Warning/condemnation*
	11:2-4a, Shemaiah
	12:5, Shemaiah
12:7a, Shemaiah	
	12:7b, Shemaiah
15:1-7, Azariah	
	16:7-9, Hanani
	19:1-3, Jehu
20:13-19, Jahaziel	
	20:37, Eliezer
	21:13-15, Elijah
	24:20, Zechariah
	25:15-16, Anonymous
	28:9-13, Oded

From this list it can be seen that ChrH's prophets have more often a word of warning and condemnation than of encouragement. In this schema, nonprophets are sometimes used to bring revelation as well, showing how loose ChrH's concept of a "prophet" really is. There were kings, a priest, a foreign ruler, and even mediums, and they used sermons, prayers, and direct warnings as their vehicles of communication. Words of encouragement are brought by them in 14:10 (*RSV* 11) and 20:5-12, and of doom in 1 Chr 10:13-14; 2 Chr 13:2-12; 26:18; 35:21. Revelational encouragement comes to good kings who stand in peril, a common scene; but far more common is the need for a revelational word of warning or condemnation when one of the kings, good or bad, is embarking on an evil course. One way or the other, ChrH sees to it that the Judahite kings are not without transcendental light. God is always present in one of his spokesmen.

Bibliography

G. Beyer, "Beiträge zur Territorialgeschichte von Südwestpalästina im Altertum. I. Das Festungssystem Rehabeams," *ZDPY* 54 (1931) 113-34; Y. Elitsur, "The Biblical Account of Shishak's Invasion: Prophetic Historiosophy versus Reality" (Hebr.), *Fourth World Congress of Jewish Studies* I (Jerusalem: World Union of Jewish Studies, 1967) 29-31, 252; V. Fritz, "The List of Rehoboam's Fortresses in 2 Chr 11:5-12," *ErIs* 15 (1981) 46*-53*;

Z. Kallai, "The Kingdom of Rehoboam" (Hebr.), *ErIs* 10 (1971) 245-56; B. Mazar, "The Campaign of Pharaoh Shishak to Palestine," in *Volume du Congrès: Strasbourg 1956* (VTSup 4; Leiden: Brill, 1957) 57-66; R. Micheel, *Die Seher- und Prophetenüberlieferungen in der Chronik* (Frankfurt a/M: Land, 1983); P. Weinberg, "Die 'ausserkanonischen Prophezeiungen' in den Chronikbüchern," *AcAnt* 27 (1978) 387-404.

IV. REGNAL RESUMÉ, 12:13-16

Structure

This material is taken from separate sections in Kings: 1 Kgs 14:21-22 and 29-31. Galling (ATD) and Rudolph (HAT) take it to be a post-ChRH addition based on Kings, but it would be strange if Rehoboam turned out to be the only king besides Ahaziah and Amon to do without a concluding resumé. One can see, to be sure, that at this point ChRH has not yet settled down to a stereotyped way of presenting these summaries. The statement in v. 13a is his own: "And King Rehoboam [honorific] established himself [*ḥzq*, hiph.] and reigned"— which is about all that can be truthfully said about him, for he spent all his energies getting himself in a safe position to hold on to his throne. The theological evaluation in v. 14 seems harsh ("he did evil and did not set his heart to seek Yahweh"), but according to the account before us he was up and down, not doing any remarkable good for the scribes to record (see Willi, p. 130). The sources referred to are again from otherwise unknown prophets, and apparently tell little more than the continual hostilities with Jeroboam, v. 15. For the first time, the death and burial notice also speaks of a burial, v. 16a.

Genre

Verses 13-16 are a REGNAL RESUMÉ, with the ACCESSION AGE FORMULA, a STATEMENT OF LENGTH AND PLACE OF REIGN, a THEOLOGICAL REVIEW, the CITATION FORMULA in the form of a RHETORICAL QUESTION ("are they not written . . .?"), the DEATH AND BURIAL FORMULA (in classical form, "And X slept with his fathers and was buried in the city of David"), and the SUCCESSION FORMULA.

REPORT OF THE REIGN OF ABIJAH, 13:1-23A (*RSV* 13:1–14:1a)

Structure

ChrH chooses to use 1 Kgs 15:1-2 and 7-8 as regnal summaries, but otherwise goes to what many scholars consider a private historical source for the rest (on the text, cf. Lemke, 142-45). V. 1 has ChrH's sole synchronism with the reign of an opposite king, a regular feature in Kings. This is because his report of Abijah's reign is completely taken up with the battle against Jeroboam at Mount Zemaraim and its effects. His mother is identified as "Micaiah daughter of Uriel," a flat contradiction of the statement in 2 Chr 11:20 that Maacah, daughter of Absalom, was his mother. This agrees with 1 Kgs 15:2, and, because the birth reports in 2 Chr 11:18 appear to be taken from a private, reliable source, this notice must be in error. V. 2 gives us the battle situation, ûmilḥāmâ hāyětâ bên . . . ûbên . . . , "And there was war between . . . and between . . ."; cf. 1 Kgs 15:7. Because Abijah makes a long, taunting address, vv. 2b-12, one gets the impression that he was the aggressor, but this cannot be determined from v. 3, which says that Abijah "took on" ('sr) a battle, since this could mean, in response to aggression; also Jeroboam's action, "draw up ['rk] a battle (line)," refers only to a formation prepared at the sight of the Judeans, and not to a defensive war as such. The striking differential between Jeroboam's 800,000 and Abijah's 400,000, plus the fact that Abijah assumed a strong point before making his address, suggests that Jeroboam was really the aggressor.

The mountain where the battle took place cannot confidently be identified with any topographical feature mentioned in the Bible. Imaginative as the story may be, it is a priori unlikely that, with hundreds of barren mountains available as candidates for the site within the border region between Israel and Judah, ChrH would find it necessary to invent one. Dalman identified Zemaraim with Ras-et-Tahune eastward of the road to Bethel; Koch claims that it was Ras-es-zemara, northeast of Bethel. It seems strange (and quite artificial) that Abijah could make his speech heard by an opposing force who should be imagined as at a safe distance from Abijah's lines. Be that as it may, his address is cleverly structured. In vv. 4b-5 he addresses both Jeroboam and "all Israel" (which here and in v. 15 has the meaning "all who properly belong to Israel," i.e., to David's kingdom, in distinction from *bĕnê yiśrā'ēl*, "the sons of Israel," vv. 12, 16, 18, referring to the opposing soldiers as individuals). What Abijah wants to tell them, thus addressed, is that they ought to know (taunt) that Yahweh has given the kingship to "David" perpetually *(lĕ'ôlām)*, having made a *bĕrît melaḥ*, "covenant of salt," with his posterity (v. 5).

Next, Abijah turns directly to the opposing soldiers, ignoring Jeroboam, of whom he speaks scornfully in the third person, informing them of how the schism came about (vv. 6-7), taunting them for their reliance on vain might (v. 8), reproaching them for tolerating a false priesthood (v. 9), boasting in Judah's orthodoxy (vv. 10-11), and appealing to them to surrender (v. 12). In short, he is attempting to separate Jeroboam from his troops. First, Jeroboam is accused of rebelling *(mrd)* from his liege lord Rehoboam, who because of his youth and weak determination *(na'ar wĕrak-lēbāb)* was taken advantage of by *'ănāšîm rēqîm bĕnê bĕlîya'al*, "scurvy fellows and mischief makers" (Williamson, comm., 112, rightly argues that *'mṣ*, hith., means "persuade," and that the persons mentioned were his youthful counselors). The TAUNT of v. 8 ridicules the idea of opposing "the kingdom of Yahweh in the hands of David" with their "mighty host" (*hāmôn* is a key holy-war term, and is seen also in 14:10), aided by Jeroboam's golden calves (it seems as unlikely that they had actually transported these cult objects to the battlefield as that the historical Jeroboam made gods of them). Abijah also reproves his hearers for expelling Yahweh's priests (cf. 11:14b), who apparently consist of both *bĕnê 'ahărōn*, "Aaronites," and Levites (... *'et* ... *'et* puts "priests" in one phrase and "Aaronites and Levites" in another). This may be a reminder of an early Levitical claim to priesthood. Be that as it may, Abijah taunts them that their priests are no priests, and their gods are no gods. V. 10 has the transition *wa'ănaḥnû*, "But we" (a rare form in ChrH). He boasts: He is our God; we have not forsaken him; we have priests, "sons of Aaron" and Levites ("for their service," v. 10, may be a corrective explication of v. 9); they are punctilious about every ritual. In short, we keep the charge you forsake. The final appeal is loaded with ideology: *wĕhinnēh 'immānû bārō'š hā'ĕlōhîm*, "And behold, with us at the head is God" (v. 12). Add to this the trumpeting priests (cf. 1 Chr 15:24, etc.). The final exhortation is "Don't fight; you cannot succeed."

Next comes the narrative of the battle, for Jeroboam's troops would not listen to Abijah's peroration. They had a strategy that could win: the main force in front, an ambush in the rear, v. 13. When Judah saw its peril it performed two effective actions from the holy-war tradition: outcry *(ṣ'q)* and the blowing of trumpets by the priests (both were designed to produce a *hāmôn*, "panic," among the enemy). Then the Judahite soldiers made the battle shout *(rw')*. Simultaneously Yahweh acted: *wayĕhî bĕhārîa' 'îš yĕhûdâ wĕhā'ĕlōhîm nāgap*, "And when the Judahite soldier shouted, God struck" (v. 15). The victims are Jeroboam and "all Israel"—separate entities in Abijah's speech, but now sharing the same fate. There is a statement that the Israelite soldiers fled *(nws)*, v. 16, and then were smitten *(ykh*, hiph.) with a *makkâ rabbâ*, "a mighty slaughter." In good holy-war story style, there is a CASUALTY REPORT: *wayyippĕlû ḥălālîm*, "And casualties fell"; they consisted of *'îš bāḥûr,* "elite soldiers," to the fantastic number of 500,000 out of the original 800,000. The concluding EPITOME, also common in the classical holy-war story, is short and contains the time designation: "So the Israelite soldiers were subdued [*kn'*, niph.] at that time," v. 18a.

Verses 18b-21a tell the results of this victory. We are told that the *běnê yěhûdâ,* "Judahites" (cf. *yěhûdâ,* vv. 1, 13-14; *'îš yěhûdâ,* v. 15 twice), prevailed through trust (*š'n,* niph.) in Yahweh the ancestral God; also that Abijah pursued the enemy and took three border cities, the best known of which was Bethel (there is no way of testing the historicity of this claim, but it seems hard to believe that the northerners could actually have tolerated interruption of worship at their special shrine, Bethel). In any event, Jeroboam remained harmless/impotent (*lō'-'āṣar kōaḥ . . . 'ôd,* "[he] did not recover [his] power," v. 20) until Yahweh struck him down (*ngp,* same word as in v. 15).

There is no more to tell about Abijah except that he kept getting stronger (*ḥzq,* hiph.). Partly as a blessing from God, and partly as a manifestation of this strength, he got numerous wives, sons, and daughters (cf. 11:21). On the REGNAL RESUMÉ, cf. Watson (3.6); on the text, cf. Lemke (p. 145). Here ChrH departs from the usual pattern, using the formula "And the rest of the acts . . . ways . . . sayings . . . ," and reporting only one authority, "the *midrash* of the prophet Iddo." See the discussion in Chapter 4 above on the presumed sources in ChrH's citations; we have identified a genre, MIDRASH, but do not know whether Iddo's *midrash* was anything like it. We note, finally, that the DEATH AND BURIAL notice for Abijah and the SUCCESSION FORMULA for Asa have been used by ChrH as a heading for his ch. 14.

Genre

The main genre is REPORT. The pericope has elements of the REGNAL RESUMÉ at the beginning and end, here alone with the SYNCHRONISTIC ACCESSION FORMULA, v. 1. There are also the STATEMENT OF LENGTH AND PLACE OF REIGN, v. 2, the CITATION FORMULA, v. 22, and the DEATH AND BURIAL and SUCCESSION FORMULAS in v. 23. The narrative core is entirely taken up with the QUASI-HOLY-WAR STORY genre (see "Setting" below), in which a TALLY and APPELLATIONS for each army, v. 3, a statement of locale, v. 4a, the account of ambush, triumph, and slaughter, vv. 13-17, and the EPITOME of v. 18a ("Thus the men of Israel were subdued at that time"), the CONVEYANCE FORMULA of v. 16b ("God gave them into their hand"), and the APPELLATION, TALLY, and CASUALTY REPORT of v. 17, properly belong. Vv. 4b-12 constitute an ADDRESS which is in its entirety an ADMONITION, by definition a type of address that is designed to dissuade an individual or group from an undesirable type of conduct. V. 4b is a CALL TO ATTENTION. V. 5 is a STATEMENT that includes the RHETORICAL QUESTION "Ought you not to know?" Vv. 6-7 constitute a REPROACH for following Jeroboam, with another of the same genre in v. 9 for expelling Yahweh's priests; it too has a RHETORICAL QUESTION, "Have you not driven out . . . ?" V. 8 is a TAUNT, "And now you think to withstand . . . ," with another of the same genre in v. 9b, "Whoever comes to consecrate himself with a young bull or seven rams becomes a priest of what are no gods." Vv. 10-11 constitute a BOAST, defined as an utterance which appraises some person or thing as superior to another. V. 12 is an APPEAL, which, unlike (→) command, prohibition, or petition, assumes no special obligation on the part of the addressee(s). Here Abijah appeals to Israel not to fight, but their response is entirely optional, depending on whether they accept his claim that they cannot win because fighting him is the same as fighting God. It contains the ASSISTANCE FORMULA ("God is with us at our head") and a concluding ADMONITION ("O sons of Israel, do not fight against Yahweh"). The STATEMENT occurs for four items in vv. 18b-21. V. 21 repeats the TALLY for the different groups within Abijah's family.

Setting

At least on one occasion, drawing from written source material, ChrH reported a real historical battle (1 Chronicles 19), but as a rule his battles are fictitious. They always have a strong parenetic tone, reflect the Jerusalem cult, and emphasize Judah's weakness in order to glorify Yahweh's power. A vigorous faith on the king's part is indispensable. Welten (Geschichte, 166-72) shows that the major battles are fought in the north (ch. 13), west (ch. 14), east (ch. 20), and south (ch. 25), reflecting the ChrH's third-century situation in which the enemies of Nehemiah's time were still remembered and were possibly still active: Sanballat in the north, Ashdod on the west, Geshem to the south, and Tobiah in the east. The central idea, then, is lasting security for the Judahite state, using the period of the kings as the model for the late postexilic situation. It stands to reason that battles involving an alliance with an Israelite or foreign king (chs. 16; 18; 22) were acts of impiety and stood under divine judgment.

Our present passage plus chs. 14, 20, 25 belong to the genre QUASI-HOLY-WAR STORY. All these narratives are artificial, schematic, and mostly devoid of historical actuality—though some kernel of fact may lie behind them. We must also say that they are saturated with ancient holy-war terminology and ideology. Von Rad popularized the term "holy war" and described it as defensive and highly theocentric (Der heilige Krieg im alten Israel [4th ed.; Göttingen: Vandenhoeck & Ruprecht, 1965]). Smend (Yahweh War and Tribal Confederation [tr. M. Rogers; Nashville: Abingdon, 1970]) argued that "Yahweh war" was more precise and descriptive than "holy war." Richter has nonetheless retained von Rad's term (Traditionsgeschichtliche Untersuchungen zum Richterbuch [Bonn: Hanstein, 1966]), isolating two separate schemata for it as a distinct genre: (1) situation, empowerment, summons/mustering, victory, annihilation; (2) situation, battle, annihilation or pursuit (never both). We are not sure whether Abijah's battle with Jeroboam was defensive or aggressive, though the weight of the arguments favors the former (see "Structure" above). Because Abijah's address is built into the narrative as an integral part of it—or, more accurately, because the whole battle account is plainly designed as a framework for the address—we have to call it both "holy-war story" and "quasi-." This is not just a traditional holy-war story, adorned with ideological speechifying; it is, from the form-critical point of view, a distinct new genre. As one studies this story and the others on this list, one will often see a highly accentuated supernaturalism. That is not so much the case here as in the others, yet it does appear in Judah's claim that God is their rō'š, "head/captain," and especially in the priests with their battle trumpets, vv. 12, 14, which not only frighten the enemy but somehow summon the power of the supernatural (cf. L. Koehler, "Archäologisches. 3," ZAW 34 [1914] 147).

ChrH shows evident concern about the causes and effects of the schism, or

THE INDIVIDUAL UNITS

breakup, of "all Israel" in vv. 5-7. Benzinger called this a midrash on 1 Kings 12. Delcor took this with Zechariah 11 as evidence at the beginning of the Greek period for the well-known but little understood Samaritan-Jewish schism. As has been shown in Chapter 1 above, this claim is now in serious doubt. It is true that Abijah is glorified far above his portrait in Kings, and that the text claims legitimacy solely for the Judean monarchy and the Judean clergy. Williamson (comm., and *Israel*) has done much to demonstrate that this is no polemic, but an *apologia* for reunification. The way in which Abijah excoriates those who miscounseled Rehoboam seems surprisingly frank in the light of the fact that 2 Chronicles 10 had no word of criticism for Rehoboam or the "newcomers" whose counsel he followed, which shows that, in ChrH's thinking, the disruption never should have happened. Of course, Jeroboam gets the blame for being a rebel against his master, quite to the contrary of the original text of 1 Kings 12. But even if ChrH had access to an unglossed Kings text, he and his fellow Judahites would have learned that Jeroboam became a rebel, whether he was present at Shechem or not. His willingness to become a counter-king to Rehoboam, his dismissal of Jerusalemite clergy, and his fabrication of cult objects which even DtrH condemned as "the sin of Jeroboam the son of Nebat" were seen more and more in the worst possible light. ChrH in his time sought the true reunification of "all Israel." It was plain that if this was ever to come about, these "offenses" would have to go: a rebel king, a rival and unsanctified clergy, and all shrines except the "house where Yahweh's name dwelt."

Intention

ChrH's rationale for King Abijah is the following: (1) his address set the terms for the reunification of the nation; (2) in the light of Rehoboam's lapses, he was the first Judahite king after Solomon to re-embody the model rule of Solomon, setting the pattern in humility, courage, and obedience for all the kings to follow; (3) his numerous sons and daughters, like those of Rehoboam, were a sign both of strength and of blessing. The STATEMENT in v. 5 tells unequivocally what Yahweh's will was with regard to the kingship. He does not have two kings, but one. "Ought you not to know that Yahweh God of Israel gave the kingship forever to David and his sons by a covenant of salt?" Assuming that the opposing army did know this, Abijah moves to isolate Jeroboam from the scene (see "Structure" above). It is better, he says, to have served a young and irresolute king (v. 7) than to serve a vigorous ruler like Jeroboam, whom God had never chosen (ChrH ignores 1 Kgs 11:31-32).

As for the priests: only the true lineage from Aaron, some of whom ChrH claims were exiled by Jeroboam, are true priests; the ones appointed by Jeroboam are idolatrous, serving gods that are no gods. There is no compromise in this polemic. The historical Jeroboam may have had priests as sacred as those of Jerusalem, though his calf-emblems were probably not designed as gods at all; but history has been cruel to Jeroboam. The kingdom he established did not survive the 8th century, so he had no one left to defend his policy. That is just as well for ChrH's late postexilic community, living in and near Jerusalem, and worshiping at the restored temple. This was the time for answers, not for questions. Addressing whomever their antagonists may have been, they too rejoiced in the assurance of being able to say, "But as for us, Yahweh is our God, and we have not forsaken him. . . . We keep the charge of Yahweh our God, but you have forsaken him" (vv. 10, 11).

295

Bibliography

G. Dalman, "Einige geschichtliche Stätten im Norden Jerusalem," *JBL* 48 (1929) 360-61; M. Delcor, "Hinweise auf das samaritanische Schisma im alten Testament," *ZAW* 74 (1962) 281-91; K. Koch, "Zur Lage von Ṣemarajim. Erkundungen zwischen *bētīn* und *eṭ-ṭaijibe*," *ZDPV* 78 (1962) 19-29; P. Welten, *Geschichte und Geschichtsdarstellung in den Chronikbüchern* (WMANT 42; Neukirchen-Vluyn: Neukirchener, 1973); H. G. M. Williamson, *Israel in the Books of Chronicles* (Cambridge: Cambridge, 1977).

CHRONICLE OF THE REIGN OF ASA, 13:23b (*RSV* 14:1b)–16:14

Structure

Rudolph ("Asa-Geschichte") believes that the chronology of these chapters is badly confused; in particular, 13:2 claims that there were ten years of peace, after which follows the war with the Cushites, 14:8-14 (*RSV* 9-15), which in turn is followed by a festival covenant in Asa's fifteenth year, 15:10. We cannot accept two different reforms (Azariah refers to none, 15:1ff.), hence we must take 15:1-15 as a literary doublet of 14:2-4 (*RSV* 3-5); vv. 15, 16, and 18 are late glosses, modifying 14:3 (*RSV* 4); also 15:3-6 is disarrayed, and the passage should read 2, 3, 5a, 6, 4, 7. Williamson (comm., 255-59) objects to Rudolph's reconstruction. To accept at face value, with Albright, Asa's thirty-sixth year as the date for Asa's war with Baasha, 16:1, would throw the entire synchronistic chronology of the kings of the two realms into confusion (see S. J. De Vries, "Chronology of the Old Testament," *IDBSup*, 161-66; E. R. Thiele, *The Mysterious Numbers of the Hebrew Kings* [rev. ed.; Grand Rapids: Eerdmans, 1965]); its counterpart in 1 Kgs 15:16 gives no date. According to the chronology in Kings, Baasha died already in Asa's twenty-sixth year (1 Kgs 16:6, 8). The best solution, according to Williamson, which we accept, is to assume that the number 36 refers to years since the schism and somehow got substituted for 16, with 15 in 15:19. This allows us to accept Rudolph's view that 14:2-8 (*RSV* 3-9) and 15:1-18 are in fact variant reports of the same reform, which ended, after the battle with Zerah, in the actual fifteenth year of Asa's reign. This view finds support in the fact that the seam that occurs at 15:10, 11 has been created by ChrH's effort to integrate the Zerah account, 14:8ff. (*RSV* 9ff.), with the second reform account (see below on these verses; see also S. J. De Vries, *Yesterday, Today and Tomorrow* [Grand Rapids: Eerdmans, and London: SPCK, 1975] 96-98). This leads to the following chronology:

> Years 1-15: reform and covenant, 14:2-7 and 15:1-18
> Year 15: war with Zerah, 14:8-14, and victory celebration, 15:11
> Year 16: war with Baasha, 16:1
> Year 39: Asa's illness, 16:12
> Year 41: Asa's death.

Taking Asa's sixteenth year as the date for his war with Baasha, we allow at the same time another ten years before the latter's death (Asa, 26), plus a large number of uneventful years (13) before Asa's illness, intended by ChrH to be understood as the fulfillment of Hanani's prediction (contemporaneous with the end of the war), 16:7-9, that "from now on you will have wars." Even though no more wars are reported, and the time before Asa's illness, v. 12, seems remarkably long, this is all supposed to have occurred after the war with Baasha. This leaves the above chronology intact. Even if ChrH himself were responsible for the number 36, there would hardly have been time for Hanani's "wars," which in any event remain unreported.

The reform report of 14:2-6 (*RSV* 3-7) is a paraphrase of 1 Kgs 15:9-14. The reform of 15:8-10, 12-15 may have occurred as described, but this is pretty much in ChrH's own words; vv. 16-18, again, are taken almost verbatim from 1 Kings (15:13-15). As has been suggested, 15:11 is the link between the two reports. It harks back to the Zerah battle, 14:8ff., which had become attached to the first reform report. ChrH himself must have taken the two reforms as one, putting the two under the same date, the fifteenth year of Asa, third month (15:10). His CHRONICLE, then, speaks first of ten years of quiet and reform, 13:23b–14:4. He then built fortified cities for an unspecified period, evidently five years (14:5-7 [*RSV* 6-8]). When Asa was prepared with a strong army, Zerah came up and was defeated (14:7-14 [*RSV* 8-15]). ChrH does not specify the year, but, judging from 15:10-11, it had to be in the fifteenth year, concluding Asa's initial period of rest. 15:1-15 includes the second reform report (which, however, records the same events as in 14:2-4 [*RSV* 3-5]), a prophetic speech, the report of Asa's reform measures, and the festival covenant in Jerusalem. The intent may be that 15:16-18 came afterward. In any event, these deeds of commitment were followed by a short (one-year) or long (twenty-one-year) period of "no more war." Then came the war with Baasha, 16:1-6, followed by Hanani's rebuke, vv. 7-10. Asa's wrath on the prophet seems excessive, raising the question, How long does it take for a king's character to change so much? The infliction of cruelties on other persons "at that time" is ChrH's concluding chronistic note, but it is ambiguous in its interpretation, for it could be looking back over a long period from the standpoint of the illness and death, or forward over a long period of innocence and obedience.

In what follows we present the structure of the constituent subelements within this CHRONICLE, which must be handled as a cunningly conceived EDITORIAL UNIT.

I. Report of fifteen years of piety and
tranquility   13:23b–14:6 (*RSV* 14:1b-7)
  A. Ten years of reform   13:23b–14:4
    1. Introduction: prevailing tranquility   13:23b
    2. Asa's pious deeds   14:1-4a
      a. Introductory summary   1
      b. Offensive cult objects destroyed   2
      c. Enjoinment of right religion   3
        1) Seeking the ancestral God   3a
        2) Keeping the law   3b
      d. Removal of Judahite cult objects   4a
    3. Conclusion: resulting quiet   4b
  B. Five years of defensive construction   5-6
    1. Building fortifications   5

2. Asa's instruction   6a
    a. Exhortation to build defences   6aα
    b. Theological rationale   6aβ
3. The people's compliance   6b

Abijah's DEATH AND BURIAL FORMULA, with Asa's SUCCESSION FORMULA, 13:23a, serve the double purpose of concluding the account of Abijah's reign while also introducing the reign of Asa. There is no clear pericope break, therefore, but we must take 13:23b, "Now in his days [LXX^BA, L explicates 'In the days of Asa'] the land had rest *[šqṭ]* for ten years" as an introductory summary and at the same time as the opening rubric for an inclusio with v. 4, "and the kingdom in his presence *[lĕpānāyw]* rested *[šqṭ].*" The following itemization of Asa's reforms follows the deuteronomistic language of Kings, but we note that 1 Kgs 15:12 is omitted in favor of language borrowed from the description of Hezekiah's and Josiah's reforms; also the statement in v. 2 that the *bāmôt (RSV* "high places") were removed flatly contradicts 1 Kgs 15:14. V. 2 makes another inclusio with v. 4a in its use of the verb *wayyāsar,* "and he removed." Although no duration of time is given in vv. 5-6, the obvious inclusio ending in v. 4b prevents us from making the phrase in v. 5, "for the land had rest" *(kî- šāqĕṭâ hā'āreṣ),* contemporaneous; hence the meaning must be that Asa decided to build forts because, and in the light of the fact that, the land was enjoying this tranquility. ChrH makes the last point emphatic: "He had no war in those years, because Yahweh gave him peace" *(hēnîaḥ yahweh lô),* a hint of the countervailing prediction toward the end of the chronicle (2 Chr 16:9), "From now on you will have wars." In v. 6 Asa encourages the building process, explaining that the land was still theirs because they had sought *(drš)* Yahweh. Because Yahweh has given them peace *(nwḥ,* hiph.), the people build and "prosper" *(ṣlḥ).*

"On that day" in 15:11 emphatically identifies the day of return with spoil (*haššālāl*) from this battle with the third month of Asa's fifteenth year, the same as the festival day on which worshipers had been gathered to Jerusalem, v. 10. This marks, then, the end of the fifteen-year period of peace. 14:7 is a transitional verse; it should not be attached to v. 6, as in *RSV*, because "So they built and prospered" is intended as a concluding summary to the preceding verses. Leaving the subject of fortifications, v. 7 tells us of the army that Asa has trained, and which will soon be engaged in the struggle against Zerah. It consists of large contingents from Judah and Benjamin. The former are "armed with bucklers and spears," i.e., infantrymen, while the latter are armed with target shields and bows and arrows. It is hard to escape the logic of Welten (*Geschichte*, 79-82) in his claim that this was a Hellenistic distinction, and that ChrH's use of it shows that he was living in a time late enough to give him a chance to observe it. In v. 7 emphasis is placed on "Benjamin" by giving it first place in its clause, as contrasted with the second position in its clause for "Judah." All are qualified with the appellation *gibbôrê ḥāyil*, "powerful champions."

That the Zerah incident is not a literary intrusion is guaranteed by Hanani's reference to it in 16:8. Unambiguously, this is to be a defensive battle. Zerah the Cushite (usually translated "Ethiopian," but very possibly the name of a Palestinian ethnic group allied with the Gerarites) has 1,000,000 men over against Asa's 580,000, plus 300 chariots—of which Asa apparently has none, v. 8. At Zerah's approach, Asa marches out and draws up his lines at a certain valley of Zephathah near Mareshah, which is in the Shephelah facing the Philistine plain (cf. Flecker, Ben-Shem). Here there is no address, for Zerah is a pagan. Instead, ChrH places in Asa's mouth a prayer (cf. Kropat, 78; Watson, 6.4, 8.1). It has a confession of the divine incomparability ("There is none like thee to help *bên rab lě'ên kōaḥ*," which has to be taken as an ellipsis meaning, "intervening against the mighty on behalf of him without power"). It is also a cry for help, with a confession of reliance (*hāmôn*: holy-war term meaning "hostile mob"). Then comes a programmatic challenge to the Deity to show that he is God, against whom man cannot prevail. With characteristic brevity, Yahweh's victory is stated; it results in the Cushites' panicky flight and close pursuit as far as Gerar, vv. 11-12aα. Plundering is also the fate of the "cities round about Gerar" and of those who had camels—thus client towns and dependent bedouin (vv. 12b-14). Contrary to the authentic holy-war tradition (→ 2 Chronicles 13), the slaughter of the enemy went with this (v. 12b, "the Cushites fell until none remained alive"; "they smote all the cities. . . . they smote the tents," vv. 12, 14). The transcendental dimension is specifically mentioned in the phrases "for they were broken before Yahweh and his army," v. 12, and "the fear of Yahweh was upon them" (the INTIMIDATION FORMULA), v. 13. This was indeed Yahweh's army and Yahweh's battle.

As has been explained, this fifteen years is the same as those of 14:1-7 (*RSV* 2-8). Rudolph ("Asa-Geschichte") is close to the truth in identifying 15:1ff. as a doublet to 14:2-4 (*RSV* 3-5)—only it is not a literary addition but ChrH's personal account from a private source, identified also by him as equivalent to the reform verses in ch. 14 (Galling, ATD, is forthright in throwing out 15:1ff. as a secondary expansion). Willi (p. 213) describes Azariah's sermon as an illustration of ChrH's "theology of time," though the elucidation of his meaning remains obscure. The use of the verb *yṣ'*, "go out," "approach," which is used of Azariah in 15:1 as well as of Asa and Zerah in 14:8, 9 (*RSV* 9, 10), respectively, is a stylistic element binding the two chapters together (on v. 1, cf. Watson, 3.6, and on vv. 2-7 see von Rad,

"Levitical Sermon," 270-71). As has been mentioned, Rudolph restores the order 2, 3, 5a, 6, 4, 7, but this cannot be accepted because Rudolph's argument lacks the indispensable explanation of how the original text got so disordered. There is the call to attention, and then the aphorism, summarizing all of ChrH's theology:

Yahweh is with you as long as you are with him;
If you seek him, he will be found by you;
But if you forsake him, he will forsake you.

This introduces two inclusios, one between vv. 2 and 4 on seeking and finding, the second between vv. 2 and 10 on Yahweh being "with" them. These aphorisms are a close quotation of Deut 4:29; Jer 29:12-13, and embody much of the deuteronomistic theology. To illustrate the point of his aphorisms, Azariah next introduces a HISTORICAL REVIEW, which cites a certain tradition to the effect that "for a long time" —evidently while Israel was in Egypt—Israel had no true God, no teaching priest, no law (cf. Watson, 7.6; Kropat, 79), v. 3. Then "in their distress" they turned, sought (bqš; cf. drš, v. 2), and were found by him, v. 4. In v. 6 Azariah describes the great disturbances that afflicted the land "in those times," v. 5, caused by the distress that Yahweh brought, v. 6. But Azariah intends this history lesson merely as an example; it is up to his present hearers to heed the exhortation to take courage and work hard, knowing that their work will not go unrewarded, v. 7 (Williamson, comm., 266, sees this as the connecting link back to 14:2-8 [RSV 3-9]). The whole point of Azariah's historical review seems to be that Israel without God can expect nothing but upheaval and distress. Vv. 5-6 seem to regress back to the situation of v. 3. V. 4 is the only positive note, and the fact that the address is allowed to culminate on a negative note can only mean that the sermon as a whole is a warning.

In any event, "take courage" in v. 7 is immediately echoed in the narrative report of v. 8 to the effect that Asa did take courage (ḥzq; cf. Watson, 3.6, 7.8), enough to "put away," v. 8a, "repair," v. 8b, and "gather," v. 9. The "words" that Asa heard were Azariah's sermonic interpretation of the aphorism he quoted in v. 2; the "prophecy" with which they are equated has to be those aphorisms themselves, Azariah's "text." A text needs expostulation and then it needs application—and that is what Asa gives it in vv. 8-9. The people invited to the covenant ceremony are of course Judah and Benjamin, but in addition sojourners from Ephraim, Manasseh, and Simeon—enough to represent "all Israel" in principle.

It is evident that although ChrH has no systematic and coherent chronology, he is fond of using dates (7:9-10; 29:3, 17; 30:13; 35:1, 16-19). In this passage he dates the covenant assembly precisely in the third month (no day is given) of Asa's fifteenth year. This is accordingly the Feast of Weeks (Shebuoth), one of the three great festivals when pilgrims came to the temple, and in late Judaism observed as a special day of covenant renewal. "On that day" in v. 11 refers to the gathering, but because the action specified is the sacrificing of animals taken as spoil, we have a virtual synchronism with the triumphal march of 14:14b (RSV 15b). The act of "entering into a covenant" (wayyābō'û babběrît, v. 12), fervently to seek (drš) Yahweh as the ancestral God, essentially continues the action of v. 10, the gathering. Their covenant was made in so zealous a spirit as to stipulate that anyone, man or woman, young or old, who would not join in it would be executed (yûmāt, form of the death sentence, e.g., Exod 22:18). The references to an oath in vv. 14, 15 seem redundant after the covenant, hence we suspect here a continuation, with v. 11, of the original victory story, for such oath making, shouting, trumpet blowing (v. 14), and rejoicing (v. 15) suits just such a situation. In any event, ChrH has successfully integrated the two narrative strands. "They sought [bqš] him with their whole desire and he was found by them" seems an appropriate inclusio for v. 2, while the phrase "Yahweh gave them peace [wayyānaḥ] round about" corresponds to 14:6 (RSV 7), "He has given us peace [wayyānaḥ] on every side." We note finally that "Judah" in 15:15 corresponds to "Judah" in 14:13 (RSV 14:14); cf. v. 14—another sign that 15:11, 14-15 continues the narrative strand of ch. 14.

Rudolph ("Asa-Geschichte") sees only 15:17 as ChrH's own borrowing from 1 Kgs 15:4, with vv. 16, 18 as late glosses from 1 Kgs 15:13, 15. This hypothesis seems unduly complex, for we see ChrH simply running out of material for his covenant-festival account and turning back to Kings for additional information. Willi (p. 158) believes that ChrH is refurbishing his Joshua typology. In the light of 14:2 (RSV 3), the statement in v. 17 that Asa removed the bāmôt, "high places," would be a contradiction except that ChrH has harmonized by specifying that the nonremoval was in "Israel"—here indicating the northern realm, beyond his control. ChrH puts this in, we understand, because it is in his Kings source. ChrH also copies the Kings statement about Asa's heart being blameless "all his days." Maybe ChrH forgot this claim when he went on to tell in ch. 16 about some very blameworthy deeds of this king (cf. Williamson, Israel, 104). In v. 19 ChrH takes the statement of 1 Kgs 15:16 that there was warfare between Asa and Baasha and gives it a new twist. His emphasis is on the peace that lasted until the war with Baasha. See above (pp. 296-97) for our reasons for regarding the numbers as faulty in 15:19 and 16:1. It does seem a little vapid to state that there was no more war until Asa's fifteenth year—which we have argued to be correct—when he had just completed the great war with Zerah in that same year. This is better than the alternative, anyway—which is to stick with MT's 35/36. Even if ChrH was actually responsible for those dates, his chronology is entirely out of kilter because, as we say again, Baasha died in Asa's twenty-sixth year (1 Kgs 16:8). Therefore "Yahweh gave them rest round about," 15:15, corresponds to "no more war" until Baasha, 15:19. The peace was evidently of brief duration; that it was so short is seen, in the eyes of ChrH, as Asa's own fault (cf. 16:9).

Apart from the suspect synchronism at the beginning, the entire account of 16:1-6 is taken almost verbatim from 1 Kgs 15:16-22. In that passage, no special blame was laid upon Asa, but here he is severely censured because he entered into an alliance with a foreign king, Ben-hadad of Aram. Willi (p. 171) believes that ChrH put this in as an explication of his later severe sickness; Lemke (p. 150) sees it rather as an opportunity to illustrate the theme of retribution. The story of the war with Baasha is quickly told: Baasha's fort at Ramah, actually within traditional Benjaminite territory, threatens Jerusalem; Asa bribes Ben-hadad, who moves his army down into Galilee, forcing Baasha to take his forces off to meet him; this frees Asa to scavenge Ramah and to build his own forts at Geba and Mizpah.

The section on Hanani's prophecy is an inclusio; the formula "at that time" introduces him in v. 7, and concludes in v. 10 the king's cruelties resulting from it. Scholars have noted several close parallels here with the book of Isaiah (cf. Seligmann). Hanani's complaint, "Because you relied on the king of Syria and did not rely on Yahweh your God," v. 7, reminds one of the language of Isa 10:20, "will no more lean upon him that smote them, but will lean upon Yahweh." There are also echoes of Isa 7:7ff.; 1 Sam 13:13; Jer 20:2-3; Zech 4:10 (see Williamson, comm., 274; and von Rad, "Levitical Sermon," 269-70). The announcement of Aram's escape, v. 7b, is to be taken proleptically, i.e., with a view to the cruel deeds that this people were destined to do to the Hebrew kingdom in an age lying in the not distant future, which is to say that Asa should have attacked Aram when he had a chance, or at least not have encouraged it to attack his fellow Israelites. That Asa did not simply trust Yahweh now, having just so recently been rewarded for his trust in the face of Zerah and his hordes (14:8-14 [*RSV* 9-15]), seems incomprehensible and utterly worthy of denunciation, v. 8. Asa cannot hide this, for the eyes of Yahweh run to and fro through all the earth. The condemnation is as with Saul: "You have done foolishly" (*skl*, niph.), v. 9a (cf. 1 Sam 13:13). His punishment is that "from now on you will have wars," v. 9aβ-b. This threat is no doubt intended as the ironic counterpoint to the beginning of the Asa chronicle, 13:23b (*RSV* 14:1b), "In his days the land had rest." Asa evidently takes it so, for he flies into a rage, locking Hanani in prison while doing cruelties to other unnamed persons, v. 10. This is the first time that we have heard of an Israelite king doing violence to a prophet, though the passage reminds us of Micaiah's treatment according to 1 Kgs 22:26 par. 2 Chr 18:26. The correct interpretation is probably not of a personal vendetta; rather, the king imagined superstitiously that by locking up the prophet he could keep his prophecy from having its effect.

In the concluding resumé, vv. 11-14, the source cited is "the book of the kings of Judah and Israel." This is the first time that this source has been cited since 1 Chr 9:1. There is reason to believe that it is as fictitious as the books of various prophets, previously seen. In any event, one has to wonder whether Asa's outrageous treatment of Hanani influenced ChrH to deny him the honor of reference in prophetic writings (see Lemke, 153-54). The item about Asa's sickness in his feet sounds like something that might have been taken out of an archive, but one readily sees that it is overladen with ChrH's biased interpretation. Asa has a severe disease in his feet (cf. Driver, "Lore"). The complaint against Asa is that "he did not seek [*drš*] Yahweh but sought *rōpĕ'îm*." *RSV* translates this "physicians"—and it may indeed be a sin to trust doctors rather than God—but something more serious must be meant. Judging from references to the *rp'm* as chthonic deities in the Ugaritic literature, we may have here an example of the meaning "medium," that is, someone like the witch of Endor (1 Samuel 28) who had access to the underworld.

Not only is the year of Asa's sickness given, but that of his death as well. This is normally no part of the REGNAL RESUMÉ pattern, so it must be seen as a carrying through of ChrH's chronistic approach to this reign. The burial report in v. 14 is very unusual too. The text does not simply say that Asa was buried in the royal tomb, but explains that he was buried in a special tomb, evidently somewhat apart from the others. Mention is also made of a bier overlaid with spices. We cannot go far wrong in suspecting that his diseased body stank so that it was almost unfit for a proper funeral. Perhaps to compensate for this sorrowful end to a sometimes magnificent reign, a great funeral fire (evidence of such fires has recently been recovered by archeologists working in western Jerusalem) was lit in his honor.

Genre

This is the first and last instance in which ChrH contrives the genre CHRONICLE, which is defined as a prose composition consisting of a series of reports, normally in the third person, of selected events arranged and dated in chronological order. The fact that ChrH has used doublets of the reform and altered the date of the war with Baasha does not affect this genre identification. 13:23b–14:6 is a REPORT, with an EXHORTATION in v. 6. V. 7 is a STATEMENT derived from a MUSTER ROLL, with the TALLY (twice) and an APPELLATION, *gibbôrê ḥāyil*, "powerful champions." The account of Zerah's defeat, 14:8-14, is our second example of a QUASI-HOLY-WAR STORY (→ 13:2-18); its structure is: (1) encounter, (2) prayer, (3) triumph, (4) punishing the Cushites, (5) plundering allies. V. 8 has a TALLY. V. 10 is a PRAYER with a DESCRIPTION OF YAHWEH that is also an INCOMPARABILITY STATEMENT ("There is none like thee . . ."), a CRY FOR HELP ("O Yahweh, thou art our God"), and an APPEAL ("Let not man prevail against thee"). V. 13 has the INTIMIDATION FORMULA, "The fear of Yahweh was upon them."

15:1-19 is another REPORT. Vv. 1-7 are a SERMON; to call it "Levitical sermon" with von Rad makes little sense—even though it does show the structure (1) citation of text(s), (2) interpretation, (3) application—because it is put in the mouth of a prophet, and the Levites have little to do with it except in the sense that ChrH, an adherent of the Levitical ideology, composed it. It has the WORD FORMULA and the CALL TO ATTENTION, vv. 1-2a. V. 2b has a triple APHORISM, featuring the ASSISTANCE FORMULA, "Yahweh is with you." Vv. 3-6 have the genre HISTORICAL REVIEW, the rehearsing of salient facts in the past experience of Israel or an individual. This present example purports to review a dark period in Asa's past (departure from Egypt and settlement in the land) which is intended as a type of ChrH's proximate past, the time of return from exile and rebuilding. Azariah's SERMON ends in v. 7 with an EXHORTATION to do Yahweh's work (see De Vries, "Prophetic Address," 25-26, 33). An echo of the ASSISTANCE FORMULA appears in v. 9b. Vv. 10-15 are a REPORT OF RITUAL, which in this instance includes sacrificing and the making of a covenant. Ending in v. 15 with rejoicing, it shows the FESTIVAL SCHEMA. V. 11 is the original EPITOME conclusion to 14:14b (see De Vries, *Yesterday, Today and Tomorrow,* 96-97). The "should be put to death" clause in v. 13 is a death sentence and belongs to the Trial genres. V. 17b is a THEOLOGICAL REVIEW, an editorial statement which reviews, states offenses, and evaluates a king. Normally, but not here, it appears in the introductory part of a REGNAL RESUMÉ.

The narrative of Asa's war with Baasha, with Ben-hadad as an ally, is another BATTLE REPORT. The date in 16:1 is a TRANSITION FORMULA. A one-sided NEGOTIATION is reported in vv. 2-3. Like 12:5, 16:7-10 belongs to the genre REPORT OF A PROPHETIC WORD. It begins with the TRANSITION FORMULA, "at that time." This presents Hanani, who begins his speech with an ANNOUNCEMENT OF JUDGMENT, a statement that some disaster, in this case the escape of the Arameans, who will be Israel's later tormentors, is imminent as Yahweh's punishment for transgression, which in this case was relying on the king of Aram in the place of Yahweh. Thence commences another HISTORICAL REVIEW (→ 15:3-6) with a RHETORICAL QUESTION ("Were not the Cushites . . . ?"), the CONVEYANCE FORMULA ("gave into your hands"), and a DESCRIPTION OF YAHWEH ("The eyes of Yahweh run to and fro throughout the whole earth to show his might . . ."). V. 9b has a REPROACH ("You have done foolishly in this") and a THREAT ("From now on you will have wars"). V. 10, recording Asa's cruelty, is a narrative of response concluding this structure (cf. De Vries, "Prophetic Address," 26-27, 33). Vv. 11-14 constitute the concluding REGNAL RESUMÉ, with the CITATION FORMULA in v. 11 and an expanded DEATH AND BURIAL FORMULA (now a REPORT) in vv. 13-14. V. 12, about Asa's sickness and spiritual apostasy, is an isolated STATEMENT that has influenced the expansion of the DEATH AND BURIAL FORMULA.

Setting

ChrH's rationale for Asa is the following: (1) he gained an astounding victory through trust in Yahweh; (2) a foreign alliance undid all the good that he had done and led him into wickedness; (3) he suffered the most personal form of retribution from God, viz., a gangrenous sickness in his feet.

Asa began his reign as the worthy successor of his father. Besides purifying the religious cult of objectionable intrusions, 14:1-4; 15:8, 16, he carried out a vigorous program for building defensive works and building up a strong army (cf. Welten, *Geschichte*, 15-19). This was an act of great piety, but at the same time the sign that he was under the divine blessing, as was evidenced in the fact that "the land had rest," "he had no war," "Yahweh gave him peace." To keep things so, it was necessary for the people to continue in the work of reform and of building, trusting in the promise "Your work shall be rewarded" (15:7b). This happy condition is put to a severe test at the attack of the monstrous army of Zerah, 14:8-14. The victory is won not by Asa's formidable army of 580,000 (14:7), but in Yahweh's prompt answer to Asa's moving prayer, 14:10, challenging Yahweh to help those who rely on him and prove that he is truly God. Zerah's attack is, indeed, a type of the cosmic menace so vividly portrayed in Ezekiel's "Gog of Magog" (cf. Welten, *Geschichte*, 125-40). A report of the victory celebration, 15:11, is integrated into the report of a Weeks festival that culminates in a covenant and an oath to "seek Yahweh," who had again given them "rest round about" (15:10-15).

For Asa's rule, ChrH had a strong chronological interest. This king's forty-one years of reign could be divided into two distinct periods: (1) fifteen years of rest/peace, interrupted only by the victory over Zerah, which only confirmed and strengthened that rest (15:11). This was the time of Asa's fervent and unmarred piety. Then, in the sixteenth (MT: thirty-sixth) year, Asa forgot to trust Yahweh and turned instead to a foreign power, Aram, which did get Baasha off his back, but at the price of encouraging this people in the policy of attacking the Hebrew kingdoms (16:1-7). The reproach of Hanani proved true, and this introduces the second half of Asa's reign. Yahweh had given Zerah into Asa's hand because he had relied on him, but he had done foolishly, so that from now on he would have wars, 15:9. We do not in fact read about any more wars for Asa, but the calamity of warfare would come in future generations. On Asa individually, who not only transgressed in summoning the Arameans, but also confined the seer and inflicted cruelty on some others, v. 10, the penalty was a disgusting, debilitating disease in his feet. Coming in the thirty-ninth year of his reign, this suited ChrH's chronology because it meant that Asa was never able to thwart Yahweh's purpose. Meanwhile, he had grown so impious that he no longer sought Yahweh, but, perhaps realizing that Yahweh was punishing him for his unrepented wrongdoing, he sought help from mediums (see the explanation in "Structure"). History was destined to repeat itself. The day would come when Judah would be attacked by Israel and Aram together (ch. 28) and the Judahite king then, Ahaz, would ally himself with Assyria, vv. 10-23, but only to the ultimate ruin of his own kingdom.

Intention

As has been mentioned, the Cushites may not be Ethiopians. According to Ben-Shem, they were an Edomite tribe living near Ma'an in the region of Petra, the ally

Gerar being no other than Jerar near Wadi Musa. This explains why Asa's plundering after the victory consisted mainly of sheep and camels, 14:14. Thus there is a likely historical basis for the story of this raid. Nevertheless, ChrH presents the attacking army as a world power, with the Cushites as actual Ethiopians having *hallûbîm,* "the Libyans," 16:8, as allies. As has been suggested, the typology of a Gog world power menacing God's people in Jerusalem must have been in ChrH's mind (Welten, *Geschichte,* 129-40). He surely intended it to typify still other world powers, viz., those that actually threatened the postexilic Jews. To them the prayer of Asa would have special poignancy: "O Yahweh, there is none like thee in treating the mighty like the weak. Help us, O Yahweh, for we rely on thee. . . . O Yahweh, thou art our God, let no man prevail against us," 14:10.

ChrH undoubtedly intends Azariah's sermon to be given a contemporary interpretation. 15:3-6 actually has little relevance for Asa's time. Following von Rad's categories, we identify vv. 3-4 as *doctrina,* vv. 5-6 as *interpretatio,* and v. 7 as *applicatio.* Azariah is speaking of a "long time" without God, priest, or law (cf. Hos 3:4), creating a situation of distress out of which they turned to Yahweh and were found by him. This seems enigmatic, but can refer only to the Egyptian bondage and wilderness wandering. V. 5, "in those times," introduces the interpretation, to the effect that during this period of ignorance and willfulness, they were troubled with every sort of distress and great disturbances. This is a retrospect, which is followed in v. 7 by an exhortation: "Take courage; let not your hands be weak, for your work shall be rewarded." The historical gap between the "finding of Yahweh" in the giving of the law and now, the reign of Asa, would seem to demand some details from the previous history of Israel, suggesting a recent apostasy or slackening of spirit, for why otherwise must the people be exhorted so strongly? The answer is that ChrH is placing the conditions of his own time back into the time of Asa. Seen from his perspective, the references to being without God or a teaching priest or the law, plus the parallel condition of being in distress, being disturbed with great disturbances along with nations and cities that were shattered by fighting against one another, all under the wrath of God, point to the imperial conquests leading up to, and flowing out of, the Babylonian exile. Now one can see how the *interpretatio* fits the *doctrina.* The "no peace," "the great disturbing of all the inhabitants of the lands," the being broken in pieces, the being troubled by God "in every sort of distress," occurs at the same time as when they were without God, priest, or law—during the nation's downfall and exile. This makes sense of the *applicatio,* v. 7. The new Israel was to take courage, not to let its hands be weak, for now more than ever, the promise "your work shall be rewarded" is destined to come true.

The same is true of Hanani's denunciation, 16:1-9. Now Israel would not be tempted to rely on Syria (Aram), for it had already experienced the Assyrians. Israel would not face Ethiopians and Libyans, but there were even more formidable foes to face. On whom would it now rely? The eyes of Yahweh still run to and fro throughout the whole earth (Zech 4:10) "to show his might in behalf of those whose heart is blameless toward him."

The lesson of Asa is clear: when formidable enemies attack God's people, their trust in Yahweh will assure them the victory. But when they use force and intrigue on their own initiative, ignoring their special calling as his people, they bring ineluctable ruin on themselves and their posterity.

Bibliography

I. Ben-Shem, "The War of Zerah the Cushite," in *Bible and Jewish History (Fest.* J. Liver; Tel-Aviv: Tel-Aviv University, 1971) 51-56; G. R. Driver, "Ancient Lore and Modern Knowledge," in *Fest.* A. Dupont-Sommer (Paris: 1971) 283-84; E. Flecker, "The Valley at Mareshah," *PEFQS* (1886) 50-52, 148-51; G. von Rad, "The Levitical Sermon in I and II Chronicles," in *The Problem of the Hexateuch and Other Essays* (tr. E. W. Trueman Dicken; New York: McGraw-Hill, 1966) 267-80; W. Rudolph, "Der Aufbau der Asa-Geschichte," *VT* 2 (1952) 367-71; I. L. Seeligmann, "Die Auffassung von der Prophetie in der deuteronomistischen und chronistischen Geschichtsschreibung," in *Congres Volume: Göttingen 1977* (VTSup 29; Leiden: Brill, 1978) 254-84; M. Weinfeld, "Pentecost as a Festival of the Giving of the Law," *Imm* 8 (1978) 11.

ACCOUNT OF THE REIGN OF JEHOSHAPHAT, 17:1–20:37

Text

A thorough inner-Septuagintal and inter-versional analysis of 2 Chronicles 18 par. 1 Kings 22 has been published in S. J. De Vries, *Prophet Against Prophet* (Grand Rapids: Eerdmans, 1978) 11-24.

Structure

I. Report of Jehoshaphat's auspicious beginning	17:1-19
II. Prophetic battle story: Jehoshaphat accompanies Ahab	18:1–19:3
III. Report of organizing the land for justice	19:4-11
IV. Quasi-holy-war story: victory in the desert	20:1-30
V. Final notations	20:31-37

This ACCOUNT of the reign of Jehoshaphat ("Yahweh judges") is arranged chiastically with relation to the CHRONICLE of Asa. There everything began wrong, but by purging idolatry and building fortifications, Asa was in a state of triumphant faith when his land was attacked by Zerah and his powerful army. But just when the land was secure in peace, Asa spoiled it by joining a foreign king, Ben-hadad, in a venture that had immediate benefits for himself but threatened continual wars in the future. Here in the Jehoshaphat account Jehoshaphat first joins in another foreign alliance (ch. 18), only this time the Syrian is the foe while the northern Israelite, Ahab, is the ally. The Syrians win again, while the Israelite allies are defeated. This means death for Ahab and a very severe rebuke for Jehoshaphat (19:1-3), threatening that "wrath has gone out against you from Yahweh." Even though Jehoshaphat personally was not stricken as Asa was, the sequel will tell that the threatened wrath does strike his sons. Perhaps the attack of the Moabites, Ammonites, and Meunites in ch. 20 is intended as divine punishment, but in this instance Jehoshaphat shows that his faith is as strong as Asa's had been against Zerah, and Yahweh rewards him with a magnificent victory. Thus the design for the two contrasting reigns is:

Asa: 1. piety; 2. trust brings victory over foreign invader; 3. war with foreign ally brings penalty

Jehoshaphat: 1. piety; 2. war with foreign ally brings wrath; 3. piety; 4. trust brings victory over foreign invader.

Part I, "Jehoshaphat's auspicious beginning," has no introductory formula, but 17:1, "Jehoshaphat his son reigned in his stead," does make an inclusio with 20:31, "and Jehoshaphat reigned over Judah." 17:5b, "he had great riches and honor," finds a link through repetition in 18:1a, "Now Jehoshaphat had great riches and honor." The temporal link between ch. 17 and ch. 18 is 18:2, "after some years." The *qeṣep*, "wrath," of 19:2 deliberately echoes 2 Kgs 3:27, where Israel (including Jehoshaphat) is condemned for attacking Moab. In substituting the completely different story of 2 Chronicles 20, ChrH makes Moab an aggressor against Jehoshaphat and suggests that wrath has been turned to joy and victory. Part III, 19:4-11, is thematically central with its development of the concept of appointing administrators of justice, of dwelling in Jerusalem, going out over the countryside, and returning to Jerusalem again. "After this" in 20:1 hardly pinpoints the great battle against the eastern alliance. It is clearly climactic, and leads to a conclusion that would suit the narrative of Asa's early reign, "So the realm of Jehoshaphat was quiet *[wattišqōṭ]*, for God gave him rest *[wayyānaḥ]* round about" (20:30). ChrH intends this account to be the substitute for 2 Kings 3. In the final notations, the order is fixed by 1 Kgs 22:41-50. In the REGNAL RESUMÉ, the DEATH AND BURIAL and SUCCESSION FORMULAS have been shifted to ch. 21 because of the intrusive appendix, 20:35-37, likewise introduced by the innocuous "after this"; the word *pāraṣ*, "break out" (20:37), is reminiscent of 1 Chr 13:11 where this uncommon word is also used.

I. REPORT OF JEHOSHAPHAT'S AUSPICIOUS BEGINNING, 17:1-19

Structure

A. Religious-political strength	1-6
1. Measures against Israel	1-2
a. Expanded succession formula	1
b. Maintained defense forces	2a
c. Appointed prefects	2b
2. Evidence of divine approval	3-5
a. Assistance formula	3a
b. Jehoshaphat's behavior	3b-4
1) His walk	3b
2) His seeking of Yahweh	4a
3) His obedience to the law	4b
c. Statement about security, riches, and honor	5
3. Statement about courage for purging Judah's cult	6
B. Year three: statement about program of religious instruction (transition formula)	7-9
1. Teachers	7-8

The SUCCESSION FORMULA for Jehoshaphat has been displaced from its normal place in the REGNAL RESUMÉ for Asa, just as the latter's was in 13:23 (*RSV* 14:1). It is followed by a statement that he strengthened himself (*ḥzq*, hith.) against Israel, which here must surely mean the northern realm (cf. Williamson, *Israel*, 104-5), with a view to the events of ch. 16. Inasmuch as Zerah had apparently done no damage to the fortress cities constructed by Rehoboam, Jehoshaphat could now strengthen their garrisons while appointing prefects (v. 2, *něsîbîm; RSV:* "garrisons") both for "the land of Judah," i.e., the tribal territory of Judah and Benjamin together, and for "the cities of Ephraim which Asa his father had taken." "The land of Ephraim" stands for the entire north, but it is of Abijah, 13:19, not of Asa, that such successes are recorded (ChrH may have been confused, thinking of 16:7, which in fact speaks about cities in traditional Benjaminite territory).

Next comes a very loose paraphrase of 1 Kgs 22:41-44. It is with high praise that ChrH speaks of Jehoshaphat in vv. 3-6. We note two distinct inclusios. V. 6, "the ways of Yahweh," is set over against v. 3, "the earlier ways of his father" (this must mean Asa; "David" is in the text, but ChrH does not distinguish between David's earlier and later morality), which were good, and (negatively) "the ways of Israel"—again referring just to the northern realm. The second inclusio is chiastically arranged (vv. 3-4):

a   He walked *[hlk]* in the earlier ways (etc.)
  b   He did not seek *[drš]* the Baals
  b'   But sought the God of his father
a'   And walked in his commandments

The normally narrative form, *wayĕhî*, introduces statements of fact at v. 3a (Yahweh with [him]) and v. 5b (he had great riches and honor). The narrative verbs, *wayyāken*, "established," and *wayyittĕnû*, "brought," in v. 5a do form a narrative sequence. The notice that Jehoshaphat removed the high places and the Asherim might seem superfluous after a similar notice for Asa in 14:2 (*RSV* 3), yet 20:33 par. 1 Kgs 22:4 denies that these objectionable cult objects were, in fact, removed. (This shows that ChrH does not always try to emend everything objectionable in his sources, but often copies what he sees.)

The list of teachers, vv. 7-8, is thought by some scholars to be of early origin. Five *śārîm*, "officials," are named, then nine Levites and two priests. We can be quite certain that the last two groups, named in vv. 8aβ + b, constitute a secondary intrusion because the *śārîm* are each named with ChrH's characteristic *lĕ* determinative, which is missing in the lists for the Levites and priests. Also, between the instruction of v. 7, "to teach in the cities of Judah," and the narrative conclusion, "and they taught among the people," v. 9b, the clause "and they taught in Judah" in v. 9aα seems superfluous. Thus vv. 8aβ-9aα should be left out of the original text, which would then read, "In the third year of his reign he sent his princes . . . to teach in the cities of Judah, and with them were the Levites, and with them was the book of Yahweh's law, and they went about to all the cities of Judah and taught among the people." This unit has the inclusio "among (all) the cities of Judah," vv. 7, 9. The reference to the "third year" can only be explained from *lĕqēs·šānîm*, "at the end of some years," which ChrH himself substitutes in 18:2 for *šālōš šānîm*, "three years," in 1 Kgs 22:1. ChrH evidently wants to depict Jehoshaphat as a paragon of piety, as well as mighty in warfare (vv. 10-19) in prospect of that king's apostate behavior as it would be recounted in ch. 18.

There is no chronology for the buildup of Jehoshaphat's military forces, but his willingness to join in Ahab's campaign, ch. 18, suggests that it occurs just prior to it. That Jehoshaphat may be free for an aggressive expedition, it is necessary that there be "no war against Jehoshaphat," v. 10. The fear of him is so great that Philistines and Arabs bring both presents and tribute. Meanwhile, Jehoshaphat built fortresses and store cities, and garrisoned them with *'anšê milḥāmâ*, professional soldiers, vv. 12-13. ChrH added to this the militia, of whom there is a MUSTER ROLL in vv. 14-18. Ordinarily, these citizen-soldiers were summoned up only in time of war, but v. 19 reports that they were in the service of the king *('ēlleh hamĕšārĕtîm 'et-hammelek)*, meaning that they had been called up to full-time duty (this is a better interpretation than that ChrH was confused and did not know the difference). It is expressly stated that these were beside the defenders of the fortresses, i.e., the regular garrisons of professional soldiers. Only the musters of Judah and Benjamin are given, and that according to the names of the respective colonels in charge (there is no agreement with the MUSTER ROLLS of 1 Chronicles 7–8). Tallies are given, with the branch of service in the case of Benjamin, plus the appellation *gibbôrê ḥayil,* "powerful champions" (v. 14).

Genre

The main genre is REPORT. The SUCCESSION FORMULA (from ch. 16) is in v. 1. V. 3a, "Yahweh was with Jehoshaphat," is the ASSISTANCE FORMULA. Vv. 5-6 belong to the genre STATEMENT, as do vv. 7-9 and vv. 10-19. "In the third year of his reign," v. 7, is a TRANSITION FORMULA whose bearing remains rather obscure, except by speculation. The NAME LIST occurs in vv. 7-8. The INTIMIDATION FORMULA is in v. 10. Vv. 14-19 constitute a MUSTER ROLL with a statement of deployment. In this kind of material we expect the TALLY (vv. 11a, 11b, 14b, 15, 16, 17, 18); also the APPELLATION (vv. 13, 14b, 16, 17) and the RANKING FORMULA (vv. 14b, 15, 16).

Setting and Intention

There is less said in this pericope about bringing rest and peace to the land than about seeking Yahweh and keeping his commandments. Jehoshaphat is not content with his personal piety, but sends *śārîm,* officials, with the aid of Levites, to teach Yahweh's law in every city throughout Judah. This teaching function of the Levites does not surprise us after having read Neh 8:8-18, but we are interested to read that Yahweh's law is comprised in a book which can be taught and learned. Yet such teaching is not carried on by Levites alone; it is primarily a task for the secular officials whose names appear on the NAME LIST, v. 7. Whether or not there is historical fact behind this notice, we must agree that it rests on a very old tradition; otherwise, ChrH would not be giving so spiritual a task to laymen. Strangely, this notice pertains only to people belonging to the tribe of Judah, apparently leaving out Benjamin. Perhaps the same teaching of the law was brought to them, and even to proselytes from northern Israel, but no record of the fact survives.

On the vigorous building program and the enlargement of the armed forces, see Welten (*Geschichte,* 19-24, 82-87). He is probably right in seeing in the fusing of the militia with the professional army an unhistorical element, but one that might have been put into practice in the late postexilic period. At this time the province of Yehud probably was allowed no standing army, making the ancient ideology of a tribal militia, to be called up in time of emergency, an attractive concept. After all, it represented the ideal tribal union, as in 1 Chronicles 2–8, and retained its reality in principle even when kings and armies had disappeared from the scene.

Bibliography

P. Joüon, "Notes philologiques sur le texte hébreu de 2 Chron 17, 17," *Bib* 13 (1932) 87.

II. PROPHETIC BATTLE STORY: JEHOSHAPHAT ACCOMPANIES AHAB, 18:1–19:3

Structure

A. Proposal to relieve Ramoth-gilead	18:1-8
1. Occasion	1-2
a. Jehoshaphat's grandeur	1a
b. Marriage alliance with the Omrides	1b-2aα
1) New relationship	1b
2) Visit to Samaria	2aα
c. Hospitality leads to incitement	2aβ-b
2. Search for revelation	3-8
a. Alliance compacted	3
1) Ahab's request	3a
2) Jehoshaphat's acquiescence	3b
b. Revelation requested	4-8
1) Jehoshaphat's demand	4
2) Report of an oracular inquiry from four hundred prophets	5
a) Request for divine approval	5a
b) Oracle (conveyance formula)	5b
3) Jehoshaphat demands confirmation	6-8
a) Need for further inquiry	6
b) Hated Micaiah identified	7a
c) Micaiah summoned	7b-8
(1) Jehoshaphat's remonstrance	7b
(2) Order to the officer	8
B. Micaiah's revelation	9-27
1. Inducement to conformity	9-13
a. The revelatory situation	9
1) August presence of two kings	9a
2) All the prophets prophesying	9b
b. Advice to attack	10-11
1) Zedekiah's symbolic act (messenger formula)	10
2) Unanimous support	11
c. Counsel to Micaiah	12-13
1) The messenger's admonition	12
2) Micaiah avows independence	13
2. Report of an oracular inquiry from Micaiah	14-15
a. The king's inquiry	14a
b. Oracle (conveyance formula)	14b
c. The king's reproach	15
3. Two unfavorable oracles	16-22
a. Vision report I	16
1) Sheep without a shepherd	16a
2) Yahweh's interpretation	16b

In the four major scenes of this story, a descriptive exposition stands at the beginning, followed by alternating narration and discourse. We shall show this pattern with the following chart:

Exposition	Narrative	Discourse
18:1-2		
	3aα	3aβ
		3b
	4a	4b
	5aα	5aβ-b
	6aα	6aβ-b
	7aα, bβ	7aβ-bα
	8a-bα	8bβ
18:9		
	10a	10b
	11a	11b
	12aα	12aβ-b
	13a	13b
	14aα	14aβ-b
	15aα	15aβ-16
	17a	17b-18a
18:18b		
		19-22
	23a	23b
	24aα	24aβ
	25aα	25aβ-26
	27aα	27aβ-b
18:28		
	29aα-b	29aβ
	30aα	30aβ-b
	$31a\alpha^1$-βb	$31a\alpha^2$
	32	
	33a	33b
	34	
19:1		
	2aα	2aβb-3

The only exposition not at the beginning of a major section is 18:18b, which is the introduction to Micaiah's second vision, a description of the heavenly court. It stands in thematic contrast to the exposition of v. 9, a description of the court at Samaria. A scrutiny of the above chart will disclose just how much discourse dominates the narrative. Not only is there more of it; it regularly follows the narrative scenes, very often continuing at length, as in 18:14-18a, where Micaiah delivers a favorable oracle, is rebuked, delivers his first vision (interpreted by the king), and prepares to deliver his second vision oracle; also in vv. 19-22, the second vision oracle; vv. 24-27, where Micaiah is rebuked and jailed; and finally in 19:2-3, where the prophet Jehu ben Hanani delivers his rebuke to Jehoshaphat. It is safe to infer that this profuse discourse carries the story's meaning.

Following up the elements of introductory exposition, the narrative elements further the action to which these sections of discourse relate. Scene I is posited on a questionable proposal made by Ahab to Jehoshaphat, leading to the identification of the one prophet who may be trusted. Scene II is the most paradoxical; in the form of retrospect, it more particularly describes the two kings surrounded by their enthusiastic well-sayers among the prophets, then of Micaiah vacillating between giving a favorable oracle and giving an evil vision, clarifying the latter by a vision of the heavenly court, and ending up the object of scorn by fellow prophets and civilian officials alike. This is the last we hear of Micaiah. Scene III describes the battle at Ramoth-gilead, leading to the death of the king of Israel; it is here that the narrative element (quite naturally) predominates. Scene IV narrates Jehoshaphat's safe return, followed by Jehu's stern rebuke. There can be no doubt in our mind that this prophetic rebuke expresses ChrH's final and most decisive interpretation on the whole story.

18:1, "Now Jehoshaphat had great riches and honor," is a deliberate echo of 17:5, "and he had great riches and honor." It is in this condition that he made a marriage alliance (*ḥtn*, hith.) with Ahab. As with Rehoboam (12:1), prosperity brought pride and self-will. We had been told that Jehoshaphat "did not seek the Baals" (17:3), but by allowing one of his sons to marry a daughter of the notorious Baalist Ahab, Jehoshaphat was opening the door to future apostasy in his dynasty. The marriage also meant the end of hostilities between south and north as the two realms united to resist Aram (Syria), who was now foe to them both.

We are to assume that "after some years" (*lĕqēṣ šānîm*, 18:2) follows "the third year" mentioned in 17:7. It may be that 18:1b is a resumptive introduction, and that we are therefore to interpret the great feasting of v. 2 as part of a wedding celebration. This supplies a motivation that is wanting in Kings and at the same time introduces a link in the chain of tragic events falling under the SCHEMA OF DYNASTIC ENDANGERMENT. Under these circumstances, Jehoshaphat allows Ahab to induce him to ally his forces with him in an attempt to capture Ramoth-gilead. These expository verses (18:1-3) constitute the introduction to ChrH's grand inclusio ending with 19:2, where Jehu demands, "Should you help the wicked and love those who hate Yahweh?" That Jehoshaphat has his "people," i.e., troops, with him is a flaw in the story, for this would have been more than a light bodyguard that he brought with him to the wedding celebration; in other words, he came prepared for war, and Ahab had only to ask him. The reluctance that is missing at the first request seems to disappear, however, as Jehoshaphat requests prophetic confirmation, and then, in the face of suspicious unanimity, goads "the king of Israel" (true to Kings, he is never again called "Ahab" until v. 19) into summoning the prophet who always speaks ill of him, Micaiah.

Verse 9 brings the scene away from a banqueting hall to the threshing floor at the gate of Samaria. The prophets who had come to them in the palace are there too. This looks like a retrospect, but it is, in fact, another serious flaw in the story. At any rate, it has the effect of delaying the action, heightening the theme of trying to seduce the one prophet who speaks ill, who, after vacillating, does give him his first vision report, v. 16, identified by the king as genuine because it bodes him ill, v. 17. This vision report contains Yahweh's own words of interpretation, containing a threat for the "shepherd/master," urging the "sheep" to "return home in peace" (*bĕšālôm*). As is seen in vv. 26-27, which interprets this phrase with reference to the king of Israel, and in 19:1, which applies them to Jehoshaphat, this becomes the leading thematic phrase for the entire story.

Micaiah then gives his second vision report, vv. 18-22, which concludes with Micaiah's interpretative announcement, "Yahweh has spoken evil concerning you"; this confirms the initial description, that Micaiah speaks only evil of the king of Israel, v. 7. This does not, however, deter the Israelite king. Having locked Micaiah in jail (i.e., to restrain the fulfillment of his evil prophecy, much as with Asa and Hanani in 16:10), the two armies march out to meet Aram. The only remaining suspense element is whether Jehoshaphat will be killed and the king of Israel spared through the subterfuge of disguise. The Aramean charioteers surround the former, but Yahweh helps him and draws his attackers away, v. 31a. The king of Israel is fatally struck, and presumably the battle is lost (ChrH omits the words that tell of the dispersal of Israel's troops, 1 Kgs 22:36-38). As 19:1 states, Jehoshaphat returns home in peace *(bĕšālôm)*, but not to escape prophetic denunciation (note that Jehu "goes out" *[yṣ']* to meet him; cf. 15:1). Here is an inclusio: Micaiah had been rebuked and locked up, but here was another prophet who could announce evil. There is a concession of "some good," but this scarcely mitigates the dread of the threat, *ûbāzō't 'āleykā qeṣep millipnê yahweh,* "But for this, upon you wrath from the presence of Yahweh."

Genre

The main genre of this pericope is PROPHETIC BATTLE STORY, defined as a type of historical story focusing on a military encounter, in which one or more prophets assume important dramatic roles and enunciate interpretative perspectives important to the author (→ PROPHETIC BATTLE STORY). A REPORT OF AN ORACULAR INQUIRY, asking, "Shall we go up to Ramoth-gilead?" is present in vv. 5 and 14-15. The ORACLE, with the CONVEYANCE FORMULA, "Go up, for God will give it into the hand of the king," is seen with slight variations in vv. 5, 11, and 14. V. 8 has an ORDER, "Bring quickly Micaiah. . . ." V. 10 is an interpreted SYMBOLIC ACT (the horns) with the MESSENGER FORMULA. V. 12, the words of the messenger to Micaiah, is an ADMONITION because he is being urged to do something he does not want to do. V. 15 is a REPROACH for disobeying the king's command. Both v. 16 and vv. 18-21 belong to the "dramatic word" variety of the VISION REPORT, defined as a type of report which recounts what a prophet or seer perceives in his inner consciousness. V. 18a has the CALL TO ATTENTION. Yahweh's word in v. 21b, "Go forth and do so," is an ORDER. V. 22 is Micaiah's interpretation of his vision, cast in the form of an ANNOUNCEMENT OF JUDGMENT. This may be an element of a (→) prophetic judgment speech, but it often occurs separately, as here. Its essence is a statement that disaster is imminent as Yahweh's punishment for transgression. Zedekiah's blow and RHETORICAL QUESTION of v. 23 constitute a REBUKE, a sharper form of REPROACH. V. 25 has an ORDER and v. 26 has instructions (→ INSTRUCTION). Micaiah's repartee in v. 27b (though not in the original Kings text) is an APPEAL FOR RETRIBUTION ("Hear, all you peoples!"). Actually belonging with the (→) trial genres, this special type of APPEAL has full juridical force, in which the appellant—here Micaiah —calls for justice and retribution when he has been unjustly punished. Vv. 28-34 constitute a BATTLE REPORT, the climax of the original story. 19:1-3 belongs to the genre REPORT OF A PROPHETIC WORD. Jehu's PROPHETIC SPEECH includes the ACCUSATORY QUESTION ("Should you help the wicked and love those who hate Yahweh?"). Especially common in ChrH, this is a brief RHETORICAL QUESTION, substituting in prophecies of punishment for the (→) accusation, or in other words of prophetic reprimand for an accusation together with the addressee's presumptive reply, taken to be affirmative when the form is "Have you not . . .?" or an unacceptable excuse when the form is "Why do you . . .?" or "Should you . . .?" (→ ACCUSATORY QUESTION). On the PROPHETIC BATTLE STORY see De Vries, "Prophetic Address," 21-22, 32; on the REPORT OF A PROPHETIC WORD see ibid., 22, 32.

Setting and Intention

There is a long tradition history behind this PROPHETIC BATTLE STORY. There was once a historical Micaiah who spoke a discouraging oracle regarding a campaign of the two Hebrew realms against the Arameans at Ramoth-gilead. The factual report of that battle and its aftermath is presently contained in 2 Kings 9–10. Around 800 B.C. an imaginative narrative was constructed around this event. The "king of Israel" was not named, but was probably Joram ben Ahab, who in our present narrative dies from a stray Syrian arrow rather than from the arrow of Jehu. In *Prophet Against Prophet*, 25-51, I have shown that this narrative must be disentangled from another Micaiah story that was composed ca. 700 B.C., then very soon combined with it to make up our present 1 Kings 22. The redactor who combined these two accounts has added material of his own to smooth over some difficult gaps. The structure of the earlier narrative was: I. The need for supporting revelation, vv. 2b-9; II. Conflict between a favoring and an evil oracle, vv. 15a-29a; III. Resolution: the evil oracle fulfilled, vv. 29-38. The structure of the later narrative is: I. The revelatory situation in Samaria, vv. 10-12; II. The revelatory situation in heaven, vv. 14, 19-23; III. Resolution: diatribe between Zedekiah and Micaiah, vv. 24-25. In connection with a thorough analysis of the many subgenres of PROPHETIC LEGEND, I was able to assign the earlier Micaiah narrative, with 2 Kgs 8:7-15, to what I called "superseding oracle narrative," in which a superseding oracle to a king is fulfilled in preference to one that it follows (pp. 52-92). The second Micaiah narrative I assigned to a subgenre titled "word-controversy narrative." Its only parallel is the Rabshakeh versus Hezekiah narrative in 2 Kings 18–19, and both narratives belong to the period of Hezekiah's rule.

The early Micaiah narrative deals with the question, Can an evil oracle supersede a favorable one? Can human subterfuge overcome it? The answer is that Yahweh is sovereign and free, and his true prophets respond accordingly. The later Micaiah narrative is concerned with the question of identity: Who speaks Yahweh's true word? The answer is that even when the court prophets and king-pleasers speak in Yahweh's name, Yahweh's spirit in them is a lying spirit, seducing their kings to evil even when their word is good. The redactor who put these two stories together did an admirable job, yet the problem of erratic sequencing and aimless duplication remains. What appears as the work of a redactor in Kings must not be scrutinized too closely for the function of each detail; e.g., why the two kings sit enthroned outside Samaria's gate (v. 9) when they have been banqueting within (vv. 2ff.). This is even more true with regard to ChrH, who can be credited for his fairly close reduplication of the Kings text, but certainly not for discerning the rich tradition history of his text.

There are just three places where the intent of ChrH in using this material can be clearly seen. After all, this is the only story where ChrH actually copies a lengthy text from Kings having to do with a northern king. We may be certain that ChrH does not do this out of interest in Ahab. He dutifully records Ahab's death, but we notice that he leaves out the bloody details of 1 Kgs 22:35-38. One of the places where ChrH shows his hand is in v. 31, where we read that Yahweh helped Jehoshaphat when he cried out, drawing the Syrian charioteers away from him. In other words, Jehoshaphat is saved, not because the Syrians recognized that he was not Ahab, but because God intervened. One would have to assume that Jehoshaphat would otherwise have suffered the same fate as Ahab. All the way through this story Jehoshaphat has placed himself on the level of solidarity with Ahab; this has been his folly. Jehoshaphat's role has not been entirely passive. He offered his army; he insisted on a confirmatory oracle; he accompanied Ahab to battle. His role has mainly been to further the action, raising the essential issue of true revelation. Strange to say, Jehoshaphat makes no protest at the way God's true prophet is badgered; he goes with Ahab in spite of Micaiah's warning. He acts just as if the confirming oracle he had insisted upon does not really matter.

The other two places where ChrH interferes with the Kings text are at the beginning and at the end. Contrary to Kings, we are told that Jehoshaphat had riches and honor, that he made a marriage alliance with Ahab, that he showed his enjoyment of Ahab's hospitality so much that he allowed himself to be "induced" to join his hazardous expedition. All of this is different from Kings, where we are simply told that he "went down" to the king of Israel for no stated reason. In ChrH Jehoshaphat seems more worldly, more self-interested. In 19:1-3 we are told that Jehoshaphat came home "in peace"—but that was because Yahweh had helped him (18:31). Jehoshaphat had shown no inclination to trust Micaiah, the northern prophet, but now he is confronted with one of his own. We are not told whether he yielded to Jehu ben Hanani, but it does not matter, because Yahweh would see to it that his word through this prophet came true. He is roundly condemned in the ACCUSATORY QUESTION, "Should you help the wicked and love those who hate Yahweh?" By his mistreatment of Micaiah, Ahab had proven this description true with regard to himself. Jehoshaphat had "helped" him—to no avail—and by giving his son in marriage to a member of the family of Ahab he had proven that he did indeed "love" those who hated Yahweh.

"Because of this, wrath hath gone out against you from Yahweh," 19:2b. This can only be a hint that Jehoshaphat's pride and vainglory had made him family to the Omrides and turned him into a trusted ally. But would the love he had shown Ahab be reciprocated? Would this alliance of family and of armed forces prove beneficial? This is the burning question raised in the SCHEMA OF DYNASTIC ENDANGERMENT. Jehoshaphat, however pious he may have been, had brought "wrath." Much blood would be shed before its course had been run.

Bibliography

S. J. De Vries, *1 Kings* (Word Biblical Commentary 12; Waco, TX: Word, 1985) 259-72; idem, *Prophet Against Prophet: The Role of the Micaiah Narrative in the Development of Early Prophetic Tradition* (Grand Rapids: Eerdmans, 1978); E. Würthwein, "Zur Komposition von I Reg 22, 1-38," in *Das ferne und das nahe Wort (Fest. L. Rost; ed. F. Maass; Berlin: Töpelmann, 1967) 245-54.

III. REPORT OF ORGANIZING THE LAND FOR JUSTICE, 19:4-11

Structure

Not only does Jehu mitigate the severity of his judgment by stating that "some good is found in you" and "(you) have set your heart to seek God," 19:3, but v. 4 is prepared as an introduction to a report of Jehoshaphat's counteracting goodness. "Jehoshaphat dwelt [yšb] in Jerusalem" would be a matter of fact, for that is where his palace and family were; ChrH therefore must mean "stayed," i.e., he went on no more dubious expeditions. This seems to contradict v. 4b, which states that he went out (yṣ') among all the people (Beersheba to Ephraim mark his outer boundaries and thereby include everyone within those boundaries) to bring them back (šwb, hiph.) to Yahweh the ancestral God. Galling (ATD) considers this verse a post-ChrH addition, but without it v. 5 would have no nominal antecedent. We simply have to interpret v. 4b by vv. 5-11, so that the appointing of the judges is what is meant by bringing back the people (cf. 7:14). The verb yṣ' echoes v. 2 (Jehu's going out to berate the king) and suggests that Jehoshaphat's going out is intended to correct and nullify it. Recognizing ChrH's fondness for puns, we should also recognize that yšb, "dwell," is balanced, though not nullified, by šwb, "bring back."

The subject of appointing judges occupies the second part of this pericope,

vv. 5-11, and one can readily see that it serves as a punning exposition based on the name Jehoshaphat ("Yahweh judges"). We can suppose that it has traditio-historical priority to the Ramoth-gilead story, and it certainly shows no recollection of that material. In order to fulfill the meaning of his name, Jehoshaphat does two things, and these subdivide the section. In v. 5 we read *wayya'ămēd šōpĕṭîm*, "and he appointed judges." In v. 8 we read *he'ĕmîd . . . lĕmišpaṭ yahweh wĕlārîb*, "he appointed . . . for Yahweh's judgment and for litigation." The difference between these two acts of appointing is as follows: (1) with respect to place: the first group has jurisdiction in "all the fortified cities of Judah" (for emphasis: "city by city"), while the second group is to serve in Jerusalem (at the end of v. 8 read *wayyēšĕbû*, "and they had their seat," with *RSV* and Macholz; *contra* Heller, reading MT as "return to God" and LXX, L, Vg., BHmg, Benzinger, Bückers, Rudolph, Buber, emending to *wĕyōšĕbê*, "and those dwelling"); (2) both groups are commanded to serve "in the fear of Yahweh" (vv. 7, 9), but the first group is admonished to decide cases fairly and without partiality (vv. 6-7), while the second group is appointed to take cases referred to them, and to return instruction so as to prevent guilt devolving on the appellants, with its resulting wrath (vv. 9-10); (3) while no identification is given for the first group of judges, v. 8 specifies Levites, priests, and clan chiefs; (4) the second group of judges must work in two distinct fields: religious ("judgment for Yahweh") and secular ("disputed cases"), and the names of the chief persons (Amariah the chief priest over "all matters of Yahweh," and Zebadiah, "governor of the house of Judah" over "all the king's matters") are given. It seems all but certain that v. 8 intends that the whole judiciary should consider both religious and secular matters, and this means that the specification of the persons named to Yahweh's and the king's matters, respectively, with the Levites assigned to serve as bailiffs (*šōṭĕrîm*, v. 11), is an interpretative expansion. Inasmuch as this material shows signs of being relatively earlier, there is no need to assign this expansion to anyone other than ChrH, who in any event is using it to furbish the somewhat damaged image of Jehoshaphat, and to prepare for ch. 20.

Genre

The main genre is REPORT. Jehoshaphat's word of vv. 6-7 has first the ADMONITION, "Consider what you do," because of the evil that might tempt the judge; the ASSISTANCE FORMULA ("he is with you") is employed more as a warning than as encouragement. V. 7a, with *wĕ'attâ*, "so now," is an EXHORTATION to do what is right, in this case, to let the fear of Yahweh be with them (→ INTIMIDATION FORMULA). The COMMAND, v. 7b, is *šimrû wa'ăśû*, "keep watch and act accordingly"; a grounding clause *(kî)* introduces a WARNING. This is a form of speech in which someone in a position to know the full ramifications of a contemplated course of action points out its dangers and urges the hearer(s) to desist. It is a common form in ChrH and other late OT literature. It may take various shapes, but here it is the statement that with Yahweh there is no perversion of justice, partiality, or accepting of bribes, implying that, since Yahweh is present with the judges in their judging, he will surely see any wrongdoing and punish. Vv. 9-11 contain other ADMONITIONS: in v. 9 ("Thus shall you do in the fear of Yahweh") and in v. 11 (*ḥizqû wa'ăśû*, "Be firm in what you are doing"). This is followed by a WISH that contains the ASSISTANCE FORMULA ("May Yahweh be with the good!"). V. 10 is an INSTRUCTION, concluded by a summary WARNING, *kōh ta'ăśûn wělō' te'šāmû*, "So shall you behave so as not to bring guilt").

Setting and Intention

It is quite evident that this passage is closely related to Deuteronomy and the deuteronomistic literature (Deut 1:17; 16:18-20; 17:8-13). It does not invoke the authority of Moses, as in Exod 18:14-26, but rests solely on the authority of the king—in this case, Jehoshaphat. It contemplates only two stages in the judicial process: (1) the hearing of cases coming before a judge in one of the fortified cities of Judah, and (2) the rehearing of cases "from your brethren who live in their cities" —thus not only the aforementioned fortified cities—but only such as concern bloodshed or the interpretation of "law or commandment, statutes or ordinances." A gaping lacuna is the process of litigation in the nonfortress cities.

Macholz has studied this question thoroughly and thinks he has the answer. Assuming that the system described here is historical and actually comes from Jehoshaphat, Macholz explains that royalty established a system of justice only in the towns where the royal jurisdiction had always prevailed through the presence of the army. The military chief held the head judicial office; Jehoshaphat appointed such persons during peacetime as well as in war. This system operated in competition with the ancient system of justice at the city gate. *Contra* Knierim, Albright, Mazar, and de Vaux, Macholz claims that a high judiciary was seated at Jerusalem, operating as a collegium for all Israel. The Levites were *šōṭĕrîm*, "administrators" (my translation: "bailiffs"). The heads of the ancestral families would hear civil cases and the priests would hear "judgment for Yahweh." The first group constituted a supreme court, using oath, ordeal, and the lot in a carefully regulated system. The "king's matters" of v. 11 were those that the king himself would decide. This entire arrangement introduced some important innovations, such as the bringing together of secular and sacral matters in a single court. Local jurisdiction was necessarily reduced; the Jerusalem court would receive all capital cases. Most local disputes would go no further than the local court, civic or military, and those that went on to Jerusalem were either without precedent or too difficult to decide locally. In cases involving bloodshed, the lower court would be expected to do the necessary investigation, but they had to be brought to Jerusalem for adjudication.

Taking the ascription to Jehoshaphat as historical, Macholz is consistent in arguing that the Deuteronomy passages have developed from this. One flaw in this argument would be that it makes no allowance for an initially separate, i.e., northern, development of the Deuteronomy law code. Another flaw is Macholz's inattention to the intensive punning on the name Jehoshaphat. What is there to prove that this judicial reform actually went back to Jehoshaphat, and not to some other king? The system of courts in fortress cities sounds old and authentic, but the combination of sacral and secular court functions is suspicious for Jehoshaphat's time because it expresses ChrH's theocratic tendency. Nothing would fit the system here prescribed better than the presumed situation that evidently prevailed in the time of ChrH, when there were hardly any inhabited cities in Judah except fortified towns on the border, and when Jerusalem was the administrative center of anything that happened, secular or sacral.

322

Bibliography

W. F. Albright, "The Judicial Reform of Jehoshaphat," in *Alexander Marx Jubilee Volume* (ed. D. Frankel; New York: Jewish Theological Seminary, 1950) 61-82; J. Heller, "Textkritische zu 2 Chr XIX 8," *VT* 24 (1974) 371-73; R. Knierim, "Exodus 18 und die Neuordnung der mosaischen Gerichtsbarkeit," *ZAW* 73 (1961) 146-71; G. C. Macholz, "Zur Geschichte der Justizorganisation in Juda," *ZAW* 84 (1972) 314-40; R. de Vaux, *Ancient Israel, Its Life and Institutions* (tr. J. McHugh; New York-Toronto-London: McGraw-Hill, 1961) 119.

IV. QUASI-HOLY-WAR STORY: VICTORY IN THE DESERT, 20:1-30

Structure

A. Preparation in Jerusalem	1-19
1. Fasting in the face of peril	1-4
a. Threatening attack (transition formula)	1
b. Official report	2
1) The enemy's point of departure	2a
2) Present position	2b
c. Jehoshaphat's reverential devoutness	3a
d. Judah assembles	3b-4
1) Proclamation of public fasting	3b
2) Gathering to seek divine help	4
2. Jehoshaphat's prayer	5-12
a. Jehoshaphat's position	5
b. Communal complaint	6-12
1) Praise	6
a) Invocation of ancestral God	$6a\alpha^1$
b) Description of Yahweh (rhetorical questions)	$6a\alpha^2$
c) Description of Yahweh	$6a\beta$-b
2) Historical review	7-9
a) Perpetual conveyance of the land	7-8a
b) A sanctuary against peril	8b-9
(1) Israel built the sanctuary	8b
(2) Israel's confession	9
(a) Before the temple, in affliction	9a
(b) Crying to God to be saved	9b
3) Complaint	10-11
a) Israel's restraint under provocation	10
b) Disinheritance as recompense	11
4) Petition	12
a) Request for divine retribution	$12a\alpha$
b) Confession of powerlessness	$12a\beta$
c) Impotent Israel turns to God	12b

The artificiality of this QUASI-HOLY-WAR STORY is readily apparent to those who observe how the numerous stilted, theologically loaded speeches precede and interrupt the action. The interplay of narrative action and discourse does not come naturally, as in ch. 18. Rather, it is as if what was to be told in the narrative sections needed first to be interpreted and announced. There is a minimum of exposition. This comes at the beginning, v. 1, and at the end, vv. 29-30. It also creates a pause, just as Jahaziel begins to deliver his oracle, v. 13, and as an introductory summary of the defeat of the allies in v. 22. There is narrative in vv. 2-4, which tells of the assembly, in v. 14, introducing Jahaziel, in vv. 18-19, which relates the liturgical response, in v. 20a, which notes the march to Tekoa, in v. 21a, telling of the appointment of the singers, and in vv. 23-28, telling of the defeat, its aftermath, and the triumphal return. Discourse of some kind interrupts this at vv. 5-12 (prayer), vv. 15-17 (oracle), v. 20 (admonition), and v. 21b (instruction).

Here are some notes on details. In v. 4 ChrH's familiar locution, *biqqēš yahweh*, is given a double meaning: *lĕbaqqēš mēyahweh* means "they sought (help) from Yahweh"; *bā'û lĕbaqqēš 'et-yahweh* means "they came to seek/do reverence to Yahweh." Petersen (*Late Israelite Prophecy,* 72), expresses the general opinion when he calls vv. 6-12 a "national lament"; this is wrong because its genre is PRAYER with a number of subordinate elements (see "Genre" below). On v. 6 cf. Kropat (p. 79). The reference to Abraham as God's friend in v. 7 is a close quotation from Isa 41:8, where "offspring of Abraham my friend" is parallel to "Israel my servant, Jacob whom I have chosen." Jehoshaphat's petition in v. 12 strongly echoes Asa's confession in 14:10 (*RSV* 14:11), and of course occupies the same relative position within the overall structure. As in chs. 14–15, "Judah" stands for those under attack (cf. 14:10, 11 [*RSV* 11, 12]; 15:15); it is varied by "all Judah" or "the men of Judah," and in vv. 5, 15, 17, 18, 20 "Jerusalem" or "the inhabitants of Jerusalem" is added. Vv. 15-17, a PROPHETIC SPEECH, is called a "sermon" by von Rad ("Levitical Sermon," 272-73); a "priestly salvation oracle" by Welten (*Geschichte,* 150) and Williamson (comm., 297); and an "oracle of mercy" by Petersen (p. 73); thus the need for careful genre definition is apparent. Parallels to "the battle is not yours, but God's" are 1 Sam 17:47 and Deut 20:3-4. Jahaziel's instruction in vv. 16-17 places the technical language of the holy war in an inclusio: "Tomorrow go down . . . tomorrow go out" (cf. S. J. De Vries, "The Time Word *māhār* as a Key to Tradition Development," *ZAW* 87 [1975] 80-105). Another *terminus technicus* from this tradition is the phrase *haškēm babbōqer,* "rise early," v. 20. One notes also the use of the verb *ys',* "go out," once in v. 17 and twice in v. 20. The command to stand still and see the victory of Yahweh echoes, of course, Exod 14:13. This allusion intends to make this battle equivalent to Yahweh's defeat of the Egyptians at the Reed Sea (see "Intention" below).

On v. 19, see Watson (4.4). Willi (p. 198) argues that vv. 19, 21-22 are secondary because they bring in the Levites and singers. On v. 20b, cf. von Rad ("Levitical Sermon," 273-74) and Seeligmann (p. 272). For the tradition behind these words, see Deut 20:1-4. Isa 7:9, "If you will not believe, you will not be established," states in negative form Jehoshaphat's EXHORTATION, "Believe in Yahweh your God, and you will be established." This is his "text," and the application is "Believe his prophets and you will succeed [ṣlḥ, hiph.]"; that is to say, believing God is the same as believing his prophets, and will bring the same benefits. On v. 21 see Watson (2.7). The element of popular consultation prior to action has 1 Chr 13:1 as a parallel. According to Ackroyd ("Notes") the hadrat-qōdeš with which the singers were to praise God means "holy splendor" (by parallelism with Keret I.iii.51, it is the glory of revelation; cf. Ps 96:9; 1 Chr 16:29). The praise psalm is Ps 136:1.

All is set for Yahweh's victory, which shall now be recounted. The transition words are ûbĕ'ēt hēḥēllû bĕrinnâ ûtĕhillâ, "And at the moment when they began to sing and praise" (v. 22). It is as though a mystical noise from God threw the enemies into a panic. In the holy-war tradition (cf. Judges 7), these turn against each other, but by the rule of mathematical proportion: two against one and then one against one until they are wiped out, with no exception (cf. 2 Kgs 3:22). The scope of the victory is told not only in terms of bodies slain, but also in terms of how much effort was required to gather the plunder (on the text of v. 25a, cf. Allen, "Cuckoos," 73). The three-day figure is influenced by Num 11:32; Judges 20. "On the fourth day" in v. 26 is transitional to the assembly for thanksgiving. The coming to Jerusalem is narrated in two stages: v. 27 tells of the rejoicing along the way and v. 28 tells of the arrival at the temple; cf. 14:14 (RSV 15); 15:11. On the return, cf. Watson (8.2); on the entrance, cf. Willi (p. 195), identifying it as an expansion. V. 29 is a conclusion to this segment (cf. Williamson, Israel, 105-6), and v. 30 is a conclusion to the entire story (cf. 2 Chr 15:15).

Genre

Not only is this ChrH's third QUASI-HOLY-WAR STORY; it is by far the most elaborate and baroque. "After this" in v. 1 is his TRANSITION FORMULA. What Jehoshaphat is told in v. 2 is an OFFICIAL REPORT, which is defined as the representation of information or of a message by a person or persons duly authorized and sent forth; here it is assumed that the king trusts the report, even though the messengers are not identified in the text. Vv. 6-12 contain Jehoshaphat's PRAYER. Following an invocation, v. 6 contains the genre DESCRIPTION OF YAHWEH, with two RHETORICAL QUESTIONS ("art thou not . . .?" "dost thou not?"). Vv. 7-9 are another HISTORICAL REVIEW (cf. 15:3-6). Vv. 10-11 have a COMPLAINT that accuses Israel's enemies of ingratitude. Following a second invocation, v. 12 has a PETITION for divine judgment on those complained about.

Verses 13-19 are a REPORT OF A PROPHETIC WORD, a favorite form for ChrH and common in late periods (cf. De Vries, "Prophetic Address," 27-28). To identify the speaker, v. 14a gives his PEDIGREE. There is a rather unusual WORD FORMULA, then a PROPHETIC SPEECH that is basically a PROPHECY OF SALVATION that is at the same time an EXHORTATION to suppress fear and witness God's victory. It has the CALL TO ATTENTION ("Hearken all Judah, etc."), the MESSENGER FORMULA, and the ASSISTANCE FORMULA in v. 15. Vv. 16-17 contain INSTRUCTION with an inclusio for what is to be done māḥār, "tomorrow." As in v. 15, v. 17 has the REASSURANCE FORMULA ("Fear not and be not dismayed") with a COMMAND and AS-

SISTANCE FORMULA ("Yahweh will be with you"). The narrative sequence that follows (vv. 18-20a) contains a REPORT OF RITUAL. Jehoshaphat's final word (v. 20b) contains a CALL TO ATTENTION (same as v. 15) and an interpretative EXHORTATION to believe the prophets. "And when they began . . ." in v. 22 is a TRANSITION FORMULA. Another TRANSITION FORMULA is "on the fourth day" in v. 26. This verse and vv. 27-28 contain REPORTS OF RITUAL. V. 29 has the INTIMIDATION FORMULA, "And the fear of God came. . . ."

Setting

Many scholars claim that this story is historical, or at least is based on a historical event. On the whole question of historicity, cf. Welten (*Geschichte,* 140-53). It is evident that the story has had earlier stages of development, and these can be identified in vv. 1-4, 16-17, 20, 24-25. Like the similar stories for Abijah in ch. 13 and Asa in ch. 14, it has a heavy overburden of theological interpretation, but nowhere else is the theme "God's is the battle" so dramatically illustrated. Noth ("Lokalüberlieferung") claims to have located the ground on which this purported battle was fought. North ("Archeology," 381-83) has found the toponomical references inadequate for establishing historical data. The OT has a number of references to conflicts with the Moabites and Edomites, but nowhere is there a suggestion to confirm the claim that these peoples, with certain Meunites (= Seirites, vv. 22-23), actually invaded Judah. This is what leads Welten to claim that the story is very late and has to do with incursions from the Idumeans (a general name for eastern and southern peoples who had taken over southern Judah during the exile) late in the postexilic period. It is indeed in the mouth of peoples once dispossessed from their land, and now tentatively in hold of it once again, that the historical review and complaint, vv. 7, 10-11, seems natural.

The reference to the temple as a house of supplication is taken directly from 6:28. We are impressed with how the canonical prophets are quoted, interpreted, and applied. At a time when these had all but died out, certain orders of the Levitical singers are given a prophetic role (1 Chr 25:1, 5); hence, it is not strange that a certain Asaphite, Jahaziel, should prophesy in vv. 14-17. Yet ChrH deems it necessary to introduce his speech by declaring, "And the spirit of Yahweh came upon Jahaziel" (cf. 1 Chr 12:18)—a locution used for the inspiration of nonprofessionals. Jahaziel's prophesying seems to be continued in the liturgical singing of the fellow members of the singers' guild, v. 19. (On the further significance of Levitical prophesying, cf. the studies by von Rad, "Levitical Sermon"; Petersen; and Booy.)

Intention

Welten's view is probably correct, to the effect that ChrH concocted these quasi-holy-war stories to assure Israel of divine security on all four sides: on the north, ch. 13; on the west, ch. 14; now on the east; and in ch. 25, on the south. The emphatic affirmation that God's is the battle must reveal a deep sense of insecurity in late postexilic Israel. Continuing weak, and dependent on imperial powers, it was subject to raids and incursions from every side. What better answer than a theological one? Like the other stories mentioned, this one probably reflects at least a minimal historical core—but ChrH, especially here, has made a grand drama of this one.

Is this narrative a deliberate substitute for the tale of Joram and Jehoshaphat invading Moab in 2 Kings 3? Yes, it is. To have linked Jehoshaphat with a northern king so soon after the severely censured expedition with Ahab would have made Jehoshaphat seem an incorrigible reprobate, just when ChrH intended to use him as a model of piety. This tradition was at hand, and, very suitably, its toponomy involved the same general area. Jehoshaphat is here a winner rather than a loser—but defensively, in the true holy-war tradition, and not as an aggressor. Or, better said, he was a witness and interpreter of Yahweh's defense of his people.

Of course, the historian *qua* historian ought to be offended. In a way, what happens in this story is like a grand pontifical mass: mostly words with a minimum of action. What does the king do? He prays; he falls down and worships. Perhaps this was precisely what was expected of the surviving Davidic leader in ChrH's own time. It is significant that not he but the Asaphite singer Jahaziel instructs the people what to do. According to the story, he moves them to a good place of observation; this is like a liturgist moving the worshipers in a procession. Jahaziel is no real prophet, and, though the Spirit falls upon him, his message has little similarity to the prophetic messages of olden times. His message is to quell fear and prepare the people to witness. In the sense that a prophet's task is to give the people the message that the present moment requires, he is a prophet, for in ChrH's community there must have been constant fear and anxiety, and the people needed to let God work with his purpose while they stood still and witnessed it.

The role of the Levitical liturgists was to "praise Yahweh, the God of Israel, with a very loud voice" (v. 19)—making a noise that would not only express the reality of their fervor, but at the same time throw a panic into the enemies (Korah's presence alongside Kohath reflects a stage of tradition development perhaps contemporary with ChrH himself; cf. Petersen, 76, with Gese). Meanwhile, Gershon has dropped out (cf. Möhlenbrink, 213). This is a model of true worship: to express pure devotion while driving away every demon that assails the faithful.

The Judahites standing by the watchtower in the wilderness and looking out toward the hostile multitude remind us of nothing less than Israel and Moses, safe on the shore of the sea, looking back to see the Egyptians dead upon the seashore (Exod 14:20). Just as Moses commanded Israel, "Fear not, stand firm, and see the victory of Yahweh which he will work for you today" (Exod 14:13), Jahaziel uses almost identical words: "Fear not and be not dismayed, for the battle is not yours but God's. . . . You will not need to fight in this battle; take your position, stand still, and see the victory of Yahweh on your behalf" (2 Chr 20:15, 17). We can see these events as in a Doré etching: there the antique figure of Moses surrounded by his huddled masses, here the figure of Jehoshaphat in his regal robes, surrounded by singing Levites, gazing into the wadi below, where the last of the enemy soldiers are chopping each other to death. In such an image one is surrounded by symbols more than by historical actualities. But in the final analysis, one understands that the symbols have more permanence than the fleeting figures of actual history.

Bibliography

P. R. Ackroyd, "Some Notes on the Psalms. 3. The Interpretation of *hadrat qōdeš* (Ps. xxix.2, xcvi.9, 1 Chron. xvi.29, 2 Chron. xx.21)," *JTS* 17 (1966) 393-96; L. C. Allen, "More Cuckoos in the Textual Nest," *JTS* 24 (1973) 69-73; T. Booy, *Godswoorden in de Psalmen* (Amsterdam: Rodopi, 1978) 63-77; S. J. De Vries, "Temporal Terms as Structural Elements in the Holy-War Tradition," *VT* 25 (1975) 80-105; R. North, "Does Archeology Prove Chronicles Sources?" in *A Light unto My Path (Fest.* J. Myers; ed. H. N. Bream, R. D. Heim, and C. A. Moore; Philadelphia: Temple, 1974) 375-401; M. Noth, "Eine palästinische Lokalüberlieferung in 2. Chr. 20," *ZDPV* 67 (1944-45) 45-71; D. L. Petersen, *Late Israelite Prophecy: Studies in Deutero-Prophetic Literature and in Chronicles* (SBLMS 23; Missoula: Scholars, 1977); G. von Rad, "The Levitical Sermon in I and II Chronicles," in *The Problem of the Hexateuch and Other Essays* (tr. E. W. Trueman Dicken; New York: McGraw-Hill, 1966) 267-80; I. L. Seeligmann, "Die Auffassung von der Prophetie in der deuteronomistischen und chronistischen Geschichtsschreibung," in *Congres Volume: Göttingen 1977* (VTSup 29; Leiden: Brill, 1978) 254-84.

V. FINAL NOTATIONS, 20:31-37

Structure

A. Regnal resumé 31-34
  1. Accession age formula and statement
    of length and place of reign 31a-bα
  2. Identification of mother 31bβ
  3. Theological review 32
  4. Apologia 33
  5. Citation formula 34
B. Appendix: Jehoshaphat's ill-fated venture 35-37
  1. Introductory summary (transition formula) 35
  2. Joint building of ships 36
  3. Eliezer's prophecy of punishment over
    an individual 37
    a. Introduction 37a
    b. Denunciation and announcement 37bα
    c. Fulfillment 37bβ

Genre

This REGNAL RESUMÉ, transferred from an initial position in Kings, has the ACCESSION AGE FORMULA (v. 31a), a favorable THEOLOGICAL REVIEW (v. 32), and the CITATION FORMULA (v. 34), referring to a book of the Jehu ben Hanani who had scolded him (19:1-3) and the old standby, "the book of the kings of Israel (and Judah)." See Lemke (pp. 161-67) on the text; Williamson (*Israel,* 106) and Willi (p. 237) for interpretation. We note a play on the word *swr,* "turn," "remove," in vv. 32-33. Because of the appendix, vv. 35-37, the elements of DEATH AND BURIAL FORMULA and SUCCESSION FORMULA have been moved to 21:1, where they form the introduction to the reign of Jehoram (so 13:23 [*RSV* 14:1]; 17:1). This appendix has a TRANSITION FORMULA, "after this," and a very brief PROPHECY OF PUNISHMENT OVER AN INDIVIDUAL, which is defined as a prophetic word announcing disaster to an individual, with two components: accusation and announcement (cf.

De Vries, "Prophetic Address," 28, 33). Here the accusation is, "Because you have joined with Ahaziah," and the announcement is, "Yahweh will destroy what you have made." Cf. Watson (6.2).

Intention

Willi (p. 173) calls this appendix a "reflection." Lemke (pp. 167-70) claims that it is an exemplification of ChrH's alleged anti-north bias and an illustration of the retribution theme. It is indeed odd that it has been inserted after the normally concluding REGNAL RESUMÉ, especially in stating that Jehoshaphat took the initiative in proposing a shipping venture to Ahaziah of Israel, "who did wickedly," whereas 1 Kgs 22:49-50 (RSV 48-49) states that it was the latter who made the proposal, which was refused by Jehoshaphat. One should note also ChrH's apologia for Jehoshaphat's failure to remove the "high places" (cf. 1 Kgs 22:44 [RSV 22:43]), blaming this on the people, "who had not yet set their hearts upon the God of their fathers." Rudolph (HAT) takes vv. 31-33 as an interpolation from Kings, but this is a poor solution from a structural point of view. ChrH always includes the initial elements of the REGNAL RESUMÉ, and there is no reason to think he would omit it here. Perhaps fearing that he had already written too much good about this king, and following perhaps a different tradition about the sea venture, ChrH takes one more opportunity to illustrate that the SCHEMA OF REWARD AND RETRIBUTION pertains also to good kings who do wrong. In 19:2-3 Jehoshaphat had received no more than a slap on the wrist. According to Eliezer, the wickedness of joining Omride kings in cooperative ventures is punished only in the wreck of the ships (v. 37b). In the light of the way in which the SCHEMA OF DYNASTIC ENDANGERMENT was soon to come fully into play, this was meant as much as a warning as a penalty.

ACCOUNT OF FRATRICIDE AMONG JEHOSHAPHAT'S BAALIST SUCCESSORS, 21:1–23:21

Structure

I. Report of the reign of Jehoram   21:1–22:1a
II. Report of the reign of Ahaziah   22:1b-9
III. Story of Athaliah's downfall   22:10–23:21

These materials are united formally by overlapping succession formulas. They are united thematically by the fratricidal episodes they record. The rationale of ChrH is to show how marriage with the Omrides endangered the Judean royal family and threatened to nullify the promise and covenant made with David through apostasy to the Baalistic practices of the Omride family.

I. REPORT OF THE REIGN OF JEHORAM, 21:1–22:1a

Structure

A. Beginning of an evil rule	21:1-10
1. Succession	1
a. Death and burial formula for Jehoshaphat	1a
b. Succession formula for Jehoram	1b
2. Fratricide	2-4
a. Name list of brothers	2
b. Paternal gifts	3
1) To the brothers	3a
2) To Jehoram (ranking formula)	3b
c. The crime	4
1) Jehoram's power secure	4aα
2) Murder of brothers	4aβ
3) Murder of officials	4b
3. Information about Jehoram's reign	5-7
a. Accession age formula and statement	
of length and place of reign	5
b. Wickedness	6-7
1) Emulation of Omrides	6a
2) Theological review	6b-7
a) Performed what Yahweh judges evil	6b
b) Spared by promise to David	7
4. Loss of territory (transition formula)	8-10
a. Battle against Edom	8-9
1) Revolt and independent kingship	8
2) Jehoram's night attack	9
b. Statement about unsuppressed revolt	10
1) Edom's perpetual separation	10aα
2) Libnah's simultaneous revolt	10aβ
3) Abandonment of the ancestral God	10b
B. Judgment on Jehoram's unrelieved apostasy	11-19
1. His sins	11
a. Built country shrines in Judah	11a
b. Led Jerusalemites into harlotry	11bα
c. Made Judah apostate	11bβ
2. Report of a prophetic word	12-15
a. Elijah's letter	12a
b. Prophecy of punishment over an individual	12b-15
1) Messenger formula	12bα
2) Accusation	12bβ-13
a) Behaving according to bad example	12bβ-13aβ
(1) Ignoring Jehoshaphat and Asa	12bβ
(2) Following Israelite kings	13aα
(3) Led Judah into Omride harlotry	13aβ
b) Murdered innocent brothers	13b

Jehoram is the first, but not the last, king about whom ChrH has nothing good to report. He has both an introductory and a concluding REGNAL RESUMÉ. The pattern is highly unusual: v. 1 has the formulas for Jehoshaphat's end, used here as an introduction. V. 5 has the formulas for Jehoram's introductory resumé. V. 20a is a reprise. 21:20b–22:1a has substitute language for the usually stereotyped DEATH AND BURIAL and SUCCESSION FORMULAS. The record of Jehoram follows two parallel themes: (1) fratricide and (2) Baalistic affiliations. It is too early for ChrH to make the interconnectedness of the two understandable, but he does put them alongside each other in Elijah's denunciation. Noth ("Chronistische Werk," 143) thinks vv. 2-4 are an addition and should be omitted, but then one should, for consistency, also omit v. 13b. The NAME LIST of Jehoram's brothers is probably taken from the royal archives. The gift even of fortified cities to these brothers at the same time shows Jehoshaphat's eagerness to treat his sons as equally as possible, and also serves to suggest jealousy as the motive for Jehoram's killing them. There is a play on the element of the "possessions" which fell to him when he murdered them, and the emphasis, further on, on the loss of possessions as one element in Jehoram's judgment (vv. 14, 17). The crime itself—the murder of brothers—becomes thematic for this whole section (cf. 21:17; 22:1, 8, 10). Jehoram's wrath is not limited to his own siblings; according to v. 4b there are also *miśśārê yiśrā'ēl*, "some of the officials of Israel," which may be identical with "the princes of Judah" in 12:5 because ChrH's practice has been to apply the name "Israel" to Judah under the theory that Judah/Jerusalem constitutes the heart and center of ideal Israel. ChrH does not worry about confusion of meaning even in a context where "Israel" has to refer solely to the northern realm (v. 13). No reason is given for Jehoram's murder of the officials; the text perhaps assumes that these were persons in charge of the murdered brothers.

One possible reason for the appearance of elements of the REGNAL RESUMÉ formula at v. 5 may be that ChrH wanted to introduce the second theme, that of Baalistic affinities, by repeating 2 Kgs 8:16-19 (cf. 2 Kings 8:20). Jehoram's sin was that he "walked in the ways" of the Omrides ("house of Ahab") because he had married into their family. The result was that he did continual evil. Nevertheless he was not struck down, says ChrH, because Yahweh would not let the house of David be destroyed. There may have been living descendants of David through collateral lines from Rehoboam, Abijah, and Asa, but Jehoram had seen to it that he was the only direct heir from Jehoshaphat, and only descent from reigning kings seemed to count in fulfillment of the covenant promise to David. Willi (pp. 107, 171) first calls this statement a specification and later an explication. Lemke (p. 171) sees it as an illustration of the theocracy theme (cf. Williamson, "Eschatology," 148-49). For the lamp image as a symbol of a surviving Davidide, cf. 1 Kgs 11:36.

The statements in vv. 8-10 about the loss of Edom and Libnah are taken pretty well intact from 2 Kgs 8:20-22. Edom's separation "to this day," v. 10, is etiological; no doubt ChrH specially regrets making this statement because of all the trouble the Idumeans, descendants of Edom, were making for the Jews of his day. The statement about Libnah's revolt seems to have a redundancy of time designation: *'āz tipša' libnâ bā'ēt hahî' mittaḥat yādô*. Here *'āz* is consequential ("so," "thus"; cf. S. J. De Vries, *Yesterday, Today and Tomorrow,* 336-37), while *bā'ēt hahî'* is purely temporal, so that we must translate, "Because of this Libnah revolted from under his power at that time." V. 10b is ChrH's interpretative addition; cf. 2 Kgs 8:22 (Willi, 173: reflection; Lemke, 172: retribution theme).

Thus far ChrH has gotten most of his material straight out of Kings. Virtually all the rest is his own, being taken from independent sources or from his own reflections. Section II tells about the judgment that fell on Jehoram because of his sins, and this judgment came first in verbal form as an oracle from the great prophet Elijah, second as an almost word-for-word actual fulfillment. But first ChrH comes back to the subject of Jehoram's sins, employing the emphatic demonstrative *gam-hû'*, "to be sure, he . . ." (v. 11). This list of sins does not at all correspond with the sins mentioned in vv. 3-6. First, he built (not just failed to destroy) *bāmôt*, "high places," in Judah (Elijah has no reprimand for this); second, he led the citizens of Jerusalem into harlotry *(znh);* cf. v. 13; third, he caused Judah to be "thrust away" *(ndḥ,* hiph.)—a term more appropriate for the time of Deuteronomy (cf. Deut 12:6, 11, 14).

While living in such sins, Jehoram receives a letter from Elijah. Elijah is chosen as the prophet because according to Kings he was living in the north just at this time, and because his ministry had been directed against the Baalism of the Omride kings. There was to be no crossing of borders, however, as in the case of Amos. Elijah stayed home and wrote a letter. Although correspondence by letter became common practice during and after the exile, it fits ill in this particular period (but cf. Huram, 2:10 [*RSV* 11]; Sennacherib, 32:17). Elijah's letter-prophecy has the regular judgment form, with MESSENGER FORMULA first (here colored by the identification of Yahweh as the God of David), then the accusation, and finally the announcement of a penalty (cf. De Vries, "Prophetic Address," 28-29, 33). Elijah's accusation against Jehoram is that he was following the bad example of his Baalistic in-laws (territorial bias is expressed in calling Asa a "king of Judah" while the in-laws were "the kings of Israel," marking the first as pious and the second as wicked). In v. 13 Elijah mentions the harlotry complained of in v. 11, and at last blames him for murdering his innocent brothers ("better than yourself" is juridical, not moral; it means that Jehoram is the one who was worthy of being murdered). The penalty (v. 14) is announced with a formula of imminent action, *hinnēh yahweh*, "behold Yahweh," followed by an active participle, meaning that even at this moment Yahweh is in the process of carrying out this action. It is to strike his family and possessions with *maggēpâ gĕdôlâ*, "a mighty blow," and to strike his own person *bohŏlāyîm rabbîm*, "with numerous illnesses" (v. 15).

From some source or other, ChrH gleans information on the fulfillment of these two terrible threats. Yahweh arouses Arabs and Philistines to plunder the royal property; this is a tradition variant to that of 22:1, which speaks only of Arabs murdering Jehoram's sons "in the camp." According to 21:17, Jehoram's wives and all but the youngest sons are kidnapped, perhaps never to be seen again. Jehoram was in extremity when none but his youngest son, Jehoahaz (here given as a familiar, or nickname, variant for the regular form, Ahaziah; cf. Willi, 186), remained alive, just as with Joash in 22:11-12. But this was not the worst. Yahweh also smote Jehoram in his body, that is to say, with an incurable disease in his bowels (according to Driver, an ulceration of a prolapsed bowel) for two years, after which he died in great agony, v. 19a. There was no funeral fire for him as there was for Asa (16:14), evidently because he was so wholeheartedly despised.

The concluding summary is not in its usual order. For some reason, v. 20a is a reprise of v. 5 (so with Jotham at 27:8). Jehoram is buried in Jerusalem, but, again, not in the royal tombs. 22:1a takes the place of the usual SUCCESSION FORMULA (on the text, cf. Lemke, 175). Since the elder sons of Jehoram had been killed by the Arabs, the Jerusalemites crowned his youngest son, Ahaziah (cf. 21:17). This fits well with other occasions of crowning by popular action after an act of violence (thus was Jehoram's death interpreted; cf. "Yahweh smote"), as in the cases of Uzziah, 26:2, Josiah, 33:25, and Jehoahaz, 36:1.

Genre

The main genre is REPORT. Elements of the REGNAL RESUMÉ are present in 21:1, 5, 20; 22:1a. 21:1a has the DEATH AND BURIAL FORMULA for Jehoshaphat; v. 1b has Jehoram's SUCCESSION FORMULA. V. 2 is a NAME LIST; v. 3b has the RANKING FORMULA. V. 5 has the ACCESSION AGE FORMULA and the STATEMENT OF LENGTH AND PLACE OF REIGN. Vv. 6b-7 are a THEOLOGICAL REVIEW. V. 8 has the TRANSITION FORMULA, *bĕyāmāyw*, "In his days." V. 10 is a STATEMENT. Vv. 12-15 constitute a REPORT OF A PROPHETIC WORD, specifically, a PROPHECY OF PUNISHMENT OVER AN INDIVIDUAL, introduced by the MESSENGER FORMULA. The expressions *wĕ'aḥărê kol-zō't*, "and after all this" (v. 18), and *wayĕhî lĕyāmîm miyyāmîm*, "and it happened after a while" (21:19), are TRANSITION FORMULAS. The ACCESSION FORMULA and STATEMENT OF LENGTH AND PLACE OF REIGN are repeated in v. 20a. The DEATH AND BURIAL FORMULA and the SUCCESSION FORMULA are given in altered form in 21:20 and 22:1a.

Setting and Intention

ChrH has Kings to follow, but evidently has other sources at his disposal as well. His one evident purpose is to illustrate the mechanism of fratricide. Evidently motivated by selfish ambition and debilitating anxiety, Jehoram murders all his brothers upon accession to the throne. This of course makes derelict the principle of trust and humility which the reigns of his father and forefathers have so urgently advocated. Here the SCHEMA OF REWARD AND RETRIBUTION comes into play. Just as Jehoram, the *bĕkōr*, "firstborn," has disposed of sibling rivals, he is in the end punished by having all but the very youngest of his sons, Ahaziah, murdered by the Arabs. Here the SCHEMA OF DYNASTIC ENDANGERMENT bursts full force on the scene. Yahweh punishes a transgression by a penalty that resembles it and is engendered by it. Soon Jehu will come to wipe out all the royal seed (the cousins), and what he has omitted to do, Athaliah, the Baalist daughter of Ahab, will try to carry through to utter extinction. Thus the promise and covenant to David find themselves in grave danger, partly because of the crass worldliness of the one who occupies the throne, and partly because the religion of Baal is so bitterly antagonistic to the staunchest representative of Yahwism, the lineage of David occupying the throne of the true Israel. How appropriate it is that ChrH reaches out to the figure of Elijah, Israel's most formidable opponent against Baalism and the Omride dynasty, to declare Jehoram's doom in a prophecy whose fulfillment cannot be undone.

Bibliography

S. J. De Vries, "Dynastic Endangerment," 68-69; G. R. Driver, "Ancient Lore and Modern Knowledge. 3. Disease and Death," in *Hommages à André Dupont-Sommer* (ed. J. Amusin, et al.; Paris: Librairie Adrien-Maisonneuve, 1971) 283-84.

II. REPORT OF THE REIGN OF AHAZIAH, 22:1b-9

Structure

The two main sections of this brief narrative are indicated formally by the designation "Ahaziah the son of Jehoram, king of Judah," vv. 1b, 6b (MT: Azariah). The first section, vv. 1b-6a, aims to tell how evil counsel gets this new Judahite king to repeat the sin of his grandfather Jehoshaphat, i.e., to accompany an Omride king to battle. The usual elements of an introductory REGNAL RESUMÉ are present in vv. 1b-4. In the place of the formal SUCCESSION FORMULA, we are simply told that Ahaziah reigned, even though the only concrete thing to report about his reign is how he got involved in this battle and how he got killed. His mother is named as the dreaded Athaliah, granddaughter of Omri. As a zealous devotee of Baal, she was also the daughter of the wicked Jezebel.

Lemke (pp. 176-80) attributes what is next said (vv. 3-4) to ChrH's anti-north bias, as well as to his desire to illustrate the principle of retribution; Willi (p. 173) is content to speak of it as an exegetical technique involving reflection. It is far more than a reflection; it is an integral part in the development of the SCHEMA OF DYNASTIC ENDANGERMENT. Nor is ChrH affected by an undiscriminating rage against the north; it is against the Baalizing Omrides in the north that he objects. Ahaziah "walks in the ways of Ahab" (22:3) because at home he is under the direct influence of Athaliah. He also does what is evil in Yahweh's sight, being influenced after his father's death by his cousins, the Omride kings. Three times in vv. 3-5 the verb y'$ṣ$, "give counsel," appears, making it thematic (cf. also 25:16). One of the effects of their counsel was to accompany Joram against Hazael at Ramoth-gilead. Although usually mentioned by his short name, in v. 5 his first mention provides the full name and title, "Jehoram the son of Ahab, king of Israel." He was wounded and returned to Jezreel to convalesce. ChrH copies 2 Kgs 8:28-29 so closely that he reproduces the DtrH gloss in v. 29a, where Ramoth-gilead is called "Ramah" and a superfluous circumstantial clause is added at the end (cf. S. J. De Vries, *Prophet Against Prophet* [Grand Rapids: Eerdmans, 1978] 67-68, 90).

Verse 6b tells of Ahaziah's visit to Joram after the battle. In the Kings account the reader might have to assume that the visit was motivated by friendliness and a sense of camaraderie, but in v. 7a ChrH tells us emphatically that it was *mē'ĕlōhîm*, "through God"; Ahaziah's *tĕbûsâ*, "downfall," was to occur precisely because of this visit (Willi, 173, speaks of this as a reflection on the source material in 2 Kgs 9:1–10:28; but ChrH is not offering exegesis, but only telling the story his own way). The course of events seems a little mixed up from 2 Kings: (1) Ahaziah goes out with Joram (healed already?) to face Jehu, anointed by Yahweh to destroy the house of Ahab, v. 7; (2) Jehu executes judgment on the house of Ahab, v. 8a, which apparently includes the event of 2 Kgs 10:12-14 as well as that of 9:30ff., i.e., he slays all who attended Ahaziah, specifically śārê yĕhûdâ ûbĕnê 'ăḥê 'ăḥazyāhû, "the Judahite princes and the sons of Ahaziah's brothers." The meaning is that all the close royal kin, including the grandsons, of Jehoram were slain. This creates a difficulty because 2 Chr 22:1 says the Arabs killed all the older sons, but sons of these brothers must have been left alive. This detail is not in 2 Kgs 10:12-14, which speaks only of Ahaziah's "kinsmen" ('āḥîm). (3) Ahaziah hid in Samaria and, when found, was executed and buried, v. 9. This is totally at variance with 2 Kgs 9:27-28 and must reflect a variant tradition unless ChrH is making a deliberate change. His version does give the adherents of Jehu an opportunity to pay a tribute to Jehoshaphat, the grandfather, "who sought [drš] Yahweh with all his heart" (cf. 2 Chr 19:3). The conclusion in v. 9b is that the "house of Ahaziah," meaning his royal establishment, consisting of his direct heirs, had no one left to take over the throne.

Genre

This is a REPORT. Vv. 1-4 have the REGNAL RESUMÉ, with a modified SUCCESSION FORMULA, an ACCESSION AGE FORMULA, a STATEMENT OF LENGTH AND PLACE OF REIGN, and a THEOLOGICAL REVIEW in modified form. ChrH seems to be in a hurry to tell his story, which of course is much abbreviated from his source in 2 Kings 8–10. Vv. 6b-9 constitute a DEATH REPORT. Its proper conclusion is, without doubt, the "Story of Athaliah's downfall" which begins in v. 10.

Setting and Intention

As has been suggested, ChrH may have had access to certain independent traditions for some of the things he writes in this pericope, but his main source is 2 Kings 8–10. It cannot be said that he is just extracting from that source; he is making a digest of it, throwing in little changes and twists of his own, with a heavy overburden of theological interpretation. ChrH has now come to the climax of his SCHEMA OF DYNASTIC ENDANGERMENT. Here is a Judahite king who not only goes to war with the Omrides and enters into occasional commercial enterprises with them, but who is totally under the evil influence of Omri's granddaughter, the daughter of Ahab and Jezebel. He wishes to be entirely like his Samaritan cousins in ruling the kingdom of Judah. He takes counsel not only from Athaliah, but from her brothers — specifically Joram. In battle at Ramoth-gilead, he is like his grandfather Jehoshaphat in escaping harm from the Syrians. It is Joram who gets wounded. But ChrH is not at all interested in telling of Joram's death, or even the death of Jezebel, the evil matriarch. He does mention that Jehu is carrying out his divine commission to destroy the "house of Ahab," but he makes sure to repeat from Kings that this includes such Judahite royalty as have descended from Ahab and have been under his influence. The entire entourage of Ahaziah, including the sons of his own brothers, are slain, and then he himself. Because of the rule of direct descent, there was no one now left to take over the throne. The promise to David of an everlasting kingdom seemed at the point of coming to nothing. Not only was the survival of the Davidic line of kings at stake, but also the veracity and reliability of Yahweh himself.

Bibliography

S. J. De Vries, "Dynastic Endangerment," 69-70; P. Joüon, "Notes philologiques sur le text hébreu de 2 Chron. 22,7," *Bib* (1932) 87-88.

III. HISTORICAL STORY OF ATHALIAH'S DOWNFALL, 22:10–23:21

Structure

A. Asylum for sole surviving Davidide	22:10-12
1. Athaliah wipes out the royal seed	10
2. Joash sequestered six years	11-12
a. Rescued by Jehoshabeath	11a
b. Protected in temple	11b-12
B. Year seven: Joash's throne conspiracy for investiture	23:1-11
1. Jehoiada's preparations	1-7
a. Secret assembly (name list)	1
1) Jehoiada's initiative	1aα
2) Plot among captains	1aβ-b
b. Chieftains and Levites summoned	2
c. Fealty to the king	3
1) Covenant of allegiance	3a
2) Jehoiada's acclamation	3b
a) Davidic claimant identified	3bα
b) Appeal to dynastic promise	3bβ
d. Instructions for the coup	4-7
1) Stations for off-duty clergy	4-5a
2) Others assigned to temple court	5b
3) Clergy to enter during worship	6
4) Levites as armed guards	7a
a) To surround the king	7aα
b) To slay intruders	7aβ
5) Protection within and without	7b
2. Jehoiada presents Joash for enthronement	8-11
a. Introduction	8aα
b. Co-opting on- and off-duty shifts	8aβ-b
c. Distribution of weapons	9
d. Stationing of guards	10
e. The enthronement	11
1) Presentation of Joash	11aα^1
2) The investiture: crowning and endowing him with "testimony"	11aα^2
3) "Making him king"	11aβ

If this were primarily the story of Joash's investiture, the covenant/cleansing scene, vv. 16-19, would not intrude before the climactic notice of Joash's enthronement. The reason why these items do take precedence is that it is primarily the story of Baalism's downfall. 22:10 is actually an exposition and belongs at the beginning; it would be wrong to attach this verse to the preceding pericope merely because it continues the theme of wiping out the Davidides. Likewise it would be a mistake to sever 22:11-12 from 23:1ff., because the sequestering of baby Joash is the narrative introduction to what Jehoiada undertakes to do in the sequel. We may also point out that the report of the reign of Joash, ch. 24, is an entity unto itself and not the structural continuation of ch. 23.

Although ChrH follows Kings closely in presenting this story, it is surprising to see how many changes and additions he makes in it. In 22:10 he adds the clarifying explication "of the house of Judah"; in v. 11 he adds "thus ... Ahaziah";

in 23:1-3 he adds "took courage . . . assembly"; also "and Jehoiada . . . David"; in vv. 4-7 he adds "of you priests . . . Yahweh. The Levites"; in v. 8 he adds "the Levites and all Judah" and "for Jehoiada the priest did not dismiss the divisions"; in v. 10 he adds "and he set . . . hand": in v. 12 he adds "the people . . . the king"; an addition in v. 13 is "and the singers . . . celebration"; in vv. 18-19 ChrH adds "under the direction . . . unclean." There are a few minor omissions and alterations, the most prominent being the substitution of "And they set the king upon the throne" in v. 20b for Kings' "And he took his seat on the throne of the kings," which makes Joash seem more active.

Lemke (pp. 180-86) considers ChrH's effort a complete rewrite of Kings and categorizes the changes he makes under four prominent themes: (1) the pan-Israelite impulse; (2) the prominence of the Levites; (3) the sanctity of the temple; and (4) emphasis on liturgy. It must be said that, even with the sizable additions that ChrH has made, the story is still intricately woven and entirely understandable. Characterizations are not prominent: Jehoiada is very active, and always the boss, yet we can scarcely see the man behind the priestly robes. Athaliah in her brief moment is more understandably human than any of the others. Truly, she looks and acts like a Medusa—or at least like a Jezebel.

Although Ahaziah was forty-two years old when he began to reign (22:2), and he had sons for Athaliah to slay (v. 11), for some reason none of these was able *la'sōr,* "to seize hold of," the kingdom, v. 9. This may actually be proleptic of vv. 10-11, which is to say that no son could rule because Athaliah had murdered them all. The details are too obscure for us to solve, though it might be proposed that Athaliah had planned to incorporate Judah with the north, and had only been prevented from doing so by the presence of Jehu on the throne. Be that as it may, for the very first time a foreigner—and a woman at that—"reigned over the land" of Judah. In effect, the Davidic lineage was severed, yet unbeknownst to her there was a Davidic heir alive, due to the promptness and courage of Jehoshabeath and Jehoiada.

The significance of the seventh year is obscure. Seeing that the time is ripe, Jehoiada calls a secret meeting of the officers of the armed guard—named here to be memorialized—who gathered all the Levites from all the cities of Judah. This addition by ChrH might seem to make quite impossible the secrecy that was necessary; ChrH's logic is that since they were the gatekeepers of the temple, they belonged there alongside the civilian guards. Although Jehoiada does not bring out Joash until v. 11, in making the covenant with the officers and Levites, 23:3, he exclaims, "Behold the king's son!" Rather than suppose that Jehoiada has actually brought Joash out before the guards, it is possible to take one of two courses: (1) read *hinnēh ben-hammelek yimlōk ka'ăšer dibber yahweh 'al-bĕnê dāwîd* as a complete sentence with indicative verb: "Behold, the king's son shall reign, as Yahweh spoke concerning the sons of David"; or (2) read Jehoiada as saying, "Behold, there is a son of the king!," establishing the identity of the pretender, and then adding either the indicative, "He shall be," or the jussive, "Let him be. . . ." We chose the second alternative because it accords with ChrH's sense of drama and with his ideology. Everyone had imagined that the Davidic line had been cut off, that there was nothing left to do except to serve Athaliah. But Jehoiada, who has kept faith through this crisis, has faith. The line of David is about to be restored.

This is the crucial scene because all else flows naturally from it. Jehoiada gives strict orders for carrying out the coup, vv. 4-7 (Willi, 198, considers vv. 4b,

6a secondary; on v. 6 cf. Watson, 10.52). It is agreeable to ChrH's reasoning that the Levites should have primary responsibility for guarding the pretender, v. 7, though he leaves to the military personnel the responsibility of arresting and executing Athaliah, vv. 14-15, 20. V. 11 is the climactic moment; we should read, "while Jehoiada and his sons were anointing him" to keep the separation that ChrH intends between the acts of Jehoiada and the acts of the people (Willi, 127, regards this clause as a theologizing addition). Next comes Athaliah's execution, vv. 12-15 (on v. 13a cf. Watson, 7.9; Willi, 198, identifies the reference to the singers as a late gloss). She cries "Treason!," is arrested and led out, and is slain (ChrH "horse gate" may be derogatory; cf. 2 Kgs 11:16). Jehoiada then makes a covenant involving himself, the people, and the king "that they should be Yahweh's people" (23:16; ChrH omits "and also between the king and the people," 2 Kgs 11:17). To ChrH this means three things: (1) immediate removal of the Baal cult (also in Kings); (2) the appointment of Levites to monitor the temple service; and (3) the exclusion of "unclean" persons from the temple (vv. 16-19). This done, an honor guard escorts young Joash through the "upper gate" to the royal palace, where they enthrone him (see on v. 20 above). The results are universal rejoicing and an opportunity for the city to enjoy security (šāqāṭâ, v. 21). The final conclusion is wĕ'et-'ătalyāhû hēmîtû behāreb, "So this Athaliah they put to death with the sword."

Genre

This is another example of the HISTORICAL STORY. It is historical, being based on an actual course of events, and it is a story because it develops thematically from problem through tension to resolution, with no irrelevant intrusions except those that ChrH has added along the way. 23:1-11 is a THRONE CONSPIRACY, a type of report which tells briefly and schematically of conspiracy against the occupant of the throne and its outcome. V. 1 has a NAME LIST of five coconspirators. Vv. 4-7 consist of INSTRUCTIONS for stations and duties in carrying out the coup (→ INSTRUCTION). "Long live the king!" in v. 11b is an ACCLAMATION, an enthusiastic greeting, expression of acceptance and loyalty, and wish for a long life and reign. Athaliah's outcry in v. 13b is a very brief INDICTMENT SPEECH, which is defined as a formal statement handed down by a juridical authority charging a person or persons with committing a crime. V. 14a contains Jehoiada's ORDER for arresting Athaliah, and v. 14b repeats "the priest's," i.e., Jehoiada's, PROHIBITION against executing her in the temple. V. 15 is a DEATH REPORT. V. 16, "that they should be Yahweh's people," is a partial and indirect form of the COVENANT FORMULA, the full form of which is "You shall be my people and I shall be your God." In v. 18a the AUTHORIZATION FORMULA is kakkātûb bĕtôrat mōšeh, "as it is written in the law of Moses"—referring to the sacrifices—together with the REGULATION FORMULA, 'al yĕdê dāwîd, "according to the order of David"—referring to the performance of the music.

Setting and Intention

The rescue of Joash and his being presented for coronation had to take place in secrecy and in a place where the Baalist Athaliah seldom came. It had to happen suddenly, with carefully chosen collaborators, and according to a well-thought-out plan. Jehoiada, being chief priest, had access to the entire temple, regulated who came in and went out, and ran the whole rigid procedure of public worship. In one bold moment he produced the boy Joash, had him anointed king, and awaited the inevitable coming of Athaliah. Her cries of treason were of no avail, for Jehoiada's guards were ready to seize both her and anyone who might come to her assistance. Taking no chances, Jehoiada's party disposes of her and her Baal cult. All who are present are sworn to a solemn covenant to be "Yahweh's people" (once more, that is, for surely Athaliah would have done everything in her power to have imposed Baal worship on her subjects). A guard is posted at the temple (v. 18), and then the whole party is ready for the final act, i.e., to install Joash on his throne, v. 20.

In this drama, just one person really stands out: Jehoiada. He is in command from beginning to end. No doubt it was he who continued as regent at Joash's side, for he who had been transported in a single day from a dark room in the temple to the magnificent throne of the palace owed everything to him. Alongside Jehoiada, it is of course the people, represented by their military captains, who take the foremost part. As v. 21 says, "the people of the land rejoiced"; "the city was quiet." Joash hardly knows what is happening to him; he is the very opposite of raging Athaliah, whose entrance is dramatic, but whose influence on this day is nil.

It must truthfully be said that ChrH has done everything possible to ruin this excellent story. He wrecks the element of suspense by having Jehoiada send out the trusted circle of officers to summon Levites and the secular nobility to a preliminary (and absolutely superfluous) covenant ceremony. Jehoiada's instructions for the coup become cluttered and confusing, with Levites at every post. ChrH has Jehoiada take time, while posting the guard, to specify the liturgical responsibilities of the Levites. The coup against Athaliah might never have come off at all if ChrH's version of the coup was historical. If we are to understand ChrH at all, we need to keep in mind that he is not writing history as it *was*, but as it *should have been*. In his time there probably were no "captains of hundreds" to guard the temple. For this, he depended on the Levitical guards. In the end, one could say that Jehoiada's coup would have had no significance if there were no Levites to "be in charge of the house of Yahweh, to offer burnt offerings to Yahweh . . . with rejoicing and singing," v. 18 (cf. Noth, "Chronistische Werk," 217, who considers this verse a gloss; also von Rad, *Geschichtsbild*, 88).

Bibliography

G. R. Driver, "On Some Passages in the Books of Kings and Chronicles," *JTS* 27 (1926) 158-60; Z. W. Falk, "Forms of Testimony," *VT* 11 (1961) 88-91; P. Joüon, "Notes philologiques sur le text hébreu de 2 Chron. 23, 9," *Bib* 13 (1931) 88.

REPORT OF THE REIGN OF JOASH, 24:1-27

Structure

In ChrH's telling, the Judahite kings so often put on the "Dr. Jekyll and Mr. Hyde" act that the reader is left astounded. Is human nature really as fickle as he depicts it—or is he presenting types of the good and evil in every man? At least when we come to the report about Joash, we have hints of some deep, inner, psychological motivation. Joash seems so docile while his mentor Jehoiada lives that we can almost predict that he will kick over the traces once the old man is gone. His resentment at being bullied and used may even account for his harshness to the prophet Zechariah, who has the misfortune to be Jehoiada's son. But let us remind ourselves that the OT seldom deals in psychological motivations. The text of 2 Chronicles 24, as it stands, informs us only of the effects and not of the causes.

This chapter in Chronicles is a very loose paraphrase of 2 Kings 12, so much so that neither can be used as a check on the other. All that can be said for certain is that ChrH had Kings before him and followed its order of narration. ChrH has been becoming skimpy in his use of concluding REGNAL RESUMÉS, probably because of the violent or odious deaths of the immediately preceding kings. Here, however, he provides an introductory and a concluding REGNAL RESUMÉ, the latter being the more remarkable because it follows a foregoing report of Joash's assassination, v. 25. In the narration proper, transitions are indicated not only by changes in theme and subject matter, but by transitional formulas: *wayĕhî 'aḥărêkēn,*" ellipsis for "And it happened

344

after this that . . . ," v. 4; *wĕ'aḥărê môt yĕhôyādā'*, "and after the death of Jehoiada," v. 17; and *wayĕhî litqûpat haššānâ*, "and it happened at the turning of the year," v. 23 (*'āz*, "then," 2 Kgs 12:18). But these only indicate narrative sequences; the central thematic break comes in v. 17b with the word *'āz*, "Then the king hearkened unto them." Heretofore he had always "listened to" Jehoiada; now he "listens to" the *śārê yĕhûdâ*, "princes of Judah." *śārê* is a term that has to be translated according to its context. It could mean "officials" or even "nobility"—and it could include members of the royal family because, even though Joash was only seven when he became king, the sons of whom we read in v. 3 could be well grown by the time Jehoiada died at the age of 130 years (v. 15).

The THEOLOGICAL REVIEW in v. 2 already hints of the drastic change to come. Though Jehoiada controlled the choice of wives, no doubt to prevent any more mismatches, the birth of sons and daughters, v. 3, was seen as a divine blessing, and at the same time that the shipwreck Athaliah had caused was on its way to being repaired. V. 4, "Joash decided to restore Yahweh's house," is the exposition for all of vv. 4-16 (Willi, 172: reflection). There is a play on the word *qbṣ*, "gather," in its twofold use in v. 5: Joash gathered the priests and Levites; they were to gather money. The motivation is provided in v. 7, a grounding clause introduced by *kî*, "for": Athaliah's "sons" had plundered Yahweh's temple for use in the shrines of Baal. The whole sequence, vv. 5b-6, is a late intrusion, as can be seen by the use of *hārōš*, "chief," for *hakkōhēn*, "the priest," used throughout for Jehoiada in v. 2 and the two preceding chapters (Kings = Chronicles); Welch (*Chronicler*, 78-80) argues for this exclusion. As for the looting of the temple, it is programmatic for ChrH: whenever the kings act wickedly, the temple is likely to suffer. Another point worthy of note is that Joash is "the king" throughout this section. When he is mentioned with Jehoiada, this practice of leaving him nameless underscores his subordination. Yet ChrH does seem to be giving Joash some independence, as witness v. 8, which allows "the king" to command in the place of "Jehoiada" (2 Kgs 12:9).

The tax of Moses that is asked for (its mention in v. 6 is a gloss) is the one prescribed in Exod 30:11-16, where, of course, it applies to the wilderness tabernacle; this only underscores our recognition of ChrH's acceptance of the tabernacle typology in application to the temple. The glad generosity of nobility and laity in their response echoes 1 Chr 29:6-9 (cf. Kropat, 79; Watson, 6.3; Willi, 198, claims that v. 11 is a gloss). According to v. 11 the factotum of *kōhēn hārōš*, "the high priest" (Kings: *hakkōhēn haggādôl*), takes part in handling the money; this can hardly be the same person as Jehoiada, who is always called just *hakkōhēn*, "the priest." With abundant funds on hand, the temple repairs are expedited, v. 13 (note that *'mṣ*, piel, exceeds *'md*, hiph.), and funds are left over for new utensils (this flatly contradicts 2 Kgs 12:13; cf. Williamson, comm.; Willi, 142, identifies ChrH's method as archaizing, i.e., writing as if the conditions of Solomon's temple were perfectly restored).

That Jehoiada is indeed ChrH's hero is clear not only from the fact that he is credited with an age as great as that of the patriarchs, v. 15, but also from the statement that he was buried "in the city of David" among the kings, v. 16, in recognition of the great good he had done "in Israel" for God and for his house. The first refers to his restoring the Davidic monarchy; the second refers to his restoring the temple. Baalism goes apace with the undermining of the Davidic covenant; Jehoiada had stopped them both.

We can identify what the *śārê yĕhûdâ,* "princes of Judah," wanted of Joash from what they and he did: *'zb,* "forsake," and *'bd,* "serve." The first verb has as its object Yahweh, and the second, the cult objects of Baalism. By so suddenly switching over to his fathers' sins, Joash introduced a period of unrelenting apostasy. This means that the SCHEMA OF DYNASTIC ENDANGERMENT is not yet played out. V. 18b announces that *qeṣep,* the same "wrath" that Jehoshaphat had engendered (19:2), was put into motion. This is proleptic; it points to Yahweh's mounting fury in the history of all the kings to come, as we can see plainly from v. 20, which speaks of a plurality of warning prophets and a plurality of heedless people.

Verses 20-22 tell of the murder of the prophet Zechariah, son of Jehoiada. This continues the theme of the persecution of the prophets, introduced with Asa in 16:7-10. Zechariah's inspiration is described in the words of 1 Chr 12:18. He brings a message of judgment (Williamson, comm., "Levitical sermon," after von Rad; cf. De Vries, "Prophetic Address," 29-30, 34). The charge (ACCUSATORY QUESTION) is transgression, the denunciation and announcement are: Because you have forsaken *('zb)* Yahweh, he has forsaken *('zb)* you; cf. Shemaiah in 12:5 and Azariah in 15:2. The reaction is a conspiracy, approved by Joash's order, to stone Zechariah in—of all places—the temple (cf. Jer 26:7-9)! This conspiracy *(qšr)* forms an inclusio with the conspiracy to assassinate Joash in v. 25; another ties the slaying *(hrg)* of the prophet, v. 22, to the slaying *(hrg)* of Joash. ChrH's footnote in v. 22a, "Thus Joash the king (as king) did not remember *[zkr]* the kindness *[haḥesed,* "act of devotion"] which Jehoiada, Zechariah's father, had shown him," plays on the victim's name.

The penalty comes at the hand of the Syrians and through conspiracy within Joash's own household, vv. 23-26. The Syrian invasion is mentioned without sufficient details to reconstruct what really happened, except of its effect. The apostatizing nobles were destroyed and much spoil was taken. Turning around an old maxim, ChrH remarks that Yahweh delivered many to few, the reasons being the general apostasy and to render justice on Joash. As with Joram in 22:6, Joash is sorely wounded (Lemke, 192-95: retribution theme). The conspirators, whose names are given in v. 26, carry out their bloody deed; Joash is killed, but is not buried in the royal tomb. That the one assassin is the son of an Ammonite woman, the other the son of a Moabite woman, has been interpreted by some commentators as adding still greater indignity to Joash's ruin. To judge from 25:3, this did not memorialize them, but confirmed their guilt.

Genre

The main genre is REPORT. The REGNAL RESUMÉ in vv. 1-2 has the ACCESSION AGE FORMULA, the STATEMENT OF LENGTH AND PLACE OF REIGN, and a THEOLOGICAL REVIEW. Its conclusion in v. 27 has the CITATION FORMULA and the SUCCESSION FORMULA, the DEATH AND BURIAL FORMULA having been borrowed for v. 25. V. 16 has a separate DEATH AND BURIAL FORMULA for Jehoiada. The TRANSITION FORMULA is seen at vv. 4, 17, and 23. V. 5a is INSTRUCTION. The expansion in v. 6 has an INDICTMENT SPEECH in question form: "Why have you not required. . .?" V. 9 is a third-person REPORT of an EDICT. V. 18b is an EPITOME: *wayĕhî-qeṣep 'al-yĕhûdâ wîrûšālaim bayyôm hahû'* (so LXX^BA), "So wrath came on Judah and

Jerusalem on that day." V. 20 is the REPORT OF A PROPHETIC WORD, with the WORD FORMULA and a PROPHECY OF PUNISHMENT OVER THE PEOPLE. This last is common in classical prophecy, and usually includes a statement of reasons for punishment, plus an announcement of God's intervention in punishment. In this instance, the denunciation is in the form of an ACCUSATORY QUESTION, preceded by the MESSENGER FORMULA.

As Zechariah lies dying, v. 22, he cries out, "May God see and avenge!" This is an APPEAL FOR RETRIBUTION, one of the (→) trial genres with full juridical force. The appellant calls for justice and retribution in his last living moment. He cries to heaven—to an authority higher than that of the apostate king who has wrongfully decreed the sentence of death (cf. Matt 23:35; Luke 11:51). Vv. 23-24 have a brief BATTLE REPORT, with the CONVEYANCE FORMULA in v. 24. Vv. 25-26 are at the same time a THRONE CONSPIRACY and a DEATH REPORT. A NAME LIST is seen in v. 26.

Setting and Intention

ChrH's rationale with regard to Joash's reign seems to be as follows: (1) Joash is a true "brand plucked from the fire," the symbol of the graciousness and persistence of the divine will; without initiative of his own, Joash is proof that the Davidic dynasty—and with it, the promise and the covenant—continues; (2) his thoroughgoing wickedness, once Jehoiada has passed from the scene, not only justifies his assassination but forebodes the nation's ruin. To put it in other words, if a king can be the object of such an amazing act of divine grace, and still sin so grievously as to slay the very son of his mentor and benefactor, Zechariah ben Jehoiada, when he censures his sin, then what hope is there, really, for the Davidic kingship and the nation of Israel? We might be tempted to psychologize, speculating on the possibility of a rigidly trained and supervised king rebelling against his well-meaning, but oppressive, mentor. That is not, however, the way to do exegesis. The point is, rather, that the espousal of Baalism has meant death to the heirs of the Davidic dynasty. Jehu has disposed of "the house of Ahab" and all that it stood for in the north. Wretched Athaliah made sure that there would be no more "sons of David," but Yahweh, through Jehoiada, had deceived her. That in itself was an act of great courage. To present Joash for crowning, giving the command for Athaliah's execution, was more courageous still. Little wonder, then, that Jehoiada took careful measures to ensure two things: (1) the purity of the temple that had been so grossly defiled, and (2) the young king's absolute loyalty to Yahwism. Since he was the tutor, Jehoiada kept a watchful eye on young Joash's upbringing. Since he lived very long, this influence must have continued well into Joash's adulthood. Joash's revolt after Jehoiada's death may not have been inevitable, but we can safely assume that whatever straight-laced piety he displayed during Jehoiada's lifetime was Jehoiada's, and not his own. We can hardly be mistaken about this, for the motif of Joash's subordination to the priest is thematic throughout the chapter.

A word needs to be said about refurbishing the temple. Throughout the book, its desolation always goes hand in hand with the wickedness of the kings. It was, to be sure, common practice in the ancient Near East for a conqueror to loot and desecrate the shrine of a conquered god. In our pericope, the Baalist priest is executed even before Joash is installed on his throne. For ChrH this is a sound principle: first the sanctuary, then the kingdom. Joash gives command (1) that the people donate freely to restore Yahweh's temple, and (2) that they do it quickly. "All Israel" is invited to contribute (cf. Williamson, *Israel,* 107). Willi (p. 159) rightly points to the Moses typology, since the tax of Moses that the people are to bring is, according to Exodus, for the tabernacle. What a fitting symbol the tabernacle is for such a time as this! No more than Israel could have done without the tabernacle in the wilderness could the Israel of this day do without the temple. In writing this ChrH was no doubt thinking of the temple, destroyed by Nebuchadrezzar and rebuilt by Zerubbabel, but after decades and perhaps centuries now more than ever in need of the generous gifts of "all Israel." The motif of repairing (cleansing) the temple appears later for Hezekiah (29:3-19) and for Josiah (34:8-18).

Joash's apostasy is a repetition of Rehoboam's. He too listened all too readily to bad advice, and then used all his energies to put it into execution. His decision was to forsake the temple of Yahweh and to turn to the Asherim and the idols. In other words, Joash had decided to undo in one moment all that he had learned in a lifetime. He decided to turn back to the ways of Joram, Ahaziah, and Athaliah. In so doing he doomed not only himself but the nation. To quote the epitome of v. 18a: "So wrath came upon Judah and Jerusalem *on this day.*" Prophets would come to them and testify against them, but they would give them no heed (v. 19). Vv. 17-19, as well as v. 27, are very vague and general. The rest, probably from independent source material, is sharp and clearly drawn. It tells us what it is like to kill a prophet. It also tells us what it is like to kill a king. Zechariah cried, "May Yahweh see and avenge!" Yahweh did see, and he did avenge. But a deep foreboding hangs over this tragic story. Will Joash's descendants someday be like him? Will Israel, itself forsaking Yahweh, be forsaken? If a person, "plucked from the burning," and so long and carefully trained, in the end forsakes Yahweh for the Baals, is there hope? We ask that question as ChrH's contemporaries must have asked it for themselves.

Bibliography

K. Budde, "Vermutungen zum 'Midrasch des Buches des Könige,'" *ZAW* 12 (1892) 37-51; J. R. Shaver, "Torah and the Chronicler's History Work" (Diss., Notre Dame, 1983); A. C. Welch, *The Work of the Chronicler* (London: Oxford, 1939).

REPORT OF THE REIGN OF AMAZIAH, 25:1–26:2

Structure

I. Regnal resumé	25:1-2
A. Accession age formula and statement of length and place of reign	1a
B. Identification of mother	1b
C. Theological review	2
II. Dealing with his father's assassins	3-4
A. Executing the culprits	3
B. Sparing their children	4

That the pericope extends from 25:1 to 26:2 is clear from the fact that the first contains a formal introduction for Amaziah, and the second, a formal introduction for Uzziah. The theme that binds this all together is enmity with the north, first in Amaziah's treatment of the northern mercenaries, vv. 6-10, 13, and then in the episode of the war with Joash of Israel, vv. 17-24. Subsidiary themes are (1) the execution of Amaziah's father's assassin, which ironically forms an inclusio with the report of his own assassination (vv. 3-4, 27-28); (2) the campaign against the Seirites (vv. 5, 11-12); (3) Amaziah's apostasy, prophetic reprimand, and abuse of the prophet (vv. 14-16). This is rather a kaleidoscope, yet it all hangs together with some logic except in v. 14, where the victorious Amaziah offers worship to the gods of the vanquished Seirites. Even ChrH's familiar habit of showing both sides is unable to give credibility to this abrupt and altogether senseless slip of logic, for who worships the gods of the people he has vanquished? In the "man of God's" warning in vv. 7-8, ChrH had made a thematic link with 13:8-12, Abijah's taunt. In the reference to Joash plundering Jerusalem and taking hostages to Samaria, v. 24, ChrH has created a forward link to 28:8-15 (return of Judean captives from Samaria).

In his THEOLOGICAL REVIEW, v. 2, ChrH is more spiritual and internal than Kings (on the text, cf. Lemke, 197). The act of executing his father's assassins, v. 3, is an emphatic reaction to the ongoing bloodletting of chs. 21–22; the verb *hrg*, "slay," is repeated from 24:25. To establish the principle of individual retribution, ChrH copies the quotation from Deut 24:16 in 2 Kgs 14:6; cf. Ezek 18:4. This is all preliminary. The real narrative begins in v. 5, with alternating narration and discourse. There is no indication of Amaziah's intent beyond the fact that he musters "Judah." LXX^{BA} has "Jerusalem," but this has to be wrong because it is the militia that is meant—not the professional army—and Benjamin is included by implication because it is an integral part of the kingdom of Judah (cf. Welten, *Geschichte*, 90-94). The engaging of a mercenary force from Ephraim spoils the theory of the holy war, if that is what this is supposed to be, and from an ideological point of view it quite upsets ChrH's ongoing theme of not cooperating with northern allies (cf. chs. 13; 18; 22). Yet this is a maverick element that is fully integrated into the main account and adds nothing to the theme of warfare with Edom/Seir. True, it does provoke a message from a "man of God" in vv. 7-9, but that would hardly have been invented just to bring in this element. There are good reasons, therefore, to accept it as historical. It is skillfully used by ChrH to introduce the main theme of the offended northerners, vv. 10, 13, 17ff., as we have said. It is interesting that neither the "man of God" of vv. 7-9 nor the prophet of vv. 15-16 is named (cf. De Vries, "Prophetic Address," 25-26, 34). The message of neither can properly be called a sermon (cf. von Rad, "Levitical Sermon," 268-69). On the "man of God's" warning that the Ephraimites do not have God with them, cf. 13:4-12; "the army of Israel" must mean the forces of the erstwhile united kingdom all together, which must fail in a "holy war" because Yahweh has forsaken the northerners (cf. Watson, p. 192 n. 1). In the dismissal of the Ephraimites, v. 10, there is intentional chiasmus in the clause *wayyiḥar 'appām mě'ōd bîhûdâ wayyāšûbû limqômām bohŏrî-'āp*, "And they were very angry with Judah, and returned to their place in hot anger." The main event, the victory in the valley of Salt, is quickly told (cf. 2 Kgs 14:7); it can hardly function as a climax from a structural point of view. Also from an ideological point of view little can be said for it. The only authentic holy-war element is the annihilation of the enemy, which, however, is carried to great excess in the throwing down of the 10,000 captives (note the chiasmus in vv. 11-12: *wayyak 'et-běnê-śē'îr 'ăśeret 'ălāpîm wa'ăśeret 'ălāpîm ḥayyîm šābû . . . ,* "And he smote the Seirites, ten thousand, and ten thousand living they brought back. . . ." This was a bloody age: the vengeful Ephraimites were at the same time killing off 3,000 Judahites from Samaria and Beth-horon, v. 13.

At this point, just where the reader would expect either a report of a reprisal against the Ephraimites or a victory celebration for decimating the Seirites, ChrH mentions Amaziah's incredibly unmotivated act of sacrificing to the gods of this defeated people. V. 14b has a doubly inverted syntax: *wělipnêhem yištaḥăweh wělāhem yěqaṭṭēr*, "and in their presence he prostrated himself, and to them he made burnt offerings." This is also the single place in the entire pericope where a temporal phrase creates a drastic transition from one kind of behavior to another (*wayěhî 'aḥărê bô' . . . ,* "And it happened after he came. . . ." This provokes the prophet's reproach, v. 15. The prophet's ACCUSATORY QUESTION ("Why have you resorted . . . ?") includes a taunt against the Seirites, and, by implication, against Amaziah: "gods of a people who did not deliver their own people." In v. 16 the

king interrupts him (theme of oppressing the prophets) with a RHETORICAL QUES-
TION, ORDER, and THREAT. Here and in v. 17 ChrH introduces a play on the word
y'ṣ, "counsel": the prophet is not a royal counselor, v. 16a; the prophet threatens
the king for not listening to his counsel, v. 16b; Amaziah "takes counsel" to fight
Joash, v. 17. Illogically, ChrH has the prophet stop talking and then puts additional words into his mouth.

From v. 17 to v. 24 we are dealing with a document, copied from Kings,
which shows the styling of an independent narrative; cf. especially vv. 17, 18, 21,
23, 25. In these verses the full, official titles of the two kings are constantly repeated.
V. 17 is the exposition for this new section. Ahaziah has challenged Joash of Israel
with the expression "Come, let us look each other in the face" (r 'h with pānîm);
cf. v. 21. On Joash's reply, cf. Watson (10.7, citing UT, 77:17). He tells a fable about
three different creatures that are found "in Lebanon": the thistle, the cedar, and a
wild beast. Its meaning is Amaziah's bravado and false pride; cf. 2 Chr 26:16. The
result is that Amaziah will not listen (cf. Rehoboam in 10:15, Ahaziah in 22:7); two
grounding clauses with kî say "it was of God" and "he had sought the gods of
Edom," v. 20. In the fight that follows, vv. 21-23, the Judahite battleground (Beth-
shemesh) is already a sign of Amaziah's weakness. To exaggerate the defeat,
"Judah" is placed in chiasmus: 'ăšer lîhûdâ wayyinnāgep yĕhûdâ, "which belongs
to Judah; and Judah was defeated," vv. 21-22 (cf. Watson, 25.22; on the plunder of
Jerusalem, p. 201 n. 2). The defeated Amaziah is brought back to his capital only
to see its walls torn down, its treasures pillaged, and hostages taken. So much for
false pride; but ChrH goes on to copy most of 2 Kgs 14:17-20, 21-22.

In v. 25 (Rudolph, HAT, suggests that this is a gloss from 2 Kgs 14:17) we
are told that "Amaziah son of Joash, king of Judah" (full official title) outlives Joash
of Israel by fifteen years. Then comes a fragment from a concluding REGNAL
RESUMÉ (Watson, 2.8; cf. Lemke, 199, on the text). V. 27 tells of Amaziah's assassination, continuing the qšr theme from 2 Chr 24:21, 25 (Willi, 714: reflection;
Lemke, 200: retribution theme). The TRANSITION FORMULA: ûmē'ēt 'ăšer-sār
'ămaṣyāhû mē'aḥărê yahweh, "And from the time when Amaziah first turned away
from Yahweh," not in Kings, shows that ChrH thought of the conspiracy as continuous, whereas Kings sees it as instantaneous. The chiasmus, Jerusalem-
Lachish/Lachish-Jerusalem, underscores the futility of Amaziah's effort to escape
his assassins. A further indignity is that he was brought home "on horses," yet he
was shown the respect of being "buried with his fathers," v. 28. On the act of the
people in installing Uzziah, cf. 22:1; 33:25; 36:1. The notice that Uzziah took Eloth,
26:2, is put here to show that Uzziah was able to accomplish the major purpose of
Amaziah's abortive war against the Edomites. "After the king slept with his fathers"
(also in 2 Kgs 14:22) is not taken from the royal annals; cf. De Vries (Prophet
Against Prophet [Grand Rapids: Eerdmans, 1978] 98). In the light of the fact that
Uzziah begins to reign at age sixteen, after Amaziah had reached the age of fifty-
six (25:1), we must ask whether a repetition is intended of the theme of crowning
the youngest (surviving) son, as in 22:1 (cf. 21:17) and 22:11.

Genre

The main genre is REPORT. In vv. 1-2 is the REGNAL RESUMÉ, with ACCESSION AGE
FORMULA, STATEMENT OF LENGTH AND PLACE OF REIGN, and THEOLOGICAL

REVIEW. V. 4b, quoting Deuteronomy, is an AUTHORIZATION FORMULA. Vv. 5-13 constitute a BATTLE REPORT, with elements of the QUASI-HOLY-WAR STORY in vv. 11-12. V. 5 is a MUSTER ROLL, with TALLY and APPELLATION (*yôṣē' ṣābā'*, "effective army-man"). Vv. 7-8 constitute the REPORT OF A PROPHETIC WORD containing a PROPHETIC SPEECH (both are familiar forms in ChrH). It contains an APPEAL ("Do not let the army of Israel go with you") with a negative formulation of the ASSISTANCE FORMULA in the grounding clause. The WARNING, another favorite form for ChrH, is seen in v. 8 (cf. v. 16). This is a form of speech in which one in a position to know the full ramifications of a contemplated action points out its dangers and urges the hearer(s) to desist. The end of v. 8 has a DESCRIPTION OF YAHWEH. V. 9b is another REPORT OF A PROPHETIC WORD, this time reassuring. V. 8b, "God has power to help or cast down," and v. 9b, "Yahweh is able to give you much more than this," are DESCRIPTIONS OF YAHWEH that answer both of the king's objections to sending away the Ephraimites. The TALLIES in vv. 11, 12, 13 belong to the CASUALTY REPORT. The TRANSITION FORMULA is seen in vv. 14 and 27. Vv. 15-16 contain another REPORT OF A PROPHETIC WORD, including the PROPHETIC SPEECH, with an ACCUSATORY QUESTION, a TAUNT, and (in the repartee) another WARNING. The king's reprimand contains a RHETORICAL QUESTION, an ORDER to stop speaking, and a THREAT. Vv. 17-24 constitute a BATTLE REPORT beginning with a CHALLENGE TO A DUEL, which is seen most often in prophetic threats, but here in the invitation "Come, let us look one another in the face," v. 17; cf. v. 21. V. 18 presents Joash's rejoinder in the form of a FABLE, which depicts a world of fantasy with the principal figures drawn typically from subhuman creatures, and in which a presumptuous character has an overblown ego pricked by a pointed moral. "Your heart has lifted you up in boastfulness" is an ACCUSATION; it is followed by another stern WARNING. V. 20 has the CONVEYANCE FORMULA. The CITATION FORMULA, referring again only to "the book of the kings of Judah and Israel," occurs in v. 26. Vv. 27-28 again combine the THRONE CONSPIRACY REPORT and the DEATH REPORT. 26:1 has an altered form of the SUCCESSION FORMULA, and 26:2 an altered form of the DEATH REPORT.

Setting and Intention

The beginning and the end, with the narrative about the war with Joash of Israel, are taken pretty much intact from Kings. Apart from the episode about dismissing the Ephraimite mercenaries, the rest looks very much like what ChrH would himself conceive. This includes the two prophetic speeches. The rationale of ChrH's Amaziah story is (1) to show the irony of first punishing regicide, and then becoming the victim of it himself; (2) to show how a "holy war" becomes an "unholy war"; (3) to show that Jerusalem itself is not inviolate against ruinous attack—and if this be at the hand of a fellow Israelite, how much more at the hand of foreign enemies of the future; and (4) how quickly the good that a king does is wiped out by his fall into wickedness and pride.

The third item mentioned is especially momentous. The image of a boastful Judean king being humiliated by his temperate Israelite colleague is a prolepsis of the whole nation's capture by the northern realm, ch. 28. This must be intended as a warning to the postexilic "ideal Israel." The special rage shown the Edomites/Seirites is probably a reflection of ongoing resentments against the

Idumeans in the postexilic period, and we may well suppose that Ahaziah's astounding stupidity in setting up, worshiping, and sacrificing to the Édomite gods is meant as a warning to Yehud not to be attracted by their continuing presence. We see that the prophet is ever the voice of God: when Amaziah is still open to good advice, they give him good counsel (vv. 7-8), but when kings show that they are no longer amenable to God's counsel, they threaten them with destruction (v. 16). In other words, God's good counsel is itself a gift, but when ignored or abused, it becomes the ground for one's condemnation.

The main lesson of this pericope is the ineluctability of retribution. Even though Amaziah far outlives his nemesis Joash, as ChrH tells it, there has been a conspiracy since the beginning of the time of his apostasy, and at last it breaks out and gets him. The regnal summary is placed at v. 26, prior to the narrative of his assassination, as if to say that all of Amaziah's deeds are now over. There is nothing to tell but his death. What irony that Amaziah is struck down the way his father Joash was! Although the sons of his father's assassins were spared according to Moses' law, this old and foolish king has to share the ignominious death of his father. Both of them went willfully and inexplicably after heathen gods (24:18; 25:14) and rejected the ordained organs of revelation, treating them as worthy of death (24:21; 25:16). Having cut themselves off from the light of divine revelation, each one came to the death of which they were worthy. Only now has the SCHEMA OF DYNASTIC ENDANGERMENT come to an end.

REPORT OF THE REIGN OF UZZIAH, 26:3-23

Structure

This pericope has an opening and a closing REGNAL RESUMÉ, vv. 3-4, 22-23, which is nearly identical to 2 Kgs 15:1-7. After the formal introduction, the main theme seems to be the preparation and manifestation of military strength, vv. 6-15; the rest of the pericope is taken up with the subject of Uzziah's leprosy, based upon 2 Kgs 15:5. There is a very noticeable inclusio for vv. 9-15, with a play on the name Uzziah ("Yahweh is strong/acts strongly"). The end of v. 8 reads: *wayyēlek šĕmô* 'ad-lĕbô' miṣrayim kî heḥĕzîq 'ad- lĕmā'ĕlâ, "And his name went as far as the entrance to Egypt, for he became exceedingly strong." The end of v. 15 reads: wayyēṣē' šĕmô 'ad-lĕmērāḥôq kî-hiplî' lĕhē'āzēr 'ad kî-ḥāzāq, "And his name spread out afar, for he was marvelously helped to become strong." This statement also has a pun on the root 'zr, "help," and this appears also in v. 13, "to help ['zr] the king against the enemy." This is sufficient to show us that ChrH wanted to capitalize on the name "Azariah," by which this king is known in the Kings parallel, but avoided here in favor of what is probably his familiar or nickname, Uzziah, which he is probably using in order to avoid confusion with the priest named Azariah, vv. 17, 20.

Here are some notes on details. We observe that v. 4 makes no mention of not removing the "high places"; cf. 2 Kgs 15:4. Uzziah is praised for showing his father's piety in spite of his father's wickedness; so also Jotham at 2 Chr 27:2. Who the Zechariah of v. 5 is, we have no idea. It can hardly be the prophet/priest of that name mentioned in 24:20-22. On teaching/learning "the fear of God," cf. 2 Kgs 17:28; evidently this means to learn all the ways of religion, at least in an outward way. The benefits certainly pertained to external things: "As long as he sought [drš] Yahweh, God made him prosper [ṣlḥ, hiph.]" (v. 5). In the public projects which he undertook, Uzziah was restoring the ruin caused by his father Amaziah's apostasy (vv. 9-10). It is apparent that ChrH got most of the material about fortifications from a special source. The mention of watchtowers (migdālîm) in the countryside, v. 10, using the same word that had been used for the fortifications in Jerusalem, shows that v. 10 comes from still another source (so Welten, Geschichte, 42-52; Williamson, comm.). The description of the army in vv. 11-13 may have some early material, but the fact that it is described and mustered like the volunteer militia (cf. 2 Chr 25:5, Amaziah) evidences confusion of actual historical methods, stemming from the situation of ChrH's own time. The APPELLATIONS show this same confusion. RSV is right in translating "army of soldiers" for 'ōśēh milḥāmâ ("professional soldier"), and "fit for war" is all right for yôṣ'ē ṣābā' ("effective army-men"), v. 11a, but then 'ôśēh milḥāmâ should not have been used for the militia troops of v. 13. In v. 13b three officials are named for preparing and registering the call-out of these troops (ligdûd bĕmispar, v. 11, means "enroll as a troop"). There were to be 2,600 rā'šê hā'ābôt, a tribal designation meaning "chiefs of the ancestral families" (v. 12). The troops, called ḥêl ṣābā', "trained army," tallied 307,500 (v. 13; cf. Watson, p. 192 n. 1). Their appropriate APPELLATION was bĕkōaḥ ḥāyil, "powerfully brave," v. 13. We do not know a great deal about the war engines Uzziah prepared in Jerusalem, but we must not miss the alliteration, ḥiššĕbōnôt maḥăšebet ḥôšēb, "machines invented by a craftsman" (v. 15).

Not only does v. 15b form an inclusio with v. 8; we also observe that a formal transition is intended in placing the word ḥāzāq back to back with the beginning of v. 16, ûkĕḥezqātô, "and when he had become strong." Pride was the effect and destruction (hašḥît) the result; cf. Rehoboam, 12:1. "He was false to Yahweh his God" reminds us of Saul in 1 Chr 10:13. The act of a king in burning incense on the altar is intended to remind us of Jeroboam, 1 Kgs 12:33; 13:1. This account may simply echo Jeroboam's fault—well known to everyone already, so not necessary to repeat—and has probably been developed imaginatively by ChrH to explain 2 Kgs 15:5. We take note of the fact that Uzziah only tried to burn the incense, and was prevented by the priests and the onset of leprosy from doing so. For the theme of leprosy in connection with controversy over priestly prerogatives, cf. Miriam in Num 12:9ff., Gehazi in 2 Kgs 5:25ff. (Cf. Shaver, who identifies Exod 30:1-10, 11-16; Num 17:5, as the literary sources for priestly prerogative.) The transition between Uzziah's repartee with Azariah and the onset of leprosy is the double use of the verb *z'p*, "be angry," in v. 19. In other words, it was not the mere attempt to burn incense that brought this blight on him, but his pride, his officiousness, his stubbornness to resist the rightful prohibition of the guardians of Yahweh's temple. "Behold, he was leprous in his forehead!" is a paraphrase of the formal declaration that a priest had been trained to make; cf. Leviticus 13. Uzziah is horrified. As he flees from the temple, he is aware that "Yahweh had smitten him," v. 20. The statement in v. 21 that Uzziah dwelt in a separate house until his death "because he was excluded from Yahweh's temple" seems an obvious non sequitur, but this religious banishment would have seemed to ChrH, who added it to 2 Kgs 15:5, to be the heart of the matter.

Verse 22 has different wording from the usual CITATION FORMULA, and is identified by Lemke (p. 202) as from a separate source. It is in the form of a verbal clause, and for the first time ChrH cites one of the canonical prophets. The notice of Uzziah's death, v. 23, uses the formula "he slept with his fathers" (present in 2 Kgs 15:7), implying a peaceable and honorable death. To reinforce his point about the leprosy, ChrH states that, although Uzziah was "buried with his fathers," it was in a burial field assigned to royalty, repeating what is in essence the priestly diagnosis, "He is a leper."

Genre

The whole is a REPORT. The REGNAL RESUMÉ at the beginning has the ACCESSION AGE FORMULA and the STATEMENT OF LENGTH AND PLACE OF REIGN. Vv. 6-8 constitute a BATTLE REPORT. Vv. 12-13 are a MUSTER ROLL with APPELLATIONS and TALLIES. In v. 18 Azariah delivers to Uzziah a REBUKE, "It is not for you, Uzziah, to burn incense to Yahweh, but for the priests. . . ." This is followed by the COMMAND, "Go out of the sanctuary," and the CENSURE, "You have done wrong *[mā'altā]*, and it will bring you no honor from Yahweh God." The CENSURE is stronger than REBUKE, involving outright condemnation; here the punishment is implied, but it can also be made explicit and be spoken by the king. The accusation that the king has committed *m'l* makes it also very similar to the (→) indictment speech. In the REGNAL RESUMÉ at the end, the CITATION FORMULA and the DEATH AND BURIAL FORMULA have been much modified. There is also the SUCCESSION FORMULA.

Setting and Intention

As we have seen, ChrH has borrowed very little for his pericope on King Uzziah: just certain items for his introductory and closing REGNAL RESUMÉ. The rest has been taken from private sources or invented. The case of Uzziah has offered him an opportunity to show how a model rule may be ruined by pride and impiety. The ignominious disease with which his sin is punished not only leads to a disgraceful death, but prevents him from fulfilling the years of his rule with the power and honor that would ordinarily devolve to him.

357

As we know, the name "Uzziah" substitutes in ChrH for the name "Azariah," which appears in Kings. The first is also the name by which he is known in Isa 1:1; 6:1; 7:1; Hos 1:1; Amos 1:1; Zech 14:5; also in 2 Kgs 15:13, 30, 32, 34. Since the last three references give patronyms for Jotham, it might be argued that "Azariah" was the familiar name and "Uzziah" the throne name. Against this we have the evidence of the Assyrian annals, which tell of the subjugation of "Azriau of Judah" in 743. It may be that his leprosy, with the resulting coregency of Jotham, encouraged the use of his familiar name or nickname in ChrH, where so much emphasis is placed on this event. Both names mean "Yahweh is strong" or "Yahweh helps." The likelihood is that 'zr-yhw was shortened in popular parlance to 'z-yhw, with appropriate changes in vocalization.

The information provided in this chapter for Uzziah's campaigns and military preparations has been much discussed. Welten (*Geschichte*, 153-63), who has given the subject close study, finds a historical core in v. 6a, in the statement that Uzziah broke down the walls of Gath, Jabneh, and Ashdod in his war against the Philistines and in v. 9, about the building and fortifying of towers in Jerusalem. According to Welten, the rest shows the common characteristics of ChrH's treatment of the subject of building (cf. 11:5-12; 14:5-6; 17:12-13; 27:3-4; 32:5-6; 33:13), which are (1) that they share ChrH's language and style; (2) that they are connected to a section about successful warfare and/or troops; and (3) that they are associated with a statement that the king in question brings rest or peace. Thus these notices about Uzziah's victories are historically suspect. V. 6b may even reflect the conditions of the Maccabean period. Somewhat more cautious is G. Rinaldi, who is less interested in the historicity of this passage than in the territorial-geographical significance of having possession of Gath, Jabneh, and Ashdod; according to Rinaldi, this secured a trade route from Uzziah's mines in the vicinity of Elat/ot (v. 2). According to Alt (*KS* III [Munich: Beck, 1953] 396ff.) "Gurbaal" in v. 7 guarded the main trade route from the Arabah. Uzziah not only drove out the Arabs (Negeb bedouin), says Rinaldi, but the Meunim as well; these came either from Maʿon in Judah or from Edomite Maʿan, 30 kilometers southeast of Petra. On the Meunites, who have been mentioned several times in ChrR/H, we are informed by a fragment from Tiglath-pileser III (Tablets from Nimrud, 400; cf. Tadmor). This fragment is from the campaign of 734-33 against Gaza and Samsi queen of the Arabs, and in a broken context refers to the *Muʿunaya* south of the Wadi Arish. At this early date this people may have already occupied most of the Negeb, even though their closest association seems to have been at Maʿan near Petra, and with the Edomites (later Idumeans) in general.

Welten (*Geschichte*, 24-27, 63-66, 87-90) discusses Uzziah's fortifications and army. We have agreed with him and Williamson (comm.) that, although Jerusalem did have *migdālîm*, "towers," and that such *migdālîm* were also part of the fortifications in the countryside (cf. 1 Chr 27:25), the mention of this word in connection with "cisterns," v. 10, has to do with the care of livestock, and that the use of this word in this context shows the verse as such to be from ChrH and not from authentic sources. Furthermore, the description of the "army," vv. 11-15, mingles the ideology of the ancient militia with contemporary military practices. Welten is also suspicious that Uzziah's war engines, v. 15, reflect a much later period than the time of the Judahite kings.

Rudolph (HAT) takes 2 Chr 26:6-15 as historical, but is skeptical about vv. 16-22. Many scholars would share Rudolph's misgivings about these verses, but recently Zeron has argued from Isa 6:5, where the prophet confesses *nidmêtî*, "I am destroyed," as somehow connecting him with the Uzziah who is said to have just died (v. 1). The point is that Isaiah has likewise entered the temple—a sinful and dangerous thing to do; cf. Exod 19:2; 3:6; Judg 13:22—and that the prophet realizes he is guilty of the same sin as Uzziah. This argument clarifies neither the historicity of Uzziah's transgression nor the consciousness of Isaiah that he is a sinner. If Isaiah were indeed as wicked as Uzziah, he would have been unfit for service, coals or no coals.

Bibliography

G. R. Driver, "Ancient Lore and Modern Knowledge. 3. Disease and Death," in *Hommages à André Dupont-Sommer* (ed. J. Amusin, et al.; Paris: Librairie Adrien-Maisonneuve, 1971) 283-84; A. M. Honeyman, "The Evidence for Regnal Names Among the Hebrews," *JBL* 67 (1948) 13-25; G. Rinaldi, "Quelques remarques sur la politique d'Azarias (Ozias) de Juda en Philistie," in *Congres Volume: Bonn 1962* (VTSup 9; Leiden: Brill, 1963) 225-35; H. Tadmor, "The Me'unites in the Book of Chronicles in the Light of an Assyrian Document" (Hebr.), in *Bible and Jewish History* (*Fest.* J. Liver; Tel-Aviv: Tel-Aviv, 1971) 222-31; P. Welten, *Geschichte und Geschichtsdarstellung in den Chronikbüchern* (WMANT 42; Neukirchen-Vluyn: Neukirchener, 1973); A. Zeron, "Die Anmassung des Königs Uzia im Lichte von Jesajas Berufung," *TZ* 33 (1977) 65-68.

REPORT OF THE REIGN OF JOTHAM, 27:1-9

Structure

C. Death and burial formula   9a
D. Succession formula   9b

ChrH follows 2 Kgs 15:32-38 rather closely in his own introductory and concluding summaries for Jotham. He has altered the theological evaluation, v. 2, so as to excuse Jotham explicitly from Uzziah's transgression, at the same time placing greater emphasis on the people's sin (cf. Lemke, 204-5). The section on his notable deeds shows the stereotypical ChrH pattern of (1) building, (2) hostilities, and (3) piety, and is felt by Welten (*Geschichte*, 27-29, 66-68, 163) to be quite artificial and probably unhistorical, in which case there is no sense in looking for special sources. ChrH has opportunity to exercise his penchant for chiasmus in vv. 3 and 4: *hû' bānâ . . . bānâ lārōb*, "he built . . . he built very much"; *wĕ'ārîm bānâ bĕhar-yĕhûdâ ûbeḥŏrāšîm bānâ bîrāniyôt ûmigdālîm*, "and cities he built in Judah, and on the rugged hills he built forts and towers." The notice of war with Ammon is very brief, concluding with the phrase *wayyeḥĕzaq 'ălêhem*, "and he prevailed against them" (v. 5), forming an inclusio with v. 6, *wayyitḥazzēq yôtām*, "and Jotham was made strong," which is explained in the grounding clause, *kî hēkîn dĕrākāyw lipnê yahweh 'ĕlōhāyw*, "for he kept his ways straight before Yahweh his God." The styling of the references to Ammon's tribute argues against this item's historicity, and may even involve an explanatory gloss in v. 5b. That is to say, v. 5bα, *zō't hēšîbû lô bĕnê 'ammôn*, "This is what the Ammonites paid him," looks like a concluding rubric, to which the references to a second and third year, v. 5bβ, would have been added at the same time that an original *šānâ bĕšānâ*, "year by year," attested by LXX *(kat' eniauton)*, must have been changed to MT *baššānâ hahî'*, "that year."

ChrH omits the reference to Rezin and Pekah found in 2 Kgs 15:37—which, however, Lemke (pp. 205-6) considers to be secondary in Kings. For the first time since 2 Chr 21:20 (Jehoram), ChrH resorts to the technique of the reprise, v. 8. Though its purpose is not apparent, there have been enough previous examples of the reprise to invalidate Rudolph's argument (HAT) to the effect that this verse is nothing but a marginal gloss to 28:1.

Genre

The main genre is REPORT, with the REGNAL RESUMÉ at vv. 1-2, 7-9. As usual, there are the ACCESSION AGE FORMULA (twice), the STATEMENT OF LENGTH AND PLACE OF REIGN FORMULA, the THEOLOGICAL REVIEW, the CITATION FORMULA (again, no prophetic authorities are named, only "the book of the kings of Israel and Judah"), the DEATH AND BURIAL FORMULA, and the SUCCESSION FORMULA. The only further formal element is a fragmentary BATTLE REPORT in vv. 5-6.

Setting and Intention

It is probable that ChrH had no other source material than what he found in Kings. We may agree with Welten's judgment that the references to building operations, to hostilities, and to tribute from Ammon are both too generalized and too stylized to lend any probability to the use of an independent historical source. It is evident that ChrH was not satisfied with previous references to punishing Ammon. In his own time the Ammonites were seen as a continuing menace to Yehud, so this record of a perfectly godly king, one of whom no single word of blame had been recorded, was composed as a model of the subservience that Israel's God had designed for them.

The record of Jotham's reign is intended as a model of what might have been. True, his son Ahaz would prove to be just the opposite: as wicked as anyone. Back to back, the two show as clearly as can be the rationale of the SCHEMA OF REWARD AND RETRIBUTION. For Jotham there was only blessing: "He became mighty," v. 6a. This was the reward for his directing his ways "as constantly in the presence of Yahweh," v. 6b. But even Jotham's piety could not save a people who still followed corrupt practices, v. 2b, nor could he keep the line of kings who were to follow him from joining this wayward people in the downward pathway to national destruction. Thus ChrH is preaching to his own generation, warning them that even the righteous have no power to make atonement for the folly and wickedness of others (Ezek 14:12-20).

REPORT OF THE REIGN OF AHAZ, 28:1-27

Structure

1. Death and burial formula	27aα
2. Entombed outside royal cemetery	27aβ
C. Succession formula	27b

Galling (ATD) identifies vv. 1-18 as secondary, but there is no sufficient reason to deny any of this material to ChrH. His use of poor transitions at vv. 16, 21, 22, with several erratic doublets, produces a confused literary composition. ChrH is more interested in expressing a clear and forceful theology than in telling a good story. To start with, his introductory summary copies parallel material in Kings, but the influence of DtrH is seen especially in vv. 3-4, as in the use of the expression *tō'ăbôt haggôyim*, "abominations of the heathen"; cf. also Ezekiel.

In vv. 5-15, which have a distinct beginning and a distinct conclusion, there are no special transitional formulas; all is in normal Hebrew narrative sequence, with the sole exception of v. 6, a resumptive EPITOME. Throughout this section, the thematic word is *wayyišbû*, "and they took captive" (vv. 5, 8), as also its cognate, *haššibyâ*, "the captivity/captives" (vv. 11, 13, 14, 15). The account appears to be about two different campaigns against the Judeans, not a single campaign as understood by 2 Kgs 16:5; Isa 7:1ff. Judah faces two enemies: Syria and Israel (Ephraim). The victory of the one in v. 5a and the victory of the other in v. 5b are put in chiasmus with the twice-repeated CONVEYANCE FORMULA, "give them into their hand." The Syrians (Arameans) take a group of Judahite captives to Damascus, and that is the last that is ever heard of them. Ahaz, at the head of his army, suffers a great slaughter at the hand of "the king of Israel." Since *RSV* "For" is not in the Hebrew text, the reader might suppose that Pekah's great victory, mentioned in v. 6, represents a different action than in v. 5, but v. 6 is best taken as a summarizing EPITOME, which normally includes a CASUALTY REPORT, as here, listing just such a fantastic number of casualties as the 120,000 mentioned. In this case, the EPITOME gives the reason for defeat as being Judah's forsaking Yahweh, the ancestral God. In v. 7 an independent note expands on the EPITOME, mentioning by name a mighty Ephraimite champion who cut down three of the most important men in the kingdom, including the king's own son (cf. Yeivin, explaining the office of "second to the king").

The foregoing notices make no cohesive, ongoing narrative of themselves, but this is what we find in vv. 8-15, the ANECDOTE of the Judahite captives. That this may indeed come from a separate tradition—even a written source—can best be argued from the fact that "the king of Israel," "Pekah son of Remaliah," vv. 5-6, plays no part; in fact, it is the chiefs of Ephraim *('ănāšîm mērā'šê běnê-'eprayim)* who make the crucial decision in vv. 12-15. In other words, this event might originally have had nothing to do with the Syro-Ephraimite war. An enormous number of Judahite captives (200,000) are being taken by the "men of Israel" to Samaria. From the reference to "their kinsfolk" *('ăhêhem)*, v. 8 and v. 15, we understand that even this 200,000 are but a token contingent. Actually, there are more persons involved, since wives, sons, and daughters go along too (v. 10). Upon seeing their approach, a prophet named Oded met the army and delivered a harsh speech of reprimand, vv. 9-11 (cf. Watson, 3.6; Seeligmann, 276). Oded speaks vigorously of God's anger, which is on victor as on victim. He concedes that God "gave them into your hand" (CONVEYANCE FORMULA) in the wrath *(baḥămat)* of Yahweh their ancestral God, yet he blames them for slaying them *běza'ap 'ad*

1 AND 2 CHRONICLES

laššāmayim higgîaʿ, "with fury reaching up to the sky." This far exceeds Yahweh's intent to punish them. V. 10 begins with *wĕʿattâ*, "so now," followed by the object for emphasis: "So now the Judahites and Jerusalemites you are intending to bind as male and female slaves for your own selves." The verse concludes, *hălōʾ raq-ʾattem ʿimmākem ʾăšāmôt lĕyahweh ʾĕlōhêkem*, "As for you yourselves, are not loads of guilt over against Yahweh your God laid upon you?" This surprisingly strong accusation against the Ephraimites is made even more emphatic when, having commanded them to send back their kinsfolk *(ʾăhêkem)* whom they have taken captive (introduced by a second *wĕʿattâ*, "so now"), Oded reminds his hearers that "the fierce wrath of Yahweh" *(hărôn ʾap-yahweh)* is upon them. Important for the exegesis of this pericope as a whole is the understanding that this wrath has been occasioned not only by their seizing the captives, but by all the deeds of guilt *(ʾăšāmôt)* with which Oded has just charged them. We take special note of the al-literation, *wĕhāšîbû haššibyâ ʾăšer šĕbîtem*, "and send back the captives that you have captured"; cf. also vv. 5, 8, 13, 14, 15, 17. (Cf. De Vries, "Prophetic Address," 31, 34.)

The word of the prophet is next supported by the Ephraimite chiefs (as has been pointed out, no king is present), vv. 12-13. Four names are given. They prohibit the army from keeping the Judahite captives. They too emphasize God's wrath: *lĕʾašmat yahweh ʿālênû ʾattem ʾōmĕrîm lĕhōsîp ʿal-haṭṭōʾtênû wĕʾal-ʾašmātênû*, "To Yahweh's wrath already upon us you intend to add to our sins and our guilty deeds." To this accusation the chiefs add a confession, *kî-rabbâ ʾašmâ lānû wahărôn ʾāp ʿal-yiśrāʾēl*, "For we have great guilt, and fierce wrath is on Israel."

The rest is narrative (vv. 14-15). The army yields up captives and booty; the "men mentioned by name" *(hāʾănāšîm ʾăšer-niqqĕbû bĕšēmôt)*—meaning the four chiefs of v. 12, not "those specially designated" (Williamson, comm.)—take charge of both, feed, clothe, and nurse the needy, and conduct them to their "kinsfolk" in Jericho, chosen as a border point, with access to both parties.

The section vv. 16-21 has neither structural nor thematic connection to the ANECDOTE of the Judahite captives. It tells of Ahaz's ineffectual appeal to the Assyrian king, "Tilgath-pilneser." This account stands in direct contradiction to the parallel account in 2 Kgs 16:5-9 (cf. Isa 7:1ff.), which relates that this king does help Ahaz (Lemke, 209-10, argues that both texts may be correct if seen as reporting different episodes). Integral to the structure of ChrH's account is the inclusio formed by vv. 16 and 21, which introduces the scene with the transition formula *bāʿēt hahîʾ*, "at that time," and then relates that "King Ahaz" (honorific title) sends to the king (LXX, Vg., Tg.; MT "kings") of Assyria *laʿzōr lô*, "to help him"; the concluding formula is in v. 21, where, having plundered the temple and the palace and the other rich houses for tribute, he discovers that *wĕlōʾ lĕʿezrâ lô*, "there was no help for him." The purpose of sending to Assyria for help is understood to be to fend off the Syrians and Ephraimites (vv. 5-7). A transitional *wĕʿôd*, "and again/moreover" (v. 17), only emphasizes the need, and does not give a hint of temporal sequence. Vv. 17-18 tell us of another exile of Judahites by Edom, then of the capture of a rather large number of cities and towns in the Shephelah (not in the Negeb) by the Philistines. The theological interpretation in v. 19 appears to apply only to these raids by the Edomites and Philistines; it explains that Ahaz was brought low *(knʿ, hiph.)* by Yahweh because he had done wantonly *(prʿ, hiph.)* in Judah and had exceedingly wronged Yahweh *(ûmāʿôl maʿal bĕyahweh)*. We note

here the use of the full legal title, "Ahaz king of Judah" (MT: "Israel") as in an indictment (cf. the full title of the Assyrian king in v. 20). V. 19 has two grounding
clauses with *kî:* "for Yahweh brought Judah low"; "for he had dealt wantonly in
Judah." The first explains why the Edomites and Philistines came; the second explains why Yahweh allowed this to happen (this verse is, accordingly, a good example of Yahweh's role as instrumental agent, effectuating a cause that a responsible human person—Ahaz—had put in motion).

As we have mentioned, vv. 20-21 are contrary to 2 Kgs 16:5-9 in stating that
the Assyrian king does just the opposite of helping Ahaz. V. 20 states that he afflicted him rather than strengthened him. V. 21 begins with another circumstantial
clause, to the effect that Ahaz looted *(ḥlq)* the temple and the homes of all the leading men (including himself), as a bribe to the Assyrian or as tribute demanded by
him, but it did not help.

The section vv. 22-25 has a formal introduction, *ûbĕ'ēt hāṣēr lô,* "and in the
time when he was afflicted." This is to be taken consecutively or sequentially. ChrH
does not much worry about such questions. All he wants to tell is that even subservience to and ill-treatment by a supposed ally do not get Ahaz to repent toward
Yahweh, but "he became yet more faithless toward him" *(wayyôsep lim'ôl bĕyahweh).* In disdain ChrH provides the emphatic identification, *hû' hammelek 'āḥāz,*
"this very same king Ahaz." He then details just how absurdly wicked Ahaz becomes. In v. 23 he tells how he sacrificed to the same Syrian gods that had defeated
him; his explanation is that since those gods helped *('zr)* the Damascenes he was
going to sacrifice to them to get them to help him. We note the chiastic parallelism:
hēm ma'zĕrîm 'ōtām lāhem 'ăzabbēaḥ wĕya'zĕrûnî, "They were helping them; to
them I will sacrifice in order that they may help me" (subject-verb-object; object-
double verb-object). But, as v. 23b states, they proved instead to be the ruin *(kšl,*
hiph.) of himself and of "all Israel"—meaning, of course, the ideal Israelite state
and not just Judah. What Ahaz does here is an ironic reversal of Amaziah's worshiping the defeated gods of Edom, 25:14. There as here, it is not the logic of
whether to worship defeated or defeating gods that matters, but the question of
loyalty to Yahweh. Amaziah went out faithful, won with Yahweh's blessing, and
worshiped the defeated gods. Ahaz goes out unfaithful to Yahweh, is defeated, and
worships the victorious gods. It is not Yahweh who has changed in either case;
going over to other gods can only bring ruin.

Having become fully apostate, Ahaz does what he can to drive Yahweh away
from his temple, vv. 24-25 (cf. 2 Kgs 16:17-18 for a more historical description
of this king's radical cultic innovations). Willi (p. 171) describes this section as
an explication, i.e., exegesis, of just how wicked Ahaz was. ChrH is actually
preparing for 2 Chr 29:5ff. when he tells how Ahaz destroys the holy vessels (cf.
Ackroyd, "Temple Vessels"). ChrH likewise prepares for 29:3, 7, when he tells
how Ahaz locks the temple doors. Again using chiasmus, ChrH connects the new
shrines of Jerusalem with those in the countryside: *wayya'aś lô mizbĕḥôt bĕkol-
pinnâ bîrûšālāim ûbĕkol-'îr wā'îr lîhûdâ 'āśâ bāmôt,* "And he made himself altars at every corner of Jerusalem, and in every city, even the cities of Judah, he
made shrines" (verb-object-prepositional phrase; prepositional phrase-verb-ob-
ject). ChrH's theological assessment, v. 25b, is that he thereby offended *(k's)* Yahweh the ancestral God.

In the concluding summary, Lemke (p. 213) suggests that ChrH would have

365

been following a separate tradition from 2 Kgs 16:19-20. A more likely explanation is that ChrH is just letting out some of his antipathy against this prototype of a wicked king. Again, no prophetic source is mentioned, only "the book of the kings of Judah and Israel." Though he had no sore sickness like Asa (2 Chr 16:14) or Uzziah (26:21), ChrH tells how Ahaz was allowed to be buried in Jerusalem, but not in the royal tombs (cf. Willi, 121).

Genre

Though this pericope is complex and somewhat lengthy, it has no other theme than Ahaz's wickedness. It is a REPORT, therefore, not an (→) account. At the beginning is a REGNAL RESUMÉ, with ACCESSION AGE FORMULA, STATEMENT OF LENGTH AND PLACE OF REIGN, and THEOLOGICAL REVIEW. The concluding REGNAL RESUMÉ has the CITATION FORMULA, the DEATH AND BURIAL FORMULA, and the SUCCESSION FORMULA. Taken in their totality, vv. 5-15 constitute a BATTLE REPORT, but the ANECDOTE of vv. 8-15 is a separate unit within it. V. 6 is an EPITOME, including the customary CASUALTY REPORT. Also germane to the BATTLE REPORT is the CONVEYANCE FORMULA, seen in vv. 5a, 5b, 9a. Although the ANECDOTE normally records an experience in the life of one person, vv. 8-15 fall under this genre because the various groupings (Judahite exiles, prophet, Ephraimite chiefs) all behave as individuals; like others of its kind, this ANECDOTE makes much of conversation and imaginative description. Truly central to this narrative is the vehement PROPHETIC SPEECH of Oded, together with the introduction constituting a REPORT OF A PROPHETIC WORD, vv. 9-11. Oded's speech features the ACCUSATORY QUESTION, "Have you not sins of your own?" and the WARNING, "Now hear me . . . for the fierce wrath of Yahweh is upon you." "Send back the captives" is a COMMAND. In the introduction to the chieftains' speech, vv. 12-13 contain a NAME LIST. This speech belongs to the genre ADDRESS (vocative omitted); it includes a PROHIBITION ("You shall not bring . . ."), an ACCUSATION ("You propose to bring upon us guilt"), and a CONFESSION OF GUILT ("Our guilt is already great, and there is fierce wrath against Israel").

Verses 16-21 form a roughly organized BATTLE REPORT. There are TRANSITION FORMULAS to introduce vv. 16 and 17, NAME LISTS of regions and cities in v. 18, and a THEOLOGICAL REVIEW, including an ACCUSATION, in v. 19. Vv. 22-25 have few formal structures, only a TRANSITION FORMULA in v. 22 and another THEOLOGICAL REVIEW in v. 25b.

Setting

Although ChrH sticks quite close to his Kings source in the introductory summary, he departs from it elsewhere. Ahaz brings something new to Judah. Not only does he fail to do what is right, like David (v. 1), walking in "the ways of the kings of Israel" (v. 2), but he practices outright idolatry. In the expansion of the REGNAL RESUMÉ (vv. 3-4), he is accused of actually making molten images of Baal (cf. 1 Kgs 16:32; 2 Chr 23:17), of introducing the abominable Molech cult, and of extending local shrine worship to "the hills and under every green tree." It seems entirely in character for him, then, to become "yet more faithless to Yahweh" by sacrificing "to the gods of Damascus" (vv. 22-23). In this king, Israel seems to be probing the depths of wickedness still remaining as possibilities for them. The SCHEMA OF REWARD AND RETRIBUTION has not been consistently applied to him, for the defeats and deportations that Ahaz experiences, vv. 5ff., 17ff., cause his people more harm than himself. All that Ahaz suffers by way of personal retribution is the apparently unmotivated dishonor of not being buried in the ancestral tomb, v. 27. It does seem true to character that such an enthusiastically eclectic king should allow the temple to be plundered (v. 21), and even close down the temple altogether in favor of heathen shrines in Jerusalem and throughout the land (v. 25). ChrH may be exaggerating Ahaz's wickedness in order to make his son Hezekiah seem the more pious, but the anger of Yahweh that he is said to have provoked (v. 25b) has little effect on him personally.

By being so unspecific on this point, ChrH seems to invite us to think of a corporate guilt, i.e., that Ahaz was inciting Yahweh's anger against the people; that the people would eventually be forced to bear Ahaz's punishment. He does have the prophet Oded declare that "because Yahweh, the God of your fathers, was angry with Judah, he gave them into your hand" (v. 9). The prominent position given the ANECDOTE of the captive Judahites, vv. 8-15, seems to suggest that ChrH's true theme is Judah's exile, not Ahaz's sin. This is already the point of the EPITOME in v. 6: "They had forsaken Yahweh, the God of their fathers." It is difficult to determine how much of vv. 5-15 is fictional and how much is from reliable historical sources. 2 Kgs 16:5 is in the background of vv. 5ff., but it does not say that Ahaz was conquered. V. 6 seems to be a concoction, but the notice about Zichri's exploit, v. 7, seems real. As for the ANECDOTE, all seems staged, including the reference to chiefs acting in lieu of a king. We are not convinced of historicity even by the express naming of four of these chiefs in v. 12. What we seem to have, rather, is a dramatized sermon on brotherly treatment of Judahite captives. Pekah may indeed have killed some Judahite soldiers and taken some captives, who were eventually restored to their land (the reference to Jericho sounds historical, but may be an embellishment). Especially questionable as an historical statement is the detailing of the solicitous care given the captives. The conclusion to which we must come is that ChrH has here created a stirring narrative for illustrating the theological point of Ephraim's guilt in common with Judah.

Any who may be inclined to credit ChrH's version of the contact with "Tilgath-pilneser" (cf. 1 Chr 5:26), preferring its statement to that of 2 Kgs 16:5-9, which claims that Ahaz did make a successful approach to the Assyrian king, should weigh especially the schematic nature of ChrH's account, with everything compressed within the inclusio, "sent . . . for help," v. 16, and "it did not help him," v. 21. A further point to consider is that this arrangement puts Ahaz in an unfavorable rather than a favorable light—just what ChrH wanted.

Intention

ChrH's rationale for Ahaz's reign hangs on the following points: (1) this king's unrelieved wickedness, extending even to outright idolatry, marks the nation for an ineluctable doom; (2) the report that Ahaz chopped up the temple vessels, and even locked the doors against would-be worshipers, is a vivid type of the temple's desecration in the coming exile; and (3) a typology of restoration from exile is set in place by two essential elements: return for the prisoners and the restored wholeness of Israel. ChrH has made much of the theme of successful warfare against foreign enemies; here that theme is reversed in the notice of Pekah's successful war, vv. 5-7, and in the notice of Edomite and Philistine invasions, vv. 17-19. The lesson is stated clearly in v. 19, "For Yahweh brought Judah low because of Ahaz king of Israel."

A new element is the theme of exile. First, there is mention of a large number of captives brought to Damascus, v. 5a. Then there is the ANECDOTE, vv. 8-15, telling of a fantastically large number of Judahite captives taken to Samaria. Fortunately, these are restored—a symbol of the return from the exile to Babylon yet to come. Thus the theme of hope does survive in this account of many calamities. But by far the most important theme is northern Israel's (Ephraim's) contrition, confession, and deed of brotherly charity. Williamson (comm.) has made a great deal of ChrH's apparent notion that the breach which was created by Jeroboam's revolt against Rehoboam, 2 Chronicles 10, and which was so severely censured by Abijah in 13:3-12, is here restored in principle. We cannot put too much emphasis on this symbolism of restoration. ChrH understood very well, just from reading 2 Kings 17, that Samaria fell and that there never was a political reunion of north and south. Yet the breach is healed in principle when northerners confess co-responsibility, and begin to treat the Judahites as brothers. We must not miss the point that the 200,000 Judahite captives leave their "kinsfolk *['aḥêhem]*" behind, leading Oded to command (v. 11) the army to "send back your kinsfolk *['aḥêkem]* whom you have taken." Truly it can be said that "the men of Israel" who seized so many Judahite captives, and intended to make male and female slaves of them, represented separated Israel before they rediscovered brotherhood, while Oded and the chiefs represent separated Israel seeking to rediscover this brotherhood (see Williamson, *Israel,* 113-18).

We cannot doubt that ChrH sees a solidarity in guilt as the key to this rediscovery. The fact that the Judahites have been taken captive is in itself proof of Yahweh's anger against them, but Oded articulates this point: "Behold, because Yahweh, the God of your fathers, was angry with Judah, he gave them into your hand," v. 9b. The God who punished is the God of their fathers, hence he is their own God, and is using them to punish the wayward. But, adds Oded, Ephraim is committing two sins of its own: (1) slaying them with "a rage reaching up to heaven"—i.e., unbounded by considerations of brotherhood, and far in excess of Yahweh's intent (Isa 40:2; Zech 1:15)—and (2) destining them for slavery, a permanent expression of Yahweh's wrath (v. 10a). The impropriety of such ill treatment is expressed in Oded's RHETORICAL QUESTION (v. 10b): "Have you not sins of your own against Yahweh your God?" Indeed they did, and they were as deserving as their captives of a cruel punishment. Therefore Oded commands them to send the captives back, adding the grounding clause (v. 11b), "for the fierce wrath of Yahweh is upon you." Whether this divine wrath is because of the aforementioned sins, or in particular because of seizing the captives, seems to be made clear in the chieftains' accusation of v. 13: "You shall not bring the captives in here, for you propose to bring upon us guilt against Yahweh in addition to our present sins and guilt." In their confession, v. 13b, these chieftains reemphasize the distinction: "For our guilt is already great, and (now) there is fierce wrath against Israel."

ChrH is using these speeches to express a deeply felt conviction of his own. First, much guilt has accumulated, especially in the north, because the kingdom was separated and kept separated. Yahweh is angry with both kingdoms for this, and punishes both peoples alike when they transgress. But "the fierce wrath" of Yahweh is reserved for those who violate brotherhood and seek to victimize one another. When did this happen? Our ANECDOTE tells that it happened under Ahaz (and no wonder, for no Judean king was as wicked as he). But ChrH means this as a kind of parable, a paradigm for his own time. Judah has gone into exile and been restored, but it still needs brotherhood with remnants of true Israel in the north. We have heard of northern enmity in Nehemiah. Although its origins remain obscure, sometime, somehow a Samaritan schism took place. There were still some in the north who would perpetuate the exile and prevent restoration. What was needed, then, was a continuing confession of sin and a return to Yahweh, who had been, and still was, the God of all their fathers.

Bibliography

P. R. Ackroyd, "The Temple Vessels—a Continuity Theme," in *Studies in the Religion of Ancient Israel* (VTSup 23; Leiden: Brill, 1972) 166-81; S. J. De Vries, "The Forms of Prophetic Address," *Hebrew Annual Review* 10 (1986) 15-36; B. Oded, "The Historical Background of the War Between Rezin and Pekah Against Ahaz" (Hebr.), *Tarb* 38 (1968-69) 205-24; I. L. Seeligmann, "Die Auffassung von der Prophetie in der deuteronomistischen und chronistischen Geschichtsschreibung," in *Congres Volume: Göttingen 1977* (VTSup 29; Leiden: Brill, 1978) 254-84; H. G. M. Williamson, *Israel in the Book of Chronicles* (Cambridge: Cambridge, 1977); S. Yeivin, "Philological Notes XI.iii. 'The Next to the King' (II Chron. 28,7)" (Hebr.), *Leš* 35 (1970-71) 172-74.

ACCOUNT OF THE REIGN OF HEZEKIAH, 29:1–32:33

Structure

I. Report of Hezekiah's reforms		29:1–31:21
A. Regnal resumé		29:1-2
B. Reforms in the first month		29:3-36
C. Keeping the festivals in the second month		30:1–31:1
D. Arrangements for distributing the offerings		31:2-19
E. Theological evaluation		31:20-21
II. Historical story: Hezekiah's deliverance		32:1-23
III. Report of further facts		32:24-33

In terms of space occupied, Hezekiah is ahead of all the other kings except David and Solomon. ChrH has a lot to tell about him. Most of it is about his cultic activities, but there are items about political and military matters as well.

ChrH's rationale concerning Hezekiah can be summarized as follows: (1) Hezekiah's vast and exemplary good outweighs the prototypical wickedness of his father Ahaz, and thereby extends the day of divine patience; (2) nevertheless, since the nation is doomed, Hezekiah's peccadillo (32:24, 31), even with his repentance, kept the nation on its fateful pathway; (3) his greatest contribution was setting firmly in place a model for the eventual restoration of Israel's cultic life; (4) he developed the Solomon typology in his devotion to the temple and its cult. Transition formulas at 29:3; 32:1; and 32:24 connect the Hezekiah material as a cohesive ACCOUNT, while the mention of Hezekiah by name, initiating successive new moves at 30:1 and 31:2, marks the major subdivisions.

I. REPORT OF HEZEKIAH'S REFORMS, 29:1–31:21

Structure

Because of the complexity of this material, it will be helpful to present our outlines and comments regarding "structure" in sections.

A. Regnal resumé	29:1-2
1. Accession age formula and statement of length and place of reign	1a
2. Identification of mother	1b
3. Theological review	2

This is virtually identical to 2 Kgs 18:2-3. The theological review to the effect that Hezekiah did right in Yahweh's eyes, according to all that David his father had done, is unusual and highly significant. Taking "David his father" in a typological as well as genealogical sense, it sets him up as a reincarnation of Solomon.

B. Reforms in the first month	29:3-36
1. Opening and repairing temple doors	3
2. Address to priests and Levites	4-11
a. Introduction	4
b. Address to the Levites	5-11
1) Call to attention	5a
2) Order	5b
a) Sanctify selves and temple	5bα
b) Remove uncleanness	5bβ
3) Indictment speech against the forefathers	6-7
a) General	6
(1) Infidelity	6a
(2) Backsides to Yahweh's "tabernacle"	6b
b) Specification: suspended temple worship	7
4) Result	8-9
a) Yahweh's wrath	8a
b) Judah/Jerusalem a laughingstock	8b
c) Fathers dead, children captive	9
5) Call to action	10-11
a) Declaration of intention	10
(1) Renew covenant	10a
(2) Avert divine wrath	10b
b) Admonition	11
(1) Prohibition against lassitude	11a

There are few formal transition points within this section. The structure of the various subunits is the most important indication of where sections take up and leave off. Although we are given a time frame, this is not sufficient itself to create the structure of a chronicle (cf. Asa). The mention in v. 3 that Hezekiah began his reform by opening and repairing the temple doors "in the first year of his reign, in the first month," almost certainly means Nisan (universally the beginning of the spring New Year in postexilic times, and the accession month for a new king), in spite of the fact that the Judahite kings were still observing a Tishri New Year at the time of the historical Hezekiah (cf. S. J. De Vries, "Chronology of the OT," *IDB*, I:595). ChrH intends to accomplish two things: (1) to put Hezekiah to work at reform as soon as the reign of his wicked father had ended; and (2) to fill up the time between the first day of this month till its sixteenth day with cleansing operations (v. 17), allowing a festival of cleansing and rededication to occur on the sixteenth, vv. 20ff. This allows ChrH to accomplish a third purpose, to provide a rationale for celebrating Passover on the fourteenth day of the second month (30:2, 15), for too many days had been spent in cleansing the temple to allow the Passover to be kept at its proper time in the first month (Exod 12:1ff.).

We are here faced with a conundrum: was it the tradition of a sixteen-day cleansing that was in place first, or the tradition of a second-month Passover? Much scholarly erudition has been spent on this problem, and it is impossible to discuss it here. After all is said and done, we must not overlook that (1) ChrH takes considerable pains to describe in detail Josiah's Passover in the correct month—the first, 35:1-19, showing that he did consider the first month correct after all; and (2) that the dedication festival described in ch. 30, at the end of the cleansing period, is to be thought of as a repetition of Solomon's festival for the dedication, narrated in 7:8-10, and that this had priority over a routine celebration of the Passover. Looking back at our description of the FESTIVAL SCHEMA (→ 2 Chr 7:7-10), we recall that the festivals of Solomon (ch. 7), Asa (ch. 15), Hezekiah (ch. 30), and Josiah (ch. 35) share four elements in the normal order: (1) notice of date, (2) identification (including purification) of participants, (3) description of ceremonies, and (4), except in ch. 35, joyful celebration. The dating of Solomon's ceremony in the seventh month does provide some basis for identifying it with Tabernacles—yet it remains primarily a feast of dedication. Ch. 29 also has the four elements of the FESTIVAL SCHEMA: (1) the notice of date in v. 3; (2) the identification and purification of the participants, vv. 4-19; (3) the description of the ceremonies, vv. 20-35; and (4) a joyful celebration, v. 36. Thus two conclusions may be drawn: first, that ChrH is making Hezekiah emulate Solomon in rededicating the temple; and second, that this ceremony of cleansing and rededication is a kind of shadow Passover, just as Solomon's dedication was a shadow Feast of Tabernacles. We can be quite certain that ChrH goes on to tell of a real Passover—be it all in the second month—for fear that he might mislead his readers into thinking that its observance was a matter of indifference. If we keep these observations in mind, we will better be able to understand the highly complex structure of ch. 29.

The internal structure of Part B, "Reforms in the first month," can be clearly seen. The beginning, v. 3, is a brief report of action; then comes Hezekiah's involved and impassioned address, vv. 4-11; next is a narrative report of the response to this address, vv. 12-19; then comes a long and involved description of the offerings, vv. 20-35a; and finally a formal conclusion, v. 35b, with a statement of the people's reaction, v. 36.

In v. 3 we have a statement of Hezekiah's first act, with an obvious play on the king's name: *pāṭaḥ 'et-daltôt bêt-yahweh wayĕḥazzĕqēm*, "He opened the doors of Yahweh's temple and strengthened them." There is no clue to what the "strengthening" consisted of; the pun is everything, and if we dared, we might translate "Hezekiahed them." On the day, see our previous remarks; it is the same day as that of v. 17. Willi (p. 171) identifies this and what follows as an explication of 2 Kgs 18:4, but the identification with the FESTIVAL SCHEMA tells us that ChrH is telling his own story. Willi (p. 199) cannot be right in marking v. 4 as a gloss, for structurally it is indispensable in telling us what Hezekiah is about as he begins his address. A problem is immediately apparent in this verse because it is "the priests and the Levites" who are summoned, yet it is solely the Levites who are called upon in v. 5 to sanctify themselves (which they are reported as doing in vv. 12-15), and what is more, to sanctify Yahweh's temple, carrying out the "filth" even from *haqqōdeš*, "the holy place." It also seems that these Levites are the ones called "my sons" in v. 11, chosen to perform the priestly duties of "standing in Yahweh's presence" and burning incense.

Petersen (pp. 77-85) analyzes this passage and finds a sharp priest-versus-Levite rivalry. Undeniably, some rivalry is present, yet, since v. 16 clearly says that the priests cleansed the "inner part" *(pĕnîmâ)* of Yahweh's temple, carrying out the uncleanness *(ḥaṭṭum'â)* to the temple court for the Levites to dispose of, we have no ground for thinking that the Levites actually usurped the priestly prerogative. A better explanation is (1) to acknowledge that ChrH is definitely a spokesman for the Levites, but (2) to recognize that in this situation the Levites actually had a more responsible role to play. True, only the priests might venture into *haqqōdeš*, "the holy place," so that the Levites needed the priests to cooperate in cleansing the temple itself. Yet the "attending" that the Levites were to do over against the priests included supervision (cf. 1 Chr 23:32)—seeing to it that the priests performed their duties as prescribed. In the present passage Hezekiah addresses the Levites as general overseers; the admonition of v. 11 is still spoken to them in a general sense, but with specific application to the priests, who must also obey the admonition not to be negligent. (The report of vv. 18-19, to the effect that the temple and the table of showbread, along with other implements and articles, had been cleansed, may be thought of as first spoken by the priests and then passed on to the king by the Levites.)

There is little ground for the claim of Williamson (comm.) that Hezekiah's speech is a "Levitical sermon" (von Rad), for it lacks the development: *doctrina, explicatio, applicatio,* and is certainly not spoken by a Levite. The charge, v. 5, is to "sanctify yourselves [cf. 29:31; 30:15, 24b] and Yahweh's house," which means removing all its uncleanness *(niddâ).* The need for this is explicated in general and specific complaints *(kî),* vv. 6-7 (Galling, ATD, discards v. 6 as a gloss, without realizing that this is ChrH's own judgmental statement). "Our fathers"—meaning Ahaz specifically but including all previous sinners—have engaged in outrageous misbehavior *(mā'ălû;* 26:18), making themselves like the elders of Ezek 9:16, turning their faces away from Yahweh and giving him their backside *('ōrep)* instead. That is Hezekiah's general complaint. The specific charges are these *(gam):* they (1) shut the doors, (2) put out the lamps, (3) neglected the incense, and (4) abandoned the burnt offering. The result is Yahweh's wrath *(qeṣep;* cf. Joash, 2 Chr 24:18), which has manifested itself in two ways: (1) Judah and Jerusalem are the laughingstock that you see, and (2) our fathers have died by the sword, while sons, daughters, and wives are captives. The answer is to make (i.e., to renew) Yahweh's covenant, so as to turn away this wrath, v. 10. Because there is no narrative of a covenant ceremony, we assume that Hezekiah is speaking of righteous acts as a covenant renewal.

There is something highly artificial about the list of Levites in vv. 12-14 (Willi, 199, speaks of this as a gloss; see also the discussion in Petersen, 81; Möhlenbrink, 213; Watson, 4.4). It is strange to read that they "rose up" *(wayyāqumû),* since they must have stood to hear Hezekiah's address. Furthermore, it is strange to read that the fourteen persons named had to "gather their brethren" —presumably their fellow Levites—if those Levites (or some of them) were already present (v. 15). Strangest of all, the Levitical families include not only the four traditional ones, but the three families of singers as well (Gese, "Zur Geschichte der Kultsänger am zweiten Tempel," in *Abraham unser Vater* [*Fest.* O. Michel; ed. O. Betz, et al.; Leiden: Brill, 1963] 226, puts the arrangement of singers in his tradition III-A, i.e., about ChrH's own time). We would expect the schematic two from each family, but it is a novelty to read (v. 15) that the king's command was "by the words of Yahweh"—in other words, revelation—a concept that is reiterated and reinforced in 30:12 (cf. Williamson, comm.).

We have commented on the separate responsibilities of the priests and Levites (Petersen, 82, speaks of Levitical glorification; von Rad, *Geschichtsbild,* 92-93, discusses the "holy place" as a priestly preserve; cf. also Watson, 4.3). Kidron as a place for disposing of cultic uncleanness is mentioned also in 15:16; 30:14. Corresponding to the two-stage removal is a two-stage time schedule, v. 17, which is strange not only in allowing just eight days for each area, but particularly in the fact that "up to the porch [*'ûlām*]," the domain of the Levites, was finished first, and then the temple itself, assigned to the priests. According to this, the Levites took eight days to cleanse the courts and then had to carry away for eight days the uncleanness that the priests found in the temple. From this we gather that the Levites worked twice as long as the priests; but we do not receive the image of the former showing subservience by performing more menial service, but rather that the latter were under Levitical supervision, and began their special task only when the Levites were ready for them to begin. V. 17 has an interesting chiasmus involving assonance; it starts out with *wayyāḥēllû*, "and they began," and ends with *killû*, "they finished." As has been said, the report to the king, vv. 18-19, has to be taken as spoken by the leading Levites on behalf of all the workers, Levitical or priestly.

An entirely new move is signalled in v. 20, with *wayyaškēm yĕḥizqîyāhû hammelek*, "And King Hezekiah started out" (not *RSV* "rose early," because no time sequence is involved; cf. Jehoshaphat, 20:20), meaning that the king now takes action. All of vv. 20-35a is concerned with the offering of dedicatory sacrifices (cf. Petersen, 92, after Hänel). First, there are to be two kinds of official sacrifices, vv. 20-29; next, there is to be congregational singing, v. 30; and then there are to be spontaneous lay offerings, vv. 31-35a. Among the official sacrifices, over which the king exercises direct authority, there are two kinds: sin offerings to atone for the people's guilt, and whole burnt offerings for praise. The interpretation of Williamson (comm.) is that these took place simultaneously. The impression that this might have been so may be created by the fact that the Aaronite priests are commanded to "offer up [*'lh*, hiph.] upon the altar" (no object is given), v. 21b, with the assumption that this refers back to at least some of the victims that have been brought in v. 21a, *lĕḥaṭṭā't*, "to make atonement," i.e., as sin offerings. We must choose either of two possibilities: (1) that the best and largest of the animals were reserved for the *'ôlâ* sacrifice that was to follow, this reference being therefore proleptic, or (2) that Williamson's claim is right, and that both kinds of sacrificing went on simultaneously. Either interpretation would be theoretically possible, but the latter is less likely. Considering both the orderliness that we might expect in an actual service and ChrH's orderly habit of mind, we find it hard to believe that ChrH intended simultaneity.

We must pay particular attention to places where the king intervenes; in addition to v. 21b, see vv. 27, 30, and 31. In the last three places the king's command (*'mr*) carries the service further. Both vv. 21b and 24b ought to be taken as asides explaining the action in progress. We must add that v. 25 has to be a secondary expansion, for the following reasons: (1) it has the only introductory verb (*'md*, hiph.) without the regular subject, Hezekiah; (2) the addition of Nathan and Gad to David (cf. v. 27) for authority, without theological rationale, is suspicious; (3) the qal of *'md* at the beginning of v. 26 can be identified as the likely takeoff point for this expansion, with its initial *'md*, hiph.; (4) v. 25b is an awkward and transparently artificial rationale: *kî bĕyad-yahweh hammiṣwâ bĕyad- nĕbî'āyw*, "for the command was by Yahweh's hand by the hand of his prophets."

There were to be seven of four kinds of animals comprising the category *lĕḥaṭṭā't 'al-hammamlākâ wĕ'al-hammiqdaš wĕ'al-yĕhûdâ*, "to shrive the kingdom and the sanctuary and Judah" (v. 21; LXX "Israel" may be correct since ChrH generally claims this name for Judah). According to v. 22 the first three kinds were to be killed. The question is by whom, because in Leviticus it is the worshiper who must kill the sacrificial victim. Here the subject is indefinite, but 30:16 suggests that the Levites are intended; they killed the animal and gave its blood to the priest, who threw it against the altar. If that is what is intended here, it is a novelty; it shows how the Levites were constantly eager to insert their presence where it had not been required before. The seven atoning he-goats are saved for last (cf. Leviticus 16); the priests are definitely the ones who kill them. The special purpose of this sacrifice is stated to be *lĕkappēr 'al-kol-yiśrā'ēl*, "to atone for all Israel," v. 24aβ (cf. Williamson, *Israel*, 126). The "aside" of v. 24b seems to be making an effort to explain this "all Israel," which is chiastically juxtaposed in the main statement and in the "aside."

As has been said, the whole burnt offerings to which we come in v. 25 are meant to follow next in sequence after the sin offerings. Galling (ATD) and Willi (p. 200) say that all of vv. 25-30 is secondary (cf. Petersen, 83; von Rad, *Geschichtsbild*, 104), but this is because of the greater prominence given the Levites. These are not nearly so prominent if we acknowledge the previous arguments that v. 25 by itself is an expansion. The section properly begins with the statement in v. 26 that Levites and priests were stationed *('md)* with David's instruments (cf. 1 Chr 15:16-24) and trumpets. Emphasis is placed on the sound these instruments made (vv. 27-28) while the *'ôlâ*, "burnt offering," was being offered at the king's command. According to vv. 28-30, the congregation *(qāhāl)* bowed in worship (1) while the sacrifice was being offered, (2) at its conclusion, and (3) while the Levites sang the praise songs of David and "Asaph the seer."

As the king and princes call for the praise psalms in v. 30, Hezekiah calls the people in v. 31 to voluntary offerings of their own (cf. Watson, 6.2). That something new is coming is signalled by *'attâ*, "Now." The king then declares that they have "ordained themselves" *(millē'tem yedkem)*, hence are now invited to present *zĕbāḥîm* and *tôdôt*, "(regular) offerings" and "thank offerings" (Lev 7:2; cf. Petersen, 84). In v. 31b they do just this, and afterward anyone who was *nĕdîb lēb*, "willing of heart" (cf. 1 Chr 29:6), would present an *'ôlâ*, "burnt offering." To demonstrate the magnitude of this outpouring, ChrH next tallies the bulls, rams, and lambs that were offered as *'ôlâ*, "burnt offering," plus the *qĕdāšîm* (a general term for all offerings; cf. Petersen, 84) of bulls and sheep (cf. 1 Chr 26:20, 26; 28:12; 2 Chr 31:12; 35:13). Then comes a section, vv. 34-35a, that Petersen calls anti-priestly, but which more probably is only pro-Levite, its point being that the Levites had to hustle to help the priests handle all these sacrifices, showing that theirs was the greater zeal.

The Solomon typology emerges even more clearly in the summary conclusion of v. 35b, *wattikkôn 'ăbôdat bêt-yahweh*, "So the ritual of (restoring) Yahweh's temple was completed"; cf. 2 Chr 8:16, at the end of a cultic section in the Solomon narrative (cf. Williamson, comm., 351). In v. 36 ChrH adds the final element of the FESTIVAL SCHEMA, telling how king and people rejoiced. Highly theocentric in its orientation, this joy was humanitarian in its emphasis; it was for what Yahweh had done for his people. Both angles are emphasized in the grounding clause at the end, *kî bĕpit'ōm hāyâ haddābār*, "for unexpectedly [spontaneously] the thing had come about."

This chapter's apparent discrepancies and conflicts with 2 Chronicles 35 have given some scholars migivings regarding its unity. Some or all of it has been assigned to later redactors or glossators. Galling (ATD) would omit the entirety. Willi (p. 200) would omit vv. 16bβ, 17b, and 21b-22 because of the prominence they give the Levites. Von Rad (*Geschichtsbild,* 104) agrees that vv. 21b-22 are secondary. Haag sees so many discrepancies that he would divide up the chapter into four separate strands, (1) the old Chronicles source; (2) the first redactor, ChrH; (3) a second redactor; and (4) harmonizing glosses. It is unparalleled to see such heavy redactional activity in ChrH. Here is a translation of the original content of the chapter according to Haag's old Chronicles source:

(1) And Hezekiah sent to all Israel and Judah that they should come to Yahweh's house in Jerusalem. (6) And the couriers went through all Israel

and Judah according to the command of the king and proclaimed it. (13) And many people came together in Jerusalem to keep the Feast of Unleavened Bread. (18) The majority of the people had not cleansed themselves, but Hezekiah prayed for them: "Yahweh, pardon!" (20) And Yahweh heard Hezekiah and healed the people. (21) And the people of Israel that were present at Jerusalem kept the Feast of Unleavened Bread seven days. (22) And they completed the feast of the seven days. (26) Since the time of Solomon the son of David king of Israel there had been nothing like this in Jerusalem. (27) Then the Levitical priests arose and blessed the people, and their voice was heard, and their prayer came to his holy habitation, to heaven.

Although this gives a tight, smooth account, this very fact must be turned against the validity of Haag's undertaking, for ChrH as we have by now come to know him loves extraneous fullness. Besides, the language and style of the omitted sections are his. Scholars have been particularly perturbed about the shifting about between Passover and Mazzoth nomenclature and practice, and also by the addition of an extra seven-day feast at vv. 23ff., which is particularly vexing because Josiah's Passover in ch. 35 includes only a single seven-day Mazzoth celebration (vv. 16-18), which agrees with the presumed ancient model in Exod 12:15. On the whole problem of the Passover/Mazzoth, here and in ch. 35, one should consider the judicious observations of Williamson (comm., 361-65). What is to be said here borrows from Williamson, while benefiting directly from our own previous study of the FESTIVAL SCHEMA. In five stories, this schema has its third element, "Ceremonies," and in all but two (chs. 15, 29), this specifies a seven-day period. Here in ch. 30 there is a seven-day duration for the regular Mazzoth (Unleavened Bread) festival, followed by a second of the same. But this is not unique. 2 Chronicles 7 (Solomon) has a similar seven-day festival, followed by a second period of the same duration (v. 9). Of course, this is not a Mazzoth festival, but a dedication feast (ch. 29); but we have already seen evidence that ChrH is constructing Hezekiah's reign on the model of Solomon's, so why should we not look for him to add a second seven-day period to the festival? The second Mazzoth week has been concocted by ChrH himself.

Inasmuch as a second seven-day festival is structurally significant in this passage, it is understandable that the first, regular Mazzoth week should predominate in ChrH's description of the combined Passover/Mazzoth celebration (note vv. 13-14, 21-22). However, since the actual Passover ceremony initiates the combined festival, it alone is mentioned in the summary's introduction, 30:1, and in the summons, v. 2. It also marks the beginning of the ceremonies, carried out in proper fashion by the celebrants, in v. 15a. Its apparent separation from the Mazzoth festivities, vv. 21ff., reflects no time delay but the complex (to ChrH) question of getting everyone sanctified for the Passover along with the Mazzoth festival that followed it.

The Passover was to be celebrated in the second, not the first, month. We have discussed the reason for this change in connection with (→) 29:17. The P legislation at Num 9:6-11 makes express provision for shifting from the first to the second month in special circumstances, and we can scarcely doubt that ChrH is taking advantage of that leniency here (see Shaver, 158-64). If we keep in mind that 30:1 is an introductory summary, we will avoid RSV's misleading "for" (wanting in Hebr.) and the pluperfect tense in v. 2, as well as the impression that the sending of the couriers in v. 6 is a doublet of v. 1; this verse intends to say that the invitation was to "all Israel," including specifically Judah, and was written in letters for Ephraim and Manasseh; this is phrased somewhat differently in v. 6, but means the same. (On the late practice of writing letters, showing special concern and urgency, see our remarks on 21:13-15.) The verbal form *wayyiwwā'aṣ,* "and [they] took counsel," occurs with *haqqāhāl,* "the congregation," also in v. 23 *(wayyiwwā'āṣû),* signifying a difficult, controversial, and binding decision (cf. 1 Chr 13:1). A joint decision is made on the impossibility of keeping the Passover *bā'ēt hahî',* "at this time" (v. 3; *RSV:* "in its time"), the reason being that it is now the sixteenth day of the first month, too late for the start in the fourteenth day of the first month (cf. 2 Chr 29:17). ChrH avoids this straightforward reason, substituting two others that seem facetious and unconvincing, v. 3. These are given in two grounding clauses with *kî:* (1) there are not enough sanctified priests (connected to ChrH's anti-priestly critique in this section), and (2) not enough people were there yet (cf. Num 9:9-12). So the decree was made to invite "all Israel" ("from Beersheba to Dan" is ChrH's way of resetting the old phrase; cf. 1 Chr 21:1). The wide distribution of this invitation, implied throughout vv. 5-11, 18, implies a theory of the return in sharp contrast to 2 Kings 17; cf. Williamson *(Israel,* 66-67, 123). Both the Passover and the Mazzoth feast, separate at first, were home celebrations according to Exod 12:1-17, but already with Deut 16:1-8 they could be celebrated only "at the place where Yahweh your God shall choose." So a pilgrimage to Jerusalem, from however far away, was demanded. The grounding clause with *kî* in v. 5b seems as facetious as ChrH's previous reasons: *kî lō' lārōb 'āśû kakkātûb,* "for they had not done it in large numbers as prescribed" (cf. v. 13); according to 2 Kgs 23:22, Israel had not kept the Passover since the days of the judges!

One can easily see why Haag has been so suspicious of vv. 6-9, for it is a sermon on repentance rather than a summons to the Passover. Williamson (comm.) calls it a "Levitical sermon," after von Rad, but it belongs to the genre of DISPUTA-TION (see "Genre" below). The addressees are called *běnê yiśrā'ēl,* "Israelites"; cf. v. 21, but according to v. 6 (cf. 2 Chr 34:9, 21), they are part of *happělêtâ hanniš'eret,* "the escaped remnant" (cf. Williamson, *Israel,* 126; and on exile typology in general, idem, comm., 367-68). A model of contrition is their repentance *(šwb),* in order that Yahweh may repent (so again in vv. 8, 9; cf. the programmatic promise in 7:14). A model of apostasy is the *ma'al,* "infidelity," of their fathers and brethren (the problem is not only historical, but contemporary). The hearers are to avoid their ancestors' stubbornness (cf. Zech 1:2-6) by coming to his eternally sanctified sanctuary, serving him in order to appease his anger. We cannot pass over this lightly, for this appeal explains ChrH's dominating anxiety about the new Israel's right adherence to the ordained customs. The couriers' promise, v. 9, is based on the Solomonic model: Yahweh is eager to do his part, viz., to relent and restore the exiles, if Israel will itself repent. In the north—as one would expect—the response is mixed, vv. 10-11: most refuse (cf. 2 Chr 36:16), while a representative and exemplary few comply (cf. v. 18). In the south ("Jerusalem" and "Judah" are placed chiastically in vv. 11-12) "the hand of God" (cf. 1 Kgs 18:49; Ezek 8:1) gives Judah one heart. Thus supernatural power intervenes to bring the people, just as it intervened to make what the king and the princes commanded "the word of Yahweh," v. 12.

The feast is introduced by the statement that *'am-rāb,* "a great people," came, *qāhāl lārōb mě'ōd,* "a congregation exceedingly large," v. 13. Immediately they got busy throwing some more of Ahaz's altars into Kidron, v. 14 *(wayyāsîrû,* "and they removed," and *hēsîrû,* "they removed," in chiasmus). So far so good, but now comes the question of uncleanness. This was a serious problem for the returned exiles (cf. Zechariah 3), and occupies all of vv. 15-20. Following an almost casual notice about killing the Passover lamb, ChrH notes that even the priests and Levites had to be shamed into becoming ritually clean before they would be fit to bring *'ōlôt,* "burnt offerings." When they did so, we read, each group of clergy took the assignment *(wayya'amědû)* given them by Moses; i.e., the Levites would hand the sacrificial blood to the priests for sprinkling on the altar (cf. 29:22; 35:11; see Willi, "Thora," 102ff., 148ff.; and cf. 34:19). (Shaver, 163, notes that this is the one regulation in ChrH claimed as Mosaic that actually has no basis in the Pentateuch, opening up the possibility that the "law of Moses" was not yet in the final form of the Pentateuch.) This is explained in v. 17, which tells us that many worshipers were not ritually clean, so that their Passover lambs would not be clean either, forcing the Levites to kill them for them and (presumably) to hand over the blood to the priests. The grounding clause with *kî* foremost appears four times in vv. 17-18: "For a great congregation . . . for a multitude of people . . . for they ate the Passover . . . for Hezekiah interceded." It is a chain of cause and effect.

The king's prayer is a remarkable one. He asks God to pardon every ritual transgression, if only the worshiper seek *(drš)* the ancestral God. One who reads this can hardly believe that ChrH is a sterile ritualist. Still less is Yahweh a God who holds rigidly to rules: "And Yahweh listened to Hezekiah and healed *[wayyirpā']* the people," v. 20. No wonder, then, that we read that the *běnê-yiśrā'ēl* (an inclusive term for "Israelites") kept the Mazzoth feast "with great gladness," and that the clergy praised Yahweh continually and "with all their might," v. 21 (Buttenwieser argues that *kělê,* "instruments," means "song," i.e., a song with the title *'ōz lěyahweh,* "Strength to Yahweh"). V. 22 seems to pick up the pro-Levite theme again in stating that Hezekiah praised the Levites for their skill. V. 22b tells the actual ritual: feasting, sacrificing, and giving thanks.

Then comes the second week (see above). It is celebrated on common agreement *(wayyiwwā'ăṣû kol-haqqāhāl);* cf. v. 2. A *kî*-clause in v. 24 mentions the justification: it was the added capabilities offered by the great availability of sacrificial victims and the fact that, by now, numerous priests had sanctified themselves (in the light of v. 15, this is a gratuitous disparagement similar to 29:34-35). In telling of the unparalleled rejoicing, vv. 25-26, ChrH first defines the four distinct groups present: Judah's own congregation, the priests and Levites, Israel's congregation, and *haggērîm habbā'îm mē'ereṣ yiśrā'ēl,* "the sojourners coming out of the land of Israel" with the settlers *(hayyôšěbîm)* in Judah (v. 25). The expression *'ereṣ yiśrā'ēl* occurs elsewhere in 1 Chr 22:2 (David); 2 Chr 2:16 (Solomon); 34:7 (Josiah); cf. Williamson *(Israel,* 123). That sojourners may also partake of the Passover/Mazzoth is permitted on the condition of their submission to circumcision, Exod 12:48-49. Following this listing, ChrH explicitly compares Hezekiah to Solomon in stating that this was the greatest occasion of rejoicing since Solomon's time, v. 26 (cf. Williamson, comm., 361). V. 27 mentions the final act, arising and blessing the people. On the possibility that "the priests the Levites" (VSS: "and the Levites") may be original, cf. von Rad *(Geschichtsbild,* 87); in any event, it is significant that the Levites bless alongside the priests. A closing word of transcendence states that their prayer came to God's holy habitation in heaven, v. 27b. At the conclusion of the festival "all Israel" — including at least Judah, Benjamin, Ephraim, and Manasseh—destroyed all the intrusive altars throughout their respective territories and then returned home, 31:1.

(3) Inclusions	16α²-b
b) For enrollment	17-18
(1) Priests: genealogical	17aα
(2) Levites: functional	17aβ-b
(3) Entire families included	18
c) Distribution to country clergy	19
E. Theological evaluation	20-21
1. Summary conclusion	20a
2. Perfect performance of the good	20b-21
a. Piety toward God	20b
b. Zeal and success in temple undertakings	21

This section certainly does not follow ch. 30 in the way ch. 30 follows ch. 29, i.e., in chronological sequence, but rather because of its topical affinity. Galling (ATD) would omit the entirety; Willi (p. 197) and von Rad *(Geschichtsbild)* would omit v. 2; cf. Watson (10.52) and Williamson *(Israel,* 122). Vv. 20-21 form their own section, intending to summarize and evaluate every spiritual service of Hezekiah from 29:3 onward. 31:2-19 has to do with soliciting and distributing various kinds of gifts from the laity for the benefit of the priests and Levites. Strictly speaking, 31:2 lies outside this structure because it states in summary fashion that Hezekiah took responsibility for regulating (*'md,* hiph.) the divisions *(maḥlĕqôt)* of the priests and Levites according to the several tasks assigned to them *('îš kĕpî 'abōdātô).* There are three different categories of such service: (1) taking care of the offerings; (2) ministering *(šrt);* and (3) praising and thanking "in the gates of Yahweh's camp" (tabernacle imagery; cf. Numbers 1–2; 1 Chr 9:18-19). What follows in vv. 3ff. goes in a somewhat different direction, yet the copula makes a direct joint to v. 2, leading us to interpret vv. 3ff. as its ideological as well as grammatical extension. This is to say that the subject of gifts for the clergy is presupposed in the summary of v. 2. How, after all, could the priests and Levites sacrifice and minister and sing praise songs unless they were properly supported by the laity? The laity could not perform these tasks for them, but by giving gifts and tithes they would be participating in them.

Though there are some elements of narration in vv. 3-19, it is all prescription rather than description. First we have a statement of what contributions the king gave, and therefore are to be expected, v. 3, followed by a similar statement regarding the laity (1) in Jerusalem, vv. 4-5, and (2) in nearby cities, v. 6. It is said that the laity bring so much that what they bring has to be placed in heaps *('ărēmôt 'ărēmôt).* After the blessing of the givers, v. 8, there is a dialogue, vv. 9-10, between Hezekiah and Azariah about this rare phenomenon. This opens up a whole new section, vv. 11-19, telling first how the gifts are more safely stored, vv. 11-13, and then how they are equitably distributed to deserving priestly and Levitical personnel, vv. 14-19.

Here are some notes on this section. Emulating Solomon (8:12-13), Hezekiah offers gifts to be used as burnt offerings, with these specifications: they are for the morning and the evening sacrifices; they are to be offered on sabbaths, new moons, and the great annual festivals; this is to be done "as written in Yahweh's law" (cf. also Numbers 28–29; Ezek 45:17), v. 3. V. 4 is programmatic; the Jerusalemites are commanded to give the priests' and Levites' portion *(mĕnāt)* "so that they might be strong in Yahweh's law" *(lĕma'an yeḥezqû bĕtôrat yahweh),* i.e., be completely and without distraction devoted to it (on the postexilic language, cf. Williamson, comm., 374). On giving the portion, see Nehemiah 13. On the unhesitating response, cf. Williamson (*Israel,* 129). The laity bring the very best *(rē'šît)* of their produce, *ûma'šar hakkōl lārōb,* "beyond a tithe of everything," v. 5. Those in Judah outside Jerusalem are called *bĕnê yiśrā'ēl hayyôšĕbîm bĕ'ārê yĕhûdâ,* "the Israelites dwelling in the cities of Judah," v. 6 ("and Judah" is a gloss); enthusiastically *(gam-hēm),* ChrH reports their two kinds of tithes: of animals and of *qodāšîm hamĕquddāšîm,* lit., "sanctified holy things"; *RSV* "dedicated things" (cf. Williamson, comm., 375, after Rudolph). Vv. 8-10 are cast in narrative style: "came . . . saw . . . blessed . . . inquired . . . answered." The blessing is of Yahweh and the people, but the king wants to know which of the two to credit for the heaps. The respondent, v. 10, is identified by name, lineage, and office. Katzenstein shows that the title "high priest" and the predominance of the lineage of Zadok are postexilic; he also shows that there were four high priests named Azariah, the last of which he dates 610-597, too early to be a contemporary of ChrH and too late to be a contemporary of King Hezekiah; the third Azariah, dated 730-710 and thus from the time of the historical Hezekiah, is probably meant. He reports that since the contributions started, there has been plenty to eat. The explanation is entirely theocentric: "Yahweh has blessed his people."

The next step is signalled by an order from Hezekiah, v. 11. First, storerooms *(lĕšākôt)* are to be built for the three kinds of gifts *(tĕrûmâ,* "offerings"; *ma'ăśēr,* "tithes"; *qŏdāšîm,* "things dedicated"); these are safely *(be'ĕmûnâ)* stored away, v. 12a. Vv. 12b-13 list the personnel in charge: there are ten assistants *(pĕqîdîm),* with Conaniah "the Levite" (cf. v. 14) at the head, assisted by his *'aḥ,* "kinsman," Shimei (Hezekiah and Azariah, representing secular and sacral authority, respectively, have given them this responsibility). Second, the *nidbôt hā'ĕlōhîm,* "freewill offerings to God," including apparently the *tĕrûmâ* and the *qodšê haqqŏdāšîm,* have to be distributed, and this responsibility is given to a certain Kore ben Imnah "the Levite"; he is called "keeper of the east gate," but cf. 1 Chr 26:14. He is given six assistants in the priestly cities. The distribution takes place (1) without cheating *(be'ĕmûnâ);* (2) by divisions *(maḥlĕqôt);* (3) and without regard to age, v. 15. There are two exceptions: (1) those genealogically enrolled, from three years and up, and (2) priests actually on duty in the temple, v. 16. Enrollment is different for the priests and the Levites: for the first it goes by genealogy *(lĕbêt 'ăbôtêhem),* but for the Levites it depends on the service performed *(bĕmaḥlĕqôtêhem),* v. 17. According to v. 18, a priest's whole family would be included on the condition that *(kî)* "they were faithful in keeping themselves holy" *(be'ĕmûnātām yitqaddĕšû-qōdeš).* To distribute portions *(mānôt)* to the Aaronite priests in country places it is arranged, according to v. 19, to have special persons designated, and they are to distribute to male priests and enrolled Levites (because of the reference to "common land," *migrāš,* v. 19, Willi, 195, argues that the whole section, vv. 12-19, is post-ChrH).

The theological review in vv. 20-21 says that Hezekiah did *haṭṭôb wĕhayyāšār wĕhā'ĕmet lipnê yahweh 'ĕlōhāyw,* "what was good and upright and faithful the way Yahweh his God said." In other words, he was the very model of complete submission to divine direction. Hezekiah prospered *(hiṣlîaḥ)* in every work that he undertook on these conditions: it was for the ceremonial service of God's temple or for the law and commandments; its aim was to search *(drš)* for his God; and it was done with all his heart.

Genre

The main genre of "Hezekiah's reforms" is REPORT. The REGNAL RESUMÉ of 29:1-2 has the ACCESSION AGE FORMULA, the STATEMENT OF LENGTH AND PLACE OF REIGN, and the THEOLOGICAL REVIEW. Vv. 5-11 constitute an ADDRESS, including the CALL TO ATTENTION and ORDER in v. 5, in vv. 6-7 an INDICTMENT SPEECH with a bill of particulars, and in v. 11 an ADMONITION to perform according to divine appointment by not being negligent (→ PROHIBITION). Vv. 12-14 contain the NAME LISTS of Levites and singers. "By the words of Yahweh" in v. 15 is an AUTHORIZATION FORMULA. Vv. 18-19 contain the OFFICIAL REPORT of those who had cleansed the temple. Vv. 20-24, 27-31 contain two separate REPORTS OF RITUAL. There are NAME LIST and TALLY in v. 21, the REGULATION FORMULA in the gloss of v. 25, and a LITURGICAL SUMMONS in v. 31. There are new NAME LISTS with TALLIES in vv. 32-33, and a COMPLAINT in v. 34.

In ch. 30, v. 5 has the REGULATION FORMULA, "as prescribed" *(kakkātûb).* Vv. 6b-9 form a MESSENGER SPEECH, which is also a DISPUTATION, with a COMMAND ("return"), two PROHIBITIONS ("do not be like your fathers . . . do not be stiff-necked"), an APPEAL ("Yield yourself"), a PROMISE ("your brethren and your children will find compassion"), and a DESCRIPTION OF YAHWEH ("gracious and merciful, and will not turn away his face"). This chapter also has the AUTHORIZATION FORMULA in v. 16 ("according to the law of Moses the man of God") and the REGULATION FORMULA in v. 18 ("otherwise than as prescribed," *bĕlō' kakkātûb).* Vv. 18b-19 constitute a SHRIVING PETITION. V. 26 is an ENCOMIUM that is at the same time an INCOMPARABILITY STATEMENT ("nothing like this in Jerusalem"). 31:1 has a TRANSITION FORMULA, "Now when all this was finished." This chapter also has the AUTHORIZATION FORMULA in v. 3. V. 10 is another OFFICIAL REPORT. Vv. 12b-13 and 14-15a are ROSTERS, the first with NAME LISTS and RANKING FORMULA, the second with NAME LIST.

Setting

ChrH may have had some fragments of narrative tradition at his disposal, and certainly he made good use of current cultic tradition, but the greater part of what he has written in these chapters is self-conceived and programmatic. The most notable novelties in this account are the rededication of the temple and the Passover in the second month. Inasmuch as Kings says nothing of Hezekiah in connection with a Passover celebration, while ChrH will follow Kings in recording a first-month Passover for Josiah, one has to wonder why our writer felt compelled to tell about it, unless it be that, having established Hezekiah as the cleanser and rededicator of the temple, he wanted to show how the rededicated temple was used. With Hezekiah, it is the temple cleansing and rededication that is important; when ChrH tells about Josiah, he will record the Passover celebration, but his big concern will be to memorialize Josiah as the king who reestablished the law and the covenant. Thus the main typology will be: Hezekiah, rededicator of the temple; Josiah, renewer of the law. Both are images that ChrH wanted to attach to the symbol of kingship as it survived into the postexilic period.

There is beyond doubt a solid historical foundation for the concept of Hezekiah as rededicator of the temple. This is firmly fixed in the brief account of

Kings. ChrH has reproduced 2 Kgs 18:2-3, but rather than repeat Kings' statement about cultic reforms in 2 Kgs 18:4, the encomium of v. 5, and the glowing testimony of vv. 6-7a, he brings in all new material (2 Chr 29:3–31:21) to show the same thing in his own way. This will mainly be in narrative form, but as has been said, its description is prescriptive; in other words, it is to be copied by contemporaries and by generations to come.

We notice that ChrH gives a large role to the priests and Levites (especially the Levites), who will be responsible at all times and in all situations for upholding the king's prescriptions. ChrH wants to hold fast to the theory that regal authority underlies the cult. This is why he has Hezekiah giving the command, not only for the work of cleansing the sanctuary, but for moving forward from one step to another in the ritual celebration. The king must always be present—at least symbolically—to represent authority and to personify the unity of God's people.

In this pericope ChrH makes heavy use of the typology of Solomon. Hezekiah is not only a descendant of Solomon—he is the new Solomon. ChrH is not interested at all in Solomon's fame for wisdom. He makes some use of the image of Solomon's riches in 30:24, where he tells of Hezekiah's generous gifts for the sacrifices. But this is not at all central. The main element of the Solomon typlogy is Solomon's great work of building and dedicating the temple. Much space had been given to that role (2 Chronicles 2–8). Not the wisdom, not the riches, but the temple of Solomon survives. It also survives in ChrH's own time, and is the object of his greatest concern. So ChrH has Hezekiah charge the clergy with cleansing the temple, and then holds a feast of rededication, for his wicked father Ahaz had defiled it and brought its sacred service to a stop. We can be sure of the Solomon typology from 29:35, "Thus the service of Yahweh's house was restored," echoing the statement about Solomon in 8:16. Hezekiah's couriers echo Solomon's dedicatory prayer in their repetition of the promise of return for those who repent, 30:9. The ENCOMIUM of 30:26 makes an express comparison with Solomon: "Since the time of Solomon the son of David, king of Israel, there had been nothing like this in Jerusalem." In the summary of 31:20-21 ChrH lauds Hezekiah for all the good things that Solomon had done: working for the service of God's house, keeping the law and commandments, seeking God with all his heart.

In Hezekiah's charge to the clergy he recalls all the sad history of Judah's kings, but especially the wickedness of Ahaz (29:6-9), even using Ezekiel's drastic image of the elders farting in Yahweh's face (probable original in Ezek 8:17). Details concerning the sacrificial system and the festivals can be traced to—or at least correlated with—specific passages in the Pentateuch, showing that it was roughly equivalent to the "law of Moses" that is constantly cited. The only exception is the apparent reference in 30:16, which claims Mosaic authority for the Levites' practice of killing the Passover sacrifice and handing the blood over to the priests for sprinkling on the altar. This is important, because it shows that there was still an oral tradition of what Moses' law was and what it required. Another novelty is the claim in 29:15 and 30:12 that the king's decree regarding matters of ritual could be regarded as revelation—as direct indications of the divine will. This goes back to David's claim that his plan for the temple was written from the hand of Yahweh (1 Chr 28:19). It explains why most of the examples of the AUTHORIZA-

TION FORMULA go back to Moses, but the examples of the REGULATION FORMULA (regarding correct ritual) go back to David (cf. 2 Chr 29:25, 27). See S. J. De Vries, "Moses and David as Cult-Founders."

Intention

As has been argued above in Chapter 1, we cannot go so far back in dating 1–2 Chronicles that we find ourselves in the time of Zerubbabel and Zechariah. The temple of ChrH's day has been long standing. Nevertheless, the problem of its defilement and possible disuse must have persisted. These chapters, accordingly, have been composed as a *Programmschrift*, a working paper, for keeping Israel's worship on a straight line. No doubt this image of a later king, Hezekiah, cleansing and rededicating Solomon's temple has itself become a type and model—in other words, a guide for renewing the temple once again, whenever it might be needed. There is ever the danger of subsiding into lassitude, hence the urging, "My sons, do not now be negligent" (29:11). Somehow the Levites show greater diligence and zeal than the priests, and this is in truth the major basis of ChrH's rather prominent critique, 29:4-11, 12-19, 34-35; 30:3. The Levites may have been a minor order, but they carried a major responsibility, part of which was to ensure that the most honored clergy, the priests, should diligently perform their duty. The kingdom of God ever needs that kind of inner or self-critique. Part of ChrH's program is to urge public generosity to the cult (29:31-33) and ample support for the clergy (cf. 31:1-10, especially as manifested in v. 5), and to regulate the equitable distribution of these gifts among the clergy (31:11-19). As is so aptly stated in 31:4, the people's giving the due portion to the priests and Levites is equivalent to giving themselves to Yahweh's law.

Surely part of ChrH's intention in this section is to inculcate a high concept of God; cf. especially 29:36, "The people rejoiced because of what God had done for the people; for the thing came about unexpectedly"; 30:12, "The hand of God was also upon Judah to give them one heart"; 31:10, "We have eaten and had enough, and have plenty left, for Yahweh has blessed his people, so that we have this great store left."

As has been noted, ChrH does not agree that exiles returned only to Judah. In Hezekiah's INDICTMENT SPEECH he declares that "the fathers" who forsook God have fallen by the sword, adding that sons, daughters, and wives are still in captivity, experiencing the fierce anger of Yahweh (29:6-10). In terms of narrative context, this may refer to 28:5, 16, but very transparently the Babylonian exile and the continuing diaspora stand in the background. Hence this generation too needs to make a covenant with Yahweh (29:10). The couriers of 30:6-9 address all would-be Passover pilgrims, north and south, as a "remnant"; that they have escaped from the hand of the kings of Assyria (v. 6) is typological for the "remnant" that has come back to Palestine, that must still be warned not to be "stiff-necked as your fathers were." So long as sin and unrepentance remain, the exile of God's people remains as a threat. So the command for every generation is, "Return to Yahweh. . . . For Yahweh . . . will not turn away his face from you if you return to him" (30:9).

Bibliography

A. Büchler, "Das Brandopfer neben dem Passah in II Chron. 30,15 und 35,12.14.15," *ZAW* 25 (1905) 1-46; M. Buttenwieser, *"biklê 'ōz lĕyahweh,* 2 Chronicles 30:21: A Perfect Text," *JBL* 45 (1926) 156-58; H. Haag, "Das Mazzenfest des Hizkia," in *Wort und Geschichte* (AOAT 18; *Fest.* K. Elliger; ed. H. Gese and H. P. Rüger; Neukirchen-Vluyn: Neukirchener, 1973) 87-94; J. Hänel, "Das Recht des Opferschlachtens in der chronistischen Literatur," *ZAW* 55 (1937) 46-67; P. Joüon, "Notes de lexicographie hébraïque, II. 6," *Mélanges de la Faculté orientale de l'Université Saint Joseph* 7 (1911-12) 413; H. J. Katzenstein, "Some Remarks on the Lists of the Chief Priests of the Temple of Solomon," *JBL* 81 (1962) 377-84; W. Meier, " 'Fremdlinge, die aus Israel gekommen waren,' " *BN* 15 (1981) 40-43; K. Möhlenbrink, "Die Levitischen Überlieferungen des Alten Testaments," *ZAW* 52 (1934) 184-231; F. L. Moriarty, "The Chronicler's Account of Hezekiah's Reform," *CBQ* 27 (1965) 399-406; D. L. Petersen, *Late Israelite Prophecy: Studies in Deutero-Prophetic Literature and in Chronicles* (SBLMS 23; Missoula: Scholars Press, 1977) 77-85; J. R. Shaver, "Torah and the Chronicler's History Work" (Diss., Notre Dame, 1983); S. Talmon, "Divergences in Calendar-reckoning in Ephraim and Judah," *VT* 8 (1958) 48-74; T. Willi, "Thora in den biblischen Chronikbüchern," *Judaica* 36 (1980) 102-5, 148-51.

II. HISTORICAL STORY: HEZEKIAH'S DELIVERANCE, 32:1-23

Structure

A. Defense measures	1-8
1. Sennacherib's invasion (transition formula)	1
2. Hezekiah prepares Jerusalem	2-8
a. Assessment of Sennacherib's intentions	2
b. Executing plan to stop water	3-4
1) Council of officers and officials	3
2) Many work	4a
3) Rhetorical question	4b
c. Preparations for siege	5
1) Strengthening fortifications	5a
a) Walls and towers	5aα
b) Millo	5aβ
2) Manufacture of projectiles	5b
d. Reassurance to the defenders	6-8
1) Appointment of commanders	6a
2) Assembly	6b
3) Address	7-8
a) Admonition	7
b) Assistance formula	8a
c) The people reassured	8b
B. Sennacherib's deputies demand surrender	9-16
1. The situation (transition formula)	9
a. Message to Jerusalem	9a
b. Hezekiah/Jerusalem as addressees	9b

This is ChrH's substitution for the extensive and complex material found in 2 Kgs 18:19–19:37 par. Isa 36:1–37:38. According to Lemke (p. 215) it has been composed to illustrate the pious king theme. Ackroyd ("Chronicler as Exegete," 11-12) shows that ChrH feels free to make adjustments to very familiar material, giving the event a somewhat different meaning in the light of subsequent events. Thus this is no "exegesis" (Willi), but a fresh composition. All the same, it does follow the order of the Kings story, with a number of rather obvious omissions. The story is about Hezekiah, and the thematic word is *ḥzq*, "be firm/strong," cf. vv. 2, 5, 7, 20. The opening transition is somewhat unusual: *'aḥărê haddĕbārîm wĕhā'ĕmet hā'ēlleh*, "After these events and these faithful acts," alluding of course to the summary at 2 Chr 31:20. In other words, Hezekiah does not still have to prove himself, but merely illustrate the effects of the fidelity he has already shown.

Sennacherib's invasion is by no means a punishment, for Hezekiah has been constantly faithful. Rather, it is an opportunity for Yahweh to show how powerful he is to help those who trust him. This is the familiar theme of the QUASI-HOLY-WAR STORIES of earlier chapters, but here it is based on a true historical account.

Verse 1 can be designated as the "exposition" for the entire story. According to ChrH, Sennacherib was merely besieging certain Judahite cities; he had not captured them, as in 2 Kgs 18:13. Hezekiah rightly assesses Sennacherib's intent to attack Jerusalem eventually, so he sets to work, with the counsel of officers and officials (*wayyiwwā'aṣ;* cf. 30:2) and the aid of many willing hands, to stop up all the springs and rivers in the vicinity of Jerusalem (cf. Watson, 2.3), vv. 3-4a. He then sets to work strengthening the walls and towers (broken down by Joash, 25:23), and also the Millo that was connected with "the city of David" (cf. 1 Chr 11:7-8). He also manufactures siege weapons (Welten, *Geschichte,* 29-31, 68-72, argues that these details are based on late postexilic conditions). In v. 6 we read that having set *śārê milḥāmôt,* "military commanders," over the people, he assembles them all in the city square (cf. 29:9) and addresses them, assuring them of victory (vv. 7-8). Although Hezekiah repeats the familiar words of calming and reassurance found in Deut 31:6; Josh 10:25, this is hardly a sermon (cf. von Rad, "Levitical Sermon," 274); he informs them that Yahweh can beat the Assyrian king: "There is one greater with us than with him. With him is an arm of flesh; but with us is Yahweh our God, to help us and to fight our battles," vv. 7-8. This is the classical language of the holy war. Hearing it, the people are reassured (*smk,* niph.).

Coming to the next section, we perceive that the story is about a duel. It is mostly a duel of words, but readiness for deeds backs them up. Hezekiah is boasting about Yahweh, but Sennacherib's emissaries will mock that boast. They will claim that Yahweh is inadequate and Hezekiah is unworthy. The emissaries appeal, understandably, to the Jerusalemite populace, for it is their fate that hangs in the balance. Omitting any reference from 2 Kgs 18:14-16 to Hezekiah actually paying any tribute, the story quickly gives the new situation (Sennacherib at Lachish, messengers speaking to Hezekiah and Jerusalem, v. 9) and then reproduces Sennacherib's taunt in much the same form as in Kings (omitted are references to a lack of troops and the failure of Egyptian aid, 2 Kgs 18:23-25). Though Yahweh will be judged as too weak to help them, these emissaries have as their major theme that Hezekiah is misleading them (cf. Curtis and Madsen, ICC, 489). Rhetorical questions abound: "On what are you relying?" (v. 10); "Is not Hezekiah misleading you?" (v. 11); "Were the gods of the nations . . . able?" (v. 13b); "Who among all the gods . . . was able to deliver?" (v. 14). V. 12 brings a blatant accusation against Hezekiah that would have meaning for the addressees, but which is an utter artificiality in the mouth of the historical Assyrians as we know them: he removed the intrusive altars and demanded worship at Yahweh's altar alone. For the Hebrews this would be a plus, yet it does touch a tender sore for any among them who might have been only halfhearted or eclectic in their Yahwism. V. 15 sums it all up in the warning: (1) Be wary of Hezekiah's deception; (2) your god is as helpless as all the others. The warning is urgent: "Don't let Hezekiah fool you . . . don't let him seduce you like this . . . don't trust him" (*'al . . . 'al . . . 'al . . .*). About the gods the argument is from the greater to the lesser: "If no other god . . . how much less [*'ap kî*] your god!" So far Sennacherib; according to v. 16, the emissaries continue to revile Yahweh and "his servant" Hezekiah (cf. Ps 2:2) on their own.

Since this did not have the immediate effect intended, Sennacherib next wrote letters, the content of which was a summary of the foregoing taunt, to be read aloud to the defenders (no mention of the Rabshakeh, 2 Kgs 18:26) in a loud voice and in their own language, trying to frighten them into revolt and surrender, vv. 17-19. In terms of structure, this is a delaying element, sustaining suspense to see whether a more direct approach would persuade the Jerusalemites. As Hezekiah has not answered Sennacherib the first time, he does not answer here. Instead, he prays to heaven, v. 20 (this is a radical shortening of 2 Kgs 19:14-34, omitting vv. 14-20 and summarizing the prayer = message of vv. 15-34). As in Kings, an angel intervenes, first wiping out (*khd*, hiph.) the enemy camp and, as a result, sending Sennacherib home *běbôšet pānîm*, "shamefaced," where *mîṣî'ê mē'āyw* ("those issuing from his loins," a mocking term for his sons) cut him down with the sword.

Verse 22 is a concluding epitome very much in the style of Exod 14:30: *wayyôša' yahweh 'et-yěḥizqîyāhû wě'ēt yōšěbê yěrûšālaim*, "So Yahweh saved Hezekiah and the residents of Jerusalem." The prepositional phrase that follows is expansive: it is not only from the Assyrians but from *kōl*, "all," that they are saved. The result is that Yahweh now secures tranquility (*nhl*, piel) all around. To this EPITOME ChrH has added a generalizing ENCOMIUM in v. 23, to the effect that (1) many bring gifts, and (2) Hezekiah is "exalted in the sight of all nations from that time onward" (cf. David, 1 Chr 14:17; Solomon, 2 Chr 9:23-24; Jehoshaphat, 17:10-11; 20:29-30; Uzziah, 26:8).

Genre

This is a HISTORICAL STORY; it is based on history and follows a clear plot. The TRANSITION FORMULA is in v. 1, where the danger first presents itself, and in v. 9, where the actual "contest" begins. The RHETORICAL QUESTION is a frequently used device (vv. 4, 11, 12, 13b, 14). Vv. 7-8 form an ADDRESS, with an ADMONITION to be strong and a classical statement of the ASSISTANCE FORMULA. Vv. 10-15 comprise a TAUNT, defined as an utterance which derides a person or thing as inferior to another. It begins with the MESSENGER FORMULA, with Sennacherib as speaker. V. 12 has an ACCUSATION, which is a charge naming the offense and (usually) a number of specifications to support it. V. 16 is a STATEMENT. The TAUNT is summarized in v. 17b. V. 22 is an EPITOME and v. 23 is an ENCOMIUM.

Setting and Intention

According to Childs *(Isaiah)*, who devotes pp. 104-11 to an analysis of this chapter, ChrH has made a genuinely new literary creation. What we have here is not legend but "midrash"—an attempt to interpret a written text (but → 1 Chr 5:1-2). There is a dialectical interrelationship between ChrH and his Kings *Vorlage*. Childs blames Wellhausen for much derogatory misunderstanding. ChrH deduces the siege of Lachish from Kings, keeping him there so as to localize Sennacherib's destruction at that place. 32:13 harmonizes 2 Kgs 18:35 and 19:12. 32:10 harmonizes 2 Kgs 18:17ff. with 18:26ff. Also, ChrH rearranges the letter of 32:17 by putting the reference to it between the speech of vv. 10-15 and the shouting of v. 18, thereby strengthening the blasphemy theme. 2 Kgs 19:8 leaves open the question whether the large army of 18:17 was still besieging Jerusalem, an impression that

ChrH strengthens in vv. 29-31, 32-34, making the army destroyed in 2 Kgs 19:35 the same as that of 18:17. ChrH also gives a positive interpretation to the action underlying Isaiah 22. He makes this action a thoroughly theological affair. Hezekiah, not Yahweh, is taunted as being unworthy of trust; Yahweh is simply charged with being unable to help. All in all, says Childs, this pericope in ChrH goes a long way in developing the blasphemy of Yahweh theme that becomes so prominent in Daniel.

Having been so selective in what he took from Kings regarding Hezekiah, ChrH shows that he is glad to have this opportunity to rework so important a text on the theme of Yahweh's help to the faithful. As has been said, this story outdoes ChrH's several quasi-holy-war stories. Jehoshaphat's people had to do nothing but stand still and see Yahweh's work (2 Chr 20:17). Hezekiah and the Jerusalemites do not even need to go out of Jerusalem, for a fervent prayer to heaven, v. 20, brings an angel to destroy the Assyrians. Living in a time when Yehud was still very weak and vulnerable, this was a powerful encouragement to trust and faithfulness. Hezekiah at least had an army, but postexilic Israelites were quite without any effective fighting force. Nevertheless, the words of 32:7-8 retained their validity: "Be strong and of good courage. Do not be afraid or dismayed before the king of Assyria and all the horde that is with him; for there is one greater with us than with him. With him is an arm of flesh, but with us is Yahweh our God, to help us and fight our battles" (cf. also 2 Kgs 6:16; Isa 31:3; Jer 17:5).

Bibliography

B. S. Childs, *Isaiah and the Assyrian Crisis* (SBT 2/3; Naperville: Allenson, 1967); H. Haag, "La campagne de Sennachérib contre Jérusalem en 701," *RB* 58 (1951) 348-59; C. van Leeuwen, "Sanchérib devant Jérusalem," *OTS* 14 (1965) 245-72; R. North, "Does Archeology Prove Chronicles Sources?" in *A Light unto my Path* (*Fest.* J. Myers; ed. H. Bream, et al.; Philadelphia: Temple, 1974) 375-401; J. Wellhausen, *Prolegomena to the History of Ancient Israel* (tr. Menzies and Black; Cleveland-New York: World, repr. 1965) 171-227.

III. REPORT OF FURTHER FACTS, 32:24-33

Structure

A. Hezekiah provokes divine wrath (transition formula)	24-26
1. Yahweh's help in deadly illness	24
a. Hezekiah's sickness	24a
b. A petition and a sign	24b
2. Hezekiah's ingratitude	25
a. Pride precludes responsiveness	25a
b. Wrath on Hezekiah and Judah/Jerusalem	25b
3. Divine wrath averted	26
a. Hezekiah and Jerusalem humble	26a
b. Postponed in Hezekiah's lifetime	26b

Williamson (comm.) lists this material under the rubric "divine reward," but this is too schematic; it is more paradoxical than that. What we have here, in terms of structure, is a random collocation of notes that ChrH found in Kings and in other sources. Ackroyd ("Chronicler as Exegete," 10-14) comments on how ChrH effectively reinterprets 2 Kgs 20:1-15 in order to state his own attitudes, and Williamson (comm., 386), following S. Talmon ("The Textual Study of the Bible—A New Outlook," in *Qumran and the History of the Biblical Text* [ed. F. M. Cross and S. Talmon; Cambridge: Harvard, 1975] 329), makes a special point of emphasizing that it has been carefully composed. Nevertheless, Lemke (p. 216) is correct in stating that ChrH's method is quite inscrutable. The statement in v. 24 that Hezekiah contracted a deadly illness and, on praying to God, was healed and given a sign *(môpēt),* though not telling us what the sign was, can hardly be called a skillful resumé of the carefully composed narrative in 2 Kgs 20:1ff. = Isa 38:1ff. The reader gets the impression that ChrH would not have included this item had it not been directly attached to the deliverance narrative in Kings; hence the rather laconic transitional formula *bayyāmîm hāhēm,* "In those days." In 2 Kgs 20:12 we read that the Babylonian ambassadors visit him because they heard that he was sick, and this then becomes the occasion for a prideful display of his riches. This is contradicted by ChrH, who states in v. 31 that they came to inquire about the sign. Nevertheless, it is that episode that inspired ChrH to attach the notice of Hezekiah's pride directly to his recovery from the illness and the giving of the sign. Willi (p. 177) describes vv. 25-26 as a reflection on 2 Kgs 20:12ff., but actually it has programmatic quality, i.e., it is a statement that expresses part of ChrH's final assessment of Hezekiah. ChrH does not say how the ingratitude got there, but he does state that it was a manifestation of pride *(kî gābah libbô,* "for his heart grew big," 32:25). On Amaziah's pride, cf. 2 Chr 25:17ff.; on Uzziah's pride, cf. 26:16.

The divine response was wrath *(qeṣep)* not only on Hezekiah, but on Judah and Jerusalem as well. ChrH again is stingy with words: he does not tell us how the divine wrath manifested itself, but only how it was averted. Hezekiah and Jerusalem humbled themselves *(knʿ,* niph.), so that the wrath of Yahweh did not come upon them in Hezekiah's days *(wĕlō'-bā' ʿălêhem qeṣep yahweh bîmê yĕḥizqîyāhû),* v. 26b. Contrast Hezekiah's rather cynical words in 2 Kgs 20:16-19. On sparing Jerusalem from divine wrath, cf. 1 Chronicles 21.

ChrH draws on independent sources for delineating Hezekiah's laudable deeds, except in vv. 30-31, where he goes back to Kings. The description of his riches, vv. 27-29, is quite elaborate in comparison with parallel statements regarding David, 1 Chr 29:28; Solomon, 2 Chr 1:12; 9:13ff.; and Jehoshaphat, 17:5; 18:1. Keeping up the Solomon typology, ChrH here makes amends for saying so little in previous sections about Hezekiah's wealth and honor (cf. Williamson, *Israel*, 122-23). There are buildings and there are cities, with structures not only for people but also for livestock (vv. 28b-29); no king before him except Uzziah (26:10) had shown so strong an interest in the propagation of animals. A grounding clause at the end identifies the source: *kî nātan-lô 'ĕlōhîm rĕkûš rab mĕ'ōd,* "for God gave him very much property." It is as if he is a new Abraham.

Turning back to his Kings source, ChrH makes use of the emphatic identifier *wĕhû' yĕḥizqîyāhû,* "Now this Hezekiah," v. 30. Here we are told how he built the famous Siloam tunnel from the Gihon spring to the pool of Siloam. He adds to 2 Kgs 20:20 the detail that the waters were brought down "to the west side of the city of David (Ophel)" (cf. Noth, "Chronistische Werk," 139; North, "Archeology," 375ff.; Dahse, 1-5). ChrH would like to list still more public works, but for want of detailed information he merely writes, "And Hezekiah prospered in all his works *[bĕkol-ma 'ăśēhû]."*

What remains is the matter of the Babylonian ambassadors, v. 31. As has been suggested, ChrH's statement is a misstatement if not a deliberate misrepresentation. But ChrH is not interested in the story as such, only in Yahweh's purpose, which he states somewhat enigmatically in the words, "God left him to himself, in order to try him and to know all that was in his heart" *('ăzābô hā'ĕlōhîm lĕnassôtô lāda'at kol-bilbābô); cf.* 2 Kgs 20:19.

The concluding summary alludes to *ḥăsādāyw,* "acts of devoted faithfulness"; this has to refer to all that Hezekiah did for the temple and cult according to chs. 29-31 (cf. Josiah, 2 Chr 35:26; Nehemiah, Neh 13:14). For sources, reference is again made to Isaiah ben Amoz (cf. Uzziah, 2 Chr 26:22), as well as to the familiar book of the kings of Judah and Israel. Alongside the usual DEATH AND BURIAL FORMULA, there is a notice of Hezekiah's honorific memorialization by all Judah and Jerusalem (Lemke, 218, judges this notation to be original here and in Kings; cf. LXX in both texts. Its omission in MT Kings is due to haplography).

Genre

This collocation constitutes a REPORT, with an ENCOMIUM in vv. 27-29. V. 24 has a TRANSITION FORMULA. The concluding REGNAL RESUMÉ has the usual elements: CITATION FORMULA, DEATH AND BURIAL FORMULA, and SUCCESSION FORMULA.

THE INDIVIDUAL UNITS

Setting and Intention

In spite of the highly laudable deeds that Hezekiah had performed in cleansing and rededicating the temple, chs. 29–31, for which he is properly praised in the death and burial notice, ChrH wishes to communicate the notion that the near-approaching exile is somehow due to some shortcoming on Hezekiah's part. ChrH's sources tell of only one fault: his apparent pride and ingratitude after his sickness. There is also his ambivalent behavior on the occasion of entertaining the Babylonian ambassadors. Without explaining why, ChrH says that Yahweh reacted to the pride and ingratitude by putting his wrath on Judah and Jerusalem as well as on Hezekiah. This is a new twist in the SCHEMA OF REWARD AND RETRIBUTION. Now it is no longer the sinner personally who must bear God's wrath, but his people as well (cf. 1 Chr 21:2-14). More enigmatically, something similar had taken place with Jehoshaphat in 2 Chr 19:2-3, "Because of this, wrath has gone out against you from Yahweh. Nevertheless some good is found in you." That apparently meant that Jehoshaphat's good deeds mitigated the wrath he deserved; but here it is first placed on his city and nation, and then put in abeyance for another generation. This notion is not new (cf. Ahab in 1 Kgs 21:29), but it is new in ChrH. Nothing evil is going to happen to Hezekiah or Judah/Jerusalem in his lifetime — but the wrath of Yahweh has been sufficiently aroused that another generation, one not too far distant, will have to bear it. Thus even good kings, exemplary kings, are now seen by ChrH as contributing to the great store of wrath that shall ere long be poured out (compare the cynically phrased statement in the parallel passage, 2 Kgs 20:16-19).

Inasmuch as v. 25 seems to make Hezekiah responsible for corporate guilt, ChrH adds v. 31 to tell how Yahweh would deal with him on a person-to-person basis. He would leave him (not forsake him) just to test him and know "all that was in his heart." In other words, Yahweh still does not know how this righteous, magnificent prince will behave if unattended by his own spirit and presence. What Hezekiah actually did according to Kings was not very laudable, but ChrH says nothing of that. Perhaps he is genuinely perplexed about the Kings passage, and does not know whether what Hezekiah did was good or bad. He believes that God knows, however. The surprising thing is the notion that God might not know all things ahead of time, but must sometimes give a man his leash in order to see whether he is really as good as everybody has been saying he is. But this should not be interpreted as an assertion of human autonomy. It is a warning against externalism. If left alone, will one whose public deeds have been all good continue to do the good on his own?

Bibliography

P. R. Ackroyd, "The Chronicler as Exegete," *JSOT* 2 (1977) 2-32; J. Dahse, "Textkritische Studien I. 1. Die Lage der Quellen von II Chr 32, 30. 33, 14. nach der LXX," *ZAW* 28 (1908) 1-5; R. North, "Does Archeology Prove Chronicles Sources?" in *A Light Unto My Path* (*Fest.* J. Myers; ed. H. Bream, et al.; Philadelphia: Temple, 1974) 375-81.

REPORT OF THE REIGN OF MANASSEH, 33:1-20

Structure

The first nine verses are taken virtually intact from 2 Kgs 21:1-9. Manasseh with his extreme apostasy forms a sort of inclusio with Ahaz, enclosing the contrasting exalted righteousness of Hezekiah; but of course ChrH gets it from Kings, whose depiction of these three kings is undoubtedly based on historical reality. Be that as it may, the Ahaz-Hezekiah-Manasseh alternation well illustrates the three-generation pattern used in Ezekiel 18: "If a man is righteous, and does what is lawful and right [v. 5]. . . . If he begets a son who is a robber, a shedder of blood [v. 10]. . . . But if this man begets a son who sees all the sins which his father has done, and fears, and does not do likewise [v. 14]"—only, with these three kings it is the righteous one who is in the middle of the generational ladder. Certainly, Ezekiel's lesson is true: "The soul that sins shall die" (v. 4); nevertheless, ChrH's arrangement suggests that Hezekiah's righteousness is enveloped and quite overwhelmed by the wickedness of his father and his son.

This pericope begins with the usual REGNAL RESUMÉ. Up until now, mothers' names have been included except in the case of Ahaz (also omitted for Ahaz in Kings). ChrH—but not Kings—omits it now for Manasseh, and will omit it for every king (including Josiah) down to the end. Lemke (p. 220) argues that the consistency of this pattern shows that they were missing from ChrH's *Vorlage,* but we should at least consider the possibility that this is ideological, if not in ChrH, then in his *Vorlage.* Most of the kings of Judah's final years were not worthy of the dignity of having their mothers' names mentioned. Anyway, ChrH is rushing on to a denouement; seemingly irrelevant details can only delay the inevitable end.

In the theological evaluation, v. 2, Manasseh is expressly compared with Ahaz (cf. 2 Chr 28:3) in the statement that he did evil according to the "abominations" *(tôʿăbôt)* of the dispossessed nations, v. 2. Hezekiah had gotten rid of all the symbols of fertility worship (30:13; 31:1), but Manasseh restores their altars while rebuilding the country shrines *(bāmôt),* v. 3. He even builds intrusive altars in (or at) Yahweh's temple, v. 4; v. 5 is probably explaining that these are "for all the host of heaven" and that they were erected in the temple's courts, v. 5. With an emphatic *wĕhûʾ,* "and this one," v. 6a, ChrH goes on to accuse Manasseh of repeating the especially shocking enormity of Ahaz (28:3), that of making burnt offerings of his sons in the notorious Hinnom Valley. But even worse, he resorted to every sort of witchery, the sin of Saul (1 Chr 10:13). Culminating all else, Manasseh ventured so far as to set up the idol of Asherah (2 Kgs 21:7; Chr is corrupt, perhaps due to a scribe's shocked piety) in the very temple itself, v. 7. To illustrate Yahweh's claim, ChrH paraphrases 2 Chr 6:6 to the effect that this is where Yahweh has put his name, i.e., declared ownership, forever. He balances this by paraphrasing from 1 Chr 29:8 the promise "never to remove the foot of Israel" from the land appointed for their fathers, but on the strict condition that they observe all of Moses' law, v. 8 (cf. Watson, 10.3). V. 9 summarizes the effect (Willi, 130: theologizing) by stating that ChrH made Judah and the Jerusalemites err (*t'h*, hiph.), with the result that they did more evil than the nations whom Yahweh destroyed to make room for them. This is the equivalent of saying that they were now back at the zero-point— where they were before the conquest, while they were still in the wilderness.

In the section on "punishment, repentance, and restoration," it is easy to find the main division point from the transition formula, *wĕ'aḥărê-kēn*, "and after this," v. 14. None of this is in Kings, and numerous scholars have questioned whether historical fact underlies the statement in v. 11 that Manasseh was taken as a prisoner to Babylon, which seems especially strange since the Assyrians who captured him would certainly not imprison him in a hostile capital. On the section as a whole, cf. North ("Archeology," 383ff.). The verses preceding the transition are roundly structured in the pattern: punishment, vv. 10-11; repentance, v. 12; restoration, v. 13. Without intimating that a prophetic oracle has been given, v. 10 states what must be considered the primal sin, a deliberate ignoring of revelation ("Yahweh spoke to Manasseh and his people, but they gave him no heed"). The "commanders of the army of the king of Assyria" come to take him, but it is Yahweh who causes their coming, v. 10; surely gross indignity as well as brutal force is intended in the expression *wayyilkĕdû 'et-mĕnaššeh baḥōḥîm wayya'asruhû banĕḥuštayim*, "and they caught Manasseh with hooks and bound him with bronze fetters" (cf. Koehler). In v. 12, a temporal clause, "and when he was in distress *[ṣrr]*," sets the condition for his change of heart (cf. Willi, 130: theologizing). The result was Manasseh's "humbling himself greatly *[wayyikkāna' mĕ'ōd]* before the God of his fathers." The result was that Manasseh prayed, Yahweh listened to his prayer, Yahweh restored him to his kingship in Jerusalem. "And Manasseh knew *[yd']* that Yahweh, he is God," v. 13b, is meant as a summary of the entire episode, but also as an EPITOME of its meaning, which is that only one god could be God, and that his deportation and restoration had convinced Manasseh, i.e., made him know through personal experience, that Yahweh is the only one that fits the description of what "God" is, and ought to be able to do.

The normal pattern for the Judahite kings is for work on Jerusalem's walls, etc., to come near the beginning, as part of the statement of the good that that king did (Rehoboam, 2 Chr 11:5ff.; Asa, 14:5ff.; Jehoshaphat, 17:2ff.; Uzziah, 26:10; Jotham, 27:3-4). In the case of Hezekiah, whose prideful ingratitude brought divine wrath, 32:26, the notice of working on defenses comes at the end, 32:27ff. So now also in the case of Manasseh. It is only after the report of his repentance and restoration that ChrH inserts information about work on Jerusalem's walls and the fortification of strong points in the country, v. 14 (cf. Welten, *Geschichte*, 31-34, 72-78). V. 15 tells us that the foreign gods with their images and altars were thrown *ḥûṣâ lā'îr*, "outside the city" (cf. "Kidron," 15:16; 29:16; 30:14). In the process, Manasseh restored Yahweh's altar and put it back into service, instructing the Judahites to "serve Yahweh the God of Israel." This was Manasseh's confession of who Yahweh truly was (cf. v. 13) and who the people's worship would likewise confess him to be. We are not told that the people obeyed, but the restrictive clause of v. 17 makes their compliance at least partially certain: *'ăbāl 'ôd hā'ām zōbĕḥîm babbāmôt raq lĕyahweh 'ĕlōhêhem*, "Although the people kept on sacrificing at the local shrines, this was exclusively to Yahweh their God."

The concluding REGNAL RESUMÉ is unusual in listing specific items which the readers might find in the two books of reference, "the book of the kings of Israel" and "the book of the seers." This is a sort of *apologia* for Manasseh, as though readers who knew about him only from Kings needed some assurance that ChrH had access to some material that they did not know about. Most of the items mentioned can be inferred from the preceding account, but not the "words of the seer who spoke to him," v. 18, for v. 10 states merely that Yahweh spoke to Manasseh. Again, ChrH is attempting to furbish Manasseh's image. He actually has no tradition about seers for Manasseh, but at this point ChrH wishes to make his previous references to revelation more traditional, assuring his readers that Manasseh was not, after all, so wicked that Yahweh's "seers" (the more authoritative title "prophet" is avoided) would no longer speak to him (cf. Watson, 9.1). The burial notice is ambivalent: Manasseh was buried "in his house" (cf. Joab, 1 Kgs 2:32); the text may be corrupt (cf. Lemke, 224), but compare 2 Kgs 21:18, "in the garden of his house, in the garden of Uzza."

Genre

The main genre is REPORT. The introductory REGNAL RESUMÉ (vv. 1-2) has the ACCESSION AGE FORMULA, the STATEMENT OF LENGTH AND PLACE OF REIGN, and the THEOLOGICAL REVIEW. The concluding REGNAL RESUMÉ (vv. 18-20) has the CITATION FORMULA, DEATH AND BURIAL FORMULA, and SUCCESSION FORMULA. "In Jerusalem shall be my name forever," v. 4b, is a snatch of LITURGY, as is also the somewhat longer portion in v. 7, "In this house and in Jerusalem, which I have chosen out of all the tribes of Israel, I will put my name forever." V. 8, "And I will no more remove . . . if only they will be careful to do . . . ," is a PROMISE. V. 13b, "Then Manasseh knew that Yahweh, he is God," echoes the RECOGNITION FORMULA, "Then you will know that I am Yahweh," which is usually the concluding element in a (→) self-disclosure oracle, but is also found in the P story in Exodus (e.g., 14:4, 18). As has been noted, a TRANSITION FORMULA occurs in v. 14.

Setting and Intention

ChrH's rationale concerning Manasseh includes the following points: (1) his unusually severe wickedness is unremittingly foreboding of the exile of the nation; (2) although his "foxhole conversion" repentance is accepted, the nation that shared in his sin continues unrepentant. It was no doubt important for ChrH in his time to say once again that however wicked one's previous life, if he truly repents, God will forgive. Not all of the returned exiles were able to believe that Yahweh had truly forgiven the Jewish people. Being deprived of political independence and an effective kingship, ever in peril and often living on the edge of poverty, it was easy to believe that Yahweh's wrath continued unabated. The nation had once complained, in the words of Ezekiel 33, "Our transgressions and our iniquities are upon us and we waste away because of them; how then can we live?" (v. 11), and "The way of Yahweh is not just" (v. 17). To this, Ezekiel had replied, "When the righteous turns away from his righteousness and commits iniquity, he shall die for it. And when the wicked turns away from his wickedness and does what is lawful and right, he shall live by it. . . . O house of Israel, I will judge each of you according to your ways" (vv. 18-20). Manasseh is being held up as just such an example; he was wicked, he repented, he was restored. The repentance and the restoration are just what ChrH adds to the story of Manasseh in Kings. There one reads nothing about repentance. Manasseh is, indeed, so very, very wicked that DtrH has to give him the specific blame for bringing the whole nation under Babylonian bondage (cf. 2 Kgs 21:10-15; 24:3-4). ChrH understands that so monstrous a sinner must "humble himself greatly"—but he does humble himself. And if such a one can deeply humble himself in order to enjoy once more God's mercies, so can everyone finding himself suffering under the fury of God's anger.

One thing though: Manasseh did set a bad example for the people; he seduced them, and two bad things followed: (1) they did more evil than the nations whom Yahweh destroyed before the people of Israel, v. 9, and (2) they gave Yahweh no heed when he spoke, v. 10. There is nothing here about the people repenting, only about them returning to the formal worship of Yahweh because Manasseh said they must, v. 16. In the end, Manasseh escaped because of his individual repentance, while the people continued to pile up wrath. So we can say that, while ChrH adds the element of Manasseh's repentance, DtrH is right in giving him the chief blame for the nation's downfall. There may not be such a thing as "corporate guilt" in ChrH, but surely this shows us the consequences of sin from generation to generation and from king to people.

While affirming the concept of Jerusalem as the divinely chosen center for Israel's worship, v. 7, ChrH reaffirms Israel's right to possess "the land which I appointed for your fathers," promising never to "remove the foot of Israel" from this land. This promise is proleptic in view of the coming exile to Babylonia, but for ChrH's community it would have been heard as a reassurance that never again would their removal occur. But only on the same condition, that they be careful to do all that Yahweh commanded them through Moses, v. 8. That is the big "if," and it always remains the same. Times may change, kings may come and go, exiles may return, but Yahweh's promise to keep Israel in his care would ever carry this condition. Whether to experience God's wrath or not, whether to go into exile or stay at home, would always depend on their *doing* God's commandments.

About Manasseh's deportation: the position taken here is that it is one of ChrH's artful contrivances, but we take note of the fact that some scholars still defend its historicity. Ehrlich, for instance, explains that Manasseh's fortifications, v. 14, were constructed as an act of loyalty to Assyria, part of a system of defense against Egypt. Manasseh was a loyal vassal of King Esarhaddon. It was while his successor Ashurbanipal was struggling to master his brother Shamash-shum-ukīn, 652-648, that Manasseh joined an unsuccessful western alliance; when it failed, he was deported, but eventually he was able to establish his fealty to the new king and was restored. His deportation is hinted at in 2 Kgs 21:10-15 and in Zephaniah, but was of too short a duration to be reported by DtrH. Since this is mostly supposition and conjecture, it is better to interpret it as a contrivance of ChrH.

Bibliography

E. L. Ehrlich, "Der Aufenthalt des Königs Manasse in Babylon," *TZ* 21 (1965) 281-86; K. H. Graf, "Die Gefangenschaft und Bekehrung Manasses," *ThStK* 32 (1859); L. Koehler, "Alttestamentliche Wortforschung. Ḥōhim Schlupfwinkel," *TZ* 5 (1949) 314; E. Nielsen,

"Political Conditions and Cultural Developments in Israel and Judah During the Reign of Manasseh," *Fourth World Congress of Jewish Studies* I (Jerusalem: World Union of Jewish Studies 1967) 103-6; R. North, "Does Archeology Prove Chronicles Sources?" in *A Light unto my Path (Fest.* J. Myers; ed. H. Bream, et al.; Philadelphia: Temple, 1974) 383-86.

REPORT OF THE REIGN OF AMON, 33:21-25

Structure

I.	Regnal resumé	21-22a
	A. Accession age formula and statement	
	of length and place of reign	21
	B. Theological review	22a
II.	His wickedness	22b-23
	A. Sacrifice to father's idols	22b
	B. Rejection of father's humbleness	23a
	C. Increase of guilt	23b
III.	Throne conspiracy and death report	24-25
	A. Assassination by his servants	24
	B. Common people take power	25
	1. Execute conspirators	25a
	2. Crown Josiah	25b

This is a virtual carbon copy of what one finds in Kings. There is an introductory REGNAL RESUMÉ, but no concluding equivalent (cf. 2 Kgs 21:25-26). In leaving this out, ChrH shows that he is growing impatient and is hurrying toward the end. A special section on Amon's wickedness, vv. 22b-23, supplements the usual THEOLOGICAL REVIEW in v. 22a. He sacrifices to his father's idols but does not repent, the result being stated in v. 23b, *hû' 'āmôn hirbâ 'ašmâ*, "This Amon increased guilt" (cf. 2 Chr 28:13). His servants conspire *(qšr)* to assassinate him in his house. The common people *('am hā'āreṣ)* punish the conspirators, and then take his young son Josiah and put him on the throne.

Genre

The main genre is REPORT. The REGNAL RESUMÉ has only the ACCESSION AGE FORMULA and the THEOLOGICAL REVIEW. Vv. 24-25 have the THRONE CONSPIRACY REPORT, which is at the same time a DEATH REPORT.

Setting and Intention

ChrH's rationale for Amon is as follows: (1) Manasseh's repentance does not carry over to save his son or the nation; (2) Amon's emulation of his father's sins shows his own unrepentance and that of the nation. In other words, it is much easier to copy a parent's sin than to share his repentance. Amon's reign is so brief and ephemeral that this REPORT seems like just another stepping-stone in the downward pathway. In the end, Amon shows himself so weak of character that his own servants have no trouble carrying out a conspiracy against him (cf. Joash, 24:25; Amaziah, 25:27-28). With the palace in an uproar, the common people *('am hā'āreṣ)* are forced to execute the conspirators (cf. 25:3) and place Josiah on the throne. This notice does not make an *apologia* for democracy or the common man; it is an act of desperation when the people are forced to take over because their kings have grown so corrupt that their own servants have to get rid of them.

Bibliography

A. Malamat, "The Historical Background of the Assassination of Amon, King of Judah," *IEJ* 3 (1953) 26-29.

ACCOUNT OF THE REIGN OF JOSIAH, 34:1–35:27

Structure

I. Report of Josiah's reform	34:1-7
II. Report of the finding of the lawbook	34:8-33
III. Report of Josiah's Passover	35:1-19
IV. Battle report: Josiah's death	35:20-25
V. Concluding regnal resumé	35:26-27

ChrH's rationale concerning Josiah can be summarized in the following points: (1) all his good deeds could not save him from an ignominious death or the nation from its imminent doom; (2) at this late hour in the nation's history he worked to promulgate the law by which the nation should live again, while putting in place the proper cultus for a time when it could be observed once more. As Hezekiah was memorialized for rededicating the temple, Josiah is memorialized for reestablishing the law and demonstrating how to worship God according to it.

Transition formulas at 34:8 and 35:20 bind the Josiah material together as a meaningful ACCOUNT. The date given in 35:1 strengthens the connection by implicitly referring back to 34:8 (cf. 35:19).

I. REPORT OF JOSIAH'S REFORM, 34:1-7

Structure

A. Introductory regnal resumé	1-2
1. Accession age formula and statement of length and place of reign	1
2. Theological review	2
B. Reform	3-7
1. Chronology	3
a. Eighth year: devotes self to David's God	3a
b. Twelfth year: cultic purge	3b
2. Purging Judah and Jerusalem	4-5

402

In his introductory summary for Josiah, ChrH repeats the theological evaluation of Kings and adds a specification of his own: he "did right in Yahweh's eyes and he walked in the ways of David his father [cf. Hezekiah, 2 Chr 29:2], and he did not turn aside to the right or to the left." This is the description of absolute rectitude.

Having thus characterized this new king, ChrH proceeds to tell of his cultic reforms, vv. 3-7. Two things are notable about this. First, the chronology is set forward in comparison with 2 Kgs 22:3 (the eighteenth year as opposed to the twelfth year of Josiah's reign), and the reforms as an event are set forward, severing them completely from the story of the finding of the lawbook. The description of the reforms is, indeed, a mere paraphrase of the lengthy and detailed account in 2 Kgs 23:4-20, where undoubtedly it is meant to be prescriptive for the deuteronomistic reform as a continuing program.

Before the reform can begin, spiritual maturity must come to evidence in the reformer's own person. Thus ChrH tells us that in the eighth year of Josiah's reign, when he was sixteen and developing into manhood, he "began to seek [drš] the God of David his father"—thus not just the ancestral God, "the God of the fathers," which carries the connotation of returning to a covenantal morality that he had not forsaken—but to Israel's God as personally known and worshiped by David, the founder of Israel's cult and nation. V. 3 goes on to tell, then, that in Josiah's twelfth year he began his purge. Summarizing details from Kings, ChrH says that Josiah first purged Judah and Jerusalem, destroying relics of Baal worship; v. 4a is in chiasmus: verb-prepositional phrase-object; object-relative clause-verb. ChrH does not neglect to insert the rather astounding note that he also burnt the bones of the idolatrous priests on their own altars. The conclusion is brief: "and he purged [ṭhr] Judah and Jerusalem," v. 5b. Next Josiah extended his purge to those "cities" in the apparently dependent territories of Manasseh, Ephraim, and Simeon, going on "as far as Naphtali," where he seems to have had only partial control; MT běhar bōtêhem sābîb is an apparent corruption; cf. RSV and Joüon. There he continued the work of violent destruction, "breaking down," "pulverizing," "hewing down," v. 7a (cf. Watson, 5.3, 7.51). V. 7b, "Then he returned to Jerusalem," is transitional.

Genre

This unit consists of a REPORT, vv. 3-7, expanding a REGNAL RESUMÉ, vv. 1-2. The latter contains the ACCESSION AGE FORMULA, the STATEMENT OF LENGTH AND PLACE OF REIGN, and a THEOLOGICAL REVIEW, and, as the chronology shows, is intended as the direct introduction to the REPORT proper.

Setting and Intention

The age of Josiah when he began his reform has been much discussed, if only because it affects the chronology of Josiah's reign. There have been advocates of the correctness of ChrH's twelfth year over against DtrH's eighteenth year, 622/21 B.C., with attempts to relate the earlier figure with events in the late Assyrian empire, but since no direct correlation is possible, there seems to be no good reason to discard DtrH's date as incorrect. On the other hand, something of ChrH's design can be discerned. He apparently wants to depict Josiah as a lifelong reformer, beginning as early as possible to undo the great evil that remained over from the reigns of his grandfather Manasseh and his father Amon. ChrH stated that already in the eighth year of Josiah's reign he "began to seek the God of David his father." As Williamson has noted (comm., 397), dating at the beginning of a reign elsewhere stands as a sign of divine approval; cf. Jehoshaphat, 17:7; Hezekiah, 29:3. We observe that, in any case, ChrH keeps DtrH's date, eighteenth year, for the finding of the lawbook (2 Kgs 22:3; 2 Chr 34:8). The twelfth year for ChrH is merely the date when Josiah "began to purge" *(hēḥēl lĕṭahēr)*, referring to the removal of cult objects and not to the finding of the book of the law. ChrH means to say that Josiah was already many years into the work of purging before the lawbook was found—that his purges were the precondition, and not the consequence, of finding the book. In his view, Josiah knew that it was his duty to cleanse the land of idolatry without, and prior to, the lawbook. As we shall see when we examine the following pericope, the purge that followed the discovery of the lawbook is briefly noted, and is to be understood as an extension and continuation of the work that he had already begun (34:33a).

Bibliography

P. Joüon, "Notes philologiques sur le text hébreu de 2 Chron. 34, 6," *Bib* 12 (1931) 89.

II. REPORT OF THE FINDING OF THE LAWBOOK, 34:8-33

Structure

The main element that ChrH adds to 2 Kgs 22:3–23:4 is the material about the participation of the Levites, vv. 12-13. In addition, the episodes of distributing the money for repairing the temple, vv. 8-11, of Hilkiah's discovery of the lawbook, vv. 14-15, and of the final acts of compliance, vv. 32b-33, are free paraphrases of Kings. Otherwise ChrH follows closely the text of Kings. In all candor it must be said that ChrH starts out badly; this is a poor case of narrative reporting as compared with Kings. The apparent temporal sequence should be seen as the following: (1) the keepers of the threshold have been collecting money from worshipers at the temple; (2) in his eighteenth year Josiah comes to the decision to repair the temple from these funds and orders the royal secretary Shaphan to receive an account of this money from Hilkiah the high priest; (3) according to the king's instructions, this money is paid out to the foremen, who distribute it to the various workmen; no account of how the money was actually used (2 Kgs 22:7) or of the repairs that were actually made is given, but it is assumed that these came in the proper order; (4) the making of these repairs somehow enables Hilkiah to recover/discover the lawbook; (5) this is immediately reported to Josiah and sets in motion the climactic episode of seeking an interpretation from Huldah. ChrH confuses this sequence at two points: (a) in reporting how and when the money was collected, vv. 9-10, and (b) in making Hilkiah's discovery contemporaneous with the bringing out (*yṣ'*, hiph.) of the money (= v. 9), v. 14. This happens mainly because ChrH has added two names to that of Shaphan in v. 8 and because ChrH has extended the building episode by inserting his lists of Levitical overseers in vv. 12-13. Far from improving the excellent Kings narration, this has only resulted in delay and confusion.

The eighteenth-year chronological note makes an inclusio with the note about Josiah's Passover in his eighteenth year in 2 Chr 35:19 (par. 2 Kgs 23:23). Referring back to vv. 3-7, the reference in v. 8 to the purging of temple and land forms another inclusio with v. 33b. Since this half-verse is summarizing and short, in no way reproducing the extensive narrative of Josiah's cultic reforms in 2 Kgs 23:4-25, it is apparent that ChrH sees the reforms as parentheses to what is central, the lawbook and its interpretation—not as in Kings, where the lawbook is prerequisite to the reforms (*contra* Willi, 174, who calls this a mere reflection). To make certain Josiah's intent, v. 8bβ states the content and purpose of Josiah's charge: *lĕḥazzēq 'et-bêt yahweh 'ĕlōhāyw*, "to bolster/strengthen the temple of Yahweh his God."

Verse 9 seems to contradict itself in stating that the king's officials "delivered" *(ntn)* the money that "had been brought" *(hammûbā')*, and which the Levites "had collected" *('sp)*; it is probable that *ntk*, "pour out/count out" (cf. v. 17), should be read for a corrupt *ntn* (so Rudolph, HAT; Williamson, comm.), and this would accurately preserve the narrative sequence previously outlined. ChrH specifies that the "keepers of the threshold" who collected the money were Levites, and he identifies the donors as coming from two groups: (1) Manassites, Ephraimites, and *šĕ'ērît yiśrā'ēl*, "the remnant of Israel" (cf. 30:6; 34:21; see Williamson, *Israel*, 230); and (2) the Judah/Benjamin/Jerusalem complex (Lemke, 230: pan-Israel, Levite bias; Willi, 107: reflection; read the Ketib and VSS over against Qere and MSS: "and he returned"). If we accept the proposal to change *ntn* to *ntk* in v. 9, we are left with a sequence of three *ntn*'s in vv. 10-11; the royal delegation delivered the money to the foremen *(hammupqādîm)*; they gave it to the workmen *('ōśê* [LXX, Vg., Syr.; MT *'ōśēh*] *hammĕlā'kâ)*, who in turn paid it to the carpenters and masons for buying stones and timber.

Next comes a statement of the workmen's diligence, v. 12, an entirely different statement than is found in 2 Kgs 22:7 (cf. Watson, 4.4). Structurally, it belongs with the rest of vv. 12-13 because of the participial styling. We might well be tempted to agree with Willi (p. 200) that vv. 12-14 are a post-ChrH addition, especially since Gershon is omitted from the family representatives and because Levitical musicians *(kol-mēbîn biklê-šîr)* are put in charge of *hassabbālîm*, "burden bearers," and *mĕnaṣṣĕḥîm*, "overseers." The description of Levitical musicians as "all understanding instruments of song" is found also at 1 Chr 25:7, a secondary passage; it may be better to accept von Rad's view *(Geschichtsbild*, 104) that only v. 12b is secondary, in which case v. 13b, introduced by *ûmēhalĕwîyim*, "and some of the Levites," in charge of scribes, officials, and gatekeepers, would make more sense.

As has been noted, the transition to the lawbook episode is weak, especially if *ûbĕhôṣî'ām* is given a temporal meaning *(RSV)*. Giving credit to ChrH, we perhaps ought to take this phrase as circumstantial: "Now in the process of their bringing out." For ChrH, the book that Hilkiah finds is more than "a/the book of the law"; it is "the book of the law of Yahweh (given) through Moses." ChrH increases suspense at this point by having Shaphan first report to Josiah all about the money for repair work, vv. 16-17; "Shaphan brought the book to the king" has to be identified as an introductory summary in the light of v. 18a. Coming at the end of the episode, this points anew to the lawbook as central and climactic.

The inquiry episode begins (v. 17b) with the statement that Shaphan read this book to the king, who shows his alarm at its contents (the curses of Deuteronomy?) by tearing his clothes, v. 17b. Immediately (v. 21) the king sends a deputation to seek prophecy (here *drš yahweh* means "seek an oracle," not "cultivate religiosity," as elsewhere in ChrH). The book in question seems to threaten him as king and *hanniš'ār bĕyiśrā'ēl ûbîhûdâ*, "the remnant in Israel and Judah" (cf. Williamson, *Israel*, 126). Josiah's urgency is motivated by the conviction that Yahweh's wrath *(ḥēmâ;* ChrH's usual term is *qeṣep)* has been caused by their ancestors' failure to keep Yahweh's word as revealed in this book. The delegation is named in v. 20; in v. 22, reporting their compliance, only Hilkiah is mentioned along with *wa'ăšer hammelek,* i.e., those belonging to the king (that the VSS and MSS differ suggests that the verb *šlḥ,* "send," is not to be supplied).

Huldah is identified along with her place of residence, v. 22, and then she delivers an oracle in classical prophetic style, vv. 23-28. It is actually two oracles, the first of which was to be reported to *hā'îš,* "the man," who had sent them—an impersonal and somewhat derogatory reference to the king; cf. v. 26. Huldah uses the messenger formula before instructing the delegation, v. 23a and again in v. 24a, to introduce the announcement of judgment, but we note that the styling varies from "Thus says Yahweh the God of Israel" in vv. 23 and 26 to the shorter "Thus says Yahweh" in v. 24. Both the announcement, v. 24, and the accusation, v. 25, are spoken by Yahweh in the first person. His intent is to bring all the curses *(hā'ālôt)* written in the lawbook on "this place" and its inhabitants. The reason *(taḥat 'ăšer)* is their forsaking *('zb)* and provoking *(k's),* which have aroused an unquenchable wrath *(ḥămâ)* "on this place."

In vv. 26-28a Huldah proceeds to deliver a personal oracle to Josiah by ordering the inquirers to report to "the king of Judah"—more respectful and sympathetic than in v. 23. She enumerates the signs of Josiah's humility: his humbling himself *(knʿ,* niph.), his tearing his clothes, his weeping (MT *wattikkāna' lĕpānay,* v. 27aβ, is a dittograph). Yahweh is speaking now, too, and he assures Josiah that he has heard, v. 27b. Yahweh then assures Josiah that he shall die in peace and shall not personally see the disaster that he will bring on "this place" and its inhabitants, v. 28a.

This is all communicated to Josiah, who does everything to show repentance. He sends, gathers, reads, vv. 29-30. ChrH offers inclusive terminology to describe the company of listeners, v. 30 ("prophets" in 2 Kgs 23:2 becomes "Levites," possibly through a slip of the pen, but more likely because in ChrH's time the Levites had actually taken the place of the prophets). This time the book is called "the book of the covenant," and we can see the reason for it in the fact that a covenant renewal ceremony immediately follows. Some kind of ritual is involved; there is a special place for the king to stand, v. 31. The text is more interested in the agreements that are made: walk after Yahweh; keep commandments (etc.) with heart and soul; do the words of this covenant book. V. 32a reports that "he [Josiah] caused all who were present in Jerusalem to take their stand [*RSV* "stand to"] in the covenant [read *babbĕrît* for MT *ûbinyāmin*]."

Once this ceremony was completed, the Jerusalemites went out to perform the covenant's obligation (Williamson, comm., inappropriately speaks of this as a "reward" in ChrH's ideology). A regnal policy to remove all the *tôʿēbôt*, "abominations," was activated; cf. 2 Chr 33:2 (Ahaz). This was to be *mikkol-hā'ărāṣôt 'ăšer libnê yiśrā'ēl*, "from all the lands belonging to the Israelites," probably a reimaging of Solomon's vast realm since *'ereṣ*, plur., can hardly mean "territorial holdings" in a local sense. By this purge Josiah removed any other choice, so that "all that were found in Israel" (cf. v. 32) were obliged to serve Yahweh as their God. This was Josiah's reward in the proper sense. Doom would come "on this place," but "all his days they [everyone in Israel] did not turn away from Yahweh their ancestral God," v. 33.

Genre

The main genre of this pericope is REPORT. The chronological note in v. 8 is a TRANSITION FORMULA. The NAME LIST appears in vv. 8b, 9, 12 (twice), and 20; these are all of individual men except in v. 9 (tribes and related ethnic groups). The OFFICIAL REPORT, a representation of the transmittal of information or a message by a person or persons duly authorized and sent forth, appears in vv. 15 (Hilkiah to Shaphan), 16-17 (disbursement of money), and 18 (finding of the book announced to Josiah). "Go and inquire," v. 21, is an ORDER. Vv. 20-28 contain a REPORT OF AN ORACULAR INQUIRY, a late narrating genre reflecting the belief that the word of a prophet must be understood as emerging out of a particular historical situation; the verses in question have a narrative introduction, vv. 20-22, and a narrative conclusion, v. 28b (cf. De Vries, "Prophetic Address," 22-24). The word of Huldah must be designated as a PROPHETIC SPEECH. It contains first a PROPHECY OF PUNISHMENT OVER THE PEOPLE, seen elsewhere in Chronicles only at 2 Chr 24:20, but very common in the canonical collection. It has the MESSENGER FORMULA twice, a COMMAND to report, v. 23b, and the announcement of judgment ahead of the accusation. Huldah's PROPHETIC SPEECH contains also a PROPHECY OF SALVATION in vv. 26-28a (cf. 20:15-17); it has the MESSENGER FORMULA, the PROPHETIC UTTERANCE FORMULA (*nĕ'um-yahweh*, "utterance of Yahweh," v. 27b), and a PROMISE of personal safety to the recipient, Josiah (v. 28a). V. 31a has a very sketchy REPORT OF RITUAL; this paraphrases in narrative style the COVENANT FORMULA, i.e., the part about Israel's obligation.

Setting

The interjection of Levites among those that repaired the temple, vv. 12-13, and taking the place of the prophets in the covenant ceremony, v. 30, has confused but hardly restructured this account. One must observe, however, that the Gershonites are now entirely absent from the list of Levitical families, only Merari and Kohath being named. A development seems to be in process in the reordering of these families, whose priority in prestige and authority is elsewhere reflected in the order in which they are named (cf. Möhlenbrink, 213). It is apparently early tradition, as reflected in Exodus, that accounts for Gershom(n) being named as the elder brother of Eliezer and son of Moses, 1 Chr 23:15-16; but also his priority as a son of Levi over Kohath and Merari in 5:27; 6:1-2. The order Gershon-Kohath-Merari appears at 23:6, where the gatekeepers attaching themselves to Levitical families are so ordered (see the Gershon genealogy that follows, 23:7-11). The singers also attached themselves to one of these Levitical eponyms, but in the order of priority, Kohath-Gershon-Merari, 6:23-27. 6:38-65 places Gershon last in the allotment of territories, and the order Kohath-Merari-Gershon is retained in 15:4ff.; 2 Chr 29:12. Apparently the Korahites, a branch of Kohath, have taken over completely in the role of singers, according to 2 Chr 20:19. Here in 34:12, not only has Gershon disappeared, but Merari comes before the one who has been long in the ascendancy, Kohath. Although we have no means for dating these developments in the history of tradition, what we see here most probably reflects a situation contemporaneous with ChrH.

The phrase šĕ'ērît yiśrā'ēl, "the remnant of Israel," is peculiar to ChrH in reference to those who have escaped exile in the northern realm (cf. also 30:6; 34:21). It is noteworthy that they too have contributed to the temple, and that Josiah is concerned with the fact that the lawbook's curses seem to apply to them as well as to their counterpart in Judah. We note, further, that Huldah's oracle is directed against "this place" (hammāqôm hazzeh), i.e., shrine site, with its inhabitants. This is a term for the Jerusalem shrine that makes itself thematic through constant recollection: 1 Chr 14:11; 15:1, 3; 17:9; 21:22, 25; 2 Chr 3:1; 5:7, 8; 6:20, 21, 26, 40; 7:12, 15; 20:26; 34:24, 25, 27, 28. Jerusalem is more than a "place" on a topographical map; it is more than a city; it is hammāqôm par excellence—the shrine site where Yahweh reveals himself, and which is now slated for destruction. Only when one understands ChrH's attachment to this māqôm can one comprehend the dimensions of the coming disaster according to his perspective.

It is only because he has copied Kings so closely in the inquiry section that ChrH retains the original form of preexilic prophecy. With few exceptions, the prophetic messages that make up ChrH's SCHEMA OF REVELATIONAL APPEARANCES are reported in the genre REPORT OF A PROPHETIC WORD. So too here with the PROPHETIC SPEECH OF HULDAH. Two things are to be observed: (1) elsewhere the prophet/seer puts in an uninvited and unannounced appearance: so Shemaiah, 2 Chr 12:5; Hanani, 16:7-10; Jehu, 19:1-3; Jahaziel, 20:13-19; Elijah (by letter), 21:12-15; Zechariah, 24:20; a "man of God," 25:7-8; a prophet, 25:15-16; Oded, 28:9-11; here, however, inquirers come to Huldah with their request for a divine response to a specific problem, making the genre a modified form of the REPORT OF AN ORACULAR INQUIRY (cf. 1 Chr 14:10, 14; 2 Chr 18:5, 14-15; 25:9), exempting Josiah's deputation from directly stating the subject of their inquiry (similar to the instances of REPORT OF A PROPHETIC WORD, listed above, is the PROPHETIC COMMISSION REPORT, seen here and at 1 Chr 21:9-13 and 2 Chr 11:1-4, in which first Gad and then Shemaiah are directly ordered by Yahweh to present their respective messages). (2) All the instances listed for the genre REPORT OF A PROPHETIC WORD are supplied by ChrH rather than taken from Kings, are relatively simple in structure, are designed to fit a specific narrative framework, and adhere closely to the theme: evil on evildoers, blessing on the righteous. It seems impossible to escape the conclusion that this "genre" is ChrH's own creation, particularly when we compare the relative complexity of such oracles as that of Huldah, taken directly from Kings and reflecting an authentically historical pattern. Huldah speaks judgment and blessing; she speaks to Josiah as "man" and as "king of Judah"; she has distinct elements of announcement and accusation; she even has the PROPHETIC UTTERANCE FORMULA, *ně'um-yahweh* (v. 27b), extremely common in the canonical collection but present only here in ChrH—and that because it is copied from Kings. All this reinforces the impression that ChrH has never actually heard a prophet speak, and that the prophets he introduces on his own initiative are fictional creations.

It is to be expected that ChrH adheres to Kings in allowing Huldah's prophecy to be followed immediately by a covenant ceremony, vv. 29-32. The fact that the prophecy interprets the lawbook raises the question whether covenant comes out of law or law out of covenant. D. J. McCarthy ("Covenant and Law") demonstrates his perceptiveness regarding the historical development of formal structures according to which ChrH's key words are first identified (*dāraš*, 137 times in the OT as "seek revelation," but 27 out of 38 times in ChrH as "cleave to God"; *kāna'*, "be humble," 17 times in ChrH out of a total of 37 in the OT; negatively, *'āzab*, "forsake," *mā'al*, "do wickedly"); next McCarthy explains that the Assyrian *adu* loyalty oaths provide a background for the covenant renewals in ChrH and Nehemiah (in Assyria this has a societal function, tying the community together through an oath administered by the king or his surrogate; in Israel the basic demand assuring communal unity is fidelity to Yahweh, the nation's true king from antiquity, so that a weak or wavering community must first purify itself, putting away other gods, honoring Yahweh alone); finally McCarthy explains that beside this functional similarity to the Assyrian texts, ChrH and Nehemiah see a ceremonial structure that includes (1) being presided over by royalty, (2) being concerned primarily with fundamental loyalty, and (3) the people taking a posture of deference and even prostration. 2 Chr 34:29-33 emphasizes these features much more strongly than its parallel in 2 Kgs 23:1-3. ChrH and Ezra-Nehemiah are going back to a very ancient concept, and, in spite of the arrangement, it is clearly the renewed covenant that has priority over the law.

Intention

In spite of this interpretation of Josiah's covenant, the priority given in ChrH to purifying the land of idols puts the finding of the lawbook in quite a different perspective than in Kings. In Kings nothing has been said of Josiah's "beginning to purge" in his twelfth year. The reader is to suppose that the evil example of Amon continues to affect the people and perhaps (despite an approving THEOLOGICAL REVIEW in 2 Kgs 22:2) Josiah himself. Hence this king's alarm at hearing the book read and ultimately the far-reaching, vigorous reform of 2 Kings 23. Not so according to ChrH, for Josiah was himself well prepared ("while he was yet a boy he began to seek," v. 3) and so were the people, all of whose intrusive idols except the *tô'ēbôt*, "abominations," of v. 33 had been removed before repairs began on the temple. The fact that the Levites are also given supervision over this work shows that cultic purification was indeed Josiah's paramount concern. Thus Huldah's stern pronouncement about a wrath coming on "this place and its inhabitants" has to be paradoxical unless understood as a carryover from previous generations. In preaching to his own contemporaries, ChrH intended this as a warning that the curses of the lawbook still stood—that the forefathers had piled up wrath in such a measure that any apostasy in the present generation could again provoke Yahweh's anger. In spite of the Passover in 2 Chronicles 35, Josiah is not seen as the great cultic reformer (Hezekiah), but as the exemplary enforcer of the covenant and of the law.

Bibliography

H. Gressmann, "Josia und das Deuteronomium," *ZAW* 41 (1924) 313-37; P. Joüon, "Notes philologiques sur le text hébreu de 2 Chron. 34, 33," *Bib* 12 (1931) 89-90; D. J. McCarthy, "Covenant and Law in Chronicles-Nehemiah," *CBQ* 44 (1982) 25-44; K. Möhlenbrink, "Die levitischen Überlieferungen des Alten Testaments," *ZAW* 52 (1934) 184-231; T. Willi, "Thora in den biblischen Chronikbüchern," *Judaica* 36 (1980) 102-5, 148-51.

III. REPORT OF JOSIAH'S PASSOVER, 35:1-19

Structure

	Original	Secondary
A. Introductory summary	1	
1. Josiah's proclamation	1a	
2. Performance on fourteenth day of the		
first month	1b	
B. Supervision of the clergy	2-5	6
1. Authorized priestly duties	2	
2. Instructions to the Levites	3-5	6
a. Sanctified teachers of "all Israel"	$3a\alpha^1$	
b. Release from "bearing the ark"	$3a\alpha^2$-b	
1) Order for deposit in Solomon's temple	$3a\alpha^2$	
2) Freedom to serve Yahweh and Israel	$3a\beta$-b	
c. Arrangement by family and service	4-5	
1) Order to organize (authorization formula)	4	
2) Command to serve by family groupings	5	
d. Ritual preparation		6
1) Order to slaughter		6a
2) Order to sanctify worshipers and prepare		
for kinsmen (authorization formula)		6b
C. Contributing victims		7-9
1. Josiah's gifts for the laity		7
a. Tally of small animals and bulls as Passover		
victims		$7a\alpha$
b. Tally of bulls		$7a\beta$
c. From royal property		7b
2. Freewill offerings by officials		8
a. Representing the laity		8a
b. Supervisors of temple		$8b\alpha$

There are two main lines of evidence that this pericope is not a literary unity (cf. Galling, ATD, omitting vv. 7-10; Willi, 197, 200, omitting vv. 2-6, 9-10). One is that in v. 4 and v. 10 the vocable *kwn,* "prepare," refers to the stations and roles assigned to the priests and Levites in preparation for the Passover, whereas in vv. 6, 14 (twice), and 15 it clearly refers to the actual work of preparing the sacrificial victims. Since burnt offerings are mentioned in v. 16 as part of keeping the Passover, covered by the phrase *wattikkôn kol-'ăbôdat yahweh,* "So all the service of Yahweh was prepared," this verse should be listed with the latter group of passages. The second item of evidence is the fact that the phrase *bayyôm hahû',* "on that day" (v. 16), marks this verse as an epitomizing conclusion, whereas v. 17 uses the parallel phrase *bā'ēt hahî'* in the statement, "And the people of Israel . . . kept the Passover at that time" (cf. S. J. De Vries, *Yesterday, Today and Tomorrow* [Grand Rapids: Eerdmans, and London: SPCK, 1975] 72-73). One should also observe that this summarizing statement in this verse duplicates at least in part "and they killed the Passover lamb," v. 11, and that v. 17 refers to the feast of Mazzoth, not mentioned elsewhere, while failing to make any reference to the sacrifices that are so prominent in vv. 12ff. In the account of Hezekiah's Passover the Mazzoth is not only present but is dominant, and the sacrifices referred to there are—except for v. 14—exclusively those that pertain to the Passover victim (2 Chr 30:13ff.), from which we may infer that the verses of ch. 35 referring to the Mazzoth, and not to sacrifices, are original. The rest is supplementary expansion, ending in the concluding epitome with *bayyôm hahû',* v. 16. "King Josiah," v. 16, compared with "Josiah," v. 1, may be a further token of the separate origin of this material.

Our listing of original and secondary materials in the preceding outline shows the contours of these two literary strands. Thus in the original narration (vv. 2-5, 10, 17-19) Josiah instructs the priests and Levites (it is typical of ChrH to give more attention to the Levites), so that each group is ready according to the king's command; then everyone present celebrates the Passover "at that time" (i.e., on the date mentioned in v. 1). This narration is introduced by an introductory summary (v. 1) and is followed by the ENCOMIUM of v. 18 and the chronological statement of v. 19. The fact that v. 18 parallels 2 Kgs 23:22, and that v. 19 duplicates 2 Kgs 23:23, shows that it is ChrH who is supplying these verses according to his usual method of citing Kings; 2 Kgs 23:21, a command connecting the Passover to the finding of the lawbook, finds its counterpart in ChrH's v. 1. Thus all that Kings has provided concerning Josiah's Passover is closely reproduced in the original strand of ChrH.

Here are notes on the structure of this pericope. In v. 1 Josiah's "making" *('śh)* a Passover is interpreted as a proclamation, since that was his actual function; cf. v. 16; "they killed" is proleptic of the entire ceremony to follow. The need for this introductory summary is to provide an opportunity to mention the date, the fourteenth day of the first month, in differentiation from Hezekiah's practice according to 2 Chr 30:2, 13. Vv. 2-5 (original) begin with narrative and continue in discourse. To "encourage" *(ḥzq,* piel) the priests may suggest criticism similar to that observed in 30:3, 24 (see Williamson, comm.). The Levites are identified in v. 3 as the sanctified teachers of "all Israel"; to this they had been appointed by Jehoshaphat according to 17:7-9 (cf. von Rad, *Geschichtsbild,* 96-98). "Bearing the ark" is meant metaphorically, for, although they had brought the ark into David's tent (1 Chr 15:14, 26), according to 2 Chr 5:7ff. it had been the priests who had placed this cult object inside Solomon's temple. Their duty now is to "serve Yahweh your God and his people Israel"; cf. 1 Chr 16:4. A possibility is that we should read a niph. or qal pass. of *ntn* in place of the impr. *tĕnû:* "has been placed"—a past event. In v. 4 a niph. impr. (Ketib, LXX, Vg., in place of Qere hiph.) continues the king's command: "and organize. . . ." The authority for this is cited in the formula *biktāb . . . ûbĕmiktab,* referring to 1 Chronicles 23–26 as a "writing" authorized by David, and to 2 Chr 8:14 as a "writing" of Solomon. V. 5 is a new command in which the king tells the Levites to "stand," i.e., to take a ritual role and position so as to represent the respective ancestral families from which each had come. Here ends the original material.

Verse 6 has a command to slaughter (cf. 30:17), carried out in v. 11, and then to prepare (*kwn,* hiph.) the flesh *la'ăhêkem,* i.e., for fellow clergy, as in vv. 14-15, and not "kinsmen," as in v. 5. For this the authority of Moses is adduced, as in 30:16. Vv. 7-15 continue the narrative; only v. 10, stating that Josiah's commands of vv. 2-5 have been fulfilled, is original. Since v. 11 states that the priests sprinkled the blood while the Levites flayed the victims, we are inclined to attribute the slaying to the actual worshipers (cf. 30:16). V. 13 is in disagreement with Exod 12:8-9 and follows Deut 16:7 in stating that the flesh was not roasted (*RSV* cj.), but boiled (*bšl,* piel); cf. Shaver, 164-67. The transition *wĕ'ahar,* "and afterward," in v. 14 is internal and of no structural significance. Unless interpreted as an (→) epitome, *wattikkôn kol-'ăbôdat yahweh,* "so all the service of Yahweh was prepared" (v. 16), is a repetition of what is in vv. 11-15 and a contradiction of v. 10—but that is what it is. Again, v. 17 would seem repetitious without the recognition that it introduces the continuation of the original material from v. 10. According to this verse, Josiah has made no special effort, like Hezekiah (2 Chr 30:1-9), to bring in worshipers in great numbers and from afar; his Passover is just for "the people of Israel who were present." On the laudatory comparison, cf. 30:26, but especially 2 Kgs 23:22. Four groups are specifically mentioned as taking part: Josiah, priests and Levites, those from all Judah and Israel who happened to be present, and the Jerusalemites themselves (cf. Williamson, *Israel,* 12-13).

Genre

This is a REPORT. The original text had INSTRUCTIONS for the Levites, vv. 3-5, with two ORDERS, "Put the ark in the temple," v. 3, and "Prepare yourselves," v. 4. It has the AUTHORIZATION FORMULA in v. 4b and a COMMAND in v. 5. The expansion in vv. 6-9 has three ORDERS, "Kill the Passover lamb," "sanctify yourselves," and "prepare for your brethren," all in v. 6. V. 6 also has another AUTHORIZATION FORMULA. The TALLY is seen in vv. 7 (twice), 8 (twice), and 9 (twice). There are NAME LISTS in vv. 8 and 9. Vv. 10-15 as they now stand are a REPORT OF RITUAL. The AUTHORIZATION FORMULA occurs in v. 12, the REGULATION FORMULA in vv. 10, 13, 14, 15, and 16, and there is a TRANSITION FORMULA in v. 14. V. 16 is an EPITOME, requiring that the original material in vv. 17-19 be designated as an epilogue. V. 17 has another TRANSITION FORMULA and v. 19 has the DATING FORMULA. V. 18 is an ENCOMIUM.

Setting and Intention

Only gradually was the Passover merged with the Mazzoth festival. They were together a family festival until the time of Deuteronomy. In Deut 16:5-6 the combined festival is called a "Passover sacrifice" and is brought to the central shrine, Jerusalem. Kings makes no mention of a Passover festival for Hezekiah, which must be seen as a secondary reflex of Josiah's Passover when reported for the former king in 2 Chronicles 30. Josiah does have a Passover according to 2 Kgs 23:21-23, but that text identifies it as required by Hilkiah's lawbook, and the description is notably brief. No mention is made of Mazzoth or of special sacrifices. Our study of 2 Chronicles 30 has shown us that, while the Mazzoth element is regarded as part of the Passover, it receives all the attention and there is only a problematical implication (v. 15) that special sacrifices (burnt offerings) were included. Our present passage is clearly modeled upon 2 Kgs 23:21-23 (see above). The original core of this narrative of Josiah's Passover is quite neutral about special sacrifices, but it does specifically mention that a seven-day Mazzoth feast was part of the festival (v. 17). There can be little doubt but that its aim was to attribute to Josiah a correct calendar over against Hezekiah's highly suspicious celebration in the second, rather than the first, month (see v. 1 and bā'ēt hahî', "in that time," in v. 17). Josiah gets a foot up on Hezekiah in that he is compared to all the kings back to Samuel, not just those back to Solomon (cf. 2 Chr 30:26). By including the dating formula of 2 Kgs 23:23, v. 19, ChrH makes the Passover part of the cultic reform, a pattern that pertains also to Hezekiah, whose purification rites (2 Chronicles 29) preceded his celebration of the Passover (ch. 30).

The secondary elements in ch. 35 evidently reflect a somewhat later period than that of ChrH, in which public sacrifices had come to expand markedly the private and familial aspects of the original practice. Inasmuch as one of the secondary verses (v. 15) refers to the Asaphite singers, reflecting Gese's tradition III-A, which is to be dated ca. 350, it is probable that the entire expansion comes from approximately this same date (cf. Petersen, 86: "tradition shift"; Gese, "Zur Geschichte der Kultsänger am zweiten Tempel," 222-34).

A final word about the FESTIVAL SCHEMA: even in its original form, this narrative has all four elements if we include the ENCOMIUM of v. 18 as indicative of the last: (1) date; (2) participants/purification; (3) ceremony; (4) joyful celebration. With the expansions, the second and third elements are made more prominent, but the essential structure remains the same. We may be certain that ChrH and his epigone intended this as a model for the continual celebration of this high holy feast.

Bibliography

A. Büchler, "Das Brandopfer neben dem Passah in II Chron. 30,15 und 35,12.14.15," ZAW 25 (1905) 1-46; L. Rost, "Josias Passa," in Theologie in Geschichte und Kunst (Fest. W. Elliger; ed. S. Herrmann and O. Söhngen; Witten: Luther-Verlag, 1968) 169-75.

IV. BATTLE REPORT: JOSIAH'S DEATH, 35:20-25

Structure

A. Confrontation with Neco (transition formula)   20
   1. Situation   20aα
   2. Neco marches to Carchemish   20aβ

2 Kgs 23:29-30, from which ChrH draws this narrative, is a sparse account mentioning five essential facts: (1) Neco marches *('lh)* to the Euphrates; (2) Josiah marches *(hlk)* against him; (3) Neco slays Josiah at Megiddo "when he sees him"; (4) Josiah's body is carried to Jerusalem and interred; (5) the people anoint Jehoahaz as his successor. ChrH keeps this order intact but makes the following major additions and/or alterations: in v. 20 he uses the transition formula *'aḥărê kol-zō't,* "after all this," thus making a sharp separation between the account of all Josiah's righteous deeds and this tale of tragedy *('ăšer hēkîn yōʾšîyāhû 'et-habbayit,* "when Josiah had prepared the temple," intends to make a direct connection to the chronological note ["eighteenth year"] in v. 19, ignoring the fact that, according to 34:1, Josiah still had thirteen years to reign); in v. 21 he inserts a message from Neco to Josiah (cf. De Vries, *Yesterday, Today and Tomorrow,* 251-52) of admonition and warning; in v. 22a he describes Josiah's preparations for combat (Willi, 121, "conjecture") and in v. 23 the manner and effect of his wounding; in vv. 24b-25 he adds his own interpretative comments on the lasting effects of this tragedy.

Genre

The main genre of this pericope is BATTLE REPORT. The only TRANSITION FORMULA is at the beginning, v. 20a. Neco's message is an ADMONITION, urging Josiah to refrain from something that, in Neco's viewpoint, he ought not to do. It contains a formula of APPEASEMENT, *mah-lî wālāk*, "What is there between us?" It also contains a WARNING, styled as a WISH, *'al yašḥîtekā*, "May he (God) not destroy you." This is also a THREAT. The narrative of the ensuing battle, with Josiah's death by an arrow, obviously borrows from 1 Kgs 22:28-29 par. 2 Chr 18:29, 33-34; its conclusion is a DEATH REPORT. The following DEATH AND BURIAL FORMULA has no "slept with his fathers" clause. V. 25 constitutes an EDITORIAL UNIT.

Setting and Intention

There has been much discussion of the death of Josiah as a historical event. There can be little doubt that ChrH's modifications to the Kings report are interpretative elaborations. Some scholars have argued that Josiah's approach (*liqrā'tô*, v. 20) to Neco was the protocol of a vassal to a recognized master, and that the Judahite king had no warlike intentions. ChrH takes pains to show the opposite, that he actually did intend to stop Neco's advance by armed force (cf. A. Malamat, "Josiah's Bid for Armageddon," *JANESCU* 5 [1973] 267-78). This is an important point for understanding the reference to revelation in Neco's message (v. 21) and in the report of Josiah's attack (v. 22). After informing Josiah whom he is attacking *hayyôm*, "today," Neco informs him that "God" (*'ĕlōhîm*) had told him to hurry, and commands him to "cease opposing God, who is with me, lest he destroy you." There is no point in Couroyer's argument that the Egyptians had a general term for Deity, which is what Neco uses and is translated "Elohim" by ChrH. For one thing, this assumes the historicity of this verbal exchange. The clue is given by the statement in v. 22 that "he did not listen to the words of Neco from the mouth of God" (*mippî 'ĕlōhîm*) but attacked Neco as he had intended. We have already observed that prophets have ceased appearing to the Judahite kings (cf. 33:10, "Yahweh spoke to Manasseh and his people, but they gave no heed"). This is an important point with ChrH, whose SCHEMA OF REVELATIONAL APPEARANCES includes the possibility that Yahweh may at last become so exasperated with Judah's unwillingness to obey that he withholds prophetic revelation altogether (cf. Amos 9:11-12). Even though Josiah has been exemplary in his righteousness, the day of revelational appearances is well nigh past, and Yahweh speaks to Josiah only through the mouth of an Egyptian king. It matters not to ChrH which Egyptian god speaks, or if Deity in general is meant. To him the revelation that Neco claims is a supernatural warning that he should heed. Josiah owes no allegiance to this *'ĕlōhîm*, yet it must have some force and authenticity because what it spoke through Neco came true.

Even though this act of ignoring a supernaturally derived warning might be construed as a misdeed on Josiah's part (cf. Frost), ChrH is unable to blame him for wickedness. The point he is anxious to make is the magnitude of the tragedy, not only for Josiah himself, but for the nation as well. In ch. 36 he will tell how Josiah's sons and grandson led the nation to utter ruin, and no doubt his editorial comments in v. 25 suggest the dimensions of the tragedy of losing a righteous king who might have prevented it. It may be true, as Williamson (comm.) claims, that "to this day" identifies v. 25 as part of a document from an earlier time; yet ChrH uses it (or composes it) to express the depth and universality of popular grief over Josiah's demise. When the good and the best cannot preserve Israel from ruin, great is the voice of sorrow!

Bibliography

B. Alfrink, "Die Schlacht bei Megiddo und der Tod des Josias (609)," *Bib* 15 (1934) 173-84; F. Buhl, "Eine arabische Parallele zu II Chr. 35,25," *ZAW* 29 (1909) 314; W. W. Cannon, "A Note on Dr. Welch's Article, 'The Death of Josiah,'" *ZAW* 44 (1926) 255-60; B. Couroyer, "Le litige entre Josias et Néchao," *RB* 55 (1948) 388-96; S. B. Frost, "The Death of Josiah: A Conspiracy of Silence," *JBL* 87 (1968) 369-82; G. Pfeifer, "Die Begegnung zwischen Pharao Necho und König Josia bei Megiddo," *MIOF* 15 (1969) 297-307; A. C. Welch, "The Death of Josiah," *ZAW* 43 (1925) 255-60.

V. CONCLUDING REGNAL RESUMÉ, 35:26-27

Structure

A. Further details (regulation formula)	26
B. Citation formula	27

Genre

This REGNAL RESUMÉ defines Josiah's other good deeds with use of the REGULATION FORMULA, "according to what is written in Yahweh's law," for whose finding and application he was chiefly to be remembered. A CITATION FORMULA mentions no prophetic writings: only the book of the kings of Judah and Israel. Vv. 24-25 make a further (→) death and burial formula superfluous. There is no (→) succession formula, nor will there be any such for the kings of Judah's downfall, ch. 36, except in the case of Jehoiachin (36:8).

REPORT: JUDAH FULFILLS ITS FINAL SABBATH, 36:1-23

Structure

I. Provoking Yahweh's irrevocable wrath	1-21
A. The reign of Jehoahaz	1-4
1. Regnal resumé	1-2
a. Crowned in Josiah's place	1
b. Accession age formula and statement of length and place of reign	2
2. Actions of Neco	3-4
a. Punishment	3
1) Deposition	3a
2) Tribute	3b

The reigns of the last four kings of Judah are told in far less detail than in Kings; items about Jehoahaz, Jehoiakim, and Jehoiachin are hurried over in order to get to Zedekiah and the day of doom for Jerusalem. The sections in the first three are markedly symmetrical, containing in each instance an introductory summary and a report about the disruptive action of a foreign king. It is stated in v. 1 that the "people of the land" made Jehoahaz king. This is a regular motif in ChrH; cf. Ahaziah, 22:1; Uzziah, 26:1; Josiah, 33:25; Zedekiah, 36:10. Items for Jehoahaz are picked out of 2 Kgs 23:31-35, but the negative theological evaluation of 2 Kgs 23:32 is overlooked. On the actions of "the king of Egypt" (= Neco), cf. Watson (4.1); Willi (pp. 100, 164) describes ChrH's method as generalizing. According to Willi (p. 165), vv. 5-10 are meant as a typology of the future, but the ordinary reader might see here only one more step in Judah's course of destruction. From the account of Jehoiakim's rule in 2 Kgs 23:37–24:7 ChrH reproduces an introductory and a concluding summary. The thing that is surprising is the statement in v. 6 that Nebuchadnezzar took Jehoiakim to Babylon (not in Kings; but cf. Manasseh, 2 Chr 33:11). Also underived is the statement in v. 7 that Nebuchadnezzar plundered the temple vessels at this time (so also at vv. 10, 18; cf. Ackroyd, "Temple Vessels," 178). Jehoiakim's notice concludes with a SUCCESSION FORMULA for Jehoiachin, which is probable evidence that he died in Jerusalem after all, as Kings implies.

The Jehoiachin notice is even briefer than 2 Kgs 24:8-17; after the introductory summary little is said except that Nebuchadnezzar came up against him *litšûbat haššānâ*, "at the turn of the year" (v. 10), and brought him with the temple vessels (a contradiction of vv. 7 and 18?) to Babylon. In the place of a (→) succession formula, there is a statement that Zedekiah "his brother" (cf. 1 Chr 3:16) was installed in his place.

On the reign of Zedekiah cf. Seeligmann ("Auffassung," 276-77). ChrH draws very little from 2 Kgs 24:18–25:12. He gives the introductory summary and then a series of complaints, first against Zedekiah personally, and then against the clergy and laity. The first complaint against Zedekiah is that he refused to humble himself before Jeremiah the prophet, even though it was the word of Yahweh; this can refer to such passages as Jer 34:6ff. Another complaint is that he broke his oath to Nebuchadnezzar, something about which we read in Ezekiel 17. Willi (p. 172) suggests that the complaint about Zedekiah's stubborn unresponsiveness to Yahweh is based on Jer 37:2. But as ChrH goes on to recount his complaints against the people, Zedekiah's sins pale into insignificance. His were mainly the sins of unresponsiveness and neglect, but theirs was the sin of blatantly denying, even defying, the ever returning word of Yahweh. ChrH heaps up the superlatives. Not just the people, but *kol-śārê hakkōhănîm*, "all the princes of the priesthood," v. 14, outrageously piled up outrages (*hirbû lim'ôl-mā'al* [Ketib]), following all the *tô'ēbôt*, "abominations," 2 Chr 33:2; 34:33) of the nations (not just of the native peoples of Palestine), even polluting (*ṭm'*) Yahweh's house that he had sanctified (*qdš*, piel) in Jerusalem, v. 14.

But that was not the worst. To stop them from this wickedness and turn them back to himself, Yahweh came again and again (*haškēm wěšālôaḥ*, "got up early and sent") with "messengers," i.e., prophets, seers, and preachers, being motivated solely by compassion (note the alliteration, *kî-ḥāmal 'al-'ammô wě'al-mě'ônô*, "for he was sorry for his people and his dwelling place"), v. 15. In response, they were *mal'ibîm . . . ûbôzîm . . . ûmitta'tě'îm*, "mocking . . . and despising . . . and scoffing"; neither his messengers nor his words nor his prophets had any but a negative effect on them. This is therefore the end. The wrath (*ḥēmâ*) of Yahweh has arisen against his own people *'ad- lě'ên marpē'*, lit., "until there was no remedy" (v. 16), but implying result: "to the point where it [God's wrath] could no longer be remedied," i.e., appeased.

Verses 17-21 inform us of what that wrath consisted. It is Yahweh himself who summons "the Chaldean king" (perhaps this title has a grimmer association than the proper name Nebuchadnezzar, vv. 6, 7, 13). To depict this king's depredations ChrH starts with the most extreme case: the best young men are slain with the sword, and that "in their sanctuary." The slaughter extends to "young men and virgins, elders and aged." According to v. 15, Yahweh had had compassion (*ḥml*), but the Chaldean king lacked it altogether, v. 17. As ChrH itemizes the ensuing plunder and destruction, he keeps using the word "all": *hakkōl*, vv. 17, 18; *wěkol*, v. 19 (twice). So the holy city is ravished. V. 20 seems almost anticlimactic: "those who escaped the sword" were exiled to Babylon to serve the kings of this dynasty until the kingdom of Persia took its place.

ChrH has stated the causes of this deportation (vv. 12-16), but his account does not end until he also tells its purpose. Even in giving up on his people and allowing his temple to be destroyed, Yahweh has a purpose, v. 21. Even over this ultimate tragedy he stands supreme. Yahweh has allowed it to happen not just to punish the wicked, but to fulfill his own prophecy spoken through Jeremiah (Jer 25:11-12; 29:10) predicting a seventy-year exile. ChrH interprets this in the light of Lev 26:34-35, 41-43, which allows the land also to have a sabbath of rest (one year out of seven). ChrH's phrase, ʻad- rāṣĕtâ hā'āreṣ 'et-šabbĕtôteyhā, "until the land should have enjoyed [or received recompense for] its sabbaths" (→ Chapter 1, "The Original Version of Chronicles," under "Intention"), shows two things: (1) to be rid of this contumacious generation would be a pleasant rest and recompense for Yahweh's own land, and (2) the plur. "its sabbaths" shows that ChrH is thinking of a pluralization of the traditional seven. ChrH clarifies by affirming that "all the days it lay desolate it kept sabbath" (šābātā), the purpose being "to fill up" (lĕmall'ôt) the seventy years with positive purpose, i.e., to allow it to make up for the sabbaths of the past (cf. Galling, ATD, 185).

On the expansion in vv. 22-23 (Rudolph, HAT: gloss), see Williamson (Israel, 7-10). As has been noted, it is the virtual equivalent of Ezra 1:1-3. In Chapter 1 above, "Introduction to Chronicles," we have argued that it is a redactional gloss designed to attach Chronicles to Ezra-Nehemiah. No other alternative seems attractive. In terms of the text itself, one should note that this addition's concept of fulfilling Jeremiah's prophecy differs significantly from that of v. 21. V. 21 uses the verb ml', "fill up," because ChrH adopts the positive stance in which the seventy years are filled with something useful and helpful, i.e., the restful and restorative sabbath(s) of the land. V. 22, on the other hand, refers to the same Jeremianic prophecy but thinks that the exile has had no significance except in its completion or termination. Thus it uses the verb klh, "complete," with reference to this word of Yahweh. Even if it could be shown that vv. 22-23 are an original part of Chronicles, it would be most difficult to explain the writer's sudden shift from the one line of interpretation to the other. But since the verbal identity with the beginning of Ezra is so obvious, we need not burden ChrH with the responsibility of reconciling this disparity. His book ends, paradoxically, on a negative note that is strangely positive. While the captives languish, the holy land, Yahweh's own land, the land of promise, recovers from years and centuries of abuse. When at last its sabbaths are complete, it may sprout new growth unto righteousness.

Genre

The main genre is REPORT. There are introductory REGNAL RESUMÉS in vv. 1-2, 5, 9, and 11-12a; all of these have the ACCESSION AGE FORMULA and STATEMENT OF LENGTH AND PLACE OF REIGN; all but the first have the THEOLOGICAL REVIEW. It is only in v. 8 that the concluding REGNAL RESUMÉ, with CITATION FORMULA and SUCCESSION FORMULA, is found. Vv. 12-16 constitute an INDICTMENT SPEECH, with specifications against both the ruling monarch and the clergy and people. The CONVEYANCE FORMULA ("gave into his hand") appears in v. 17b. The secondary expansion, vv. 22-23, creates a new EDITORIAL UNIT by expanding its foregoing context. The proclamation of v. 23 has the MESSENGER FORMULA, a PROTOCOL stating how Cyrus got his authority and how he came to the decision to rebuild Jerusalem, and an EDICT ("let him go up") with the ASSISTANCE FORMULA ("May Yahweh his God be with him").

Setting and Intention

For more detailed discussion concerning the secondary character of 36:22-23, the reader should consult Chapter 1 above, "The Ezra-Nehemiah/Chronicles Collocation," under the subheadings "Structure" and "Intention." Our treatment of the sabbaths issue as the theme of the entire ChrH is justified more fully in another part of that same chapter, "The Original Version of Chronicles," under the subheading "Intention," where it is argued that ChrH sees the exile as the last sabbath cycle in an extended series of sabbaths for the land, comprising in the end a jubilee (cf. the far more idealized structure of the apocalyptic book of *Jubilees*, dating from ca. 190 B.C.). See also De Vries, "Lord's Sabbath," 96-103.

In Chapter 5 above, on the pericope 1 Chr 10:1-14, we have argued that Yahweh's wrath on Saul, leading to removing him from kingship, is a type of the wrath of God poured out on the last four kings and the people, resulting in the Babylonian exile. Here we have found much merit in the arguments of Mosis and Williamson. To be specific, 1 Chr 10:13-14 produces with 2 Chr 36:14-16 the ultimate inclusio upon which ChrH has been structured. In other words, the entire period of the kingship from David to Zedekiah is a failure that Yahweh had endeavored to preclude in exchanging David for Saul, then in extending David's kingship through Solomon to a long lineage of Judahite kings. 1 Chr 10:13-14a reads:

> So Saul died for his unfaithfulness *[běma'ǎlô]*, in that he was unfaithful *[mā'al]* to Yahweh with respect to the word of Yahweh, which he did not keep, and even consulted a medium for obtaining an oracle instead of inquiring of Yahweh.

2 Chr 36:14-16 lays emphasis on both elements: the unfaithfulness and the rejection of Yahweh's messengers:

> [And] even all the chiefs of the priests, with the people, multiplied being unfaithful in deeds of infidelity *[hirbû lim'ôl-ma'al* (Ketib)], as with all the abominations of the nations; and they defiled Yahweh's house which he had sanctified in Jerusalem. And Yahweh the God of their fathers eagerly sent *[haškēm wěšālôah]* to them through his messengers because he had compassion on his people and his dwelling place, but they just kept on mocking God's messengers, despising his words, and scoffing at his prophets, until Yahweh's wrath arose against his people to the point where there was no appeasing it.

Here is where the SCHEMA OF REWARD AND RETRIBUTION crosses paths with the SCHEMA OF REVELATIONAL APPEARANCES. We have observed that prophetic warnings to the people have been coming further and further apart. Now we are told the reason: Yahweh had kept trying to communicate with his people about the ultimate consequences of their *ma'al*, "unfaithfulness," but they either would not listen, or they quickly forgot. It came to the point where, far from gaining their repentance, God saw his revelation through "messengers," "words," and "prophets" mocked and laughed at. There had been no dearth of the word of God: he had spoken to comfort them in their distress, and he had spoken to warn them of a coming "wrath" if they would refuse to repent. Yahweh still had compassion on his people and his "dwelling place" among them—but there was no remedy because they would no longer listen. ChrH retells the story of how they had provoked divine wrath by refusing to listen, hoping that such wrath would never be provoked again.

Bibliography

P. R. Ackroyd, "The Temple Vessels—a Continuity Theme," in *Studies in the Religion of Ancient Israel* (VTSup 23; Leiden: Brill, 1972) 166-81; idem, "The Theology of the Chronicler," *Lexington Theological Quarterly* 8 (1973) 101-16; I. L. Seeligmann, "Die Auffassung von der Prophetie in der deuteronomistischen und chronistischen Geschichtsschreibung," in *Congrès Volume: Göttingen 1977* (VTSup 29; Leiden: Brill, 1978) 254-84; H. G. M. Williamson, "Eschatology in Chronicles," *TynBul* 28 (1977) 115-54.

Glossary

SCHEMATA

FESTIVAL SCHEMA (Schema einer Festfeier). A pattern dividing the religious festivals into (1) date, (2) identification of participants, with preparation and purification, (3) description, and (4) rejoicing. 2 Chr 7:8-9; 15:9-15; 29:3-36; 30:13-27; 35:1-19; cf. Neh 7:33–8:18; 12:43.

QUESTION AND ANSWER SCHEMA (Frage und Antwort Schema). A literary device which projects a question and its answer as a means of describing a future situation. 2 Chr 7:21-22.

SCHEMA OF DYNASTIC ENDANGERMENT (Schematische Erzählung von dynastischer Gefährdung). A narrative structure featuring the tension between the fulfillment of the dynastic promise to David and an insatiable bloodlust among the Omride Baalists and their Judahite in-laws. 2 Chr 11:18–25:3.

SCHEMA OF REPRIEVE (Schematische Darstellung von Begnadigung). A description of sinful behavior followed by divine punishment and/or the mitigation of this punishment. 1 Chr 21:17.

SCHEMA OF REVELATIONAL APPEARANCES (Schema von offenbarenden Erscheinungen). A pattern in which the bringers of revelation offer assurance and encouragement to good kings and threaten condemnation on bad kings.

SCHEMA OF REWARD AND RETRIBUTION (Schema von Lohn und Vergeltung). A repeated cycle of virtue and reward, apostasy and retribution, throughout 2 Chronicles 11–36.

SCHEMA OF TERRITORIAL CLAIM (Schema von territorialem Anspruch). A pattern stating (1) how a group came into possession of a given territory, (2) affirming that its occupation had been continuous, and (3) stating that the occupation is still in force. The time expression 'ad hayyôm hazzeh, "until this day," is characteristic. 1 Chr 4:41, 43. → ETIOLOGY.

GENRES AND GENRE ELEMENTS

ACCOUNT (Bericht). A narrative form similar to (→) report but generally longer and more complex. It often consists of several briefer reports, statements, or

426

descriptions. 1 Chronicles 13–16; 18–20; 21:28–2 Chr 9:31; 2 Chronicles 10–36; 13:26–16:14; 17–20; 29–32; 34–35.

ACCUSATION (Anklage). A charge, naming the offense for which the accused deserves to be brought to trial, often with specifications. 1 Chr 10:13-14; 2 Chr 25:15; 28:10, 13; 32:12.

ACCUSATORY QUESTION (Anklagefrage). A form of (→) rhetorical question, always brief, substituting in prophecies of punishment for the accusation, or in other words of prophetic reprimand for an accusation together with the addressee's presumptive reply, either an affirmation if the accusatory question is in the form "Have you not . . .?" or an unacceptable excuse in cases where the form is "Why do you . . .?" Ezek 13:7; 16:43; 42:2, 18; Mic 2:7; Nah 3:8; 2 Chr 19:2; 24:20; 25:15; 28:10.

ADDRESS (Anrede). A political, military, or religious (→) speech in which the addressee is named. 1 Chr 21:17; 28:2, 7; 2 Chr 1:7; 5:3-11; 7:12-22; 13:4-12; 29:4-11; 32:6-8.

ADMONITION (Ermahnung gegen . . .). A genre of address designed to dissuade an individual or group from a certain type of conduct. 1 Chr 12:18; 22:11-13; 28:9-10; 2 Chr 13:4-12; 14:6; 18:12; 20:20; 28:11; 29:11. → EXHORTATION; PROHIBITION.

AFFINITY SAYING (Verwandtschaftsspruch). A clipped, rhythmic affirmation in which one who belongs to Israel by birth or heritage is emphatically accepted as the object of a pure and full devotion. 1 Chr 11:1; 12:19.

ANECDOTE (Anekdote). A report that records an event or experience in the life of a person, often including conversation and imaginative description. 1 Chr 4:8-10; 11:1-3, 13-14, 15-19, 23; 12:17-19; 20:4-8; 2 Chr 9:1-12; 28:8-15. Subgenre: → EXPLOIT REPORT.

ANNOUNCEMENT OF DIAGNOSIS (Ankündigung einer Diagnose). Seen especially in the priestly legislation, this form of (→) priestly declaration is uttered by a priest to a person who has come to him for inspection, or is otherwise recognized as ill. 2 Chr 26:20 (cf. v. 23).

ANNOUNCEMENT OF JUDGMENT (Gerichtsankündigung, Gerichtsansage). Commonly an element in a (→) prophetic judgment speech, this may constitute an independent type of (→) prophecy. Calamity of some sort is announced as Yahweh's punishment for transgressions. 2 Chr 16:7-9.

APHORISM (Lehrspruch). A terse saying, embodying a general truth or a characteristic typical for the addressee. 1 Chr 28:9; 29:5; 2 Chr 10:10-11, 14; 15:2; 20:20.

APPEAL (Berufung). Similar to (→) command, (→) prohibition, (→) petition, (→) admonition, and (→) parenesis, this form of speech urgently aims to incite a certain kind of conduct, but without the assumption of any special obligation on the part of the addressee. 2 Chr 13:12; 25:7; 30:8.

APPEAL FOR RETRIBUTION (Berufung auf Vergeltung). An abrupt and urgent cry for justice and retribution by the victim of official injustice. 2 Chr 18:27; 24:22.

ASSURANCE OF VICTORY (Zusicherung eines/des Sieges). The promise of victory on the basis of Yahweh's help and presence. 2 Chr 20:15-17; 32:7-8. → AS-SISTANCE FORMULA.

BATTLE REPORT (Schlachtbericht). A schematic recounting of a military encounter typically containing (1) the confrontation, (2) the battle, and (3) the consequences. 1 Chr 4:39-41, 42-43; 5:9-10, 18-22; 10:1-7; 11:5-6; 14:9-12, 13-24; 18:1-6, 12-23; 19:14-15a, 16-19; 20:1-3; 2 Chr 12:2-4; 15:19–16:10; 24:23-24; 25:5-13, 17-24; 26:6-8; 27:5-6; 28:5-7, 16-21; 35:20-26. → BATTLE STORY; QUASI-HOLY-WAR STORY.

BATTLE STORY (Schlachterzählung). Following the theme of a military encounter, this genre shows narrative exposition, characterization, and plot. 1 Chr 19:1–20:3. → BATTLE REPORT; QUASI-HOLY-WAR STORY.

BIRTH REPORT (Geburtsbericht). The recording of a birth in narrative style, with special notice of the mother. 1 Chr 2:3-4, 17, 18-24, 26, 29, 34-35, 46, 48-49; 4:6, 17-18; 7:14-17, 18, 23; 8:8-9, 11-13; 2 Chr 11:18-20. → GENEALOGY.

BOAST (Prahlrede, Prahllied). An utterance which appraises some person or thing as superior to another. 1 Chr 11:5; 2 Chr 13:10-11. → INCOMPARABILITY SAYING; ENCOMIUM.

CALL FOR DIVINE ATTENTION (Aufruf zur göttlichen Beachtung). The summoning of the Deity for special and direct help. 2 Chr 6:40. → PETITION.

CALL TO LOYALTY (Aufforderung zur Treue). A challenge delivered by a leader to those offering to be his followers. 1 Chr 12:18 (*RSV* 17).

CASUALTY REPORT (Verlustbericht). The (→) notice or (→) report of the number of slain, always on the enemy side. Although this regularly appears in a (→) battle report, it is based upon and presupposes an actual (→) official report as this might have been communicated to the chief officer or king. As the final element in the battle report, it often has an epitomizing function (→ EPITOME), particularly when it includes the temporal phrase "on that day" (*bayyôm hahû'*). The tendency is toward highly exaggerated, schematic numbers. It occurs without *bayyôm hahû'* in 1 Chr 18:5, 12; 19:18; 2 Chr 13:17; 25:11-12; in 2 Chr 28:6 it appears with the locution *bayyôm 'eḥād*.

CASUISTIC REVIEW (Kasuistische Nachprüfung). Modeled after the (→) casuistic lawcode, this is a form of speech arranging related cases in a series of conditional clauses or sentences. 2 Chr 6:21-39.

CATALOGUE (Katalog). A list that enumerates or labels specified items or names according to a particular system of classification. 1 Chr 6:39-66.

CENSURE (Verurteilung). Going beyond (→) rebuke/reproach, this involves outright condemnation, with the punishment implied or directly stated. 2 Chr 26:18.

CENSUS ROLL (Zensusliste). A listing pertaining to a population group, organized by traditional or legal subgroupings and with tallies for each subgroup and for the total population (→ TALLY; MUSTER ROLL). 1 Chr 12:25-38.

CHALLENGE TO A DUEL (Herausforderung zum Duell). Although most biblical instances of this genre involve Yahweh in opposition to Israel, these are based on actual military encounters in which one person demands that another person confront him in combat. 2 Chr 25:17-19.

CHALLENGE TO PIETY (Aufforderung zur Frömmigkeit). A speech in which one of notable piety invites and demands unusual acts of piety. 1 Chr 29:5.

CHRONICLE (Chronik). A prose composition consisting of a series of reports or selected events arranged and dated in chronological order. 2 Chronicles 14–16.

CLAN ETIOLOGY (Sippen Ätiologie). An (→) etiology about and transmitted within a particular clan. 1 Chr 4:10.

COMMAND (Gebot). A direct commission based on the authority of custom, law, or decree, expressed in imperative verb forms and often accompanied by a motive clause. 1 Chr 21:18-19; 28:9-10; 29:20; 2 Chr 26:18; 28:11; 30:6; 32:7.

COMMISSION (Sendung, Beauftragung). An authoritative charge given by a superior to a subordinate. 1 Chr 22:6-16. → COMMAND; ORDER.

COMMISSIONING OF A MESSENGER (Aussendung eines Boten). A narrative representation telling of the sending of a messenger with his message. 1 Chr 21:10.

COMPLAINT (Beschwerde). A statement describing personal or communal distress. 1 Chr 13:12; 2 Chr 20:10-12.

CONFESSION OF GUILT (Schuldgeständnis, -bekenntnis). A statement in which a defendant formally acknowledges his guilt and often discloses his action and/or the circumstances. 1 Chr 17:16-17; 21:8; 2 Chr 12:6; 28:13. → PLEA OF GUILTY; SHRIVING PETITION.

CONSTRUCTION REPORT (Baubericht). A type of report which tells of the building, manufacture, or fabrication of cult and/or state objects and edifices, based ultimately on archival records or related documents. 2 Chr 3:1-2, 3-13; 3:15–4:10.

DEATH REPORT (Todesbericht). A special kind of report in which all interest is focused on a violent death according to the pattern (1) causes, (2) the death, (3) the effects. 1 Chr 2:3; 7:21-22; 2 Chr 22:7-9; 23:15; 24:25-26; 25:27-28; 33:24-25; 35:20-24. → THRONE CONSPIRACY.

DEDICATORY DECLARATION (Widmungserklärung). Solemn words of dedication and/or consecration, cast in exalted and poetic style and marking the transition of the previously profane into the realm of the holy. 1 Chr 22:1; 23:25-28; 2 Chr 6:1-2; 7:12.

DESCRIPTION OF YAHWEH (Yahwebeschreibung). A partly doxological and partly didactic characterization of who Yahweh is or what he does, occuring mainly in hymns and prayers. 1 Chr 17:20; 21:13; 29:11-12, 17; 2 Chr 14:10; 16:9; 30:9. → INCOMPARABILITY STATEMENT.

DISPUTATION (Streitgespräch). A dispute between two or more parties in which differing viewpoints are aired. 1 Chr 21:3; 2 Chr 30:6-9.

DOXOLOGY (Doxologie). A highly lyrical, pithy acclamation of the divine glory.

DREAM EPIPHANY (Traumerscheinung). A brief and schematic report in which Yahweh appears in a dream in order to give a message or engage in dialogue with the recipient. 2 Chr 1:7-12; 7:12-22. When reported in narrative form, the genre is modified as a (→) DREAM REPORT.

DREAM REPORT (Traumbericht). A type of (→) report in the first- or third-person style that recounts the principal elements of a dream experience. 2 Chr 1:7-13 par. 1 Kgs 3:4-15; 2 Chr 7:12-22 par. 1 Kgs 9:2-9.

EDICT (Edikt). A proclamation carrying the force of (→) law, issued by an authority acting in an executive capacity. 1 Chr 15:2; 2 Chr 30:5; 36:23.

EDITORIAL UNIT (Redaktionelle Einheit). Two or more pericopes, with or without editorial comment, drawn together under a new framework of interpretation and forming an enlarged literary unit. 1 Chr 13:1; 23:1, 2, 6, 24, 27; 24:3, 6, 30-31; 2 Chr 35:25.

ENCOMIUM (Lobrede). An extended praise oration, exaggerating to the point of wild adulation. 1 Chr 29:25; 2 Chr 1:15; 9:5-8; 12:13; 30:26; 32:23, 27-29; 35:18. → PRAISE SPEECH.

EPITOME (Auszug, Abriss). A succinct distillation and summation through authoritative interpretation, usually at the end of a pericope and employing the time designation "on that day." 1 Chr 11:5; 12:41; 18:6, 13; 29:22; 2 Chr 13:18; 32:22; 35:16.

ETIOLOGY (Ätiologie). A narrative set in primordial or historical times, involving gods and/or men, and designed to explain for a particular society the origin of certain elements of its shared knowledge, experience, practice, custom, or belief. This genre name is reserved for those narratives whose intrinsic goal is etiological, which should be distinguished from narratives that are broadly explanatory or contain etiological motifs or appendices. The connection between the thing being explained and its etiological explanation commonly depends on assonance developed between key words in the two respective structural elements, often with use of a special (→) etiological formula.

EXHORTATION (Ermahnung zu . . .). A form of urging different from (→) admonition in that it makes no particular assumption regarding a rule of conduct and urges the addressee(s) to a new, perhaps risky, endeavor. 1 Chr 22:16; 28:8, 20-21; 2 Chr 15:7.

EXPLOIT REPORT (Bericht einer Heldentat). A brief note closely related to, and derived from, the exploit (→) anecdote, mentioning a hero's name and parentage, his rank or standing, and the exploit itself. 1 Chr 10:8-12; 11:11, 20, 22. → ANECDOTE.

FAMILY SAGA (Familien-Sage). A narrative of an event or events composing the past of a family unit, often exemplified in the affairs of the patriarchal head of the family. → SAGA.

FAREWELL SPEECH (Abschiedsrede). A speech in the first person delivered by a notable person at or near the time of his death and containing (1) a reference to the coming death, (2) admonitions, and (3) directives. 1 Chr 29:1-9.

GENEALOGY (Stammbaum). A list enumerating individual and tribal descent from the originating ancestor. A linear genealogy traces a single line from father to son, but a collateral genealogy branches out to list siblings. 1 Chronicles contains thirty-eight examples of this genre; 2 Chronicles has none. → BIRTH REPORT; MUSTER ROLL.

HEROIC SAGA (Heldensage). A type of (→) saga which focuses on events in the life of one central figure who is significant for the people who remember him.

Typically, heroic saga includes some account of the hero's birth, marriage, vocation, and death, along with displays of virtues and heroic deeds. The heroic figure has importance for people more widely defined than the limitations of the family unit, and thus moves toward a national consciousness. A heroic saga appears in 1 Samuel 31 par. 1 Chronicles 10.

HIEROS LOGOS (Heiligtumslegende). A sacred recital pertaining to the origin of a holy place; cultic legend intended as an account of the foundation of a sanctuary by a depiction of the event marking the sanctuary as holy and legitimizing it for the official cult. → LEGEND. 2 Samuel 24 par. 1 Chronicles 13.

HISTORICAL REVIEW (Geschichtlicher Rückblick). The rehearsing of salient facts in the past experience of Israel or an individual, generally with a parenetic concern. 1 Chr 17:5, 7-8; 2 Chr 15:3-6; 20:7-9. → FAREWELL SPEECH; TESTIMONY; PARENESIS.

HISTORICAL STORY (Historische Erzählung). A self-contained report recounting how a particular event happened, developing a rudimentary plot with the purpose of recounting events as they occurred. 2 Chr 10:1-19.

HISTORY (Geschichtsschreibung). An extensive, continuous, written composition devoted to a particular subject or historical period. 1 Chr 9:35–2 Chr 36:21.

HYMN OF ENTRANCE (Einzugshymnus). Hymnic liturgy for the entrance of Yahweh and/or his surrogate (the ark) into the temple. 2 Chr 6:41-42; 7:1-3.

HYMN OF PRAISE (Hymnus, Loblied). A psalm extolling and glorifying God. Rooted in worship, it takes a variety of forms. 1 Chr 16:8-36.

INCOMPARABILITY STATEMENT (Aussage von Unvergleichlichkeit). Closely related to the (→) encomium and using the syntax of the superlative, this is a statement to the effect that its subject is beyond comparison with anything else in its category. 2 Chr 2:4; 6:14; 9:9, 11, 19, 22; 30:26; 35:18.

INDICTMENT SPEECH (Anklageerhebung). A statement formally handed down by a judicial authority charging a person or persons with committing an act punishable under the provisions of the law. Although Yahweh is not always directly quoted as making such a speech, the writer so presents the words of the indictment. 1 Chr 22:8; 2 Chr 23:13; 29:6-7, 34; 36:12-16.

INSTRUCTION (Instruktion). Guidance given to an individual or group, setting forth values, giving rules of conduct, answering questions, and providing details for carrying out a contemplated procedure. 1 Chr 21:18; 22:13-16, 17-19; 23:3-5; 28:11-21; 2 Chr 18:26; 19:10; 20:16-17; 23:4-7, 14; 24:5; 35:3-6.

INVENTORY (Inventarium). A list that either tabulates related items or classifies items by character and quality. 2 Chr 4:12-15, 19-22. → LIST.

JOB DESCRIPTION (Arbeitsbeschreibung). A detailing of work assigned to a group or individual. 1 Chr 9:14-33; 23:25-26, 28-32.

KING LIST (Königsliste). A type of (→) list which enumerates successive rulers within a particular state. Besides the royal names, it may include epithets, regnal years, and filiation, although its emphasis is on succession rather than on linear kinship. 1 Chr 1:43-51.

LEGEND (Legende, Heiligen- oder Wundererzählung). A narrative concerned primarily with the wondrous, miraculous, and exemplary. Legend aims at edification rather than at entertainment or instruction. A legend may instill awe for a holy place, ritual, or holy man.

LIST (Liste). A simple sequence of items, usually according to some principle of order or affinity. 1 Chr 1:43-51a, 51b-54; 29:2-6. → INVENTORY; NAME LIST.

LITURGICAL PARAPHRASE (Liturgische Paraphrase). The recasting of a standard liturgical model to suit the purpose of the narrator. 1 Chr 16:36 (cf. Ps 106:48b).

LITURGICAL SUMMONS (Liturgische Aufforderung). An urgent invitation to worship spoken by a person in authority. 2 Chr 29:31; cf. 1 Chr 13:2-3; 2 Chr 15:9; 20:3.

LITURGY (Liturgie). Complexes of cultic acts and words set in a stylized pattern and sequence. 2 Chr 6:1-2, 11; 33:4.

MESSENGER SPEECH (Botenspruch, Botenrede). The oral message delivered by a messenger, repeating literally the words given him upon his commissioning. 2 Chr 2:2-9; 30:6-9.

MIDRASH (Midrasch). An exposition of the authoritative word of Scripture according to the needs and viewpoint of the times. 1 Chr 5:1-2; 15:5-6; 27:23-24.

MUSTER ROLL (Musterungsliste). A list of fighting men, often with (→) tallies, (→) rankings, and (→) appellations, kept as a record to be used in preparation for battle. 1 Chr 4:34-38; 5:7-8, 13-15, 18, 24; 7:1-5, 6-12, 34-40; 8:39-40. Cf. narrative reports in 1 Chr 12:24-41; 2 Chr 25:5; 26:11-13. → GENEALOGY.

NAME ETIOLOGY (Namensätiologie). The explanation of a name by association with an event, commonly involving wordplay or punning (alternate name: ETYMOLOGICAL ETIOLOGY). 1 Chr 1:19; 4:9, 14; 7:23; 13:11; 14:11; 22:9; 2 Chr 20:26. → ETIOLOGY.

NAME LIST (Namensliste). A (→) list consisting purely of proper names, whether of persons, cities, or countries. It occurs 61 times in 1 Chronicles, 13 times in 2 Chronicles.

NEGOTIATION (Verhandlung). An exchange of speeches moving toward agreement or disagreement and focused on a particular issue. 1 Chr 21:20-25; 2 Chr 2:3-16.

NOTICE (Notiz). A very brief (→) report similar to a simple (→) statement.

OATH (Eid). A pronouncement binding one to a particular course of action, attitude, or stance by invoking sanctions of the Deity. 1 Chr 11:19.

OFFICIAL REPORT (Amtlicher Bericht). Representation of the transmittal of information or a message by a person duly authorized and sent forth. 1 Chr 21:5-6; 2 Chr 20:2; 29:18-19; 34:9, 14-15, 16-17, 18.

ORACLE (Orakel). A communication from the Deity, unsolicited or in response to an inquiry (→ ORACULAR INQUIRY). 1 Chr 14:10, 14-15; 21:9-10; 2 Chr 1:11-12; 18:5, 14, 16; 25:9.

ORACULAR INQUIRY (Gottesbefragung, Gottesbescheid). A report telling of seeking and receiving an (→) oracle. 1 Chr 14:10, 14; 2 Chr 18:5, 14-15; 25:9.

ORACULAR REPORT (Bericht eines Orakels). A message from God quoted or closely paraphrased in a report from the receiver of the message to a third person. 1 Chr 22:8-10; 2 Chr 6:5-6, 8-9.

ORDER (Befehl). A forthright, direct expression of will from someone in authority to one subject to his will. 1 Chr 21:2; 22:16; 2 Chr 11:2-4; 18:8, 21, 25; 19:6-7, 10; 23:19; 29:5; 31:4; 34:21; 35:4. → COMMAND; INSTRUCTION.

PARENESIS (Paränese). An address seeking to persuade toward a definite goal. 1 Chr 28:8. → ADMONITION; APPEAL; EXHORTATION.

PEDIGREE (Abkunft, Stammbaum). A (→) list in which a descendant traces his direct lineage to a remote ancestor, naming all the males in the line of descent. 1 Chr 5:14; 6:18-32; 9:16. → GENEALOGY.

PETITION (Bittrede). A request or plea, usually to the Deity, asking for some definite response. 1 Chr 29:18-19; 2 Chr 1:8-10; 2:6-8; 6:16-17, 18-20; 14:10; 20:12. → PRAYER.

PLEA OF GUILT (Schuldgeständnis). An element of the (→) confession of guilt in which the suppliant states, "I have erred/sinned" (ḥāṭāti), sometimes with a designation of the person sinned against and the circumstances. It is found in Exod 10:16; 1 Sam 15:30; 26:21; 2 Sam 12:13; 24:10 par. 1 Chr 21:8; 2 Kgs 18:14.

PLEA OF INNOCENCE (Unschuldsbeteuerung). A statement formally declaring that one is not guilty of allegations or accusations made against him. 1 Chr 29:17.

PRAISE SPEECH (Lobrede). A brief and somewhat elaborate formulaic utterance praising and thanking God for some good fortune or happy circumstance. 1 Chr 17:24; 29:10-13; 2 Chr 2:10-11; 5:4; 6:14-15; 9:7-8; 20:6.

PRAYER (Gebet). A direct address to one's god. 1 Chr 17:16-27; 29:10-19; 2 Chr 6:12-42; 14:10; 20:5-12; 32:20.

PRAYER OF INTERCESSION (Fürbittegebet). Prayer by one individual for another, by the community for an individual, or by an individual for the community. 1 Chr 29:18-19; 2 Chr 6:21-39.

PROHIBITION (Verbot). A direct forbiddance of an action or thing, based on the authority of custom, law, or decree. 1 Chr 11:5; 17:4; 28:3; 2 Chr 11:4; 23:14; 28:13; 29:11; 30:7.

PROMISE (Verheissung, Versprechen). As an independent genre, this is a spoken or written commitment to a specified form of action. 1 Chr 11:2; 17:9-14; 22:4-10; 28:6-7. It is a sub-element in a (→) negotiation (2 Chr 2:9), in a (→) covenant (2 Chr 7:13-16; 30:9; 33:7-8), and in an (→) exhortation (1 Chr 28:20; 2 Chr 15:7).

PROPHECY OF PUNISHMENT OVER AN INDIVIDUAL (Prophetische Gerichtsankündigung über den Einzelnen). A prophetic announcement of disaster to an individual for an offense; it usually contains the elements of accusation and announcement. 2 Chr 20:37; 21:12-15.

PROPHECY OF PUNISHMENT OVER THE PEOPLE (Prophetische Gerichtsankündigung über das Volk). Same as above, but directed to a people. 2 Chr 34:22-25.

PROPHECY OF SALVATION (Prophetische Heilsankündigung). A prophet's announcement of salvation, health, healing, or restoration. 2 Chr 34:26-28.

PROPHETIC BATTLE STORY (Prophetische Schlachterzählung). A (→) battle story in which a prophet assumes an important dramatic role and enunciates interpretative perspectives. 2 Chr 18:1–19:3.

PROPHETIC COMMISSION REPORT (Bericht einer Prophetensendung). A report that tells of God's commissioning a prophet to speak or act. 1 Chr 17:1-5; 21:9-13; 2 Chr 11:1-4.

PROPHETIC SPEECH (Prophetische Rede). Any speech by a prophet, usually without the traditional, clearly marked sub-elements. 2 Chr 11:4; 12:5, 7-8; 15:2-7; 16:7-9; 19:2-3; 20:15-19, 37; 24:20; 25:7-9, 15; 28:9-11.

PROTOCOL (Protokoll). A declaration made at the beginning of a king's reign, in which are set forth the ways in which he came to be king, the task(s) with which he is burdened, and his plans for fulfilling it (them). 2 Chr 6:4-11; 36:23.

QUASI-HOLY-WAR STORY (Quasi-Heiligekriegserzählung). An artificial, rigidly schematic, and highly imaginative imitation of Israel's primitive holy-war narrative. 2 Chr 13:3-21; 14:8-14; 20:1-30; 25:5-13.

REBUKE. → REPROACH/REBUKE.

REGISTER (Register). A writing that officially records items or persons with regard to the identifying characteristics by which they are subject to control within institutions or corporate bodies, the purpose of which is to document the basis on which such items or persons may be administered.

REGNAL RESUMÉ (Abriss einer königlichen Regierungszeit). The formulaic summary of a king's reign, usually in both introductory and concluding sections. Drawn from Kings, it occurs in 1–2 Chronicles 31 times, always containing most or all of the following formulas: (→) accession age, (→) citation, (→) death and burial, and (→) succession; also the (→) statement of length and place of reign and (→) theological review.

REPORT (Bericht). A brief, self-contained prose narrative about a single event or situation in the past. 1–2 Chronicles has at least 42 of these. → BATTLE-, BUILDING-, THEOPHANY-, BIRTH-, and DEATH REPORT.

REPORT OF ORACULAR INQUIRY (Gottesbefragung). A short narrative about seeking and receiving an (→) oracle. 2 Chr 18:4-23; 34:20-28.

REPORT OF A PROPHETIC WORD (Bericht eines Prophetenwortes). A late genre in which narrative contexting serves to help communicate a prophetic message as related to a historical situation or event. 1 Chr 17:3-15; 21:10-12; 2 Chr 11:2-4a; 12:5; 16:7-10; 19:1-3; 20:13-19; 21:12-15; 24:20; 25:7-8, 15-16; 28:9-11; 34:22-28.

REPORT OF RITUAL (Bericht eines Ritualgeschehens). A brief description of procedures followed in the performance of public worship, all of which has been regulated by ritual. 1 Chr 13:6-14; 15:25–16:6; 29:20-22; 2 Chr 1:2-6; 6:12-13; 7:3-10; 15:10-15; 20:18-19, 26, 28; 29:20-33; 35:10-15. → LITURGY.

REPROACH/REBUKE (Vorwurf, Tadel). A sharp reprimand for indecorous conduct or not performing as expected, delivered by one claiming authority or supervision over the person being criticized. 1 Chr 15:13; 2 Chr 12:5; 13:8-9; 18:15, 23-24; 19:1-3; 25:16; 26:18. → CENSURE.

REPUDIATION SAYING (Verwerfungsspruch). A rhythmic political ditty designed to make the maximum possible impact on the person being repudiated. 2 Chr 10:16.

REQUEST FOR SHRIVING (Bitte um Beichte). An impassioned plea for divine forgiveness without consideration to one's worthiness. 1 Chr 21:8; 2 Chr 30:18-19.

RHETORICAL QUESTION (Rhetorische Frage). Structured as an ordinary question, but allowing only one answer, either yes or no, and thereby functioning as a dramatic statement. 1 Chr 11:19; 17:6; 2 Chr 1:10; 16:8; 32:4, and frequently. → ACCUSATORY QUESTION; WARNING.

RIDDLE (Rätsel). A question or proposition that is worded in an ambiguous or intriguing way so as to provoke conjectural interpretation or solution. 2 Chr 25:18.

ROSTER (Ordonanztabelle). A list of all the names within a related group together with the duties or offices assigned to each. 1 Chr 6:18-33; 11:26-47; 12:3-8, 10-15; 15:5-10, 16-24; 16:4-6; 18:15-17; 24:20-30; 25:1-7; 26:1-11, 20-28; 27:16-22, 25-31, 32-34; 2 Chr 31:12-15. → TABLE OF ORGANIZATION; ROTA.

ROTA (Dienstliste). A fixed order of rotation, as of persons or duties. 1 Chr 24:7-19; 25:8-31; 27:2-15. → ROSTER; TABLE OF ORGANIZATION.

ROYAL NARRATIVE (Königsnovelle). Narrative portions of Egyptian (→) royal inscriptions that represent the king as an ideal figure of strength, piety, and success. Cf. 2 Chr 1:2-17.

SAGA (Sage). A traditional narrative having an episodic structure developed around stereotyped themes or objects, recounting deeds or virtues from the past insofar as they contribute to the composition of the present narrator's world. It appears frequently in primitive narrative such as that of Genesis. Elements of saga appear in 1 Chr 7:22-23.

SCHEDULE (Terminplan). A (→) list correlating persons, times, and tasks. 1 Chr 9:25. → ROTA.

SERMON (Predigt). A formalized address in a liturgical setting rehearsing the past in the light of present conditions and obligations. 2 Chr 15:1-7.

SHRIVING PETITION (Bittrede um Beichte). An element in the (→) confession of guilt requesting that God overlook, cleanse, or set aside a specific offense. 2 Sam 24:10 par. 1 Chr 21:8; 2 Chr 30:18-19.

STATEMENT (Aussage). A brief oral or written notation or description of a situation or circumstance. 2 Chr 1:14; 2:1, 17-18; 8:1-6, 7-10, 11, 16, 17-18; 9:10-11, 13-21; 12:10-12; 13:20-21; 14:7; 17:5; 21:10.

STORY (Erzählung). A sophisticated narrative that creates interest by arousing tension and resolving it during the course of narration. 1 Chr 21:1-27; 2 Chr 10:1–11:4; 22:10–23:21; 32:1-23; 35:1-19. → HISTORICAL STORY.

GLOSSARY

SUMMONS TO WAR (Aufforderung zum Kampf). A genre used by a leader to call the fighters to battle. The constituent parts are (1) the summons proper and (2) the motivation, which usually refers to the imminent intervention of Yahweh. It is used especially in the holy-war narratives and imitated by the prophets in the (→) announcement of judgment. It occurs in 1 Chr 19:13 par. 2 Sam 10:12.

SYMBOLIC ACTION (Symbolische Handlung). A report in which a prophet uses a symbolic action as an instrument and interpretation of his spoken message. 2 Chr 18:10.

TABLE OF ORGANIZATION (Organisationsverzeichnis). An administrative instrument in which various jobs or reponsibilities are listed in relationship to one another, often with identification of the person(s) who are to fill the various slots. 1 Chr 23:3-14; 26:12-18. → ROSTER.

TAUNT (Verspottung). An utterance which derides a person or thing as inferior to another. 2 Chr 13:8-9; 25:15; 32:10-15.

TESTIMONY (Bezeugung). A form of speech in which an individual person makes a solemn declaration concerning himself in relation to the community. 1 Chr 29:2-5.

THEOPHANY (Gotteserscheinung). A type of (→) report, occasionally poetic, which recounts the manifestation of God. In 2 Chr 5:13-14 and 7:1-3, this is in the form of a cloud of glory casting awe on the people. In 1 Kgs 18:38; 2 Kgs 1:10, 12; 1 Chr 21:26 it is in the form of fire from heaven.

THREAT (Drohung, Bedrohung). A grim and menacing speech spoken to or about the intended victim by someone who has the authority and often the means to carry it into action. 2 Chr 7:19-22; 10:14; 16:9; 25:16; 35:21. → PROPHETIC JUDGMENT SPEECH.

THRONE CONSPIRACY (Verschwörung gegen den Thron). A brief report telling of (1) a conspiracy, (2) the king's murder, and (3) its effects. 2 Chr 23:1-15; 25:27; 33:24.

TRIAL GENRES (Gerichtsreden). A collective term for genres (or formulas) related to legal procedure within the court situation, whether at the gates or the sanctuary. Genres used in the dispute prior to official court action are the extradiction request, the formula of imputation, the appeasement question, and the petition for a trial; those relating to speeches of litigants in court are the speech of the accuser, the speech of the defense, and the acknowledgment of guilt; those relating to the conclusion of a trial are the statement of acquittal and the conviction. For details, see FOTL XXIII.

VISION REPORT (Visionsbericht). The report of what a prophet or seer hears and sees in a visionary experience. 2 Chr 18:16, 18-22.

VOCATION ACCOUNT (Berufungsbericht). The formal structure of an (→) account or (→) oracle reporting a commitment to a particular vocation, usually with the structure: (1) call to attention, (2) commission, (3) objections, (4) reassurances, and (5) commitment. In 1–2 Chronicles it appears at 1 Chr 22:6-16 and 28:9-10, both of which are speeches by David to Solomon.

WARNING (Warnung). A form of speech in which one who is in a position to know

436

the ramifications of a contemplated action points out its dangers and urges the hearer(s) to desist. 2 Chr 25:8, 16, 19; 28:11; 32:15; 35:21.

WISH (Wunsch, Verlangen). A form of speech in which one expresses a strong desire to have something or see something done. 1 Chr 11:17; 22:12; 2 Chr 35:21.

FORMULAS

ACCESSION AGE FORMULA (Formel für das Thronbesteigungsalter): "X was Y years old when he began to reign." 19 occurrences in 1–2 Chronicles.

ACCLAMATION FORMULA (Akklamationsformel): "Long live king X!" 2 Chr 23:11.

ACCUSATORY QUESTION FORMULA (Anklagefrageformel). A question, usually with "were you (not)" or the like, substituting as a formal accusation. 2 Chr 19:2; 24:20; 25:15; 28:10.

ADOPTION FORMULA (Adoptionsformel): "I will be your father and you shall be my son," with variations. 1 Chr 17:13; 28:6.

APPEASEMENT FORMULA (Beschwichtigungsformel): "What have we to do with each other?" 2 Chr 35:21.

APPELLATION FORMULA (Benennungsformel). An honorific term of distinction usually conferred on military personnel and presented in a (→) muster roll or related structures. 1 Chr 5:18, 24; 7:2, 7, 9, 11, 40; 8:40; 9:13; 11:22; 26:6; etc.

ASSISTANCE FORMULA (Beistandsformel): "I am/will be with you" and similar expressions. 1 Chr 9:20; 11:9; 12:9; 14:15; 17:2; 21:16, 18; 28:20; 2 Chr 13:12; 15:2, 9; 17:3; 19:11; 20:15, 17; 32:8; 36:23.

AUTHORIZATION FORMULA (Ermächtigungsformel). A formula for identifying the proper authority for a given cultic procedure, always in the form "as Moses/David/the prophets spoke/wrote/commanded (in the law), etc." 1 Chr 6:34; 9:22; 15:15; 16:40; 28:19; 2 Chr 8:13; 25:4; 30:16; 31:3; 35:6, 12, 15, 16. → REGULATION FORMULA.

BLESSING FORMULA (Segensformel): "Peace, peace," or "Blessed be . . ."; a formula of devout praise or well-wishing, whether to men or to God. 1 Chr 12:19; 29:10.

CALL TO ATTENTION FORMULA (Aufmerksamkeitsrufsformel): "Hear me," followed by the vocative. 1 Chr 28:2; 2 Chr 13:4; 15:2; 20:20; 29:15.

CALL FOR DIVINE ATTENTION FORMULA (Aufruf zur göttlichen Beachtungsformel). A special form of the (→) call to attention addressed to the Deity and initiating or repeating a (→) petition for special and direct help. 2 Chr 6:40.

CALL TO LOYALTY FORMULA (Aufforderung zur Treueformel). A challenge delivered by a leader to his followers, demanding their loyalty and warning them of betrayal. 1 Chr 12:18.

CASUALTY REPORT FORMULA (Verlustberichtsformel). Usually at the conclusion of a (→) battle report, this element states an unusually exaggerated number of enemy casualties; with the time designation "on that day," it constitutes an (→) epitome. 1 Chr 18:5, 12; 2 Chr 13:17.

CHALLENGE TO PIETY FORMULA (Herausforderung zur Frömmigkeitsformel). In question form, an urgent invitation to perform extraordinary deeds of devotion to God. 1 Chr 29:5.

CITATION FORMULA (Zitationsformel): "And the rest of the acts of X are written in Y," or the like. This occurs 12 times in 2 Chronicles as an element of the (→) regnal resumé.

CONVEYANCE FORMULA (Übergebungs-, Übergabe-, Übermittlungsformel): ". . . gave/will give unto your/his hand," i.e., put into the power of. 1 Chr 22:18; 2 Chr 13:16; 16:8; 18:5, 11, 14; 24:24; 25:20; 28:5 (twice); 36:17.

COVENANT FORMULA (Bundesformel): "You shall be my people and I shall be your God," with variations. 1 Chr 17:22; 2 Chr 15:12-13; 23:16; 34:31.

DEATH AND BURIAL FORMULA (Tod- und Bestattungsformel): "X slept with his fathers and was buried in . . ." occurs 14 times in 1–2 Chronicles as an element in the (→) regnal resumé.

FAMILY FORMULA (Familienformel): "X and his sons and his brothers," an element in the (→) roster or (→) rota. 1 Chr 25:9-31; 26:8.

FULFILLMENT FORMULA (Erfüllungsformel). An explicit reference to a previous prophecy, identifying an event as its fulfillment with use of "just as X spoke," "according to the word of X," or the like. 1 Chr 11:3, 10; 12:23; 22:11; 2 Chr 10:15.

HYMNIC REFRAIN (Hymnischer Kehrreim): "For he is good, for his devotion is forever," a response triggered by the acclamation "Praise Yahweh." 2 Chr 5:13; 7:3, 6.

INTIMIDATION FORMULA (Einschüchterungsformel): "and the fear of God came upon . . . ," regularly the concluding statement in a (→) battle story or (→) battle report. 1 Chr 14:17; 2 Chr 14:30; 17:10; 20:29.

MESSENGER FORMULA (Botenformel): "Thus says X (usually Yahweh)." 1 Chr 17:4, 7; 2 Chr 12:5; 20:15; 21:12; 24:20; 32:10; 34:23, 24, 26; 36:23.

PROPHETIC UTTERANCE FORMULA (Prophetische Offenbarungsformel): "says Yahweh," lit., "oracle of Yahweh." 2 Chr 34:27.

RANKING FORMULA (Rangordnungsformel): "first (chief) . . . second . . . third, etc.," identifying a person in terms of rank in relation to his fellows. Asyndetically, the ordinal is placed in direct juxtaposition with the personal name. 1 Chr 9:17; 23:19-20; 26:1-3, 4-5.

REASSURANCE FORMULA (Beruhigungsformel): "Be not afraid and do not be dismayed," and the like. 1 Chr 22:13; 28:20; 2 Chr 20:17.

REGULATION FORMULA (Verordnungsformel). Designed to assure that a given cultic procedure is fully and correctly carried out, this formula begins with the comparative kĕ, "as," and follows with "the word/writing/ordinance (of David/the king/the book [or law] of Moses/Yahweh)." 1 Chr 28:19; 2 Chr 4:7; 23:31; 24:19; 29:25; 30:5, 6, 18; 35:4, 10, 16. → AUTHORIZATION FORMULA.

SELF-ABASEMENT FORMULA (Selbsterniedrigungsformel). A formula that makes the speaker less significant or worthy because he measures himself over against some greater or more notable person or being. 1 Chr 17:16.

SELF-DISCLOSURE FORMULA (Erweiswortformel): "Then you shall know that I am Yahweh," with variations, stating that a given event will make a person aware of Yahweh's being, presence, and purpose. 2 Chr 33:13.

STATEMENT OF LENGTH AND PLACE OF REIGN (Angabe der Orts- und Regierungsjahre). A prepositional phrase such as "in Jerusalem" accompanying the (→) accession formula and a statement of the length of reign as an element of the (→) regnal resumé. It occurs in 1 Chr 29:27 and 16 times in 2 Chronicles.

SUCCESSION FORMULA (Sukzessionsformel): "And X his son reigned in his stead," the closing element in the REGNAL RESUMÉ. It occurs twice in 1 Chronicles and 13 times in 2 Chronicles.

SYNCHRONISTIC ACCESSION FORMULA (Synchronistische Thronbesteigungsformel). An element in the introductory (→) regnal resumé, this formula states the date of one monarch's accession with reference to the regnal year of his counterpart in the northern or southern kingdom. It occurs in 2 Chr 13:1 and regularly in Kings.

TALLY (Summierung). A cardinal number attached asyndetically (frequent in Chronicles in the [→] genealogy, [→] battle report, [→] muster roll, and other administrative forms) to (→) lists of persons, towns, or animals, and syndetically (in 18 Chronicles passages) as part of a complete syntactical structure.

THEOLOGICAL REVIEW FORMULA (Theologische Begutachtungsformel): "And X did good/evil in the sight of Yahweh" (often with specifications and details), an element in the (→) regnal resumé. There are 22 occurrences in 2 Chronicles.

TRANSITION FORMULA (Überleitungsformel). A variety of temporal or circumstantial phrases employed to introduce a new phrase or episode in narration. 1 Chr 2:22; 20:1, 4; 21:28; 29:21; 2 Chr 1:7; 7:8; 16:7; 18:2; 20:1, 35; 21:8, 18-19; 24:17, 23; 25:14, 27; 28:16; 32:1; 33:14; 35:14.

WORD FORMULA (Wortereignisformel): "And the word of Yahweh came to X," and the like. 1 Chr 17:3; 21:9; 22:8; 2 Chr 11:2-4; 15:1.